The Maya World

The Maya World

Yucatec Culture and Society, 1550-1850

∾

Matthew Restall

STANFORD UNIVERSITY PRESS, STANFORD, CALIFORNIA

Stanford University Press
Stanford, California
© 1997 by the Board of Trustees of the
Leland Stanford Junior University
Printed in the United States of America

CIP data appear at the end of the book

licil in kubic lay in hun tin uatan Helen u kaba

Preface

The Mayas of Yucatan were a subject people of the Spanish Empire from 1542 to 1821. During that time they kept legal and other records, written in their own language but in the roman alphabet; dated between 1557 and 1851, extant examples of material written by Maya notaries exist in libraries and archives in the United States, Mexico, and Spain. These records have received little scholarly attention, and this book is the product of an effort to locate, translate, and analyze the documents that survive.

My principal academic debt is to the teacher and mentor who provided the original advice, support, encouragement, and inspiration without which this work would not have come to fruition: James Lockhart. I profoundly value his guidance. I am also grateful to other scholars for their support and for their example: Howard Tomlinson at Wellington College, and Felipe Fernández-Armesto at Oxford University; at UCLA, it was an honor and a pleasure to work with the late E. Bradford Burns, H. B. Nicholson, Geoffrey Symcox, and José Moya; at Tulane University, Victoria Bricker and the late Martha Robertson of the Latin American Library were extremely helpful to my research, as was Philip Thompson; Frances Karttunen, of the University of Texas, has been extraordinarily generous in her support and has contributed greatly to my understanding of the Maya language, as has William Hanks, of the University of Chicago. I value their friendship and generosity, as I do that of Kevin Gosner, Ruth Gubler, Marta Hunt, Susan Kellogg, Karen Powers, and Susan Schroeder. I should like to add a specific additional word of gratitude for detailed and extensive comments made on various drafts of this study by Victoria Bricker, Frances Karttunen, and James Lockhart. As copy editor, Shirley Taylor has made important contributions to the final product, as have Stanford's Norris Pope and John Feneron.

I also wish to thank the staffs of the Archivo General de la Nación in

Mexico City and of the Archivo General de Indias in Seville (where Manuela Cristina García Bernal was especially welcoming), as well as those in Yucatan who offered me their assistance and friendship: the staffs and directors of Mérida's notarial, state, and local archives (ANEY, AGEY, and CAIHY/CCA), especially Piedad Peniche Rivero, Michel Antochiw, Patricia Martínez Huchím, Yolanda López Moguel, and William Brito Sansores; Yucatan's most notable scholar, Sergio Quezada, and its most hospitable couple, Carlos Villaneuva Castillo and Rocio Bates Morales; Fernando Peón Molina; and in Telchaquillo, don Rufino, doña Esmeralda, and their children.

I have greatly appreciated the encouragement and comradeship of the peers and colleagues with whom I have studied and worked, especially Alice Araujo, Jim Braun, Margaret Dunaway, Richard Huston, Dana Leibsohn, Tim Mullane, Steve Patterson, Terry Rugeley, Eric Selbin, Pete Sigal, Bob Snyder, Kevin Terraciano, the members of the Southwestern University History Department (Martha Allen, Weldon Crowley, Steve Davidson, Jan Dawson, and Bill Jones), as well as Jim Cronin, Deborah Levenson-Estrada, and Larry Wolff of the Boston College History Department. The research for and writing of this study were accomplished with the financial support of various UCLA grants (1988–92) and Southwestern University Cullen Faculty Development grants (1993–94), and with the generosity of Dr. and Mrs. Orion L. Hoch. I thank my parents and my family—especially my mother, Judy, my father, Robin, and my sister Emma (the latter two authors themselves), Mariela, Milly, and the two Davids—for their understanding and for the confidence they have given me. Without the spiritual support of my wife, Helen, her love, her patience, and her undying faith in me, these words would not have been written.

M.B.R.
Georgetown, Texas
Belmont, Massachusetts

Contents

Maps and Figures

Maps

Figures

Tables

The Maya World

·❧·

CHAPTER ONE

Introduction

The indigenous people and civilization of the Maya area have attracted a great deal of attention, both academic and popular, ever since Stephens and Catherwood "discovered" abandoned pre-Columbian cities in Yucatan, Guatemala, and Honduras a century and a half ago. Since that time, our understanding of Maya society before Europeans reached the New World has grown considerably, just as the living Maya have been so thoroughly studied that an anthropologist can now be found in or near most of today's Maya communities.

The fate of the Mayas in between ancient splendor and modern observation has remained more obscure, partly because the lack of monumental architecture and hieroglyphs and the absence of living witnesses made the Mayas under colonial rule seem less accessible and less romantic, and partly because students of the period relied on Spanish sources. Spaniards believed themselves racially and culturally superior to subject peoples such as the Mayas, who could be turned into collaborators of colonial oppression if they could only be convinced of that fact; in the past, scholars tended to believe either in Spanish superiority or in the indigenous people's acceptance of their own inferiority.[1] It is now clear that neither was true—certainly, as this study demonstrates, not of the Mayas, whose society and culture remained far more complex and potent and had a greater capacity for localizing introduced concepts, than has previously been thought.

Spanish Conquest and Maya Reactions

In these provinces there is not a single river, although there are lakes, and the hills are of live rock, dry and waterless. The entire land is covered by thick bush and is so stony that there is not a single square foot of soil. . . .

The inhabitants are the most forlorn and treacherous in all the lands
discovered to this time. . . . In them I have failed to find truth touching
anything.
                              —Francisco de Montejo, 1534

May [the Spaniards] suffer the penance for the evils they have done to us,
and may our descendants to the fourth generation be recompensed the
great persecution that came upon us.
                              —Francisco de Montejo Xiu, 1567

The conquest and colonization of the peninsula of Yucatan has long
been symbolized by the founding of the Spanish city of Mérida on the
ruins of the Maya city of Tihó. The image of destruction and construction,
of Spanish Yucatan as phoenix rising from the ashes of Maya civilization,
was modified in the iconography of the celebration of Mérida's 350th
birthday in 1992, in which a bearded conquistador made way for an indigenous warrior in resurgent pose. This interpretation says as much about
the old historiography of New Spain as it does about the political potency
of indigenous imagery in modern Mexico, but it has little to do with the
history of the postconquest Maya.

A more accurate metaphor would be that of colonial-era Tihó, a Maya
community neither destroyed nor unaltered by the conquest. In such settlements the indigenous people of Yucatan continued to speak and write
their own language, now supplemented by a sprinkling of Spanish words
to describe the new objects and institutions that affected their lives, and
officially written with the Latin alphabet in formulas and formats borrowed from Spanish legal procedures. The Maya of Yucatan continued to
produce consumable and woven goods, a good deal of which went in
tribute or forced sales to Spanish settlers and officials. They still chose their
own leaders and administered their own affairs, though only at the community level and sometimes along guidelines laid down by the colonial
authorities. Above all, the Maya maintained a sense of identity and affiliation with the communities in which they continued to live, the integrity
and internal structures of which were sanctioned by a Spanish regime
dependent upon indigenous mechanisms of tribute and labor provision.
The Maya called such communities *cahob* (in the singular, *cah*).

Second only to the cah as a social unit determining Maya identity was
the patronym group or extended family lineage, the *chibal*. These two
social foci helped determine not only how the Maya reacted to colonization but also how they reacted to the military phase of the conquest.

A regional federation of some kind centered on the cah of Mayapan
had broken up, following a massacre of Cocom nobles by the rival Xiu
chibal, a half-century before Christopher Columbus traded with Maya
merchants off the Yucatec coast in 1502. Although Columbus never set foot

on the peninsula, within a decade Spanish survivors of a Caribbean ship-
wreck were washed ashore. Their fate was a symbolic one. Most were soon
killed—sacrificed, according to one of two survivors, Gerónimo de Aguilar, who in 1519 was able to join Hernán Cortés on the Yucatec island of
Cozumel and subsequently to take part in the conquest of central Mexico.
The other survivor, Gonzalo Guerrero, has a place in Mexican legend as
the father of the first mestizo; by Aguilar's account, Guerrero had "gone
native," marrying a Maya woman, wearing a warrior's earplugs, and leading a successful attack on a Spanish expedition at Cape Catoche in 1518—a
feat he repeated through the 1520's. Guerrero's appeal today is romantic
and figurative, the prototypical Maya-saving non-Maya whose twentieth-
century successors might include Felipe Carrillo Puerto and Subcoman-
dante Marcos; yet it was ultimately Aguilar who came to represent the
future of Spanish-Maya relations.

The Maya resistance to Spanish intrusion was effective for another generation, with expeditions under one or more of the Francisco de Montejos
(father, son, and nephew all bearing the same name) turned back between
1527 and 1535. Because Maya loyalties were localized rather than centralized, the invaders were unable to match the collapse of the well-
organized Nahua resistance that followed the destruction of Tlatelolco-
Tenochtitlán. Nonetheless, owing to a number of favorable conditions, the
elder Montejo, styled *adelantado* after his conqueror's license, was able to
establish a permanent colony in the 1540's. Many of these conditions were
a direct consequence of the Spanish invasions—the damage wrought by
repeated invasions and the economic disruption caused by the collapse of
long-distance trade following the conquests of first the Nahuas and then
the Guatemalan Mayas, and the demographic devastation of the Maya by
smallpox epidemics (a population reduced by some 70 to 80 percent in the
early sixteenth century was halved again in the first three decades of
colonial rule). There was also a period of drought exacerbated by a plague
of locusts. The Spanish use of large numbers of Nahua auxiliaries (who
feature prominently in the Calkiní account of the conquest, for example)
was added to the ongoing interregional conflict, highlighted by the Cocom
taking their revenge on the Xiu in 1536 both for Mayapan and for the
friendly Xiu reception given to Montejo.

The Xiu were not the only ruling chibal interested in making common
cause with the Spaniards; the Pech were likewise persuaded to cooperate
with the founders of the colonial settlement at the southern end of the
region they dominated. The Spaniards were thus able to turn around what
had been the disadvantage of Maya decentralization and to combine this
divide-and-conquer strategy with periodic and systematic violence, ex-
emplified by the brutal suppression of a Maya "rebellion" in 1546–47 and
what one Xiu leader would later call "the great persecution" of 1562 in

which four and a half thousand Mayas were tortured, many to death. The
end of this inquisitional campaign of fray Diego de Landa concluded what
might be called the military phase of the conquest of Yucatan. By this time,
the colonizers had grown strong enough to turn violently even upon
leaders who had become allies in the conquest, such as the Xiu; and one
noble related to the Xiu chibal, Gaspar Antonio Chi, had become a symbol
of early acculturation and cooptation, acting as Landa's assistant and
interpreter.[2]

Some of the leaders who had cooperated in the conquest later drew up
and may have presented to Spanish authorities their own accounts of their
roles in the conquest. Such accounts, combined with references in other
Maya-language sources to the coming of the Spaniards, suggest various
Maya perceptions of the conquest that provide some background to Maya
reactions to colonial rule.

According to the Pech nobles of Yaxkukul and Chicxulub, their role in
the Spanish conquest was one of allies of equal standing against a "Maya
people unwilling to deliver tribute to these first foreigners" (*manan Maya
uinicob ti kuchi yolob u kube patan ti yax dzulob*); these intransigent Mayas are
accordingly blamed for the violence and calamity of the conquest, including warfare and slaughter, torture by fire and dogs, heavy taxation, im-
prisonment of Maya officials, and the seizure of people to build and work
in houses in Mérida. This attempt to distance the Pech ethnically from
other Mayas and assert a historical affinity with the Spaniards is best
illustrated by the claims of the supposed authors of the Titles of Chicxulub
and Yaxkukul to be "I, the first of the hidalgo conquistadors" (*yax hidalgos
concixtador en*, and *ten cen yax hidalgo concixtador*)—using not only the exclusively Spanish term *conquistador* but also the Spanish term for noble,
hidalgo. Although the Pech were granted *indio hidalgo* status in return for
their cooperation in the conquest of the eastern end of the colony, the
naming of both Spanish and noble indigenous conquerors implies a closer
association with the very first settlers.[3]

Other references in the Title of Chicxulub to "Maya people" as a group
distinct from the Pech chibal imply that this group consisted not only of
those communities and their leaders (such as the Xiu and Cocom) to the
east of the Pech area (the colonial La Costa) but also of commoners under
Pech rule. If the Maya nobility perceived the conquest in class as well as
ethnic terms (the intersection of the two reflecting the late-colonial origin
of these accounts), the view of less-privileged Mayas may have been similarly class-based. In the Chilam Balam of Chumayel, the formulaic phrases
used to describe the miseries of conquest give the impression that the
arrival of the Spaniards represented not so much a disruption as an augmented perpetuation of the daily hardships of Maya life. One of these
hardships was social inequality. The conquest added church dues (*limosna*)

to the age-old burden of tribute (*patan*), and it also added Spaniards (*Españolesob*) and colonial public prosecutors (*fiscalob*) to the list of preconquest officers who required services (*meyahtabal*)—priests (*ah kinob*), cah governors (*batabob*), and teachers (*camzahob*). Such officials, Spanish and Maya, abuse the humble community Mayas (*u palil cahob*, literally "the children of the cah"), and act as "the community leeches that suck on the poor commoners" (*ah picil cahob yah ɔuɔil otzil mazehualob*).[4]

Similarly in the conquest-era violence against Maya communities described in the Tixchel title, Spaniards are largely incidental to encounters involving Christianized Chontal Maya campaigns to bring other Maya groups into the colonial system. In this and other sources (primarily land documents) that refer to the conquest period, Spaniards tend to be distinguished from Mayas by their names but not by their actions: they are simply among the prominent protagonists in the drama of past events. Otherwise, the coming of the Spaniards is no more than a temporal point of reference, merely implied by way of explaining at what time somebody acquired a Christian name or his older brother or father still had a pre-Christian name. The emphasis is on continuity in terms of indigenous rulership and indigenous landholding.[5]

The conquest could thus be seen either as the beginning of class relations or as the start of rivalries between communities and their dominant dynasties (cahob and *chibalob*); colonial rule could be seen as confirmation of social inequality or as the opportunity for confirmation of social, political, and economic privileges (the Titles were intended to win continued Spanish recognition of Pech hidalgo status and of the territorial boundaries claimed by Calkiní, Chicxulub, and Yaxkukul).

The Chilam Balam's class-based commentary on the harshness of everyday existence and the Pech vision of the conquest as a civil war with indigenous winners as well as losers reflect a Maya reordering of the violence and permanence of the conquest in two ways. One is rooted in the fact that the Maya are well aware of the ethnic dimension of the conquest but choose to reinterpret it in terms of the centrality of cah, chibal, and class in Maya society. The other is the willingness of the Maya to engage their own history with irony and satire, as well as self-interest and a determination to manipulate the past in order to create a better present.

Historiographical Context and the Structure of This Book

Thus he put down his name . . . because he knew how to write a document.
—Title of Calkiní

The traditional tendency of colonial Yucatec historiography to treat the Maya as a hidden and silent culture devastated to the point of anomie by the conquest, after which they sullenly harbored thoughts of resistance and revenge for three centuries, is rooted in the perspective of the colonizers themselves. Even the emphasis placed on the 1546 rebellion, the Landa investigations of 1562, the 1761 Canek revolt, and the Caste War of the 1840's reflects more the fundamental fears of Yucatan's minority rulers than any balanced historical perspective. The reluctance of the international scholarly community to accept the assertion by John L. Stephens 150 years ago that the ruined cities had been built by the ancestors of the current natives indicates the cultural void into which the Spaniards had assigned the people whose language and culture they themselves had to some degree adopted.[6] The early Mayanists, drawn to the mysterious potential of preconquest sites, treated the living Maya as the Spanish Yucatecans had—as useful, but ultimately irrelevant to their own pursuits.[7] Even the historians who turned to the sixteenth century and beyond were trapped by the contemporaneous norm of the chronological-institutional approach, following a sequence of political and ecclesiastical events and prominent figures that took little account of Spanish society, and none at all of the Maya in any guise.[8]

The roots of the intellectual rescue of the postconquest Maya lie in the sixteenth-century ethnography of Diego de Landa—a considerable irony in view of his destruction of perhaps 90 percent of the Maya books that survived the conquest—and also in the annotated translation of Landa's work by Alfred Tozzer; Daniel Brinton's translation of some colonial-era Maya manuscripts and Tozzer's Maya grammar were also important early contributions.[9] But Yucatan's true historiographical golden age began under the auspices of the Carnegie Institution of Washington in the 1930's and 1940's. While France Scholes and Robert Chamberlain worked on sixteenth-century Spanish documentation, with Eric Thompson "ranging everywhere,"[10] Ralph Roys turned to postconquest material written by indigenous notaries in their own language. His collaboration with Scholes on the material from Acalan-Tixchel is still an ethnographical standard; but Roys's independent work, some fifty articles, monographs, and books published between 1920 and 1965, made him, in J. Eric S. Thompson's words, "by far the greatest gringo scholar in Maya."[11] The achievement has yet to be equaled. Roys was the first and only scholar to acquire a knowledge of Yucatec Maya sufficient to transcribe and translate a substantial corpus of colonial literature in that language, from medical and botanical tracts to the almost impenetrable Ritual of the Bacabs and the Books of Chilam Balam. The sum of these efforts is an ethnography of the Maya, yet Roys never produced an analytical synthesis or magnum opus that adequately reconstructed Maya society in the colonial period.[12] An example of the extent, and the limitation, of Roys's contribution lies in his transcription and translation of the 250-year municipal records of the cah of Ebtun, published almost sixty years ago. This was an invaluable gift to future scholars. But Roys's characterization of the Yucatec Maya as simply a "tribal group," rather than as a collection of complex entities (of which Ebtun was one), indicates the conceptual infancy of his analysis.[13]

Not that Roys can be fairly faulted for his failure to identify and emphasize the cah as the principal sociopolitical unit of the Maya; in the final years of Roys's life Charles Gibson published his seminal study of the "Aztecs" without actually identifying the equivalent central Mexican unit, the *altepetl*, the significance of which was not fully understood until James Lockhart began to study Nahuatl notarial sources a decade later.[14] Since then, although great advances have been made in the ethnohistory of central Mexico, Yucatan has remained as much on the fringes as it was during its relative marginalization under colonial rule.

A new generation of scholars of Yucatan that emerged in the mid-1970's built only indirectly upon the foundations laid down by Roys. Three important works of this period, by Manuela Cristina García Bernal and Marta Hunt, did much to unveil social and economic patterns in colonial Yucatan—Hunt's study in particular gives a richly textured portrait of *encomendero* society—but their perspective remained Spanish, as did also Robert Patch's in his analysis of changes in landownership and use at the end of the colonial period (an expert use of documentary evidence that has since been rewritten into the major contribution to our understanding of Yucatan's economy after 1650).[15]

More recently this problem of approach has been acknowledged—most notably by Inga Clendinnen, Nancy Farriss, and Grant Jones—as a methodological challenge posed by the use of Spanish-language colonial documentary sources to reconstruct certain aspects of the Maya historical experience.[16] Recognizing that Spanish texts treat the Maya as "objects," these scholars have attempted to reinterpret the sources emphasizing the Maya as "subjects"—that is, scholars' subjects.

The results of this reinterpretation are mixed. Clendinnen sets out to present both Spanish and Maya viewpoints of the conquest, but she focuses her discussion on Diego de Landa and his persecution of the Maya in the 1560's, using Spanish-language sources. A comparison with Nelson Reed's Caste War account is instructive: both books treat the difficult subject of racial-cultural conflict in Yucatan by dividing their text into two parts, but the first parts, dealing with the wars from the Spanish point of view, are longer and more convincing than the second parts, which attempt to analyze Maya viewpoints without the support of Maya-language sources.[17] Similarly, Farriss's monumental monograph, although it comes much closer to the Maya, especially on religious matters, is partly defined by her reliance upon Spanish (especially ecclesiastical) sources. Both scholars recognized the limits of the Spanish interpretations: Clendinnen concluded that what characterized Spanish-Maya contact most was a lack of mutual understanding; Farriss remarked that the "Spanish observed only part of what the Indians were up to, and understood even less."[18] These conclusions may also be a reflection of how far our understanding of postconquest Maya society has to go.

Farriss succeeded in doing for Yucatan what Gibson had done for the Valley of Mexico, and just as Gibson left for Lockhart the opportunity to approach the same subject from an indigenous perspective, so did Farriss provide future scholars with a similar opportunity. Farriss's work is Gibsonian in scope, in its historiographical significance and in its comprehensive attention to every aspect of the indigenous experience under colonial rule, and a study such as the present one would not have been possible without Farriss's work as an invaluable tool of reference—regardless of whether new evidence confirms, qualifies, or contradicts her conclusions.[19]

Nevertheless, whereas Lockhart has sought to demonstrate that indigenous societies constituted a "partly autonomous sector" that had to be "studied on its own terms," Farriss's title, *Maya Society Under Colonial Rule*, reflects the fact that the Maya were being viewed from the perspective of colonial, not cah, bureaucracy.[20] Lockhart's work therefore offers a methodological counterbalance as well as a framework for locating Yucatan in the quilt of Spanish provinces. What had been missing from our comprehension was not only an awareness of the ability and capacity of the Maya to function without continual reference to the colonial context but also a sense of the normalcy of indigenous social patterns in the Yucatan of this period—for just as Maya society had been similar in many ways to Nahua society before the conquest, as indeed had all Mesoamerican societies, so did it continue to exhibit these common traits during the colonial period.

It is from the perspective of native-language documentation that some of the most exciting contributions since Roys to the historiography of the postconquest Maya have come. The categories and formats of the documents are still largely Spanish, but the Maya themselves are undeniably both the executors and subjects of these sources, making them "Self"-oriented, and in that way bringing us far closer to the "Other."[21] Victoria Bricker, already a pioneer in the field of hieroglyphic studies, first forged intellectual ties between the language of pre- and postconquest texts, demonstrating that imaginative textual analysis could be invaluable in the recreation of Maya culture. Meanwhile her colleague Munro Edmonson reopened the debate on the meaning and nature of the Chilam Balam literature. The best reinterpretations of that literature (though limited to certain passages only) have come from Allen Burns and from William Hanks, who used his perspective on "language and lived space" among the modern Maya to produce a series of articles analyzing colonial-era Maya texts.[22]

It is rather astonishing, however, in view of the usefulness of this anthropological work in shaping an ethnohistorical approach to Maya notarial documents, that the first analysis of this material was the 1978 dissertation of Philip Thompson, significantly enough a Bricker student. Thompson took a corpus of Maya-language testaments and land sales from the eighteenth-century cah of Tekanto (sources also featured in the present study) and added to them Tekanto's post-1750 parish records to create a "documentary ethnology" of the community that reconstructed key elements of Maya social and political organization. Two aspects of Thompson's work were quite original: his presentation of kinship terminology, and his presentation of the marital and kin links among Tekanto's ruling families at the end of the eighteenth century. Three additional aspects—inheritance patterns, class structure, and political office—fall more fully within the outlines of this study and thus receive a more critical scrutiny with a view to arguing for conclusions that confirm, modify, or contradict Thompson's own.

The historiographical roots of this book, then, are twofold. One is Roys, whose translation and tentative analysis of colonial-era Maya documentation threw out a challenge picked up by Thompson, who applied with fruitful rigor an anthropological methodology to the corpus of Maya notarial material from Tekanto. The other is Lockhart, who led the historical literature on central Mexico toward what he has called a New Philology. This recent "vein of ethnohistory" is characterized primarily by its foundation upon indigenous-language sources. The development of this school from the social history of the late 1960's and early 1970's represents a shift of emphasis from "establishing patterns through synthesis of the diverse action of individuals and small organizations" to paying "attention to key concepts appearing as words and phrases in the sources relating to those individuals and organizations."[23]

Part One of this book introduces and defines the key concepts of the cah and the chibal, before turning to the political manifestations of organization and identity in cah society. Part Two explores the ways in which cah members were differentiated from each other, in terms of status, gender, inheritance practices, and daily life; these internal boundaries are also examined and modified with respect to the function of sexual attitudes and religious expectations in cah culture. Part Three discusses the ways in which the Maya perceived, acquired, and parted with land and other material items, with some context provided by a look at patterns of settlement and land use. Part Four is a more conscious analysis of the Maya-language sources of the book, including a presentation of both general characteristics and some specific genres, complemented by a study of the written use of the Maya language in the colonial period.

The purpose of this book is, if the reader will permit such a conceit, to give a voice to the Maya. It is a retort to Montejo's frustrated insistence that the land was useless and its people forsaken—and it comes unwittingly from the Maya themselves, in their own words.

PART ONE

◌

Identity and Organization

CHAPTER TWO

The Cah: Identity

The cah is ubiquitous throughout the Maya notarial record; it was the fundamental unit of Maya society and culture. Every cah had its place in the geopolitical framework of Yucatan, just as every individual Maya still tied to indigenous community society was a *cahnal*, "cah member," in the general sense, as surely as she or he lived on a cah house plot with relatives of the same, or an associated, patronym group. More than that, the cah-centricity of the Maya world view tended to be tied to one particular cah, always named in the documentary sources; all Maya men and women were rooted by family and friends in the specific cah of their birth (or, in a few cases, of their choosing). That affinity was the basis of Maya society. That being so, before viewing the cah as a geographical, political, and organizational entity, I wish to place it within the context of Maya self-identity.

"Maya"

How will he understand us if he has no grasp of the Maya language?
—cabildo of Bacalar, 1838

The term "Indian" does not appear in this study. It is sometimes claimed that the term is too useful to be abandoned, that it is here to stay, that there is no substitute. These arguments could, indeed have, been used to justify any number of racial epithets. In this case, "Indian" is objected to less because it is a political statement (akin to calling Columbus's contact with the Americas a "discovery") or a misnomer (the misunderstandings of history cannot be undone, although their repetition can be avoided), but because it unnecessarily reflects the colonists' point of view. Not once in all the body of extant Maya documentation seen so far does the term *indio* appear. Neither the Nahuas nor the Mayas imitated this generic category used by Spaniards to describe indigenous peoples in the Americas.

I use the more neutral but equally broad (adjectival) term "indigenous," and the all-purpose "Maya" or "Mayas" (with "Mayan" only to describe the broader language group). We cannot be sure how the word Maya would have been understood by the colonial-era Mayas. The term appears in the Maya notarial record almost always in reference to the language, and in the form *maya than*, "Maya speech": for example, *ma tu nuctic maya than*, "he does not understand the Maya language," as one cah complained of their priest. Occasionally, the term appears as an adjective to a material item—such as *maya pom*, where *pom* is "copal incense."[1]

The use in postconquest Maya material of the word Maya to mean a person appears primarily in quasi-notarial records, and even then it is not widespread. In the Book of Chilam Balam of Tizimin, for example, the word appears just once, between *uchben* and *xok* ("the ancient Maya count"), but it is used to refer to people nine times in the Chumayel, eight of them with *uinicob*, "men, people."[2] Munro Edmonson suggests that "the Maya" are here seen as the Xiu, or westerners of the peninsula, as distinct from the Itza, or easterners. If there was such a regional designation of the term, it is paralleled by its usage in the Title of Chicxulub. In this Pech account of the conquest, the *Maya uinicob* are those non-Pech Maya who resisted the putative conquering alliance of Pech nobles, Spaniards, and Christianity.[3] This, of course, reverses the east-west distinction in terminology that may be present in the Chumayel, although the Pech author of the Chicxulub text also refers to the commoners of that cah as "Maya people," implying a prejudice based on class as much as on region. The sole self-reference of the term that I have found among notarial material is in a 1669 petitionary phrase, *coon maya uinic*, "we Maya men," referring to the members of the municipal council (or *cabildo*) who drew up the document.[4] The context—formulaic opening sentences couched in the highly reverential language typical of Maya petitions (see Chapter 19)—suggests that the phrase is intended to be self-deprecating and indicative of an attitude of humility, even subservience.

The key point is that not only was the use of the term Maya as an ethnic designation rare, but it was even more rarely used as a term of self-description. That it was primarily used as a term of ethnic reference in quasi-notarial texts and not in mundane documentation, and even then in a qualified or compromised sense, suggests that this usage was seen as an archaic or literary term not common to everyday speech. Present-day usage is actually not dissimilar: "Maya" refers to language, not people, except in literary or academic contexts, or sometimes with respect to the inhabitants of Quintana Roo's beyond-the-pale cahob.

It also seems probable that the term was viewed by the Mayas as potentially derogatory—as can be the case today—hence its use by indigenous authors seeking either to humble themselves or to demean others. It is not clear whether the roots of this are preconquest or colonial, but the way in which the term is used certainly does not seem to indicate an ethnic homogeneity of self-perception among colonial-era Mayas. This is not to suggest that the Mayas did not view themselves as distinct in some ethnic sense from non-Mayas (Spaniards obliged Mayas in all kinds of ways to be aware of Spanish ethnocentrism), but they clearly did not recognize that distinction as primary or even legitimate from their cultural perspective. More than that, the Spanish emphasis on ethnic categories was strongly resisted by the Mayas, evidenced not only in the limited use of Maya as an ethnic term but also in the overwhelming importance of deeply rooted nonethnic categories of identity and description. The fact that these categories—cah and chibal—carried ethnic connotations after the conquest reflects not a continuity or profundity of Maya ethnic consciousness but rather the racist constraints of a colonial system that imposed such a consciousness while paradoxically encouraging its weakness by offering partial social mobility to those who collaborated economically or biologically with the colonizers.

Cah and Chibal

The money is to be given to the members of this cah, not to any Spaniards.
—cabildo of Hunucmá, 1819

It is thus fair to say that the Maya lacked a common term of ethnic self-description. Nevertheless, the us-and-them ethnocentricity of the Spaniards was in a sense mirrored in the Maya concept of the outsider, embodied in the Maya *dzul*, "foreigner," a term that had been used in the past to describe intruders from central Mexico and elsewhere, and today is still used to describe non-Maya, Mexicans included.[5] The Spanish term *vecino*, "resident," appears in Maya records as a specific reference to a Spaniard, the indigenous equivalent being *ah cahnal* . . . "he who resides (or was born in) the cah of . . ." When the cabildo of Ebtun remark that *minan besino mix huntul uaye*, "there is no vecino, not one, here," they are saying "there is not a single Spaniard here."[6] Or when the cabildo of Hunucmá state that certain funds "are to be distributed to those of this cah, not to any Spaniard of the cah," *utial c tħox ti ley h cahala mix utial uamac vesinoil tet caha*, they are making a specific distinction between two ethnic groups who, by the time of this particular example (1819), are living in a form of segregated coexistence.[7] Such distinctions are also implicit in Nahuatl statements that, for example, lands are to be sold not to Spaniards but to *nican altepehuaque*, "inhabitants of the altepetl here."[8]

Vecinos and cahnalob (*-ob* is the Maya plural) had been residing in the same towns since the turn of the eighteenth century, not only in *cabeceras* (regional centers designated by the Spaniards) such as Hunucmá or Itzmal/Izamal, or in the *cahob-barrios* (defined below) of Mérida, but also in smaller cahob such as Tekanto. However, the two groups belonged to separate communities, differentiated by race, wealth, culture, and their relationship to the power structure of the colony. Within the "us" group of cah dwellers, Maya self-definition was class-based, with society being divided into *almehenob*, "nobles," and *macehualob* (a loan, possibly preconquest, from the Nahuatl *macehualli*), "commoners," a term that in Yucatan came close to acquiring its colonial central Mexican meaning of "indigenous people." This is indirectly illustrated in a Maya testator's reference to the two varieties of fowl that he is leaving the parish priest in partial payment for a mass to be sung for his soul: *hunpok maseual U lum capok ah castilla*, "one macehual [i.e., indigenous] turkey, two of the Castile variety."[9]

Because the ethnic division in New Spain was also a division between ruler and ruled, macehual could simultaneously mean "commoner," "subject," and "native." This was reinforced by the aforementioned fact that one of the common stylistic aspects of Maya address to high-ranking Spaniards was its overtly deferential and self-deprecating character, so that petitions and similar documents give the impression that macehual was used to describe all Maya. However, though the Spaniards may have fallen for Maya claims of universal poverty, the Maya aristocracy were fully aware of the rhetorical irony of calling themselves commoners instead of nobles, *mehenob*, the "children" of the Spanish addressee, instead of al-mehenob, and *otzil uinicob*, "miserable men," instead of the *noh uinicob*, "important men, elders," that they truly considered themselves to be. The term *uinic*, often adjectivally qualified, was, like *almehen*, only used to describe the Mayas, and was thus an ethnic term by implication.

The ethnic grounding of "cah" is stronger, and the term has deep linguistic roots. There is a semantic and functional connection between the cah and residency, for another *cah* also functions as a verb "to be." It is not clear whether the two words have a common derivation, but they are semantically complementary. The phonetic *ká'ah* (as opposed to *kàah*) can be used verbally in two closely related ways: to mean residency itself—*yn cah lic*, "I live here," "I am here" in an existential sense—or as an auxiliary verb to convey the continuous present indicative—*cimil yn cah*, "I'm dying," a phrase found not surprisingly in testaments.[10] A parallel term to *ah cahnalob* was *ah otochnalob*, similarly indicating residence in the cah but specifically meaning "householder, homeowner" (*-nal* is an agentivizing suffix). When Maya testators state the home cah of their parents, these two terms are used interchangeably.

TABLE 2.1

Maya Terms of Self-Description Containing Ethnic Implications

Term	Variants	Meaning	Context of usage
ah cahnal	cahnal, (ah) cahal / cahalnal, h cahala [late]	cah member, resident	all genres, nonrhetorical, often juxtaposed to vecino ("Spaniard")
ah otochnal		householder, native	same as ah cahnal
macehual	masehual	commoner	rhetorical usage implying "Maya"
mehen		(man's) children	same as macehual
almehen		noble	only to describe Maya nobility
uinic		man, person	sometimes means (Maya) person
kuluinic	u nucil uinic, noh uinic	a principal, or elder	Maya person only
maya uinic		Maya man / person	rare; quasi-notarial sources only
maya than		Maya	the language
ah [cah name]		person of [cah]	Maya person only
ah [patro- nym]		person of [chibal]	Maya person only

SOURCES: Colonial-era Maya-language notarial and quasi-notarial sources.

A further element, that of the patronym groups, or *chibalob* (plural of *chibal*), completed the nexus of Maya self-identity. In addition to the non-specific collectives ah cahnal and ah otochnal, there were two types of specific collective terms of identification: *ah* [cah name]-*ob* and *ah* [patronym] -*ob*. These are pervasive in Maya notarial texts, most often used to describe the holders of particular parcels of land in testaments, bills of (land) sale, and boundary disputes or agreements between cahob. The term *chibal* is rarely used; the chibal is almost always named. Within a given cah, members of a chibal—those of the same patronym—formed a kind of extended family, most of whose members seem to have pursued their common interests wherever possible through political factionalism, the acquisition and safeguarding of land, and the creation of marriage-based alliances with other chibalob of similar or higher socioeconomic status. Such marriages were in part necessary because chibalob were exogamous, a principle that seems to have been applied across cah lines, although after the conquest there was no formal organization of chibal members beyond the cah level. Chibalob were closer to exogamous clans than to lineages, bearing similarities to both, although the Maya term more accurately reflects their particular combination of characteristics.[11]

Table 2.1 summarizes the various terms of Maya self-description. It is clear that cah, chibal, and class primarily determined the way in which the

Maya saw themselves. Chapter 3 will show how naming patterns reinforced these criteria and reflected one more important criterion: gender. In all these, ethnicity is not explicit, only implied by the fact that the Maya maintained their own terms in their own language in contrast to those of the colonizers.

The Maya sense of ethnic self-identity remained far more fragmented than that of the Spaniards not only because the two senses differed in extent at the time of contact but also because the Spaniards of Yucatan were until the late nineteenth century a small, tightly knit group aware to the point of paranoia that they were outnumbered. The community Maya continued to live in the world of the cah, and though this world now existed within the colonial context, on the whole the cultural and administrative links between the cahob and the world of the *dzulob* had little impact on the Maya contextual sense of self.

A comparison with the colonial-era Mixtecs and Nahuas suggests a certain degree of ethno-geographical determinism. As we have seen, Nahua identity tended to focus on the altepetl, in parallel with Maya cah-centrism; both speakers of Nahuatl and Yucatec Maya lived in relatively homogeneous language areas that did not necessitate frequent contact with other indigenous ethnic groups. In contrast, the Mixtecs had a strong sense of ethnic consciousness; those from the Mixteca Alta and Valley of Oaxaca consistently referred to themselves in their own language as *ñudzahui*, "the rain people" or "people from the rain place" ("Mixtec" means "people of the cloud place" in Nahuatl). If this pattern was influenced by the fact that the Ñudzahui have as close neighbors a number of other ethnic groups (there were five distinct languages spoken in the colonial jurisdiction of Teposcolula alone), it would help to explain why the language of ethnic reference of the Yucatec Maya, who lacked close neighbors, had evolved differently. Whereas the Ñudzahui lacked a word for "foreigner," referring to others by their place of origin, the Maya referred to others with the blanket term for "foreigner," dzul.[12]

Whether or not some Mayas felt a sense of macroregional loyalty and identity before the conquest, it is clear that after the imposition of Spanish colonial government Maya self-identity, definition, pride, and loyalty focused on the cah. It was not until the early nineteenth century, when oppressive and hostile activities by the dzulob began to affect more Maya more harshly than ever before, that a real sense of ethnic self-identity was fostered; even then it was Hispanic Yucatecans or Ladinos who redefined their civil war of the 1840's as a caste war. The Spaniards' indiscriminate grouping together of all Maya (with other indigenous peoples of the Americas) as indios had not created a sense of collective identity, but this was achieved by the later indiscriminate labeling of all Maya as the enemy.

Thus in letters from Cruzob leaders to the state governor and other Ladinos, old terms are used in a way quite different from the colonial period—such as *in uinicilob*, or *in masehualob*, to mean "my people," that is, "the Maya." Yet even at this point, neither indio nor Maya appear as a conventional ethnic term in the Maya written record.[13]

CHAPTER THREE

The Cah: Entity

Having established some sense of the conceptual role of the cah in the Maya self-view, we now turn to the cah as a geographical and sociopolitical entity—thus continuing to build the foundations for subsequent discussions of the function of naming and political patterns in Maya identity and organization.

Geography

There is a forest plot at the entrance to the cah, on the road to Dzemul.
—will of Antonia Coba, Ixil, 1767

The cah was a geographical entity, contained within a specific boundary that enclosed the *solares* (house plots) of the community and also included land that could lie many miles from the house plots of the cah. The entity that might be termed the residential cah was thus a well-defined core quite separate in a geographical sense from what would then be the territorial cah. This division is important, in part because it has not so far been emphasized in the historical literature, but primarily because it provides a strong contrast to Nahua patterns, which did not include such a marked distinction.[1]

The core settlement may have been conceived of as a square with four entrances, which were four gates to the four roads that divided the cah into four parts as they converged upon a central plaza. If this was the ideal, as has been suggested, there is little colonial-era evidence for it.[2] Indeed, town plans were not very consistent, and they seem more likely to have been determined by the presence and accessibility of subterranean water. Only the plaza was a consistent feature, not only of preconquest Mesoamerican settlements but also of medieval and early-modern Spanish towns. In both cases the buildings facing the plaza were the religious and administrative centers, as well as the residences of the most important families in the community.[3]

The outlying parcels of land were held according to a variety of tenure types, but land owned by a cah resident was considered as much a part of the cah, to be defended by its officers, as cah land itself, owned by the community and administered by the cabildo. Because of the extended and scattered nature of cah holdings, community border disputes were frequent, and throughout the colonial period the Spanish courts were inundated with inter-cah litigation and related petitions and agreements. Such documentation may have equaled Maya-Spaniard land litigation, even exceeding it prior to the eighteenth-century increase in Spanish land acquisition.

The territorial extension of the cah beyond the cah itself was a consequence of the topography of the peninsula. Farming on a flat limestone shelf covered by a thin topsoil requires frequent fallow periods in order to maintain productivity, and this necessitates access to larger areas of land; this feature may be a source of the common interpretation of preconquest geopolitics, a subject to which we shall shortly return. Ownership of land within the confines of cah territory signified membership in the cah, and the land owned by a cah member helped to define a cah's territory. The cultivated plots that lay outside the residential cah were therefore an important part of the entity, and their names evoke a whole toponymic world particular to each cah. Table 3.1 gives an example of such a world; note that the term *kax*, usually meaning "forest" (i.e., uncultivated, as opposed to "field," usually termed *col*), is used in Ixil to refer to all nonsolar land.

It is to be noted also that although references to the cah and its entrances in descriptions of kax locations show a strong cardinal orientation (see Chapter 15), they do not seem to indicate any quadripartite division or four entrances. It may be that such a division was taken for granted by the cahnalob (cah members) of Ixil, but the indirect evidence of preconquest and modern community settlement patterns makes such an inference unlikely. In thirty years of studying the Maya, Evon Vogt has advanced a number of hypotheses regarding settlement patterns. Three of these, having to do with swidden agriculture, patrilineages, and community layout, that are relevant to the colonial period add up to a picture of Maya settlements consisting of ceremonial centers and outlying dispersed hamlets, with "the bulk of the population living in extended family compounds in the hamlets." This pattern was found to exist even in dense cities such as Tikal, only in compressed form, being still further compressed in Mayapan (which is closer in time and space to our subject of study).[4]

Related to this question of the layout of the cah is that of the layout of family settlement, that is, the house plot (which Vogt calls the extended

TABLE 3.1
Toponymic World of Ixil

Named locations of kax described in testaments

kax "at":

Subinche	Tzucya	Ixculix
Ixku	Ixlochchen	Ixtohil
Ixtucilna	Ixuaytok	Ixualahtun (thrice)

kax "on the road to":

Bena	Chicxulub	Cudzila
Dzemul (twice)	Kaknab	Pacchen
Ixku (twice)		

kax "west of," "north of," "south of," or "southwest of":

Kulche	Ixlochchen (twice)
Ixculix (twice)	

Locations of kax in relation to the cah

tu nohol cah, "south of the cah"
tu nohol be yan lae nak cah, "south of the road that is next to the cah"
tu xaman cah, "north of the cah"
tu chikin u hol cah, "west of the cah entrance"
tu hor cah ber ɔemul, "at the entrance to the cah, on the road to Dzemul"

SOURCE: TI (1765–68); kax location phrases from TI: 7, 15, 30, 36, 55; Restall 1995a.

family compound). The fact that in all the colonial documentation the Maya consistently use the introduced term *solar,* when all other Spanish loans in testaments are used to describe introduced items and concepts only, strongly suggests that the Spanish imposed the house plot upon the cah in an effort to tidy up its layout and make it conform to the early modern urban ideal. Furthermore, the layout instructed in the 1573 Laws of the Indies included the division of the central urban blocks into four sections, called solares.[5] In the poor Cacalchen of the seventeenth century the word solar is not used, but neither are house plots mentioned or bequeathed at all, in contrast to the ubiquity of solars in all eighteenth-century Maya wills.[6] Cacalchen's wills do mention individual trees, chickens, and other objects normally connected with the solar, so presumably houses were located at certain distances from each other on plots without clear borders.

This interpretation is supported by Vogt's precolonial evidence, as well as by the evidence in Edward Kurjack's study of Dzibilchaltun. This community consisted of a central group of buildings (where such features as vaulted structures and roads, or *sacbeob,* were concentrated), around which were residential clusters containing terraces or platforms, which themselves typically supported two to four structures (most of them houses). The striking feature of this Late Classic pattern, from the perspective of the colonial period, is that its organizational principles so much resemble those of the solar-based layout. The central group becomes the plaza onto which

face the church, audiencia buildings when later they are built, stores, and
the most prestigious residential plots; the clusters become the large blocks
of the grid; the platforms or terraces they contain become the solars; which
themselves support a similar number of structures as in preconquest times
(subject to the demographic turbulence of the colonial period). This conceptual correlation would have facilitated a rough and gradual physical
transition from one layout to the other, a transition evidenced by Robert
Redfield's observation that when Chan Kom became a "pueblo" in the
1930's it reorganized its layout into a grid of solars. Chan Kom does not
appear to have existed in the colonial period; for those cahob that did, this
process would have taken place long before the twentieth century.[7]

The layout of the modern cah—visible in aerial photographic maps
better than on the ground—is thus a reflection of the partial imposition of
the urban grid onto traditional less-structured Maya settlement patterns.
Map 3.1 is a stylized reproduction of the aerial view of modern Ixil, a cah
chosen not only because its colonial documentation is the source of much
of this study but also because the lack of modern buildings and apparently
little twentieth-century growth suggest that Ixil looks from the air today

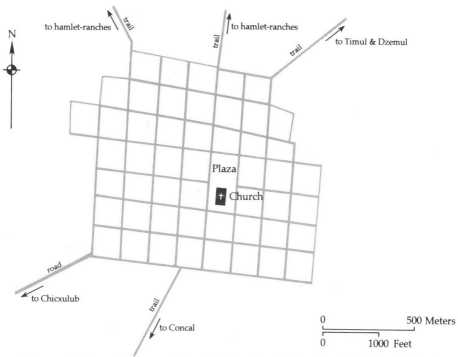

Map 3.1. Modern Ixil. Source: Map "F16C42 Conkal Yucatan," Instituto Nacional
de Estadistica Geografia e Informatica.

much as it did two centuries ago. The squares of the map are blocks, divided into four solars each according to the Spanish model; this division can be observed throughout the peninsula today, and it is supported by colonial documentation—although in colonial-era material, as well as in Ixil and other cahob today, solars are often further divided or linked to neighboring plots.[8]

Sociopolitical Organization

Here in this cah . . . the subunit barrio of Santiago.
—cabildo of Santiago Tihó, 1782

The geographic shape of the cah, and the balance of indigenous and Spanish settlement patterns, bear directly on the question of its internal sociopolitical structure. An elemental part of the Spanish city was the *barrio*, sometimes translated today as "suburb" but in early-modern times more properly meaning an urban subdivision. More apropos, in central Mexico the concept of urban subdivisions facilitated the continuation of a well-developed indigenous subunit system; the altepetl of the Nahuas was divided into (most typically eight) *calpolli* or *tlaxilacalli*, which shared the duties and responsibilities of the altepetl under a system of strict sequential rotation. Similarly, the *ñuu* of the Ñudzahui (Mixtecs) consisted of subunits—termed, according to regional variation, *siqui, siña,* and *dzini*—whose social, political, and economic function was much like that of the calpolli although there were usually more than eight per unit.[9]

The Yucatec arrangement is far less clear. Some scholars have asserted that Maya communities before the conquest were divided into wards called *cuchteel* or *tzucub* or *tzucul*, presided over by an *ah cuch cab*. Another has claimed that *tzucub* was not a geopolitical unit at all but a social system based on gubernatorial lineages, and that *cuchcabal* was not a microunit of the cah but a macrounit, that is, a province made up of various cahob.[10] Indeed, the dictionary definition of *tzucub* is both macrounit ("provincia") and microunit ("parcialidad"); *tzuc* also means a hill or mound, which suggests some relation to preconquest temple mounds as well as to the "hill" (*tepetl*) element in *altepetl*, the Nahua equivalent of the cah.[11]

The confusion stems both from the paucity of preconquest indigenous sources and from the subsequent dependence by historians on comments by Spaniards who did not necessarily understand indigenous arrangements. For the Maya, a cah was a cah regardless of its size and importance, from the tiniest hamlet to the largest town. The Spaniards saw not cahob but *repúblicas indígenas*, which were either *pueblos* (settlements or villages) or *parcialidades* (sometimes wards of pueblos, sometimes relocated or reduced pueblos) or *barrios* (suburbs) of a Spanish town; and if pueblos they were either *cabeceras* (head towns or regional capitals) or their *sujetos* (subject towns). The Spanish perception of a gradation of settlements was not altogether inaccurate, since the size of a cah influenced the nature of its cabildo, and the presence of Spaniards likewise served to undermine indigenous control over political office, prime land, and centrally located residences. On the other hand, Spaniards were so few in number that the acculturative process tended to work in both directions, and differences between cahob as a result of Hispanization can be seen as just some of the many criteria of cah variation. In most of the colonial-era written Maya sources, Spaniards are not mentioned at all; it is the cah that is overwhelmingly important, as a geographical, political, and social unit, indissoluble in the face of variation and change.

If the Spaniards saw in cahob merely pieces of the puzzle that made up *their* Yucatan, they had even less interest in the indigenous organization within the cah (beyond the stipulations and duties of cabildo government). Scholars have created something of a riddle out of the question of the sociopolitical macrounits and microunits of the Late Classic and post-conquest Yucatec Maya. This is, of course, partly owing to the inexact nature of the sources—with historians relying on Spanish-language documentary evidence that is vague and inconsistent, itself based on a poor Spanish understanding of Maya sociopolitical structures—and partly also to the fact that the Maya sociopolitical units were different in construction from both Spanish and Nahua systems. The view evolved, for which evidence was slight, that at the time of contact the Maya were grouped into eighteen dynastic "provinces," consisting of a variable number of towns, each of which was probably subdivided into four. The Spaniards replaced the macrounits (the dynastic provinces) with centralized colonial rule, and the municipal subdivisions somehow disappeared also, leaving "Indian" towns ("pueblos," or "repúblicas indígenas").

Although Gibson grasped the nature of Nahua sociopolitical structure through Spanish sources, it took an analysis of documentary material in Nahuatl before such structures could be understood in depth and detail.[12] Owing to this precedent, it seemed likely that Maya units would also be better understood through the translation of postconquest indigenous notarial documents.[13] That material reveals the cah as the sole central and indisputable unit of Maya sociopolitics, but it provides no direct evidence either of the macrounits that supposedly existed before the conquest or of the subunits of the cah that supposedly existed until the seventeenth century. Therefore a reappraisal of these units is needed, and an outline of such can now be made using the indirect evidence, both old and new.

In both Yucatan and central Mexico, colonial organization outside

Spanish cities and towns was firmly based upon already existing indigenous units, the cah and altepetl, respectively. This organization consisted of
the encomienda, the rural parish, the indigenous (but Spanish-style) municipality, and the system of administrative jurisdiction. As its foundation,
the cah, like the altepetl, far from being diminished by the conquest, gained
in importance during the colonial period.[14] The correlation between indigenous units and those of Spanish rule was not always simple anywhere in
New Spain. Large multi-cah encomiendas in Yucatan, for example, were
broken up into single-cah grants early in the seventeenth century (with
cahob being very rarely divided between encomenderos), although governmental and parish structures remained tied to the cabecera-sujeto system of regional organization. This complex process has been examined in
some detail elsewhere; my concern here is simply to add the perspective
offered by the Maya sources, whose viewpoint reflects the broad outlines
rather than the details of the imposition of the colonial administrative
structure and emphasizes not macrounits but the continued centrality of
the cah.[15]

If, at the cah level, the building of Spanish structures was relatively
straightforward, at the broader level of imperial and ecclesiastical administration, the loose nature of indigenous provincial structures meant that
colonial districts only partly coincided with preconquest ones. Nancy Farriss has suggested that the parish unit was "the one exception to the total
fragmentation of Maya society into separate and equal communities."[16] I
wish to offer a slightly different emphasis, based on three considerations.
First, the traditional centrality of the cah as a sociopolitical unit and the
lack of evidence for well-developed multi-cah units before the conquest
suggest greater continuity, calling into question any "total fragmentation"
after the conquest. Second, the cabecera structure was as much a unit of
provincial government as it was an instrument of the church. Third, the
evidence that this structure neatly correlated with preconquest "provinces" is circumstantial, as Farriss has shown in her attempt to match
parishes to Maya provinces, and as Quezada demonstrated in his mapping
of the so-called *batabil* ("governorship") to the cabecera system.[17] The fact
that some correlation can be made is easily explained by the existence of
certain communities that were larger (and therefore wealthier, more important to the Maya, and more influential among Spanish authorities) than
others both before and after the conquest; the number and regional power
of these dominant cahob would not have been static in either preconquest
or colonial times.

All Maya terms that potentially could apply to sociopolitical subunits
are found for the most part only in dictionaries, where they are given
multiple meanings, or they are used in colonial-era Maya sources to mean

a nonspecific "province." *Cuchcabal*, which would seem to be the Maya term closest in meaning to the Nahuatl subunit term *calpulli*, is used in Maya documents as though it meant "subunit" in general. It could refer to Yucatan itself (i.e., as a subunit of New Spain and a translation of *provincia*), or to a region of Yucatan, or to an entire cah that was a subunit to a broader Spanish entity (e.g., *u cuchcabal bario santigago*, Mérida's "subunit suburb of Santiago"); the use of the agentive term *ah cuch cab* was equally unspecific.[18] Another possible parallel term, used in the Title of Chicxulub, is *cacab*, which Daniel Brinton takes to describe two districts of the cah of Chacxulubchen. But cacab, which can be seen in some Yucatec toponyms, simply means "settlement"; besides which, the same source also calls Chacxulubchen itself a cacab. The text implies that Chacxulubchen (Chicxulub) and the other cacab, Chichinica, were both cahob, with the latter dominated by the former.[19]

The Spanish term that specifically seems to refer to subunits of a cah is *parcialidad*, or ward, but this term nowhere appears in Maya documents, and even in Spanish records it disappears around the mid-seventeenth century—probably not, as has been claimed, because such units themselves disappear, but because the acculturative drive of colonialism had in this sense been halted and even partly reversed.[20] In other words, the concept never had much meaning in Maya society, as the Spaniards of Yucatan came to realize.

The parcialidades that are referred to in late-colonial Spanish records are the cahob that were the subject of *congregación* campaigns instituted periodically from about 1550 to 1750 with a view to concentrating the Maya population in larger towns where they could be more easily controlled as parishioners and tributaries. These campaigns were problematic from the start. For example, of the seventeen cahob that were reduced in 1565 onto the cabecera of Maní (the focus of the Yucatec campaign at that time), eight had been "reconstituted" by 1582—meaning that the Spanish authorities were forced to recognize the effectiveness of Maya resistance to forced resettlement, while apparently never understanding the patterns of land use and social organization that fueled the resistance. The fact that the Maya continued to treat "reduced" communities as independent cahob (often maintaining the territorial cah even when the residential cah now occupied the same site as another), at the same time that Spaniards perceived them as distinct, indicates both why congregación largely failed in Yucatan and the different perceptions that Mayas and Spaniards took of sociopolitical units in the colony.[21]

This is not to say that the cah was a monolith without any kind of subdivision; naturally there were areas that we might call neighborhoods, and there would have been parts of a cah that were considered more desirable residence sites than others. There are also signs that larger cahob acquired more than one patron saint, possibly reflecting either *cofradía* organization or the building of smaller secondary churches.[22] Furthermore, the colonial authorities would have divided a cah according to administrative necessity. For example, a tax and census record of 1795 for cahob in the Izamal region includes opening and closing statements in Maya, referring to the community charges and head tax for Izamal's *"barriob"* and cuchcabal. But the *matrícula* does not offer any clues about Maya sociopolitical organization; although it lists the householders in groups, the place names inserted among the patronyms do not correspond to the groups, and there is no clear indication of who belongs to a barrio of Izamal of who to a cuchcabal, the latter apparently referring not to any subunit of the cah but to the colonial multi-cah jurisdiction of which Izamal was the cabecera.[23]

There was, however, a Maya unit of social organization that was structured between the levels of cah and family and was of great cultural importance to the Maya—the chibal, or patronym group. The chibal was in many ways a substitute for a calpolli-type subunit in that it formed a partial basis for identity, economic organization, and sociopolitical faction within each cah. Patronym groups may also have been part of the basis for the supra-cah organization of the Late Classic "provinces." Although there is no evidence of postconquest chibal organization above the cah level, by the colonial period there was an established tradition of recognizing fellow chibal members from other cahob, possibly aiding them if they were in need, but definitely not marrying them. Furthermore, each "province" consisted of an area of cahob over which an extended ruling family or group of families within one chibal had achieved dominance; the cahob of the Ceh Pech area, for example, were linked by the fact that 90 percent of them were ruled by a Pech batab (cah governor). The role of chibal is reflected in the names of most of these macrounits; for example, the four that encircled Mérida were Ah Canul, Ah Kin Chel, Ceh Pech, and Tutul Xiu, dominated respectively by the Canul, Chel, Pech, and Xiu. The Cupul dominated the area named after them, and the Cocom ruled the cah of Sotuta and neighboring cahob.[24] But there is no evidence that these chibalob (or any other persons or groups thereof) controlled every cah within each "province," nor did they rule the area by means of a system of centralized government.[25] Tsubasa Okoshi has denied the existence of any sort of Late Classic Yucatec political unit based on clearly delineated territories and suggests instead that political power was based on the control of human resources.[26] Carried further, this interpretation is certainly valid in its questioning of the very existence of provinces. Perhaps cahob engaged in rivalries and alliances that, because of the dominance of particular chibalob in some areas, reminded sixteenth-century Spaniards of the provinces or city-states of Europe.

At any rate, if the chibalob effectively created social subdivisions within the cah, they did not constitute geopolitical and sociopolitical subunits like the calpolli subunit of central Mexico; the calpolli subunit, which along with the altepetl is as ubiquitous in Nahuatl notarial records as the cah is in Maya sources, has no parallel at all in comparable Maya documentation.

The riddle of subunits and the Spanish reference to parcialidades in the cahob is further illuminated by the existence and functioning of what might usefully be termed complex cahob. These will be discussed in two groupings: those that I call cahob-barrios, that is, cahob that were seen by the Spaniards as suburbs of a Spanish municipality; and twin cahob, that is, pairs of Maya communities whose relationship was longstanding and perhaps also the product of congregación.

The existence of cahob-barrios throughout the colonial period indicates the persistence of the cah both as a political unit recognized by the Spanish authorities and as the focus of Maya self-identity. Just as the Nahua population of Tenochtitlán-Tlatelolco maintained their own indigenous sociopolities (including governors, cabildos, and geographical jurisdictions), so did the Maya maintain their own cah organization and structure in Mérida, Campeche, Valladolid, and Bacalar (the Spanish *ciudad* and three Spanish *villas* of Yucatan), as well as in administrative cabeceras such as Izamal. In the case of Mérida, Valladolid, and Izamal, the indigenous municipalities maintained their Maya names—Tihó, Saci, and Itzmal.[27] These communities within communities were not absorbed until the nineteenth century, a process that can be traced beginning in the documentary record of late-colonial-period Mérida. Thus "the high degree of continuity" reported by Ida Altman for the Mexico City area, "despite the massive demographic, political, economic, and ecological changes the Indians . . . experienced during and after the conquest," is also found in the Mérida-Tihó area.[28]

In the case of Bacalar and the cabeceras, a notarial document in Maya that contains a list of Maya cabildo officers proves the existence of cah structures (i.e., Maya self-government) in this town.[29] Because there is no sign of more than one cah in such places, these Maya communities might more accurately be termed parallel cahob, rather than cahob-barrios. In Valladolid and Campeche, there were clearly multiple cahob; the number and their toponyms (patron saint names, not Maya names), as well as Spanish references to these communities as barrios, characterizes them as cahob-barrios. Valladolid's notarial records were apparently burned in the Caste War, and no Maya documents from Saci have survived in other archives. Fortunately, census documents from the end of the colonial period indicate that Valladolid had a number of barrio communities, at least one of which, San Marcos, contained a largely Maya population and was probably a cah.

The same census lists five extramural barrios for Campeche, recording details of both the non-Maya ("Europeans," "Spaniards," "Mulattoes," and "other castes") and Maya ("Indians") populations of Guadalupe, Santa Ana, San Francisco, Santa Lucía, and San Román. The detailing of separate records for "Indians" and "Castes" implies that some of these, if not all, were cahob-barrios. The existence of at least three cahob that became suburbs of Campeche is confirmed in Maya-language notarial documents recording a 1737 petition to sell (and the subsequent sale) of cah land that is written and ratified by three separate Maya cabildos. Only the name San Francisco is mentioned in this source, perhaps because he was the patron of the Spanish villa, but the three cahob-barrios of these documents were presumably San Francisco itself and two others from among the remaining four.[30]

What little has been written about the history of Campeche has taken the inevitable Hispanocentric attitude toward its postconquest indigenous communities, emphasizing their role as convenient sources of domestic labor—the very reason, presumably, for the founding of these indigenous satellites by the Spaniards. The sources for such assumptions are vague and intrinsically unreliable. One historian, for example, cites a 1579 *relación* by a Juan de Urrutia to the effect that Campeche's barrios were founded as repositories for Mayas (San Francisco and Santa Lucía) and for "*naboríos mexicanos*" (San Román), but later cites a Spanish source of 1566 stating that Santa Lucía was a barrio of mulattoes, Santa Ana contained "naboríos," and San Román "mexicanos" (as though the two categories were now mutually exclusive).[31]

There are two reasons for such inconsistency. First, Spaniards, from a largely utilitarian perspective, looked upon "Indians" as a single group, generally crediting themselves with all aspects of colonial organization that facilitated the use of these "Indians." Colonial commentators on Yucatan's Spanish municipalities naturally assumed that all barrios had been established by the conquerors to serve their purposes (and also that the repúblicas indígenas were a Spanish creation, which they were, but only as a veneer that covered cah organization). Second, no clear dates for the alleged founding of these barrios can be given, and it seems likely that they were cahob already in existence at the time of the conquest. In the case of Campeche, the link between preconquest and postconquest indigenous communities cannot easily be determined; in all likelihood, communities were moved closer to the new Spanish port-villa, and some were reconstituted to include dependents of one ethnicity or another.

The case of Mérida is more complex, but in many respects more easily clarified. The ethnic classification and listing of barrios by colonial-era Spaniards (and by most historians) is as inconsistent for the capital of the province as for Campeche, for precisely the same reasons.[32] However, our knowledge of Tihó (Mérida) can now be greatly enhanced by the reading of over 200 eighteenth-century indigenous-language notarial documents from Tihó's cahob-barrios.[33] The more coherent history of the city that thereby emerges also helps to illuminate the nature of the cah—in its manifestation as cah-barrio just minutes' walk from the very heart of the Spanish province.

Map 3.2 is a simplified ground plan of Mérida-Tihó as it looked throughout most of the colonial period (and, with slight differences, as the city center looks today). Mérida was founded in 1542 upon the site of the Maya complex cah of Tihó, which consisted of five independent but associated cahob (as the name would imply if we were to take *ti* as the locative prefix and *ho* as "five"). Several of the Books of Chilam Balam and the Title of Chicxulub use the long version Ixcan Tihó or Ichcanziho, glossed as "heaven-born Mérida" by Edmonson and "the place of five serpents" by Brinton, the latter presumably a reference to the iconography on the temples that stood on the five mounds that the Spaniards allegedly found at the site.[34] In fact, only two mounds (marked on Map 3.2) were of a substantial height: one was not cleared or reduced until the 1620's; the other became the foundation of the Franciscan convent that was completed around this same time.[35] The name Tihó therefore probably came not from the mounds but from the number of communities that surrounded the preconquest ceremonial center. There is no direct evidence of how these five cahob functioned in relation to each other before the conquest, although there are some colonial-era instances of five-cah cooperative action.[36] These documents drawn up by more than one cah suggest that Tihó was the sum of its parts, rather than being a sixth entity dominating five subordinates, as Spanish Mérida was to become.

The substitution of the pre-Christian ceremonial core by the *traza* (or urban core) of Spanish Mérida indicates a certain semiotic as well as geographical continuity in urban layout; one form of dominant center was replaced by another. And in spite of the fact that the new center was not only more parasitic than its predecessor but also subject to expansion, there was also a sociopolitical continuity that lasted into the nineteenth century. The five cahob of Tihó continued to function as Maya communities, complete from their *batabob* (batabs) to the structures of their central plazas, although they are all a short walk from the plaza mayor of Mérida, and were considered by the Spanish to be barrios of their city.

Whereas Spaniards invariably referred to these five Maya municipal-

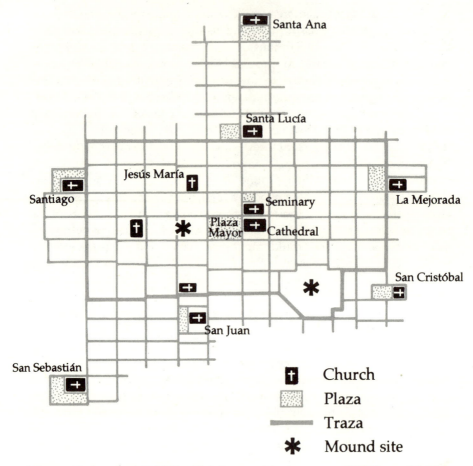

Map 3.2. Early-colonial Mérida-Tihó. Sources: Hunt 1974: 244; INEGI map "F16C52 Mérida Yucatan"; field notes, 1992.

ities as barrios, almost all references in Maya-language material classify them as cahob. The typical identifying phrase is the classic formula for all cahob: *uay ti cah san sevastian*, "here in the cah of San Sebastián." In the second half of the eighteenth century, the proximity of Mérida and the influence of Spanish classifications produced fuller descriptions, such as *uay tu cahal san sebastian tu bario san sebastian nak lic u noh cahal cuudad de Mérida*, "here in the cah of San Sebastián, the barrio of San Sebastián, here beside the great cah, the city, of Mérida." Mérida was thus a separate entity, whereas Tihó not only included the cahob-barrios but was, as it had always been, the sum of the five communities, with in many cases the center as well; a resident of San Cristóbal was also *ti noh cah ti hoo*, "in the great cah of Tihó (or Ho)."[37]

The assertion that Santa Ana, La Mejorada, San Cristóbal, San Sebastián, and Santiago were all preconquest cahob requires some justification, particularly in view of the fact that there are few surviving Maya documents from these communities earlier than 1713 and none before 1665. Four points can be noted. First, these sources survive in an archive where very few pre-1713 (and no pre-1689) Spanish documents are extant. We know from Spanish references elsewhere that such communities existed in the early colonial period; it is their nature that is in question.

Second, the possible "five" in Tihó and the survival of Maya documents proving that there were five colonial-era cahob encircling the traza seems too much of a coincidence, particularly considering the even distribution of the five around the core area—with Santiago and La Mejorada equidistant from the preconquest-colonial central square, which is located within a pentagon that would be created by drawing imaginary lines between all five cahob (see Map 3.2 above and Map 3.3 below).

Third, the five cahob-barrios were not the only barrios of colonial Mérida; there were also San Juan and Santa Lucía. These were not cahob-barrios, however, but were of a much later date and quite unrelated to the Maya community. There is not a single Maya record in any archive from either of these barrios; Spanish records make no mention of any Maya cabildo in either place; and in Spanish-language records of sales in these barrios going back to the 1660's there is not a single mention of the involvement of a Maya person. The communities grew up around chapels built in 1552 and 1575, respectively, to accommodate a Spanish population that soon after 1600 began to outgrow the traza, both being located closer to the plaza mayor than the five cahob-barrios; both were populated not by community Maya but at first by fringe elements of Spanish society (poor Spaniards, persons of mixed race, and black and Maya domestics) and later by Spanish vecinos and their auxiliaries. Moreover, both communities were subordinate to the city center in civil and ecclesiastical organization, unlike the cahob-barrios, which from the onset were politically self-governed and were either parishes in their own right or ecclesiastically subject to another cah-barrio. Other Maya communities eventually became suburbs of Mérida; but these were not among the original five, being far too distant to have been directly included in the preconquest settlement, even though the early loss of Maya toponym by a community such as Santa Catalina implies heavy Spanish influence from the start.[38]

Fourth, remarks such as fray Alonso Ponce's 1588 statement that San Cristóbal was inhabited by naborías from central Mexico does not mean

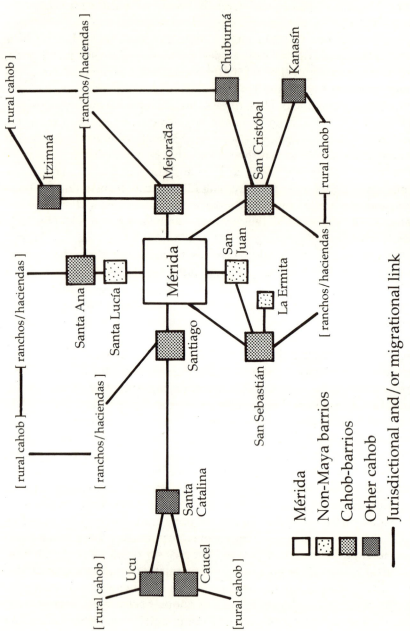

Map 3.3. The jurisdictional and migrational sphere of Mérida-Tihó, late-colonial period. Sources: Hunt 1974: 243; AGEY-CP, 1, 1 (Census of 1809); Maya notarial documents in ANEY.

that a Maya cah did not exist before the arrival of Nahuatl speakers. Had the barrio been founded by Spaniards and Nahuas, we might logically expect it to have developed sociopolitical forms that were not so typically Maya. Seventeenth-century references to Mexican elements in some Maya barrios are probably a more accurate reflection of the original situation.[39] In fact, there is no evidence at all that any of the cahob-barrios did *not* exist before the conquest. The lack of sixteenth-century references to San Sebastián, for example, simply places that cah in a category with many other cahob invisible at first owing to the paucity of extant records from earlier decades; as document survival picks up after 1650, and as Mérida's direct influence expands, San Sebastián begins to appear in the notarial record—immediately as a fullfledged cah. That the first church construction at La Mejorada is not recorded until 1610 does not mean that the community did not exist before this date; indeed, a fullfledged cah is implicit in the seventeenth-century documentation.

The reason that the notarial records of the cahob-barrios begin to show up in numbers after the year 1725 is not simply a matter of less deterioration of the written page; rather, it is an apparent consequence of the expansion of Mérida by the Spanish population's (technically illegal) purchase of property and settling in the cahob-barrios.[40] This process, captured well by Marta Hunt from the perspective of the Spanish-language sources, is reflected similarly in Maya-language bills of sale (see Chapters 16 and 17 below). San Sebastián's location on the road to Campeche exposed it to Spanish incursions sooner than Santa Ana, to the north of the traza; Santiago and San Cristóbal, larger and closer to the traza, were drawn into the Spanish world earlier still. The importance Hunt gives to Santa Catalina can be misleading; as she herself recognizes, it was simply one of a number of more distant communities subject to the cahob-barrios, through whom the cahob themselves received Spanish influence.[41] The traffic went both ways: Mayas were drawn into Mérida in a relay system that began in the rural cahob and ran through the cahob-barrios' satellites and into the city (although this was just one of a number of different Maya migration patterns).[42] These inter-cah relationships and the ethnic-organizational status of the communities in the Mérida-Tihó sphere of influence are illustrated in Map 3.3.

Map 3.3 (not to scale) is a schematic representation of the approximate location of Spanish and mixed-race residential areas in relation to the rings of cahob that spread out from the Spanish capital in the late-colonial period like ripples in a pond. (La Ermita, for example, is a suburb not included in Map 3.2.) The lines that connect the communities on the map also convey the manner in which rural Maya migrated into satellite cahob or (in the late-colonial period) onto *haciendas*, and from there into the suburbs. The satellite cahob in the map have been chosen because these became subject to certain cahob-barrios, which acted as cabeceras with jurisdiction over them as well as over several dozen haciendas, *ranchos*, and *sitios* (Spanish-owned estates) in the Mérida-Tihó environs (listed in the census records mentioned earlier).

It is worth emphasizing here a point to do with Maya migration made more fully in Chapter 13: in the colonial period, as today, Maya movements were not necessarily permanent; slash-and-burn agriculture had long produced a model of permanence coupled with itinerancy, reflected in the manifestation of the cah as both residential core and territorial spread. The work opportunities of colonial and modern Mérida accord happily with that model, enabling migrants to maintain ties with their rural cahob. Thus the evolution of Mérida-Tihó was and is far more complex than mere growth and acculturative melting.

In spite of the inevitable intrusion of the Spanish world on the cahob-barrios, it remains important to emphasize the survival of cah organization and identity to the very end of the colonial period. As Hunt pointed out, by looking solely at Spanish sources, "it is difficult to determine whether the Indians of San Cristóbal had preserved any corporate identity as late as 1700."[43] Maya sources can now show us that San Cristóbal and its neighbors certainly had preserved their corporate identity, as we shall see in chapters to follow where use is made of the Tihó documents; suffice to say a few words here on the form and content of this material.

The documents are overwhelmingly bills of sale for urban solares, or house plots, with a minority being sales of cultivable land outside the residential cah. Even in this sense these communities conformed to the cah model; the documents follow the formulas and formats used in cahob throughout the province.[44] The very existence of such documents confirms that a sense of corporate identity in all five communities clearly survived not only 1700, but 1800 and beyond—yet the intrusion of the Spanish language into the notarial business of the cahob-barrios is a symbol of an increased Spanish residential intrusion by the turn of the nineteenth century. The first extant example of a solar sale by a Maya to a Spaniard, conducted by a cah-barrio cabildo but written in Spanish, is from Santiago in 1759; such records do not become common, however, until after about 1795, and even then the hand is still distinctly Maya, as is the form, including the cabildo officers' names listed at the bottom. By 1809 (the example is from Santa Ana) a solar sale in Spanish no longer even necessarily involves a Spaniard: the Canul family are selling to a Pool before a body of witnesses, cabildo included, that is entirely Maya except for two mestizos. The last extant sale in Maya from any of the five is dated 1809; the same process continues in Spanish to at least 1840.[45]

Perhaps a still more evocative symbol of Mérida's increasing embrace of the cahob-barrios lies in the startling discovery that Spaniards were using the very batab of the cabildo in Santiago as a property-purchasing agent. Sometime between 1793 and 1797 don Marcelino Bacab succeeded his father, don Marcelo Bacab, in the batabil of the cah; as soon as he appears in the record as cabildo head, presiding over the sale of plots in Santiago to Spaniards, he also appears as some sort of real estate broker—acquiring, for example, the power of attorney for one Josef de Acosta, to enable the Spaniard to buy land from Manuel Chan in 1802. Clearly, whatever don Marcelino's sense of community loyalty was, it had no ethnic dimension. In not perceiving a conflict of interest between the responsibilities of the batabil and the role of estate agent for outsiders, don Marcelino may not have been alone. Yet the sudden frequency with which sales in Santiago to Spaniards appear in the record during this particular batab's term of office implies that he helped open the doors to a Spanish invasion that had been delayed for 250 years.[46] Under Mexican rule this invasion was to be fatal to Maya corporate identity, not only in the cahob-barrios but also in a satellite cah such as Itzimná.

Complex cahob have been defined here as those that existed or functioned in significant relation to others, taking as examples (because they are documented) the cahob-barrios of Mérida and Campeche; by the same definition, twin communities such as Uman and Dzibikal were also complex cahob.[47] Cahob were drawn together during the colonial period by the growth of Spanish communities, by the resettlement policies of congregación, or by the sheer proximity and competition for resources. Whatever the colonial impact was, the integrity of these communities as cahob survived in spite of Spanish attempts to reduce some of them to some form of mere subdivision. The grouping of communities had preconquest precedent, and the conquerors' choice of Tihó as the site for their provincial city ensured the survival of the five preconquest Tihó cahob; but there were presumably other groupings that did not survive the upheaval and demographic decline of the mid-sixteenth century. Indeed, pre- and postconquest evidence points toward a pattern of paired communities—what might be termed "twin cahob."

On a large number of lowland Maya sites archaeologists have uncovered causeways—sacbeob, "white roads"—that linked two ancient communities. These range in length from a few kilometers to the 16 kms of the Uci-Cansahcab sacbe, to the 32-km Ake-Itzmal causeway, to the longest of all, the 100-km sacbe between Coba and Yaxuna. Scholars have speculated that the ancient Maya would normally have traveled by shaded trails, leaving the causeways primarily for ceremonial purposes.[48] Significantly enough, the ceremonial pairing of Maya towns in modern Yucatan is widespread, often involving the sharing of a revered Virgin or other saint image or the ranking of one image over another, making it necessary to transport the image in the annual holy procession from one community to another. One such pairing, between Tetiz and Hunucmá, is infamous throughout the peninsula, owing in part to the huge market and fiesta of the ceremonial day and in part to a running feud between the two towns.[49] Other ceremonial or celebratory modern pairings are Ekpedz and Chikidzonot, and Dzoncauich and Buctzotz.

The long survival of pairings suggested by this evidence is confirmed in colonial-era Maya documentation. Pairs of cahob drew up petitions and land sales that formed single documents but were written and ratified by two separate and complete indigenous cabildos. The motivations behind such relationships were apparently not only common interests but also shared land boundaries, but though these considerations produced joint petitions and border agreements ratified by more than one cabildo, the pairings themselves were not necessarily long-term and consistent. Tetiz and Hunucmá, and Ekpedz and Chikindzonot, are among such pairs. The documents they produced are similar to the multi-cah land sale of the cahob-barrios of Campeche, but these twin cahob were never subject to absorption from larger Spanish communities, nor did they ever become physically linked as a result of urban growth.

One pair, Uman and Dzibikal, is an example of a slightly different phenomenon. Although the two communities were separate organizational and territorial cahob, they were as a result of Spanish policy both located on the same residential site. One document from these twin cahob refers to them significantly as *ca tzucil cah*, but this is not the *tzucul* or *tzucub* that was allegedly a subunit of the Post Classic cah, and that might suggest a glossing of "the two wards of the cah"; rather it is ɔuc (*dzuc*), a numeral classifier used for settlements, giving the phrase the meaning "the two cahob." Uman and Dzibikal were also connected geographically and in Spanish eyes to a third cah, Dzibikak, which was the subject of reduction attempts and survives today as a small settlement a few kilometers from Uman. Subordinate communities may have lacked their own batab, as a Dzibikal record of 1669 implies, but they had their own cabildos and were viewed by the Maya as cahob in their own right, regardless of colonial designations; in a land treaty of 1815, where the Maya uses "cah" in reference to Dzibikal and Dzibikak, the accompanying Spanish translation uses "parcialidad." Uman may have dominated Dzibikal and Dzibikak, but they were not its subunits—just as Calkiní claims in the Title of that name that it dominated (but did not consist of) Nunkiní, Mopila, and Pakam. Also paired were Espita and Tzabcanul, the latter termed a parcialidad by

Spanish officials but apparently considered a fullfledged cah by the Maya, complete with its own batab and cabildo.[50]

Congregaciones, or forced resettlements, by the Spanish authorities shortly after the conquest had an important effect on twin cah traditions, but the fact that such traditions existed at all needs to be emphasized in this context. The ability of the Maya to maintain independent cah identities within multi-cah relationships, combined with the mobile nature of Maya settlement patterns, undermined the ultimate impact of relocation policies. The congregación campaign of the early 1550's was no doubt traumatic and disruptive to Maya life. Yet so were many other aspects of the conquest, including warfare, religious persecution, and massive epidemics, none of which destroyed the basic institutions of the Maya community. This was due not only to the tenacity of the cah but also to the fact that adaptation and manipulation—not destruction—served Spanish ends. For resettlement programs to be successful in the long run, they must be reinforced for many generations.[51] Yucatan's colonial authorities not only failed to reaffirm congregación consistently after its initial application, but also, as mentioned above, permitted the reversion of the original campaigns. Between 1565 and 1582 (when a second minor round of congregación was enforced in the Maní and Tizimin areas), nearly 40 percent of the communities previously relocated were returned to their original sites, and during the early seventeenth century cahob around Tizimin, Calkiní, and other areas continued to return to original sites, with or without Spanish supervision. Subsequent efforts to reduce cahob in 1688–89 likewise failed, and Yucatec authorities refused to obey royal edicts of congregación in the early eighteenth century.[52]

Reduction reversal was consolidated by the Maya themselves in three ways. One was the maintenance of cah structures of social and political organization by the resettled community, which ensured a continuation of identity and function that bridged the period of geographical dislocation. Second, although the residential cah may have been transplanted, the territorial cah was left intact, allowing the cabildo and landowning families of the cah to continue working and exchanging the same fields and forests. Third, landholding continuity stimulated an old pattern—the creation and growth of satellite communities that eventually become cahob themselves—because it necessitated travel back to the original cah site.

These aspects of continuity in Maya settlement have been recognized by historians, but there has been little emphasis on their combined implication, that in the long run congregación was but one aspect of a Maya settlement tradition that featured both mobility and an enduring attachment to the cah as an entity and a source of identity.[53] Certainly a number of cahob disappeared after the conquest; but this was neither the first nor the last time such a thing had occurred. More significantly, the vast majority of cahob survived both the conquest and the colonial period. This emphasis on persistence (and preconquest precedents to complex cahob) is the Mayacentric perspective; an emphasis on congregación (and its use to explain complex cahob) would have been the Spanish perspective.[54]

Some of the issues surrounding a fuller definition of the cah have now been addressed, particularly questions relating to geopolitical and sociopolitical macrounits and subunits, as well as the existence of what I have called complex cahob. But the cah was more than simply the Maya municipal community. What remains to be discussed is what these minority variants had in common with the rest of the cahob—the workings of cah society.

CHAPTER FOUR

Names

The naming system of a social or cultural group can be an indicator of so-cial status; a person's name can communicate to others within (and, under certain circumstances, outside) the group where that person ranks in rela-tion to them. Such information invariably includes gender, but potentially also covers age, descent, and ethnic or regional origin. The evolution of personal naming patterns among the Maya of colonial Yucatan not only reflects broader postconquest social relations but also provides additional evidence of the determinatives of Maya identity and social organization.

Change

He was ruling as batab when he was given a name here in this cah.
—description in the Title of Yaxkukul of the christening
of Macan Pech as don Pedro Pech

The information available to us on preconquest naming patterns is derived from documentation drawn up after the arrival of the Spaniards that identifies persons (almost all males) alive in the sixteenth century, such as the books named after Chilam Balam, the Titles of Calkiní, Chicxu-lub, Yaxkukul, and the Xiu, and a few early-colonial notarial sources. The consistency of this information enables us to be fairly sure of how the Maya named their children, and what, therefore, they gave up or kept when they accepted christening. Simply put, a man received two formal names, the first being his mother's matronym, to which he prefixed a *na* (meaning "mother"), the second being his father's patronym. A woman was named likewise, the difference being that her maternal name was prefixed with an *ix*. Thus the son of Namay Canche and Ixchan Pan was Nachan Canche.[1] Had the couple had a daughter, she would have been called Ixchan Canche.

TABLE 4.1
Evolution of Maya Naming Patterns

Name types	Preconquest	Postconquest	Present day
nickname	✓	✓	✓
Christian name		✓	✓
father's patronym	✓	✓	✓
mother's matronym	✓		
mother's patronym			✓

SOURCES: Maya-language notarial documents; Roys 1940; Sullivan 1989; Hanks 1990; Everton 1991; 1991–94 Yucatan field notes.

On the face of it, such a system would seem to lack any potential for creative flexibility or imagination on the part of the parents, besides the fact that brothers would all be named identically, as would sisters. These considerations are doubtless the root of the appellations ascribed to pre-Christian Mayas that do not fit the above pattern—their "given" names. In the only published study of Maya names, Ralph Roys places these other names into three categories: "boy names," "jesting names," and "unclassified names" (the latter being those that he was unable to interpret). Because the distinction between these categories is slight, in Table 4.1 I have elided them into one—"nicknames"—all the names therein being descriptive in some sense or another. Many are humorous: Ah Xochil Ich, "owl face"; or Ah Tupp Kabal, "he whose belly button resembles a potter's wheel."[2] Most were probably granted in childhood; Landa remarks that the Maya "tradition was to call their children by different names until they were baptized or somewhat grown up, after which they dropped those names and began calling themselves after their fathers until they were married, when they took the names of both father and mother."[3]

Although there is no documentary evidence that nicknames persisted after the conquest, I suggest that they did, for several reasons. First, such names would not have been placed on record anyway; by definition, written documents would only have listed "formal" names. Second, the tendency to bestow upon one's offspring the same Christian name as oneself meant that two men in the same family might have the same formal names, necessitating abbreviations or nicknames.[4] Third, the use of nicknames that satirize a person's physical or behavioral traits is common among the Mayas today; this does not prove continuity, but it seems unlikely that such a practice would disappear and reappear in conjunction with our chronological designations.[5] In fact, as we shall see, colonial-era Maya nicknames may also have taken on a new form resulting from postconquest changes in the formal naming system.

With the adoption of a Christian first name, the Maya abandoned the *na/ix* name, but retained the patronym. Although a woman did not change her patronym upon marriage (nor, indeed, did early-modern Spaniards), her children of both genders would bear the appellative mark of only their father. This would appear to imply the destruction of maternal lines of descent and the lineal or dynastic importance of women, but in other respects the female role in Maya society was of considerable significance and it does not seem to have been seriously damaged by Spanish colonialism (see Chapter 10). There is not one instance in the colonial record of a Maya using his or her maternal patronym (i.e., the Spanish practice, not the preconquest Maya system) in addition to the paternal patronym, although that has become Maya practice today.

Such practice, presumably an example of Spanish influence rather than a partial resurfacing of the preconquest Maya recognition of matrilineality, may have begun in the nineteenth century, at least in the Maya communities around Mérida. A don Pedro Nolasco Camal is batab of San Cristóbal in 1815, a single example that suggests the diffusion of a Spanish last-name system down from those most subject to Spanish influence, the Maya elite in the capital of the colony. Indeed, it is in the cahob-barrios of Mérida, in the final half-century of the colony, that the strict model of two names is broken to accommodate a second Christian name, almost always following "Juan." This is not the same as two surnames, but it could be a step in that direction, especially in the case of a name such as Juan Ramos Canche.[6]

Of tangential relevance here is the fact that the Nahua use of Christian names appears to have been prejudicial to women, in that the early colonial naming of females was seemingly "conservative and also not very important" (in S. L. Cline's words), whereas male Christian names were far more varied—although the first names of Nahua women became equally varied later in the colonial period.[7] This was not the case in Yucatan; Maya-language evidence shows a variety in Christian names equal among both genders. In choosing Christian names for their children, men did not appear to favor sons over daughters: a Francisco or Pasqual was just as likely to name a daughter Francisca or Pasquala as to name a son after himself. More often, in fact, a man was named after his grandfather. The Maya seemed to have had more of a liking than either the Spaniards or the Nahuas for Christian names that had male or female counterparts, such as Pasqual-Pasquala, or Bernardino-Bernardina. One Mayanized Christian name, xpab, appears to feminize a Spanish name by using a Maya female prefix, although it is not clear whether the original name was Fabiana or Pablo (made, as it were, into Pabla).[8]

The Titles of Calkiní, Chicxulub, and Yaxkukul all recount the moments when the dynastic leaders whose causes the documents trumpet accepted baptism and acquired a Christian first name.[9] The impression given is that the process was significant and symbolic (of the acquisition of status within the colonial social system), but not difficult or traumatic. This reflects the Titles' somewhat distant perspective on the conquest period, partly as a result of the post-sixteenth-century date of extant versions. Yet the same impression with regard to Christian names is given by documentation whose early date is not in dispute. In a land document of 1569 a Juan Pox refers not only to his father in pre-Christian nomenclature (Nadzul Pox) but also to his elder half-brother (Napuc Pox), while in a 1628 record Melchor Mex remarks that he is selling the lands of his grandfather, Napuc Coba; it is as though one's name was simply determined by one's age relative to the arrival of the Spaniards.[10] One almost imagines the Maya population changing names with the ease with which we might file a change-of-address form at the post office.

Yet this was surely not the case. There is abundant evidence of the ambiguous acceptance of other aspects of Christianization by the Maya, particularly during the first two generations after the conquest, and the Mayanization of some of these forms over the subsequent centuries.[11] What probably did not exist was a temporary system that mixed preconquest and Christian practice—a transition stage like that of early colonial central Mexico.[12] Certainly there is little documentary evidence for this, limited to one Spanish source, Bishop Gómez de Parada, who claimed in 1722 that "the Indians" were still "calling themselves by their names from pagan times . . . to the extent that we have seen husbands who do not know the Christian names of their own wives."[13] Furthermore, the simplicity of exchanging a *na* name for a Christian name while retaining the Maya patronym did not lend itself to a Nahua-style transition. In a sense, of course, the postconquest Maya practice is a bicultural mixture: Maya nicknames must have persisted, but at the same time Maya acceptance of Christian names was not straightforward; in fact, these foreign first names were Mayanized, following a largely subconscious process whereby the Maya heard, repeated, and consolidated Christian names according to the principles of their own phonological system.

The evidence for this contains no surprises. The orthographic variations employed by Maya notaries in writing Spanish Christian names (see Table 4.2) are similar to such variations found in the writing of the surnames of Spaniards from outside the community, or the names of Spanish legal procedures, or indeed Spanish loanwords in general (see Chapter 22). One infers that the Maya had an uncertain notion of what these names should sound and look like, since Spaniards wrote them one way and the Maya pronounced them another way (sometimes hypercorrecting themselves); and because cah residents, especially notaries, seldom heard these

TABLE 4.2

Colonial Maya Spelling Variants and Modern Maya Usages of Some Christian Names

Spanish	Colonial Maya renderings	Modern Maya usage
Alejandro	alegadro	
Antonio	antoyo	Anto
Aparicio	apalaçio, ablasio [could be Ambrocio]	
Baltesar(a)	Bartessara, Batisar, Blatasar	
Bartolome(o)	Baltolomen, Bartorome, Bardoromen, balturme	
Basilia	bassia	
Bautista	Bap^{ta}	
Bernabe	Belnaber, benaber	
Bernard(in)o/a	Ber^{na}, ber^{na}da, belnaldino, berdino/a	
Blas	balas	
Carlos	calos, caras	
Cipriano	Sipirian	
Clemente	cremete	
Cristóbal	xtouar, xpoual, xpual	Tobal
Dionisio	Donisio	
Esteban	esstevan	Es
Eugenio	Uhenio	
Evaristo	Eb^{to}	Eb
Fabiana	xpab, pabiana	
Felipe	pelipe, felip	Fi [could be Fidelio]
Félix	felis, felisto	
Gabriel	gravier, grabyer, grabrier	
Gerónimo	gelonimo	
Gregorio	glegolio	
Hernando	Jernado, He^{do}	Nado
Hilaria	Ylalia	
Isabel	Ysaber, Sabel	Isa
Isidro	zidro	
Jacinto	Jasintho, jassinto	
Joaquin	juachin, Ju^{o}chin, juanchim	
José(ph/f)	Joseh, Josep, Juysep, Ju^{o}phe [could be Juan Felipe]	
Juan(a)	Ju^{o}, Jauana	
Juan de la Cruz	Ju^{o} de z, Ju^{o} caras	
Juan Espiritu Santo	Ju^{o} espitu s^{n}	
Poncia	lipansia, yliponsia, liponsa	
Leonardo	elnardo, leonno, leuudano, laurianodo [could be Lauriano]	
Lorenso/a	Rorenso, Rorenssa	Lol
Luisa	luuissa	
Magdalena	madalen^{a}	
Manuel(a)	man^{ra}	Man
Maria [etc.]	marlia, malia crus, marianebes	Mali
Maria Candelaria	ma^{a} can^{d}, mali^{a} candelalia	
Mateo	mathe^{o}	Mate, Teo
Matias	mathais, Martias	
Melchor	mechor	
Miguel	ming^{l}, minger	Minguel
Nicolás(a)	Micolassa	Nico
Pablo/a	pabro, xpab	Pab
Pasqual(a)	Pasguara, Pas, py^{ra}	
Rosa	Rosasa, Rossa, lossa, lohça	Losa

TABLE 4.2
Continued

Spanish	Colonial Maya renderings	Modern Maya usage
Salvador(a)	sar[ol], sarua[or], sarua[a]	
Sebastián	sebas	
Silvestre	silbes[te]	
Teodora/o	teudora, thenidoro	
Ursula	ulsula	
Ventura	Bentula, Bon[ra], vyula	
Victor	Bicto	V/Bicto
Viviana	Bibi[a], bibiyana	

SOURCES: Maya notarial documents; for modern attestations: field notes 1991–92; Sullivan 1989; Hanks 1990; Everton 1991.

Christian names as pronounced by Spaniards and had no model or standard spelling for them, they either attempted to reproduce the names as accurately as possible, or they reproduced them in such a way that reflected local pronunciation. In other words, the Mayanization was a straightforward phonological process.

I have not systematically counted and dated these variants, but it is my impression that there is a shift in the late eighteenth century toward conventional Spanish spellings of Christian names, although notarial sources point to a less thorough and slightly later change (with early-nineteenth-century variants easily found) than that observed by Frances Karttunen in baptismal records of 1740–80.[14] Versions of Spanish Christian names consistent with Maya phonology can still be seen in correspondence between Mayas and anthropologists in the field in the 1920's and 1930's, and many are still in use today. Table 4.2 lists some of these modern usages; no doubt many others are common, but since they are not unique to Maya, they must reflect conventional Spanish abbreviations and diminutives as well as the persisting logic of (or assimilation to) Maya phonology.

One additional aspect of colonial-era Maya names was a postconquest innovation. The use of *don* (and its feminine counterpart, *doña*) as a prefix indicating noble status was a rigidly conferred Spanish practice that became increasingly flexible during the colonial period (among Spaniards and Nahuas too), evolving toward today's usage of *don* in the Spanish-speaking world as merely a common term of respect. The Mayas, on the other hand, maintained their own strict application of the prefix during colonial times, granting it only to *indios hidalgos* (a class of indigenous nobility recognized by the Spanish authorities) and to batabs past and present. Effectively the don functioned as a substitute for many of the preconquest titles of high status and office that under colonial rule fell into disuse or—like *halach uinic*, "the true man"—became applied to high-ranking Spaniards such as Yucatan's governor.[15]

Continuity

> All of them live on this house plot: Dominga Cab and Maria Cab, Fran-
> cisca Cab, Rosa Cab, and Francisco Cab; and the children of the deceased
> Josef Cab, Isidro Cab, Ana Cab, and Simona Cab.
> —cabildo of Ixil, 1767

A comparison of Maya, Nahua, and Ñudzahui practices, pre-Christian
and colonial, illuminates the other main aspect of postconquest Maya
names: the indigenous patronym. The lack of lineage surnames in pre-
Columbian central Mexico (even ruling dynasties bore sets of names
rather than surnames) carried over into the early colonial period. The
Nahuas adopted Spanish names but not the Spanish system of hereditary
or family nomenclature. Until about the 1620's many Nahuas still had
indigenous last names that were not patronyms but reflected a preconquest tradition of naming a child after its birthdate: Acatl, for example
(Reed), or Quauhtli (Eagle).

Yet the prevailing Nahua trend was to use Spanish names as a complex
denotation of social status. Thus Juan Diego, having two first names, or
simply Juan, would be at the opposite end of the scale from don Hernando
Cortés, of whom there were many among the central Mexican indigenous
aristocracy owing both to the proliferous sponsorship of the conquistador
and to the mark of nobility that his name represented long after his death.
In between (in order of ascending social status), were surnames taken from
the saints, surnames taken from Christian doctrine, such as "de la Cruz,"
and Spanish surnames of varying social prestige. The passing of a surname
from parent to child was relatively rare.

The Ñudzahui system in the Oaxaca region was similar to that of the
Nahuas. Preconquest Ñudzahui names were calender-based and did not
constitute lineage or family surnames. The Ñudzahui adopted Spanish
Christian names shortly after the conquest (as did indigenous peoples
throughout Spanish America), but maintained calendrical surnames into
the seventeenth century, when they gradually adopted Spanish surnames
(in a more prolonged and slightly later version of the similar transition
among the Nahuas). Again, as in central Mexico, the Ñudzahui naming
system conveyed social status through the types of Spanish saint names or
surnames chosen, with the system still based on choice, not on lineage.
Although this summary does little justice to the evolution of these systems
over time, to regional variations, or to the subtlety with which they reflected social differentiation, it does provide the basis for a comparison.[16]

First, the Maya already had and continued to retain their patronyms.
For example, a high-ranking Maya noble sponsored by the conquistador of
Yucatan was renamed at baptism don Francisco de Montejo Xiu; the pre-

conquest patronyms in Yucatan carried a lineage and organizational significance too important to be abandoned. In fact, the example of don Francisco de Montejo Xiu is a rare one, in that even the adoption of Spanish patronyms as extensions of first names was an early colonial phenomenon limited to those dynastic leaders involved in the conquest or to their sons. Even in this case the full form does not seem to have survived, for a Maya noblewoman of Tekax referred to her grandfather in her will of 1689 as "don Montejo Xiu."[17]

Second, the Maya chibal system was not used to denote social differentiation in the same way; a particular patronym indicated status in a particular cah, but patronyms were not borrowed or granted. Therefore the Maya did not borrow Spanish surnames as Nahuas did. The mass of notarial documentation in Maya reveals that the only Mayas who had Spanish patronyms were residents of Mérida's cahob-barrios in the final decades of the colonial period; their names almost certainly reflect the biological colonialism at work in the capital's suburbs at that time. In Yucatan, it appears, there was very little deliberate adoption of Spanish surnames by indigenous persons as an indication of upward mobility, as occurred in central Mexico. In eighteenth-century Tekanto two mestizo families, the Castro and the Miranda, claimed hidalgo status and were very wealthy, but, and this is a significant point, such families were not a true part of the cah community, and they appear rarely in the Maya notarial record as full participants in the drama of cah life (and death), being in a sense the vanguard of Spanish infiltration of the cahob in the early nineteenth century. In other words, these families do not represent the acquisition of Spanish surnames by Maya as signs of upward mobility, but instead represent the downward mobility of low-ranking Spaniards into the Maya community, Spaniards who attempted to use marriage into relatively well-off Maya families to mitigate a downward slide in socioeconomic status.[18]

Diego de Landa asserted that the Maya "make much of knowing the origin of their lineages . . . and they boast much about one of their lineage who has distinguished himself . . . [they] consider all those of the same name to be related and treat them as such. Thus when anyone goes to a part of the country where he is unknown and in need, he makes known his name, and anyone of the same name receives him and treats him with good will and kindness. Thus no man or woman marries another of the same name, because they regard this as a great infamy."[19] To what degree the colonial Maya still considered themselves related to each other by patronym is not known, but the notarial evidence confirms with very few exceptions indeed Landa's observation on chibal endogamy.[20] As we shall see, this taboo necessitated marriage alliances between patronym groups.

These informal alliances and other such group activities show that chibalob were considered important throughout the colonial period, from dynastic lineages such as the Pech in the La Costa area, to lesser chibalob that dominated fewer or single communities such as the Camal of Ebtun, to the hundreds of other chibal groups scattered across the peninsula.

A Maya chibal certainly included all those of a given patronym within a given cah; beyond that, there is evidence of a perception of common identity and interest only at the dynastic level. Still, if all Maya of the same patronym were indeed descended from common ancestors, for which there is indirect evidence, one would expect some traces in the geographical distribution of patronyms.[21] Such traces are remarkably strong, considering the depletion of the indigenous population and the tendencies toward flight emphasized by scholars of the colonial Maya.[22] Roys first noted them more than half a century ago, based primarily on his review of the 1688 tax lists.[23] Some of his observations have been correlated with other data above, and others are worth repeating: the Cochuah were confined c. 1688 to the area around Tihósuco, once the center of a region named after the dynasty; the Cupul, along with at least fourteen other patronyms, were rarely found in the west of the province, and an additional seven patronyms have only been found on Cozumel (courtesy of a 1570 census of the island); in the west alone are found the names Chel and Iuit; the Pech and Xiu are concentrated c. 1688 in the areas they traditionally dominated.

Appendix B is an attempt at a more systematic contribution to our knowledge of this pattern. I have chosen five communities from among those that have the strongest documentary representation in notarial sources, and have simply noted which patronyms appeared in these cahob. Neither relative sizes of each chibal in each cah, nor fluctuations over time, could be reliably drawn from the sources. The list of patronyms is based upon Roys's 300 found in the 1688 tax lists, with the addition of a dozen that I encountered elsewhere in the colonial record.

The table must include a certain margin of error, smaller for Ebtun and Tekanto, from where wills, land sales, and other genres of documents are extant, than for the Tihó cahob, from where only land sales have survived, and for Cacalchen and Ixil, whose data are based overwhelmingly on wills. Nevertheless, a basic pattern of limited distribution or diffusion is discernible, implying that, in spite of patterns of demographic fluctuation, flight, and geographical mobility, cah ties remained strong enough to ensure a long-term stability and continuity in settlement. The geographical location of the cahob in relation to each other, particularly the proximity of Cacalchen, Ixil, and Tekanto (see Map 18.1), implies that marriages tended to be patrilocal; this is confirmed by the pattern of cah endogamy evidenced in the Ixil testaments of the 1760's. (However, the pattern is complicated by further evidence relating to settlement patterns, as discussed in Chapter 13.)

The relatively high number of patronyms appearing in the cahob-barrios of Tihó is only partly explained by the fact that five communities have been lumped together in the table; the names in these communities not only include those of the inhabitants at the onset of the colony, but may also reflect the process of Maya immigration into the capital, a process that intensified in the late eighteenth century, the period from which the Tihó data are drawn.[24] Cacalchen shows fewer patronyms probably because its data are all from the seventeenth century, when the cah was small, whereas the list of names from the other cahob is drawn from eighteenth-century documentation.

This evidence suggests therefore that the concentration of patronyms in certain cahob and regions would have encouraged the myth of common chibal ancestors, regardless of the degree to which that myth reflected the true extent of demographic evolution. This theme of continuity is substantiated by the persistence of such concentrations into the late-colonial period; evidence from other sources of increasing Maya mobility at this time is only strongly reflected in the late-colonial Tihó data.

CHAPTER FIVE

Government

The Maya of colonial Yucatan enjoyed a high degree of self-rule at the municipal level, as exercised by the cabildo of each cah. The cabildo was the town council, or municipal authority, an institution that was introduced by the Spaniards but was adapted by the indigenous peoples of Spanish America according to their own traditions. Just as the indigenous unit of the cah (or altepetl in central Mexico) became the basic unit of colonial organization—pueblo, parish, encomienda—so too did the indigenous body of elders, the *kuluinicob* or *principales*, assume the official roles of the cabildo. In some instances indigenous titles and functions were inserted into the structure of the institution. As the governing body of the cah, the cabildo had a hand in every aspect of community life.

Administration

I withdrew community funds at the end of the year, 1814, at Christmas, to buy one iron well pulley for six reals.
—batab and cabildo of Ebtun, 1815

The administrative functions of the Maya municipal authorities can be organized into three groups, as determined by the degree to which each function is derived from either internal or colonial obligations. The first group consists of duties entirely dictated by the demands of the Spanish authorities. Such demands were not always regular, often being determined by the greed of local Spanish secular and clerical officials (or that of a colonial governor such as don Rodrigo Flores de Aldana in the 1660's).[1] The geographical location of a cah might also affect the nature and extent of these demands.

For example, one of the basic duties of the indigenous cabildo was to provide runners for the *cordillera*, the mail and communications system that ran throughout the colony. The cah of Tahnab, however, claimed in 1605 that its position along the *camino real* between Mérida and Campeche was a crippling disadvantage to the community. Being *uay tu yol be*, "here at the heart of the road," *hach yabil numya lic ca mançic*, "we experience extreme misery," asserted the cabildo of Tahnab. That meant incessant obligations to carry goods and mail and to transport horses, for a Spaniard wishing to change horses en route from Mérida to Campeche would require someone to return the horses to the capital, and the chore would naturally fall upon the inhabitants of the most conveniently located Maya settlement.[2]

The Tahnab petition (presented more fully in Chapter 19) also complained about two other basic demands placed upon indigenous communities and their cabildos: the delivery of civil and ecclesiastical tribute, and provision of the *mandamiento*, or labor service, which was also a form of taxation. As we might expect, Spanish officials went to some length documenting the record of tribute payments and debts, and scholarship based on Spanish sources has devoted considerable space to the subject.[3] Although Maya cabildos recorded their deposits in the central granaries (and may have recorded other tribute payments), most mentions of tribute in Maya sources are either indirect, such as the testamentary itemization of the tribute blanket or *manta* called *yubte* by the Maya, or in the form of petitions of complaint. Such petitions, though dramatically phrased in language that ought to arouse the skepticism of the historian, support statistical evidence of the highly onerous nature of colonial taxation.

Another clue to this effect is the existence of the *caja de comunidad*, the community treasury, and the *pósito de granos*, the community granary. Although both benefited members of the cah, both were mandated by the colony, whose demands they served. Thus, although the caja de comunidad was used to pay local salaries and maintain the cah church and audiencia, it was also insurance against seasons when crop failure and demographic loss prevented the cah from meeting tribute demands that were usually not adjusted to catastrophe. In the event that the caja failed the cah, the cabildo might resort to the sale of community property; three of the cahob-barrios of Campeche, for example, cited debts to the Spanish authorities in a 1737 request to sell a tract of forest valued at a staggering 260 pesos.[4]

Similarly, the community granary was intended as insurance against shortages brought on by drought or locusts, but its existence was periodically exploited by the Spanish authorities. The colonists, most of whom lived in Mérida or in a handful of villas and nearby cabeceras, were always concerned that food supply lines from the countryside might be cut off.

This paranoia was not just a part of the siege-mentality collective psy-chosis that produced such fantasies as those surrounding the 1761 Jacinto Canek "revolt," and seasonal rumors of conspiracies among Maya house servants to murder their masters in their sleep.[5] It had its basis in the expe-rience of regular shortages, and it produced a whole network of pósitos de granos, with Mérida at the pyramidal apex.

All cahob in the colony were required to make regular deposits in their local branches of the central granary, and each deposit was duly recorded on paper. Extant examples of these documents reveal a formula of record, to which, typically, each cah applied its own variants. Maní tended to be briefer than most; in this example, seed, rather than maize, is being deliv-ered, to a Spaniard who was probably a local hacendado:[6]

ton con Batab yt Justisyas yt Regidores yt essⁿᵒ Uay ti cah Mani lic ɔaic u conosimientoil u chic kamic semilla diesiocho cargas ti ca noh tzicbenil yum Senior Dⁿ Bizente de agilar Sargento mayor y cappⁿ ynterino lic ɔaic u hahil than bin kube yt utz u lak diesiocho tu pachi hecen bix u yutzil u yacunah cu mentic ti tane utial thox lam tabal ti le cahob lae u hahil tumentah ton hunpel utz hecen Bix u yacunticon ca yumil ti Dˢ utial cu kantalnal utiale habe yanil laee kubic u hel halili u xul than helel en 29 de mayo del 1771 ã	We the batab, magistrates, reg-idors, and notary here in the cah of Maní certify that our much-respected lord Señor don Vicente de Aguilar, sergeant major and acting captain, re-ceives 18 loads of seed, and we give our word that later [he'll receive] the other 18 [loads] also. It is good that this [seed] shall take root in the cahob, and through the love of our lord Dios it shall ripen in the year it is delivered. Here ends the statement, today, May 29, 1771.

The main reason for the Spanish-imposed granary system was, of course, to guard against the starvation of the Spanish population; seed was redistributed to Maya communities so that indigenous farmers could pro-duce corn for the central granaries. A key cabildo administrative duty was therefore the acquisition of corn when cah production or Spanish re-distribution was insufficient. Two late-colonial examples of this kind of cabildo activity are petitions from Tihólop and Tetiz, both requests for just and prompt payment of corn for work mandated by colonial authorities and carried out by cah members.[7]

A second group of cabildo functions consisted of administrative duties that were required by the Spaniards but primarily affected the cah popula-tion and in some form were a continuation of governmental functions performed by preconquest principales. The cabildo was, for example, the local court of justice, which resolved and pronounced judgment on disputes within the cah. These proceedings were presumably mostly spoken testimony, for little record of them remains except where a person sought redress in a higher court, namely, the Spanish legal authorities at the nearest cabecera or in Mérida. If any Spaniards were involved in a dispute, the case was certain to be drawn into the Spanish system; and since this was always heavily documented, we tend to infer that the Maya often came into conflict with Spaniards but seldom fought among themselves—surely a false inference, given that the vast majority of Maya human contact was with fellow Mayas.

In fact, the few incidences on record of intra-cah disputes that were brought before the Spanish courts give some idea of the kind of cases the cabildo dealt with on a regular basis, from the Ebtun man who beat his wife (and was jailed for twenty-four hours by the cabildo), to the heirs in Ixil, Tekanto, Tekax, and elsewhere who went before their cabildos in order to gain possession of inherited property, to the protagonists of political factionalism discussed in Chapter 6. One man from Dzan claimed that his batab had adjudicated an alleged inheritance dispute with prejudice to the petitioner, for the batab coveted his wife and hated him—a rare example of an intra-cah dispute, possibly factional, passing into the written record.[8]

Related to its judicial function was the cabildo's central role in the production of written documentation. First, the cabildo saw to the continuation within the cah of the skill of reading and writing by choosing the apprentices to support the *maestro* (choirmaster) and assume the mantle of *escribano* (notary). Both maestro and escribano were prestigious community titles and positions, and they were conferred on persons according to the local status of their families. Some cabildos titled the apprentice *escribano segundo* or *mahan kab*, "hired hand"; others appear to have used the office of *tupil doctrina mandamiento* for that purpose. The tupil doctrina mandamiento, the notary, and the maestro were the only three offices that commanded a salary. Second, in notarizing documents—giving them the authoritative stamp of the "signatures" (the notary signed the officers' names for them) of the batab, alcaldes, and regidors—the cabildo also legitimized them, so that these officers were officially recognized and ratified in their posts by the Spanish authorities. Third, the cabildo functioned as the cah archive, maintaining records on whatever local business required documentation. There was probably a system of record keeping in separate books by genre that in the late eighteenth century collapsed into a single book containing all cah business (see Chapter 18). The Spanish authorities required a book of wills to be kept as evidence that the correct fees were being collected for posthumous masses and that the Maya were dying more or less in a state of grace; they also expected the cabildo to deliver the notarized record of its annual election.

The last cabildo function that falls within this the second of our three categories of duty—colonial obligations that were also traditional indigenous duties of government—was the maintenance of the audiencia, the plaza, the church and atrium, the jail, and all streets and public walls, as well as the *mesón*, or public guest house. The cabildo also took responsibility for the annual fiestas that were celebrated in the public spaces of the cah. Religious celebrations were often sponsored by Maya *cofradías*, though the officers of these brotherhoods were drawn from the same pool of principales as cabildo officials (see Chapter 12). Unfortunately, cabildo minutes such as those from sixteenth-century Tlaxcala have not survived from any cah, but there are a few late-colonial records of mundane council actions. For example, Ebtun repaired its mesón in 1811, using funds from the community caja; in 1831 Tixpeual sold several community house plots, including a mecate of land fronting the cah plaza, to finance the casting of iron doors for the new municipal hall, or audiencia. As in the central Mexican altepetl, the audiencia and especially the church buildings were symbols of the prestige of the cah, and the cabildo was therefore inspired to keep them in as good a state as possible. There are signs that in smaller, poorer cahob the audiencia was not a separate structure but was no more than a room, or even a table, in the church; Tixpeual's new audiencia doors may have been for the first such structure in that cah's history.[9]

By way of concluding the above, we might turn to an example of annual expenditure from a particular cah in the capital's jurisdiction: Cħapab.[10] "We withdraw community funds for the year 1800," *ca hokzic u takinil comunidad utial u habil 1800 años*, state the cabildo officers, who go on to confirm that the priest performed the duties (mass, confession, and extreme unction) for which he is being paid. It is significant that an arrangement that Spaniards would have seen as one of tributary obligation, the Maya viewed as one of employment; a relationship originally forced upon the indigenous population had been turned by them (at least conceptually) into a contract of mutual benefit. "Therefore," continues the treasury record, using the representational pronominal first person of the batab:

tin manah yxim utial u gasto ca yum Padre liccil u ɔaic Misa amal Domingo, hunhumpel tumin u mutil uchic ca manic: Bay xane heix takine uchic ca manic lay yxim, treinta pesos u taknil	30p^s
Bay xan tin manah zachun utial Audiencia cħapab lae u takinil	12p
Bay xan tin botah u salario Escribano, u takinile	8p
Bay xan tin botah u salario Maestro de capilla ti santa Iglesia u takinile	6p
Bay xan tin manah Agaya y Alcaparrosa utial ɔib ti Audiencia cħapab	1p
Bay xan tin ɔah u taknil uchic in manic cib licil u manel correo y akab y xan licil u ɔabal Patan y akab y u tzabal comunidad y Hoolpatan u takinil	3p
Bay xan kubil takin ti contaduria Tihóo	74p

I bought corn for the cost of our lord the priest giving mass every Sunday,
    one tomin [real] for each measure [almud] that we buy: here then is
      the money for the corn purchased, thirty pesos   30 pesos
Also I bought whitewash for the Chapab courthouse, at a cost of   12 pesos
Also I paid the notary's salary, at a cost of [literally: its money]   8 pesos
Also I paid the church maestro's salary, at a cost of   6 pesos
Also I bought quill and ink for the Chapab court written business   1 peso
Also I gave the money for buying the hand-delivery mail service with
    which the tribute, the community charge, and the head tax were
    delivered by hand, at a cost of   3 pesos
Also the delivery of money to the treasury in Tihó   74 pesos

Besides enumerating many of the administrative elements of council duties, this account also demonstrates the burden of taxation upon the cah budget. The Chapab budget is much like those of other cahob at the end of the eighteenth century (from which decades records are extant); Pixilá's 1795 expenditure of twenty pesos, for example, consisted of eleven pesos in payments to priests, eight pesos to cover the notary's and maestro's salaries, and one peso for white paper.[11]

We might also include among this aspect of cabildo responsibility the maintenance of cah lands, which the cabildo rented out (for community income) or allocated, while safeguarding the integrity of their borders and their inalienability, to the point of litigation if necessary. In the case of land litigation against Spaniards the cabildo was filling a role sanctioned by the colony but seldom actively supported by it. The tenacity and energy with which the Maya could engage the Spanish legal system potentially places this aspect of cabildo duties in my third category of cabildo functions: those not mandated by the colonial authorities. This category essentially constitutes one function: representation of the cah within the bureaucratic and legal system of the colony, the only effective forum that was available to them. The irony of this was that the Maya, as already noted, displayed considerable skill in manipulating this system to their partial advantage, even though the conquering power arguably intended it to be an instrument of colonial exploitation.[12]

Representation

On behalf of all the members of the cah.
—cabildo of Bacalar, 1838

From the Spanish perspective, the function of the Maya cabildo was to perform the various administrative duties listed above, to act in many ways as an extension or instrument of Spanish administration. But from the Maya perspective the cabildo served a more vital purpose: to represent every member of the cah, collectively and individually, before the extra-cah world. Hence the officers signed petitions and other records *yoklal tulacal u cahal*, "on behalf of the whole cah," or "for all the members of the cah."[13]

In fact, the entire corpus of notarial documents in Maya is telling evidence of the representative role of the cah cabildo. Indigenous testaments are a fine example, and the point is underlined in the case of intestate deaths, when a cabildo goes beyond ratification of a testator's claims and wishes and actually determines the wishes of one who is deceased.[14] The cah residents not only did not question that as part of the cabildo's function, they expected it. Far from being the product of one person's dictation to the notary, a Maya document such as a will involved the entire community, either directly as witnesses or indirectly through cabildo participation. An integral part of the oral-notarial record-keeping dialectic was thus its communal nature, expressed in the multiple authorship of the document and the role of the audience. In land sales, the cabildo, the seller, and purchaser are all contributors to the ritual of valid exchange; in wills, both authors and audience function as authenticating witnesses, and are actors and participants in the ritual. In what was surely preconquest tradition, testaments were communal and public, dictated *tutan batab yetel justisias lae*, "before these the batab and magistrates."[15] In other words, before the entire community—not necessarily literally, but certainly symbolically, as manifested by the presence of the officers of the cabildo, and the executors, who are themselves always prominent locals, often titled *almehen*, noble, or *don* (reserved among the Maya for batabob, ex-batabob, and indigenous hidalgos). Named executors of wills, and witnesses to land sales, were drawn from the same social group as members of the cabildo, and are an indication of the persistence of the traditional preconquest ruling body usually referred to as the principales (in Maya, the *kuluinicob* or *u nucil uinicob*; see Table 7.1). The cabildo thus served the interests of the kuluinicob, while the cabildo-kuluinicob represented those of the mass of residents (the cahnalob).

In his study of the colonial-era Nahuas, Robert Haskett noted "a marked tendency for the groups pursuing litigation before the Spanish authorities to be made up of current council members, past officers, and members of the greater ruling group . . . or principales."[16] This was certainly true in Yucatan for reasons having specifically to do with the nature of political authority within the cah; indigenous witnesses were far more than mere "testigos." The format of the Spanish testament required the presence of witnesses, and in Spanish wills these can even be whatever virtual strangers could be found at the time. This is never the case in any Maya wills. Most Maya wills begin with a formulaic opening that states the presence of the cabildo officers, and end with a similar formal statement, followed by the names of the officers. Intruding statements by relatives support the impression that the testator's kin were also present; in some Ixil wills relatives adopt the pronominal first person to make their contribution to the peaceful transfer of property, and in one will of 1700 from Dzan, family members are listed as *testigob*.[17] The content of each will was public information, as every testator states: *lay bin ylabac u hunil yn testamento*, "this the document of my will shall be seen," that is, "read, made public." The purpose of these officers and relatives is not simply to witness the ceremony but to attest to the truth of the statement, that the testator claims property that is really his, and allocates it justly—"the batab and magistrates will verify this," testators declare, or "as m'lord the batab and magistrates know."[18] The fact of knowledge—the verb *ohel*—possessed by the cabildo is per se a validation of the claim or statement being made.

From this perspective, then, we see the cabildo as author, validator, representative, and witness, all in the form of ordinary bureaucratic business (primarily wills and land exchange). The cabildo also functioned in this way through the presentation of petitions. Indigenous stylistic elements in extant examples of Maya petitions suggest that this genre's expression of the cabildo's representative role had some preconquest precedent (see Chapter 19). Whether this was true or not, Maya officers were skilled strategists and accomplished fighters in the arena of the Spanish legal system, defending cah interests against onerous taxes and obligations, and against abusive Spanish officials and priests.

Finally, Maya cabildos also served as witnessing bodies whose escribano could be hired to perform personal business of Spaniards, with the cabildo being employed to ratify that business—even to the point of a cabildo statement in Maya, complete with a list of officers. Two dozen such ratifications, all dated mid-eighteenth century, have surfaced so far, although more must surely have perished and still others must be languishing in estate archives.[19] The extant examples ratify Spanish wills, Spanish land sales (that is, vendor, purchaser, format and language of record, all Spanish), a court order obliging a Spaniard to pay an outstanding debt to a compatriot, and, most frequently, Spanish documents providing power of attorney.

Not surprisingly, all these records come from communities quite distant from the capital, places where presumably a Spanish notary could not be found. The *poder* traveled a two-way street between Mérida and the colony's hinterlands. In 1759 a don Lorenzo de Lorra, resident priest in Tihólop and the *teniente de cura* of Ichmul, a cah on the edge of the colony that was an indigenous pilgrimage site, gave power of attorney to a don Andrés Fernández de Armas in Mérida to pursue the matter of a thousand-peso inheritance that was supposed to have arrived from Mexico City. Conversely, Spaniards resident in Mérida looked to local priests—the obvious candidates—to manage their business affairs in, for example, Chunhuhub (1745), Tekax (1760's), and Oxkutzcab (1770).[20]

A ratification from Chikindzonot in 1775 provides an example of the kind of business that Spaniards were mostly concerned with out among the cahob: land. It also shows the formula a cabildo used in ratifying a Spanish document. The formula is similar to that used to ratify copies of Maya records: it asserts true and correct notarial practice, and briefly describes the act or event being notarized:[21]

ton con Batab y Justias ɔayc u	We the batab and magistrates assert
hahil u Bicil tanil tu ɔibtah yn	the truth of that written before my
tzicbenil yum Cura y uupel	respected lord the curate and six
textigoob lay hun lae licil u ɔic	witnesses; this document now gives
y u chucil ti in yum Bʳ Dⁿ	power to Bachiller don Pantaleón
paⁿtaleon Rosado utial u conil	Rosado regarding the sale of the
hunpel u estancia cacalchen	estate called Cacalchen to m'lord
u kaba ti in yum Dⁿ ygnacio	don Ignacio Anguas. This is the
Anguas bey u hahil ɔayc ca	truth. We sign in the year and
firma tu habil y tu yuyl ɔiban	month written above, here in
te canala uay chikinɔonot Dⁿ	Chikindzonot: don Matias Tuyu,
Matias tuyu Batab Bentura yupit	Batab; Ventura Yupit, Alcalde;
Alcalde fermin cob Noh Řegidor	Fermin Cob, Head Regidor. Before
tin tanil Matias yama essⁿᵒ cah	me, Matias Yama, cah notary

Not all notaries were this thorough. At the other end of the scale was Ignacio Ake, escribano of Tihólop in 1759, who could only muster a brief note in a half-legible half-sensible scrawl:[22]

tin tanil y xtin tanil yn yum	Before me and also before m'lord
Batab y tzesob lay u hahil ci	Batab and witnesses; this is the
chi uɔaci u chu ti yn yum pader	truth; power is given to m'lord
Br Lorens Lara kabal ma	father Br. Lorenzo Lorra; not
ygnasio ake essno	below [?]; Ignasio Ake, notary.

In its role as witness for hire the Maya cabildo functioned in a seemingly untypical manner: instead of fulfilling its administrative obligations to the Crown and to its cah subjects, it acted as a private business, even facilitating the penetration of Maya landholdings by Spaniards. But this was just another way in which the Maya cabildo functioned as part of the Spanish-indigenous governmental system. Although there is no record of the fee charged for this service (and there may have been payment in kind, in the form of ritual drinking, for example), it would seem more typical of Spanish practice that cabildos be paid for their witnessing services. If they were, the revenue would have passed into the community treasury, where most of it would ultimately benefit the cahnalob, or cah members. In other words, the cabildo did what it could to fulfill the primary obligation of rulership: to protect the cah, much as (in the language of Maya petitions) the branches of a sapote offer protection from the sun.

Whereas this position of authority may at one time have inspired Maya principales to exploit their subjects, as in some cases they continued to do (particularly the batabs), the burden of colonial rule forced cabildos to act as intercessors, not only between cahnalob but also between cahnalob and colonizers. This latter role is best illuminated by the various types of cabildo petitions, and these documents open small windows onto Maya life in these centuries. Some of the characteristics of this genre appear ironic in the colonial context: the rhetoric of rulerly address now used by the Maya nobility to address Spanish bureaucrats; the self-deprecating language of that address, its protestations of misery and destitution, now potentially reflecting the burden of colonial rule; the repressive sexual stance of the Catholic church used by the immodest Maya as a weapon against the church's own cohorts; the expert manipulation of the Spanish legal system by Maya cabildos defending themselves and their people against the masters of the system.

Yet the ethnohistorian must avoid the pitfall of approaching the sources with too much credulity. Although Maya petitions, taken together, seem to offer a monolithic Maya vs. Spaniard view of indigenous life, they were no more than isolated cases whose common patterns must ultimately be placed in the broader context of all Maya documentation. Much of cabildo activity focused on rivalry between cahob, and much of it focused narrower still, on the dynamics of intra-cah relationships. Furthermore, cabildos themselves were not monoliths but bodies composed of men with particular concerns and ambitions.

We have been looking at the cabildo as a single functional unit, emphasizing its role as the representative before the outside world of either individual cah members or the cah as a whole. These two categories are not, of course, mutually exclusive; given the pervasion of the system of representation in cah society, they are in a sense mutually inclusive. Thus, for all the seemingly exclusive nature of Maya politics, the function of political office in the cah served to include all its members in some sense. However, only a select group within the cah participated in political life. These were adult males from the same families that enjoyed the greatest economic and social status in the community—the cah elite. The following chapter discusses the offices and officers of the Maya cabildo, particularly with a view to illuminating patterns of cabildo composition and the career patterns of individual cabildo officers or groups thereof.

·◌·

CHAPTER SIX

Politics: Faction, Office, and Career

The indigenous municipal councils of New Spain, responsible as they were for both internal and external affairs, took on the role of the preconquest indigenous ruling bodies. In the colonial period this meant, as we have seen, administering the relationship between indigenous community and Spanish authorities. Colonial rule also meant that political structures within indigenous municipalities were altered to suit Spanish models. However, throughout New Spain (and wherever possible in Spanish America) Spanish civil and ecclesiastical units were based on existing indigenous units so as to facilitate the profitable administration of initially large subject populations by small cadres of officials and settlers. The other side of this coin was that indigenous cabildos interpreted aspects of the Spanish system, as well as their roles within and outside it, according to the traditions of local political practice and organization.

Cabildo Composition: Mayanization and Localization

> In the presence of the batab, the magistrates, the escribano, and the other principal men and witnesses.
> —cabildo formula, Tekanto, 18th century

The cah, like its Nahua cognate, the altepetl, became the basis of the encomienda, the parish, and the pueblo—the respective organizational instruments of economic, religious, and political control. By 1546, when the Spaniards had "pacified" what then became the colony of Yucatan, a number of ordinances and central Mexican precedents had already established that indigenous municipalities were to be self-ruled by a governor and a body of nobles who would hold the offices of the cabildo: alcalde (judge), regidor (councilman), and escribano (notary).[1] Four Spanish cabildos were thus set up in Yucatan (in the city of Mérida, and in the villas, or towns, of Campeche, Valladolid, and Bacalar), but the cahob, who would eventually number about two hundred, were granted their own cabildos. On the surface, the Spaniards appear to have been successful in imposing an institution of their own onto indigenous society; indeed, in terms of function, the cabildo structure served the colony well. Yet there is also evidence that new Maya communities, created in the eighteenth century in response to population growth, turned themselves into cahob complete with cabildos of officers and parallel church and cofradía hierarchies—without colonial authorization.[2] Furthermore, from the onset, the Maya shaped the institution of the cabildo to suit local needs and traditional practices.

In localizing the cabildo the Maya of Yucatan were not unique. Regional studies have shown that indigenous communities in central and southern Mexico similarly reversed the Spanish ranking of alcaldes and regidores, and similarly made independent selections of offices and their numbers. The most comprehensive of these studies, covering what is now Morelos, revealed variations in council composition not only between altepetl but also within each altepetl over the course of the colonial period. I have found an identical pattern in Yucatan, although, appropriate to the broader picture, the details of those variations differ between the Maya and the Nahuas, most notably in the role of the governorship.[3]

The *batabil*, or "batab-ship," was the senior and governing office of the cah, a post held by a noble and ranked above the cabildo. The position had no Spanish precedent, but was grafted onto the indigenous cabildo in Yucatan as part of the Spanish strategy of coopting indigenous leadership into the structure of colonial rule. Although the municipal governorship was intended to reflect indigenous dynastic traditions (traditions that were also powerful in early modern Europe, but not at so local a level), it was also supposed to be an annually elected position so as to restrict the power of individual indigenous rulers. In central Mexico's first postconquest generation, the dynastic ruler (the *tlatoani*, an equivalent title to batab) filled the governorship, but thereafter crises in succession led to a bifurcation of the senior office in the altepetl. Colonial authorities presumably encouraged this split, for if the tlatoani could not hold the governorship every year, he would be forced to some degree to share power in the altepetl. Yet Spanish attempts to exploit the situation and weaken indigenous dynasties failed to recognize that Nahua rulers had always been chosen from a pool of eligible candidates who belonged to an elite group of between one and four families.[4]

In other words, the Nahua nobility were able to hold on to their dominant position as a group within altepetl society. A similar manipulation of the system by Ñudzahui nobility meant that dynastic rulership in the Mixteca was largely maintained.[5] The same is true of the Maya nobility. Inevitably (as in central Mexico, or indeed in Europe), the dominance of subgroups, families, and individuals was finite, but as a group the Maya ruling classes continued to rule. There was, however, a fundamental difference between the Nahua transition of office from tlatoani to tlatoani-gobernador and the Maya transition from batab to batab-gobernador. The comparison is important not simply for comparison's sake, but because the Nahua pattern has, I believe, become the basis of a misinterpretation of the Maya pattern. In his attempt to illuminate this transition, Ralph Roys (in 1943) turned to the central Mexican example, which even at that time clearly indicated that in some cases the tlatoani and gobernador were two separate persons, and projected it onto a few vague remarks made by Spanish officials. The resulting analysis quite unnecessarily entangles the terms batab, gobernador, and *cacique* into a knot of obfuscation. Roys's examples alone show clearly that all three terms were being used more or less interchangeably, and that the Spaniards were using both gobernador and cacique—a Spanish word of Caribbean origin meaning hereditary lord—as translations of batab.[6]

Forty years later Nancy Farriss avoided this entanglement by dismissing attempts to trace the separate ancestry of colonial offices as "futile," yet her description of the batab-gobernador transition betrays Roys's influence nonetheless. The "prestige and functions" of the gobernador are said to be "similar to those of the batab," and the two posts "eventually merged"; the interpretation is made visual in a figure that shows batab and gobernador as separate sixteenth-century offices but as a single seventeenth-century office that, by the eighteenth century, is termed only batab.[7]

This interpretation by Roys and Farriss, the two major authorities on Yucatan's "colonial Indians," is the accepted one, but it presents a number of problems. First, I have not come across any instances of a cah that has a separate governor and a separate batab. Neither did Roys, as a careful reading of his examples reveals. Likewise, the sources cited by Farriss that I have looked at do not seem to prove that the governorship and batabil were ever separate or rival posts.[8] Second, the annual election of indigenous governors, which became established in central Mexico from the late sixteenth century, never took root in Yucatan.[9] Consequently, if the batab was not required to surrender the office of governor at year's end, the batab had no reason to maintain the batabil as a separate office.

If the batabil and governorship ever were separate offices, it was for a brief moment at the onset of colonial rule, a moment for which there is slim documentary evidence.[10] There was no evolution of office or of terminology beyond the simple acquisition of the title gobernador as a synonym for batab. A systematic reading of extant Maya notarial evidence reveals no pattern beyond that of cah-to-cah variation (this pattern emerges in almost every facet of Maya society under study) coupled with the fact that batab is used more than gobernador. There is room for speculation on isolated examples—perhaps Cacalchen's usage of both batab and gobernador in 1653 and 1654 is related to the fact that the cah appears not to have had a batab in the early part of the century; most of Tihó's cahob-barrios use gobernador in late colonial times when most other cahob use batab, implying possible Spanish influence—but for each example there is another to contradict or qualify it. A significant example is found in a Santiago sale record of 1741, in which don Manuel Poot is titled "batab" in the text and "governor"—*g°rsantiago*—after his signature.[11]

A related question is that of the *halach uinic*, the preconquest officer said to have been senior to the batab. In the first postconquest generation such a lord could surely win the governorship over the batab. Yet there is no evidence that the preconquest halach uinic did not himself hold the post of batab in the dominant cah of the region. On the contrary, colonial evidence implies that the batab of a cah that achieved dominance over a region became halach uinic: the halach uinic based in Sotuta, Nachi Cocom, became don Juan Cocom, batab-governor of that cah, and halach uinic Kukum Xiu assumed the batabil-governorship in Maní; the batabs of the Pech chibal in Motul claimed descent from the former halach uinic of the so-called Ceh Pech province centered on Motul, and the Iuit batabs in Hocaba made a similar claim.[12] In other words, halach uinic was an honorific term for an especially powerful batab. Logically, the Spanish provincial governor became halach uinic after the conquest, with Mérida as the dominant "cah," and it is to that Spanish official that the title is granted in Maya petitions. Perhaps as a result of this colonial application of halach uinic, the batab of a cah perceived by the Mayas as still dominating its neighbors after the conquest was called *noh batab* (as Calkiní styled its late-sixteenth-century batab, don Miguel Canul, for example).[13] The same formula was also applied to cabildo titles (*noh regidor* was the "regidor mayor").

A second question related to the continuity of the batabil is that of a ruler's legitimacy. This point was emphasized by Roys, who translated the so-called "Language of Zuyua" passage in the Chilam Balam as a test of rulerly legitimacy, although it has recently been interpreted as more of a scurrilous satire on ruling class pretensions, and by Farriss, who focused on assertions by Maya petitioners of the illegitimacy of the person they were trying to oust.[14] However, the question of legitimacy to rule relates not only to the context of factionalism but also to that of the criteria of eligibility suggested by mundane documentary evidence. According to this evidence, eligibility to rule was determined by a complex but not totally rigid system of interrelationships of class, patronym, wealth, and political experience. In a sense, attaining the batabil indicated legitimacy in itself, for although batabs were, as far as can be told, of almehen (noble) class, the batabil carried with it the Spanish title don used by the Maya as the ultimate indicator of status. Thus accusations of illegitimacy were largely factional attempts to exploit Spanish ignorance of Maya politics. Similar opportunities for the advance of once-subordinate Maya factions were presented by demographic decline, and by Spanish policies such as congregación. Disputes over the batabil are therefore treated below in the section on factionalism.

The only systematic attempt to establish patterns defining the batabil was conducted by Philip Thompson in his study of Tekanto.[15] His findings are clear enough to allow evidence from other cahob to confirm or qualify them. Two conclusions stand out from Thompson's work: the term of the batabil was apparently twenty years; and the kin connections between batabob were the ties that bound together what was in effect an eligibility-group of elite families within the cah. The pages below on career patterns present evidence of cah variation on batabil terms, although there are signs of hereditary rule within an elite group and even within single chibalob. The existence of an elite within the cah with privileged access to political office is further confirmed by a case study of Ixil presented in Chapter 7.

Meanwhile, let us turn from the batabil to look at the offices of which Maya cabildos were composed. Early-seventeenth-century Spanish laws aiming to standardize indigenous cabildos in Spanish America were more of an indicator of the problem than a solution to it. Not only was the horse long gone, but such laws failed even to bolt the stable door. Indigenous municipalities continued to fill alcalde and regidor posts in the numbers they chose, while lesser posts, unregulated even under Spanish law, were filled by the remainder of the body of local notables.[16]

The office of teniente is typical of this pattern as manifested in Yucatan. Like the batab, the teniente was not elected, and the office is never included in the list of officers in election records. The lieutenant periodically appears at the foot of regular notarized cabildo business, beneath or sometimes in lieu of the batab's name. This role befits the office's European origins, and indeed the only lieutenant who appears in the long run of Tekanto election records (1683–1707; a Gerónimo Cach in 1703) appears to be acting batab in lieu of a Spaniard from Izamal who has been appointed cah governor by the colonial authorities pending the resolution of a local political dispute.

This, however, was a case of unusual circumstances. Indeed, in 1706, with the Spaniard still as nominal governor, Gerónimo Cach appears as alcalde mayor, normally the senior ranking post after batab. A similar example comes from the cah-barrio of La Mejorada, where there was no lieutenant before the 1790's, at which point there is no longer a batab: clearly, the one office has simply supplanted the other. Yet this too is unusual, for the other four cahob-barrios of Tihó show lieutenants more often than not, but apparently for one-year appointments. Thus, although the teniente may sometimes have been personally linked to the batab or acted as a batab substitute, I believe the position was in most instances not filled through appointment by the batab but instead was filled as a result of the factional jostling that controlled other offices.

An attempt to define this office should not lead us astray from the central fact of cah variation. Late-colonial Ixil and Tekanto offer a comparative example. There were just seven tenientes in Tekanto between 1703 and 1820 (of whom one, Gerónimo Cach, has already been mentioned): four previously served as alcalde; two went on to become batab; one, Pedro Chan, worked his way up from third regidor in 1799 to lieutenant for twelve years under a batab from Dzemul (he may have served as acting batab) before finally acquiring the batabil in 1833. The office in this cah was clearly a significant rung on the political ladder.[17]

On the other hand, interrupted records from Ixil of 1765–1807 imply that the lieutenant was most often the kind of man who served as a testamentary executor: a noble whose regular cabildo career was peaking or had just peaked and who as part of the ruling classes enjoyed the right to political involvement. Accordingly, the post was not always filled (Cacalchen seems never to have had a teniente). In other words, it was often a post of indirect political importance, being filled by a man whose social stature in the community derived from his wealth or chibal connections, or from both.

The batab, on the other hand, though by necessity also being a man of such social standing, would have increased his stature a good deal simply by acquiring the batabil. To illustrate this batab-teniente contrast, let us compare some specific Ixil officers (see Table 6.1). Gaspar Coba was lieutenant in 1766, and an executor the following year, when Andrés Tec was lieutenant, having been an executor the previous year. Neither man is recorded as holding another post. Josef Cob, on the other hand, who was batab from at least 1773 to 1779, had been an executor in 1769, but was escribano in 1765; he was a literate career officer who presumably held other positions before 1765 (for which there are no records).

This example also illustrates some of the general similarities and differences between the lieutenant and the notary. Both seem to have been on a similar tier between batab and alcalde, often powerful stepping-stones to the batabil; both were nonelective posts that were not even cabildo posts

TABLE 6.1
Careers of Some Ixil Cabildo Officers, 1765–1807

Pasqual Canche	Regidor 4⁰	1765, 1768	
	Regidor 1⁰	1769	
Pedro Canul	Regidor 4⁰	1766	
	Alcalde 2⁰	1773	
Josef Pech[a]	Alcalde 1⁰	1766	
	Regidor 4⁰	1773	Executor 1779
Sebastián Chim	Regidor 3⁰	1767	
	Alcalde 1⁰	1779	
Gaspar Yam	Alcalde 2⁰	1767	
	Regidor 1⁰	1773	
	Alcalde 1⁰	1777	
Marcos Poot	Mahan Kab	1765	
	Escribano	1767, 1777	
Pablo Tec	Escribano	1766, 1768	
(Don) Josef Cob[b]	Escribano	1765	Executor 1769
	Batab	1773–(1779)	
Don Gaspar Canul	Batab	(pre-1765)	Executor 1766, 1767, 1768
Gaspar Coba	Teniente	1766	Executor 1767
Andrés Tec	Teniente	1767	Executor 1766
Juan Matu	Regidor 1⁰	1768	Executor 1767
Pedro Mis[a]	Alcalde 1⁰	1807	Executor 1766
Francisco Coba[a]	Teniente	1798	Executor 1767

SOURCE: TI; Restall 1995a. Data are comprehensive 1765–68, sporadic through 1807. Full lists of cabildo officers from Ixil, Cacalchen, Tekanto, and the five cahob-barrios of Mérida-Tihó are in App. C; also see discussion of career patterns below.

[a] There may have been two men with each of these names.

[b] Only don after he became batab; was still batab in 1779, but not by 1786.

proper under the Spanish model, yet seem to have been considered such by the Maya; and both were subject to variations of term limit, being strictly annual posts in some cahob (e.g., Ixil), posts of several years' duration with possible return appearances in others (e.g., cahob-barrios of Tihó), and long-term if not lifetime posts in other cahob (e.g., Tekanto). However, as seen, there was not always a lieutenant and the post does not seem to have commanded specific duties.

The notary, or escribano, by contrast was a vital salaried official with specific skills. This function was quite different from that of the escribano in the Spanish cabildo; the latter kept the records and affirmed their authenticity, but he was not invariably of noble rank, and he would not necessarily go on to assume a voting cabildo office. The Maya notary's prestige was visible only to his own people, but the authenticating power of his signature was recognized by the Spanish authorities, thereby validating documentation produced by his cah. Occasionally the notary is referred to, or describes himself as, *ah ɔib(al) hu(u)n*, "the writer of the document," suggesting preconquest precedent of practice, if not specific office. His skills were self-perpetuated within each cah, and sometimes the signature of the apprentice—the escribano segundo or mahan kab—

appears below that of his teacher. In Tekanto and no doubt elsewhere the post of tupil doctrina mandamiento may have functioned as an apprenticeship to the escribano or maestro (or to both): these were the only three offices of the cah that required literacy, and in the Tekanto election records they are listed together in a separate section. The tupil doctrina had responsibilities for the teaching of catechism similar to those of the maestro; Lucas Camal, notary in Tekanto from 1703 to 1705, had been tupil doctrina in 1685 and 1693; he held no other posts, and indeed the office of tupil doctrina seems to have circulated among a small group who rarely moved into other cabildo positions, perhaps because maestro and escribano in Tekanto were long-term positions that were seldom open.

In smaller cahob, the maestro may have assisted the notary. A 1759 Maya cabildo ratification of a Spanish record of power of attorney is written in the fine Maya-looking hand of a man who declares: *ten cen Martias cuxim Maestro Tihólop,* "I who am Matias Cuxim, maestro of Tihólop." This maestro then lists six Maya witnesses, and the officers of the cabildo of Tihólop. What is unusual is that the document is not drawn up by the escribano. A clue to the mystery is provided by a brief statement in the bottom left-hand corner of the manuscript, in the awkward hand of Ignasio Ake, Tihólop's notary. Without further records from the Tihólop of that time, one can only imagine why Ignasio Ake performed so poorly on the job that the maestro had to stand in for him. Old age, arthritis, even intoxication, might explain the bad handwriting. Whatever the reason, Ake's few words of validation were still considered necessary to assure the full legality of the document; when the escribano's skills failed him, the authenticating power of his office remained.

Indicative of their rank and concomitant with their status as literates (unique after the turn of the seventeenth century), the notary and maestro received salaries from the community treasury. According to Spanish sources, the escribano also charged a fee for preparing "private" documents such as wills, and the maestro skimmed a cut for himself off the top of parochial fees for baptisms, weddings, and funerals. Maya notarial records contain no evidence of this additional income, although records of cah cabildo expenditures and election records do indicate annual salary rates. These were more varied than was previously realized, as shown by Table 6.2.[18]

The offices of alcalde and regidor became the staple of the Maya cabildo. It has been suggested that, although alcalde had no preconquest equivalent, regidor was seen as a substitute for the Maya office of *ah cuch cab*. A petition of 1578 lists its signing officers as one batab and three ah cuch cab; a similar document from 1589 lists a gobernador, an alcalde, and two regidors. This evidence could suggest that the temporary switchover

TABLE 6.2
Some Examples of Escribano and Maestro Salaries

Cah	Year	Escribano's salary	Maestro's salary
Tekanto	1683–1706	6 pesos and 12 cargas of corn	6 pesos and 12 cargas of corn
Pixila	1795	5 pesos	3 pesos
Itzmal	1795	12 pesos	6 pesos
Chapab	1800	8 pesos	6 pesos
various	1790–1805	12 pesos and 12 cargas of corn	12 pesos and 12 cargas of corn

SOURCES: Tekanto: AGEY, 1, 1; Pixila and Itzmal (the Maya cah within Spanish Izamal): AGN-IN, 82, 1, 158, 169–71; Chapab: AGN-CI, 2052, 6, 9; various: reports by Spanish officials cited by Farriss 1984: 470, n. 56.

from batab to gobernador alleged by historians was accompanied by a parallel rapid shift from preconquest to colonial among other titles.[19] But this was not necessarily the case; just as batab and gobernador are used at different times by different cahob in a way that reveals no temporal pattern, so do preconquest offices such as ah cuch cab, *belnal*, and *chun than*— general terms for officers ranking more or less at the regidor level—crop up right through and beyond the colonial period, though less often than in the sixteenth and seventeenth centuries.[20] The main difference between the batab-gobernador and regidor–ah cuch cab usages is that the former are always the same office, whereas the latter are not; mid- and late-colonial denotations of ah cuch cab tend to refer to one person who is granted what may have been a temporary floating title to give dignity and importance to his participation in cabildo business.

The notion that the ah cuch cab was the predecessor of the regidor is tied to the assumption that the cah was divided into four wards, each with its own ah cuch cab, and that this facilitated the transition to a Spanish-style cabildo with four regidors. The evidence for such a preconquest arrangement is tenuous, however, and there are signs of a historiographically created myth resembling the myth about the evolution of the batabil.[21] Furthermore, the colonial-era evidence of varied numbers of regidors undermines the quadripartite theory for the postconquest period, in addition to which there is an absence of any Maya reference to the alleged subunits, while the title ah cuch cab is used sometimes as a synonym for regidor and sometimes as a separate designation.[22]

The apparently unsystematic use of ah cuch cab and other floating titles, both Maya and Spanish, in fact reflected a thoroughly systematic attempt to maintain the traditional practices of community government and the participation of the cah elite. Community principales who lacked official posts in any given year were often still present at the moment of cabildo business, all in accordance with traditional Maya government: *u hahan kuluinicilob u t[e]s[tig]oil*, "the other leaders and witnesses."[23] The

TABLE 6.3
Variations in Maya Cabildo Composition

	Xecpes	Dzaptun	Dzan	Cacalchen		Tekanto	Pustunich
	1578	1605	1651	1647	1653	1683–1702	1740
batab	1		1	1	1	1	1
escribano	1	1	1	1	1	1	2
alcalde		3	1	3	4	2	2
regidor		3	1	6	5	4	2
procurador		1	1				
ah cuch cab	3						
tupil			4				
nucil uinic	2	2					4

	Santiago		Santa Ana	Ixil			Sicpach	Mejorada
	1741	1797	1748	1765	1766	1767	1786	1791–93
batab	1		1	1	1	1	1	
teniente	1		1		1	1		1
escribano	2	1	2	2	1	1	1	1
alcalde	2	1	2	2	2	2	2	1
regidor	11	3	6	4	4	4	2	3
alcalde col							1	
ah cuch cab						1		
nucil uinic							2	

SOURCES: AGN-I, 69, 5, 199; AGN-CI, 2013, 1, 6; T-LAL-TT, 22 and 41; CCA, Chichí, III, 21; cabildo tables in App. C. Officers are those appearing as ratifying witnesses to notarial business, not those listed in election records. These examples are a small percentage of total colonial-era variations. Santiago, Santa Ana, and (La) Mejorada are Tihó cahob-barrios.

Maya used numerous formulas to record this fact, including Spanish collective titles such as *justicias*, "magistrates," and *cabildosob* (usually *cabidosob*), a Mayanization of "cabildo" to mean "cabildo officers," as well as traditional Maya collectives such as *belnalob*, "elected officers," *kuluinicob*, "principal men," and other variants referring to the intelligence, importance, or age of the principales.[24]

Nonetheless, in relation to the system across the whole colony and colonial period, this tendency to vary the roster of offices obscures the fact that in every cah, the importance of each office and its ranking must always have been clear. Besides using Spanish ordinals to denote rank, the Maya tacked their own terms for size onto the titles to produce such offices as *noh regidor* and *chichan alcalde*.[25] The order in which offices were listed at the foot of notarial documents is clear in most cases and gives some idea of rank. Table 6.3 provides some examples of such lists. These were not comprehensive lists of all cabildo officers for that cah and that year; on the contrary, they represent those chosen to ratify the business at hand either for reasons of convenience or because these officers were neighbors, relatives, or associates of the testator or vendor. (Just as a document dealing with cofradía land might choose officers with positions in the brotherhood, or at least mention their cofradía rather than cabildo titles—for example, a record of 1708 from Dzan, witnessed by one escribano, four *priostesob*, four *diputadosob*, and two additional untitled officers.)[26] This table also illustrates the variety in numbers that characterized Maya cabildo composition, as well as a use of titles that was unconventional from the Spanish perspective, all of which had the effect (one hesitates to infer intention) of continuing the preconquest practice of including the body of principales in cah business.

Below the rank of regidor were what might be termed extracabildo officers. Whereas a cabildo of the Spanish model included no offices below alcalde or regidor, the larger ruling group of the cah consisted of thirty or more officers, who in some sense were part of a greater Maya cabildo. Extracabildo officers rarely appear as signatories to regular cabildo business, and when they do no consistent patterns are apparent. However, it is clear that these junior offices were often rungs on the same ladder of political advancement that featured the batabil as its highest step (although, conversely, they may sometimes have been emeritus titles to senior notables who had stepped down from whatever office had been their career apex). As we have seen, the apparent confusion with which the Maya operated the Spanish-imposed municipal political system was in fact a manifestation of endemic regional variation. What all these cahob did have in common was their concern to maintain the governmental participation of a larger body of principales. Members of this ruling body had access to the various offices listed in Table 6.4. These offices do not seem to have been a set structure of posts over which the principals could fight and negotiate but were instead offices that were assigned as needed in each cah and in each year.

Table 6.4 is modeled on the officer lists (which can be found in Appendix C) from Tekanto's election records of 1683–1707. To the Tekanto list a few variations have been added, notably a second escribano and tupilob (constables)—titles that appear periodically in the written record. Testigosob (witnesses) and albaceasob (testamentary executors) do not appear on election documents, but executors were usually nobles, and both executors and witnesses were often former high-ranking cabildo officers. They were therefore part of the broader ruling group. An idea of how varied full officer rosters might have been, extracabildo posts included, is given by the previous table (6.3).

The ranking is based on the order in which officers are listed in the Tekanto election records, slightly adjusted by the evidence of over one hundred career patterns drawn from those records. The tier structure is justified by various criteria: as made clear above, the batabil was a tier unto itself, and the escribano and teniente were on a rung above the standard

TABLE 6.4
The Offices of the Cah by Tier and Rank

Civil	Civil-religious	Religious
1. batab-gobernador		
2. teniente		
escribano publico (salaried)	maestro (salaried)	
[assistant] escribano		
3. alcaldesob (2)		sacristán mayor
regidoresob (4)		fiscal mayor
4. alcalde mesón		
procurador		
mayordomo		
alguacil mayor		cantoresob
alguacilesob (6)		fiscalesob
mandamiento mesón (2)	tupil doctrina mandamiento	
5. tupilob / tupil mesónob		cananob
(offices of varying rank with Spanish titles)		
albaceasob (executors)		
testigo mayor / testigosob (witnesses)		
(offices of varying rank with Maya titles)		
ah cuch cab (sometimes similar to regidor-alcalde)		
ah ɔib hun (notary)		
alcalde col ("field" alcalde)		
belnal (officer)		
chun than (officer or "speaker")		

SOURCE: Maya-language notarial records from Tekanto and other cahob.

cabildo offices of alcalde and regidor; the gap between the latter and the bulk of extracabildo officers was reflected in the fact that in most extant examples the regidor is the most junior named officer to ratify notarial business.

The maestro and tupil doctrina mandamiento are placed in a civil-religious category because they were included in Tekanto's (civil) election roster; the Cacalchen election record of 1690 includes maestro and fiscal, but I have followed Tekanto's choice because of documented instances of the maestro performing a civil notarial function, and because the tupil doctrina mandamiento seems to be a potential apprentice to either escribano or maestro. The other religious offices included are just those that I have seen in Maya notarial documents, although there were also Maya *músicos* and *acólitos*, and sometimes a body of fiscales and sacristanes.[27]

Career Patterns

He has served as Alcalde Mesón, Regidor Mayor, and also as Lieutenant.
—cabildo of Xcupilcacab, 1812

One central characteristic that the Maya and Nahua cabildos had in common, as distinct from the Spanish model, was the treatment of offices as rungs of a ladder—posts that could be held by noblemen without loss of status. This was qualified by the fact that only nobles became indigenous governors, and few non-nobles even became alcaldes. Yet in Yucatan most batabs began as regidors, and an alcalde might have started his career thirty years earlier as an alguacil at the bottom of the ladder. The system was therefore more fluid—it took "a broader view of prestigious office," in Haskett's words—than the Spanish system, which tended to restrict minor offices to men of lesser social rank.[28]

The following discussion is based on the data in the tables in Appendix C, which present the mid-seventeenth-century Cacalchen cabildo (garnered from wills), the late-seventeenth-century full roster of officers from Tekanto (listed in election records), Ixil's cabildo in the 1760's (also drawn from wills), and finally the cabildo officers of the cahob-barrios of Tihó at the end of the colonial period (taken from records of the exchange of urban property). These tables offer patterns that provide enough individual biographical data to enable the construction of officer careers, and give us some idea of what was common, and what unusual.

The best database for this analysis is the body of election documents from Tekanto, which list all twenty-one officers over a twenty-five-year span (1683–1707), with gaps in only two years at the start and end of the sample period. A partial study of this data has already been included in unpublished doctoral work by Thompson, who added the names of alcaldes and regidors (from testaments) for most years through to 1820, to create an arresting theory of office cyclicity.[29] I have returned to this data because Thompson chose not to look at the careers of officers below the rank of regidor, and because this data and data from other cahob (albeit more patchy) suggested pattern possibilities not emphasized by Thompson. Indeed, Thompson himself recognized the limited applicability of the cyclical pattern; the following pages place those limitations in a more comprehensive perspective.

A computer-assisted survey of this data, aimed at detecting patterns in these cabildo lists of twenty-five years, produced one important preliminary fact—the sample contains exactly 200 names of which two-thirds are multiple-officeholders displaying career patterns—and two cautionary facts: some careers must begin or end outside the sample period, and the same name may be held by two or even three different persons. This leaves us with an estimated 112 men whose careers can be largely or entirely reconstructed.[30]

The overwhelming pattern is one of ascension through the ranks, with each position acting as one rung of the same ladder. There were a few exceptions: the batab, lieutenant, and notary were superior offices whose holders do not appear below the rank of regidor; the notarial position required a special skill that associated it with the offices of maestro and tupil doctrina mandamiento (whose placing at the foot of the table represents their tangental, not subsidiary, relation to the main ladder); alcaldes and regidors are a separate tier, being the offices of the original Spanish cabildo, and those whose holders' names appear most frequently in the ratification formulas of notarial business—yet regidors and alcaldes for the most part still had to work their way up the lower rungs of the ladder.

It is also clear from the start that a person seldom held office two years in a row, even less seldom the same office for consecutive years. These gaps are a potential window onto general patterns, and indeed for the first two decades of the nineteenth century the regularity of the gaps drew Thompson's attention to the fact that regidor and alcalde offices had become monopolized by an elite group who had begun to circulate the positions among themselves according to a quadripartite roster. But this pattern only begins to take shape in the 1780's, and is not evident a century earlier. Instead these career gaps reveal two alternative patterns.

The first of these is the shape of a successful career, as opposed to that of a flawed one. A classic success story is that of Feliciano Dzib, who worked his way up from alguacil (1684) through mayordomo (1687), procurador (1689), regidor mayor (1691), and alcalde segundo (1694, 1698), to alcalde mayor (1701). The course of his career is smooth, without a setback in rank or an exceptionally long hiatus, culminating in the holding of junior alcalde twice, a sign of eligibility for alcalde mayor. Similarly holding the post of alcalde mayor twice implied eligibility for the batabil, a fact to which we shall shortly return. On the other hand, holding lesser posts (such as alguacil) consecutively implied that one's career was stalling. Juan Baz, for example, was mandamiento mesón in 1689, then alguacil twice (1692, 1699), after which he is not seen again. The seven-year gap between his two alguacil terms also indicates that Juan Baz is not destined for high office. Similarly Bernardo Dzib was alguacil twice (1693, 1696), and then rises to alguacil mayor in 1700, but does not reappear in the election lists.

A final sure sign of a faltering career is a demotion; nine times out of ten an officer who drops a rank or more subsequently disappears from the roster of officers. Francisco Canche climbed from alguacil mayor (1690) to fourth regidor (1692), but then fell back to mayordomo (1694) and is never heard of again; Pedro Ppol's cabildo service takes him from mandamiento through alguacil and regidor mayor to alcalde segundo (1701), but a drop to regidor segundo in 1703 spells the end of his sixteen-year career.

The second pattern indicated by gaps in individual careers takes us to the heart of the political system in Tekanto at this time. Possibilities lay in the spacing of these gaps, or a connection between them and patronyms, but no such pattern is apparent. The key, rather, was the batabil. From before our sample period begins until 1698 don Juan Dzib was governor. The absence of a governor in 1699, followed by the mere three-year term of don Antonio Camal and the subsequent imposition by colonial authorities of a Spaniard from Izamal, don Agustín de Valenzuela, onto the governorship for at least four years, all confirms the history of a dispute over Tekanto's ruling office (see "Elections and Factions" below). Thompson's observation, that the apparent rivals for the post, Antonio Camal and Mateo Ppol (who becomes governor sometime after 1706), both served multiple terms as alcalde mayor and were therefore establishing eligibility for the batabil, jibes well with general patterns. Only two other names appear twice as alcalde mayor: Francisco Canul, who was in fact two if not three different men; and Gerónimo Cach, who seems to have been something of an interim governor during the dispute, appearing as alcalde mayor (1699, 1706) and teniente (1703) only in hiatus years. The question, then, is whether a change of governor at a time of intense rivalry in the upper ranks signals a change in the lower ranks, as though one regime were being replaced with another. This indeed does appear to be the case.

If we take the career officers from alcalde to mandamiento of 1700, don Antonio Camal's first year as governor, we find that thirteen out of the fifteen do not appear as officers after Camal's fall from office (or death), and the careers of the remaining two are unreliable anyway because more than one officer seems to carry each name. Of the thirteen career officers serving in 1701, five do not appear again, and three appear in 1703 as demoted officers, after which they also disappear, and three reappear only in 1707, when it is unclear who is governor. The statistics for 1702 are similar to those for 1700, except for the appearance of three new names at the very bottom of the ladder, men who go on to serve in the post-Camal years. Perhaps these most junior offices represented too loose an affiliation with the governorship to be of potential damage to one's career. If we therefore exclude these three, and look at Camal's three-year term as a whole, we find that the careers of 75 percent of officers serving under Camal appear to have been damaged by association with him. If we also exclude men whose careers are unreliable owing to repetition of names, that figure rises to 87 percent. Furthermore, officers from pre-1700 who do not serve under Camal resume their careers in the 1703–7 period.

There is no record of who became governor in 1707. The change of escribano, which also occurred after Camal was deposed or died, indicates that the Valenzuela interregnum may have ended. There is also an unusually large number of officers in 1707 who have not served at all since

1699 or earlier, including a few who served when Mateo Ppol was last alcalde mayor in 1692. It may be, then, that Ppol, who was governor by 1714, began his term in 1707.

The fact that there were factions of officers organized around men eligible for the batabil comes as no surprise: factional disputes were central to postconquest Nahua politics.[31] What is significant is that we find no apparent principles behind this organization, in the sense that there is no mention of sociopolitical subunits or wards let alone ward affiliation by faction, nor can we establish or detect from the Tekanto data alliances of chibalob (patronym groups). However, Thompson has shown that the eighteenth-century governorship in Tekanto was controlled (to use the terminology of this study, not his) by an elite group of dominant chibalob in the cah who were interlinked by marriage and commanded a dispro-portionate share of community wealth.[32] Ixil in the 1760's was dominated by a similar chibal elite, with cabildo representation diminishing as one moves down the socioeconomic ranking of chibalob. What emerges, then, is a complex picture in which access to political office is determined by broader considerations of status within the community, and these consid-erations help determine the shape of a person's political career. Yet one's political destiny was not written in stone. It appears that within the larger confines of class choices were available, so that the officers who hitched their wagons to don Antonio Camal might have guaranteed for them-selves a political environment of reduced political competition for many years. As it turned out, for most, the decision was fatal to their careers.

Both Thompson's analysis of late-colonial upper-tier politics in Tekanto and fragments of evidence from other cahob bear out this view of Maya politics as being structured on a kind of factionalism in which factions were contained within class and the hierarchy of offices was part of the larger and less scalable ladder of socioeconomic hierarchy. Cabildo lists of senior officers drawn from testament collections show ladder-climbing ca-reer patterns in mid-seventeenth-century Cacalchen and Ixil in the 1760's; and the same is demonstrated by officer data taken from bills of sale from Tihó's cahob-barrios (see Appendix C).

In the latter there are clear signs of the batabil being held alternately by factions, and of a hereditary factional representation: Don Juan Espiritu Santo Chable is batab of Santiago in the 1760's, don Marcelo Bacab by 1778, and don Silvestre Chable from 1779 to at least 1782. By 1786 don Marcelo has regained the position, and ten years later he is able to pass it on to his son don Marcelino Bacab. The latter ceded the post at least in 1802, but is still batab in 1806. This relatively rapid exchange of the senior cah office seems to have represented a sharing of power among factions, rather than an ejection of an entire regime with each change of batab: senior officers such as tenientes and escribanos are able to survive from one batabil to the other; in one year of don Marcelo's batabil (1786), both alcaldes and the regidor mayor are Chable, implying an attempt to balance the cabildo between the two factions. There is a similar rotation, or to-and-fro sharing, of the batabil between Camal and Chan in early-nineteenth-century Tekanto, and also in Santa Ana, visible even though records are extant for only seven years, with the office bouncing between a Canche and a Kauil from at least 1748. Dionisio Kauil's appearance as regidor mayor eighteen years before he shows up as batab implies the existence of ladder career patterns here in Santa Ana too; and in 1822 (when the batabil no longer exists in the cah) the fact that the senior alcalde is a Canche implies considerable continuity in the handling of faction and in the heredity of rulership.

A central ramification of the creation of a ladder of offices by the Maya is the minimalization of specific function, and the flexible usage of titles. What separates the notary, maestro, and whatever apprentices they might have from other offices is an exceptional skill not demanded in any other post. For other posts, what mattered most was rank and inclusion, and therefore additional numbers of regidors could be created (as in Santiago, 1741) so as to include the desired number of principales; or designations such as testigo could be distributed for the same reasons (for example, San Cristóbal, 1830). The title ah cuch cab was a similar means of inclusion with meaning no doubt specific to each cah at each moment it was applied (such as Xecpes 1578; Cacalchen, 1649; Ixil, 1767).

Mid-seventeenth-century Cacalchen seems to have added alcaldes and regidors at will, perhaps dispensing with the distribution of lesser offices. The use of "don" by the alcalde mayor in 1646 as well as the consecutive holding of the same post for three years by Pedro Chi imply that the lack of any mention of a batab meant that the cah, being small and poor, did not have one. By 1653 a batab existed, but the alcalde mayor is described as don Gerónimo Pat, and the number of alcaldes (four) and regidors (five) is unusual. An election record of 1690 shows that by this date Cacalchen has begun designating a consistent list and number of offices to its principales along the same lines as contemporaneous Tekanto. This treatment of the alcalde mayor as a batab equivalent in seventeenth-century Cacalchen is mirrored at the end of the colonial period by an identical use of the alcalde mayor position by cah-barrio principales. In San Cristóbal, for example, a don Pedro Nolasco Camal, who was batab between at least 1810 and 1815, was out of office in 1819, but in 1820 reappears as head of the list of *alcaldes auxiliares*; although he seems to have lost his "don," Camal is still the senior officer in the cah.

Thus, in spite of the imposition of foreign structures of government and in spite of the annual electoral requirements of the colonial authorities, the Maya pursued their own view of how politics functioned and how politicians interacted. Just as the offices and meaning given to such cabildo posts were, in a broad sense, Mayanized, and in many instances localized by an individual cah, so too was the electoral process—to which we now turn.

Elections and Factions

M'lord batab is weak of mind and no longer desires to represent us. Therefore, we request as a favor . . . that there be a change of the lord batab that governs us here in this cah.
—cabildo of Xcupilcacab, 1812

As with other aspects of the sociopolitical structure of the colonial-era Maya, the outward form of cabildo elections was Spanish, but their practice and expression were in many ways indigenous. It is not known whether Spanish electoral procedures were imposed along with the initial establishment of cabildos in the repúblicas indígenas of New Spain; a royal cédula dated October 9, 1549, categorically stated that all indigenous cabildo officers were to be elected annually or biennially. This election procedure was confirmed with respect to Yucatan in the sixteenth-century ordenanzas promulgated by López Medel, Céspedes, and Palacios.[33]

Most extant Maya election records date from a twenty-three-year period at the end of the seventeenth century, and almost all of those come from Tekanto. Nevertheless, it is clear that by the turn of that century some conventional procedure for annually selecting cabildo officers had been established in the cahob. By the 1680's that procedure included elaborate opening and closing formulas similar to those found in election records in Nahuatl.[34] Probably for most of the colonial period Maya cabildos kept formularized election records either in separate books—*u libroyl* (1690), or *u libroil elecon* (1801)—or with other notarial material.

The use of a full Maya vocabulary to describe the process in such formulas suggests that the procedure was based to some extent upon a preconquest precedent in which selection, as well as birth, played an important role. After the conquest, although the titles of office changed, the offices still represented positions of rulership and government in the cah. And though the exact date and place of election changed to suit colonial preferences, the date remained constant and calendrically significant (the end of the year), and the place was, as before, public and monumental (the church, until courthouses were built in the eighteenth or nineteenth centuries).

In contrast to cabildo elections in Nahua communities, elections in colonial-era cahob do not appear to have involved a named electorate of voters. A document from Ebtun records the selection of nine electors and their subsequent selection of six cabildo officers, but the document is in Spanish and is dated 1823. In Maya-language sources before Independence, the absence of any mention of either voters or ballot-taking may mean that the body of cah principales simply chose the officers from among their number, in a single process that combined nomination and election. Indeed, although Independence may have brought a change in outward procedure to Ebtun and other cahob, the essence of elections remained the same: in 1823 both the electors and the new cabildo officers are chosen unanimously.[35] In other words, competition, maneuvering, and dissent among factions and individuals was played out prior to the public ritual of selection recorded on paper. This process is essentially what also took place in central Mexico, the only difference being that the Nahuas were less vague about the electing process, sometimes referring to electorates and voting.

Some idea of the qualifications considered necessary to serve as batab—and thus by extension in any post—is given by a petition of 1812 from Xcupilcacab. More accurately, the petition tells us what the Maya thought the Spaniards thought were necessary qualities: a strong record of service on the cabildo, a reputation for defending the cah well, being intelligent and of sound mind, or simply being a "good man," *malob uinic.* Yet these were surely merits that the Maya themselves would have emphasized, especially the ability to protect or defend the cah, which, as we shall see later, is brought out clearly in the language of rulerly address in Maya petitions. In addition, the emphasis on cabildo service sits well with the evidence of colonial-era Maya career patterns.

Such patterns illustrate the complexity of what ultimately determined a man's political destiny: the subsystems of rotation based on calendrical cycles and chibal alliances, overlaid with the maneuvering and factionalism fundamental to all political organizations. The documentary evidence has left us with two sample cases of electoral conflict and factionalism, from which we can make a number of deductions. A record as dry and brief as that of Ticul's 1611 election shows not an inkling of political wheeling-and-dealing, but the petition of 1812 from Xcupilcacab tells an interesting, and revealing, story.[36]

The petition requests that the batab of the cah be retired, and goes on to present three replacement candidates for the governorship of the town. This method of candidacy is the sole sign that the post-1770 viceregal regulations on elections, which sought to alter central Mexican practice and within a generation had imposed Spanish as the language of election records, may have had some effect in Yucatan. The new law required the "voters" to submit three names under supervision of the local priest or Spanish official.[37] In fact, almost all nineteenth-century cah election records are in Spanish, and the parish priest or *juez de paz* (or both) submitted a *terna*, or trio of candidates. The first name was almost always chosen.[38] The Xcupilcacab petition implies that the terna system had been introduced into the cahob in the late-colonial period, and that the Maya had soon learned how to minimize the changes and work the system to their advantage, for the dice are clearly loaded in favor of Rafael Tzin:

... cantul Reg°res y u nuctacil uincob ti lay cah bicil yn yum Rafael tzin katic u yatzilil ca yanac u yocol u mektanton ti lay cah tumenel ɔoc kaholtic u yacuntah ɔoc u menti[c] u alcalde mesónil ɔoc umenti[c] u Reg°r mayoril ɔoc u mentic u tenienteil xan lay u nucul ɔoc kaholtic bicil hach malob u yacuntic cah u caɔice yum felipe tzab Bay xan ɔoc u mentic u Reg°r mayorlil lay u nucul ɔoc kaholtic u yacun tic cah xan u yoxɔice Benito Puc Bay xan ɔoc kaholtic bicil malob uinic y cuxolal ...

... the four regidors and other principal men in this cah ask the favor that m'lord Rafael Tzin govern us in this cah, because he is of sound mind and has served as Alcalde Mesón, Chief Regidor, and also Lieutenant. It is understood and remembered how very well he protects the cah. Secondly, lord Felipe Tzab also served as Chief Regidor. It is understood and known that he also protects the cah. Thirdly, there is Benito Puc. He too is known as a good man and an intelligent one ...

The underlining of Tzin's name was presumably made when, several months later, Tzin was confirmed as the replacement batab. The Spanish documentation that has survived with the petition dates from between January 27 and April 20, 1812. The earliest date refers to a previous petition by Xcupilcacab requesting the removal of the batab, don Manuel Na, on the grounds of age and also his alleged treatment of all the inhabitants as though they were his personal vassals. This latter accusation no doubt gets closer to the truth, introducing as it does an internecine element, but perhaps for this very reason it does not make it to the petition of February 15. The earlier petition also mentions the same three replacement candidates and also in a way that favors Rafael Tzin, who by April 17 is approved in office. The Xcupilcacab Maya achieved their end via the Spanish legal system with unusual speed. Spanish officials knew little of local Maya affairs and were not motivated to complicate local politics, or their own jobs. Thus the Maya petitioners got their way, and the Spanish authorities could continue to enjoy the three-century-old delusion that they understood and controlled indigenous politics.

The petition of 1812, along with similar records running into the 1840's, indicates remarkable continuity in a number of ways, not least of which is the implication that the Maya are still choosing officials for their own cabildo, and submitting them to the Spanish authorities for ratification, and still engaging in a factional politics that periodically disturbs the surface of the system. Spanish records show that Maya claims of senility among their batabs were common in the early generations after the conquest.[39] There is no doubt that the Maya immediately learned how to work within and exploit the Spanish legal system to their advantage. It seems that in the early nineteenth century they may have still been employing the same tactics. If so, the allegedly senile batab of Xcupilcacab did not have enough power to muster a petition of protest. The Rafael Tzin faction seemed to have won the support of all the town's alcaldes and regidores, whose names appear at the foot of the petition. Of course the cabildo officers were illiterate, so it would have been an easy trick to write in their names as though they were party to the petition, but there is no direct evidence in the Xcupilcacab file of such duplicity.

Maya factionalism did not always avoid disturbing the calm surface of colonial administration. Tekanto at the turn of the eighteenth century succeeded in creating waves so significant as to prompt the colonial authorities to intervene and actually impose a Spaniard as governor. Don Juan Dzib had been Tekanto's governor from 1683 or before, through 1698. During this time two Mayas, Mateo Ppol and Antonio Camal, had both served consecutive terms as senior alcalde. As argued earlier, this violation of the norm indicated that, as early as the 1680's, these two were being considered, groomed perhaps, as future governors. Then in 1699 the election record leaves a blank space where the governor usually "signs," and the opening formula reads simply s^r $guer^{or}$; the post still existed, but it was vacant. The calendrical timing of this anomaly prompted Philip Thompson to argue that Tekanto was attempting to adjust the traditional calendar-based term of office for the batab to the European century-cycle.[40] If this was so, the internal debate over this decision must have taken on factional overtones: from 1700 through 1702 Camal is governor; in 1703 a Spanish official from Izamal, don Agustín de Valenzuela, is imposed as the cah's nominal ruler, with a Maya as his lieutenant; sometime between 1707 and 1712 (from which period no records have survived) Ppol finally wins the governorship.[41]

During the four years or more of Valenzuela's term, Camal and Ppol must have campaigned and petitioned fiercely for Spanish approval, for Valenzuela's presence, although it would have been nominal rather than physical, shows that the selection process had passed from Maya into Spanish hands, no doubt an instructive experience for Tekanto's ruling class. Fortunately for us, the dispute caused two decades of Tekanto's election records to be sent to Mérida, where they still sit, the only known surviving continuous run of such documents from Yucatan. Unfortunately, none of the petitions that must have accompanied the dispute has surfaced.[42]

A number of other disputes involving batabob have survived on paper, and most, if not all, seem to be factional to some degree. Farriss convincingly discusses two of them—the so-called rebellion in Tekax of 1610 and a successful 1670 campaign by a faction in Tzotzil to have their batab removed—in the context of "social strain" and "class struggle," but also "elite factionalism"; indeed, the evidence of these examples, along with that of the cases presented above, suggests that these were largely factional disputes whose nuances escaped the Spaniards, who exaggerated the element of popular unrest because this was a chief concern of the colonists. There are two important contextual bases to the 1670 case—the fact of social hierarchy in the cah and the potential therein for class antagonism, and the investigation into the Flores de Aldana governorship encouraging several such attacks on batabs as representatives of the *repartimiento* (forced purchase) system—but, as Farriss observes, the episode itself was provoked by the Tzotzil batab's clumsy handling of cah factionalism.[43] A third case, alluded to earlier, claims to be a personal petition aimed at reversing an unjust settling of an estate by the batab of Dzan; the petitioner claims that this batab hates him, and has attempted to rape his wife, and that therefore his decision is not objective but is based on personal animosity. This case may also be a factional dispute, in which one faction has opportunistically exploited an otherwise uncontroversial decision made by the batab.[44]

The electoral process, then, was often far more Machiavellian than a simple election record shows. In the vast majority of cases, the machinations of the selection process, and consequently any factional battles that may have occurred, were hidden from Spanish officials (and future historians); in cases such as Xcupilcacab (1812), the Spaniards were either fooled or oblivious; in cases like Tekanto (c. 1700), the colonial powers are obliged to step in and reimpose the *pax hispanica*.

By virtue of the paperwork they generate, disputes within any area of recorded activity tend to give an impression of instability in that area. In fact the colonial-era Maya political system was notably stable, especially compared with the similar indigenous system in central Mexico. The well-documented frequency of election disputes in Nahua towns might be taken to suggest that, because in general there are more records in colonial Nahuatl than in Maya, there must have been much internecine political conflict in the cahob for which we have no evidence. I believe this was not so, for one crucial reason: election disputes in altepetl and cah alike always centered on the office of governor-batab; Nahua governors were elected annually along with the other cabildo offices, whereas Maya governors-batabs remained in office for up to twenty years.

No doubt the colonial authorities tolerated long batab terms of office partly because they fostered stability, even if they did defy colonial law and encourage the perpetuation of dynasties. In fact, Spanish bureaucratic involvement in the Maya electoral process appears to have been pro forma, as indicated in two ways: the dispatch of Maya electoral records to Mérida, and the inspections of these records by Spanish officials. That election documents traveled to Mérida each year is indicated by two pieces of evidence. One, Francisco Crespo also signed off on Cacalchen's 1690 election record, making the usual marks in the margin. Two, an ordinance translated into Maya and dated October 9, 1789, of which a copy addressed to twenty-six cahob in the jurisdiction of Valladolid has survived, orders that the cahob elections for the coming year be held in three weeks and the records of them be brought in with the head tax, at which time the Governor—*ca yum halach uinic*—will give his approval to the documents.[45] Thus the statement by the Ticul cabildo in 1801 that they were taking their copy of the 1612 election record into Tihó not only provides evidence relating to a lawsuit in which they were engaged but also proves an annual obligation at least two centuries old.

Spanish concerns regarding the Maya electoral process are clearly indicated by the marginal ticks made by the officials who reviewed Tekanto's election documents from 1683 to 1706—Francisco Crespo through 1689, and Ceverino ("Zepherino") Pacheco from 1690. Both officials tick, or mark with a bracket that resembles the number 3, the same six offices: the alcalde mesón, the two tupil mandamiento mesón, the maestro, the escribano, and the tupil doctrina mandamiento. The first three of these ran the mesón, the guest house that was lodging for Spaniards who had to travel in rural Yucatan on official or private business. The last three were vital to Maya literacy and to the church, both of which were an essential part of the colonial system of indirect rule. The skills of the maestro and escribano allowed the Spanish paper-intensive legal and administrative system to function at the indigenous level, and the maestro and his subordinate, the tupil doctrina mandamiento, helped maintain the faith by ensuring attendance at catechism. The latter may also have collected the *higuerilla*, one of the taxes upon which the local priest relied. In other words, Spanish preoccupations were practical, centered on the efficient and profitable function of provincial administration to a degree that allowed the Maya with their relatively stable cah system to practice local politics more or less undisturbed.

PART TWO

Society and Culture

ᴕ

Class

The fallacious notion that colonial Mexico's indigenous communities were so culturally and economically impoverished by Spanish rule that all inhabitants were reduced to the level of commoners tends to be rooted in the misapplication of a sense of outrage over the injustice of colonialism, in the adoption of a Spanish point of view as a result of approaching indigenous society via Spanish sources, and in a literal reading of indigenous claims that they were indeed reduced to the equalizing poverty of the lowest common denominator.[1] Much has been made of the differing fates of those Maya dynasties who were early collaborators (especially the Xiu), and those who offered some resistance (especially the Cocom).[2] This view, too, reflects Spanish perceptions, which were themselves influenced by the propaganda advanced by Maya collaborators and by Spanish blindness or indifference to the fate of other leading Maya families. As late as 1821 the Cocom were still important figures in the cah of Sotuta, their "capital" at the time of the conquest.[3] Another dynasty, the Pech, was still a dominant noble chibal in the late eighteenth century, in spite of one historian's suggestion that they had fallen off the map more than a century earlier.[4] The primary concern of the colonial authorities was stability; as long as the system was running smoothly, the colonists could pursue their own ambitions of acquiring wealth and status. And the system depended for its smooth running on the indigenous nobility and their intermediary role in the power structure of colonial relations. In Yucatan—indeed, wherever Spaniards ruled indigenous peoples—colonial rule facilitated rather than depressed class differences in indigenous society. By the same token, it was clearly more advantageous to the Maya nobility to provide a façade of stability, behind which the new system could be reconciled to the old and traditional privileges could be maintained as much as possible. The Maya soon perceived and mastered this challenge, and under colonial rule most of the elite families continued to hold their positions at the top of a society still based on class differentiations.[5]

Individual status within the structure of Maya class society was determined by several mutually dependent factors. These included not only one's chibal and connection to the traditionally dominant families, but also gender, wealth, and, for men, a record of political or religious office. This was not a caste system: there was social interaction between classes, as well as some possibility of social mobility, in both directions. Nor was the exercise of the power and influence accruing to one's status in cah society based simply on what Foucault has called "the interplay of nonegalitarian and mobile relations."[6] Rather, it depended on predetermined expectations of behavior in every aspect of life, from cabildo relations to land use to marriage choices to the settling of an estate, in which both individual and private action has certain communal and public implications. In cah society, the public modified the private in such a way as to blur the line between the two and blend the individual and communal ramifications of the determinatives of social status.

Social Differentiation

I, don Lazaro Uitz, batab, with the notary, exchange one plot of forest with the nobleman, Gregorio Chi.
— batab and cabildo of Sicpach, 1750

Maya notarial documents reveal various terms of class differentiation, listed here in Table 7.1. The Maya term for nobility, *almehen*, survived through the colonial period. Its semantic origins are the words *al*, "the child of a woman," and *mehen*, "the child (usually son) of a man," implying that the person so titled is the child of a man and woman, meaning, that is, a man and woman of importance—similar to the Spanish *hidalgo* (*hijo de algo*, the child of someone, that is, someone important) and also the Nahuatl *pilli* (*-pil* [possessed], "offspring"; *piloa*, "to depend"). Philip Thompson, observing an increased use of the word almehen at the end of the colonial period in Tekanto, suggested that this was an attempt by Maya nobility there to stall their descent into macehual or commoner class. This has been taken as evidence that the Maya use of almehen was "erratic" and that indigenous designations of nobility were vague and inconsistent.[7] This may have been true in some cahob toward the end of Spanish rule, but on the whole I believe almehen was used quite specifically—more or less the way the Spaniards used hidalgo and the way the English used "knight" or "squire," terms that lost weight as they became more common but in the

TABLE 7.1
Some Maya Terms of Class Differentiation and Social Category

Term	Translation	Comments
almehen	noble	[M] Maya class designation, not an office
colel	lady	as above
hidalgo	noble	[Sp] designated by colonial authorities; *indio hidalgo* if speaker is Spanish
yum	father, lord	[M] term of respect and deference
batab	ruler	[M] cah governor; also *gobernador*
don	similar to British "sir"	[Sp] precedes Christian name; used by Maya only for batabob and indios hidalgos
doña	lady, madam	possibly for wives of the above; all Maya doñas appear to be independently wealthy
maestro	teacher	[Sp] an office that commanded class status
macehual	commoner	[M] comes to mean "Maya person"
uinic	(Maya) man	[M] sometimes means "(Maya) person"
kuluinicob	principal men [Sp. *principales*]	[M] traditional ruling body of the cah; also *u nucil uinicob* and *noh uinicob*
chibal	patronym group	[M] properly *chibal*; effective social subunit of the cah
kilacabil	ancestry, lineage	[M] *kilacabilob*, "ancestors"

SOURCE: Maya-language notarial documentation.

early modern period were usually unambiguous. A person either was or was not of such status. This was certainly true in the cah of Ixil in the late eighteenth century.

This is not to say that the use of class terminology or class relations was entirely static. Yet the characterization of Maya class differentiation as vague is unsatisfactory, in part because it reflects the treatment of the term almehen by Spanish officials, who usually translated it as hidalgo. Strictly speaking, the Spaniards were right, but the terminology is confused because the colonial powers had granted to certain indigenous groups the title *indio hidalgo*, a status that afforded certain privileges, most notably exemption from tribute taxes. Partly out of prejudice, the Spaniards misleadingly lumped together almehenob and indios hidalgos.

When a Yaxkukul land document (part of the Pech title named after that cah) lists the sons of the cah's batab, they are described as *ydalgosob*. Inevitably it was this part of the title that was important to the Maya, whereas to the Spaniards *indios* was the descriptive noun carrying more weight than its adjective, *hidalgos*.[8] To the Maya, there was a noble class termed almehen, within which was an elite termed hidalgo; the latter group was exclusive, yet contained within the former. Neither designation was office-related, but both were selectively hereditary; the sons of don Alonso Pech, the aforementioned Yaxkukul batab, were all hidalgos bearing the don prefix, but not every person of the Pech patronym was of that status. Most Pech, however, especially in the Ceh Pech area, seem to have been almehenob. The role played by prominent Pech men disproves the

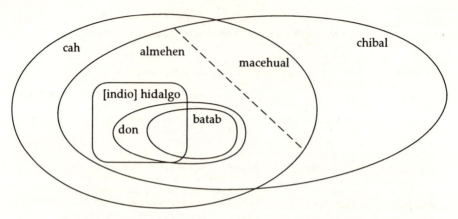

Fig. 7.1. A Maya class model.

notion that indios hidalgos were somehow set apart from local Maya hierarchies, forming "an Indian subcategory" of Spanish society.[9] Twenty-
one of the twenty-five cahob in the Ceh Pech region were governed by
Pech batabs in 1567; there were Pech batabs in Yaxkukul, Ixil, and other
cahob in the region in the seventeenth and eighteenth centuries; and Pech
involvement in Ixil's politics, society, and economy in the 1760's was
extensive.[10]

Figure 7.1, suggested by Philip Thompson's Ven diagram representations of almehen and hidalgo, includes two other titles that also indicated
status but were not, on the face of it, hereditary.[11] The office of batab, the
municipal governor, was not normally passed from father to son (although
there are cases of such), but neither was it annually elected—a batab might
hold office two decades—nor was it even considered a true cabildo office;
but it was usually controlled by a group of upper-class families, such as the
Bacab and Chable in late-eighteenth-century Santiago Tihó, and the Canche and Kauil in nearby Santa Ana in the same period. Of the 33 chibalob
in the Ebtun written record, just 9 had batabs between 1600 and 1823, with
over a third of them Camal; of Tekanto's 36 colonial-era chibalob, 13 produced batabs (in broken records of 1581 to 1856), but 6 chibalob were
represented by 70 percent of those batabs (22 percent of the total were
Camal). The Camal also dominated the batabil in Sisal, as did the Xiu in
and around Maní and Peto, the Cocom in and around Sotuta, the Iuit in
Hocaba, the Euan in Caucel, the Cupul in Cuncunul and Xecpes, and the
Pech in Chicxulub, Chuburna, Ixil, Motul, and Yaxkukul.[12]

Access to the batabil indicated and perpetuated privilege not just in cah
society but within the local cluster of noble chibalob. Both the Spanish
authorities and the cahnalob recognized the batab as the community rep-

resentative, and with this social and political prestige came economic opportunity. In times of relative prosperity, the batabil could be a lucrative office, but when Spanish demands far outstripped Maya productive capacities, the role of colonial intermediary made the batabil a potential political liability. This uncertainty, along with the class differences and tensions that existed in the Maya world, is well illustrated by two periods in Yucatec history. During the period of gubernatorial exploitation by don Rodrigo Flores de Aldana, as records of the subsequent investigation (his *residencia*) reveal, in many cahob the cabildo blamed their batab for repartimiento excesses. Cahnalob normally accepted their batab's (sometimes profitable) role in these forced purchases, but in times of great hardship batabs ran the risk of violating the expectations of the moral economy and rendering class differences intolerable. A similar situation prevailed in the period before the outbreak of the Caste War, when the increasing failure of the neocolonial economy and authorities to allow batab participation and profit became a causal factor in the conflict; in other words, it was not during, but after, the colonial period that power structures in the province seriously threatened the maintenance of class differences in the Maya community.[13]

The batab's colonial-era position was reflected in the Maya usage cf the prefix "don," which was conservative compared with the usage in central Mexico. At the time of the conquest only the highest Spanish noblemen enjoyed the don prefix, although most women of hidalgo rank were doña. The Nahuas almost immediately adopted the title, but with an important difference: it was less hereditary than indicative of high office, and thus the equivalent of the Nahuatl *teuctli*, "lord." This gradually changed, so that, whereas in the 1540's only the governor of Tlaxcala was a don, by the 1620's the title had spread to include the whole cabildo. This process had not reached Yucatan by Independence, with only an election document of 1821 showing alcaldes and regidors as don. Even today the title is used far more conservatively in Yucatan than in central Mexico.[14]

Although the office of batab afforded noble status, conversely only nobles could hold that office. The use of "don" strongly suggests as much, for the Maya granted that title only to batabob and former batabob, or to hidalgos. Surely if a nonhidalgo almehen did not merit a don, then a batab, whose office was signified by the don prefix, could not originate below the level of almehen. One reasons, then, that batab and don, although potential designators of office, always designated class; in terms of class groups, though not necessarily in terms of individuals, both designations were hereditary.[15]

By "class groups" I refer not only to "almehen" as a hereditary class group within which "don" becomes accessible, but also to the class role played by Maya patronym groups or chibalob. These important social units lay between the cah and the household, and were referred to with one of the few such collective terms in Maya—*ah pootob*, "the Poot family or chibal"; *ah uhil uinicob*, "the Uh people"—comparable to the cah collective term *ah mocochaob*, "those of Mococha."[16] To be outside the chibal system was to be outside Maya society—that is, non-Maya in the cah, or Maya entirely removed from the cah; thus Maya society existed within the intersection of cah and chibal systems. Within the chibal system one's status was potentially determined by one's patronym and that of one's mother. The maintenance of the Maya taboo on intrachibal marriage reflects the maintenance of the practice of interchibal marital alliance, which created multi-chibal households. The combination of these households was a cah-wide network of chibal interest-groups. The effect was to help perpetuate the class system, since chibal interest groups tended to consist of families at similar socioeconomic levels. In Ixil, for example, the second through fourth tiers of chibalob formed a primary such group with affinal connections to the first tier (the Pech), their interests combining to perpetuate their domination of the cah (see Table 7.4 and others below).[17]

Links between chibalob also extended into the ranks of the better-off commoners: for example, in Ixil, the Tec were tied to the Canche and Chan. Outside the circle of almehenob in Figure 7.1 were the macehuales, the commoners. The line between them is dotted to indicate that this distinction was porous in terms of the relative potential status of an almehen of modest means versus that of a wealthy macehual; also, economic upward mobility made it possible for almehen status to be acquired by a commoner chibal over generations, possibly even by somebody within his own lifetime. The figure does not show the variation in status (or the subclasses) within the greater macehual class, but this can be illustrated by a detailed look at relative wealth (and its correlation with other factors) in Ixil, a cah chosen partly because relevant documents have survived but also because the time frame of the sources—the 1760's—helps to support a thesis of class persistence. Supportive and comparative evidence is provided by data from mid-seventeenth-century Cacalchen.

A Class Case: Ixil

Thus will end the prayer for the soul of this noble.
—cabildo of Ixil, 1767

One of the key questions examined in Part Two of this book is that of the relationship between kinship and property. The question has been the subject of much debate among anthropologists. One scholar, for example, has remarked that "the transmission of property to children of both sexes" arises when parents are concerned with maintaining the social status of their children, particularly daughters, and thus "is likely to appear in societies in which status is based on economic differentiation."[18] Indeed, as Chapter 9 will show, the Maya did bequeath property to both sexes, and, as the database that is Appendix D reveals, there was certainly economic differentiation in Maya society. Nonetheless, Maya sources reveal a general overlapping of categories that transcends merely kinship and property.

We need not attempt to reconcile the notion of social status based on wealth with that of social status based on heredity, for the two already coincide in Yucatan, as we shall see in the case of Ixil. And if economic differentiation is a factor determining status, it should function as an incentive toward increased productivity and the diversification of wealth (including the acquisition of prestigious goods). The sources in Maya do not yield data on productivity—even detailed tribute records would unreliably provide such information. We can, however, examine to some degree (see Tables 3–6 in Appendix D) the diversity of wealth in two cahob in different centuries (seventeenth-century Cacalchen and eighteenth-century Ixil), especially among the wealthier testators, as well as the importance of property items introduced by the Spaniards (horses, for example, some tools, some furniture, religious objects, coinage, and men's clothing).

Although we cannot rank these testators by the total value of their estates because the pecuniary worth of items is rarely mentioned, and when it is, values differ, depending no doubt on the quality and condition of the item, we can give an approximate indication of relative prosperity within the two cahob. Tables 1 and 2 in Appendix D are indexes of the testators that enable the reader to put a name and date to the will numbers listed in the preceding four tables. Note that the wealth tables do not include all testators, since 15 percent in Cacalchen and 30 percent in Ixil only itemize property to pay for their burial and posthumous mass (corn and chickens in the former; money in the latter), a group that can be placed at the lower end of the social scale.

Cacalchen's wealthiest male testators were Alonso Couoh (folio number 11), Francisco May (14), Francisco Kuk (18), and Juan Eb (22); and female testators, Ursula Ake (16), Clara Che (21), Juana Eb (24), doña Francisca Uitz (31 and 32), and Ana Xul (33). Table 3 in Appendix C (cabildo officers of Cacalchen) shows that the same patronyms were prominent in the rosters of political officers during the same time period—there are Couoh, May, and Kuk as alcaldes and regidors, for example, and Eb and Ake also as regidors.

The data for Ixil can be analyzed more systematically: more wills are extant for this cah; the wills name neighboring landowners, which was not done in Cacalchen; and the Ixil cabildo was not irregular in its composition and rotation as was Cacalchen's. The Ixil male testators who appear to be the best off, based on large holdings of trees, bees, livestock, or land, are Felipe Coba (will number 10), Diego Chan (14), Pedro Mis (30), Josef Yam (33), Antonio Huchim (37), and Pasqual Ku (54). Female criteria are clothing and trees, producing Pasquala Matu (29), Juana Tun (48), and Luisa Tec (56) as the cah's wealthiest women.

This data can now be compared with other evidence of social differentiation in Ixil. First, let us look at who appear to be the hidalgos and almehenob in this cah. The designation hidalgo is not used at all in the Ixil wills of the 1760's, although we know from other sources that a good part of the Pech chibal were hidalgos; almehen, on the other hand, is appended to one testator's name, and it is used to describe most of the executors named. Four Pech are executors, and three of the Pech mentioned in the texts of wills are given the don prefix. As already stated, "don" was used only by batabob, former batabob, and important members of hidalgo chibalob. There are only three non-Pech dons in Ixil (for the will period, 1765–68), one the batab (don Ignacio Tec) and the other two possibly former batabob (don Clemente Tec, and don Gaspar Canul). Although not every person in a given patronym group or chibal was an hidalgo or almehen, the existence of one or more such nobles in a chibal indicated that the chibal held a certain class status in that cah. With this caveat in mind, we can say, therefore, that the Pech were the hidalgos in Ixil, the prominent almehenob (possibly also hidalgos) were the Tec, and the other almehen chibalob were the Canul with the seven others that included executors referred to as almehenob (listed in Table 7.4).

Second, it is possible to tabulate the landowners in Ixil at this time by using donor information in testaments and the naming of neighbors by these donors. Table 7.2 necessarily reflects the data from the testaments, rather than the total number of kaxob in Ixil at this time, which, one must assume, totaled more than the ninety-four listed here.[19] Yet we can also assume, considering the vagaries of human mortality, that this is a random sample of dying landowners and their neighbors, and thus the table effectively identifies the landowning class of a given Maya community, and, in particular, demonstrates the high status of the Pech.

The names of testators are italicized in this table because their ownership status appears more complicated than that of neighbors, which is

TABLE 7.2

Landowners of Ixil, 1765–1768

Total number of kaxob per chibal	Chibal members on record; number of kaxob owned in parentheses; kax-owning testators italicized
18 Pech	Baltesar, don Bartolome, Cristóbal, Diego, Felipe, Joaquín (2), Josef (3), don Juan (2), Juan (2), Manuel, Marcos, Mateo, Pasqual
12 Tec	*Gabriel* (3), *Luisa* (2), *Micaela*, *Nicolasa*, Andrés (2), don Clemente, don Ignacio, Miguel
10 Yam	*Josef* (3), *Mateo* / Mateo (3), Agustín (2), Andrés, Jacinto
9 Coba	*Felipe, Juan de la Cruz* (2), Gaspar, Ignacio, Juan, Nicolás, Salvador (2)
6 Huchim	*Antonio* (4), Ignacio, Pedro
6 Mis	*Pedro* (4), Josef, Juan
5 Canche	*Mateo*, Andrés, Felipe, Pasqual (2)
5 Couoh	*Pedro*, Juan, Nicolás, Sebastián (2)
4 Canul	*Diego, Ignacio* (2), Francisco
4 Poot	*Jacinto, Salvador*, Gaspar, "the Poot family or chibal"
2 Chan	*Diego* (2)
2 Matu	*Mateo*, Juan
1 Ake	Agustín
1 Bas	Ignacio
1 Cante	Agustín
1 Cime	Marcos
1 Cob	Andrés
1 Cutz	Manuel
1 Itza	Juan
1 Ku	*Pasqual*
1 Piste	Gaspar
1 Uh	*Sebastián*
1 Un	Sebastián

SOURCE: TI.

always unambiguously stated. For example, Juan de la Cruz Coba appears in the table as the owner of two kaxob. One of these is:[20]

in mul matan kax ti in Na catalina coba–yan tu xaman ti xculix lae–cin patic tu kab yn uixmehen pasq^{la} coba y yn uiɔinob phelipe coba–y Nicolas couoh–y in tillo Agus^n coba–u matanob tu cantulilob lae	my kax jointly inherited from my mother, Catalina Coba; it is to the north of Xculix; I leave it in the hands of my daughter Pasquala Coba, my younger siblings Felipe Coba and Nicolás Couoh, and my uncle Agustín Coba; all four of them are heirs together

The complexity of Maya joint inheritance that this reflects is not included in Table 7.2; I list the piece of kax under the testator's name alone, not those of his benefactor or heirs. This is in the interests of consistency: if the kax in the quote above, bequeathed to four heirs, were subsequently to be mentioned in the will of a neighbor, its owner would be recorded as only the senior male in the group. In other words, with the ninety-four parcels in

TABLE 7.3
Correlation of Ixil Landowners with Cabildo Officers and Will Executors, 1765–1769

Chibal	Kaxob	Offices
Pech	18	3 alcaldes, 2 regidors, 4 executors
Tec	12	1 batab, 1 teniente-executor, 1 notary, 1 regidor
Yam	10	1 alcalde, 1 executor
Coba	9	1 teniente, 1 alcalde, 2 regidors, 3 executors
Huchim	6	1 regidor
Mis	6	1 ah cuch cab-executor, 1 executor
Canche	5	1 regidor
Couoh	5	1 alcalde, 1 regidor
Canul	4	2 regidors, 2 executors
Poot	4	1 notary-executor, 1 executor
Chan	2	1 regidor
Matu	2	1 regidor-executor
Ake	1	
Bas	1	
Cante	1	1 alcalde, 1 executor
Cime	1	
Cob	1	1 notary, 1 notary-executor, 2 executors
Cutz	1	
Itza	1	
Ku	1	
Piste	1	
Uh	1	
Un	1	
May		2 alcaldes
Coot		1 alcalde
Na		2 regidors
Chim		1 regidor
Ek		1 regidor-executor
Euan		1 regidor
Kinil		1 regidor
Chale		1 executor

SOURCE: TI; kaxob numbers from Table 7.2 (1765–68); offices from App. C (1765–69).

TABLE 7.4
A Social Hierarchy of Chibalob, Ixil, 1765–1769

Tier	Status	Chibal
1	[indios] hidalgos	Pech
2	upper almehenob	Tec
3	middle almehenob	Cante, Canul, Cob, Coba, Mis, Poot, Yam
4	lower almehenob	Ek, Ku
5	upper commoners	Canche, Couoh, Chan, Huchim, Matu
6	upper-middle commoners	Cot, Chale, Chim, Euan, Kinil, May, Na
7	lower-middle commoners	Ake, Bas, Cab, Cime, Cutz, Itza, Piste, Tun, Uh, Un
8	lower commoners	Balam, Mas, Mex, Mo, Mukul, Tacu, Uitz

SOURCE: TI; Tables 7.2 and 7.3.

the table, each of the ninety-four owners represents as many as seven other family members in whose hands the kax has been placed.[21] Thus the real gap in landed wealth between the Pech and the Tec is numerically greater than the numbers listed in the table, although if the sample is indeed random, the Pech should still control 50 percent more land than the Tec, 80 percent more than the Yam, and so on.

Third, we can now take these chibalob and compare their ranking according to kax holdings with their cabildo representation. This information is presented in Table 7.3. Although at the lower end we find officers whose chibalob do not appear as landowners—explained by the fact that our data rely solely upon the random incidence of death over a given three years, and thus we know all the cabildo officers but not all the landowners—the upper end shows a satisfying correlation between wealth and political office.

Drawing these four threads together—title, overall wealth, kax-owning, and office—a chibal-based class hierarchy of class can be constructed for Ixil (see Table 7.4). At the lower end are chibalob who do not appear in any of these categories but whose existence in Ixil is known because even testators without property to bequeath are named, as are their parents. Of greater status are those who have estates to settle at life's end but do not appear on the cabildo; above them are lower-level officers, and above them is the group of almehenob, who also have high cabildo status and impressive kax holdings. Interestingly, the hierarchy is not pyramid shaped, but more rectangular, with a small pyramid shape at the top. At the apex are the Pech, who dominate every category except that of wealth among testators—no Pech die in Ixil in 1765–69.[22] Thus in opening this window onto the Maya world at a particular point in time and space we find that the chibal that dominated the area after which it was named (Ceh Pech) before the conquest and shortly after it, is still, in the late-colonial period, overwhelmingly dominant economically, politically, and socially in at least one community in the region.

CHAPTER EIGHT

⌒

Daily Life

By looking at the implications of Maya terminology for family, kin, and the household, and by reviewing the material objects of work and home life, we can come as close to "thick description" as the sources will allow, and can learn something of what it was like to live in a cah of the colonial period—of what stuff the material, cultural, and semiotic environment of a Maya family was made.

Household and Family

We are all now gathered together to deliver this house plot with its well to the children of Josef Cab and to his younger siblings.
—cabildo of Ixil, 1767

There is no Maya word in the documentation that can be accurately translated as "family." There is an abundance of kinship terminology (see Table 8.1), including catchall terms such as *on*, "parent, relative, kin," and *kilacabil*, "forebear, ancestor," as well as the patronym system whose effect, if not function, was to separate the Maya people into large identifiable groups. But collective expressions are rare and often vague; *lakob*, for example, might be interpreted as "relatives" when used in Tekanto,[1] but it literally means "others," and in Ixil is used to mean "neighbors" without necessary implications of kinship. The patronym or chibal collective mentioned earlier, *ah* [patronym]-*ob*, appears to refer to family in the broadest sense, possibly including all those of that patronym in a given cah. The four terms in Maya that refer to each element of the quadripartite kin system—*yumlal*, "paternal relative"; *naalal*, "maternal relative"; *idzin sucunil*, "fraternal relative"; and *mamil*, "affinal relative"—are dictionary terms that I have not encountered in the textual record in either singular or collective form. This does not mean that such terms were not used, but this is part of a general picture of the lack of emphasis both on large groups and on groups bound by stated kin or affinity.[2] Furthermore, if that only leaves us with the nuclear family, none of these terms adequately describes it either. Does this mean that such an entity did not exist?

Of course not. The Maya failure to categorize some form of nuclear family in a single term in their notarial records may inconvenience us, but it did not them; it does not signify the nonexistence of some sort of family concept any more than the failure to mention houses in Maya wills means that Yucatan's indigenous families slept under their sapote trees. Maya houses did not require mention because they were taken for granted, in part because houses were relatively easy to create, dismantle, adapt, or move. Likewise, family was taken for granted, but its definition was also broader than the notion of family that we still take for granted (that is, the nonlateral small nucleus that probably originated in early-modern England and became bigenerational in the postindustrial West).[3] For example, there were greater lateral and affinal possibilities, symbolized by the sometime use of *mehen*, "son," to refer also to one's nephew or son-in-law. It is significant that there were also specific terms for such relatives: *achak*, for "nephew," used in eighteenth-century Tekanto, and the term for "father-in-law," *haan*, used to mean "son-in-law" in seventeenth-century Cacalchen and late-colonial Ebtun.[4]

Yet there was more to it than that. A key fact might serve to differentiate a son-in-law who was one's haan, and one who was one's mehen: residency. As with the Nahuas at this time, the terminology that brings us closest to the family is that of habitation.[5] When the cabildo of Ixil, in a testimony of 1767, remarked *lic oc lic ychil lay solal tulacarlob*, "they all already enter this house plot," a statement was being made about family life. The "they" of the quote was a man and his three sisters, their nephew, and two nieces; the elder generation of this example, if not both generations, were of an age to have spouses, perhaps children, whose inclusion would have been assumed. This one solar, then, may have supported up to a dozen residents or more, with as many again using the plot for everyday social and economic activities.

To tie family to residency is consistent with the semantic variants of "cah," which meant not only the Maya community but also functioned as a verb, "to reside." (A similar word, spelled the same in colonial-era texts, was a verb "to be" and an auxiliary verb to indicate the continuous present.) In other words, the two primary units of social organization, cah and household, were residency based. I use the word household instead of family because a term that *does* appear in the documentary record is *otoch*, "home." Indeed, to complete the cah-otoch parallel, the two terms are interchangeable where, in the opening formula of Maya wills, testators state their parents to be *cahnalob* or *otochnalob* of that particular cah.[6] Otoch is distinct from *na*, "house," which refers to the structure rather than to the social space occupied by human beings and the objects and animals of their cultural-material environment.[7]

Of course, it is not always clear which and how many family members lived in which houses. In one unusual case, Pedro Mis of Ixil, when settling his estate upon his deathbed, left one house to his wife and the other to his "illegitimate" son (and thus perhaps his mistress too).[8] However, he adds:

. . . hunpel chen y u solaril u	. . . I leave one well and its solar in
pach lae cin patic tu kab yn uatan	the hands of my wife, Pasquala Coba,
pasg^la coba y lay yn tzenpal	and this my adopted child, Josef
J^ph pech lae u yal ix lay phelipa	Pech, the son of this Felipa Pech;
pech xane canupob xani	[it goes] also to both of them

This seems to mean that both houses were on the same site, so that all three—wife, mistress, and son—lived on this one solar. In other cases, there appear to be half a dozen or more residents on each house plot. A Spanish source of 1548 commented that each house contained two to six residents; the 1583 census of Pencuyut revealed an average household of eight to eleven people.[9] Maya wills show that the average number of adult (that is, surviving) children per couple was about three, making a nuclear family of five. Add to this the evidence of individual wills, and a picture is presented of solar occupancy of six to twelve people who made up the larger Maya family or household. This picture is supported by the range of kin who appear as heirs in Maya wills, all of whom are listed in Table 8.1.

Table 8.1 shows three things: the kin relations between testators and heirs in these three cahob, information that is tabulated against types of bequest items and by donor gender in Appendix D, as discussed in Chapter 9; the cah-to-cah variations in kinship terminology (such as the term for "wife"); and Maya kin terminology as a whole, although the list only covers terms used in extant wills (hence, for example, fewer terms by female speakers), and is not therefore necessarily comprehensive. Something of the chief characteristics of Maya kinship can be seen in the table, although a detailed review of such is not my purpose here; suffice to point out that a distinction is made between cross and parallel kin, and that generation is one of the fundamental principles of the system (note the terms linking cousins to Ego).[10] More distant kin do not appear in the wills, but note that recipients are sometimes named without kin relation being specified (this is especially common in seventeenth-century Cacalchen); their patronyms indicate only that they are not consanguineal near-kin, so such recipients could be affinal kin, distant consanguineal kin, related

TABLE 8.1

Maya Kinship: A Comparative Terminology

Kin	Cacalchen	Ixil	Tekanto
kin of a male:			
grandfather		mam	(nuxi)sucun, mam
father	yum	yum	yum, tata
godfather	conpadre		compadre
uncle		tillo, tata	tio, tyo
maternal uncle	acan		acan
brother	[context]	sucun	sucun
younger brother		iɔin	
brother-in-law			bal
elder cousin			sucun
cousin			mam
son	mehen	mehen	mehen
nephew		mehen	mehen, achac
son-in-law	haan	mehen	han
adopted son		tzenpal	
grandson	mam	iɔin, mam, mekpal	mam
grandmother			nuc colel
mother	na	na	na, mama
mother-in-law		ixhaan	
wife	chuplil	atan	chuplil
mistress		tzenpal	
sister		cic	cic, iɔin
daughter	al, ixmehen	ixmehen	ixmehen
niece		ixmehen	ixmehen, achac
granddaughter	chich	iɔin, mam	
child(ren)	pal(ilob)	pal(ilob)	pal(ilob)
kin of a female:			
grandmother			chich, mim
mother		na	
aunt		tilla	
sister	[context]		
elder sister	cic		
younger sibling	iɔin	iɔin	iɔin
younger cousin			iɔin
cousin			mam
daughter	al, chuplal	al, chuplal	al
daughter-in-law	ilib	ilib	ilib
niece			al
granddaughter	abil	[context]	abil
grandfather		mam	sucun, mam
father	yum	yum	yum
paternal uncle	ɔeyum		
husband	icham	icham	icham
son	al	al, al xib	
son-in-law	haan	[context]	han
elder brother		sucun	sucun
brother-in-law	mu		
elder male cousin			sucun
children	alob	alob	alob

SOURCES: LC; TI; DT; P. Thompson 1978: 151–53. Orthography and spelling follow Maya sources. Where kinship is indicated by context rather than by terminology, I have entered [context] in the table.

through co-parenthood, or unrelated creditors or friends. General inheritance patterns would suggest affinal kin.

Note that the only Spanish terms in use were *tío/tía*, and one of the obverses, *sobrino*.[11] This borrowing of Spanish terms for uncle / aunt / nephew may have been late colonial, for they do not appear in seventeenth-century Cacalchen. Unlike Nahuatl (which also borrowed these terms), Spanish, or English, Maya differentiated between paternal and maternal uncles and aunts, which would explain why this borrowing was considered necessary. The Spanish term *compadre* (which I include although it is not strictly a kin term) also appears—in Cacalchen, for example, in a will of 1647, in the form *conp^e*; the kin relation of the godfather named is not clear, but seven years later he appears as a regidor of the cah, so perhaps his standing in the community was the criterion upon which he was chosen as compadre and (in the 1647 will) as guardian of the testator's daughter. The few references in Tekanto to godparents are likewise by males to males, naming these compadres simply as minor recipients.

The connection between kinship and residency will be explored further below. For now, I wish to mention two examples from Ixil that indicate something of the mutually supportive nature of household interaction and of cah life. Luisa Tec, in passing on her share of her father's solar to her son, Pablo, mentions that *u kahsic en yokol cab lae*, "he remembered me on this earth." Pablo Tec was escribano in 1766 and 1768 and no doubt in other years; perhaps Luisa was grateful that, in spite of his cabildo responsibilities, Pablo had still found time for his mother. Marta Mis, on the other hand, did not appreciate the neglect shown to her by her daughter. In her will of 1769 Marta decided to leave her ungrateful child nothing, "because she does nothing on my behalf"; what's more, "she is not ashamed of it."[12] These examples are two poles, if you will, one representing unexpected support, the other support expected but unrealized. In between lay the unstated norm, wherein the fluid family of common solar residents shared property and produce, and assisted each other in the endeavors of daily domestic life.

The Possessions of Daily Life

I give to my son one mare that I bought for my cornfield, and one cow with its calf that I bought for five tostóns, and one house door with its frame that I bought for one peso of henequen, and one chest and one silver spoon, both inherited from my mother.
—Juan Cutz, with cabildo of Motul, 1762

There was in Maya society an interrelation and equation between "family," "home," and "cultural-material environment." Appendix E,

"The Material World of the Cah," does not quantify material culture by adding up the numbers of chests or horses or images of the Virgin (although such numbers are included, cah by cah, in the tables on wealth in Appendix D), but it does give some idea of the symbolic role that these material items may have played in Maya social intercourse. From this perspective, society and culture do not exist on different levels but are simultaneously the home of the symbolic world of the cah.[13]

Let us approach these symbols in the form of a journey that makes use of the material objects—animal, vegetable, and mineral—of Appendix E to take us from the land where Maya men toiled daily, back home to the land to which they returned nightly. Although today Maya cultivation emphasizes citrus fruits and avocados, as well as corn, squash, and beans, colonial-era Maya documents prove that only corn, cotton, henequen, and a number of non-citrus trees were grown on the kax (forest) or col (field) that were the mainstay of Maya wealth (technically speaking, kax became col once under cultivation, but Ixil and some other cahob continued to use kax to describe all nonresidential land). Most of the cornfields and forests lay some distance from the cah, but orchards were just as easily sited adjacent to, or within the confines of, house plots, and indeed they are described as such in many records. Those orchards with the greatest number of trees usually contained species that were relatively small in size, such as the fifty-plantain orchard in an Ixil testament.

The work of a Maya man was the manual toil of a farmer, the cutting, digging, fixing, pulling, branding, extracting, shaving, hammering, attaching, and repairing of life on the land. The principal tools of male workers were the machete and ax, although there were a variety of other tools that were preconquest in origin but were modified by the introduced and invaluable item of iron. Regional variations in tool types reflected cah-to-cah variations in cultivation and animal husbandry—beekeeping equipment was common in apicultural Ebtun, whereas only cattle-rearing Tekanto recorded the possession of branding irons—and these were paralleled by differences in terminology.

If a family's land was far from the cah, there were shacks or even *tocoyna*, "abandoned house[s]," on site for overnight stays, and some kaxob had wells (making possible more substantial secondary residences, as is still the case today); alternatively, horses are virtually ubiquitous in wills from all cahob, suggesting a common form of transportation, as well as a means for a woman (usually a widow) to support herself by hiring out the animals. The frequent mention of mares, sometimes pregnant, and juvenile horses, is evidence of a culture of horse breeding, as well as cross-breeding (mules and donkeys, but only in the eighteenth-century data).

The existence of so many of these domestic animals is one of two glaring examples of the violation of Spanish laws against "Indian" possession of certain property; the other is the not infrequent appearance in wills from Cacalchen and Tekanto of shotguns, the earliest such example being in 1647. The Spaniards forbade the Maya firearms for fear they would be used on the colonists (as, in the nineteenth century, they would be, although those weapons were mostly given to the Maya in the 1840's civil wars among the Ladinos), but shotguns in the cahob were no doubt used for hunting wild animals, many of which (the tapir, for example) have not survived.[14]

Arriving now at the solar, we find a potential variety of flora and fauna, from palm and plum trees to raised vegetable gardens, from bees to geldings to turkey chicks. The botanical world of the Maya is given more detailed treatment in Chapter 15; suffice to say here that testamentary evidence lends support to the conquistador Montejo the Elder's remark that "every town is an orchard of fruit trees."[15] Likewise, there would have been a multitude of animals not only in the house-plot compounds, but often loose in the streets between solar boundaries—a noblewoman of Bolompoyche, doña Marta Sel, claimed she missed catechism one day because she was retrieving the animals that had wandered from her solar.[16] The quantity and variety of animals in a particular cah at a particular time depended upon five related factors: the relative poverty of the community, its location in the province, the incidence of disease among the animals, a famine that would result in their being eaten, and the fact of the steady increase in the number of introduced animals during the colonial period, especially in the first century after the conquest.

The solar was the scene of the various elements of the Maya domestic economy. Animals provided a variety of foods; trees and plants provided fruit, vegetables (cultivated in the raised benches, still used today, to protect them from pigs and fowl), henequen fiber, cotton, palm leaves for weaving hats or making roofs, and medicinal herbs; beehives were a source of wax and honey, items that were locally consumed but also served as valuable tribute and trade goods.

The Spanish conceived of a solar as bordered and square or rectangular; the Maya appear to have loosely adopted that notion, as the Spanish authorities wished them to do, when they appropriated the word. As discussed in Chapter 3, the solar was an essential part of the urban grid-plan introduced by the Spaniards. In that plan it consisted of a quarter block: Maya land sales in the colonial period indicate that this was the model size at that time, although solares were frequently halved or joined to adjacent plots; the practice today is identical.[17] Because there is not a single Maya term equivalent to solar in all the documentary evidence, it is likely that the concept was introduced; solars are ubiquitous in eighteenth-century wills, but absent from those of Cacalchen seventeenth-century testators, although solar-based items of flora and fauna are bequeathed.[18]

Cacalchen's houses may have been located at certain distances from each other on uneven plots whose borders were marked by stone mounds at corners or at regular intervals (or both) in the manner of kax boundaries. There is no evidence bearing on the development of the stone walls that surround modern-day house plots, although it is logical that they evolved as part of the centuries-long process that gave solares to the cahob. Perhaps the small stone mounds that were an essential part of Maya boundaries gradually evolved into solid walls, beginning with the eighteenth-century rise in cattle ranching. Loose enclosures around cattle, or, for that matter, small orchards, could have doubled as solar "walls." A Spanish source refers to fences of bursera (the *chacah* tree willed in Cacalchen) that take root once in place.[19] Fences made from tree branches or palm fronds or henequen would not have left any archaeological trace. A final aspect of this question is that of roads. A record of 1582 states that, after three years of construction under a fray Pedro Peña Claros, the road ("*calla*") was opened in Calkiní; this construction may have been the laying of the cah's new grid plan, the framework into which the realigned house plots would fit.[20]

The layout of houses on the solar is not conveyed through floor-plan illustrations in the documentary sources such as those that have aided historians of the Nahuas, yet we can reasonably speculate that the modern siting of Maya houses in series, with front and back doors aligned to allow air and light to pass through two or more houses, goes back to the colonial period. This careful placing of structures in series does not seem European in origin; moreover, the fact that one house is usually sited at the edge of the plot so that one must enter the solar through the house suggests that the practice originated with or soon after the introduction of solares. Many of the stone bases of the thatched-roof stucco Maya houses still in use today may not have been relaid for several centuries (during which time the non-stone portions of a house may have been rebuilt many times).

Like contemporaneous Nahua houses, the structures on a single solar were not isolated from each other, reflecting the ties of blood, marriage, and labor that bound all residents, yet each had its own entrance. Like Nahua buildings, Maya houses were almost always fully detached separate units, but unlike the Nahuas, the Maya only built single-storied houses.[21] As is the case today, and as was the case before the conquest, although some houses were rectangular in shape, many (unlike Nahua dwellings) were apsidal.[22]

Testament data from Ixil indicate that the normal number of houses per plot was no more than two. It is possible that smaller, older, or doorless structures would not have been considered worthy of mention; there is no sign that buildings were designated exclusively for holding religious images (as in central Mexico), or storing corn, although I have seen on modern plots the structure closest to the street being used to store corn at one end and other valuables at the other end (including religious statues and pictures, colonial-style chests, and agricultural tools), at the same time functioning as a reception area, an interim space between the outside world and the inner domestic world.[23]

The most revealing aspect of house bequests in Maya wills is the fact that, as already noted, houses were almost never actually mentioned. Or, put another way, they were indirectly mentioned, for the testator willed "my house door," often "with its frame." In poor (seventeenth-century) Cacalchen only frames were mentioned; in (eighteenth-century) Ixil and Tekanto some testators included a key with the door and frame. One Ixil testator also itemizes a beam.[24] This practice was common in central Mexico, though not as general as it seems to have been in Yucatan, which perhaps suggests that Maya structures were considered even more temporary and even more subject to regular renewal than Nahua ones. The principle, however, is the same—perhaps yet another Mesoamerican culture trait—and indicates that stucco skills were common and unspecialized, whereas woodworking was a specialized skill that produced items of a lasting intrinsic value that was greater than that of the actual houses.

A glance at the items listed in Appendix E under "furniture" and "valuables" gives the impression that Maya furnishings were varied and potentially extensive. Set against this evidence, the paucity of property inside the houses of the ringleaders of the 1610 Tekax uprising (used by one historian as proof of the general poverty of Maya interior surroundings)[25] surely shows that the rebel leaders had in fact managed to hide their valuables before the Spanish raid. Alternatively, considering that testamentary evidence is largely late colonial, Maya material life may have become a good deal richer as the period wore on. Furniture was described in both Maya and Spanish terms, in some cases ("bed," for example) a bilingual usage that may have indicated different objects rather than double terms for the same object.[26] In general, household furnishings of value were European in origin, the usual items being beds, tables, chairs, and the *caja* or chest that was equally common among the Nahuas at this time.

The chest, a sturdy wooden trunk that usually came with a metal lock, was used to store smaller items of value, such as jewelry, money, silver cutlery, or clothing and cloth not being worn, washed, or woven. These items may be summarized under three activities: eating, adornment, and worship. The first and second may have overlapped, if valued crockery and cutlery was ever displayed openly in the home; a silver spoon may, in fact, have been considered a valuable rather than a piece of cutlery, rarely, if ever, to be used for eating.

Adornment and worship undoubtedly overlapped, for saints images (and perhaps rosaries also) were positioned prominently either on tables or in tabernacles—the niched or recessed covering described in wills using the Spanish term *tabernacula*. Most such images were of the Virgin Mary, *ca cilich colebil*, with a few male saint images also bequeathed in wills. Such bequests tended to be by men, whose role as household head paralleled that of the saint as protector and representative of the household. Image-owning households tended to be in the upper socioeconomic ranks of a cah, suggesting that such images, while lacking the detailed adornment of precious metals and cloth often described in the wills of Spaniards, were nevertheless items of some value.

The representative assumptions that allowed a religious image to be both owned by a single male and owned collectively by the family of house-plot residents are indicative of the nature of Maya property holding in general. As will be made clear in Chapter 16, the concept of simultaneous individual and group ownership was fundamental to the Maya land-tenure system. The same concept may also have determined attitudes toward most of the material items in the home, however, since it strengthened, if not created, the need to share property where there were insufficient goods to go around. One should not be misled by the form of colonial testaments into assuming that a man who declares his machete in his estate was the sole user of that tool; that would have been contrary to the whole nature of Maya society. Two related aspects of Maya culture are worth mentioning here: the practice of even and joint distribution of property as inheritance, discussed in Chapter 9; and the porous or blurred division between the private and public spheres.

Thus the only material items that may have been truly personal were money and clothing. Maya dress and the use of money are treated in greater detail in Chapter 14, so only a few words on clothing will be said here. Men wore a Spanish-style shirt and trousers, sometimes with a cloak, and possibly a belt or sash around the waist and a blanket (either of the rough-cloth or tribute *manta* kind) over one shoulder. Female dress was more conservative in that it reflected continuity from preconquest times, and indeed is still common in Yucatan today; a Maya-style petticoat is worn under a *huipil* dress (*ypil* in Maya), over which a shawl might be draped. As will be detailed later, women devoted much of their time to the production and care of items of cloth as well as clothing—for family consumption, for sale, and to meet tax payments. Footwear is absent from the notarial record; perhaps women went barefoot, as they mostly do today when on the house plot, and men were buried shod, as is also today's custom among Nahua and Maya men.

I have suggested that the material environment of the cah, more specifically, the solar, was a symbolic world in which possessions represented the importance of status, gender roles, sustenance, beauty, and life itself in the Maya community. In doing so, I made an assumption that the Maya shared these symbols as surely as they lived together in any given cah. This assumption requires qualification, because, methodological considerations aside, there are signs in the documents that some members of the cah either read the same symbols differently or chose different symbols. The range of attitudes and opinions that percolated through this world are, to paraphrase Serge Gruzinski on colonial central Mexico, not adequately represented by the monolithic image of the indigenous community often presented by ethnologists.[27]

In other words, it must be remembered that, although the above depiction of Maya household life may appear as a static model, all historical moments are transitional. At any point in the colonial era, Maya society was in transition from precolonial to neocolonial or between whatever two points the reader chooses. Ixil in the 1760's, for example, was a Maya world acutely aware of Yucatan's Hispanized world, upon which it touched like the overlapping eggs of the Ven diagram in Figure 7.1. To illustrate how the whites of these metaphorical eggs flowed and mixed, is the case of Pedro Mis, who died in Ixil in the summer of 1766.[28]

In some ways Pedro is a good example of a well-off and well-connected member of his cah. Earlier in the year he appears in the record as an executor and almehen. Although his mother was a Tun, whose chibal members are not recorded as landowners in Ixil at this time, Pedro's father was a Mis, he was married to a Coba, and he seems to have fathered a son by a Pech—three patronym groups that ranked among the better-off in the cah. At first, Pedro seems exceptional because he is the only testator to claim a child that, from our and the Spanish perspective would have been considered illegitimate—the use of *tzenpal*, "adopted child," likewise thinly veiling his extramarital relationship to the mother. We can only guess at the situation here, but the existence of other wealthy men bearing their mother's patronym implies that it was socially acceptable to form an adulterous sexual union, at least under the circumstances on record (that is, union between a man and a woman from prominent families leading to the birth of a son).

Nevertheless, Pedro is exceptional. He bequeaths two of the three houses mentioned in the Ixil corpus, and the only house that comes with a *mac*—"a lid or door that shuts or locks"—as opposed to the standard *hol na*.

Equally unusual, both Pedro's houses feature locks. Not only the structures, but also their doors, are clearly more substantial than regular Maya houses. Some of Pedro's lesser items of property are also unique: his *banco* or bench is *ħuch*, "polished"; he owns a rare tool, *ɔopatancochbol*; one house comes with a *nuc*, possibly a seat of some kind or even a patio; he has the only writing desk in the testamentary record (although he does not appear in the record as a notary), a *papirera*, that is, *papelera*; and, most notably, he is the only Ixil testator from this period to leave in his will the statue of a named male saint (San Diego).

Pedro Mis is more than just another wealthy Maya farmer with five pieces of land and over a dozen other material possessions. He is by no means Hispanized, but his material and thus symbolic environment is meaningfully different from that of his fellow cahnalob. His affinities are not typical of Ixil; his orientation is slightly toward the colonial world; his perception of what is important, what signifies status, has been more markedly influenced by the world beyond the cah.

CHAPTER NINE

Inheritance

The principles of Maya land tenure, in particular the relationship between communal and private possession, are given comprehensive treatment in Chapter 16. However, two of the central principles of property ownership, *cetil* and *multial*, or "even distribution" and "joint ownership," will be discussed here; these principles form the basis of indigenous inheritance patterns, which in turn are an articulation of the way in which possessions expressed personal relations, both familial and societal, in Maya culture.

Cetil and Multial

The intent of his ancestors was to protect, not break up, the house plot.
—cabildo of Ixil, 1767

The most striking general inheritance pattern that emerges from a study of indigenous testaments is the Maya tendency to provide evenly for one's spouse and children, at the expense of other relatives, and without excessive prejudice toward either sex. Although movable goods were largely bequeathed according to gender, and land was not, in both cases there remained a concern for a balanced distribution of the overall wealth of one's estate. What may be a simple theoretical model was not always easily translated into practice. One problem in particular arises: how to distribute land evenly without cutting it up into pieces and diluting its utility. The solution: land was collectively, or jointly, owned, sometimes being placed nominally in the hands of a familial group representative.

The will of Viviana Canche, dictated to the escribano of Ixil sometime before her death on April 26, 1766, is a useful example with which to open this discussion. After providing for her burial and a said mass to speed her soul through purgatory, and after bequeathing two horses to her immediate family, she states:[1]

bay xan heix yn parte chen y solal
tu patah ten Yn Yum ychil u
testamento ca cimi lae cin patic ti
yn uicham xan y Juan cante–te bin
ylabac tu testamento yn Yum lae
bix yanili ca Yumil ti Dˢ bin ɔaic
u nucul y ca Yum Jusᵃˢ tu kinil
tumen oxac lay chen y solalae
heuac multialbil licil yn patic tu
kab uicham y yn ual y yn tio y
yn sucunob y u iɔinob lae

here also is my share of the well(s)
and house plot given to me by my
father in his will when he died, which
I leave to my husband and to Juan
Cante also; it may be seen in the will
of my father—who is with our Lord
Dios—his intention, given to our
Lord Magistrates, why today I leave
these three wells and their house plot
jointly with my husband, my son, my
uncle, my older brothers and their
younger siblings.

Because the Maya text does not indicate whether *oxac* ("three," with a numeral classifier) extends to *solalae* ("that, or their, house plot") as well as *chen* ("well"), it is not clear whether Viviana Canche is leaving three wells and three house plots, or a plot with three wells on it.[2] In the absence of morphological evidence, the latter is suggested by the fact that Viviana's only other declared wealth is a mare and its filly; there are also other instances of plots in Ixil containing more than one well. Assuming she is leaving one solar, then, there are three aspects to this bequest that are representative of general patterns of inheritance in Ixil and elsewhere.

First, there is the simultaneous emphasis on both joint inheritance and even distribution. Not only does Viviana mention the bequest twice, the second time listing a contingent of five beneficiaries, but she adds the word *multial*, "jointly, together as one," strengthening it with *heuac*, which can mean "but, yet, however" or can simply act as an intensifier.[3] Presumably all five males, perhaps with wives and children, live on the plot, its three wells implying size and multiple residency. This is further suggested by Viviana's statement that she is leaving only "my share"—*yn parte*—of the property. But this does not necessarily mean that the number of people sharing ownership of the solar is increasing. If Viviana's will-pattern is consistent with her father's, some (even all) of her heirs, such as siblings and uncle, would have been her corecipients of the same plot under her father's will.

This brings us to the second aspect of Viviana's declaration: if these four, possibly five, named male heirs do have families, the testator is making an indirect statement about male representation of familial groups; and not only is it sufficient to name only the men, but two men in particular are more significant than the others—her husband (identified earlier in her will as Marcos Cante) and Juan Cante (identified by her earlier as her son). The hierarchy implied is (i) male kin of the nuclear family, (ii) male kin of the extended but still consanguineal family, and (iii) whatever female and dependent male relatives, consanguineal or affinal, if any, of (ii).

Third, Viviana is concerned to validate the ordering of her estate with reference to the testamentary wishes of her father. This is significant on a number of levels, some discussed earlier. In citing three legitimating authorities, the testator is drawing upon to validate her own will—and thereby contributing to the validating power of—three institutions: paternal authority, testaments (the insertion of Viviana's in the contextual series of cah wills being emphasized), and the cabildo or cah "magistrates" (as guardians of the wills). My concern here is to highlight the first of these three points and draw attention to the continuity of joint inheritance and the multiplicity of ownership and residency thereby indicated.

An individual will, of course, can only be an anecdotal revelation of the general picture. It may be, for example, that Viviana feels the need to mention her father's wishes because the general tendency in Ixil at the time is to divide up estates into separate units. However, other wills from the Ixil of the 1760's, and from other cahob at other points in the colonial period, support the above impression of even and multiple inheritance as conventional Maya practice. As for the potential contradiction implied—can property be evenly distributed and jointly inherited at the same time?—the evidence suggests that Maya practice was to use joint inheritance as a form of even distribution, and that the Maya use of the terminology of inheritance (see Table 9.1) shows conscious efforts on the part of Maya testators to make this fact clear.

In his study of wills from Tekanto, Philip Thompson refers to the practice of even distribution, or cetil, as indicative of a trend from group ownership to individual ownership.[4] I should like to suggest that the evidence supports a different pattern. Such a trend was not a cause of the depletion of Maya resources in the late-colonial decades—the depletion was the direct result of Spanish incursion onto indigenous land and the rise of large estancias—and indeed such a trend may not have existed. On the contrary, cetil was employed by the Maya as a means of perpetuating group ownership of property.

So far this discussion has been about land (and also wells, which are explicitly linked to land, and houses, which are implicitly linked to house plots). The following examples show that the even-and-joint distribution of such property tends to be accompanied by an even distribution of other goods that is less often simultaneously "joint." This reflects the connection between ownership and residency; clothing and tools, on the other hand, tend to be gender-specific and their use is more practical in individual hands. The examples below are wills from Cacalchen, Ebtun, and Ixil; data are included in the inheritance tables in Appendix D, which provide the reader with an overview of inheritance patterns. All tables are organized by gender; Tables D.3–6 feature the types and items of property left by

TABLE 9.1
Some Terminology of Inheritance Used in Maya Testaments

Term	Meaning	Source
cetil	even distribution	Tekanto
lahcetcun	to make equal or even	Ebtun
u multialob	their joint property	Ebtun, Ixil, Cacalchen, Tekanto
ca[ox etc.]tulob	both [all three etc.] together	Homun, Ebtun, Ixil
erencia	inheritance	Tekanto
yn mul matan	my joint inheritance	Ixil
mul [kax]	jointly owned [forest]	Ixil, Cacalchen
mul matan [kax]	jointly inherited [forest]	Ixil, Cacalchen
mul man [kax]	jointly purchased [forest]	Ixil, Cacalchen
parte [solar]	[house plot] share	Ixil
xeth [solar]	portion or division [of a plot]	Ixil
-ac [solar &c.]	numeral classifier for things inanimate and whole	all the above

SOURCES: AGN-T, 1359, 5, 19; DT: 5, 31,61,65, etc.; P. Thompson 1978: 182; LC; TE: 195, 234; TI: 23, 36, 40, etc. Kax and solar are the items mostly commonly associated with the terms shown with them above, but they are otherwise interchangeable with each other and with *chen*, "well," and (in the case of *mul* and *mul matan*) *col*, "field." Also see the dictionaries (Pío Pérez 1866–77; Barrera Vásquez 1991), and Chap. 16 below. The classifier -*ac* may have originally been a specific measurement (see Chap. 15).

each testator, and Tables D.7–12 show which types of property went to specific kin of the testator.

Francisco Un of Ebtun left his two solars to his three daughters, "and also the well I bored, which cost me 25 pesos, as their joint property." His wife and three daughters also received twenty beehives each, and the wife inherited a fifty-mecate col (field) "for her to support herself." The daughters got as balanced an inheritance as possible. The three doors-with-frames and three beds (one of each to each) may have represented the houses in which the women were already living with their husbands. Francisco only had two cows, but the third daughter was given his goat. Arguably the distribution of Francisco's chest, table, and stool was not quite fair to all daughters, but there was only one of each item; perhaps the women appreciated their father's good intentions.[5]

Another Ebtun testator, Rosa Camal, had similar intentions, but either could not be bothered to apportion the goods or trusted her children to do it justly and peaceably themselves. Or perhaps a degree of even-and-joint ownership was assumed, for Rosa declared that the items, including two horses, ten beehives, a chest, and a flask, should "be distributed equally among my four children." Without some sharing of ownership, this would have been something of a mathematical challenge.[6]

Another body of Maya wills, from a cah several days' distant from Ebtun, and from an earlier point in the colonial period—mid-seventeenth-century Cacalchen—is replete with examples similar to the above two. Francisco May, who died in 1649, left his largest field as the joint property of his seven children; two smaller fields were left to the sons alone, but the daughters each received an even share of their father's beehives. Aside from his horses, Francisco's declared movables numbered seven, enabling a balanced bequest to his seven sons and daughters.[7]

The year previously Baltesar Puc had died, leaving behind him three fields and two children. The mathematics were solved by the fact that one child was a married daughter, whose husband thus became recipient of the third col, or milpa field.

The concern over cetil by another Cacalchen resident, Francisco Kuk, extended to the fate of even unborn livestock:[8]

licix in kochbeçic in mehen ti p°	I also charge my son, Pedro Kuk,
kuk he cabin yinac yal tzimin tin	that when the foal is born of the
ɔah tie ca u ɔab ti u yiɔin ti	horse I am giving him, that it be
mag^na kuk–hex cabin alnac	given to his younger sibling, Mag-
keken tin ɔah ti in chuplile [ca]	dalena Kuk; and when the pig I gave
u ɔab ti in uixmehen ti m^da kuk	my wife bears its piglet(s), it / they
	be given to that same daughter of
	mine, Magdalena Kuk

As with many of Cacalchen's other testators, Francisco Kuk's three fields matched the number of his children. One might be led to suspect that large plots are simply being divided up into shares as needed, save for the fact that, as in Ixil over a century later, the vast majority of these bequests of land are named or otherwise identified or located, with each testator tending to own land in a variety of spots.

That is not to say that no divisions of land took place. Sebastián Uh bequeathed his solar in two halves, split between his four children; yet he still speaks of it as one, not two, and his wife's name is put on both halves. When Juan Eb left a col of 120 mecates to his son, and one of 160 mecates to his daughters, it may be that subsequently the daughters' field was divided between their two husbands.[9] We cannot know the fate of this particular field, although we do know that six generations later cetil was still being practiced in a neighboring cah.

The will of Pasquala Matu of Ixil is a clear example of the even distribution of movable goods and the donation of land to heirs in toto. Aside from a pair of necklaces, which go to her husband's sister, Pasquala's wealth consists of a large quantity of clothing, which is distributed, item by item, to her husband, five children, and four daughters-in-law. Thus Manuel gets a shirt and trousers, his wife a huipil and petticoat, Roque and his wife the same, likewise Domingo and spouse, and so on. Their mother's sole piece of land, a house plot with two wells—inherited, she tells us, from her father in his will—is left to all five children as *u multialob*, "their joint property."[10]

Perhaps Pasquala's children were all living on her solar; considering that it had two wells, this is possible. There was a potential obstacle to cetil in a testator's offspring not all being resident on his or her house plot. Perhaps this was why Josef Yam sold one of his house plots to his eldest son, Pasqual, for ten pesos, and then left two pesos each to his five children—Pasqual included. In other words, Pasqual got the plot he lived on, but the custom of cetil required that he buy out his siblings to avoid the joint ownership that was the expected arrangement. The children also received roughly even quantities of other goods from Josef Yam's estate, including seven beehives each to four children, although Pasqual (the clear favorite) was given twenty, and Josef's wife thirty.[11]

Other families used similar arrangements to solve the problems arising from the common practice of joint inheritances from the previous generation, coupled with expectations of same by the next generation. Manuel Chan of Tekanto not only left his estate solely in money, leaving twelve reales to each of his three sons and four daughters, but each heir entered into Manuel's will an identical statement acknowledging receipt of the money.

Likewise, shortly before her death, on July 18, 1767, members of Pasquala Tec's family, along with Ixil's batab and his lieutenant (both of whom were also Tec), and the six cabildo officers, gathered around her on the solar she was to leave to her children, to hear her dictate her last will and testament to the cah notary, Marcos Poot. After dispensing with a few valuables, she stated:[12]

Bay xan hunperl u hol Na yl u marcoyl cin patic tu kab yn uar Ambronsio cante catun u ɔaab uacper tumin yn uar Ambronsio cante utiall u parte u lakob Bay xan ten clemente cante cin ualic minan yn than ti lay u hor na cu cutar tu kab yn uiɔin Ambronsio cante lae Bay xan ten Agus[n] cante helay u hor na lae cinualic u hahil yn than minan yn than y hele lae tumen yn Mul matan y yn sucun gaspar cante cachi tu ɔah ten yn Sucun gaspar cante yn parte lae yoklal lay u hor na lae

Item: One house door with its frame I leave in the name of my son Ambrosio Cante, who has given six *tomin* for the other shares. Thus I, Clemente Cante, state that I have nothing to say about this house door, which from now on is in my younger brother Ambrosio Cante's name. Also I, Agustín Cante, tell the truth, that I have nothing to say about this house door, which was jointly inherited and given to me with my older brother, Gaspar Cante; [I shall say nothing] about my share of this house door

This is a clear indication of customary practice: a testator can only bequeath her or his share of joint property, necessitating the insertion into this will of statements by Pasquala's two brothers; all children have a claim on parental property, thus requiring that a justification for disinheritance be given, or that the excluded children be recompensed with other like property or with money (as in the case above). In a few instances, disinheritance is justified in terms of personal relationships—such as the aforementioned woman who cuts out her daughter because, she says, she does nothing for her mother; the failure to conform to one expected pattern of behavior justifies an exception being made to another expected practice.[13]

One way to test this thesis on the Maya assumption of joint inheritance would be to scrutinize how the community settled the estate of a person who died before his or her wishes could be recorded. Extant Maya wills include a number of examples of intestate deaths. One of these intestates was Josef Cab of Ixil (see Appendix A), whose house plot the cabildo granted to his five younger siblings, his son, and his two daughters. His movable goods were easily distributed, for they were all male items (an ax, a machete, a man's outfit of shirt, trousers, belt, and blanket) and Josef has only one son. Another Ixil intestate, Pasqual Ku, is an almehen, and wealthier than Josef Cab. Still, most of the estate is given as joint property—U multiallob stated every time—to Pasqual's two sons, two daughters, and two grandsons. This includes a house plot and a half, with well, a parcel of kax, a door with its frame, a chest, and a small table. Pasqual's male items, an ax and machete, go to his eldest son, and an orchard of fifty plantain trees is granted by the cabildo to Pasqual's widow—typical of a tendency by men to leave their wives a single income-producing item (an orchard, beehives, horses), while land and other movables are distributed to offspring.[14]

The cabildo of Ebtun distribute the property of an intestate among his wife, son, and daughter with like uniformity in mind, as does the eldest son-in-law of another intestate from that cah who is too sick to dictate his wishes.[15] The pattern is further confirmed by evidence from outside these bodies of wills, in a dispute over the distribution of the goods of an intestate by the cabildo of Dzan around 1580, in which the eldest son contends that because he had settled his late father's debts he was eligible for more than the even share that custom would normally allow him.[16]

Statistical patterns from Ixil support the pattern suggested by the intestate examples. Only one-third of all the land willed in this cah over a three-year sample period went to individuals (90 percent of them the testator's children), while two-thirds went to groups (90 percent of them groups including children of the testator). Movables are bequeathed as joint property, or, in most cases, distributed as evenly as possible among children (with most items gender-associated, as discussed in Chapter 10).

In support of my interpretation of these patterns I suggested above that

Viviana Canche's listing of male heirs showed an assumption by the Maya that males were nominal heirs representing their dependents or nuclear family members; inheritance by such men thus actually meant joint inheritance. I believe this was so widespread that in most cases it was just that: an assumption, which, considering the local nature of testaments' intended audience, did not require enunciation. Such assertions are by nature hard to substantiate. In this case, however, the assertion is consistent with evidence presented in other chapters of this study on the nature of representation in Maya society. Furthermore, first, enough testators referred to residential arrangements that it is clear to us that usually (if not always) more than just a single male heir already lived on the property in question; second, a few testators considered it necessary to describe the assumed arrangement; and third, as mentioned above, wills drawn up by cabildos for cah members dying intestate indicate what arrangements were considered customary.

When Josef Cab's solar is given by the cabildo to his eight siblings and children, the testimony states *lic oc lic ychil lay solal tulacarlob*, "they all already enter [i.e., live on or use] this house plot." Mateo Yam inherited a solar with his brother Clemente; he willed it to his two daughters "and also to the sons of my aunt Marta Canul, Josef Cob and Martín Cob, who live on this solar and use this well." This plot's greater household would have included at least four potential nuclear families, headed by Mateo, his brother, and his two maternal cousins.[17] Multiple residency and joint ownership are thus mutually supportive, being two faces of the same institution. Or, in some cases, single ownership is the face, behind which lies joint ownership (beneath which lay de facto subdivisions that had no time to upset the pattern of joint ownership because the plots under cultivation were continually shifting).

In other words, if some of the references in Ixil to individual ownership are really disguised references to group owners represented by one individual in the record, then the 2:1 balance of land inheritance in favor of groups could in fact be artificially weighed in favor of individual ownership. Of all the references to kax owners in Ixil only one is collective—*ah Pootob*, "the Poot family"—but collective references to solar owners are frequent—for example, *ah chucob*, "the Chucs," *ah chimob*, "the Chim family," and so on. Indeed, the use of the chibal collective is common throughout Maya sources and is often a clear indicator of group holdings. But it is also clear that, by virtue of the principle of representation, individual and group ownership are not always mutually exclusive. On his deathbed Sebastián Uh, dictating to the cah escribano, made explicit the coincidence between individual male and group ownership:[18]

Bay xan hunpet kax–yan ti xku
lae cin patic tu kab yn mehen
Mar^n uh lae Mul kax utial ah Uhil
uinicob lae

Item: One forest, which is at Xku,
I leave in the hands of my son,
Martín Uh; this jointly owned forest
is the property of the Uh people.

References to residency in the Ixil wills are common, with the testator and relatives declared to be living on the solar itemized. Simón Chan's statement on his solar implies that before his father's death at least three generations of men (representing unstated women and children) lived on the plot, including Simón's siblings and sons.[19] With house plots, joint ownership is generally tied to residency, whereas with workable land— kax and col—the issue is usually one of labor and sustenance.[20] In both cases the issue is one of a tradition of familial-chibal ownership, as Sebastián Uh demonstrates.

This brings us to the third point raised at the beginning of the chapter by the testament of Viviana Canche, when she cited the wishes of her father made in *his* will. Supportive evidence again comes from *testimonio Utial Joseph Cab . . . Ma tu yalah u than lae cimi tijoo*, "the testimony regarding Josef Cab . . . who had not made his statement when he died in Tihó." Josef's father, it turned out, had also died intestate; luckily for the Ixil cabildo of 1767, Josef's grandfather and namesake, who passed on in 1726, *had* dictated a will, which, being in the cah archives, could be consulted by the officers. "The intent of [Josef's] ancestors was to protect, not to break up, the solar," state the cabildo, "this we see in the will of [grandfather] Josef Cab with regard to his descendents." The style is distinctly Maya, with ancestors and descendents juxtaposed to and complementing each other, each one its own semantic couplet—*u kilacabillob rae u yummob*, "his forebears, his fathers"; *u yarl u mehennob*, "his children (of a woman), his children (of a man)." Such language lends force to the subject, its style consistent with its content.[21]

Other references to previous generations are more prosaic, but they reinforce the point. Almost all are made in reference to land and the fact that the property was inherited from parents, in some cases showing a continuity of tenure over at least four generations. "There is also a kax," Micaela Tec stated in her will, "that was jointly inherited by my father from his father . . . I leave my share with my three children" (*Bay xan caac U mul matan kax yn yum ti u yum . . . yn parte lae cin patic tu kab oxtur yn uarlob lae*). Testators from Cacalchen, Ebtun, and Ixil all differentiate between property that is bought and property that was inherited, sometimes adding that it is a joint purchase or joint inheritance, often stating from whom it was bought or inherited.

The above examples have been presented in order to illustrate an inter-

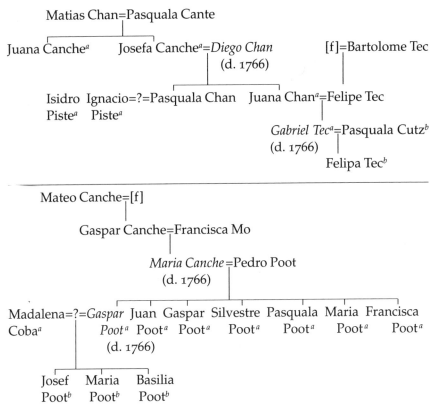

Fig. 9.1. Family trees showing kin links between two pairs of Ixil testators. Sources:
Top: TI: 14, 15. [a] Heirs of Diego Chan; [b] heirs of Gabriel Tec. Bottom: TI: 12, 19.
[a] Heirs of Maria Canche; [b] heirs of Gaspar Poot.

pretation of Maya inheritance that includes the larger picture as well as
three of its central elements. Another way to see this picture is literally to
see it: Figure 9.1 visually represents, in family tree format, the kinship and
inheritance ties between two pairs of testators, enabling the reader to grasp
at a glance upon whom property was settled. (A third such family tree, Figure 10.1, is presented in the chapter to follow.) Two testator preferences are
immediately conveyed by these examples: the preference for children over
other kinds of kin, and the preference for consanguineal over affinal kin.
Add to this picture the facts that both sexes inherited from both parents,
that spouses (or children) sometimes looked after property for children (or
grandchildren), and that responsibility for executing the testator's wishes
was placed in the hands of prominent (mostly noble) males in the community, and the Maya pattern looks similar to the Nahua and Spanish patterns.

    This is not to say that indigenous inheritance practices in Yucatan and central Mexico were entirely Spanish-influenced; we have seen that there was no significant borrowing of kinship terms among the Maya (although a chronological pattern of such borrowing among the Nahuas has been shown), and in both areas indigenous practices remain more or less consistent throughout most of the colonial period (notwithstanding both the lack of extant sixteenth-century Maya wills and the case of Nahua Mexico City).[22] Moreover, Maya wills have an important trait in common with Nahua wills that separates both from Spanish wills, namely, that the overwhelming Spanish emphasis on children is tempered somewhat in indigenous wills by the inclusion of other types of kin. The tables in this chapter, for example, show grandchildren, siblings, and in-laws benefiting from estates, albeit to a lesser extent.

    In regard to a second trait of inheritance in which Nahua and Spanish wills differ, Maya testaments do not seem to fall so easily into either category. James Lockhart has observed that Spanish wills were concerned with "attempts to maintain family status," whereas among the Nahuas "inheritance is used not for the benefit of a certain household or a certain lineage, but for the welfare of certain individuals."[23] The evidence already presented on family and chibal, in addition to the evidence on inheritance, suggests that the Maya may not have perceived a clear distinction between the welfare of individuals and that of the larger kin group. This is not simply a question of the good of the whole being the sum of the good of the parts, but an example of the role played by representation in Maya culture. The even distribution of material wealth was intended primarily to benefit offspring, but it was also an attempt to strengthen the network of household and inter-chibal alliances that protected those offspring within the broader protective shield of the cah.

◌

CHAPTER TEN

Gender

Two considerations justify giving particular attention to matters of gender and the roles played by women in Maya society: first, the marginalization of women, until very recently, by scholars, and the accompanying assumption of such a marginalization in the societies under study; and second, indications in the documentary sources of institutionalized sexism in post-conquest Maya society—such as female exclusion from cabildo politics, and the male role as household representative—together with contrary evidence of the active and central participation of women in the society and economy of the cah. Indicative of several of the key themes of this subject is the remark made by Marta Mis in her will of 1769:[1]

Bay xan hetun lay Yn chupulAl Agustina Yam ma bal tin ɔah ti tumenel ma tu mentah in quentail y y icham yohel Yn yum Batab y Justicia u ma subtalil lae	As for my daughter, Agustina Yam, I've left her nothing, because she does nothing on my behalf, [nor does] her husband; m'lord the Batab and magistrates know that she is not ashamed of it.

The symbolic significance of the passage is threefold: one, Marta is an independently wealthy woman; but two, her chastising of her daughter implies an expectation of, perhaps even a need for, gender solidarity; and three, in the end she must turn to the all-male officers of the cabildo to legitimize her complaint.

Hierarchies

It was all just tale-telling and women's gossip.
—cabildo of Tetzal, 1589

In a letter of 1589 to the governor of the province, the cah of Tetzal apologized for prior complaints made by the community against their

priest, dismissing such protests as *canxectzil y[etel] c̆hupulchi,* "tale-telling
and women's gossip." The Interpreter General's accompanying translation glosses the phrase as *algunos chismes de yndios,* "some Indian gossip."[2]

Such are the tiny threads from which social portraits are woven. The
impression given by this anecdote—that colonial Yucatec society was
structured along racist and sexist lines, and that together Spanish and
Maya men subscribed to a class ideology that was genderized and ethni-
cized—is supported by a cursory glance through the archival evidence of
the times. Women's names are absent from the lists of the political officers
of the Maya cabildos. Female Maya testators disclose less wealth than their
male counterparts, who in turn appear sadly impoverished beside the
colonists, whose wills often include many pages of inventory.

Yet there is nothing new in the statement that colonial society in New
Spain was racially stratified, and perhaps it is not surprising to find a sexist
remark in a Maya document. A more complex picture is revealed by delv-
ing deeper into the source material, further from Spanish influence; here,
just as the indigenous communities are seen actively pursuing their own
affairs within (and even oblivious of) the larger colonial context, so too are
Maya women witnessed participating actively (even independently) in
these communities. Furthermore, the system of representation evident at
all levels of Maya society meant that the question of female wealth relative
to male wealth was somewhat irrelevant.

Two analogous anecdotes from the secondary literature suggest why
there may be more to the picture than the Tetzal anecdote implies. First, a
study that compared ranking by race in Spanish American society with
Spanish perceptions of phenotypical order revealed a discrepancy between the two. Spaniards saw mulattoes and Africans as inferior to "Indians" in some ways, yet the latter occupied the lowest position in colonial
organizations.[3] Similarly, Maya women may have been perceived by Spanish and Maya men as subordinate for reasons of gender, but in certain
cultural and organizational respects Maya women played primary roles.
For example (the second anecdote), an anthropological study of some
Maya women in modern Yucatan recounts the story of a meeting between
campesinos and agricultural loan officials. The farmers are enthusiastic
about the proposal, but not a single loan is taken out, because campesinos
and officials alike failed to invite the farmers' wives, who control the purse
strings.[4]

Mary Elmendorf, the author of this latter work, which is based on field
research in the cah of Chan Kom in the early 1970's, fears for the future of
her subjects, Maya women who may be drawn away from "a subsistence
economy where they have been part of a mutually dependent relationship
with their husbands" and into an urban environment "where their role is

undefined, uncertain, undignified."[5] The implication is that before the late twentieth century, Maya women enjoyed a defined, certain, and dignified role in society. To define a woman's social role and make it certain does not necessarily imbue it with dignity, but in the case of the colonial-era Maya, female social position and activity do not appear to lack any of these characteristics. The documentary evidence shows the Maya woman quite capable of operating successfully within the ethnic hierarchy of colonial society and the sexist hierarchy of cah society. The indigenous woman is not necessarily a passive object of male action, but can often be an active participant, an actor in her own right, in the social drama of Maya life. If we accept that sexual status is the result of the interplay of three factors— "productive relations, social relations, and ideology"[6]—we must also accept that although the direct evidence on Maya gender ideology is somewhat murky, it is clarified considerably by what the sources reveal of economic and social relations.

Whether a dignified but delimited postconquest role represents a decline from a pre-Columbian Golden Age of Maya gender equality is not known, but it seems unlikely. The only evidence of a matrilineal descent system that was equal to the patrilineal is lexical and structural: the term for noble, almehen, which had evolved before Contact, includes both the word for a woman's child (al), and that for a man's son (mehen); the pre-Hispanic naming system, discussed in Chapter 4, also gave equal importance to the female line as represented in the nal name—which was replaced after the conquest by a nonlineal Christian name. However, there is an implicit sexism in the Maya terminology just mentioned: there is a single term for a woman's child, al, whereas a man's child is defined as a son, mehen, or a daughter, ixmehen, as though gender differentiation of offspring was only relevant in relation to the father.

That the operation of matrilineal descent was fundamentally different from colonial-era inheritance patterns has yet to be demonstrated; the evidence of hieroglyphic texts, to the degree that they can presently be read, indicates that female participation in society and politics was active but circumscribed by gender-specific roles, just as it was after the conquest. Evidence of royal female lineages is tentative, and the concern of Classic rulers in Palenque and Yaxchilan with maternal ancestry seems secondary to preoccupations with patrilineage.[7]

Moreover, there is colonial-era evidence that the primary social unit of the Maya, the household, was a patriarchy. Maya society contained a structure of representation, whereby the batab represented the officers beneath him and by extension the people of the community. A Maya document that begins ten cen batab, "I who am batab," is immediately defined as a cah document. Similarly, the head of a family represented its members—the collective use of the pronominal first-person singular among the Maya today has been well documented.[8] The patriarchal connection between cah and family is underscored by occasional self-references by Maya women as "a daughter of the cah."

Patriarchal representation functioned not only in speech and in official action, but also legally, in terms of land tenure (as discussed in the preceding chapter). Although women are recorded as buying, owning, and selling land, as well as inheriting and bequeathing it in wills, a woman is never described as the owner of a col or kax when descriptive reference is being made to that land by a neighbor. For example, a testator from Ixil locates a section of kax by stating its neighbors: "Francisco Canul to the south, Manuel Cutz to the east," and so forth. Francisco Canul is not physically to the south, unless he happens to be working his plot, nor is he the sole owner of the kax, but he represents it, linguistically and perhaps legally, in his role as patriarchal representative of his family. Female participation in tenure is revealed in the example of the sale of ancestral land by the Noh chibal of Homun in 1804, in whose record ten Noh women joined eight Noh men in petitioning for a sale permit. In this case the circumstances required the named participation of all the chibal; normally the patriarchal system of representation and reference applied. Land description by the colonial-era Maya was notably indigenous in style and technique, so it seems likely that its patriarchal implications were not a postconquest innovation.[9]

Division of Labor

I am declaring the items of cloth that are mine.
—Pasquala Matu of Ixil, 1766

Perhaps the primary defining feature of gender roles in Maya society was the division of labor by sex. Our chief source in this respect is again the inheritance information of Maya-language testaments, principally those from Cacalchen, Ebtun, Ixil, and Tekanto.[10]

The predominant effect of the division of labor by sex was to reinforce the tendency of gender roles to remove men much of the time from the domestic sphere. In this respect, Maya society was certainly not unique; as a scholar of the Southern Bantu has remarked: "There are two widely recognized conditions relevant to sex roles and sex-differentiated spheres of action that appear to be widespread in human populations. First, men in a great many societies occupy the principal positions of dominance and power. Second, men act in the public sphere, while women are often restricted to the domestic sphere, at home."[11] Indeed, the evidence from a study-base of over two hundred wills confirms that Maya men were more likely to work away from the solar, tending the milpa or cutting the kax, whereas Maya women tended to work within the confines of the solar.

This can be demonstrated in a number of ways by a cross-reference analysis of Tables 7 and 8 in Appendix D, whose axes are bequests set against recipients (organized by gender and kin relation to donor) for Ixil's male and female donors, respectively. The same information is given for Cacalchen in Tables D.9 and D.10. Additional supportive evidence is then provided by Table D.11, which tabulates nine Ebtun wills, the axes being donors set against bequests, with recipients (by kin relation to donor) indicated within the chart, and by Table D.12, which is based on eight wills from Bokobá, Cuncunul, Homun, Itzimná, Maní, Motul, Santiago (Tihó), and Tekax. In the discussion to which we shall now turn, the findings of these tables will be compared with testamentary information from Tekanto. The reader might also find it helpful to refer back to Tables D.1 through D.6, which tabulate wealth in testaments from Ixil and Cacalchen, emphasizing material types of bequest from male and female donors, respectively, but without any information on recipients.

First, Ixil women were twice as likely to bequeath a solar as they were a parcel of kax, whereas men were marginally more likely to leave kax to their heirs. Because recipients of both solares and kax were just as likely to be male as they were female—or, most often, a mixed-gender sibling combination—the implication is that during the course of a lifetime land gravitated into the hands of the gender that worked it. In other words, if the sons and daughters of a testator all jointly received a solar and a parcel of kax, for their wills to adopt a typical pattern the kax must in time be considered the sons', and the solar the daughters'. One way in which this might work is via marriage, with a woman's kax interests passing into her husband's hands, and a man's solar share passing into his wife's control.

What is significant, then, is not so much that there were patrilineal tendencies in the inheritance of workable land, but that women were undoubtedly a part of that land-tenure system. Indeed in Ebtun men and women displayed no land preference to either sex. In Cacalchen, house plots are not mentioned in wills, only kax and col; men bequeath and inherit over 89 percent more of these lands than women, but women are not excluded from the system, and, in keeping with Ixil patterns, the only two pieces of kax in the Cacalchen corpus are owned by women—but left to men.

Second, most of the flora and fauna willed in Ixil were situated on the solar. Although the men appear to have the edge in terms of ownership of orchards, trees, and vegetable gardens, note that every single bequest of such property by male testators went to a wife or a daughter, or both. Of the many variations of livestock only two, pigs and chickens, would not leave the solar (except in the cases of theft, sale, or escape). Significantly the only mention of these creatures occurs in wills by women. The Cacalchen information is not so clear-cut, especially for pigs and fowl, which seem to have been more central to the cah economy, yet women still inherit twice as many botanical items as men, almost twice as many fowl, and three times as many pigs.

The majority of bequests of Ixil's beehives, which would have been located at the back of the solar as they are today, also went to wives and daughters. The others went to sons, who would eventually, if not already, have their own wives and daughters to tend to the family's apicultural interests. In Tekanto, too, there was a decidedly matrilineal bias to beehive inheritance. In Ebtun, however, there was no gender preference shown in the bequeathing of hives and related equipment. This was probably because the primary economic activity on the solar was apiculture, apparently to the complete exclusion of arboriculture and the virtual exclusion of cattle raising, thus producing greater male participation. Similarly, Cacalchen had no cattle and seems to have depended largely on apiculture, so that although women are the chief beneficiaries of beehives from men, men do better from female donors. This peculiar pattern is partly explained by the uneven numbers of beehives in each estate; if we discount the numbers of hives, and count each bequest as one item, Cacalchen's general pattern is far closer to one of gender balance (as in Ebtun).[12]

As for beasts of burden, the female ownership record is poor: only three donor women in Ixil owned horses or mules, and none of the female testators in Ixil and Ebtun owned cattle. Male ownership of horses in Cacalchen outnumbered female holdings by 3.4:1. It is tempting to conclude that these animals were therefore the preserve of men. But when we look at Ixil's bequest patterns, we see that horses and mules were almost twice as likely to go to female heirs (more than twice if we include wife-with-children) than to males, and with cattle the odds were even. This was presumably because livestock was seen as an effective means of support for a widow.[13] Still, by the time these women drew up their wills, the animals were in male hands. In other words, cattle and beasts of burden *were* ultimately a male preserve, being passed on by daughters to their husbands (no doubt often as dowries), and distributed by wives to male family members mostly during women's lifetimes but in a few cases at the end of them. The same process must have occurred in Cacalchen a century earlier, only in less pronounced form, since the gender gap between ownership and inheritance was smaller here than in Ixil, although still clear.

Third, if we accept that, as a general rule, only men labored in the field and forest, we would expect to find only men owning the appropriate tools, and for such tools to be ubiquitous among the wills of such farmers.

Sure enough, the only tools mentioned by any of Ixil's or Ebtun's female testators are the loom—*akal kuch* (literally, "yarn cage")—and what appears to be a "bronze stone-breaking tool" (*bronso licil u pabal tunich*).[14] In contrast, about half Ixil's male testators have at least one of five tools, the common ones being a machete and ax, some examples of rarities being a *xul mascab*, "iron-tipped digging stick," a *lobche mascab*, "iron-tipped wooden stick," a *ɔopatan coch bol*, "blunt digging or planting stick." Note that no testator seems to own more than one of any given tool type.

Tool patterns in Cacalchen are very straightforward: although 3 tools are owned by women, men own 28 tools, and all 31 without exception are willed to men. However, when it comes to men bequeathing Ixil's tools, the pattern appears less tidy. Of the 26 tools bequeathed in this cah, all of which are left to children, 11 went to daughters. The wills in question provide the explanatory details that the tables lack: 8 of these 11 tools going to daughters are left by men who have no male heirs.[15] The other 3 are accounted for by two testators, one of whom, Mateo Yam, has no sons but mentions two male cousins, to whom he leaves his solar jointly with his daughters because the cousins use it and its well—in other words, a special case.[16] The other testator, Pasqual Huchim, is unique in leaving tools to his daughters although he has a son.[17] But his situation is also a special case. He and his children must be young, lending his passing away added poignancy:

Bay xan cin ɉatin yn palillob tu kab yn yum y yn na utiall u yilabbob bix bin manebarl u cuxtar yokol cab tumen ɉatin cah yokol cab rae Bay xan hunper yn pax gerga cin ɉatic tukab yn yum u ɔoc bote oxper pesso u biner ɔoc yn botic caper pesso⁵ . . .	Thus I leave my children in the hands of my father and mother who will see to them. There is nothing left for me of life on this earth, for I am leaving the world. And so my one cloth-debt I leave in my father's name. He must pay three pesos to end it; I've paid two pesos [so far] . . .

Pasqual leaves behind a debt, and no solar of his own. But the meager possessions that are his to bequeath are evenly distributed in accordance with cetil (as we have seen, one of two primary Maya inheritance patterns): his bed to his wife, his blanket to his son, his machete to one daughter and his ax to the other. Furthermore he is thereby able to provide his daughters (who are presumably still too young to be married) with a male object of value to bring as dowry into marriage. Thus a bequest that is an exception to one pattern actually conforms clearly to two others.

The fourth way in which division of labor by gender is shown in wills from Maya communities is the evidence of cloth and clothing. Every single female testator of Cacalchen owned at least two items of women's clothing, mostly in balanced sets of dress-petticoat-shawl or dress-petticoat; just over half the men left behind male clothing. Twenty-eight male testators of Ixil bequeath 37 items of cloth and clothing; 18 female testators bequeath 82 such items. Thus women from this cah owned and left proportionately four times as many such items as did men. One Ixil woman, the aforementioned Pasquala Matu, was particularly well off in this respect, itemizing forty items of cloth and clothing in her will. Her pool of heirs, five men and five women, was only slightly larger than average, so there can be no doubt that Pasquala was a businesswoman who manufactured and perhaps also traded in clothing—especially since she dies with eleven complete male outfits (eleven shirts and eleven trousers), and five complete female outfits (five dresses and five petticoats). Similarly, Felipa Couoh of Ebtun leaves behind four clothing items, as well as two large pieces of cloth and six smaller ones.[18] It is possible that much of the weaving done by Maya women was to fulfill tax quotas,[19] but tribute products would never have included Maya apparel.

Of all cloth and clothing items bequeathed by men in Ixil, 81 percent are male items: shirts, trousers, cloaks, the men's blanket called a *sarga* by the Maya (a Spanish word for a type of cloth), and one instance of a *tzotz* (fur [blanket]). Of the four items of female clothing willed by men, one is a shawl that Simón Chan says he has not yet finished paying for (an intended gift, perhaps), and one is a slip left by Gaspar Poot, a father who never mentions his wife, suggesting that she may have died leaving the slip in her husband's care.[20] This theory is strengthened by the fact that the remaining two female items willed by men, a dress and a petticoat, are specifically described as being *canan* (guarded, looked after) by Bernardino Cot, likewise a widower father:[21]

Heix yn canan pic lae y[etel] Ypil lae cin patic tu kab luuissa cob ca u kub ti la ypal pasguala cot u kaba lae bax bic u matan Ychil u testamento Yn uatan Dominga tec lae–lay tumen cin kochbesic yn uixmehen luuisa cob u kube lae lay tumen	Also I have looked after this slip and dress, which I leave in the hands of Luisa Cob, for her to deliver to her child, named Pasquala Cot. It was given to her in the testament of my wife, Dominga Tec, which is why I charge my daughter[-in-law], Luisa Cob, to deliver it to her

This may explain why so many women of Cacalchen left female clothing to men; the arrangement, unstated because it must have been obvious to them, was that the recipient was to pass the item on to his wife or daughter when such a person joined the household or became adult.

In other words, special circumstances aside, men owned and left to their sons male items of cloth and clothing. Women, on the other hand, owned and left a wide range of such goods pertaining to both sexes. This implies that women were responsible not only for washing clothes (one female testator leaves a washing bowl) but also for making them, a suggestion strengthened by the fact that three items—the loom (*akal kuch*), yarn (*kal kuch*), and lengths of cloth called *hebal nok*—that appear in women's wills are not mentioned in men's. A few men from Cacalchen own lengths of cloth, but of the women, one owns nine items of cloth and yarn, another at least eight, and another 120 measures of yarn. If women in this cah also made men's clothing, they were not still in possession of it at the time they dictated their wills. In general, mention of weaving equipment in Maya wills is surprisingly infrequent, considering the importance of weaving to the cah economy, and compared with Nahuatl wills from Culhuacan, for example.[22]

The overall gender balance of inheritance patterns for male donors in Ixil is roughly level. Sons do benefit more than daughters (by 30 percent to 18 percent of all recipients), but if we divide recipients strictly by sex, adding wives to the scale (21 percent), women come out on top. This compares tidily with equivalent data from the wills of Tekanto: sons are 29 percent of all recipients, daughters 20 percent, but wives come in with 11 percent to tip the scales back. In Tekanto there was a tendency to bypass daughters in favor of grandchildren, of both sexes in even proportions, thereby maintaining the gender balance.[23] In Cacalchen men benefit more than women, even if sons are matched against daughters-and-wives.

I do not believe this reveals a tendency from the seventeenth to eighteenth centuries toward gender egalitarianism of property ownership. As a basic principle, such a balance is always present, regardless of cah or decade. However, as we have seen, many items are gender-specific; what skews the Cacalchen data is the fact that, for example, there are so many (exclusively male) tools in these wills compared with house doors (i.e., houses) and valuables such as jewelry and religious images (items in Ixil that go to both sexes). The difference, in short, was that Cacalchen was poorer than Ixil and Tekanto, and the greater the material variety of the cah, the more women benefited materially. Still, a specific example from Cacalchen can serve as a good illustration of the gender-balance pattern: Alonso Couoh left behind 50 beehives, of which he willed 25 to his son, 20 to his wife, and 5 to his daughter.[24]

The pattern is similar for female donors: Ixil's figures correlate closely with those from Tekanto, whereas Cacalchen's are more male-biased, in this case largely because Cacalchen women give female clothing to men, as explained above. In Ebtun, Ixil, and Tekanto women tended to favor female kin, although in Ixil this is largely because a high proportion of female movables consists of women's clothing. Then if husbands are added to sons, the gender balance is almost restored in all three cahob.

There is another aspect of the division of labor, one that is unrelated to

TABLE 10.1
Number of Children per Testator in Some Maya Wills

Cah	Time period	Testators	Average per testator
Cacalchen	1646–78	25	2.0
Ixil	1765–69	46	3.0
Ebtun	1785–1813	9	4.2

SOURCES: LC, TI, TE.

inheritance patterns, namely, reproductive (as opposed to productive) relations. Obviously only women could bear and nurse children, an activity that must have consumed a good part of a Maya woman's adult life. We have no figures on infant mortality, and very rarely does a testator refer to a deceased child,[25] but we can make some estimate of the sizes of nuclear families by computing the numbers of children mentioned by testators. This information is listed in Table 10.1.

I include in the table only testators who name heirs, so there are a few zeros in the raw data. Since we cannot be sure that testators named all their offspring, and since most households would have contained children who were destined to die before one or both parents, these figures must represent minimum numbers. What is interesting is the change over time—an exponential increase in adult children—which I have made clearer by eliminating the first will in the Ebtun corpus (1699; testator mentioning one child); if we discount the two Cacalchen wills from 1678, leaving those of 1646–56, the figures for that cah drop to 1.96 from 2.04. The pattern in this table must have been the result either of a rise in birth rates or of a drop in infant mortality, or a combination of the two; it is confirmed by a general increase in Yucatan's Maya population in the eighteenth century.[26]

Independence and Interdependence

> My daughter does nothing on my behalf, nor is she ashamed of it, as m'lord the batab and magistrates know.
> —Marta Mis of Ixil, 1769

It was stated earlier that one's status and influence in Maya society were determined by a collusion of interlocking factors, including individual and family wealth, one's connection to traditionally powerful families, and one's record of political office. Because of their sex, women were excluded from office, and therefore they were illiterate, since only the offices of escribano and maestro required literacy and gave certain access to books. Women did, however, fully participate in the exchange and bequeathing of property, and, through marriage, they engaged in the practice of interfamily alliance and the acquisition of land without purchase.

Pasquala Matu is an example of a well-off and well-connected Maya woman in colonial Yucatan (see Fig. 10.1). She was one of the wealthiest women in Ixil at the time of her death in 1766, when she left behind some land, two wells, and some forty items of clothing.[27] The Matu, though not nobility, were among the important chibalob in Ixil at this time. A Juan Matu served as an executor the year following Pasquala's death, and in 1768 he was the senior regidor on the cabildo. Although to be an executor of a will was not to hold office, only men of importance were chosen. Pasquala's executors included don Andrés Pech of the still-powerful Pech chibal.[28] Pasquala's husband, Sebastián Yam, was also an executor the year his wife died. The Yam family were represented on the cabildo too: by 1777 they had an alcalde and a regidor, and ten years later two more Yam men were in the same posts. A third family made up the triple alliance with which Pasquala Matu was affiliated: the family of her mother, Luisa Coba. The Coba were an important Ixil chibal, attaining the number two office of lieutenant on the 1766 cabildo, filling alcalde and regidor posts other years, and revealing considerable landed wealth in the testamentary record. Two of Pasquala's four sons married women named Coba. Because it was strictly taboo in Maya society to marry someone of the same patronym, this was as close as one could get to keeping it in the family.[29]

Through the will of Pasquala's cousin-in-law, Mateo Matu, who died the previous year, we can extend this network even further. Pasquala's third son married a Couoh—no shabby connection either—and we find that cousin-in-law Mateo's mother was also a Couoh. If these four families (Matu, Yam, Coba, and Couoh) were a marital alliance group, they had cabildo representation every year from 1765 to 1769, the five years covered by Ixil's extant testaments. The wills show other marriages within these four families, as well as incidences of adjacent landholdings. Of course, there are a limited number of Maya patronyms, and alliances were not so tight as to make every marriage a strategic or political one. Yet there is a clear pattern in Ixil revealing several alliance groupings, above which were the Pech, who seem allied to almost everyone.

There is evidence of a similar process at work in seventeenth-century Cacalchen. To judge by a run of wills from 1646 to 1679, two of the wealthiest families in the cah were the Couoh and the Uitz.[30] The two patronyms in the corpus that are instantly recognizable as old ruling dynasties are Pech and Cocom. In the will of Cecilia Couoh we find these four names come together. Cecilia's sister is married to a Pech; she herself is married to a Cocom. Of her two daughters, one is married to a Uitz. The other daughter is married to an Yuiti; although no Yuiti testaments have survived, the patronym appears among the lists of cabildo officers and executors along with Couoh, Uitz, Pech, and Cocom. Not only is Cecilia a

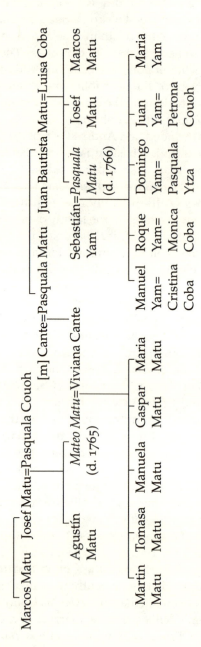

Fig. 10.1. Family tree showing the kin link between two testators of Ixil, and the marital linking of the Matu to the Coba, Couoh, and Yam. Source: TI: 1, 29.

TABLE 10.2

Debtors of Ana Xul of Cacalchen, as Listed in Her Will, 1678

Debt	Debtor	Ana Xul's comments
2 pesos, silver	Lorenso Camal	"of Nolo"
1 . . .	Lorenso Camal	
5 pesos	Lorenso Camal	
2 tomin	. . .	
2 pesos	Mateo Can. . .	
1 tostón	Ursula Pech	
5 tomin	Francisco Matu	"of Cheelmax"; "has yet to pay for one tribute manta"
. . .	Francisca Chan	"of Cheelmax"
3 tomin	Juana Chim	
2 tomin	Hernando Chable	"and his wife Beatriz Puc"
1 tomin	Antonia Yah	
1 tomin	Francisco Couoh	
1 tomin	Pas. . .	

SOURCE: LC: 33.

vital part of the family alliance, but her individual wealth, which includes twenty beehives, two pieces of land, and a horse, suggests that she was no pawn of a male-dominated network but an active participant in her own right.

A key aspect of a woman's role presented by the evidence so far has been her relationship to her husband. Via her husband she is connected to the primary social unit of Maya society, the chibal, consisting of families of household residents, and from there to the power politics of the primary sociopolitical and geographical unit of that society, the cah. The implication is twofold—that, one, a woman depended upon her husband, and two, without the institution of marriage, a woman's position was severely weakened. This was often, but not necessarily, the case.

Women were part of the cah networks of interdependency (the household, the chibal, the cah), but they could also be remarkably independent social and economic figures. This apparent paradox is well illustrated by the case of Ana Xul. Ana took advantage of the legalistic occasion of her will in 1678 not only to dispense with her property but also to draw up an accounting of her finances. She seems to have functioned as a local bank, lending out considerable sums of money in her home cah of Cacalchen as well as to borrowers from other cahob (see Table 10.2). Ana's will is badly damaged and some of the entries in the list above are incomplete, but the list covers about 80 percent of what she was owed when she died. Judging from the material nature of her estate, exclusively cloth and clothing, Ana's income originated in the sale of tribute mantas and women's clothing, with interest earnings from loans presumably enabling further growth of her money-lending business. Although Ana was married with children, this was clearly her own business, and she must have contributed at least in part to the support of her family.

As for the fate of a woman without a husband, widows do not seem to have been at an economic disadvantage; unmarried women received property more or less evenly with their brothers and could use it for support should they not get married. Nor was a woman apparently put at a disadvantage by an extramarital relationship with a man. The aforementioned Pedro Mis of Ixil provides in his will for a woman and her child, both of whom he claims to have adopted. It is clear that the woman is his mistress: Pedro Mis's wife is still alive, and the mistress's child has his mother's name; there is no question of charity, for the woman was a Pech; and the use of "adoption" to cover extramarital relationships occurred likewise among the Nahuas of central Mexico. Pedro Mis leaves his mistress only as co-owner of a solar, bequeaths a little more to his wife, while the bulk of his estate goes to his illegitimate, and only, son. Another Ixil testator, a woman, has a son who bears her patronym, implying that he was born out of wedlock. A third testator from this cah, Juan de la Cruz Coba, fails to mention his father's name, though it was customary to do so in that cah, and bears his mother's patronym. If he was illegitimate, it is significant that his will shows him to be a wealthy man by Ixil standards, with some of that wealth inherited from his mother.[31]

One advantage that community women had over those Maya women who had moved into the fringes of Spanish society was the protection of the cah cabildo. This body did not record on paper its adjudications of local disputes, but some notes written by Ebtun's senior officer in 1824 imply that in Maya society the private mistreatment of women was considered a public concern, and unacceptable. In that year Ignacio Camal was jailed for twenty-four hours "for beating his wife while he was drunk," and Buenaventura Cutis was thrown in jail on two separate occasions for wife abuse and for beating a second woman.[32]

A potential weakness of the system, and also a means whereby local disputes involving women were recorded on paper, lay in cases where the abuse was committed by a Maya official with enough authority to prevent cabildo action against him. This was the context of accusations made in late-sixteenth-century Dzan in a petition against the batab drawn up by the cah notary but lacking cabildo ratification. *U lobil u beel*, "the worst of his deeds," claims the petitioner, was that:[33]

can muc u kuchul ychil u otoch u	four times he came inside my house
chochopayte in chuplil u pakic	to grab my wife by force to
keban yetel u kati ti lolob maix	fornicate with her. He wished it in vain;
tan u ɔocabal yolah	he was not to fulfill his desire.

Even if this accusation was contrived, as a result of a factional dispute, by a petitioner aware of what kind of offense might arouse Spanish interest, it still indicates something of the sexual values of cah society—interestingly in contradiction to the modern-day situation in which a Maya woman alone, even on her own property, is susceptible to rape without recourse.[34] Where the cabildo system failed a woman, she could fall back on the social values of the cah and rely on her husband to protect her through the Spanish courts, although that still did not free her from dependency on male representation.

Under normal circumstances, however, the Maya concepts of community and of representation meant that the individual Maya enjoyed access to the opportunities of the colonial legal system via the authority that his or her cabildo had within that system. This included the benefits of some of the documents already discussed, such as wills and bills of sale. But it also allowed for the presentation of petitions and grievances—without prejudice to sex. Thus the cabildo could come to the rescue of the women of the cah in toto. In 1589 Tixmeuac complained that their priest had been refusing to confess women unless they "give themselves to him . . . and recompense him sinfully."[35] The men of Tixmeuac's cabildo were of course protecting their own interests in this case, but it would be cynical to suggest that the women of the cah were not also being defended for their own sake. The apparent relish with which a later petitioner (1774) describes the sexual excesses of local priests suggests that neither was this a question of Maya moral outrage based on general attitudes toward sexual matters.[36] One of the key differences between the petitions of 1589 and 1774 is that in the latter the women in question are clearly not of that cah and appear not even to be Maya; the petitioner of 1774 is concerned not to defend the women at all, but on the contrary to poison their reputations along with those of their priestly lovers. Thus gender as a determinant of status was strengthened or offset by two other determinants: cah affiliation, and possibly, by implication, ethnicity.

In other words, as we have seen in many other ways, cabildo preoccupations were highly localized. Defenses made on behalf of the women of the cah were really defenses of specific local women, and indeed in most such legal action the offended women are named. One of the best examples of this is the lengthy petition filed by Bolompoyche in 1812, in which a dozen victims (of which a third are women) are each given a *bay xan*, or item by item, entry. In another example, the 1811 cabildo of Ebtun drew up a notarized complaint on behalf of Valentina Un, whose daughter had suffered an injury to her arm at the hands of doña Rafaela Rosado when in the kitchen of don Pedro Cantón.[37] In the colonial world Valentina's daughter was endangered, but her connection to the world of the cah gave her recourse via the Maya authorities to, ironically, Spanish law.

Maya Women Outside the Cah

> A slave woman named Ixchen Uitzil was delivered
> to Pacheco, our first *señor*.
> —Title of Calkiní

If the men of a Maya cabildo were only concerned with defending women of their cah, the implication is that a woman who left her community also renounced its protective benefits. It is worthwhile, therefore, to take a moment to look at the way in which Maya women engaged the outside, Spanish, world, for herein lie further signs of an active, not passive, gender. Not only were Maya women crucial preservers of indigenous culture, but they acted as key links to Spanish culture. If many Maya women learned Spanish ways they also taught their ways and language to many Spaniards, to the extent that Mérida could be labeled a "mestizo" society, culturally as well as racially, by the people of Campeche in the latter part of the nineteenth century.[38]

This process of the penetration of colonial society by Maya women, with all its acculturative consequences, occurred two ways. First, it resulted from illicit or marital liaisons with Spanish colonists. At one end of the socioeconomic scale, the indigenous woman would be from a semi-Hispanized family, already had an *apellido* (as opposed to a Maya patronym), and boasted a substantial dowry. For example, doña Inés de Viana of Motul brought to her Spanish husband a 1,500-peso dowry that launched his successful career as a merchant. Of lesser status was Maria Chaueb, but she must have provided her husband, Captain Juan Rodríguez de la Vega, with significant wealth, for he and their son were prominent merchants in late-seventeenth-century Mérida.

When a Spanish merchant named Ulibarri fathered a daughter by his Maya servant, and subsequently took his (legitimate) family to Mexico City, he left the mestiza girl his apellido and a lot with a house, and he entrusted a priest with her education. Upon the priest's death this Angela de Ulibarri received enough additional property to make a dowry that would afford her upward mobility in urban society. As we shall see, such treatment of illegitimates was paralleled in cah society; the Ulibarri example, however, demonstrates that counterpatterns existed to offset the sexist and racist grain of colonial society.

A second illuminating example of the apparent respect granted to a Maya mistress by a Spaniard is that of an indigenous woman in the cah of

Yaxcaba. She took care of business matters for a Spanish merchant when he was elsewhere, and was his lover whenever he was in Yaxcaba. This alliance was not only illicit and interracial, but part-time, yet the woman and their four daughters were bequeathed substantial wealth, including debts of livestock owed by batabob between Mérida and Valladolid, and—most important—a house and four lots in the city.

The other avenue that brought Maya women into the colonial world was personal service. Throughout the colonial period large numbers of weavers, flour grinders, wet nurses, and maids were brought into the city and the villas for short periods of one, two, or three weeks at a time. Many stayed on as long-term servants, and eventually, some became independent city dwellers in their own right. In leaving her cah, a Maya woman suffered the loss of cah social support only in the long run; before that happened, she might acquire official status as a nonresident of a república indígena, thus excusing her from tribute obligations and giving her, at least temporarily, the potential social benefit but not the economic burden of cah membership. For the vecino a permanent servant was a reliable presence that could be incorporated into the household. Testaments often record the gratitude of the colonial employer: Doña Melchora Pacheco left money to her Maya maid for nursing her through a prolonged illness; other doñas left lots with houses to female Maya servants.[39]

As with the Ulibarri example above, it is not always possible to distinguish between rewards for domestic service and provisions made for Maya mistresses and illegitimate daughters. Take the case of Captain Francisco Domínguez. He left a city lot and some money to a Juana Domínguez and her sister, the children of Catalina Chable; presumably the girls were his daughters born out of wedlock. Domínguez also provided a lot with a house for another Maya girl, for when she came of age. She is described as the daughter of a couple who had worked in his house; either she was in fact the Captain's child, or his servants were being rewarded for years of service with a dowry for their daughter.[40]

That women were at the forefront of contact between the colonists and the colonized—and responsible for the partial reciprocation of that process—is also revealed by documentary evidence from the cahob-barrios of Mérida.[41] Toward the end of the colonial period an increasing Hispanization is seen in the original five communities of Tihó (San Cristóbal, San Sebastián, Santa Ana, Santiago, and La Mejorada): More and more Spaniards appear as purchasers of property; growing numbers of indigenous participants have Spanish patronyms; bills of sale start to become notarized in Spanish. Women feature as an integral part of this pattern of change.

On record as property owners, vendors, and purchasers in these communities were Spanish women, Maya women, and women who appear to be indigenous but have Spanish patronyms—mestizas, reflecting the process of ethnic mixing that must have been thriving here. In Mejorada in 1770 Josefa Chan bought a house plot, with a well and orchard, for ten pesos from her elder brother Manuel; in 1782 Simona Chan sold a plot in Santiago to Sergeant Carlos Pinto, whose new neighbors included Sebastiana "Pacheca" and "Yliponsia Solisa"; and the following year in San Cristóbal "teudora" Pérez sold a thirty-peso inherited plot that bordered on property owned by her kinswoman "yliponsa" Pérez.[42] Only one of the Pérez women is identified as a *besino* (vecino); the Pacheco and Solis women of Santiago were most likely not considered Spaniards.

In apparent paradox, this interaction between the two ethnicities that gathered pace in eighteenth-century Mérida and its environs was not typical of the colony as a whole. After 1650 Spaniards stray less from the city, the villas, and cabecera centers (although after 1750 there is a renewed assault upon indigenous landholding), and—from the perspective of documentary evidence of liaisons between Maya women and Spanish men— cah society becomes correspondingly more isolated and independent. Maya families with apellidos are less common. We can turn to cah records to find evidence of Maya women improving their circumstances within their own communities, but it is more and more rare to find them engaging and benefiting from the Spanish community.

One example, based on a will of 1692, perfectly illustrates the earlier trend of upward cross-racial mobility, and the later trend whereby even semi-Hispanized Maya emphasized and maintained cah connections.[43] It is an anecdotal bridge, if you like, as well as being a tale of much dramatic potential. Doña Maria Cristina Chuel was the daughter of don Francisco Chuel and doña Catalina Pat of Dzibikak. Her first husband was a Maya notable of Samahil, in which cah she resided. He bequeathed property to her, as did her father; it included land, which she gave to an uncle to tend for her, later placing cattle there with formal permission from the authorities to create an *estancia de ganado mayor*. When doña Maria married a second time it was also in Samahil, but to a *mulato pardo* in a Spaniard's employ. When her second husband died, she took her valuables to Mérida, where she was able to marry a petty merchant named Manuel de Flores Jorge. He was not a man of status and may have been of some Maya, African, or mixed descent (his relatives or friends who witnessed doña Maria's will were illiterate), but he was Hispanized and lived in the city; they had probably first met in Samahil, where he did business from time to time. Doña Maria outlived this third husband too, and by the time of her will she was a rich woman. Her land all went to the uncle in Samahil, as did most of the rest of her wealth, which included town lots, houses, furniture, beehives, carved statues of saints, silk embroidered *huipiles*, and gold jewelry. Thus the property of the Chuel and Pat families of Dzibikak remained in their hands, and indeed was significantly augmented.

"Where the house-hold or lineage is central," observed one anthropologist of non-Maya societies, "as it is among the Hopi and the Bontoc, or where the economic system involves more or less equal tasks and decision-making roles, as on the Barbadian plantation or in the Israeli kibbutz, the relation between the sexes tends to be balanced and complementary."[44] In the postconquest Maya cah the domestic sphere was female-dominated, though incomplete without the presence of a husband. It was also the central site of social organization, each home one in a series whose links were the marital chains of interchibal alliances; at the same time, economic activity on that site—the solar—was vital to the sustenance of the household and to its tax obligations. If these requirements led to gender relations being balanced and complementary, the balance was somewhat offset by the fact that men dominated political and religious office as well as the tenure of, and production on, agricultural land, both key aspects of social status and power in the world of the cah.

The essential determinants and differentiating factors of cah society were not unique to Yucatan; among the Nahuas, too, class, wealth, and gender contributed to one's status. However, the role of women in the altepetl so closely parallels that of the cah that the conclusions of this chapter might profitably be placed in a comparative context. Nahua women, like Maya women, "would have been expected to follow the work patterns of their gender," in S. L. Cline's words. "They would have been excluded from high office. . . . They would have been illiterate. In Culhuacan, they tended to dress in traditional clothing rather than Spanish styles. But women were not pawns without property, mere vessels for producing children. They received wealth in the form of land and house by inheritance . . . and asserted their claims to property through the Spanish judicial system."[45] The evidence from the Mexica is similar, revealing that, as Susan Kellogg has put it, "women received equal rights to houses and landed property, though their ability to use such rights, in relation to land especially, must be seen as more limited. The descriptive evidence shows women less frequently used as links or as the focal ancestor to whom a claim was traced. They also had rights to alienate property in the most general sense, i.e. buying, selling and leaving it as inheritable."[46]

This was precisely the social situation in the cahob of Yucatan, with women playing a complex role in a class society composed of a ruling nobility and commoner subjects. One outstanding difference between

Maya society and that of the altepetl is the fact that nobility in the cahob was closely tied to wealth, implying that a decline in economic fortune would signal the loss of noble status. Another contrast with gender implications lies in the importance given to patronyms by the Maya, and the function of the chibal as a socially cohesive force as well as the intermediary level of social subdivision between household and cah—much like the calpolli in Nahua society. Although land practices were in many ways different between the two areas, the relationship of women to land was very similar in Maya and Nahua society.

CHAPTER ELEVEN

Sexuality

The legalistic and mundane nature of Maya notarial documents would seem to make them an unlikely source of information on Maya attitudes toward sexual behavior; and indeed they are, save for a few Maya-language petitions of complaint in which sexual activity is mentioned in specific and revealing contexts. Some supplementary evidence can also be drawn from the Books of Chilam Balam.

Modern ethnographies of the Maya detail a vivid and pervasive culture of sexual humor. A study of Hocaba in the 1970's revealed that men and women lived in very different sexual cultures, with ribald humor being a strictly male preserve. A more recent Oxkutzcab study found that, although sexual humor was not exclusive to men, it primarily occurred among men away from the female-oriented solar; furthermore, male play speech or joking (*baxal tħan*) is frequently infused with sexual double entendres. This may well have been true in the colonial period too, in which case our written sources would reflect the distinctly male sexual perspectives of their authors (while at the same time providing insight into the status of women to complement the findings of the preceding chapter).[1]

Sexual Boundaries

When the English come, may they not be fornicators equal to these priests, who stop short only at carnal acts with men's arses. God willing, let smallpox be rubbed into their penis heads.
—anonymous petition against four priests, 1774

In 1774 an interpreter of the Holy Office in Mérida was given the task of translating into Spanish an anonymous Maya petition alleging scandalous public sexual behavior by four Spanish priests in unidentified cahob of the region. The Inquisitional official was so offended that he added to his translation his own opinion to the effect that the accusations were "scathing, audacious" and "grossly excessive," particularly in view of the fact that it was well known how the clergy treated the "Indians" with "respect and veneration."[2]

Our concern here is neither with the veracity of the interpreter's statement, nor with that of the petition (which we shall never know), but with what this petition tells us about how the Maya used sexuality, and for what purpose. One context of the document is the corpus of Maya petitions from throughout the colony and the colonial period seeking a variety of redresses for a wide range of grievances; yet, significantly, accusations of sexual offenses are extremely rare. The initial impression given by the document might be one of clerical misbehavior and indigenous outrage; is this therefore an unusual Maya expression of moral protest? Another related context is that of the broader body of notarial records in which the Maya engaged and attempted to manipulate the Spanish legal system to their own advantage; was this petition thus a dramatic waving of a red flag before the ecclesiastical bull? There is some relevance to both these perspectives, although a closer look at the text reveals hints of more complex Maya motives.

First, the 1774 petition is anonymous, lacking the usual hallmarks of notarial literature in Maya—opening and closing formulas, and the names of the cah and its cabildo officers. Even the date is recorded only in the accompanying Inquisition records. *Ten cen ah hahal than*, "I who am the informer of the truth," begins and ends the document. This indicates that the petitioners knew full well that their allegations would be judged by the Spaniards to have crossed a line of acceptability and credulity, and to be more likely to invite recrimination than redress. Thus the usual direct purpose of Maya notarial records, to advance and defend the interests of the cah, becomes an indirect purpose and is subordinated to other concerns.

Second, the possibility that humor was at the heart of these other concerns is suggested by the phrasing of the accusations, in particular the timing of exaggeration, insult, and indignation. When these four priests say mass, the petitioner claims, transubstantiation does not take place, because the priests have erections—apparently because:

Sansamal kin chenbel u chekic ueyob cu tuculicob he tu yahalcabe manal tuil u kabob licil u baxtic u ueyob he p^e torrese chenbel u pel kakas cisin Rita box cu baxtic y u moch kabi mai moch u cep	Every day all they think of is intercourse with their girl friends.... Fr. Torres, he only plays with the vagina of that really ugly black devil Rita.

| ualelob ix ɔoc cantul u mehenob ti lay box cisin la | He whose hand is disabled does not have a disabled penis; it is said he has up to four children by this black devil. |

Maya humor characteristically turns on puns and double entendres, which are not clear here to the non-Maya reader, although the cah of Pencuyut (which really exists) as the origin of one priest's mistress may have been selected because the word can also be read as "fornicating coyote." Possible puns aside, the accusations play on particular words and are structured around a series of internal punchlines.

| pᵉ maldonadoe tunɔoc u lahchekic u mektanilobe uay cutalel u chucbes u cheke yohel tulacal cah ti cu talel u ah semana uinic y xchup ti pencuyute utial yoch pelil pᵉ maldonado | Fr. Maldonado has just finished fornicating with everyone in his jurisdiction. He has now come here to carry out his fornication, as the whole cah knows. When he comes each week, a woman from Pencuyut provides Fr. Maldonado with her vagina. |

The priest's regular round of clerical duties here is satirized as a regular sexual foray through all the cahob of his visita. The use in a sexual context of *ah semana uinic*, "a weekly man"—normally used to describe Maya workers traveling to perform domestic labor in the city, for example—may also have been intended as a humorous allusion—with the accused priest "coming weekly" and performing a different kind of domestic labor. After a series of sexually explicit accusations, the petition ends with two punch lines, whose secondary meaning to the petitioner and his peers can only be guessed at, followed by a final word that seems singularly inappropriate, potentially to the point of hilarity: "God willing, when the English come may they not be fornicators equal to these priests, who stop short only at carnal acts with men's arses. God willing, let smallpox be rubbed into their penis heads. Amen."

The modern Maya culture of sexual expression takes great delight in satirical jokes aimed at the alleged excesses, or their opposite, of targeted individuals. If such a culture is reflected in this petition, the document becomes not a sincere expression of outrage but a deliberately ironic exploitation of the repressed sexual values of Catholic dogma by the Maya as a weapon against the perpetrators of that dogma, all the while providing the Maya a humorous opportunity to send sexually explicit written material into the heart of the Spanish church. The true gripe may be the clerical double standard mentioned in the complaint:

chenbel Padresob ian u sipitolal u penob
matan u than yoklalob ua ca u ment utzil
maçehuale tusebal heleac ium cura u ɔaic
u tzucte

Only the priests are allowed to
fornicate without so much as a
word about it. If a good Maya
does it, the curate always
punishes him immediately.

The petition is thus the Maya revenge against that double sexual standard, its format, anonymous and scandalous, reflecting the petitioners' belief that their complaint would not be given a sincere hearing however seriously presented. What is significant is that the Maya chose explicit sexual satire as their means of protest, with satisfaction being derived from a joke that was very much to their taste and very much not to the taste of the intended ecclesiastical audience.

The third hint of unusual motives comes in the comparison between the 1774 petition and other references to sexual activity in notarial records. The latter are not anonymous, but conform to Maya notarial conventions; they are not blatantly explicit, avoiding the references to sexual body parts that pepper the 1774 petition; and there are no signs of intended humor. The reason for this contrast clearly lies in different purposes. The examples I wish to focus on—a 1589 petition by five cahob against a priest, and a complaint of about this time by a Maya man of Dzan against his batab—do not present sexual excess as humorous because the female protagonists or victims of this excess are subjects fit not for community scorn but for protection.[3] The sexual partners of the priests in the 1774 case are outsiders, neither women of the cah nor even indigenous, judging by their names, but rather mulattas or mestizas—Black Rita, Antonia Alvarado of Bolonchen, Manuela Pacheco, and Fabiana Gómez of Pencuyut. On the other hand, Diego Pox of Dzan complains of sexual advances made against his own wife, alleging that his batab, don Jorge Xiu, hates him. In phrases also quoted in the preceding chapter, Pox claims:

yan u lobil u beel uicnal can muc u
kuchul ychil u otoch u chochopayte
in chuplil u pakic keban yetel u kati
ti lolob maix tan u ɔocabal yolah

He committed the worst of his deeds
when four times he came inside my
house to grab my wife by force to
fornicate with her. He
wished it in vain; he was not to fulfill
his desire.

Similarly, the cahob of 1589 will not even name the women involved, since they are presumably the wives and daughters of the petitioning cabildo officers:

hahilae he tilic u ɔaic confesar ti
chuplalobe tilic yalic ua matan a

This is the truth: When [the curate]
gives confession to women, he then

ɔab aba tene matan y ɔab confesar
tech lay licil u payic chuplalti matan
u ɔab confesar ti ua matan u talel
chuplal tamuk u pakic u keban
chuplalob matan u ɔab confesarti
lay u hahil tulacal baix u coilob
tu ɔacan chuplal

says, "If you do not give yourself to
me, I will not confess you." This is
how he abuses the women: He won't
confess them unless they come to
him, unless they recompense him
with their sins. This is the whole
truth about how the women are so
disturbed.

In both cases, there is no statement that sexual acts have occurred, only that such acts have been attempted; indeed, Pox emphasizes that the batab failed to rape his wife, after four attempts. These women are subject not only to cabildo representation as cah women but also to the representation of their husbands or male heads of their households, for whom it is clearly important that these women have demonstrated their sexual integrity through repeated acts of resistance.

The specific accusations of these examples are not unusual, and with respect to complaints against priests they fit into the three most common allegations: siring children by housekeepers or mistresses, public lewdness, and attempted or actual rape or seduction. But the contrasting contexts between examples reveal a male sexual culture with clear boundaries between acceptable targets of lewd humor and mandatory candidates for serious protection.

This fact is reflected in the sexual language employed. In the 1774 petition, words for sexual organs, *kep*, "penis," and *pel*, "vagina," are repeated regularly through the text, and sexual encounters are described in violent terms; one woman's vagina is "repeatedly poked before the whole cah," and another's is "bruised all night." These phrases are used instead of one-word terms for sexual intercourse, just as the term for erection is replaced with the longer "stiff penises" (*tutucħci*) and "sodomy" is substituted with "carnal acts with men's arses" (*u topob u yit uinicobe*), all apparently intended to maximize the explicit nature of the text. However, in the 1589 petition, the word *chuplal*, "woman" ("wife" in some cahob) acts as a marker of repetition to emphasize that precious aspect of cah society under attack; and the terminology to describe that attack is somewhat vague: *ɔabab*, "to give oneself"; *tal*, "to come"; and *pay*, "to pull, extract, borrow, deprecate, call," which I gloss here as "abuse," and which in Diego Pox's complaint is the stronger *chochopay*, "to grab by force." The phrase *pak keban* is ambiguous in that Maya notaries did not always follow orthographic conventions; it means "fornicate," but, if the *k* were a nonglottalized *c*, it would mean "recompense sinfully." The final phrase of the 1589 petition is similarly euphemistic: *u coilob tu ɔacan*, is "they are poisoned with madness" (or "so disturbed"), but *co* can also mean "lust" or "prostitute," so the realization of sexual acts between priest and confessant would be implied by the gloss "they are made to prostitute themselves." If this was the intended sense, *co* is a far less explicit term than those used in the 1774 text, *pen* and *chek*.

The boundary in both a physical and conceptual sense is omnipresent in the Maya notarial record, from the stone-mound boundaries between plots of land, to the psychological boundaries that separated each cah from outsiders, to the porous boundaries between private and public, or between individuals (as determined by relationships of household, chibal, class, and gender). Not surprisingly, the boundary of acceptability that divided the Maya sexual world intersected with the boundaries that the Maya set up around their communities; there was an inevitable dialectic between Maya sexual values and the priorities of cah, cabildo, and male household head.

This division of sexual matters into two arenas, one where lust and sexual activity are to be controlled, and one where sexual jokes and insults are appropriate, is apparent also in the Books of Chilam Balam. In the texts from Chumayel and Tizimin, excessive fornication (*ppen cech*) and lust (*co*) are treated as ill omens and precursors to the fall of leaders and the decline of eras into disorder and political turmoil (*xaxak*). In failing their people, to some degree because of their behavior, these leaders cross the sexual boundary and become fitting subjects for sexual insults. They are now adulterors, fornicators, pederasts, and sodomites; and, as if to underscore the status as outsiders, as sexual exiles from the world of the cah, Nahuatl terms are used to phrase some of these insults—*tecuilu* (from *tecuilontli*, "sodomite"), *u mehen tzintzin* ("sons of the anus," using the Nahuatl for "anus," *tzintli*), and, with the same term, *tu kin yan tzintzin bac toc*, "in those days there were robbers of children's anuses."[4]

This is not to say that sex is frowned upon in the Chilam Balam texts. In one passage of riddles in the Chumayel there is clearly some delight taken in the sexual puns and the satirical depiction of sexual activity of various kinds. On one level this passage is an explanation of the nature of the foods of the Maya diet through a series of metaphors and jokes, many of them sexual. The peeling of one fruit, for example, is seen as a seduction. "Bring to me here . . . ," says the reciter of the riddles:[5]

ah canan col chuplalobe bin çaclah	the women who guard the fields.
chuplalobe ten ix bin luksic u picob	The women shall be white-faced, for
yokole ca tun in hante lay chicame	I shall lift up their petticoats so as to
	eat them. This is the gourdroot.

Likewise, the alleged activities of the four priests in the 1774 petition are described with a relish so apparent that it tends to undermine the indignation and outrage that the text pretends to project. The insults can be enjoyed because the priests are outside the social systems of the cah, and thus beyond the sexual pale.

So too are the priests' mistresses, whose status as subjects for sexual mockery is determined by four significant aspects of their identity: first, they are not cah members; second, they are women, and thus, lacking the protective and status-giving mechanisms of the cah, are doubly vulnerable; third, the ethnic status of at least one of these women, Rita, who is *box*, "black," is treated deprecatingly by the Maya petitioner; and fourth, they have engaged in sexual activity with Spanish priests, an activity that may strike the Maya as reminiscent of attempts to seduce confessant women, and certainly symbolizes the hypocritical sexual double standard of these clergymen that so galls the Maya.

◦

CHAPTER TWELVE

Religion

The following discussion of some of the religious aspects of the Maya world could have been included in the first part of this study, in that the practice of religion was closely bound to the organizational and political practices of the cah; and indeed this is a topic to which some attention will be given. On the other hand, the cultural context is crucial to understanding the role played by religion in Maya society, and it is upon this context, rather than such details of worship as the correlation between the old gods and the new saints, that I wish to focus.

Conversion, Politics, and Economics

Suffering was introduced when Christianity was introduced.
—The Book of Chilam Balam of Chumayel

Scholarly discussions of what the Maya believed in the colonial period and how they expressed those beliefs have tended to center on the question of conversion: when and to what degree were the Maya Christianized? This question has been a part, not coincidentally, both of the historiography and of the historical perspective of the Spaniards. The events of the 1560s—the persecution and the debate surrounding it—might be seen as a metaphor for different ecclesiastical approaches to Maya faith during the colonial period, with Francisco de Toral insistent that the indigenous population had accepted Christianity and Diego de Landa convinced that the Maya were deceiving the likes of Toral with a clandestine "idolatry." Yet both Franciscans viewed the Maya from the same moral vision in which these inferior subjects had either embraced the soul-saving truth or were still beneath the sway of Satan. In the same way, for all the sophistication both of attempts at a Mayacentric perspective and of interpretations of compromised conversion, historians have been unable to throw off the influence of Spanish sources fully enough to question the veracity of Maya confessions, made under torture, of widespread "idolatry" and human sacrifice.[1]

In order to get out from under Spanish, especially Franciscan, sources, it may be more productive both to view the famous torture-extracted confessions with skepticism and to pose a different set of questions that take us further from the Spanish world and closer to that of the cah. There are three reasons for this. First, the circumstances of the confessions of 1562–64—Spanish assumptions of Maya guilt, the framing of questions in a way that proposes the answers, the continual threat or application of pain until a confession was extracted and detailed, the correlation between Maya confessions and fifteenth-century tales of Jewish ritual murders in Spain[2]— all these suggest that such testimony may tell us more about Spanish fears than about Maya deeds.

Second, the various Maya views of the conquest period are consistent with an interpretation of 1562–64 as a milestone in a series of imaginatively paranoid and usually violent reactions by Spaniards to a cultural environment that they tended to misunderstand. Because the connections between persecution and religious conversion were primarily created and imagined by the Spaniards, such tortures were, for the Maya, part of a sequence of catastrophes that included smallpox and other epidemics, as well as theft, the firing of guns, and other violence (the view of the Chilam Balam); or featured political divisions between Maya leaders and their chibalob during the conquest (the view of the Pech Titles). The Chilam Balam of Chumayel laments the suffering introduced by Christianity, but the list of woes includes daily hardships that predate the conquest, with the Catholic Church appearing only as a new source of tax demands; the Pech of Chicxulub deride those Maya who failed to accept "Dios" for prolonging the war of the conquest period.[3]

Third, therein lies an indication of Maya concerns, which are primarily to do with physical and material well-being. It is the coming of Christianity, not Christianity itself (the timing and nature of its arrival, not its spiritual implications), that is associated with these catastrophes; and acceptance of or resistance to Christianity stands for alliance with or opposition to the Spaniards during the conquest. In other words, conversion was for the Mayas, as with all Mesoamerican peoples, an assumed consequence of conquest. Because military victory and political dominance were evidence of spiritual strength, the acceptance of a new system of rituals was a logical, political decision.

The trauma of realizing that the Spaniards demanded a religious monopoly—the new god replaced rather than joined the old ones—may have been exaggerated.[4] Such trauma would have been part of, and mostly limited to, the immediate postconquest period of disruption and adaptation. Two further points are relevant. One, the Spanish religious monopoly was entirely consistent with the fact of Spanish settlement and the creation of a monopolistic provincial administrative and legal system. Two, the Maya were able to localize important aspects of those monopolies, in terms both of meaning and of participation. Just as continuity in self-rule was possible at the cah level, with the offices and structure of the cabildo interpreted according to local practices and needs, so was most of religious expression and organization still in indigenous hands at the cah level.

The civil hierarchy of the cabildo had a close parallel in the religious hierarchy in each cah, who effectively took on the status of the old priesthood. The same families who dominated these two hierarchies also controlled local indigenous sodalities. It was even possible, indeed not uncommon, for a man simultaneously to hold offices in the cabildo, the church hierarchy, and a local cofradía (see Table 12.1).

I have ranked the maestro, or *maestro cantor*, level with the escribano, because both were usually the only fully literate members of the community, and one was usually also the cofradía notary. Maestros were also salaried at the same level as cah notaries, if not a tad below (see Table 6.2). However, in other ways the maestro was probably on a par with the *patrón* of the cofradía, and second only to the batab. The office of maestro inherited much of the duties and prestige of the preconquest teacher, *ah cambezah* (as he was sometimes called in the first decades of the colonial period), and priest, *ah kin*; he was responsible for education in the cah, including music, catechism, and the liturgical training of young lay assistants, as well as the duties that would otherwise have been performed by a priest.

These included some relatively mundane tasks, such as recording births, marriages, and deaths in the parish register (in the later colonial period maestros increasingly made notes for priests to copy into the register), and interviewing those who wished to receive the sacraments of confession, communion, confirmation, marriage, and extreme unction (conversations not recorded, unfortunately for us). However, also included were roles of great political and social significance in the cah: the selection of lesser officials in the religious hierarchy (made, no doubt, in conjunction with the factional maneuvers discussed in Chapter 6); and, most important of all, the supervision of the Sunday and holy-day church services, complete with processions, vestments, music, and a liturgy that lacked only the performance of the ritual of eucharist.[5] In other words, to the members of the cah, their priest or practitioner of organized religion was one of their local principal men; the official priest, the padre or curate, was a visiting

TABLE 12.1

Ranked Civil, Religious, and Cofradía Offices of the Cah

Civil	Civil-religious	Religious	Cofradía
1. batab/gobernador			
2. teniente			patrón
escribano publico (salaried)	maestro (salaried)		escribano cofradía
[assistant] escribano			
3. alcaldesob (2)		sacristán mayor	priostesob (2)
regidoresob (4)		fiscal mayor	mayordomosob (4)
4. alcalde mesón			
procurador			
mayordomo			
alguacil mayor		cantoresob	
alguacilesob (6)		fiscales	mayoral
mandamiento mesón (2)	tupil doctrina mandamiento		
5. tupilob/tupil mesonob		cananob	

See Table 6.3 for a complete list of civil offices and variations in numbers (those given here in parentheses are examples). Information from Maya-language sources is supplemented, with respect to religious and cofradía offices, by Farriss 1984: 234.

Spaniard with a supervisory role who offered additional ritual services in return for some steep fees and taxes. And the Maya were concerned to get their money's worth from this outsider.

Alongside the effective continuity in personnel, in the Maya world as elsewhere in Mesoamerica, the prestige of the preconquest temple was transposed onto the colonial parish church. The relationship between local Maya elite and parish church is vividly illustrated not only in the sheer size of these structures, which were intended to project the status of the community, with towers designed to be seen from the road often as far away as the neighboring cahob, but also in the dedicatory plaques. These stone-carved plaques above the doors to cah churches invariably name, in Latin, Spanish, or Maya, the batab governing at the time the building was finished: examples are at Hocaba, Ichmul, and Pixila; in the parish church of Itzimná cah the batab's name is on the baptismal font.[6]

Herein lies something of a paradox in Maya attitudes resulting in part from the imposition of monopolistic Spanish priests. On the one hand, the connection to the colonial authorities and to powerful outsiders contributed to the prestige of the local church, some of which accrued to the batab whose name may have been on the building. On the other hand, the exclusion of Mayas from the official priesthood motivated local elites to foster a corresponding religious structure that enjoyed both legitimacy within the cah and some connection to the official church—a structure manifested in the maestro and other religious officers, in the maintenance of community saint cults, and in the running of Maya cofradías.[7]

By interweaving the religious with the social, political, and economic, the Maya were better able to maintain independent organized life. This is well illustrated by the role played by the Maya cofradía as an effective manifestation of the cah, devoted to the care of the saint or saints of the cah, administered by the same chibalob if not by the same men who filled the cabildo posts, and representing the economic interests of the community and its principal families. Maya cofradías were markedly different from the Spanish model of urban burial societies supported by alms and the dues of voluntary members. The local cofradía or cofradías, to which every cah resident belonged, were an arena for both community politics and collective economic enterprise; most of them produced beef for the local and city markets in competition with Spanish-owned cattle ranches.[8] That cofradías were a mechanism for pursuing profits and investing in enterprises unseen by rapacious Spanish officials (except perhaps for local curates who collected fees on cofradía-sponsored fiestas) suggests that these institutions were primarily economic, rather than religious, in purpose and conception. Yet, to divide activities into separate camps such as economic and religious may hinder our understanding of the Maya cultural perception of their function; both religious worship and ritual, and cofradía activities (from cattle ranching to fiesta organization), contributed to the maintenance of the social fabric of the cah and the defense of its interests.

Faith and Piety

When our lord Dios wishes to end my life here on this earth, I want my body buried in the home of our holy house, the church.
—testamentary formula, 18th-century Ixil

If organization is one aspect of religious life, the other is faith. Questions of faith are often difficult to answer, especially since our sources are either remarks made by Spaniards, who tended to be ethnocentric and suspicious cultural outsiders, or legal documents in which Maya individuals or communities profess their belief in Christianity in formulaic phrases appropriate to such documents. The few extant Maya-language texts that directly address matters of religious doctrine are patently the work of Spanish ecclesiastics concerned with communicating the details of Christian dogma to indigenous parishioners—fray Herrera's Brevario, for example, or the few sermons in Maya that have survived from the colonial period.[9]

Nevertheless, Maya notarial sources do appear to support the evidence of Spanish sources to the effect that the Maya soon integrated key aspects of Christianity, especially saint cults, into the traditional patterns of community ritual and worship.[10] The mention of saints is widespread in notarial documentation: they are prefixed to every cah name, cofradías are named after saints, and images of saints are bequeathed in wills. The smaller images of the home, nurtured so as to protect its inhabitants, were microcosmic versions of the larger images of the cah and cofradía, which would be borne around the community in procession on their saint's day—more or less according to Spanish tradition, but with a more Mesoamerican emphasis placed on the ritual consumption and offering of food and drink. The officers of the cahob—civil, religious, and cofradía—appear to have spent a great deal, perhaps most, of community funds on adorning their saint images and financing their fiesta days. This was not so much because the care of the saint was a collective activity on which the coherence of Maya society depended, but rather because the saints, like the churches—or "homes"—in which they were housed, were representations and expressions of their cahob; the more extravagant the image and its celebration (and the larger and more elaborate the church), the better the projection of cah pride and importance. It was the centrality of the cah that inspired such devotion to its representative images, cults, and structures.[11]

The Maya devotion to their religious images was no doubt also an expression of faith in the potency of their saints, but that potency was social and economic as well as spiritual; furthermore, the saints were theirs—always named with the pronominal ca, "our"—with the purpose and meaning of the cult entirely localized. Household images, too, were maintained for reasons of piety as well as for reasons of social prestige, and because they were items of material value (often adorned and accompanied by niches and small tables) and could be sold or bequeathed to family members—as reflected in their appearance primarily in the wills of better-off Maya men.

That most such images are found in men's wills probably reflects their association with the home that was protected and represented both by the saint and by the male household head; the link between home and image macrocosmically expressed in the reference by some testators to the cah church as otoch, "home."[12] This localization of saints to the levels of cah and of home may partly explain the higher incidence of Virgin Mary household images than male saints; the latter are usually named—ca yum san diego, "our lord San Diego," for example, or ca yum santo when referring to the patron of the cah—but the Virgins are always referred to with the entirely Maya phrase ca cilich colel, "our holy lady," or ca cilich colebil, "our holy virgin," with almost never a mention of Mary or the use of a loanword.[13] Likewise, cabildo officers sometimes state that they have gathered tu kuna cah noh ahau ah tepal, "in the temple of our great lord ruler," a phrase that contains no lexical indication that the lord in question (the god, Dios, or the patron saint of the cah, the boundary between the two perhaps being blurred from the Maya perspective) was anything other than indigenous in origin and purpose.[14]

The social role of these images, then, was to represent more than simply the divine power of the Catholic deity; they also signified the role as household head of the male in whose name the image was officially placed (via the testamentary record), and the social status of image-owning households in the cah. This multiple significance was, of course, possible only because the community at large perceived the images as representers of divine authority and thus as symbols of social status. In keeping with the pattern of representation in Maya culture, images may have effectively served not just a nuclear family but a larger social group consisting of chibal members and their affinal allies (in the same way that community images sometimes served a pair of cahob).[15] Nor, perhaps, would it be going too far to speculate that the cultural process that infused divine power into pre-Columbian rulership is reflected in colonial times by the acquisition of household images of the divinity by leading families in the Maya community.

The relationship between piety, social status, and economic activity in the complex of motives that lay behind Maya religious ritual and expression can also be seen in other elements in testaments. Maya men and women willingly dictated testaments to their community notaries for a variety of reasons. The ritual was a public one both literally (cabildo officers were usually present along with family members and other interested parties) and symbolically (the will was, like all notarial Maya documents, a communal product of cabildo authorship), which, according to Diego de Landa, drew upon preconquest precedents.[16] Testators also understood that wills could become important records of land ownership, tantamount to titles, and many were later brought out to confirm tenure or boundaries before a sale or during a dispute.

That the Maya valued testaments for nonspiritual reasons does not alter the fact that they were required to draw up wills by the ecclesiastical authorities.[17] Although the Council of Trent made testamentary visits an explicit episcopal duty, reiterated by royal cedula half a dozen times before rescission in 1801, we might well doubt whether the prelate of Yucatan ever made it out to the small indigenous communities of his diocese. But among the Maya testaments of Tekanto appear two brief reports (1737 and 1746) of approving inspections of the "libro de testamentos" by the Bishop of Yucatan and the Interpreter General, who certify the book as good and complete. These were followed, in 1751, by a third, less felicitous inspection. The bishop's complaint concerns the lax way in which the system of fees for posthumous masses is being administered.[18] Although he does not criticize the wills themselves, it is clear that they had to some degree to conform to the dictates of the dominant culture.

Yet there is no reason why these dictates could not have coincided with indigenous desires and priorities. For example, wills were religious as well as legal documents. Under Catholic belief a testament was a sacred rite, a prerequisite to dying in a state of grace and to burial on sacred ground; two-thirds of Ixil's testators asked for a church burial. Also, all Maya testaments began with formulaic religious statements, and about a third consisted of these formulas alone. Indigenous belief in Christianity was most commonly expressed in writing in these religious preambles, and we have no reason to believe that these portions of Maya wills were not, for some testators at least, expressions of faith—even if the frequent errors and truncations in the composition of these phrases, far more than the usual variations of spelling and abbreviation, indicate that the notary treated this portion for what on one level it clearly was: formulaic legal preamble.

This religious formula, or series of formulas, is presented in Table 12.2 in the sequence in which it appears in the Ixil wills of 1765–68 (the model is based on one will and represents the variants of three others). The formula is divided up so as to indicate subject matter (for example, 5 deals with burial arrangements), phrases within those subjects (a, b, and so on), and paradigmatic alternatives (in roman numerals).

Using the phrase numbers of this model, we can describe the formula of, say, the will of Antonia Cante of Ixil, as following the pattern 1a-1b-1c-2-3a-3bii-3ci-4aii-5a-5bii-6a-6b-6c-6dii-7a-7b, a total of sixteen phrases as opposed to the full twenty phrases of the model. Without going into further detail, it suffices to observe that every will follows a formula that can be placed within a simple model, which in turn can comprehensively demonstrate the variations between individual wills as well as bodies of them.

Furthermore, that model can be of use in a comparative context. Table 12.3 applies it first to wills from cahob other than Ixil, second to colonial-era Nahuatl wills, and third to contemporaneous European wills. Selected wills from these areas are analyzed, and, because of the phenomenon of variation between individual wills, the table also contains remarks on the general features of wills from each cited corpus. The point is not so much that the formula is clearly European in origin—that is not surprising—but that transatlantic variations are almost equaled by regional variations within Yucatan itself, reducible to individual cahob (note that Ixil and Tekanto are less than an eighteenth-century day's journey apart). This formula then is not only made Maya, but is appropriated and locally reworked by the escribanos of Cacalchen, Ebtun, Ixil, Tekanto, and no doubt other cahob besides.[19]

TABLE 12.2
Opening Religious Formula in the Testaments of Ixil

1a	tukaba Ds yumbil y Ds mehenbil y Ds espiritu santo
	In the name of God the Father, God the Son, God the Holy Spirit
1b	oxtul personas huntulil hahal Dios
	three persons [united in] one true God
1c	uchuc tumen tusinil
1d	maix pimobi
	Almighty [power over everything, however great]
2	lay bin ylabac uhunil yn takyahthan tin testamento
	it will be seen [i.e., made public] the paper of my final statement in my will
3a	hibicil tenil cen [testator]
3b	u Mehen [father] u yalen [mother]
	as I who am [], the child of [] and []
3ci	ah otochnalob
ii	ah cahalnalob
	residents/householders
3di	uay ti cah Yxil lae
ii	uay tumektan cahil cacilich yum ah bolon pixan sabernaber lae
	here in the cah of Ixil or of our Holy Lord the blessed St. Barnabus here
4ai	bacacix cimil yn cah lae
ii	Bay xan cuxul yn cuxtalic
	although I am dying and/my life is ending
4b	tohuol tin pucsikal y tin nat uetsihcilae
	content is my heart and my understanding is sound
4c	ti ualac yn nucticcilae maix mac bin u loh u ba ti cimil lae
	at this time my understanding [is] that nobody shall free himself from death
5a	ua tu yoltah ca yumil ti Ds V xules yn cuxtal uay yokol cab lae
	when our lord God wishes to end my life here on this earth
5b	Volah mucul yn uinicil
	[I] wish the burial [of] my body [to be]
5ci	ychil yotoch santa nabil Yglesia lae
ii	ychil santa ygressia
	in the (home) holy (house) church
6a	Bay xan cin uoktic ynba ti ca pixanil yum padre guar.an
	therefore I supplicate our blessed lord the Padre Guardian
6b	ca u yalab hunpedz missa [mass type] yokol yn pixan
	that he say one [said/sung] mass for my soul
6c	y caix V masen tu payalchi ychil u missa ca sebac u manel yn pixan
	and also that he send up for me a prayer in the mass so that quickly my soul pass
6di	tu numyayil animas purgatorio
ii	tu numiayayl pulgatolio
	through the suffering (of the souls) in purgatory
7a	Bay xan bin dzabac ulimosnayl [number] [coin]
7b	y [number] [coin] Jelusalem lae
	therefore will be given [] in alms and [] for that Jerusalem

SOURCE: TI: 35, variants from TI: 2, 32, 41. Minor variants, such as *cah lae/cahe*, are not noted. For spelling variants on loanwords, see Chap. 22.

TABLE 12.3
Comparison of Opening Religious Formulas in Wills

(a) Yucatan (Maya)

Ebtun, 1811: 1a-1b-x-3a-3c-3d, where x is an addition that Ixil wills lack—*lay ocan tin uol,* "this has been my belief." Ebtun formula is generally truncated, and the long phrase 4a–c is either omitted or reduced to *tohauil in uol,* "right my mind," i.e., "being sound in mind."

Cacalchen, 1647: 1a(incorporating 1c)-1b-m-2-3-4b-//-4(a)-6a-6b-6(c/d)-7, where m is a reference to the Virgin: *cilich colel ti cuhuy santa m^a.* The // indicates where a break is made that divides the formula in two, an aspect standard in Cacalchen and, as far as the extant wills go, unique to that cah. A second break, likewise indicated by a line drawn from the last word to the page edge (and not unique to Cacalchen), marks where the bequests and/or closing phrases begin. 4(a) is a Cacalchen variant on the phrase declaring one's state of mortal illness: *uayx bin cim cen ti chapahal in yanil lae,* "if I die here of the illness I now have." 6(c/d) is this cah's far shorter version of the Ixil phrases, avoiding reference to purgatory: *yokol in pixan in matab yoklal dios,* "so that my soul be received by God." Within the Cacalchen corpus there is only very minor variation.

Tekanto, 1732: 1a-3c-2-3a-3c-3d-4y-x, with 4y a variation on the Ixil 4 phrase (same words as, usually in different order to, Cacalchen's 4(a)), and x the same as the Ebtun x phrase, though in Tekanto usually lengthened to *lay ocanil yn uol ca cilich na ti santa yglesia,* which is a fuller translation of the European/Latin original. This example typifies not only the Tekanto wills of the early-to-mid-eighteenth century, but is also found in a 1661 testament from the same cah, with only the final phrase (4) varied—a sign that differences between cahob were stronger than those between centuries.

(b) Central Mexico (Nahuatl)

Culhuacan, 1581: 1a-2-3a-3c-3d-4-x-2, with x as the affirmation of faith used in Tekanto and Ebtun, the standard Culhuacan phrase being "I believe all that the Holy Church of Rome believes." It is common for Jerusalem to be mentioned in wills from some cahob, but Rome never appears in a Maya testament. Note that the 3b phrase in Ixil stating parents' names is never found in Nahuatl wills. The opening formulas in this (essentially three-year) corpus in Nahuatl is notably consistent from escribano to escribano, more so, for example, than the Ixil wills written by only three different escribanos.

(c) Europe (Spanish; English)

Malaga, 1706: 1a-2-3a-3c-3d-3b-4b-x-1a-z, where z is half a dozen additional religious phrases that I have not seen in any colonial indigenous-language wills, whose opening formula tends to be much shorter than that of these Spanish wills. This long formula is also standard in the wills of Spanish colonists in Yucatan.

York, 1578: 1a-4-2-5. This will, in which an Alexander Adam bequeaths a few old clothes, a cow, and half a dozen beehives, is remarkably reminiscent of the Ixil wills. Or perhaps, far from being remarkable, such similarities alert scholars to the trap of believing that one's own area of study is unique. The Malaga wills, being of wealthy urban Spaniards, would naturally be more comparable to the wills of Spanish *Merideños.* This York corpus, however, covers the parishes of the countryside around the city, and thus better compares to rural indigenous Yucatan. Note that the brevity of the English formula is only partly explained by the dropping of some Roman Catholic phrases as a result of the birth of an independent Church of England in the mid-sixteenth century, for a pre-Reformation example (1521: 1a-4-2-m-5, where m is a reference to "our Lady Saynte Marie and to the blessed company of heven") is still brief even by Maya standards.

SOURCES: Ebtun (Roys 1939: 343 and database of 10 wills, 1699–1813); Cacalchen (LC 17 and database of 35 wills, 1646–79); Tekanto (DT 145v and database of 420 wills, 1661 and 1724–1833); Culhuacan (Cline and Léon-Portilla 1984: 188 and database of 65 wills, 1579–99); Malaga (Reder Gadow 1986: 224 and database of 8 wills and *escrituras,* 1701–24); York (Cross 1989: 98 and database of 72 wills and inventories, 1520–1600). Spanish wills from Yucatan are prevalent in most volumes of the ANEY. For references to wills from other cahob, see the tables in App. D.

The substantive passages of the formula—requests for church burial and for said or sung mass—may have satisfied the requirements of the ecclesiastical authorities, but these practices also served to maintain a tradition of public religious ritual within the cah. We may surmise that the Maya supported the Christian mass both because it was an acceptable ritual outlet and because they believed in its spiritual efficacy (the balance between these two no doubt differed from one person to the next). Likewise, Maya testators were willing to pay double for a sung (rather than a said) mass to speed their souls through purgatory both because they believed in the power of the mass and because it was culturally desirable and socially prestigious to be posthumously remembered in song.

Maya concern for public religious ritual also had a direct bearing on the relationship of a cah to its parish priest. The Maya reaction to Christianity was a long-term struggle not to reject its beliefs but to control the expression of those beliefs; in other words, religious hostility took the form not of paganism but of anticlericalism, often with Maya parishioners judging local Spanish priests for failing to live up to official standards of public behavior and professional practice. The maestro and the members of a cah could appropriate the church, saints, public celebrations, and much of the daily religious ritual, but the parish priest could not so easily be controlled. Most cah-priest relationships were probably based on mutual tolerance, with the priest trying to spend as little time as possible in each cah, and the Maya trying to pay as little as possible in the fees and taxes that went into the pockets of the Franciscans or secular clergy.

That the attitude of Maya parishioners toward Spanish priests contained a latent resentment and antagonism is borne out in two ways. First, when in 1812–14 the liberal Spanish government temporarily abolished all forms of tribute and personal service in the empire, Yucatec curates complained bitterly that "the Indians fled from the church as though it were a gallows." In Uayma, Maya children ceased attending catechism classes, and their parents stopped paying fees of any kind to the curate or performing any personal services in his house or stables. In Cusumá, Espita, Ichmul, Izamal, Tihólop, Tinum, and other cahob children no longer came to catechism classes, parishioners refused to pay fees, and priests were denied traditional food provisions and labor services. Attendance dropped or fell off altogether at services held by Spanish priests, from whom the Mayas turned their faces in the streets. Predictably, these priests, shrill with indignation and fear, ranted that the Mayas had abandoned civilization and religion, returned to "idolatry, witchcraft, and other diabolical abuses," and taken up "quarreling, thieving, and public concubinage," as though failure to show due respect and deference to the local priest had brought a relapse to some natural native barbarism of the Spanish imagi-

TABLE 12.4
Types of Complaints in Some Examples of Maya Petitions Against Priests

Year	Cah	Complaints of		
		Violence	Sexual abuse	Malpractice
1578	Xecpes			✓
1589	Tixmeuac et al.		✓	✓
1774	[anonymous]		✓	✓
1794	Tihósuco	✓		
1812	Bolompoyche	✓		✓
1813	Pustunich and Tinum	✓		✓
1838	Bacalar			✓

SOURCES: Xecpes and Tixmeuac, AGN-I, 69, 5, 199/277; anon., AGN-I, 1187, 2, 59–61; Tihósuco (which may have originated in a smaller neighboring cah and then been presented by their cabildo before the Subdelegate in Tihósuco), AGN-CR, 335, 1, 56, 15; Bolompoyche, AGN-BN, 21,20,2–8; Pustunich/Tinum, AGEY-V, 1, 16; Bacalar, AGN-BN, 5, 35, 4–5.

nation. Yet it is clear that the Mayas were boycotting not Christianity, but the Spanish priests and their system of monopoly and exploitation.[20]

Second, under normal circumstances open hostilities still occasionally erupted, some of which are preserved in extant records. Cah complaints about particular clergymen reflect the specific nature of Maya concerns, as well as the kinds of concerns that Maya cabildos thought were held by ecclesiastical authorities. In seven sample petitions against priests ranging from 1578 to 1838 (see Table 12.4), five include accusations of violence (usually against cah officials) or of sexual misconduct, and six allege the malpractice of specific sacerdotal duties—baptism, confession, mass, and last rites.[21] Maya petitioners were particularly concerned with a priest's failure to serve the ritual needs of the community because of absenteeism or inability to speak Maya.

These accusations were not unique to the Maya; complaints by parishioners against their priests appear to have been widespread in the early modern Roman Catholic world, and anticlerical grievances were, of course, a major cause of the Reformation and of attempts by the papacy to effect internal reform beginning in earnest with the Council of Trent. Although much ink has been spilled over these events, and over European manifestations of anticlericalism as both a local and general phenomenon, little attention has been given to the incidence and nature of indigenous accusations of clerical abuse in the Americas.[22] The subject appears worthy of study, for there are common threads to such complaints, from sixteenth-century central Mexico to nineteenth-century Paraguay.[23]

Accusations of violence tended to name or indicate the office title of the Maya victims, who may have been tied up, whipped, and stabbed (as in Tihósuco—*cat hopi u colcolpayticob cat u ɔahob bayoneta tu xaxachalotil le al-*

gualsilo), or tied up and beaten (as in Bolompoyche). Such acts are presented not as random outbursts of violence but as premeditated and systematic campaigns of physical abuse. José Gregorio Canto is alleged by the cabildo of Bolompoyche to have beaten sixteen named persons, some of them after taking them to jail in Samahil, a journey for which (to add insult to injury) Canto apparently charged each victim a real.

The causes for these acts of violence appear to be the ill character of the priest (according to the petitioners), or (to be more objective) poor relations in general between priest and parishioners. Canto beat Saturnino Balam over a personal debt—*yoklal oxɔac col u paxma ti yn yum padre*, "over three mecates of milpa he owed m'lord the padre"—and he beat Gregorio Piste and Valentín Tun on separate occasions for protesting the beating of relatives of theirs (an example of the layers of family and cabildo representation in the cah).

Conflicts over religious matters are only hinted at: doña Marta Sel missed catechism because her pigs or chickens had escaped from her solar, so the priest at Bolompoyche beat her; the cabildos of Pustunich and Tinum accused their local curate of giving a dozen blows to each boy in catechism class. The teaching methods of these priests aside, catechism classes, when not held by the maestro and thus a religious obligation outside Maya supervision, may have held less attraction than Maya-controlled duties. Certainly when a priest infringed upon rituals that cah residents considered theirs, the response was more than mere indignation—Bolompoyche complained at length of what must have seemed to the Maya a highly symbolic and ritual humiliation of an ex-batab when fray Canto seized from him the ceremonial staff and hat (*u Baston y u poc*) of the Assumption Day fiesta.

Maya allegations of sexual misconduct by priests have already been treated in Chapter 11 (and are further discussed in Chapter 19). Suffice to remark here that the three types of sexual accusations made in complaints of this kind in Spanish America (siring children by housekeepers or concubines, public lewdness, and attempted or actual rape or seduction of parishioners) are all represented in the Maya record. Although many or all Maya accusations may have been true to a degree, it is also clear that indigenous cabildos developed hostility toward certain priests for reasons that they were not always willing to disclose, and sex may simply have been an ace card to lay down at a strategic moment in a campaign to be rid of an unsatisfactory priest.

In 1589, for example, the batabs and other officers of Peto, Tahdziu, Tixmeuac, Oxtzucon, and Tetzal together submitted a petition of complaint against their parish curate, Andrés Mejía ("Mexia" in the orthography of the day). The document is primarily a plea in conventional reverential language for assistance from a commissioner of the Holy Office, fray Hernando de Sopuerta, who was apparently assigned the Mejía case as a result of previous complaints. The twist in the tale comes in a final paragraph, which accuses the curate of attempting to force the women of these cahob to prostitute themselves in return for having their confessions heard: Mejía "won't confess them unless they come to him, unless they recompense him with their sins."

Those few lines may represent the archetypal anticlerical complaint: the abuse of the confessional, the proximity of priest and female parishioner recounting her sins, was one of the prime causes of the creation of the confessional box.[24] But the fact that a complaint against Mejía by the cah of Xecpes of eleven years earlier fails to mention any sexual misconduct in a list of grievances suggests that such accusations were seen as reserve ammunition if all else failed, perhaps because they risked ecclesiastical displeasure (and indeed in 1589 Tetzal also issues an apology to Mejía), or because they were often exaggerations or misrepresentations.[25]

Certainly the most sexually explicit of these accusations against priests, the anonymous petition of 1774 discussed in Chapter 11, appears to be a deliberate and elaborately constructed joke that satirizes sexual activity in general as well as priestly activity in particular, the latter seen not as a tour of cahob to attend to sacramental needs but as a tour of cahob that features public sexual display as well as sexual intercourse with (and the siring of children by) named mulatta or mestiza mistresses. The purpose of this document is not only to humiliate the four priests in question, and to place a startling piece of sexual literature on the desks of colonial ecclesiastical administrators (in fact the document made it to Mexico City), but also to exact some form of revenge against what the Maya perceive as the hypocritically punitive reaction of Spanish priests to Maya sexual activity (any details of which are significantly absent). Again, the issue is ultimately one of control; the Maya view priests as outsiders without the authority or status to pass judgment and demand punishment over this aspect of Maya life.[26]

Two further points of relevance emerge from these sources. One is the fact that curates are named as incompetents, bullies, and perverts with a frequency disproportionate to their numerical presence in Yucatan, where for most of the colonial period they were a small minority outnumbered by Franciscans.[27] Seculars may indeed have been more worldly, but unless they were significantly more susceptible to lapses into violence, sexual depravity, and malpractice than clergy of the Franciscan order, Maya petitioners must have generally resented seculars for other reasons. This supports the notion that some of these specific grievances were manufactured or exaggerated as part of the efforts by Maya cabildos to maintain the independence of (and their control over) the social life of the cah. For example, the curate of Tinum and Pustunich may or may not have beaten boys in catechism, but the petitioners must have felt that what seems to have been their real grievance—being deprived of their sons' labor every Thursday—was on its own unlikely to win the sympathy of colonial authorities. Likewise, priestly hypocrisy must have been seen as a difficult charge to make stick, especially if the evidence was based on unchaste relationships between priests and housekeepers (which were not uncommon), but an allegation of predatory or public sexual behavior was obviously far more potent (hence the survival of such documents in Inquisition files).[28]

Second, the impression of Maya parishioners projected by their cabildos is not surprisingly one of *utzil maçehuale*, "good commoners" or "good Maya subjects," modest and pious victims of clerical abuse whose concern is with high standards of sacramental performance and process. Most of the abuses already discussed are in some way also examples of malpractice (solicitation of female penitents is obviously a misuse of the sacrament of confession), and we have seen how these complaints should not be taken completely literally. On the other hand, petitions contain additional grievances that appear to be more than mere manipulations of the concerns of ecclesiastical authorities.

For example, the Xecpes petition of 1578 notes that their priest "gives mass here in a twisted fashion"—*u tzaic misa kechaante uaye*. If the Maya faithful were not at this point accustomed to hearing mass in Latin—and indeed the postconquest Maya (like the Nahuas) used the verb *il*, "to see," not *ub*, "to hear," to describe the experience of the mass—two and a half centuries later they still expected a parish priest to understand Maya: *bix u bin u nat on ua ma tu nuctic maya than?*—"How will he understand us if he has no grasp of the Maya language?"—demands the cabildo of Bacalar in 1838.

Three sacraments in particular are highlighted by Maya petitioners: mass, confession, and the last rites. It is no coincidence that records of annual expenditures by indigenous cabildos mention only these three services; the Mayas were concerned with getting their money's worth, and that meant being offered a performance of these sacraments perceived as adequate and appropriate by the cahob.[29]

The two allegations of a Bacalar petition are that the priest speaks no Maya (no doubt true) and that he is incessantly drunk (*hilan yoklal calanil*, "wretched with inebriation"—a possible artifice or exaggeration to strengthen the case), and thus unable to perform Holy Unction or mass, or hear the sins of the parishioners. The 1774 petition accuses the four priests in question of "saying false [*ma hahal*, "not true"] baptism, false confession, false last rites, false mass," but it is the last of these that is mentioned twice again in the document. The Bolompoyche petition, whose depiction of numerous beatings at the hands of the priest was discussed earlier, goes on to list half a dozen cah residents who called as they lay dying for a priest who never came or came too late. For example:

Bay xan tu hatzah ylario pech
chichan Alcalde tumen tu tuchitah
chabil utial u ɔa confesar ti hunpel
kohan xipale Lasaro puc u kaba
tumen hach manal chichil chocuil
yan tie cat bin chabil he cat tale ɔoc
u sistal ɔeɔec le tumen tu hatzah

Likewise [the priest] beat the junior alcalde, Ylario Pech, for fetching him to give confession to a sick boy named Lazaro Puc, because his fever was so high; by the time he came, [the boy] was a little cold (i.e., dead); this was why he beat [Ylario].

Another way in which a priest failed to perform the duties of concern to the Maya was through absenteeism. The Xecpes cabildo of 1578 offered an explanation for their priest's long absences:[30]

xane maixtan yulel tumenel uiih
yok manan uinic uay ti cah tumenel
uihe laix u chum matan yulel u
tibon uaye tumenel mananil hanal
toon maixbal bin ka tzab ti u
hantan te

he also doesn't come because of eating, for there is nobody here in the cah, because there's no food, and thus His Goodness doesn't come here, for we have no food, nor [if we had] food would we charge him for it

The lack of nutritional offerings in Xecpes—or the refusal of the cabildo to feed a priest who said mass "in a twisted fashion," and possibly owed them money to boot (*mabal tach u ɔaic ca paxab*)—was part of the broader effects of famine in postconquest Yucatan, and of sixteenth-century attempts to service the parishes of the province with a handful of priests.[31] Andrés Mejía had responsibility for at least the five communities who petitioned against him, and probably four more cahob too, covering an area of at least one hundred square miles north of the cabecera of Peto. Fray Hernando de Sopuerta, the Franciscan *provincial* to whom the Maya appeal in the Tixmeuac document in the Mejía case, listed in a letter of 1580 the *visita* towns of each cabecera.[32] The average was 8.3. Making the rounds must have been an arduous process, especially in the high humidity of the Yucatec summer.[33] Even today there is only an unpaved road from Peto to Tahdziu, and beyond that point, through the scrub forest, only trails.

Whatever Andrés Mejía's excuse, he seems to have held on to his position. A letter from the bishop of Yucatan to the King in 1582 names the cleric of Peto as a Pedro de Acosta, a Portuguese, a recent appointee and not a "lengua" (a Yucatec speaker). Mejía therefore may have been re-

moved following the Xecpes complaint of 1578, and then reinstated between 1582 and 1589, the date of the five-cahob petition against him.[34] That
same year (1589) another cah in the district, Tetzal, filed a statement of
apology, indicating that it too had been in on the campaign to remove
Mejía. When the campaign failed, reconciliation must have seemed the
prudent alternative. Hernando de Sopuerta may have acted as arbitrator;
Peto was a secular curacy, yet it is to the Franciscan provincial that the
Maya principales appeal in the Tixmeuac complaint. The scarcity of priests
was presumably a factor. In the last resort the desire of these Maya communities for a priest was strong enough that a bad one was preferable to
none at all, and if that bad priest could not be removed, continued hostility would only make matters worse. Therefore, declared the cabildo of
Tetzal:[35]

... yoklae xpianoil on mahunah ca
leppolae yetel yet hibal ti calah
yokol pᵉ lae cuchilae ti maiibe
maixbal ca katti maix than yokol
xan tumen ti manii lae Hohil lic
calic lae mabahun bin ca kahez tu
caten tumenel mabal cohel xan
chembelcan xectzil y. chupulchi

... because of Christianity we gave up
our anger with the padre and that
which we previously said about him.
Nor do we ask anything of him. Nor
do we have anything else to say about
it, because it is all over. We tell the
truth. We'll remember none of it a
second time, because we know
nothing about it except tale-telling
and women's gossip.

As this cabildo recognizes, "telling tales about priests is [a] bad [idea]
when their truth is not clear"—*cantabal u pectzil padresob ti ma chacan u
hahil*—or rather, when the case cannot be won.[36] For all the persistent and
masterful management of the petitionary tool by indigenous cabildos in
their labor as representatives of the cah populace, some of this literature in
the end served no purpose other than unwittingly to offer future historians an insight into life in the Maya world.

While we must be aware, then, that Maya petitioners were skillful at
exploiting Spanish fears and concerns, which may have meant hiding the
real gripe and inventing scandalous accusations, such complaints against
priests nevertheless offer a pattern of Maya preoccupation with keeping
religious ritual comprehensible. The mass may have been a required sacrament, but it also contributed to the continuation of public religious ritual
within the cah, fulfilling a spiritual purpose for many indigenous parishioners. Testators paid double for sung masses either because they believed
such performances sped souls through purgatory (however such a place
was perceived) or because they were socially prestigious, or both. The
Maya testament itself satisfied not only ecclesiastical stipulations but also

local religious, social, and economic needs, just as religious images were acquired and valued in the cah for spiritual, social, and economic reasons.

The initial Maya reaction to Christianity was thus not a question of ready conversion or of spiritual resistance, but a question of the degree to which the potency of the new religion could be appropriated for Maya purposes. As many aspects of that religion as possible were soon localized in terms of meaning, participation, and supervision. Actively and opportunistically, the Maya wove Christian symbols, rituals, and organizational practices into the complex fabric of political, social, and economic life in the cah.[37]

PART THREE

᠑

Land and Material Culture

CHAPTER THIRTEEN

ᘏᄋᘏ

Settlement

Land played a central role in postconquest Maya society, whose economy revolved around agriculture, animal husbandry, and cloth production on a cottage-industry level. Food production, much of it based on the solar, was important to the tribute economy, and vital to the subsistence economy of the cah. These and other aspects of Maya land use, introduced in the preceding chapters, will in the pages to come be placed in the context of how the Maya perceived, owned, worked, bought, and sold land.

Landholding Patterns

> There is my share of a well and its house plot . . . also a plot of forest at Xculix that I purchased with my younger brother . . . and my share of the other forest at Tzucya.
> —Pedro Couoh of Ixil, 1765

The cah has been presented above as a dual entity in terms of land—consisting of a residential core area, and a larger territorial unit. This territory was usually a patchwork of plots, some lying many miles from the residential cah and possibly closer to neighboring residential cahob. These lands would have been largely, if not exclusively, held by individual cah members, but that membership placed the lands under the jurisdiction of the cah authorities. This created a dialectic between private and communal control over land, to which we shall return in Chapter 16.

Three key conditions contributed to the nature of this settlement pattern: Yucatan's geography, the Spanish policy of congregación, and the existence of the unpacified or "despoblado" zone. I wish to play down the impact of the "extraordinary" circumstances of the colonial period and to argue that the first of these three conditions had determinative significance whereas the other two merely stimulated existing patterns.

The particular geographical features of Yucatan are relevant equally to preconquest and to postconquest Maya land use—and even, to a qualified extent, to today's practices. Because the sparse and stony topsoil above the flat limestone shelf of the Yucatan peninsula cannot sustain continuous long-term cultivation, a family in Yucatan, and certainly a community of families, required access to a larger tract of land to sustain themselves than did the contemporaneous Nahuas. New land must annually be slashed and burned to allow old plots to recover from use. These conditions are more severe in the north and northwest, where Maya settlement before and after the conquest was relatively light, than in the more fertile southeast, where the indigenous population has tended to be more dense; access to coastal resources explains some exceptions to this pattern.[1]

The Maya practice of separating family holdings into the solar and the kax/col (illustrated by the examples of Table 13.1)—a microcosm of the division of the cah into residential and territorial—was a more pronounced division than in Nahua land use. The Nahuas maintained many more different categories of land tenure than the Maya, and the indigenous nobility in particular enjoyed extensive and scattered properties, but a central Mexican family's landholdings consisted primarily of *callalli*, "house land."[2] This emphasis on callalli was made possible by the fertility of the land; it was made necessary by land restrictions imposed by lakes and mountains and by a relatively dense population. Yucatan has neither lakes nor mountains worth speaking of, and demographic pressures were not really significant until the late eighteenth century.

Judging by the land sites named in Table 13.1 that can be located on modern maps, the plots of the farmers in the three sample communities were all within a day's walk of the residential cah; indeed, a 1700 census of Franciscan parishes showed that 10 percent or less of the tributaries of these cahob lived outside the residential cah and on kaxob, or, in Spanish terminology, on estancias, sitios, or ranchos. However, where the Maya population was dense and in an urban area of Spanish settlement and landholding (as in Mérida-Tihó, or nearby in Muna), or where the soil was relatively poor (as in cahob north of Saci-Valladolid, such as Espita, Calotmul, and Chancenote), up to half or more of the tribute-paying farming population lived on lands that were by necessity distant from the residential cah. As a general rule, such farmers were still cah members, bound to the unit by ties of property and kin, even if they were able to make use of their frequent absence to avoid community tax obligations; still, some distant plots evolved from satellites into hamlets and eventually into cahob in their right—a process that also took place in central Mexico.[3]

Because the conditions most influencing highly dispersed and distant

TABLE 13.1
The Maya Dispersed Landholding Pattern: Examples

Juan Cutz	—1 solar (his home), with well and orchard
(d. 1762 Motul)	—3 solares (ancestral land through his mother), at the entrance to the cah, on the road to Cibalam
	—1 col beside the cah, north of Bom
	—1 col east of the cah estancia
	—1 col west of don Francisco Ake's land at Yaxleula
	—1 col (bought by his mother from Lorenzo Kuh, notary) north of Chenkelem
Felipe Noh	—1 solar (his home)
(d. 1763 Homun)	—1 solar (with sapote trees), on the road to Hocaba (with neighbors of the Noh chibal to the east and west)
	—1 kax, with well and plantain orchard (all ancestral property) at Ticheb
	—1 kax at Kochola
Gabriel Tec	—1 share of a solar and well (inherited from his paternal grandfather)
(d. 1766 Ixil)	—1 kax with well, north of the cah, on the road to Bena
	—1 kax north of the cah, on the road to Pacchen
	—1 kax (inherited from his maternal grandfather) next to the cah and west of Andrés Cob's land, on the road to Kaknab

SOURCES: ANEY, 1796–97, 205; AGN-T, 1359, 5, 19–22; TI: 15.

landholdings—population density and poor soil—also existed before the conquest, Maya descriptions of the founding of satellite plots have the ring of ritual and formula that accompanies oft-repeated actions. This is best seen in early records, such as the following:

En 21 de Ablil de milquinientos y
sesenta i uno años lay u kahlay u
kinil u hic u kuchul ca col koch lae
. . . ton cantul on ili lic heɔic lab
cah kochila

caix tu ppictuntahob u pach kax lae
caix ti xoti u chi u kaaxob yan
chiche balas pox . . . u yum . . .
napuc pox u kaba u nohol u mehen
naɔul pox lay cimi tu pach ahpulha
lae u nohol uinic lay yax cahiob tu
chun mul tixhumɔitkuk tijili
cahanob ti manan u tal u kin yulel
españores ah kaaxilobi tubatzilob
lay naɔul pox t ah tocoy na yax
cahi tixhumdzitkuk lae canppel
u tocoy naob yani ychil u kaaxob
lay u yax chun u uinicil naɔul
pox lae . . . ych cah mayapan u

This is the story of the day—21st of
April of 1561—upon which this our
cornfield claim was established . . .
the four of us are founding it at the
uninhabited cah of Kochila.

Then they placed stone markers along
the edge of that forest, and marked
the forest borders at Chiche, which
belongs to Blax Pox, whose father
was called Napuc Pox, the eldest son
of Nadzul Pox, who died at Ahpulha.
He was the oldest man of the first
settlers at the foot of the mound at
Tixhumdzitkuk. They settled there
before the time of the coming of the
Spaniards; the forest men were alone.
Nadzul Pox was the first to settle at
the place of abandoned houses,
Tixhumdzitkuk; there were four

talel ca u heɔah lum chichican
ca ti liki chichican ca bini
tinum yicnal u mulil ppuluzuoo . . .

abandoned houses in the forest;
Nadzul Pox was the first man . . . he
came from Mayapan cah, when he
established territory at Chichican;
when he left Chichican he went to
Tinum, near Puluzuoo mound . . .

The first example is relatively straightforward—four men from Ebtun clear a kax for milpa at the site of a preconquest cah—but in the second (dated 1569) this simple act has acquired something of the mythological tone that is seen in a stronger form in the descriptions of ancestral migration and settlement in the Titles, and in similar descriptions in Chilam Balam texts. The claim to the land is established not just through a hereditary chain of owners, but as originating in the preconquest period. This is evoked and invoked by the pre-Christian names, by the myth-memory of ancestral migration, by Mayapan, and by the ancient mounds and four buildings (Nadzul Pox also had four sons, we are told). In other words, the territorial claim is contextualized in a claim on Maya heritage and history.[4]

It was this potency of tradition in indigenous settlement patterns that the Spaniards came up against in their attempt to impose Iberian notions of city and settlement on the Maya. This second of the aforementioned settlement conditions originated with efforts by Spanish colonial administrators to facilitate the control and conversion of the subject peoples by means of congregación. It was seen in Chapter 3 that indigenous communities were resituated less easily than the Spaniards anticipated or wished, and that the disparate nature of Maya land use facilitated the maintenance of pre-congregación territorial boundaries, land use, and even residential patterns. Still, cause and effect can here be argued both ways. If indigenous settlement practices enabled the Maya to live more easily with congregación, even to undermine its intentions, congregaciones must in some instances have served to magnify the dispersed nature of those practices. In the end, the two are indistinguishable, and we are left with the patterns without being able to determine the precise significance of each root. The Maya-language colonial-era record makes no mention of congregación, neither the word nor the process; the "abandoned houses" (*tocoy na*) and "uninhabited towns" (*lab cah*) that are a feature of boundary descriptions just as likely became uninhabited as a result of plague and famine rather than as a consequence of Spanish policies in the early colonial period.[5]

The dispersed nature of Maya landholding patterns was influenced not only by the low growth rate of both Maya and Spanish populations for the first two centuries of the colonial period, but also by (the third and last condition) the existence of what the Spaniards called the "despoblado." As

Maya petitions demonstrate, the colonial authorities were fully aware of the loss of tribute that accompanied mass flight into the "unpacified" zone; furthermore, a reference to a Spaniard illegally purchasing wax and honey from Mayas living in the despoblado shows that the economy across the frontier was tied not only to the pacified cah economy but also to the colonial black market.

In terms of access to land and its produce, therefore, the Maya economy transcended the political borders of the province; the dispersed pattern of individual landholdings symbolized the scattered trans-peninsula nature of indigenous economic interests. It is one thing to find a whole cah threatening to flee into the forest unless tribute demands are lightened, or to find a plot vendor grateful to a purchaser for buying at a time of famine when the people of the cah had already gone to the forest to live on fruits and berries (*u binlah . . . kaax u tzent ubaob y u uich cheob*). But it is quite another to be given a glimpse of Maya nobles managing a regular cacao trade between Maní and Bacalar, between which communities must have stood numerous unpacified cahob for which there is no written record.[6] For even the nobility, that segment of society with the greatest vested interest in their cah as a social and physical entity, nurtured connections beyond—and regularly traveled from—their cah.

Population and Migration

I am Josef Uitz, the son of Miguel Uitz and the child of Juana Chulim, residents of that cah of Tihó.
                    —a testator of Ixil, 1765

The despoblado is also relevant to the question of Yucatan's demographic changes, which in turn affected aspects of Maya landholding (to be discussed in Chapter 17). The relative size of the Maya population has already been alluded to in this study (for example, in the presentation in Chapter 10 of evidence of increasing numbers of surviving children per Maya family). Figure 13.1 renders in graph form statistics culled from previous studies and supplemented by data from some archival census materials. The graph shows something of the massive decline in Maya population even before the conquest, as well as the beginnings of an early recovery (in contrast to every other region of New Spain and the Caribbean); it also shows the halts in this recovery in the seventeenth and early eighteenth centuries (caused largely by famines and epidemics, including yellow fever plagues in 1648–50, 1711–15, and many years in between, with the demographic low point around 1688); and the steady recovery of indigenous population levels at the end of the colonial period—a recovery

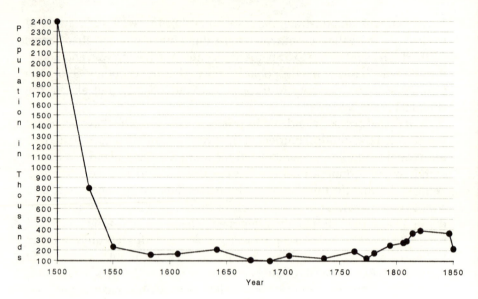

Fig. 13.1. Maya population (in thousands), 1500–1850. Sources: Farriss 1984: 57–65; García Bernal 1978: 163; Hunt 1974: 163–67; Reed 1964: 127–28; Rodríguez Losa 1985; BNM-FF, 468, 51, 59–78 (Census of 1794); CCA-III (Census of 1846). The years given are all those for which I could find estimates and sources. I have averaged values where estimates vary.

cut dramatically short by the Caste War. In the late eighteenth century there was a simultaneous growth in the Spanish population. The resulting pressure for land was eventually to change the agricultural and social face of the province altogether. This process, various aspects of which have been studied by Terry Rugeley and by Robert Patch, is visible in its early stages in late colonial Maya documentation; Maya land losses helped set the peninsula on the road to the Caste War, the henequen boom, and the "second conquest."[7]

Maya population movements, then, did not necessarily represent responses to extraordinary circumstances. A certain mobility, in fact, was the norm, and the "types" of movement that Nancy Farriss describes as "flight, drift, and dispersal" may only reflect varying analytical approaches to the phenomenon.[8] Mobility is still the norm, and new work opportunities as well as the shrinking of the peninsula by communications and transportation technology are only the latest factors to stimulate an ancient settlement pattern. A recent study of contemporary movements concluded that the extension of individual families from city to town to village has the effect of strengthening rather than weakening family ties, largely because mobility is nothing new and the institution of family has thus by necessity and as a result become stronger.[9] The cah-family parallel seen earlier in this study seems to be applicable here too; age-old patterns of extended settlement (stimulated in the colonial period first by congregación and later by the growth of satellite settlements around estancias and ranchos) similarly speak of the strength of the cah as a socially binding unit. The regional distribution of patronyms (see Chapter 4 and Appendix B) supports the notion of movement as temporary or tempered by an underlying pattern of allegiance to a cah or subregion of cahob.

This would appear to belie the suggestion that colonial-era Maya population movements show that "a tendency toward physical fragmentation emerges whenever social cohesion weakens at the center."[10] On the contrary, I would argue that the center's very existence as a force for social cohesion is partly determined by the omnipresent tendency toward physical fragmentation, and that the fragments are bound together into a meaningful whole by the defining strength of the cah. It may be that this pattern traditionally hampered the evolution of larger units, but at cah level it was formative rather than divisive. Indeed, cah size and structure were determined by the need for a permanent, residential core in the midst of shifting cultivation and dispersed territorial holdings. Thus Maya land use—settlement and agriculture—and the cah are fundamentally interrelated.

At the heart of this discussion is a methodological question relating to the theories of anthropologists and archaeologists on Maya settlement patterns (based on ancient-site analysis and on contemporary observation) and the approach of historians to colonial-era patterns (based on documentary Spanish perceptions of "Indians" as being either within or outside colonial control). What are essentially three methods applied to three time-periods clearly need to be reconciled. In spite of Spanish-influenced changes to the actual layout of the residential cah, the dispersal of settlement and landholding in the colonial period is strongly reminiscent of the patterns placed within various hypothetical frameworks by Evon Vogt and other anthropologists.[11]

The recent lament of one Andeanist, Ann Wightman, that "Too often the complex mechanism of Indian migration [has been] reduced to a simplistic duality of Indians fleeing to areas beyond Spanish control or seeking sanctuary in the employ of private landholders and mineowners," also has some bearing here.[12] The statement applies to Yucatan as much as to any area of Latin America, but with the following caveat: in Peru indigenous migrations may have been fundamentally disruptive to traditional patterns of settlement and land use. Mayas could not escape tribute obligations through migration as easily as could Peruvian *forasteros*. More importantly, migration in Yucatan was neither as random as might appear nor as tied to colonial circumstances as has been assumed.[13] Rather, it was largely a traditional pattern of movement that depended on extended economic and landed interests, annual agricultural cycles, and longer cycles of famine and plenty, all of which allowed unbroken but elastic ties to the cah.

Certainly much of Maya migration was permanent, in that nuclear families seeking opportunities moved and settled in a different or new cah for the rest of their lives. But a long-term look at such examples shows them to represent the same pattern of seasonal movement in generational terms; as the fortunes of a cah changed over decades, subsequent generations would be inspired to move back to the ancestral cah, or on to another cah where relatives or fellow chibal members resided. Examples of high percentages of residents born in other cahob—29 percent in Sotuta and 57 percent in nearby Cantamayec in 1721—are offset by examples of fully native cahob, such as Cholul, Sicpach, and Tahmek, at that same time, and this pattern of variation by cah, rather than region, is consistent with the patterns of variation in other areas of Maya society. David Robinson's analysis of parish registers to determine the patterns of migrants' source-communities showed that migration was neither random nor subject to a gradual shift from small to larger communities, but a result of individual cah variations—which were themselves a result, I would suggest, of family and chibal relationships developed between particular cahob. Sotuta, for example, had ties to Teabo and Tihó in the eighteenth century; and most nonnative women marrying men in the cah-barrio of San Sebastián came from Tecoh, Ticul, or Homún.[14]

A more typical case that lies between such extremes is that of Ixil, which had a nonnative Maya population of 8.1 percent in 1721. This statistic is reflected in testament-based data that suggest a high degree of cah endogamy in the eighteenth century; of 68 pairs of parents (of all persons dying between 1765 and 1768), only two (2.9 percent) were from outside Ixil (one pair from Tihó, one from Hoctun), with the man and woman of each couple born in the same cah as each other. Of those 68 testators, two died outside Ixil (one in Tihó, one in Mamá), a 2.9 percent that is actually far more significant than the 2.9 percent of nonnative parents, since the nonnative status was permanent, whereas being caught mortally ill in another cah was subject to chance. In other words, Ixil residents were more likely to be spending time in another cah than they were likely to have been born in another cah, supporting the notion that migration was seasonal or cyclical.[15]

To argue convincingly that Maya society was tightly bound by the cah, and yet the cah was a dispersed entity in terms of the land and even the people who belonged to it, one must understand the nature of boundaries within and around that society. It has been observed that community and ethnic boundaries "may persist despite what may figuratively be called the 'osmosis' of personnel through them."[16] I propose that Maya land boundaries, as they existed and as they were described in the colonial period, represented the Maya cultural perception of boundary as by definition permitting osmosis from one zone to another without compromising the integrity of each zone. One aspect of Maya society that allowed this osmosis was the importance of the chibal, whose members resided in more than one cah. Thus Maya land descriptions—to which I shall turn in Chapter 15—symbolically, as well as literally, represented the boundaries that surrounded the world of the cah.

CHAPTER FOURTEEN

Economic and Material Culture

Previous chapters have described in some detail the social and cultural context of the material objects that were used, valued, and bequeathed by the Maya of the cahob. The purpose of the following pages is to summarize that information and expand upon some of it, with a view to outlining the way in which the Maya used land and the extent to which the cah was economically linked to outside markets, all as a prelude to a detailed treatment of the Maya conception and exchange of land.

The Material World of the Cah

I give my son Leonicio Un six of my beehives and one bottle and six measures of cloth and one spoon and one chest and one scarf and one plate.

—Felipa Couoh of Ebtun, 1813

Land was essential to the way in which the Maya sustained themselves. Residential plots, or solars, were the site of houses and wells and orchards, as well as the small-scale cultivation, animal husbandry, and weaving that were overwhelmingly in the hands of women. The reordering of house plots into square or rectangular solars on a grid was most likely a colonial innovation, but the Maya apparently were quick to adopt its quadripartite layout, and then gradually to have developed urban stone walls from traditional stone-mound boundaries.

In the colonial period, Maya houses seem to have been positioned more or less as they are today, with front and back doors aligned to allow air and light to pass through two or more structures. As in central Mexico, the number and alignment of buildings on a house plot probably changed over time according to the needs of the extended family, with separate structures inhabited by nuclear families bound to each other by blood, marriage, property, and labor. Unlike the Nahuas, the Mayas built only single-storied dwellings, most rectangular, but some apsidal. Solars rarely had more than one house, although there are indications of lesser structures used for storage (of corn, for example) or for animals, or even as a reception area adjacent to the street. In a practice similar to that of the Nahuas, Maya testators very rarely mentioned houses as such, instead leaving to their heirs the parts of the structure considered most permanent and valuable—beams, doors, and door frames (with a simple frame at one end of the economic scale, and a frame and door with lock and key at the other).

Maya furnishings were varied, increasingly so as the colonial period wore on, and mostly Spanish in style, though it is the same few items that were common to most households—beds, tables, chairs, and the *caja* or chest that was also ubiquitous property among the postconquest Nahuas. These wooden chests stored smaller items of value, such as jewelry, money, silver cutlery, or clothing and cloth not being worn, washed, or woven. On the other hand, images of saints (and perhaps rosaries also) were positioned prominently either on tables or in the niched or recessed coverings called tabernacles. Their religious significance aside, these images—which seem to have been held by households through the representative ownership of the male head—were of considerable material value, and may have been a form of economic investment for those families who could afford them.

Men tended to work away from the solar on cultivated or cattle land, using horses and other introduced animals as beasts of burden and labor; farmers sometimes spent days or weeks on plots remote from the residential cah, sleeping in shelters or tocoyna, that were sometimes the ruined structures of the preconquest ancestors.

The introduction of iron had an enormous impact on the Maya ability to work land, especially to clear it as part of the swidden process. As a result, the machete was a treasured item in cah society, usually passed by men down to their sons, but sometimes given to unwed daughters as a future dowry item. It is the most common tool appearing in the Maya-language record, described with the Spanish loanword, which was frequently clipped to *mache* or *chete* (although today a machete is just as likely to be called a *mascab*, literally "iron tool," as may have been the case in colonial times). The most common tool with a Maya name was the ax, or *bat*, although it too would have been modified from its precolonial form to include an iron blade, and indeed in eighteenth-century wills the Spanish "hacha" is more often used. Other Spanish tools used in the cah were the pick, "pico," and hammer, "martillo," Mayanized to *matilo*.

Regional variation in the many other types of tools used by the Maya reflected different cah economies. In apicultural Ebtun, for example, bee-keeping equipment was common; but only cattle-rearing in Tekanto recorded the possession of branding irons. Cacalchen's use of the Maya *xolal*, a digging stick probably used for planting corn seed (from *xol*, "to affix or place something"), and Ixil's apparent ignorance of that term in favor of *lobche mascab* (literally, "iron-tipped wooden stick"), probably did not indicate different tools used by the men of those two cahob, but rather regional variation or temporal changes in terminology. Also used in eighteenth-century Ixil was a *xul mascab*, "iron-tipped digging stick"; a *ɔopatan coch bol*, which contains the elements *ɔop*, "to thrust, stick in," *coch*, "wide," and *bol*, "blunt, to dent," and might thus be glossed as a "blunt digging or planting stick," unless it is a carpentry tool such as a chisel; and a *bronso licil u pabal tunich*, a "broken bronze-tipped digging stick," or more likely a "bronze tool for breaking stones." At about this time Ebtun's beekeepers were making use of a *lomob hobon mascab*, a "metal beehive-scraping or honey-extracting tool." The inclusion of metal in some of these terms, as well as their descriptive nature, suggests they are neologisms of the kind created but soon abandoned by the Nahuas more than two centuries earlier.[1] The actions they describe certainly evoke many aspects of rural labor in the colonial period—the chopping and chipping, digging and planting, scraping and stabbing, cutting and pounding—that would have been shared by most Maya men regardless of wealth and status.[2]

Another tool featuring introduced technology and valued by Maya men was the firearm. Shotguns, which, though relatively rare, do appear in the earliest extant wills, would have been used for hunting game, a practice that continues to this day and has contributed to the reduction of the number and variety of wild animals in the peninsula. The Mayas did not use a loanword to describe guns but had a term of their own, *ɔon*, which may have originated in a term for "throw"—an interesting parallel to the usage by the first postconquest Nahua generations of the verb *tlequi-quiztlaça*, "to throw or let go a fire trumpet" (i.e., to fire a gun). An indication of the value of guns to the Mayas is the occasional appearance in testaments of bullets, in the form *bareta*, "baleta."[3]

The colonial-era Maya were, of course, forbidden to possess firearms; but they blatantly ignored this regulation (modern-day hunting regulations are also often ignored). They also ignored the ban on "Indians" below hidalgo rank owning horses, to the extent that the ban may not have been common knowledge in the cahob. Mayas not only kept horses, but bred and cross-bred them; mares, sometimes pregnant, and juvenile horses, are frequently mentioned, and in the late-colonial period mules and donkeys too. The Maya terms for saddle (*sia tzimin*) and bridle (*pleno tzimin*) are an interesting mix of loanwords ("silla," seat; "freno," brake, bit) with the indigenous term for tapir, *tzimin*, which was applied to "horse" in the colonial period; similarly, the Maya term for something stuck or fixed to something else, *pakam*, became the colonial term for a shoe iron.[4]

The keeping of animals for food was also a vital aspect of the domestic economy within the cah, as well as being one of the cah's economic links to the outside world. Trees, plants, and animals provided not only food but also fibers, leaves, and skins to make clothing, rope, saddles, roofs, and other objects. A number of spatial and temporal factors determined what animals were common in which cah at a particular moment. Such contrasts are illustrated by a comparison of seventeenth-century Cacalchen with Ebtun, Ixil, and Tekanto in the eighteenth century. Cacalchen had no cattle, but Ebtun, and especially Ixil and Tekanto, had many; Calcalchen had many pigs, chickens, and turkeys, whereas the other cahob apparently had none (pig and cockrel are mentioned just once each in testaments from Ixil). Obviously, both time and size are important here: the data on Cacalchen are relatively early, when that cah was small and poor and the rearing of cattle in the cahob was still fairly uncommon. The characteristics of the larger region are not a factor, since Cacalchen is close to Ixil, and not far from Tekanto, in an area whose rural economy is today cattle-intensive; Ebtun, on the other hand, was the other side of the colony. The mention of pigs and domesticated fowl in the Cacalchen wills can be taken as another indication of the relative poverty of that cah, where, unlike the other cahob, these animals were not plentiful and therefore were considered sufficiently valuable to warrant bequeathing. Perhaps, as today, diseases decimated pigs and fowl so regularly that the animals were eaten as soon as they were old enough; either way, a testator on his sickbed might well outlive one or more of his chickens.[5] A further indication of the value accruing to the animals bred in Cacalchen (and therefore of the cah's relative material poverty) is the fact that only testators from this cah go to the trouble of making bequests of the unborn offspring of pregnant mares and pigs, and even bequests of turkey chicks.

Just as cattle were a source of food as well as the source of leather, a valuable product that could be sold outside the cah, so did bees provide honey for the local diet as well as honey and wax for trade and tribute payment. Beeswax from Yucatan was needed for the production of candles in colonial Mexico City; the two indigenous products most sought after by the Spaniards, as shown in the forced sales termed *repartimientos* in Yucatan, were cotton mantles and wax.[6] All cahob represented by more than a handful of testaments include bequests of beehives, although Ebtun is unique in that, of the nine testators (1785–1813) documented, all own beehives (an average of thirty each), three leave their heirs quantities of wax, and three mention apicultural tools (wire masks and a honey-extracting tool).[7]

Money and Clothing

I sold a forest plot at Tixcacal to Josef Canul. However, I returned three tostones to his son, Martín Canul, who then ran away. Let it be recorded today that when my daughters have fully returned his money, the three pesos, to that Martín Canul, then this forest will be placed in my daughters' hands.

—Mateo Canche, with cabildo of Ixil, 1766

I suggested in Chapter 8 that the only truly personal material items in the cah would have been money and clothing. The coined money introduced by the Spaniards no doubt brought with it into the cah the European concept of personal wealth as symbolized in coin, and the Maya easily adapted the concept to their multifaceted view of wealth and property. During the colonial period they continued to exchange property by barter, but they also used Spanish money, particularly as a system for evaluating goods in barter exchanges; both types of exchange are illustrated in this remark by Juan Cutz of Motul, in his will of 1762:[8]

cin ɔaic ti lay in mehen lae hunpok yeua in manɔil na yxim col y hunpok baca y u yal in man yoklal hopel toxtones y hunpel u hol na y u marcoil in man yoklal hunpel peso u ci y hunpel caja in matan ti ina y hunpel cuchara takin in matan ix ti in na xan . . .

I give to my son one mare that I bought for my cornfield, and one cow with its calf that I bought for five tostóns, and one house door with its frame that I bought for one peso of henequen, and one chest inherited from my mother, and one silver spoon also my inheritance from my mother . . .

Likewise, when, in 1750, the batab of Sicpach, don Lazaro Uitz, signed his forest plot over to a nobleman of the cah-barrio of La Mejorada, Gregorio Chi, he made it clear that this was not a sale but rather an exchange in return for a house plot of Chi's—*ma conbili yanil tu kabi kexbil y u solalil.*[9] Yet in a way the exchange depended on the evaluation of the two pieces of property in pesos. Indeed, this case is a rare one; the overwhelming majority of land exchanges involving Maya owners are not literal exchanges, but sales featuring pesos, tostóns, and reals.

Besides using money as the primary means of purchase in the cah, the Maya also used money to advance or acquire credit, to divide property (by selling it and dividing the cash proceeds among heirs), and to save—Gaspar Poot of Ixil left his son *uacpel cueta de oro a medio u tohol,* "six gold coins, fifty percent pure in value." They also used cash to pay mass fees, especially in the later colonial period, and civil taxes; as James Lockhart observed with the respect to the Nahuas, it was probably the spread of money through the indigenous economy that made cash taxes possible, rather than Spanish cash demands forcing money into the cahob, since money was in common use in the cahob before tribute in cash became the convention.[10]

The Maya commonly used the denominations peso and tostón, but they usually called the real (an eighth of a peso) *tumin*, from the Spanish term for coin, *tomín*. These three loans are attested for the turn of the seventeenth century but were probably in use before then. Maya sources mention other coins, such as the "cuenta de oro a medio" above, but they were not normally part of daily business in the cah. It is not clear exactly when, but certainly by the mid-seventeenth century, almost every adult member of a cah saw money pass through his or her hands during the course of a year. As we saw in Chapter 10, Ana Xul of Cacalchen, who died in 1678, had been acting for years as a banker of the cah—perhaps the sole banker—dealing in tribute mantas and, above all, lending out cash. On the other hand, Pasquala Matu, who had acquired a small fortune in cloth and clothing before her death in Ixil in 1766, neither mentions money owed her nor bequeaths cash.[11] This would seem to confirm the suggestion of the mid-eighteenth-century examples from Motul and Sicpach above that money functioned as a key part of a system that still included barter. Considering the small size of the internal economy of most cahob and the fact that large quantities of coins were not readily available (even to Spaniards in some parts of their empire), the continuation of barter is hardly surprising, but it certainly does not imply that the Maya were primitive in their economic dealings.

On the contrary, there is evidence of complex financial dealings in the cahob, including short- and long-term loans, pawning (examples are late and mostly in Spanish), and investments (which is essentially what the cattle ranches of Maya cofradías were). Sales involving serial payments were not uncommon, although they involved the risk of an incomplete transaction—as Mateo Canche of Ixil discovered when he gave half the money for a kax to the vendor's son, who allegedly ran off with the cash, leaving Mateo on his deathbed with neither the plot of land nor its value in pesos. Although I can find no evidence of the continued use of cacao beans as small change for Spanish coins, as was the Nahua practice in central Mexico, the widespread use of indigenous terms for buy (*man*), sell (*con*), pay (*boot*), owe / debt (*pax* and *koch*), and exchange (*kex*) indicate that the culture of transaction was well established in Yucatan before the Spaniards arrived with their coins.[12]

In reference to the Spanish exploitation of Maya labor to produce textiles for export, Robert Patch remarked that Yucatan had, by the late seventeenth century, "become a sweatshop."[13] We have seen the connection between money and the cotton blankets, or mantas, used for tribute—in the dealings of Ana Xul the banker, for example, and in the use of the phrase *yn pax gerga*, "my cloth debt," in Ixil.[14] We have also seen how women were the primary producers of cloth items such as mantas, although it is men who sported blankets over their shoulders as an item of dress—referred to as *yubte* in seventeenth-century Cacalchen, and *sarga* (of rough-cloth) or manta (of cotton) in eighteenth-century Ixil. Before turning to the question of cloth production for export, I shall add a few more details about Maya clothing, based on Maya sources.

Clothes were passed down from generation to generation, since outfits were highly standardized and repair and refitting would have been easy. Male dress consisted of a shirt, trousers, sometimes a cloak, and possibly a belt or sash around the waist and a blanket over one shoulder. The shirt was a Spanish introduction (*camisa*), as were the trousers, despite being called *es* or *ex*, the name of the pre-Hispanic loincloth; the persistence of the Maya term throughout the colonial period implies that trousers may have been adopted later than shirts, as was the case in central Mexico. Perhaps the loincloth evolved toward the Spanish trouser, just as the Maya cloak may have evolved toward a Spanish model; Cacalchen uses a Maya term, *ziyem*, but a century later Ixil is using the Spanish *tilma*, although, as suggested by the fact that this term is itself a loan of the Nahuatl *tilmatli*, some degree of indigenous style was still involved.

Women wore a petticoat (*pic*) under an indigenous-style dress (*ypil*), over which a shawl (*boch* or *box*) might be draped—essentially the same outfit worn before the conquest and still common today in rural Yucatan. The Maya ypil was similar to the central Mexican *huipil*, a term borrowed by Spanish from the Nahuatl *huipilli*; the Maya term was probably borrowed from Nahuatl in precolonial times. The high incidence of introduced flowers, where their depiction allows identification, on contemporary ypil floral designs implies that such embroidery originated in or was altered during the colonial period; perhaps the preconquest tradition of tattooing was transferred to the ypil.[15] There are rare mentions in wills of a *kub* (dress), and a *toca* (head scarf)—perhaps the former was just an older way of describing an ypil, the latter a reference to a Spanish-style *boch*. By far the most common item of female adornment in both the seventeenth and eighteenth centuries was the necklace, with earrings also mentioned in testaments. Shoes are not listed in either men's or women's wills; if colonial practice was that of the Maya of today's rural cahob, women went barefoot and men took their shoes to their graves.

Markets

Four times I went to trade in Bacalar, that I might bring back cacao . . .
—Diego Pox of Dzan, c. 1580

The variety of terms describing cloth as well as clothing in Maya notarial sources, and the frequency with which those items appear in women's
wills, indicates something of the importance of the domestic textile industry and women's role in it. There is evidence of considerable trade of
such items within cahob and even between neighboring communities, but
Maya-produced textiles were not exchanged at central markets of the kind
maintained in the highlands of Guatemala and central Mexico before and
after the conquest. In fact, such markets do not appear ever to have existed
in Yucatan, as suggested in part by the oidor Tomás López's unsuccessful
attempt to introduce the central Mexican market or *tiánguiz* (the Spanish
loan of the Nahuatl *tianquiztli*) in 1552, and largely explained by the relative uniformity of the peninsula's ecosystem.[16]

Spanish sources indicate that itinerant traders, still in evidence today in
parts of Yucatan, were in the colonial period a substitute for large indigenous markets, with these non-Maya but nevertheless marginal figures
acting as middlemen between distant cahob. These merchants relied upon
indigenous business and thus maintained close contacts with certain communities, even to the extent of marrying a Maya woman from a chibal of
status in the cah.[17]

Still, there is evidence that the Maya engaged in a certain amount of
long-distance trade, though in the form of individual contacts and transactions rather than large, open markets. The general mobility and itinerancy
of the Maya population, together with the tendency to maintain contacts in
the home cah, would have provided opportunity as well as an acceptable
cultural context for such trade. When a Maya man died in one cah but had
his testament drawn up in his home cah, where his estate lay and where he
requested to be buried (as was the case of Gabriel Tec of Ixil in 1766), we
can only guess at that man's economic motivations for being in another
cah (Mamá) when taken ill. But when Diego Pox of late-sixteenth-century
Dzan made a claim on his father's estate, he stated quite clearly:[18]

tin tzentah ix in yum xan can uaɔ in	I have also sustained my father, for
benel ti ppolmalte bakhalale licix	four times I went to trade in Bacalar,
uulçic cacau tancoch ix lic in ɔaic	that I might bring cacao, half of
tin yum ohelan tumenel u nucil	which I gave to my father, as the
uinicob tin cahal	principal men of my cah well known.

Interestingly, Pox was not a specialized merchant, but a farmer with
various agricultural enterprises typical of the better-off male residents

of a cah. Along with this diversity of economic activity, including long-distance trading, there was an enthusiastic Maya involvement in what was to the Spaniards the black market—a widespread evasion of taxes that so worried the colonial authorities that a lengthy report on the problem was submitted to the Crown in 1766.[19]

Sometimes the movement of Mayas out of the colony and into the southern and eastern despoblado areas was a result of famine—as reflected in Pascuala Chi's gratitude to Marcos Mo for buying land from her at a time when the residents of Ebtun had fled to the forests to find food; and in the 22,000 Mayas forced back into the colony by a 1652 *entrada* in the wake of the first great yellow fever epidemic. The Maya testimonies in the files of the investigation into don Rodrigo Flores de Aldana's governorship of the 1660's are full of references to temporary flight into the despoblado to escape gubernatorial agents.[20]

Sometimes, however, Maya economic motives were not quite so desperate. The cabildos of Dzaptun and Tahnab in 1605 threatened to move out of the colony unless taxes and other burdens were lightened, and Tahnab fingered a Francisco de Magaña for purchasing black-market wax in the despoblado, pointing out that "the money [Magaña] gives the [Maya wax collectors] really belongs to the Governor."[21] Not only were Spaniards worried about the black market, but Maya cabildos were well aware of that concern and tried to exploit it in their own interests.

Another way in which cah resources passed into Spanish hands more or less without the undermining of Maya profits by heavy taxes was through the mechanisms of the cofradía. Typically, prominent local men would invest in a cofradía venture by "donating" land or water access, the few cattle it took to launch a cattle ranch, and some other basic necessities. As the business grew, the unpaid work contributions of family members would evolve into a labor and administrative structure like that of Spanish estancias, with the cofradía officers acting as mayordomos and their staff and paying the taxes of weekly salaried ranch workers. The primary product of the business, meat, went to the Spanish urban market. In the east, cofradías estates tended to be smaller and centered on apicultural operations; in the south, near the end of the colonial period they supplied beef to the military posts in Bacalar and the Petén. The beauty of indigenous cofradía operations was that they avoided royal taxes, either because they were unlicensed and thus escaped notice (save from local priests who benefited from fiesta fees), or because as cofradías they enjoyed the exemptions of "spiritual property."[22]

Much of Maya labor, however, was subject to colonial exploitation, and it ultimately benefited Spaniards more than Mayas. Such labor broadly falls into two categories: agricultural labor, done primarily by men, producing maize for the indigenous and Spanish markets; and textile labor, done primarily by women (once men had harvested the raw cotton), producing cotton blankets and thread. In both cases, the markets that drove this production were Spanish or Spanish-controlled.

At the turn of the seventeenth century the Spanish authorities established a centralized granary system to draw maize out of the cahob and into Mérida, Valladolid, and eventually all communities where Spaniards began living. In typical fashion, agents from Mérida (who contracted to buy grain from up to half the cahob under colonial rule) would pay the cabildo of a particular cah up to a year in advance for a certain number of *cargas*; those funds would then be distributed to the farmers of the cahob who contributed to the deposit after the harvest. Maya-language records, consisting of formulaic receipts for grain deposits, drawn up by the cah notary and validated by the cabildo officers, indicate the regularity of this process by the eighteenth century. Spanish sources record many of its details (beginning with the mid-seventeenth century), such as the profitable monopoly on grain transportation by indigenous muleteers, and the fact that over half Mérida's maize was supplied by Ticul, Maní, Oxkutzcab, and the other cahob of the Sierra Alta.[23]

Although the Maya seem to have participated willingly in the centralized grain market, their participation in Yucatan's textile industry was less voluntary. Cotton and woven cotton blankets, or mantas, were acquired from Maya communities both as tax payments and by repartimiento. Patch has estimated that repartimiento was the principal Spanish mechanism in Yucatan for extracting a surplus from the Mayas, and that most of this surplus consisted of cloth-related products—66 percent textiles, 7 percent thread, and 27 percent wax, according to a Franciscan report on the repartimientos of 1700. Maya farmers were paid four reales per carga for raw cotton, even when the market price was as high as twelve reales (as in the 1670's). The high Spanish profits were shared by officials of the colonial administration, especially the governor, and the prospect of even greater profit inspired some governors and their agents to devise other ways of cheating Maya vendors (such as redefining the weight of a carga, or selling back at a profit crops ruined by drought and never even harvested). The high cost of importing European textiles ensured a steady and lucrative market in Spanish America for Yucatec cotton products.[24]

The Maya gained little from Yucatan's link to the international market. On the contrary, the promise of profit for Spanish officials forced the Maya to provide virtually free labor on their own land and drained off most of the cloth products that would otherwise have been of value in the cah market. As Patch has pointed out, even though the Mayas by and large retained control over the means of production—land—they had practically no say in the relations of economic exchange between themselves and the colonial authorities.[25] That this system of exploitation relied so much upon the stable functioning of indigenous society, making the Spaniards dependent upon the "Indians" in Yucatan and elsewhere, helps explain the persistence of indigenous culture. But the Mayas themselves must be credited with far more than a merely passive role in the process. That the social and cultural integrity of the cah was maintained in spite of the pressures of the colonial system is indicative of the cah's fortitude and adaptability.

CHAPTER FIFTEEN

Land Description

The many extant examples of postconquest Maya land descriptions in wills, bills of sale, and material relating to land litigation make these documents a rich source for an analysis of Maya land culture—by which is meant Maya cultural perception and description of land, and the relation between the natural environment and its exploitation by the Mayas. The variations that these sources display are sufficiently consistent to allow certain key patterns to be detected. I wish first to present two characteristics of land description common to most such documents (repeated phrasing, and references to the cardinal directions), and then to offer an analytical division of such descriptions into two forms ("stationary" and "ambulatory"), before turning to three final aspects of these descriptions (trees, maps, and measurement).

Repetition and Cardinal Direction

Its neighbors are Juan Mis to the south, Marcos Cim over in the west, don Bartolome Pech to the north, Ignacio Bas to the east.
—Pedro Mis of Ixil, 1766

Repetition is a fundamental aspect of Maya discourse: One linguistic anthropologist has already pointed out the periodic repetition of particular grammatical forms in the boundary descriptions of part of the Yaxkukul chronicle or title,[1] but repetition is the central element of much of the land description in indigenous documentation from throughout postconquest Yucatan. The exact nature of this rhetorical convention will become clearer through the examples presented under the two forms of description below. First, however, it can be explained through discussion of the cardinal directions, which occur in a repeated rhetorical fashion in land documents.

Cardinal directions were central to the way the Maya visualized and described land. Unlike the Nahuas, who began to adopt Spanish cardinal terms in the late seventeenth century, the Maya retained their own terms through to the present century. Furthermore, these terms—*xaman*, "north"; *nohol*, "south"; *lakin*, "east"; *chikin*, "west"—suggest that the Maya had been preoccupied with cardinal directions longer than the Nahuas, whose phrases for east and west (*tonatiuh iquiçayampa*, "toward where the sun comes up"; *tonatiuh icalaquiyampa*, "toward where the sun goes down") and method of indicating north and south (references to prominent places in those directions, such as *mexicopahuic*, "toward Mexico City," or *yn ihuicpa huey tepetl*, "toward the great mountain") seem inefficient by comparison, though similar in concept.[2] Indeed, in one Nahua community whose land culture has been studied, Coyoacan, cardinal directions cease being used in land descriptions as early as the first decades of the seventeenth century,[3] whereas they are the focus of Maya land descriptions in most cahob throughout the colonial period. This may in part be explained by the fact that, compared with highland areas, Yucatan is fairly featureless.

The sequence of directions in land descriptions depicted in Tables 15.1 and 15.2 may at first glance appear to be random, and certainly the pattern is far less clear and tidy than that of similar descriptions in Nahuatl—in early Coyoacan, for example, such descriptions always began with the east (the second sequence in Table 15.2).[4] Yet in Maya descriptions there are still discernible patterns to the cardinal sequence, which reflect variations between cahob as well as variations (on what may have once been a model) within each cah. One direction stands out in both tables. Of the 18 examples culled from the testaments of Ixil, 11 mention the south, 11 the west, 11 the east, and all 18 mention the north. Of the 50 examples taken from Mérida-Tihó's Maya communities all but one mention the north. This suggests a predominance given to this direction, though what significance the Maya placed on it is not clear; in preconquest iconography the primary direction was the east, not the north, although preconquest sites tend to have a northeast tilt (and the Maní map of 1557 is oriented east-northeast). We do know which colors, deities, and trees were associated with each direction, but there seems not to have been a tradition of negative or positive association that would shed light on colonial-era practice.[5] The favoring of north may suggest Western European influence, although the shift from east to north as the primary direction did not occur in Europe until the early-modern period.

TABLE 15.1
*Sequence of Cardinal Directions in Stationary Kax
Descriptions from Ixil*

"Model" sequence	Sequence example and source
N W — E S	SWNE 30 WN 37, 40, 56 NE 20 S NE 36 S N 56, 61
N W — E S	WSEN 33, 64 SEN 33 EN 37
N W — E S	ENWS ENW 7, 14 NWS 33 N S 37
N W — E S	SEWN 7, 54

SOURCE: TI (1765–68; source numbers are testament numbers).

The Ixil descriptions are evenly divided between clockwise and counterclockwise sequences, and there is no pattern in the choice of initial or terminal directions in the sequences. However, as Table 15.1 shows, the Ixil examples can be grouped under three "model" sequences (although the members of each group do not all begin at the same point or include every direction). The examples from the five cahob-barrios of Mérida-Tihó are listed by frequency of occurrence, revealing a preference for a counterclockwise round of the directions beginning in either the west or the east (with a total preference for counterclockwise of 74 percent).[6] The clearest pattern is the overwhelming decision to respect the circle or round of directions (98 percent), rather than jump across the center as in the final and unique example. The use of all four directions is not really surprising, but the fact that all are mentioned in 94 percent of the descriptions from the cahob-barrios strengthens the circular nature of the description.

TABLE 15.2

Sequence of Cardinal Directions in Stationary Solar Descriptions in Bills of Sale from the Five Cahob-barrios of Mérida-Tihó, 1741–1825

Sequence	Date	Cah-barrio	Source in ANEY / variation
N / W E / S	1741	Santiago	1776, 256
	1741	[illeg.]	1812ii, 9
	1744	Santiago	1822–23, 102
	1753	Santiago	1812ii, 8
	1755	Santiago	1797ii, n.f
	1762	San Sebastián	1813ii, 12
	1764	San Sebastián	1761–65, 631 · WSE
	1764	Santiago	1818i, 173
	1769	Santiago	1818iii, 145
	1779	Santiago	1794–95, n.f
	1782	San Sebastián	1812ii, 2
	1783	San Cristóbal	1810ii, 91
	1786	Santiago	1835, n.f
	1815	San Sebastián	1827, 222
	1820	San Cristóbal	1822, n.f
N / W E / S	1767	San Cristóbal	1790–91, 301 · ENS
	1770	[illeg.]	1822–23, 179
	1781	Santa Ana	1813i, 43
	1781	Santa Ana	1814ii, 22
	1781	Santiago	1811ii, 186
	1782	Santiago	1822–23, 9
	1793	Mejorada	1814ii, 111
	1794	Santa Ana	1812ii, 72
	1807	[illeg.]	1824, 200
	1809	San Sebastián	1810ii, 99
	1819	San Cristóbal	1823ii, 30
	1825	Mejorada	1836–39, 17
N / W E / S	1770	Santa Ana	1769–72, 370
	1775	San Sebastián	1813ii, 198
	1784	San Cristóbal	1814–15, 71
	1789	Santiago	1834, 31
	1802	San Cristóbal	1806, 9
N / W E / S	1756	[illeg.]	1822–23, 20 · NW
	1776	Mejorada	1838, 99
	1778	San Sebastián	1826i, n.f
	1778	Santiago	1814–15, 35
	1782	Santiago	1797ii, 146
N / W E / S	1752	San Sebastián	1813ii, 13
	1766	San Cristóbal	1814ii, 148
	1766	San Cristóbal	1820, 75
	1770	San Cristóbal	1820, 75

TABLE 15.2
Continued

Sequence	Date	Cah-barrio	Source in ANEY / variation
N, W, E, S (diagram)	1766	San Sebastián	1814–15, 2
	1769	Mejorada	1814i, 76
	1770	Mejorada	1815–16, 87
N, W, E, S (diagram)	1770	Mejorada	1818ii, 50
	1781	San Sebastián	1811, 16
	1783	Mejorada	1806–9, 223
N, W, E, S (diagram)	1790	Mejorada	1814–15, 56
	1791	Mejorada	1823i, 100
	[illeg.]	[illeg.]	1814–15, 70
N, W, E, S (diagram)	1782	Santiago	1828, 7

Stationary and Ambulatory Forms

Here are the principal stone mound and the line mounds of this forested
land named Chichí.
> —cabildos of Dzibikal and Uman, 1735

Examples of descriptions from the two sources above (Ixil and Tihó)
illustrate the circular effect of the directions, as well as some of the characteristics of what I have termed the stationary form of description, taken
from a fixed central point. Unlike ambulatory descriptions, whose perspective is that of someone walking a boundary, Ixil's kax descriptions do
not mention stone mounds or tree markers, nor do they give any measurements. A plot of kax may be "to the west of Ixculix" or "on the road to
Xku,"[7] but the main identifying points of description are the owners and
the cardinal directions of the neighboring plots. For example:[8]

u tzayale chikine sebastian couoh	Its neighbor is to the west Sebastián
ti nohole layli sebastian couoh lae	Couoh['s kax], to the south that same

ti lakin Andrez canche ti xamane Agustin Yam	Sebastián Couoh, to the east Andrés Canche, to the north Agustín Yam.

The descriptions from Mérida-Tihó tend to be less spare, perhaps because they are land sales rather than wills also listing other types of property, but the circular effect remains the same. The following two examples have been selected from different cahob-barrios four decades apart (Santiago, 1753; La Mejorada, 1793) to emphasize the characteristics common across this particular subcorpus of documents.[9]

yan tu chikin u solar marselo chac Calle Real chumuc y tu nohol u solar micaela sarmiento y tu lakin u solar Ben^ra may humpakte u chi u lumil y tu xaman u solar cah cah lic felis pot Calle Real chumuc tan noh be bel cauquel	There is to the west, across the street, Marselo Chac's solar, and to the south Micaela Sarmiento's solar, and to the east Ventura May's solar, an orchard included, and to the north, across the street to the Caucel highway, a cah solar where Felix Poot is living
he ti lakine u solar Juana sapata he ti xamane u solar tomasa col heix ti chikine u solar Maria dolores domiges heix ti nohole u solar maria paula tapia caye rial chumuc	Here to the east Juana Zapata's solar, here to the north Tomasa Col's solar, also here to the west Maria Dolores Domínguez's solar, also here to the south, across the street, Maria Paula Tapia's solar

Such descriptions produce two effects, one aural, one visual. All Maya notarial documents were oral performances—not only wills, which were obviously dictated—since few if any people in a cah besides the notary were literate; and a number of cabildo officers and other interested parties witnessed the production of each document. Read aloud, stationary descriptions contain a rhythm derived from the repetition of the formulaic naming of the cardinal directions. The formula varied from cah to cah— Tekanto efficiently combined the names of neighboring plot owners and the siting of the streets into, for example, *tu nohol u calleil Luis Bacab tu lakin u Calleil Man^la hau* . . . , "to the south Luis Bacab's street [i.e., the street bordering his plot], to the east Manuela Hau's street"—but the reciting of the cardinal directions was as fixed as the earth and sky.

The immutability of the directions not only allowed variations while keeping descriptions unambiguous, but also facilitated the visualization of the five plots in question, the fifth being the central plot under exchange. The simplicity of the descriptions, avoiding mention of size or subdirections (southeast, etc.), prompts a visual image in which each plot is a square. Put together, these squares form a Maya cross, a visual representation that correlates with the preconquest Maya world model, which was

TABLE 15.3
*Comparison of Nonsolar Stationary Land Descriptions from
17th-Century Cacalchen and 18th-Century Ixil*

	Cacalchen	Ixil
land term used	col	kax
measurements of plot given	72%	0%
plot site named	97%	25%
plot "next to [road etc.]"	0%	47%
cardinal directions used	16%	67%
neighbors named	0%	64%

SOURCES: LC; TI. Percentages indicate incidence of given descriptive element in 32 Cacalchen examples (1646–56) and 35 Ixil examples (1765–68).

likewise not only quadrangular but also concentric. The cardinal directions were conceived in relation to the center, wherein grew (in preconquest iconography) the World Tree that held up the sky or (in land descriptions) any trees present on the plot of land under exchange. These five directions or spaces formed a quincunx, which was the cultural form or mnemonic framework of not only the Maya but also the Mesoamerican world view.[10]

Thus the kax or solar being bequeathed or sold became the microcosmic center of the world because the quincunx would have been at some (sub)conscious level instantly accessible to the Maya mind. In the precolonial cosmos, each direction had its color, wind, god, and tree; now, from the perspective of the holder of every plot of land, each direction had its owner, who was a neighbor and perhaps also a relative. The relationship between plot and direction was strengthened by the fact that Maya directions were not fixed compass points, but spaces or sections of the world.[11] Whether the plots in question were actually square or not (most were at least rectangular) was not important, for, as with the variations of descriptive formula, the universal model ensured universal understanding, at least within the world of the cah.

The model worked best, of course, within the grid of the residential cah, and most examples of the stationary form describe solars (as with the Tihó and Tekanto examples above). The use in Ixil of an uncluttered stationary formula to describe kax was therefore unusual; in nearby Cacalchen nonsolar land (there known as col) was described by a technique more familiar to *our* culture, with the principal anchors being toponyms and measurements. The contrast between these two is presented in statistical terms in Table 15.3. Because cah-to-cah variation was so endemic, we can be sure that this in itself helps explain this particular Cacalchen-Ixil difference. However, the example is also useful in that a century separates the sources from each cah. Solars are never referred to in Cacalchen, whereas they are ubiquitous in Ixil, so it is possible that stationary land descriptions were a Maya response, based on their own world view, to the introduction of the Spanish urban grid. If we also had early-colonial sources from Ixil, we might find that it too had lacked a fullfledged cabildo, showed no mention of solars, and did not use stationary land description—in other words, that the cah had yet to adopt, absorb, and localize the introductions of the colonial period.

The descriptive technique characteristic of the ambulatory form that is most often used in documents relating to Maya land sales walks the reader, visually, along the boundaries of the property. The cardinal directions remain as principal anchors of description, and stone mounds (often numbered, sometimes arranged as line mounds), and other landmarks such as trees, wells, or roads, are also identified. Actual distances are rarely mentioned, and there can be an apparent vagueness or paucity of detail, no doubt because, as one Maya landowner remarked, "my son knows the stone mounds."[12]

As in the stationary form, the numbering of the markers creates an internal rhythm of repetition, formula, and the directions, except that the four cardinal directions do not determine the limits of the rhythm: rather, the rhythm grows out of an accumulation of border markers; the description in a sale from Uman of 1735, for example, runs to fifty-three stone mounds.[13] Some extant descriptions appear to bridge this difference between the two forms; for example, when Marcos Chan of Ebtun sold a parcel of kax in 1696 he remarked that *yan tac u multunil tu can titzil,* "its stone mounds are at its four corners." This representation of a plot as quadripartite clearly evokes the world model, yet it is not the parcels on all four sides that Chan describes, but the location of the corner markers. Furthermore, the reader is taken along the line that runs from corner to corner:[14]

bay binbal ti nohol u yoxppel u noh multunil tu multun don lucas tun cuncunul u canppel u noh multun bay binbal ti lakin tu chun konoc habin yan multun tu chumuc u col in yum senor don antto peles bay binbal ti xaman hoppic same y tu chun uayam tu can titzil	it runs south to the 3rd large stone mound at don Lucas Tun of Cuncuncul's stone mound; the 4th large stone mound is east to the foot of a deformed habin tree; there's a mound halfway down m'lord don Antonio Pérez's field; it goes along north to where the four corners began a little while ago at the foot of a uayam tree.

This example introduces two important elements that identify the ambulatory form: the notion of a line (here conveyed by the suffix *-bal,* indi-

TABLE 15.4
Repeated Connecting Phrases in Ambulatory Descriptions: Examples

Phrase	Translation	Provenance of example
heex tet	here is	Tekax
caix ti bini on	and then we went	Tekax
bay (tun) binbal	then it goes	Ebtun, Hunucmá
tan cacatil u binel	it runs along a while	Itzmal, Tahcabo
caye chumuc	across the street	Dzibikal and Uman, Tihó
kuchuc yicnal	one arrives at	Ebtun, Pustunich

SOURCES: AGN-T, 1419, 2, 1–5; ANEY, 1826ii, 9 and 243v; ANEY-P, Izamal, 1814–21, 42, and Hunucmá, 81–85; MT: 15; TE: 221; TT: 41. These citations are examples, taken from the many that occur in Maya land sales.

cating something in a series or along a thread); and the use of verbs, usually to denote movement (here *bin*, "to go," made *binbal*, "to go or run along"). The visual journey reflects an actual journey that was required of large-scale sales or boundary agreements, of which there are many examples, from right after the conquest (the Nachi Cocom 1545 survey of Sotuta lands, written down in 1600) to right before Independence (a Maní border treaty of 1815 that took two days to walk).[15] Yet even in agreements between individuals over relatively small tracts of land, the formula of description indicates that a literal and ritual procession took place, with the verb *ximbal*, "walk," occasionally used, and perhaps too the Spanish *procesión*. For example, Pedro Ceh of Saclum *chicanpahi titon yoklal c binel ximbal te u pach u prosecioonil*, "appeared before us [the cabildo] in order to go along, to make the walk, of taking possession," or possibly "to walk behind in procession." And in ambulatory description from Pustunich *ximbal* is sometimes inserted into the formula that takes the reader-walker from one marker to the next. In a possession ritual in Tekanto shortly after the conquest, cah nobles not only walked the boundary but also placed stone mounds. The formal processions of boundary surveys and agreements must have been mirrored in the daily walks of Maya farmers along narrow trails to and along forest plots and fields.[16]

I have called these pieces of formula "repeated connecting phrases," and have recorded some of them in Table 15.4. Such phrases can be quite long; the full version of the example above from Itzmal goes *cu binel* [or *sutpahal*] *nohol* [etc.] *tan cacatil u binel*, "then it runs [or turns to the] north [etc.] a while it runs." Despite being somewhat idiomatic, most of these phrases are self-explanatory, although *caye chumuc* bears a few words. This is a partial calque, being a direct half-translation of the Spanish idiom *calle en medio*. Put literally in English, this would be "street in the middle," but the idiomatic meaning is "across the street." Caye chumuc was originally a formula of stationary descriptions of house plots, in which a street is literally between two plots, but the Maya also use the phrase for ambulatory descriptions outside residential areas (where "street" becomes "path"); it is common in solar descriptions from Tihó and other cahob, but its use in a lengthy ambulatory description from the twin cahob of Dzibikal and Uman is a fine illustration of how connecting phrases act as discourse markers, tying the boundary markers together and contributing to the rhythm of the description and the walk. They function, if you like, as footsteps:[17]

u uuctukal alcab multun tu chun sucte caye chumuc chikin tan u binel / u uax-actukal alcab multun tu chun sucte xan caye chumuc chikin tan u binel / u bolon-tukal alcab multun tu chun chulul caye chumuc chikin tan u binel

the 27th line mound runs to the base of a sucte tree, across the path, going west-ward, / the 28th line mound runs to the base of a sucte tree also, across the path, going westward, / the 29th line mound runs to the base of chulul tree, keeping to the path, going westward

This brief and deliberately repetitive excerpt (the full description in-cludes one series of thirty-five line mounds and a second of eighteen mounds) also contains other typical features of ambulatory description. In addition to the phrasing, and the use of cardinal directions to help mark the rhythm, the description has a vivid linear sense that comes from the exact placement of the mounds of stones in a series. The number of mounds in each series often followed a pattern; a plot described in Tekax in 1787, for example, contained line mounds that featured series of only threes and fives.[18]

I have separated Maya techniques of land description into two forms here for analytical reasons; the two forms have much in common, not least the element of repetition, and the Maya did not distinguish them as forms or types by terminology.[19] Nonetheless, there may have been some distinc-tion in the Maya mind, as suggested by two passages in a quasi-notarial source, the Book of Chilam Balam of Chumayel. The segment grandiosely titled by Ralph Roys *The Ritual of the Four World-Quarters* is in fact a refer-ence to and reflection of stationary and ambulatory land descriptions. It may be ritual (this systematic play on mundane activity might even be taken as a definition of ritual), but there seems to be an element of humor that cannot be ignored: where the names of neighboring owners are usu-ally inserted, this passage inserts chibal names that are puns on topo-graphical features typically used as border or land markers, all within the usual circular naming of cardinal directions:

ix noh uc u hool u poop ah lakin . . .   Ix Noh Uc rules [is the head of the
batun u hol u pop ti xaman . . .   mat] to the east . . . Batun rules to the

iban u hol pop ti chikin . . .   north . . . Iban rules to the west . . . Ah
Ah Yamas u hol pop ti nohol . . .   Yamas rules to the south . . .

In recognition of the fact that owners and objects play similar marking roles in Maya land description, the Chilam Balam passage turns the two into one, or, put another way, makes objects of landowners and humanizing features of the land. In the passages that follow, the same punning technique is used to identify markers on what is now a stylized border walk, with the names of markers or cahob being turned into events so as to create a tale, a mythological ancestral journey (by comparing the Maya text with my translation the reader will see that Tixchel contains the word for "prolong," and so on):

ca talob tixchel ti chelhi u thanobi   Then they came to Tixchel to prolong
ti chelhi u canobi catun kuchob   their words, to prolong their conver-
ninum ti num hi u thanobi ti num   sation; then they arrived at Ninum, to
hi u canobi . . . catun kuchob   have many words, to have many
chikinɔonot ti chikin tan hi   conversations. . . . Then they arrived
u uichobi . . .   at Chikindzonot, where they turned
                                          their faces to the west.

This ancestral journey in turn mirrors the very first journey of man in a creation myth that is also recorded in the Chumayel. In this passage the *uinal*, the twenty-day count presented as taking the form of the first male, "began to walk by his own effort alone," before being joined by female relatives to continue an eastward journey, stopping only to measure footsteps (a metaphor for counting off the day). In other words, the markers of the walk have been changed from physical to metaphysical and temporal.[20]

There is a certain similarity here between these mythological ambulatory rituals and the tales that Australian aboriginal peoples use to describe the land and particular pathways across it—the "songlines."[21] The Chilam Balam tale may not have been used as a mnemonic in the way that songlines are, but if the Maya reference can be said to work in the other direction—from mundane description to mythical description—then every time land is described in a sale or will, a ritual recollection is made of the (mythological) original settlement of the land. In fact, these references *must* work in both directions: the toponyms of the land and the mythological tale of first settlement mirror each other, for they have contributed to each other's cultural evolution; the ritual descriptions of the Chilam Balam and the formulaic descriptions of notarial documents mirror each other in the same way. The point is not only that the Maya methods of land description were so developed as to make this kind of reference recognizable (to us and the Maya), but that the Chilam Balam literature and notarial materials can be used to illuminate each other (a comparison that is further expanded in Chapter 21).

Maps and Measurement

The boundary runs for one *payab* and four *dzac* . . .
—cabildo of Ebtun, 1791

The importance of stone mounds in Maya land description is further illustrated by the use of maps in such documentation. These usually take a bird's-eye view of the land, in which the boundaries are broken or full lines that are marked by circles representing mounds in series or as large numbered markers, rather resembling a string of beads. Circles indicating large stone mounds are sometimes drawn so as to encapsulate a description such as *Noh multun tu chi ek lum*, "Large stone mound at the edge of (or surrounded by) black earth." The lines between mounds are always straight, sometimes idealizing a plot as a square, even when measurements are included that make it mathematically clear that the area is not square.

In some of the few extant early Maya maps, the circular rendering of stone mounds is paralleled by a larger circularity. One of the versions of the map accompanying the 1557 Maní land treaty is the best example: Maní itself sits in the center; lines connect it to its immediate neighbors, which are represented by drawings of churches in sizes corresponding to each cah's importance, and the more distant cahob are spaced along a circular horizon, their names written, and thus read, as though the map were being revolved. That this is an indigenous map characteristic is suggested first by the fact that the effect of this circular perspective is precisely that of written stationary descriptions—centrally positioned, one sees each feature before one on the horizon as one turns—and, second, by the fact that this circular perspective is replaced by a stationary perspective probably in the seventeenth century (certainly by the eighteenth). Indeed, even in some versions of the Maní map the cah names are all written from the same angle.

Otherwise, colonial-era Maya maps lack such striking indigenous features as the footprints of pre- and early-colonial Nahua maps, although we cannot be sure that Maya maps ever included that kind of feature. Of course, the way in which the Maya described land in writing in the colonial period is effectively cartographic in its heavy use of visual landmarks and the techniques of narrative journey. This fact, along with the absence of any surviving precolonial Maya maps, may indicate that the Maya before the conquest did their mapping in words. Postconquest Maya maps

TABLE 15.5
Maya Measuring Methods

Measure	Literal meaning	Equivalent	Occurrence
kal	20	20 kan	Cacalchen, Ebtun, Tekanto
kan	rope, cord	1 mecate	Ebtun, Tekanto
dzac	to count, add	1 mecate	Ebtun, Tekanto
payab	cry, shout	5 mecates	Ebtun
bak	400	400 mecates	Tekanto
sap	arm span	braza	Ebtun
lub	resting place	league	Dzaptun

SOURCES: LC, TE, and DT (Cacalchen, Ebtun, and Tekanto occurrences based on multiple findings); AGN-CI, 2013, 1, 6 (Dzaptun, one document only). Sources span 17th and 18th centuries.

are usually referred to by the Spanish loan *mapa*, typically in the phrase *u mapail u hochbilanil*; because of the ambiguity of *hoch*, which means both "image" and "copy," this could be either "the copy of the map" or a bilingual semantic couplet, "the map, the image"—or both. Maya references to maps are too few for variations between cahob to be seriously determined.[22]

The writing down of measurements in land documents, however, clearly varied according to the practice of each community. The solares and kaxob bequeathed in wills from Ixil never mention measurements of any kind. On the other hand, three-quarters of the fields bequeathed in the extant wills from Cacalchen state the measured size of the plot (see Table 15.3). The Cacalchen method, also used in Ebtun and Tekanto (see Table 15.5), was the standard Maya measure, the *kal*. Or, put another way, the *kan*. If this seems confusing, it certainly seems to have confused Roys, who glossed *buluc kal* as "nine score" with the footnote "probably the land unit, a mecate," while elsewhere he stated that the kan was the mecate.[23] Philip Thompson showed he understood what the Maya were doing; he presented a key in which 1 kal equaled 20 kan, 5 kal made 100 kan, and so on.[24] What both Roys and Thompson never quite state is the simple fact that the use of kal was merely an abbreviated reference to kan. For kal, of course, means "twenty." Thus 1 kal is really 1 unit of 20, which is really 20 kan, which means the unit all along is the kan; put differently, *hokal col*, "a field of five twenty-units," is shorthand for *hokal kan col*, "a field of five twenty-units (one hundred) kan (mecates)."

Although numbers in Maya must have counter suffixes (numeral classifiers) and thus properly speaking hokal cannot be glossed as simply "100" but as five (number) kal (counter), the effect of the abbreviation is to leave a number naked, with its classifier assumed. One Tekanto testator refers to the two kinds of land he leaves behind in a way that illustrates well these methods of measure and description: *hokal yn matan kax ti An-*

drea ake, which we might translate as "my hundred-mecate inherited-from-Andrea-Ake forest"; and *hunPet yn matan soralal ti Bern^na Bas*, "my single-item inherited-from-Bernardina-Bas house plot."[25] The kal, then, acts as a numeral classifier in the same fashion as *pet*, but its meaning is twenty kan (i.e., mecates).

The kan was a mecate in terms of specific colonial-era measuring standards but was at root a generic term for size similar (in terms of semantic origins) to the Nahuatl *quahuitl*; the Maya term means "cord, rope," the Nahuatl "rod, stick." The Spanish term mecate was of course itself derived from a Nahuatl word, *mecatl*, which also meant "cord" as well as being a term of measurement. Despite the linear implications of the literal meaning of mecatl and kan, the former was often used by the Nahuas to denote an area or square unit, and the latter was always used by the Maya to describe area.[26] The significant difference between the quahuitl and the kan is that the Nahua term is essentially a reference to a unit a twentieth the size of the kan, a unit the Maya did not have a term for because there was no need. The Maya vocabulary of measurement is specific at a larger scale than its Nahuatl equivalent. This is a logical reflection of the aforementioned shifting nature of Maya cultivation, which requires farming tracts larger than those of the Nahuas.

The Maya use of *dzac* as a counter or numeral classifier was another way of referring to the kan as a "count," or a square unit of twenty; there was no term for the twentieth subunit. The use of *ac* has been described as an abbreviation of *uinic*—as in *hun uinic col*—to indicate a field cultivated by one man, a field of twenty kan.[27] However, my interpretation of its colonial-era usage is as a numeral classifier meaning "unit" without any specific indications of size, although it would not be surprising to find that *ac* was a specific unit in a few communities; some cahob seemed to favor as counters -*ac*, some -*pel*.[28]

In Tekanto over a third of plots whose sizes were given in the notarial record were a hundred mecates (a five count); another third consisted of whole multiples of five (ten, fifteen, and twenty counts, the last being a *bak*). This suggests that a hundred mecates was the standard plot size, although in seventeenth-century Cacalchen col sizes conformed less closely to this pattern. The range in this cah was from twenty to 160 mecates, with most falling below a hundred. Here again, the contrast seems only to indicate Cacalchen's poverty relative to the Tekanto of a century later; one hundred mecates may have been the ideal in Cacalchen too, but few households could attain that sort of affluence.[29]

The clearest fact that emerges from these variations is the predominance of a unit of twenty. This was likewise the case in central Mexico, and in both regions the unit is tied to the indigenous vigesimal system of counting and, we may suppose, harks back to preconquest practices of land division and measurement. It has been suggested that the twenty-unit measure may predate the arrival of the Nahuas in central Mexico;[30] indeed it seems logical that such a unit would have become fundamental in Mesoamerica in conjunction with the evolution of the counting system, and that a plot deemed adequate for the sustenance of a household would have been divided into twenty-by-twenty pieces of stick or rope in order to create a base unit of measure.

A more obvious method of measuring had also evolved in Meso-america in a similar way to the development of our "foot." The Nahuas used their terms for arm/hand, forearm, elbow, armpit, shoulder, ear, heart, bone, foot, and nail as distances of measurement.[31] The Maya were apparently less thorough in taking advantage of the measures offered by the human body. The Maya for "ear"—*xicin*—appears in the Ebtun material not as a linear measurement but to mean width (the word for length—*uaan*—meant height). Of the preconquest measuring system in which feet (*oc*) and hand (*kab*) measures were subdivisions of a *sapal* (a full arm span), only the latter (as *sap*) appears in the colonial-era record.[32] Furthermore, only in notarial documents from Ebtun have I found the linear measures *sap* and *payab* (listed in Table 15.5), and even there examples are scarce. Not only is the payab, which Roys suggested was equal to five kan,[33] used far less often than the kan/mecate in Ebtun, but measurements are, generally speaking, a secondary and infrequent aspect of Maya land description.

The Role of Trees

The border then runs to the east, to the base of a large oak, where a stone mound has been set; then it joins the edge of the savannah, where a stone marker has been placed at the base of a button mangrove.
—cabildo of Dzan, 1569

The use of trees in ambulatory descriptions emerges as a significant aspect of the close Maya relationship with their ecological environment. Unlike stone mounds, trees cannot be easily moved, but, unlike wells, they can be planted or left standing during a slash-and-burn specifically because of their use as identifiable markers. There is no direct evidence in the notarial record that this was done, but it is strongly suggested by the tendency of the Maya to name trees, rather than refer to them with the generic *che*. Although the naming system was by no means scientific, often referring simply to the color of fruit or leaves and in that way perhaps ambiguous, it is striking how many different kinds of trees are mentioned in border descriptions as well as in testaments, and how few fall into both categories.

TABLE 15.6

The Botanical World of the Cah

Maya	English (common)	Latin (scientific)

Plants bequeathed as property or mentioned in Maya testaments

Maya	English (common)	Latin (scientific)
abal	hog plum	*Spondias mombin*
bom	palm for hats	*Carludovica palmata*
xan	palm for roofs	*Nypa fruticans*
cacau	cacao, chocolate	*Theobroma cacao*
canal che	tall tree	
chacah	gumbo-limbo	*Bursera simaruba*
chacal haas	red mamey	*Pouteria sapota*
ci	maguey, henequen	*Agave sisalana*
halab	castor oil plant	*Ricinus communis* [?]
haas	banana	*Musa* or *Mammea* sp.
prantano	plantain	*Musa* sp.
ox	breadnut [Spanish: ramón]	*Brosimum alicastrum*
pom	copal	*Protium copal*
yxche	tree [female]	
yxim	corn	*Zea maiz*
ɔin	yucca, cassava	*Manihot esculenta*
tanam	cotton	*Gossypium* sp.

Trees used as boundary markers in Maya border and land descriptions

Maya	English (common)	Latin (scientific)
bec	oak [Spanish: roble]	*Ehretia tinifolia*
chacte	brazilwood	*Caesalpinia platyloba*
chechem	burn wood	*Metopium brownei*
chi	[Yucatec Spanish: nanche]	*Malpighia glabra*
chobenche		
chonlok		
chucum	wild tamarind	*Pithecellobium albicans* or *P. arboreum*
chulul	sweetsop [?]	*Annona squamosa* [?]
habin	[Spanish: barbasco amarillo]	*Piscidia communis*
yaxnic	boxwood [?]	*Vitex gaumeri* or *V. umbrosa*
subinche		
sucte		
tzalam	[Spanish: jobico]	*Lysiloma bahamense*
tamay	cuffey wood	*Zuelania roussoviae*
huhub		
uayam	[Spanish: guaya / cotoperiz]	*Talisia olivaeformis*
yaxek		

Trees in both categories

Maya	English (common)	Latin (scientific)
copo	fig	*Ficus* cf. *carica*
kanche	button mangrove	*Conocarpus erectus* or *C. sericeus*
ya	sapote	*Manilkara zapota*

MAYA SOURCES: wills and land documents, most in TI, LC, DT, TE, TT, ANEY, and AGN-T. Maya terms are as originally written; *prantano* is a loanword (platano); terms are common, not "scientific," and thus English and especially Latin equivalents are tentative.

ENGLISH-LATIN SOURCES: Gubler 1991; Roys 1931, 1939; Marcus 1982; personal communication from Steven Patterson, and D. J. B. Restall (of the Royal Horticultural Society, Wisley, England). Note that only Ricinus and Musa are introduced (Patterson 1992).

Table 15.6 lists the plants found in these two genres of document. The data presented here, combined with remarks in preceding chapters on the inclusion of plants in Maya wills, contribute to the discussion on colonial Maya plant usage opened by Joyce Marcus fifteen years ago. Her monograph was based exclusively on published sources, primarily the *Relaciones de Yucatán* and the colonial dictionaries, which tell us only what certain Spaniards thought the Maya were doing. By adding information based on Maya-language sources, some of Marcus's generalizations can be modified, others given a firmer base. For example, first, categorizing certain trees as being of one century or another is not historically meaningful, because Yucatec Maya basic plant categories have not altered since the sixteenth century, and colonial terminology remained consistent. Second, sharply separating col and kax and the types of plants cultivated in them is misleading, on account of regional variations on the use of such terms, and the fact that Maya-language evidence points to a (partial) separation between solar and nonsolar cultivation. Third, orchards (*pakal*) were not so much "located near houses," but were either on solar land or not, usually the former.[34]

Looking specifically at trees from a sociological perspective, we might generalize their use as falling into five categories. One, trees were cultivated for their fruit; this is particularly apparent for trees grown on the solar and left in wills, although trees used as border markers may also have been valued for the nourishment of their fruit or leaves. Two, trees provided protection, literal and symbolic. This included on the one hand wood and palm fronds for construction, and on the other hand shade from the sun, an image used to symbolize the role of rulers (as discussed in Chapter 19). Three, trees and other plants played an ornamental role, which is only implied in the Maya documentation; however, Steven Patterson's recent study on this subject has detailed much of the ornamental value given to plants by the Maya today (and, to a lesser extent, during the colonial period).[35]

Four, trees had a ritual significance. The sources of this study provide no information about trees in religious rites (the subject is also tackled by Patterson), but they show clearly that in terms of tenure rituals, specifically the "walk of possession," trees were an essential part of the dotted line that was a Maya boundary. Five, again with respect to land description, trees represented order in that they were more distinct and less easily placed or removed than stone mounds. Trees were virtually invaluable to the Maya. They represented a harmonious interaction with the environment that was, perhaps for man and plant, mutually beneficial.

CHAPTER SIXTEEN

Tenure and Exchange

We have already learned something of the ways in which the Maya owned
and exchanged land, particularly in Chapter 9 with respect to inheritance
patterns and the central principles of cetil and multial, or "even distribution" and "joint ownership," whose complementary functions were to
ensure the rights of private property within those of group ownership.
However, because Maya land tenure has received uneven treatment in the
historical literature, and the Maya-language sources are rich in relevant
information, the subject will be treated here in some detail.[1]

Land Tenure

I deliver its document so that I may sell half my inherited house plot.
—Francisca Canche, Tekanto, 1807

The Mayas had a straightforward classification of land according to
types of use and tenure. Whereas the Nahuas used many categories, the
Mayas divided land into two categories of use: the solar, which was the
land on which the family house or houses sat, and on which various social
and economic activities took place, most of them female-dominated; and
land that was used exclusively for cultivation, variously termed kax, "forest," or col, "field." The generic term *lum* (or *luum*) rarely appears alone in
the notarial record, but it was often used in conjunction with a more specific term—as in *u kax lumil*, "the forested land," or *u pak lumil*, "the planted
or orchard land."[2] The solar-kax/col division is well illustrated in Table
13.1 above.

Maya land was also divided in two according to basic notions of tenure: cah land, which was rented out, allocated, or sold only by the cabildo,
and private land. Cah land was described simply by adding the word cah
to the appropriate term, by reference to the patron saint of the community

(*ti chikine utial Patron San Miguel*, "the property of the patron San Miguel is to the west"), or in a few instances by using a Spanish loan (*lay solar lae utial comonidad*, "that solar is community property").[3] The strong land-controlling role played by preconquest community authorities throughout the New World, combined with early interpretations of indigenous North American (and to some degree Andean) land tenure as communal, contributed to the traditional perception of Mesoamerica as an area of communal landholding. In fact, both pre-Columbian and postconquest tenure practices were mixed, with an emphasis on the working and inheritance of land by individuals and households. This has been demonstrated for central Mexico, where practices were similar to those in Yucatan; as this study details, the Maya held and exchanged property as individuals, while the broadly communal nature of much social business ensured the inclusion of the cabildo as the representative body of the community. In addition, the treatment of much private land as household property or as ancestral-chibal land—a category that the Spanish authorities seem sometimes to have considered as equivalent to community land—meant that the dividing line between private and communal land was not as sharp as it might sometimes appear. Indeed I have discovered no Maya term meaning "private" in the documentary evidence; the Maya either specified private land by category, or simply pronominalized it—*in solar*, "my house plot."

In its representative role the cabildo not only presided over all land exchanges (by sale and inheritance), validating their records and holding them in the cah archives, but also acted as proprietor of cah lands, buying and selling, as well as allocating such plots to cah members as needed. A fine illustration of both the acquisition and the administration of cah land by the cabildo comes in the form of a sale acknowledgment of 1670 from Ebtun.[4] One Cecilia Uc appeared before the cabildo to testify as to the sale of a house plot to the cah and the consequent formation of a new community solar—*u soral cah*. Presumably Cecilia had been married to the vendor of the plot, which . . .

ton tu ɔaah Alonso Noh tu tanil yn yum padre uardian lahcapis peso u tohol soral tu kubah Alonso noh ti cahob Bay xan ua yan mac tu yoltah cahtal tu hunalei ca u ualkes lahcapis peso . . . hetun uamac bin xetlantabac ti ma minan u soralob utial u cahlahbalob	was given to us by Alonso Noh, before the Father Guardian. The solar that Alonso Noh delivered to the cah cost 12 pesos. Thus if anyone wishes to reside there alone, let them return the 12 pesos. . . . For [the solar] is to be divided among those cah residents who lack solars.

The implication of this statement is that cah plots could be alienated (to cah residents) as readily as they might be purchased by cabildos, and indeed this is confirmed by an entry of 1803 appended to the above document. In the intervening 133 years this particular cah house plot or *u solar cah* must have fallen into private hands, for a Felipe Benito Pech claims to have redeemed it on behalf of the community, and he is now being repaid:

cin kubic u hunil u Soral cah Bay	I deliver the document for the cah
bic ɔoc yn kamic capel peso u hel	house plot. For I have just received 2
in takin u chic yn lohic hecen	pesos, reimbursement of my money
	used to redeem [the plot].

The 1803 cabildo of Ebtun appear to have made an effort to consolidate the municipal holdings, for also in that year they certified and repaired a 1763 document acknowledging the sale to the cah of a forest plot by don Feliciano Kak, a former batab.[5] Although don Feliciano had inherited the land from his grandfather, prior to that it had changed hands twice through purchase. This fact the ex-batab is sure to point out, thus proving his claim of ownership as well as supporting the unclassified status of the forest, which of course is now made *u kax cah*, "a cah forest plot."

References to cah land located both within the residential cah and far from it are frequent enough to suggest that it was normal for every cah to control such property. Some cah lands were of considerable value; take, for example, the three tracts of cah forest sold by the Maya cabildos of Campeche in 1737 for 260 pesos.[6] The disparate nature of the sources on land—surviving wills, sales, and litigation records that come from a wide range of cahob and decades—does not allow us to calculate the balance of cah land as opposed to private land. Wills not surprisingly seldom mention communal plots; Maya cabildos do not seem to have made notarial records of cah land allocations, and cah land changed hands less often than private land almost by definition (each cah had only one cabildo but a large pool of private owners). In spite of this source bias against information on cah land, it is safe to say that the vast majority of landed property was in private hands.

Private ownership was also divided two ways, into purchased land and inherited land, which we might also call ancestral land, since the Maya often emphasized ownership by chibal ancestors, although the term usually used—*matan*—means simply "given, inherited." Table 16.1 presents these terms as used in two different cahob in order to demonstrate variations between communities. The same terms were used by other communities, with the addition of *cot* ("stony ground," usually in the form *u cotil lum*, applied to all land types; also *tzekel*) and *chakan* ("savannah," applied only to nonsolar land) used not as classifications like solar or kax, but simply as qualifiers that described the terrain of the land.

Some of the tenure terms have Nahuatl equivalents, although, unlike Maya, Nahuatl consistently employed a generic word for land—*tlalli*—to

TABLE 16.1
Maya Land Terminology

Eighteenth-Century Ixil

Land types

solar	house plot
kax	forest, parcel of land

NOTE: Two other terms, *sitillo* (*sitio*, lot), and *col* (milpa, cultivated field) are used only once each in the entire body of extant documentation from Ixil.

Classifications of tenure

mul kax	joint-group forest (i.e., for family use)
man kax	bought forest
mul man kax	jointly purchased forest
matan kax	given-inherited forest
mul matan kax	jointly inherited forest

NOTE: classifications also appear with *solar* and *chen* (well).

Descriptive qualifiers

hun xeth kax	one forest portion, in contrast to *hunac kax* (*xeth* and *ac* are numeral classifiers denoting "portion" and "wholeness, immobility," respectively)
tanbuh kax	half a forest parcel
parte	share, as in *hunpet kax yn parte lae*, "my share of one [joint] forest."
u lak kax	the other forest
u tzayal kax	the adjacent or neighboring forest

NOTE: All the above except *tzayal* also appear with *solar*.

Eighteenth-Century Tekanto

Land types

solar	house plot
sitio	lot, land for cultivation or cattle but more likely to contain a well and/or a corral and/or a hut. Valued higher than kax, but less than col
col	milpa, cultivated field
kax	forest, uncultivated land

Classifications of tenure

col cah	community milpa, owned by the cah, for the use of community members as designated by the cabildo
man solar	purchased house plot
matan solar	inherited house plot

NOTE: *man* and *matan* also used with *col* and *kax*.

Descriptive qualifiers

hun ɔac solar	one additional plot, where *ɔac* functions like *ac* (see above), but denotes something additional, possibly in a series.
hun ɔac col	one field that is about a mecate in size (the same *ɔac*, when associated with milpa, may have indicated measurement, probably a mecate)
tanbuh col	half a field

SOURCES: Ixil: TI (1765–68) and ANEY, 1819iv, 19–20, and 37 (1738, 1769, 1779). Tekanto: DT; P. Thompson 1978: 40, 112, 126; Pío Pérez 1866–77.

create compound terms. *Tlalcohualli*, "purchased land," was a fundamental category that, like *man kax* or *man solar*, distinguished such property from inherited plots, which were far harder to alienate. In both Maya and Nahuatl bills of sale, the vendor tended to indicate the land type not only by term but also by a brief description of how the land was acquired, sometimes recounting the history of exchange back over a generation or two. The Maya *matan kax* (and so on) carried the same sense of permanence and family attachment as did the Nahuatl *huehuetlalli* (literally "old land," but essentially meaning "inherited," or "patrimonial").

Other Nahuatl terms lack corresponding Maya terms owing in part to differences in social organization. *Calpullalli*, for example, was land pertaining to the municipal subunit, the calpulli, an entity that had no clear equivalent in Yucatan, although as a specific municipal holding we might compare it to cah land (altepetl land, or *altepetlalli*, was simply the sum of all calpullalli). The Maya neither allocated nor described land specifically obligated to tribute payment (unlike the Nahuas: *tequitcatlalli* and related terms), nor as the exclusive property of the nobility (as indicated by several Nahuatl terms that fade out after the sixteenth century in most altepetl).[7] Another Nahua classification whose origin and application remain somewhat unclear—*cihuatlalli*, "woman land"—lacks a Maya equivalent.[8]

The contrasts in land classification between these two indigenous areas reflect not only different organizational practices—although they are part of a general picture of organizational contrast—but also the different ways in which the two languages create descriptive terminology. The (Culhuacan) Nahuatl term *teopantlalli*, for example, "church land" (meaning land used to support indigenous religious activity, not necessarily Church property), has no equivalent term in Maya, yet there are references in Maya notarial material to land that appears to have been used in this manner, such as a sale of 1810 from Tekanto that lists among the neighboring plots *tu chikin u solar ca cilich colebil*, "to the west the solar of our Holy Virgin."[9] This reference to the Virgin Mary is inserted in the formula where the other neighboring plot owners are named, as though the Virgin were just another landholding cah member like, in this case, Felipe Couoh and Esteban Yam. Most probably the plot was not cah land (the patron saint of Tekanto was San Agustín), but was either owned by a cofradía whose patron was the Virgin, or was private land dedicated in part to paying for the upkeep of a particular image or shrine or for the costs of a particular saint's festival day; in fact, the Nahuas, too, used this last form of "saint's land."[10] In other words, in spite of the apparent lack of a categorizing Maya term that we can compare with a Nahuatl term such as teopantlalli, and the lack of multiple examples of "saint's land" to compare with those from central Mexico, the Maya did conceive of certain lands as fulfilling a specific role, and that, by definition, places those lands in a distinct category.

When we look at the details of the exchange of private land the characteristics of Maya tenure become more complex. Two points stand out. One, the references in land descriptions to male individuals as owners of plots are misleading; as argued earlier, men were the household heads and as such represented family landholding interests. This fact becomes clear through the appearance in land sale documents of couples or even entire families as vendors or petitioners. This is particularly true of inherited land, and there is something of a correlation between the extent of family involvement in a sale and the number of generations a family claims to have held a plot.

Two, despite the firm terminological distinction made between inherited and purchased land, plots changed categories surprisingly often. That purchased plots were later bequeathed to children is something that might be expected, but sometimes inherited solars were sold within a family (even though private landownership tended to have familial implications), and sometimes a matan kax was sold to a Spaniard—the ultimate alienation—without apparent objection or petition. Thus, although the discussion that follows presents typical formulas and common patterns, the fact of variations and exceptions must be taken into account, as well as the broader context of the eighteenth-century increase in the loss of Maya land to Spaniards (to be treated in Chapter 17).

Exchange

> Not one commoner [Maya] can be found to buy this solar.
> —cabildo of La Mejorada, 1771

As the dual terminology of Maya land tenure implies, there were two primary means of exchange in cah society: inheritance, and sale. The process of inheritance and the patterns revealed in Maya testaments have been discussed earlier. Because heirs to land were almost always close relatives, usually children, exchange by testament tended to confirm the status of inherited land rather than alienate it, removing the necessity for petition to exchange. In a few rare recorded cases, land was literally exchanged for other land, without any money passing hands. For example, don Lazaro Uitz, while batab of Sicpach in 1750, swapped a kax parcel on the road to Nolo for a solar in La Mejorada; and in 1777 two Canche brothers from Ixil exchanged a sixty-plant henequen orchard for half a house plot, well included.[11]

Sales often appear to have been equally straightforward, subject to a simple title such as *u carta de bentail hunxeth luum*, "the bill of sale of a segment of land," or a simple formula such as *hunac in solar tin conah ti almehen Juan martines*, "one whole solar of mine that I've sold to the noble Juan Martinez," followed by a few details of price and location, and the ratification of the cabildo officers.[12] The immediate transfer of property was sometimes reflected in the language of the bill of sale, with "give" in the present tense in the first half of the record—ɔaic—and in the passive past at the end—ɔabal, "has been given."[13]

Yet sales could be more complicated, for even privately owned land could sometimes not be alienated from a community without official authorization from the cabildo or indeed from the Spanish administration. Thus, although the central role played by the cabildo in cah affairs, sanctioned as it was by the colonial authorities, provided individuals and families with assistance in getting through the legal process, it must also have prevented cah members from disposing of their land as they wished. We cannot presume that unofficial trading did not take place, although it would seem that such sales could not have escaped the notice of the cabildo in communities of this size; besides which, such sales surely ran the risk of eventually being declared invalid, to the expense and inconvenience of all involved.

The characteristics of official sales are best presented by outlining a series of typical cases. First, for example, let us take Juana Paula Couoh and her husband, Ventura Chan. The couple appeared before the cabildo officers of Tekanto in September 1812, in order that *Yn hokes u hunil u chic yn Manic holhunkal kax ti yn yum Agust*[n] *bacab*, "I have the document drawn up recording my purchase of 300 mecates of kax from m'lord Agustín Bacab."[14] The buyers "dictated" their statement, in fact merely contributing the details to a long-used formula of record. Having briefly described the location of the forest under transaction, Juana Paula (apparently the effective purchaser) stated its price—*uucpel peso catac hunpel toxton tin botah*, "seven pesos and one tostón that I paid"—and mentioned that the forest was given to the vendor by his father, as recorded in the father's will. This comment was intended to validate the sale by confirming the tenure of the vendor, but it also was a typical linking of the document being drawn up to the body of the cah archive. Following Juana Paula's first-person statement there is a gap—a pause—after which the cabildo appropriates the pronominal first person, to repeat and thus certify that Juana Paula and her husband indeed appeared before them to buy a forest of stated size from a named individual. In short, and in a standard ending phrase, *ylah u hahil*, "the truth was seen."

The interrelationship (perhaps ambiguous to us) between ancestral or family property and private land meant that an owner might seek to sell a plot that he or she inherited but that other members of his family might conceivably make claim to. By having such family members attest before the cabildo to the tenure history of a plot, two birds (current ownership; and future claims) could be killed with one stone. In a case such as this the two-step sale process often became three steps. The sale of Pech land in Motul is a classic example.[15] The first step was the assertion of ownership:

chicpahi Dⁿ Basilio Pech utial u
hokes solar ychil tixtamento utial
u chich Dᵃ Andrea Pech y Dⁿ
Lucas Pech ɔaan ti tumen u yum
Dⁿ fernado Pech ychil u tixtamento
kat cimi tu yuil en 8 de septiembre
de 1721 ã heix lay solar kub chah
ti lay yan tutan pakil na tu nohol
minan mamac bin luksic lay u hahil

Don Basilio Pech appeared in order
to have drawn up the solar in the will
of his grandmother, doña Andrea
Pech, given to her and don Lucas
Pech by her father, don Fernando
Pech, in his will, when he died on the
8th of September, 1721. The
solar to be delivered faces the adobe
thatched house to the south. Nobody
shall take it. This is the truth.

By "have drawn up the solar," the cabildo meant that the vendor had a document drawn up with proof of ownership included or contained in other records (in this case, family wills) copied from the cah archive. The second step of the sale was the confirmation by the other prominent Pech nobles—don Diego, don Andrés, don Esteban, don Lorenzo (given the title escribano, although a Mateo Pech was the notary that year), and *alférez* don Gregorio—of the inheritance history of the plot. Its location is also given by a standard four-point stationary description (in which yet another Pech noble is named as a neighbor). This step, like the first above, is ratified with a formulaic ending and the listing (the "signatures") of the cabildo officers. The third step was the sale itself, though only of the northernmost portion of the plot adjacent to the convent wall; a Spaniard paid twenty silver pesos.

These three steps took on a slightly different form when two Balam brothers of Maní wished to sell a portion of ancestral land "of the Balams" (*ah Balamil uinicob*). In October 1815 five Balam men, two nobles of the Dzib family (relatives by marriage), all their wives and children, and the local *Juez Español* appeared before the cabildo to draw up a title to the land and confirm its borders. The next day the protagonists returned for the second step, in which Santiago Balam and his wife bought out his brothers for ten pesos. Step three was not until July 1817, when Santiago and his wife then sold the land, before the exact same cast of witnesses, for twenty pesos, to *colel D.ᵃ fran.ᶜᵃ de Paula Carrillo vesina ti cah oxkutzcab*, "lady doña Francisca Paula de Carrillo, Spanish resident of the cah of Oxkutzcab."[16]

Yet another step in the sale process was necessary if the transaction violated laws regarding alienation of property. In order to secure the indigenous tribute base the Spanish authorities not only recognized cah landholdings but also required a Maya cabildo to justify their sale. For similar reasons it appears that ancestral or chibal property also fell into this category. The precise nature of these laws is not apparent either from the primary sources or from the secondary material, although what was officially on the books at any given time could no doubt be uncovered; not that it matters, since such laws were not universally enforced. For example, the sale of ancestral Maya land to a Spaniard (the Motul Pech case above) would seem to violate Spanish laws regarding the alienation of indigenous communal property to Spaniards. This partly explains why the plot in question is asserted to be the private property of just one Pech noble, although Maya practice and tradition meant the blatant involvement of all the Pech nobility of the local chibal in the process.

Furthermore, cabildos had evolved at some early stage conventional justifications for such sales that became mere formula. The history of a solar in Itzimná (now a suburb of Mérida) is illustrative.[17] The solar was originally a cah-owned plot, but the cabildo sold it in 1756 to one Alonso Mena (a mestizo, not a Spaniard), who in turn sold it eight years later to Antonio Puch and his wife, Antonia Coyi. By 1771, when the couple wished to sell to a Spaniard—*yn yum Alferes Dn feliphe santiago caxtiyo*, "m'lord Ensign don Felipe Santiago Castillo"—the plot seemed to have fallen under the jurisdiction of the Maya cabildo of the cah-barrio of La Mejorada, just south of Itzimná, who entered the following in the bill of sale:

ton con Batab y ess[no] lic ɔaic u	We the batab and notary hereby
hahilil Bicil minan mix huntul	give the truth, that there is nobody,
masehual yan yalan Barrio	not one commoner [i.e., Maya], below
mejorahada utial Maníc lay solar	in the barrio of Mejorada, to buy this
lae cu conic lay Antonio Puch y u	solar that this Antonio Puch and his
yatan Antonia coyi lae	wife here, Antonia Coyi, are selling.

Strictly speaking, a vendor wishing to alienate land broadly considered communal had to petition the Spanish authorities for permission to sell. According to effective definitions of the cah, the broadest definition of "communal" might include all land owned by the cah or any of its members; in her study of Nahua landholding, Rebecca Horn observed that the Spaniards in central Mexico tended to recognize only noble holdings as private and considered the formal title of commoner holdings as "resting with the corporate unit rather than the individual."[18] I have taken this Spanish attitude to apply potentially to noble land as well, especially if it was classified by the Maya as ancestral. For example, in two petitions to sell land (both are discussed further in Chapter 19)—one a 1737 request by three Maya cabildos from Campeche to sell cah forest tracts, the other an 1804 petition by the noble Noh family of Homun—the reason for selling was formula. In these cases, the justification is not that no Maya could be found to buy the land, but "poverty and bankruptcy" on the part of the cah and "misery and poverty" on the part of the Noh chibal.

A similar reason was given in the sale of a mere half-solar that appears

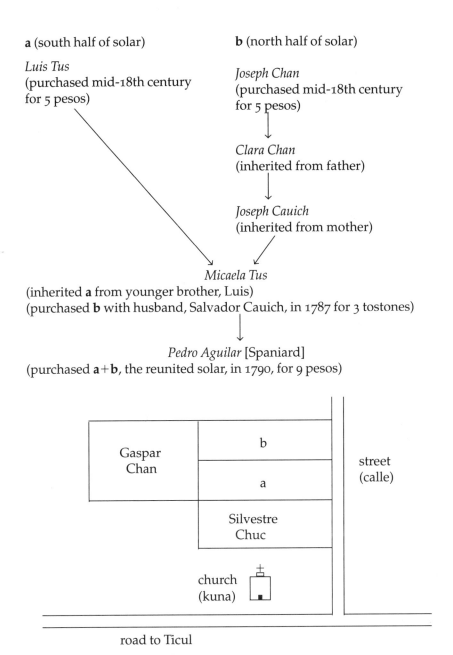

a (south half of solar)

Luis Tus
(purchased mid-18th century
for 5 pesos)

b (north half of solar)

Joseph Chan
(purchased mid-18th century
for 5 pesos)

Clara Chan
(inherited from father)

Joseph Cauich
(inherited from mother)

Micaela Tus
(inherited **a** from younger brother, Luis)
(purchased **b** with husband, Salvador Cauich, in 1787 for 3 tostones)

Pedro Aguilar [Spaniard]
(purchased **a**+**b**, the reunited solar, in 1790, for 9 pesos)

Gaspar
Chan

b

a

street
(calle)

Silvestre
Chuc

church
(kuna)

road to Ticul

Fig. 16.1. The history of a house plot. The upper section shows the tenure history of a solar in Chapab, with owners italicized and the means of exchange in parentheses. The map shows location in Chapab of the plot, whose two halves (a and b) are reunited in 1787. Source: ANEY, 1826ii, 340–41.

to have been owned not by a cah or a chibal, but by one man, representing his nuclear family.[19] Juan Asencio Pech of Tekax asserted that he was selling his half-plot . . .

u chic yn cuxcintic ynba y yn uatan	so that I can keep myself alive, and
y in lak Palalob Manic xma yximil	my wife and children besides, [who]
y uchic Yn botic yn Patan y	went by without maize; and so that I
limosna y in lak Palalob y	can pay tribute and church taxes for
tumen kohanen cachi	myself and my children; and because
	I have been sick.

This example suggests that there was in cah society a tradition of justification when it came to land sale, which may have had indigenous roots and perhaps cannot entirely be explained by Spanish concerns over the sale of communal property.

The mixed used of sale and inheritance in the exchange of land is illustrated in Figure 16.1, which is a visual representation of the information contained in a pair of late-eighteenth-century sale documents from the cah of Chapab. This particular case history demonstrates a number of tenure traits that emerge in records of sale: the frequent division of plots, especially solars, into two or four parts (never thirds: three parts would be described as two quarters and one half) and their later reunion; the sale of land within families; the fluctuating values of plots, sometimes resulting in apparent losses; and the eventual acquisition of prime-location solars in cahob close to Mérida (such as Chapab) by Spaniards.

The process of sale was, as we have seen, closely tied to the process of proving legitimacy of ownership. To sell inherited land, the Maya used testaments as such a proof, and then offered previous bills of sale to confirm the boundaries and tenure of purchased land. Nevertheless, cah variations, together with the pressure from Spanish authorities and would-be landowners to conform to the colonial legal system or risk losing property, meant that more genres of documents than wills and bills of sale were resorted to by indigenous notaries. These other genres, and the litigious context that made them necessary and ensured their survival, are the subject of the next chapter.

‹❂›

CHAPTER SEVENTEEN

Conflict and Conquest

The frequently imprecise nature of Maya land description, and its apparent reliance upon what was common knowledge in the community, raised two types of legitimacy issues in the colonial period, both of which could and often did lead to litigation. One was a discrepancy over what common knowledge actually was concerning a particular boundary, the result more likely to be litigation between two Maya families or two cahob. The other was the failure of Maya land documents to stand up in a Spanish court, the result of this more likely to be an opportunistic attempt by a Spanish landowner to extend his holdings at Maya expense.

The population increase in late-eighteenth-century Yucatan aggravated both these tendencies, thereby stimulating the outpouring of land sales and land disputes represented well in the documentary record. At the same time, Maya cabildos became more careful about recording land ownership and exchange in accordance with colonial legal requirements. Thus, although indigenous landholding became as potentially precarious in late-colonial Yucatan as it had become by the turn of the eighteenth century in central Mexico, the result was not, as among the Nahuas, the loss of exhaustive indigenous record keeping and surveying. With no easy or fully satisfactory way to settle serious disputes, Nahua landowners were often in a position to interpret evolving community norms to suit themselves.[1] This was not the case in Yucatan. This contrast between provinces was based on the fact that Yucatan did not experience a process equivalent to the fragmentation of the altepetl until well after Independence. The ongoing strength of the cah meant that people could still acquire binding local judgments on disputes and also rely upon cabildo representation in the Spanish legal system; and it meant that cah cabildos continued to litigate against each other and against Spaniards with a relentless faith in the efficacy of the colonial legal system, while indigenous record keeping became more, rather than less, exhaustive.

Legitimacy and Litigation

So that no discord shall arise, they all speak with true hearts in the holy
name of Dios.
—18th-century Yaxkukul record of a 16th-century border agreement

The late-colonial increase in competition for land is reflected in the
changing nature of Maya land records through the colonial period. Although borrowed Spanish terms for "title," "acknowledgment," and "petition" appear in Maya sources of the sixteenth century, "bill of sale" appears not to have been borrowed until the seventeenth, and only in the
late eighteenth do we find sales recorded by both a "bill of sale" and an
"acknowledgment" that include a ratifying statement by the cabildo that
repeats all the pertinent information of the transaction. Indigenous testaments appear always to have been of primary importance to the cah system of tenure legitimation, but in the late eighteenth century wills began to
be kept with land documents instead of in a separate book; the whole cah
archive, in fact, appears to have become land oriented.[2]

Thus, although the various types of Maya notarial land documents
increasingly follow Spanish models, there are still identifiable indigenous
traits, as with all Maya document genres. Most of these have already been
mentioned in the discussions of the characteristics of land description and
the significance of the presence of the cabildo. The evidence does not
directly prove that Maya rituals of land exchange involved some of the
activities common in central Mexico, such as eating and drinking and the
throwing of stones in the four directions by the buyer, but the inclusion of
community notables and descriptions of the "walk of possession" along
boundaries, sometimes including the placing of stone markers, all point to
an indigenous ritualization of exchange.

In addition to the bill of sale—*carta de venta,* usually Mayanized along
the lines of *u carta de bendail*—Maya cabildos drew up various land documents to legitimize ownership. The *conocimiento,* or "acknowledgment,"
which in its Spanish origin was usually an unnotarized acknowledgment
of debt, was adopted by the Maya as the title of a sale record in Ebtun,
Tekanto, Tekax, and many other cahob in between.[3] In some cases the carta
de venta recorded the initiation of a sale, whereas the conocimiento emphasized receipt and recorded the completion of a sale; in cases of immediate payment, only the latter document was needed. In their desire to use
the right term (valid in the Spanish courts) Maya notaries produced con-
structions such as *u hunil titulo concosimyento u kaba lae,* "the title document
whose name is conocimiento," or they simply peppered documents with
legalistic loanwords.[4] Documents that simply confirmed claims (though
they might be used later as the first step toward a sale, as discussed in

Chapter 16) were termed *u tituloil hun*, or *u certificacionil hun*, or sometimes just the generic *hun*, "document," which could refer to any of the above (including wills). Sometimes this type of document bore a descriptive heading, such as *U titlo lum kax pedro ceh*, "The title to Pedro Ceh's forest land."[5]

In spite of the ratification of sales by cabildos, the small size of most cahob, and the marital interlinking of chibalob (who thus might know each other's business), sales did produce disputes that sometimes entered the Spanish legal system and were therefore recorded on paper. The conflict might be family-based, or it might not reach the written level for decades, possibilities both at evidence in an example from 1790. In that year, Félix Balam appeared with his eldest sister before the cabildo of Tekax to make a sworn statement—a *juramento*—to the effect that a sale twenty-three years previously of *hunAc kax ek lum* ("one black-earthed forest plot") by three deceased Balams to a deceased noble was carried out with invalid papers—*conosimientoob falso*; the Balam siblings then went on to give their version of the boundaries of the tract.[6]

We shall never know the outcome of this dispute—perhaps the petitioners waited until the protagonists of the transaction were dead for a good reason—but other land disputes between Maya are well documented. This is especially so of conflicts between cahob. Multi-cah border agreements are among the earliest extant Maya documents, being both continuations of indigenous ritualized treaty-making and important aspects of the colonial attempt to impose a pax hispanica. The cahob were no longer able to field armed men in battle, but their pursuit of protracted and relentless lawsuits against each other over often petty tracts of land represents the continuation of centuries of indigenous inter-cah warfare. Perhaps in lending indigenous cabildos access to the legal system (under some circumstances at subsidized rates), the colonial authorities unwittingly provided the Maya with a safety valve, a legal way to express aggression.

Some of these inter-cah disputes are known to us as a result of border agreements that appear to have been brokered by local Spanish officials. These range from a series of treaties of 1600 between Ebtun, Cuncunul, Kaua, Tekom, Tinum, and Yaxcaba—initiated by the Spanish provincial governor and part of a series of border quarrels in the Sotuta region that ran through the colonial period—to an eight-Spaniard, four-cah, five-day walk of an estancia in 1786, to an agreement of 1815 between Abala, Bolompoyche, Chochola, Dzibikak, Dzibikal, and Uman, in which the local curate and the Juez Español joined the batabob and cabildo officers of all six cahob in the border walk.[7]

Less frequently recorded in the archives are entire cases documenting disputes between cahob. The best extant example of such is the Tontzimin dispute contained within the corpus of documents from Ebtun.[8] Without going too deep into the details of this conflict, which lasted from 1638 to

1820 and involved cahob, individual Maya, and Spaniards, I wish to make two analytical observations. First, the Tontzimin affair illustrates both the means by which the Maya engaged in postconquest territorial conflict (including the significant parts played by Spanish attorneys hired by indigenous cabildos and by the "Protector of the Indians"), as well as the genres of documentation used by the Maya—mainly petitions (to initiate legal action or win favorable decisions), wills, Maya-style acknowledgments, and border agreements (submitted as evidence of ownership and boundary claims).

Second, the Tontzimin dispute reflects certain key elements of Maya land tenure (discussed in the preceding chapter), demonstrating how the dual principles of private and communal land ownership could generate conflict. The trouble began when an Ebtun landowner, Diego Chay, sold the Tontzimin kax to Diego Cupul of Cuncunul. Chay's sale was legally valid—the land had not been Ebtun's cah land. But the kax lay on the Ebtun side of a line that separated the lands of the two communities, and in selling it, Chay had effectively alienated it from Ebtun's indirect jurisdiction and placed it under the indirect territorial control of the neighboring cah of Cuncunul. As a result of this confusion, the people from Ebtun and Cuncunul began to encroach upon each other's lands in and around Tontzimin.

It may be tempting to blame the Spaniards for this tension—Roys refers to the introduction of "an aggressive economic individualism," and to the effects of congregación on the distribution of Maya landholdings—but there was probably always an ambiguous perception of private and public in the Maya tenure system. We have seen that both individual and cah landownership had preconquest roots, and that dispersed and distant landholdings were determined long before the conquest by the need for shifting cultivation. Similarly, it would be a grave disservice to the Maya to credit the Spaniards with bringing economic aggression to Yucatan; even the Spaniards recognized the persistent and pugnacious way in which the Maya, individually or collectively, engaged in legal action over land from the onset of colonial rule.[9]

Conquest by Purchase

> I, the batab, with the magistrates, regidors, and notary of the cah . . . affirm the truth . . . of the border to the kax estancia of Chichí, owned by our lord don Rodrigo Chacón.
> —cabildos of Itzimná, Sicpach, and Cholul, 1786

The Tontzimin case also illustrates an additional dimension of Maya land tenure and land litigation in the colonial period: the indigenous response to incursion by Spaniards. Until 1711 the only involvement by Spaniards in the Tontzimin dispute had been as legal officials, but in that year a Spanish landowner was taken to court by a Maya noble, don Diego Jacinto Tun, who succeeded in having annulled the Spaniard's illegal purchase of the tract from a Maya couple from Kaua. Just three years later, however, don Diego turned around and sold Tontzimin to another Spaniard. The Maya response was interesting: three cahob in the area, Cuncunul (where don Diego was maestro), Tekom, and Tixcacalcupul, submitted petitions of protest.

Two points are worth emphasizing here. First, the three communities do not appear to have objected to the sale simply because the purchaser, Gabriel Virgilio, was a Spaniard. Their concern was similar to that of Ebtun when it objected to the sale of Tontzimin by one of its own to a Cuncunul man: the land was being removed from the territorial sphere of the community; the vendor . . .[10]

u conic lay c kax yan ti xtontzim-in yoklal helay kat lae yume oxtzuc cah yoklal ychil u mapail utial u tzentic uba[ob] cahob tulacal: cacal y ti cah tikom y cah cuncunul	is selling this our kax at Tontzimin, which these three cahob question, lord, because it is in their map, so that all the cahob may sustain themselves: Cacal (Tixcacalcupul), Tekom, and Cuncunul

The citing of all three cahob here was an artifice; the intrusion of Spaniards onto Maya land in the eighteenth century did not produce a concerted effort to resist the foreigner any more than the original conquest had done. Maya concern and perspective continued to be cah-centric.

Second, Gabriel Virgilio legally purchased the tract. It was not acquired through seizure, by bullying indigenous officials, or by manipulating legal procedures (although he may have tried such tactics). Presumably Virgilio was unaware of the quagmire of indigenous hostilities into which he was buying. He was sued by the three cahob, who in 1717 were able to compromise his position considerably; he was forbidden to place cattle on the land, while Cuncunul was given limited farming rights there, and the three litigant cahob were given first refusal should Virgilio ever sell—in fact he died in 1720 and his son sold the land to Cuncunul at a loss of nearly 20 percent.

The Maya were not always this successful at using the Spanish legal system to defend their claims, especially when they themselves were divided. Yet even when Spanish claimants triumphed in the courts, the Maya were often able to resist for prolonged periods, thereby postponing the arrival (or at least minimizing the effect) of Spanish-owned cattle on kax and col. The four-decade dispute over lands bordering the ranch at Sabacche is a case in point. In 1785 a Spaniard from Maní, don Juan de

Avila, purchased the ranch from the Keb chibal (the vendors from which were one man and six women, along with three of the women's sons). Within a year several Maya landowners appeared before the cabildo of Oxkutzcab (within whose jurisdiction Sabacche lay) to testify to incursions made by Avila south and west of his boundaries. In particular the Spaniard had begun using the land and water of Sacnicteil, a ranch owned by the Tzakum chibal in Ticul. In 1791, following a petition filed by the Ticul cabildo on behalf of the Tzakum, Avila was ordered off Sacnicteil. However, the Spaniard continued to appeal for the rest of the colonial period, during which time his cattle may have periodically strayed onto his neighbors' property (in 1802 a Tzakum was jailed for stealing a cow on the disputed land).

In 1820 the decision against the Spaniard was finally overturned; Avila had succeeded in extending his purchased land at the expense of the local Maya, but it had taken him thirty-five years.[11] In this battle he was confronted with Maya records from five different cahob in the region, including petitions, past testaments, bills of sale, and even (inexplicably) an election record nearly two hundred years old. These Maya cabildos did not conspire to defend Maya land, but the Tzakum were able to defend their claim because of the cah systems of representation and land tenure, the perpetuation of local government through the Spanish-style cabildo structure, Maya access to the Spanish legal system, and, it must be said, their own tenacity. In Avila's favor was one overwhelming circumstance: the pattern of Spanish population growth and expanded landholdings, which in retrospect can be seen as the foundation to the estate system that was to disrupt the world of the cah in the nineteenth century to an unprecedented extent.

Indeed, just as inter-cah land conflict was in a sense the colonial-era expression of an indigenous tradition of interregional conquest, so was the gradual Spanish acquisition of Maya lands, private and communal, an expression of the conquest that was ultimately more damaging to cah society than the violence and innovation of the mid-sixteenth century. This process was so effective because it was so insidious: as we have seen, despite some spectacular Maya-Spanish land litigation, Spaniards by and large acquired land through peaceful, legal purchase; further examples will serve to illustrate the role played by factors such as the encomienda, plot location, demography, and the pattern of piecemeal purchase.

A major source of late-colonial examples of land sales by Mayas to Spaniards is the notarial archive in Mérida. The several hundred Maya-language documents in volumes of this archive were connected by various legal procedures to the many thousands of Spanish documents among which they are bound, giving the impression that Maya land, especially solars in prime locations in the cahob that were colonial cabeceras, was falling into Spanish hands with extraordinary rapidity.[12] Of course, all these documents have survived precisely because the plots in question ended up in Spanish hands. This is also true of sales recorded in Spanish estate papers. Having said that, such cases do illustrate a gradual (though statistically hard to tally) transfer of land from indigenous to Spanish hands, particularly in or near Spanish urban centers and the more lucrative encomiendas.

Naturally most of the urban sales were in Mérida, followed by Campeche and Valladolid, although in the late-colonial period Spaniards took over the centers of major cahob such as Itzmal (which the Spaniards called Izamal) in the north, and Oxkutzcab, Tekax, and Ticul in the south. A typical example comes from the estate created by José Bonifacio Guzmán, a Spaniard who in 1833 sold for 18 pesos a house and its solar adjacent to the church on Ticul's central plaza. To prove his ownership of this property, Guzmán had retained copies, made by the Maya cabildo of the cah, of four separate purchases. These were the four subdivisions of the solar that Guzmán had acquired bit by bit: buying two of the quarters (pieces of solar land—*xoth u lumil solar*) in 1809 from Juan Agustín Ku and Feliciano Xece, respectively; another quarter in 1811 from Gerónimo Poot; and the final portion in 1815 from the Poot family, all of whom (male and female) appeared before the cabildo to make the sale. The circumstances of Guzmán's 1833 sale (to another Spaniard) are not given, but the reunified solar may have been worth less than the sum of its parts, since Guzmán paid 5 pesos for three of the quarters, and 13 pesos 4 reales for Gerónimo Poot's parcel (which may have contained the best, if not only, water access).[13]

Whether Guzmán paid over value for any of the parcels or not, he certainly does not seem to have underpaid, nor is there evidence that the Maya vendors were intimidated off their land. Yet these sales illustrate a process that had been occurring for centuries throughout New Spain—Spaniards effectively pushing indigenous families out of the centers of their own towns to create Spanish communities within cahob, altepetl, and the communities of other indigenous peoples.

A similar process was taking place in Yucatan's countryside, especially around Mérida and along the camino real to Campeche. A classic example is that of the estancia of Chichí, located, according to a 1653 record, a league and a half east of Mérida, three leagues west of Nolo, two leagues south of Sicpach, and one league north of the smaller estancia of Pacabtun, with lands belonging to the cahob of Cholul and Itzimná also adjacent; today it is in part a suburb of Mérida called Chichí Suárez. Chichí illustrates three dynamics of the process of conquest by purchase.

One is the part played by encomiendas. For the first two centuries of

TABLE 17.1

The Expansion of Estancia Chichí
Purchases of Kax from Maya Vendors, with Cah Ratification,
by the Encomendero don Lucas de Villamil y Vargas, 1691–1714

Year	Vendor	Cah	Comment
1691	four Ake men	Nolo	
1693	Pedro Dzul	Sicpach	kax inherited from Dzul's mother, Clara Cuxim, in 1680
1694	two Chan men	Sicpach	
1697	Luis Ku	Nolo	
1697	Francisco Canche	Sicpach	kax inherited from Chan family
1699	Andrés Canul	Itzimná	kax bought by Canul in 1694; he makes a profit and in 1699 he buys another kax plot in Itzimná, from the Poots, father and son
1699	Andrés Chi	Itzimná	kax bought by Chi from Pedro Montalvo (Spaniard) in 1690; Montalvo inherited plot from his father, who bought it from Juan Canche in 1668; Chi turns a profit
1702	Cristóbal Chan	Sicpach	kax called Petenceh
1703	Cristóbal Dzul	Sicpach	kax beside "Estancia Chichí Petenceh"; inherited from Pedro Dzul (see 1693 entry)
1706	Gaspar Cituk	Sicpach	
1710	[Onofre Díaz]	[Mérida]	plot called Xuxà, or Xuxac, sold in 1628 to Andrés Uicab by Melchor Mex, both of Cholul; had been lands of Mex's grand-father, Napuc Coba, before the conquest; Andrés Uicab and sons sell to a branch of the Rosado family (Spaniards) in 1629; cattle permit acquired 1643
1711	Luis Canche	Sicpach	kax inherited from father, Juan Canche, in 1680
1714	Diego Euan	San Cristóbal	kax inherited from mother, Clara Canche, through father, Luis Euan, in 1709

SOURCE: CCA, Chichí (uncatalogued), 1: 49–110 (all sales and accompanying wills were recorded in Maya).

the colonial period most of this estancia's owners, and all its most active ones, were local encomenderos—from the original grantee of 1558, the conquistador don Alonso Rosado, to the purchaser of 1626, don Juan de Montejo Maldonado (great-grandson of Yucatan's conqueror and the owner who first put cattle on the estancia), to don Lucas de Villamil y Vargas (see Table 17.1). For these owners, the cattle, horse, and beehive operations at Chichí were a way to maximize the labor and tax exploitation of an encomienda, while the Mayas under trust were a way to maximize the profit potential of the estancia. Because encomiendas were not land grants, estancias were vital to the business operations of encomenderos, a fact that has been well established for Spanish America in general.[14]

The second dynamic was location. Close to Mérida, Chichí and the plots around it were desirable to Spaniards, who preferred to live primarily in the city or at least to be able to reach their residence there within a day. As a result, Maya landowners and cabildos near Mérida easily found buyers at favorable prices, and they were willing to sell because a decimated indigenous population could not work all the Maya-held land that lay between cahob—until the indigenous demographic recovery of the eighteenth century ran headlong into a Spanish population that had been growing in size and increasing its landholdings. By the time famine began repeatedly to hit the cahob in the late-colonial period, the communities southwest along the camino real, southeast toward Maní, and east toward Itzmal, had already helped to create dozens of Spanish estancias,[15] just as the cabildos and families of Cholul, Itzimná, Nolo, Sicpach, and the cahob-barrios of San Cristóbal and La Mejorada had helped to create Chichí.

The third dynamic was the nature of Chichí's growth. Spanish estancias grew in fits and starts, booming and crashing, sometimes crumbling, but for the most part growing gradually through piecemeal purchases into the vast landed estates of the nineteenth century. Chichí's value rose and fell, and it changed hands roughly every generation, but as the result of concerted and systematic acquisition campaigns like that of don Lucas de Villamil at the turn of the eighteenth century (see Table 17.1) the estancia grew, so that a border walk of 1786 involved eight Spanish estanciero neighbors and four neighboring cahob and took five days; by 1912 the estate consisted of almost two thousand hectares.[16] Don Lucas's expansion—thirteen purchases over twenty-three years of inherited and purchased land, chibal, and individual or family land, in sales ratified by four different Maya cabildos—was far from unique; it was indicative of how plots of various origins and sizes, some of which had passed between Spanish and Maya hands several times, and most of which represented profits for the Maya vendors, contributed to Yucatan's changing landscape. Within this pattern lies a startling contrast between the short-term gains and the long-term losses for the Maya of the cahob.

PART FOUR

Literacy and Language

CHAPTER EIGHTEEN

᠊ᢒ᠊

Notarial Purpose and Style

Though scholars may react to Bishop Diego de Landa's infamous bonfire of books with lamentation, as did those sixteenth-century Mayas who watched their codices burn, it is now becoming increasingly clear that after the conquest the Maya soon acquired the Spaniards' skills of paper, ink, and the alphabet. Indigenous scribes put these skills to good use, generating several thousand legal and other documents through the colonial period and into the mid-nineteenth century. This quantity of written Maya material indicates a certain cultural persistence (Yucatec Maya is one of the indigenous languages still widely spoken in Mexico today);[1] it also reflects the fact that postconquest Maya literacy drew upon the preconquest traditions of hieroglyphic writing and oral discourse as well as on the introduced documentary traditions of Spanish legal practice. Maya records contain a significant nexus of indigenous characteristics that can be identified as such because they either diverge from Spanish norms or seem to echo pre-Hispanic practice.

Origins, Intentions, and Implications

I state my will for it to be written down before the batab and
the magistrates.
—Rosa Balam of Ebtun, 1812

Because of the destruction of written Maya records by the colonizers, our knowledge of preconquest traditions in writing (including such aspects as style, genre, and purpose) is tentative, but there are a few clues. The most obvious is the fact that the Mayas took so quickly and ably to alphabetic notarized record keeping. The strong literary tradition of the Mayas is the singular element most commonly identified with their pre-Columbian culture—the plethora of hieroglyphic texts in wood, bone, plaster, bark paper, and stone has for long seized the popular imagination and challenged the academic community. Complex numerical, calendrical, and writing systems gave the Mayas a sophisticated medium of communication. It is now clear that Maya hieroglyphs are neither purely pictographic nor solely (nonpictographic) logographic, but a sophisticated combination of the two that includes, most significantly, a syllabary of glyphs that could be used phonetically.[2] In other words, the Maya already had the conceptual apparatus required to grasp the function of the roman alphabet.

Some preconquest texts may have come close to an extended narrative form of expression—the 2,000-glyph Hieroglyphic Stairway at Copán has this potential—and the most significant nonmundane texts written down in the colonial period, such as the Popol Vuh of the Quiché and the Books of Chilam Balam in Yucatan, were probably copied from pre-Hispanic antecedents.[3] Most hieroglyphic texts, however, were records (or alleged records) of dates, personal and place names, and historical, mythical, and cosmological events. This tradition translated well into Spanish legal formats, which insisted on the recording of place, date, authors, witnesses, relevant events, intertextual references, and often item-by-item entries.

As advances are made in decipherment, the grammatical and stylistic links between preconquest texts and postconquest spoken Maya become more apparent. Victoria Bricker has demonstrated that some of the conventions of hieroglyphic writing are reflected in the alphabetic usage of the Books of Chilam Balam, and she suggests that traces of "the logosyllabic principles of consonant insertion, vowel insertion, and consonant deletion" in the Chumayel and Chan Kan texts are evidence of "scribal syncretism."[4] Those conventions, in particular that of consonant insertion, can also be seen in the spellings in mundane notarial texts such as testaments and land records.[5] Also the propagandistic dimension of preconquest texts proposed most notably by Joyce Marcus can be seen in some postconquest material, as argued in Chapter 21 below.[6]

The earliest extant colonial Maya manuscripts date from the 1550's and 1560's, but the close similarity in style and format between these and later colonial Maya documents would seem to indicate that Maya notaries were being trained within a few years of the founding of Mérida.[7] The Mayas had no difficulty with vocabulary to describe the notarial process, using ɔib for "write," *hun* for "document," and thus *ah ɔib hun* to describe the notary himself, or even *mahan kab*, literally "hired hand," to describe the assistant notary.[8]

The basic job of adapting Maya to the roman alphabet must have been done by Franciscans and their indigenous informants in the 1540's, for the standard orthography used throughout the colonial period with only minor and regular variations, including the elegant reversed *c* (ɔ) for what later became *dz*, is fully in use in all the early examples.[9] Although the Spanish-based Maya alphabet creatively included ways to indicate the glottalized consonants (unlike the Spanish-based Nahuatl alphabetic conventions, which for the most part left Nahuatl's glottal stop unwritten; see Tables 22.2 and 22.3 for a comparison of the two), the orthography left Maya very much underdifferentiated with respect to vowel sounds. Maya has a five-vowel system, as does Spanish, but the Maya system includes distinctions not represented in the colonial orthography—a short series, a long series with a high tone, a long series with a low tone, and a series with glottal interruption. However, most alphabets undernotate some aspect of the language, and the Spanish-based Maya orthography was more than adequate to the task of capturing, recording, and communicating Maya speech for native speakers.[10]

The products of Maya literacy in the colonial period can be divided into two categories: notarial documents, which were primarily mundane, legal records; and what I have termed quasi-notarial documents (discussed in Chapter 21). A notarial document is defined as such by virtue of the escribano or clerk-notary employed and empowered to draw it up. As we have seen, this notary was a salaried official attached to the Maya cabildo. He recorded all official cah business, and because the authenticating power of his signature was recognized both by the Maya community and by the Spanish authorities it validates documentation produced by his cah. There was, however, a crucial distinction between the function of the Maya escribano's signature and that of his Spanish counterpart. An individual Spaniard might hire a public notary to draw up a legal document, adding the witnessing signatures or marks of other individual Spaniards. Notarial documents in Maya were never generated in this manner. The person requiring notarial services gained them by virtue of his membership in his cah, and the escribano performed the service as a part of his cabildo duties. The witnesses therefore were the body of cabildo officers, representing the entire community, including the resident selling land or making his will. Thus these documents are by definition community—cah—products. This may be true for all indigenous-language notarial material in Spanish America, but it certainly cannot be said of the abundant documentary production of the colonists.

Because notarial documents in Maya were cah products, they open an ethnohistorical window not simply onto the indigenous peoples of colonial Yucatan but onto the community Maya, the people of the cahob. This would seem to exclude a significant segment of the indigenous population—those living on Spanish estates and the hamlets they spawned, and those working as domestic servants in Spanish houses. In fact, most of the domestic servants in Mérida lived in the well-documented cahob that ringed the Spanish city, and hamlets fell under the jurisdiction of the nearest cah, until they acquired municipal status themselves.[11]

Though the authors and actors of notarial documents form an ethnically homogeneous group, in some sense these records do not represent all the people of this group. Sixty-five wills from twenty-six months in the lives of Ixil's thousand-odd inhabitants cannot, even including the lists of named relatives, neighbors, and cabildo officers, be said to represent the whole population. Even less representative are a dozen scattered documents from Oxkutzcab, a cah of some 13,000 souls by the time of Independence. The bias of numbers is compounded by an age bias. Except during times of plague and famine, testators tended to be mature, if not old, and the correlation between age (as indicated by the number of children and grandchildren as opposed to parents) and wealth in wills implies that most of the vendors and purchasers in land documents were also mature. Furthermore, the ladder pattern of cabildo careers suggests that officers were only young when on the lowest rungs.

A third bias, that of gender, is less pronounced. The number of male testators outnumbers female ones by a ratio of 1.34:1 in Cacalchen, 1.33:1 in Ebtun, and 1.33:1 in Ixil, identical to the 1.33:1 male bias of testaments from the altepetl of Culhuacan. Although a run of Tekanto wills showing women outnumbering male testators 1.1:1 would seem to ruin this tidy pattern, the anomaly can be reconciled.[12] In the Tekanto example, where all members of the community are making wills, the 1.1:1 balance reflects the gender bias sometimes exhibited in human reproductive patterns; in the case of the other three cahob and the altepetl, the remarkably close statistical correlation is coincidental but significant. If all the men in the community are drawing up wills, only two-thirds of the women are. Was this due to an assumption that a woman's goods would go to her husband? As we have seen, inheritance patterns were more complicated than this. The answer has actually to do with wealth. I believe that not all men were making wills, and marginally fewer women were doing so, for the simple reason that women were less wealthy, as indeed testaments prove.

In other words, the gender bias of testaments is really a wealth bias; and this is paralleled in the male bias of land sale documents. The group that is most closely represented in these sources is not so much men as it is the wealthier segments of society. Because of the significant difference in wealth shown in the documentation, from the richest testator or vendor to the widow with nothing but a few reales for a mass, and because of the statistics just presented, we can assume that the sources do at least represent most of Maya society. This is supported by the importance of Maya society of the extended family and of alliances of patronym groups or chibalob, a system that would have provided a support network for most residents of a cah.

Other aspects of the Maya system of representation become important when we turn to the evidence of other genres of record. Election documents are concerned only with the privileged male group that had access to political office. Similarly, petitions, by definition (as cah products) presented in the interests of the whole cah, in reality served as a legal mechanism of defense for the Maya ruling classes, and in practice they might advance the agenda of only one political faction. Still, in a case in which an oppressive priest was removed, or tribute or obligatory service lightened, less privileged residents would benefit. In the same way, cabildo action to defend cah lands, through petition or litigation (or both), would also be for the good of a larger section of the population, in spite of signs that communal land was worked by those with good connections rather than by those most in need. Indeed, the Maya concept of representation in general, from the family level to that of the cah, meant that the actions of the cabildo were necessarily communal in terms of legitimacy and intent. Ultimately the bias of notarial sources is pro-cah, and that includes every last member of the community.

The slant of Maya notarial material is thus reflected in the purpose behind it. These documents are a bridge between the Spanish and Maya legal and authoritative worlds, in some sense helping to create of them a single world. A document drawn up in a small indigenous Yucatec community might travel through the provincial capital in Mérida to the viceregal capital in Mexico City and even on to the seat of the Council of the Indies in Seville. Documents such as land sales, wills, and records of cabildo elections played practical and legitimating roles within Maya communities; they also indicate the active and strategic way in which Maya communities participated in colonial society.

For example, the document type *carta de venta*, bill of sale, appears only to have been used for land sales (as was the case with notarial records of this genre in Nahuatl).[13] Except for a few mentions of sales in testaments, the regular exchange and purchase of other goods that must have been carried out by the Maya is not reflected in notarial documents; lesser goods would be exchanged at market, and were insufficiently valuable to justify notarial expenses. Land, however, was a crucial point of contact between Maya and Spaniard, and a proof of ownership that was recognized as legal by the Spanish authorities was vital to the defense and sale of Maya-owned land. The Maya therefore drew up notarial records not only because in some cases they were required to do so by the colonial authorities, but also because they were a weapon of defense or litigation that could be used within the colonial context.

Many Maya notarial documents were drawn up for litigation purposes, or were preserved within subsequent lawsuit files. The Nahuas
inundated the colonial Mexican courts with lawsuits,[14] and the Maya documentation that continues to emerge represents increasing evidence of a
comparable abundance of litigation by the Yucatec Maya. Since the one
commodity worth the cost of litigation was land, most of this material
relates to land disputes, either between Maya (which invariably meant
between cahob), or between Maya and Spaniard. Some of the best examples of land litigation among the Maya are found in the Ebtun corpus,
which contains classic cases both of the border disputes that characterized
the century after the conquest and of the prolonged litigation that characterized conflict over land in subsequent centuries.

Such litigation often reveals the masterful use of the Spanish legal
system by the Maya to defend their lands from colonial encroachment.
Indeed, even though the Spanish estancias established in the mid-colonial
period were usually acquired by piecemeal and peaceful purchase, the
expansions of the mid-eighteenth century onward were not achieved
without frequent Maya resistance. A typical example of this process is the
1785–1820 legal file from Sabacche, discussed in the preceding chapter. It
is significant that: first, the litigants were a Maya family, the Tzakum, aided
by the cabildos of Ticul and Yotholim, cahob that bordered on the Sabacche
estancia; second, the Tzakum family persisted for three decades, although
the estanciero was ultimately able to uphold his claim to the disputed tract;
and third, in prosecuting their case the Maya were able to pull and copy
documents from as far back as 1596 (a land title and a petition from Maní),
as well as wills of 1726 and 1736 (from Pustunich and Ticul).[15]

The example of land documents shows that the Maya document motive, in revealing an ambiguous mix of the voluntary and obligatory, goes
to the very heart of cah action and legal engagement in colonial Yucatan.
The indigenous tradition of ritual and record, intertwined and mutually
supportive, coincided with the requirements of community defense and
could often be reconciled with colonial administrative demands. Using the
sample genre of testaments, four topics can be isolated that relate to the
motive or purpose behind Maya notarial writing.

The first is this: Were the preconquest Maya in the habit of making
written deathbed statements? There is no evidence of written wills, but
there must have been some form of pre-Hispanic testamentary institution
because so many of the conquered Mesoamerican peoples took to the
Spanish juridical form without apparent resistance.[16] Diego de Landa remarks that when a minor became old enough to take possession of inherited property, the transfer was made "delante de los señores y principales," and the bishop's informant, Gaspar Antonio Chi, stated that all

preconquest legal proceedings took place under oath and before wit-nesses.[17] Indigenous testamentary antecedents were thus in all likelihood oral and communal, hardly different in fact from the process going on in cahob up to the nineteenth century, save for the addition of an escribano's record. The colonial-era testator also dictated his will before the principal men of the cah; in the words of one, *cin ualic u ɔibtabal in testamento tu tanil in yum Batab y Justicias* . . . , "I state my will for it to be written down before the batab and the magistrates."[18]

But if the Maya willingly drew up written, notarized wills, we must also remember that they were required to do so by the Church (my second category of motive).[19] Gonzalo Gómez de Cervantes claimed in the late sixteenth century that parish priests forced Nahuas to make wills that benefited church coffers, although the "model wills" by Alonso de Molina in 1565 and Martín León in 1611 reflect considerations of faith and concern for legal process as well as an interest in pious donations.[20] From the time of the Council of Trent until 1801, bishops were required to inspect the testaments of their prelacies. Although it is hard to imagine every Maya will passing before a bishop's eyes, there is evidence that the prelate and the Interpreter General of Yucatan did make occasional tours of the cahob, where will books were inspected and sometimes criticized.[21]

Yet, thirdly, Spanish requirements and Maya priorities were not neces-sarily mutually exclusive; as we saw in Chapter 12, testaments were also religious texts. All wills began with formulaic religious statements, and about a third consisted of these formulas alone, while two-thirds of Ixil's testators in the 1760's, for example, asked for a church burial. Indeed, we have no reason to believe that religious portions of Maya wills were not, generally speaking, expressions of faith, or were even, in specific terms, motivated by a belief in the testament as a sacred prerequisite to dying in a state of grace.

The fourth and final possible motive lies in the fact that testaments also served practical purposes beyond the basic need to ensure the peaceful distribution of the wealth of the deceased. Some of these had nothing to do with colonial circumstances but were part of the internal functioning of the cah—for example, the consultation of past wills by the cabildo when a resident died intestate, or when a testator wished to confirm that he or she legally owned the property being bequeathed.[22] In relation to the be-queathing of land, however, wills were not only a vital cog of stability in the machine of Maya landholding but also a legal way for the Maya to sell and protect their lands. The symptoms of the expansion of Spanish estan-cias through the province in the late eighteenth century were extensive purchases by Spaniards as well as much litigation against Spaniards al-legedly occupying more than they had purchased.[23] In both instances the

Maya protagonist needed to prove ownership before colonial law; notarized wills did this, at least as far as naming tracts or plots of land, often situating them beside identified roads or named neighbors. But the lack of exact measurements in wills—only bills of sale gave those, although a plot may have been transferred solely by inheritance for centuries—opened a window onto the border disputes that characterized the majority of land litigation in colonial-period Yucatan.

The decision to write Maya-language notarial records was therefore not an exclusively Maya one, nor was it solely a colonial obligation. In fact, it was both, with the two sides of the colonial power structure perceiving the process differently from their own perspectives. To illustrate the point, we may turn briefly to a final genre, election records. When a Spanish official certified an election record as valid, he ticked off in the margin the offices important to the colonial authorities (escribano, and the officers in charge of catechism and the guest house); for the Maya, the paper was not only a record of the electoral process but a legitimating part of its ritual, complete with opening and closing phrases and a long list of officers, most of whom were of no concern to the Spanish.[24]

To argue that because Maya notarial documents died out in the nineteenth century the colonial-era Maya were forced to write them by the Spanish authorities is to miss two crucial details. One, notarial produce was as much a continuation of the pre-Columbian literary tradition as were the Books of Chilam Balam, perhaps more so in that the escribano's work, like that of the hieroglyphic authors, indirectly if not directly advanced the standing and interests of the cah and its dominant families. Two, the postindependence repúblicas indígenas are repeatedly assaulted as legal entities by the Federal Mexican authorities, who attempt to remove their batabob and effectively proscribe their written language; thus, long before the nineteenth century Maya writing in the roman alphabet had become so vital to Maya social function that the Mexicans had virtually to suppress it. Indigenous writing, in all its forms, may have been one of the few major media of resistance to Spanish rule and culture that had initially been taught and encouraged by the Spaniards themselves.[25]

Genre, Style, and Format

Nobody shall come to make light of it.
—Don Lucas Tun of Cuncunul, 1699

The Maya notarial documents that have come down to us fall into broad Spanish categories such as petitions, wills, records of testimony, election records, receipts, bills of sale, titles, agreements, and ratifications.

TABLE 18.1
Incidence of Indigenous-Language Notarial Genres

Genre	Maya	Nahuatl	Mixtec
Testaments	abundant	abundant	abundant
Land transactions	abundant	abundant	abundant
Sales of other property	very rare	common	common
Petitions	common	common	common
Election records	common	common	rare
Criminal records	very rare	common	common
Community budget records	rare	rare	rare
Tribute records	rare	rare	rare
Census records	rare	rare	none
Records of church and cofradía business	rare	common	rare
Church-sponsored texts	rare	abundant	rare
Ratifications of Spanish records	common	none	none

SOURCES: An earlier version of this table appeared in Restall and Terraciano 1992. Nahuatl genres are described in Anderson, Berdan, and Lockhart 1976; Karttunen 1982; and Lockhart 1992. Mixtec genres are described in Terraciano 1994. I have omitted another category, that of proclamations, edicts, and ordinances by the colonial authorities but translated into indigenous languages, because they originated in the Spanish world rather than in the indigenous communities. Of course, as more and more indigenous-language sources are uncovered, the incidences of each genre will change.

The genre categories used in Table 18.1 are those that are most useful to ethnohistorians; the table includes a comparison with notarial documents in Nahuatl and Mixtec, as well as indications of genre incidence using five broad categories (none, very rare, rare, common, and abundant). Although most of the differences in genre incidence among the three languages are probably due to patterns of record survival, it also seems likely that Yucatan's marginalization in New Spain was a contributing factor to the paucity of Church-sponsored texts—Landa was not in the same ethnographic league as Sahagún, and Herrera's work cannot match that of the friars Olmos and Molina. In addition, the small Spanish population in Yucatan no doubt explains why Maya cabildos were needed to ratify Spanish business records in rural areas.

These genres break down into further subcategories. For example, wills also contain testimonies relating to intestates, which are relatively rare. Petitions may be requests for permission to alienate inherited land, or cah land, or they may take the form of complaints against secular priests or complaints against the overburden of taxation and service requirements from the Spanish authorities (see the tables in Chapter 19). I would include as petitions the famous "letters" of 1567 to the King of Spain. In my estimation the extant colonial Maya documentary base is close to 2,000 documents; of the 1,600 that I have seen almost half are wills, and over a third are land documents that fall into the subcategories of bill of sale, receipt, acknowledgment or *conocimiento*, title or *título*, and boundary agreement (see Fig. 18.3 below). Because most of the wills contain land bequests, it could be said that land is the primary preoccupation of Maya notarial documents.

There may be regional and temporal variations of category, both Spanish and Maya in origin, revealing blurred intercategory delineations. Certainly within categories there are regional variations of format and style, just as there are dialectical variations within Yucatec Maya. These regional variations may be more pronounced than temporal developments.

In his examination of some sixteenth-century Maya land documents William Hanks identified five "constructive features" of this genre.[26] In fact, all five are evident, variations allowing, in all Maya notarial material; despite cah variations, Maya documents from this period share features in common because they draw upon a common cultural background and a common colonial experience. The first constructive feature is a date of completion. It is extremely rare to find an undated document. Most dateless examples are sufficiently damaged as to suggest that the date has faded, been obscured, or rotted off. In the rare instance in which a date appears to have been omitted, a document will show other signs of being hurriedly executed. Testaments are a slightly different case in that their date is that of the testator's deathday, which was not always the same day that the will was dictated and notarized.

The second feature is provenance. The cah of origin was essential to the validation of any Maya document; it is identified not only by name but also by the list of cabildo officers. In particular the batabob, being prominent locals and serving as they did for up to twenty years, would have been instantly recognizable symbols and representatives of their cah, their names identifying documents then and now. Only under unusual circumstances did these identifying factors contradict each other. For example, a resident of Ixil, Gabriel Tec, fell mortally ill in Mamá in January 1766. Sensing that God was calling his soul—"*tu payah yn cuxtul ca yumil ti D[io]s*"—Tec drew up his will "before the batab and magistrates of the cah of Mamá." But he identifies his cah as Ixil (in the way normal for Maya wills: stating the mother cah of his parents), and it is the cabildo of Ixil, not Mamá, who certify the document. The confusion is revealing: had Tec been a Spaniard he would have had his will notarized where he fell, and the provenance of the document would have been unambiguous (Mamá). But being Maya, his will is not just his own, but the product, responsibility, and property of his cah (Ixil), as surely as if he had died intestate, in which case the cabildo of Ixil would have drawn up his will for him.[27]

Signatures or names identifying authors and witnesses are the third constructive feature. As discussed elsewhere in this work, the persons mentioned in Maya documents did not play exclusive or discrete roles. In wills, family members or the cabildo—all also witnesses—could appropri-

ate the role of author. In bills of sale, the cabildo, the seller, and the purchaser are all stated protagonists and may all enter the document in the
pronominal first person. Maya notarial documents cannot exist as such
without at least one author-witness name, and typically they affirm a
collective-cah authorship via the representative role of the cah officials.

The fourth and fifth features are an elaborate opening and an explicit
ending. These ritual phrases have been discussed above with respect to
land documents and wills, and they receive further attention below, with
respect to election records and petitions. It is worth remarking here on one
petition that is a notable exception to the pattern of constructive features—
the aforementioned anonymous attack on four Spanish priests, accusing
them of public sexual excesses in graphic detail.[28] The scandalous nature
of the petition necessitated the absence of a conventional opening or closing, so there are no signatures, no cah of provenance, no date (accompanying Spanish records are dated 1774), and no reverential phrases of address.
But the author, clearly feeling the need for some kind of anonymous substitute construction, identifies himself as "the informer of the truth," and
closes (with an irony that was no doubt deliberate) with "Amen."

Although handwriting styles varied among Maya escribanos as much
as among Spaniards, there remained a distinctive quality to the Maya hand
that makes it instantly recognizable (see Fig. 18.1). Any scholar who has
flipped the pages of archival legajos looking for Maya documents knows
that one's eye is caught by the hand before the language. That hand—tidy,
clear, lacking the florid almost feverish festoons of Spanish notarial produce—makes reading the Maya of this period often more pleasurable than
paleographing the Spanish. There is of course a huge difference between
sixteenth- and late-eighteenth-century Spanish handwriting, whereas
Maya hands exhibit so little change over these centuries that differences
are inseparable from notary-to-notary and cah-to-cah variations.

The Maya notarial hand, however, its legibility hampered neither by
the vagaries of fashion nor by the exigencies of time, can sometimes prove
a *faux ami*. Toward the end of the colonial period the Maya escribanos of
the cahob-barrios of Mérida began recording in Spanish, in a style of presentation, down to the neat margins and consistent columns of cabildo
officers, that remained unquestionably Maya. It is worth adding that notarial documents in other indigenous languages—of which I have seen
only Nahuatl, Mixtec, and Cakchiquel—exhibit hands that are closer to the
Yucatec style than to the Spanish, and that what I describe here as being
Maya may also be Mesoamerican. At the risk of suggesting some sort of
genetic style proclivity, I note that the detail and order of hieroglyphic text
is aesthetically closer to the tight and tidy hand of Maya escribanos than
are the cursive scripts of contemporaneous Europe.[29] There are a few other

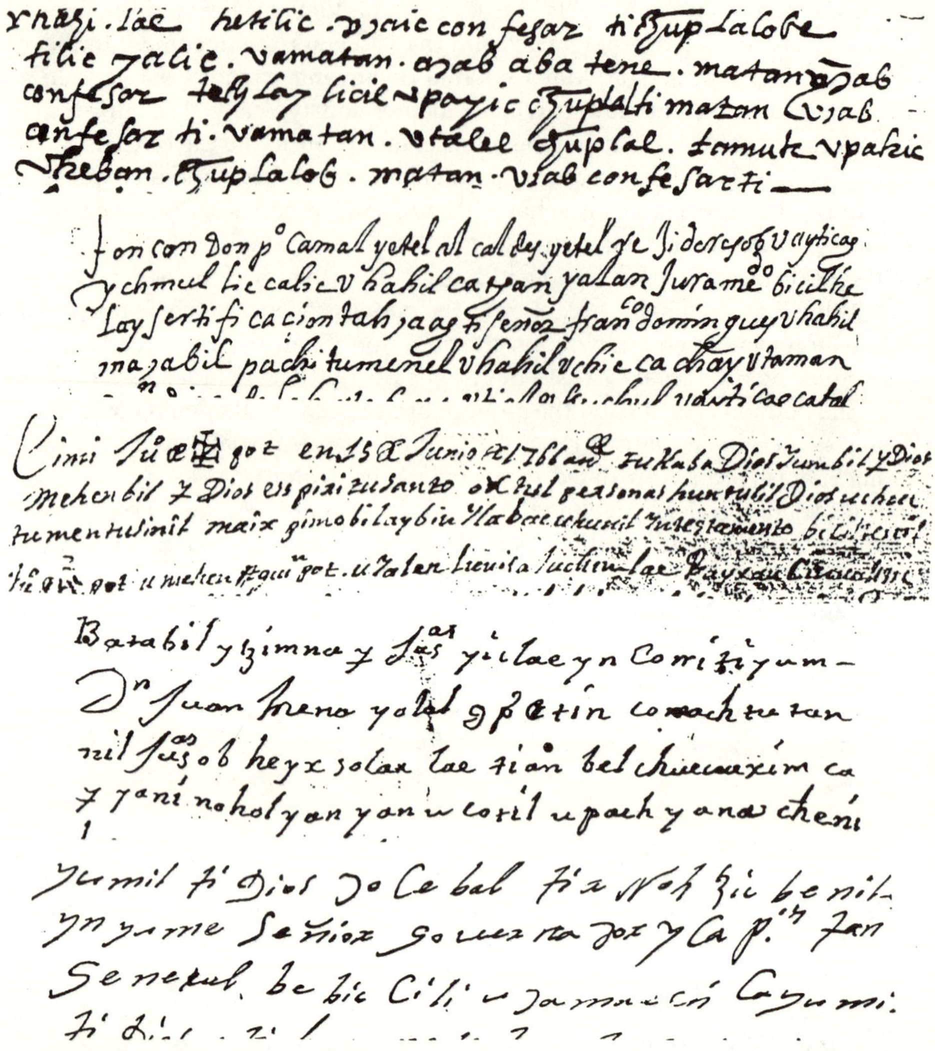

Fig. 18.1. Some examples of Maya notarial handwriting. Sources: (a) Tixmeuac, 1589, notary's name on destroyed portion of document (AGN-I, 69, 5, 277); (b) Ichmul, 1669, notary: Lorenzo Tzimil (AGI-E, 315b, 17, 180); (c) Ixil, 1766, notary: Pablo Tec (TI: 28); (d) Itzimná, 1790, notary: Domingo Mex (ANEY, 1825, 208); (e) Hocaba, 1825, notary: Pablo Yah (CCA-VIII, 1811, 09).

factors to consider: the relative newness of alphabetic script might have encouraged a more careful rendering of it; the original influence of the Franciscans and, outside Yucatan, other orders, could have had a similar effect, clerical writing being tidier in general than secular script; and the Maya notary could write at a more leisurely pace than his Spanish counterpart, who was compelled by the sheer volume of work to use abbreviations and rapid strokes.

The rhetorical style of Maya notarial documents is marked by a strong oral component, the hint of a possible pre-Hispanic linkage. In a sense, all these documents were necessarily oral, in that the escribano's role was to record the dictated statements of illiterates—batabs and testators, persons selling or receiving land, and any witness with a few words to contribute to the document. It is worth remarking that the pre-Columbian population was likewise illiterate, being dependent upon an official elite to record events and read them, perhaps publicly; the link between the written and spoken language was thus necessarily and traditionally tight. As a result, Maya notarial records contain rhythms of speech that are formal and ordered, as well as numerous moments of conversational or colloquial speech.

One of the most striking examples of ordered speech is the use of *bay xan* to separate the constituent parts of a statement and introduce the bequests of a will or the sections of a forest boundary. It translates as "likewise" or "also"—or, when in the form *bay tun*, as "then, thus"—and is often the equivalent of the Spanish *ítem*. Between the *bay xan* markers are the descriptions of property or the lay of the land; put together in sequence these sections form a narrative of one's property. This is exactly the way that the Lacandon Maya equivalent, *pay tan*, functions today as a marker in oral narrative.[30] The Yucatec Maya today still use *bay* in a number of narrative and descriptive configurations, although it seems to me that *bay xan* has been replaced by *entonces*.

Formal speech was also made manifest in the formulas of the periodic commands, or admonitions, presented in Table 18.2 in a comparative context. These perorations are standard fare in Nahuatl wills, often repeated after each item as though part of the marking formula; in Maya wills they tend to act as a finalizer, a formal break between the final item and the regular closing formula, or else they serve as emphasizers within the text, highlighting one item in particular. They are rarely found in Spanish testaments, which were private affairs, lacking the public audience of the indigenous equivalent.[31]

A third formal stylistic feature of these sources is the use of semantic couplets. These have been observed in other Mayan languages and in a few nonnotarial Yucatec sources.[32] The full corpus of postconquest Maya

TABLE 18.2
Comparison of Admonitions in Maya and Nahuatl Wills

Maya	Nahuatl
mamac bin luksic tiob nobody shall take it from them	*ayac quicuiliz* nobody is to take it from him
mayxmac bin tac ti baxa nobody shall come to make light of it	*ayac quelehuiliz* nobody is to covet it of him
hebin u ɔab ti minan kexolali it shall be given without dispute	*ayac quichalaniliz* nobody is to dispute with him about it

SOURCES: Maya, (1) TI: 35, TE: 230; (2) TE: 30; (3) LC: 11; Nahuatl, Lockhart 1992: 368.

notarial literature can now be added to that list. Examples of such couplets, especially in the form of pairs of synonymous verbs, can be found in many of the excerpts from the sources transcribed and translated in the present study. What the analysis of these sources also adds to our knowledge of this phenomenon is the use of bilingual couplets, often with bicultural implications. The most abundant of such were place names: San Agustín and Tekanto were two names for the same town, each carrying a culturally distinct historical baggage; together they were a postconquest cah, San Agustín Tekanto. Likewise, Mérida-Tihó was *U noh cahal siudad*, "the great cah, the city."

The introduction of Spanish legal terminology also produced phrases representative of the dual role played by Maya-language documentation—for example, *in takyahthan in testamento*, "my final statement, my testament," or often *in takyahthan tin testamento*, "my final statement in my testament," as though the Maya term represented an indigenous form that continued to exist within the Spanish form. The phrase, like the testament itself, is whole, yet the context and purpose of the terms used are dual. An example of an all-Maya semantic couplet in the same sentence as a bilingual one would be *u binbal ximbal . . . u pach u posesionil*, "the going along, the walk, of possession, of possession."[33] This use of Spanish to add a new dimension to a traditional technique of discourse is symbolic of the creative and active response of the Maya to colonial rule.

These ordered features often appear alongside colloquial ones. One scholar of the modern Maya, in an analysis of a Chilam Balam passage, observed that conversation is the very basis of Maya linguistic expression. Whereas European thought might be termed "monologocentric" (if such a neologism is allowed), Maya thought and literature are "dialogocentric."[34] While still recognizing the influence of Spanish forms of legal record, it may be helpful to think of Maya notarial documents as traditionally interactive in this way, with the conversationalists being the testator or vendor, and the heir or purchaser, with the cabildo playing a floating role in the dialogue. Maya testaments, in spite of their formal structure based on pious opening formulas and the listing of bequests, give the impression of being dictated in the testator's home before an assembly of the testator's relatives and the principal men of the community. Thus the pronominal reference is usually the first singular of the testator, but it will shift if the cabildo make a collective statement, or if a relative appropriates the first person to make a promise to respect some aspect of the will.[35] In one will from Tekanto every member of the family makes an identical statement confirming their acknowledgment of the testator's wishes.[36]

In other wills, colloquial asides give an impression of informal narrative. In a testament from the Ixil corpus of the 1760's the notary begins the closing formula when the testator suddenly remembers a piece of unfinished business, the memory of it literally interrupting the formula: "*halili u xul yn than kah ten xan ...*," "this is the end of my statement—also I remember ...," and he goes on to tell the story of a piece of land he sold and then tried to reclaim by returning half the money to the purchaser's son, who then ran off with the money. "On this day let it be recorded ...," says the testator, using the occasion of his will to settle the affair before the whole community.[37] In another Ixil will, quoted and discussed earlier, Marta Mis feels the need to justify why she is leaving nothing to one of her daughters, Agustina Yam, who, she says, "does nothing on my behalf, nor does her husband, as m'lord the batab and magistrates know." The Maya phrase used, "*ma tumentah in quentail*"—"she does nothing on my behalf"—is a colloquialism that is still used today.[38] The colloquialisms are especially rich in the graphic complaint of 1774 against four secular priests, mentioned above. This testimony comes across as an oral account, using slang and explicit terms to refer to sexual acts and parts of the body, avoiding any of the niceties and euphemisms that a similar Spanish complaint might use.[39]

There is thus a stylistic element to Maya record keeping that we might call communal. Because of the representative nature of Maya social structure—discussed earlier with respect to the cabildo, the chibal, and the family—the symbolic and often literal presence of community members is evident in the records of their affairs. Far from the dry legalese of much of their Spanish equivalents, the style of these documents has a very human, often personal, quality that is apparent in spite of the elements of formula and formality.

The features of genre, style, and format may appear to be simple examples of Spanish-Maya syncretism, containing as they do elements that are preconquest survivors and others that were introduced or influenced by the conquerors' culture. Yet it may be more useful to think of those features neither as separate Maya and Spanish nor as one hybrid mix of the two, but as something more complex—colonial-era Maya, in which indigenous elements existing within the framework of documentary forms originating in Spain are now used unequivocably by the Maya for their own purposes.

Maintenance, Survival, and Distribution

I entered the copy of the acknowledgment into the book of wills.
—notary of Ebtun, 1817

The slight balance of extant documents in favor of wills could simply be an accident of survival, but among cognate documents in Nahuatl, which have been uncovered and studied for a far longer time, there is also a balance in favor of testaments. The implication then is that what is extant is more or less representative. If wills are the most common genre, perhaps that was simply because Mayas died more often than they sold land, elected cabildos, and petitioned against excessive taxes and bad priests. Almost as many land documents have survived as wills (see Fig. 18.3), and since most testaments can in a sense be categorized as land records, it could be said that some 80 percent of Maya notarial material is concerned with land—a reflection of its overwhelming importance to indigenous economy and society.

The other determining survival factors revolve around the question of what happened to Maya notarial documents after they were written, and where, if anywhere, they were preserved. Documents addressed to senior colonial officials, such as petitions, were necessarily sent to Mérida, from where they might travel to Mexico City along Inquisitional channels; two-thirds of Maya documents currently preserved in the Archivo General de la Nación in Mexico City are petitions complaining of malpractice by Spanish ecclesiastical or administrative officials, or documents related to complaint cases. Examples of such petitions drawn up by cah authorities, translated in Mérida and passed through the Spanish bureaucratic network to Mexico City, are the Xecpes complaint of 1578 and the Tixmeuac of 1589, both against the same priest; or, at the other end of the temporal and regional scale, the priest-removal request from the Maya cabildo at Bacalar in 1838.[40] Colonial inquiries were also responsible for the survival of Maya-language material; almost all such documentation extant in the archive devoted to "the Indies" in Seville relates to the Crown's long investigation into the late-seventeenth-century governorship of don Rodrigo Flores de Aldana.

Alternatively, the will of a Maya landowner might be copied and submitted by a Spanish landowner as evidence of the boundaries of a piece of land purchased from the testator's grandchildren. Examples of this are found in the manuscript collections from the estates of Tabi and Sabac-che.[41] Similarly, Maya cabildos were able to submit as evidence in land litigation copies of testaments and bills of sale that were often generations' old—centuries' old, in the case of the Sabacche dispute. Most extant Maya wills, however, are contained in the contiguous collections from Cacal-chen, Ixil, and Tekanto.[42]

Submitting old wills as legal evidence could not have been possible, and will collections would not have survived, had cabildos not preserved their records in some fashion. Were there books maintaining the minutes of cabildo meetings to compare to the Tlaxcalan *Actas de Cabildo*? None has survived, and I believe such a thing would have been untypical of Yucatec Maya practice. More typical would have been a model of record keeping— discrete books for election records, wills, land transactions, and so on— that varied in actual practice according to regional and temporal variants. What has survived are segments of these discrete books, some of which contain samples or extraneous material from other books. It seems that particularly toward the end of the eighteenth century different types of records began to be kept together. The Ebtun material consists exclusively of land documents up until this time, when wills and complaints and ordinance translations begin creeping in. The two earliest wills in the Eb-tun corpus (1699, from Cuncunul, and 1785) are later copies from what was presumably a *libro de testamentos*; the other wills are part of an 1811–13 run of mixed-genre documents, implying that by this time discrete books in Ebtun had collapsed into one. Indeed in 1816 the Ebtun cabildo noted the purchase of a well pulley for the cah in the testament book—*cin chicbesic t Libro Tesm^to*, "I mark it down in the book of wills"—and the following year the notary mentioned a land document written into the same volume—*u hochol conosimiento cin ɔaic ti Libro testamento*, "I placed the copy of the acknowledgment in the book of wills."[43]

The corpus of wills from Tekanto, too, are discrete and genre-specific from 1724 to 1759, after which date the wills become less regular and are interspersed with land sales and acknowledgments and other records of cabildo business. There are even nine inserted documents dated between 1590 and 1698, all seemingly original and time-damaged. They may per-haps have been saved from decaying earlier volumes, or perhaps the in-crease in land documents, created by increased competition for land at the end of the colonial period, provided the impetus for change. Another possibility is that the information on tenure contained in wills made it logical for other land documents to be stored with them. In any case, after 1770 the system of separate books appears to have collapsed in Tekanto, as it did a bit later in Ebtun.[44]

In Ixil at this time testaments were still being kept in a separate vol-

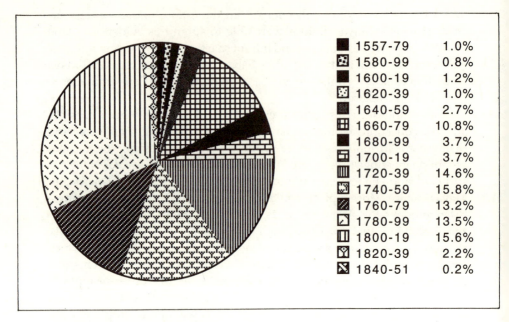

■	1557-79	1.0%
▦	1580-99	0.8%
■	1600-19	1.2%
▨	1620-39	1.0%
▬	1640-59	2.7%
⊞	1660-79	10.8%
■	1680-99	3.7%
⊟	1700-19	3.7%
⦀	1720-39	14.6%
▨	1740-59	15.8%
▧	1760-79	13.2%
◿	1780-99	13.5%
⫘	1800-19	15.6%
▨	1820-39	2.2%
⊠	1840-51	0.2%

Fig. 18.2. Temporal distribution of sources.

ume—a tantalizing twenty-six-month section of which has survived—and one of them illustrates the utility of such a system. In 1767 Josef Cab died intestate in Mérida-Tihó, leaving the settling of his estate to the cabildo of Ixil, who declare that they have consulted the testaments of Cab's forebears. They discover that his father also died intestate, but his grandfather, also named Josef Cab, left a will in 1726, forty years earlier. In accordance with the spirit of the grandfather's will the cabildo order the Cab family house plot not to be either sold or broken up.[45]

Other evidence for genre-specific books of records comes from two sources. One relates to election records, to the survival of a small corpus of such from Tekanto, and to references in Maya election records to *u libroyl,* "its book," *u libroil elecon,* "the election book," and *u libroyl ca noh ahau,* "the book of our great lord" (see Chapter 20). The other source is in the body of Tekanto wills: the three aforementioned reports in Spanish of episcopal visits to inspect the *"libro de testamentos"* (1737, 1746, and 1751). No doubt then the extant fragments of will books—Cacalchen, Ixil, Tekanto—are the tip of the iceberg that once was.

A further point on the maintenance and survival of Maya notarial records involves an intriguing link between epidemics and extant wills. Not only is there a correlation between colony-wide epidemics or famines and concentrations of eighteenth-century wills from Tekanto, but the dates of the surviving Ixil wills (December 1765–January 1768) coincide exactly with such a famine, and the Cacalchen wills also date exactly from a period of severe yellow fever and smallpox, followed by severe famine (1648–53).[46] It comes as no surprise that there are more wills generated during these periods of high mortality, although that fact does suggest cause of death (a detail never recorded in Maya testaments), and shows that normal legal procedures were maintained during a time of crisis. However, this correlation also implies that wills were more likely to survive when many were concentrated in a brief period of time. In other words, bookkeeping may have become sloppy in years when there was only a dribble of notarial records going into cabildo files, so that unbound documents were exposed to the higher risks of removal or loss.

Figures 18.2 and 18.3 and Maps 18.1 and 18.2 indicate the temporal, geographical, and genre distribution of the extant notarial documentation in Maya.[47] The documents run from 1557 to 1851, but they are far more numerous in the later colonial period, not only because more documentation inevitably survived but also because of several interrelated factors— the gradual extension of the colonial frontier, the sporadic population growth of the seventeenth and eighteenth centuries, the acquisition of pueblo and cabildo status by increasing numbers of cahob, and the steady diffusion of literacy to new indigenous notaries. In addition, greater competition for land (within and between ethnic groups) stimulated increased

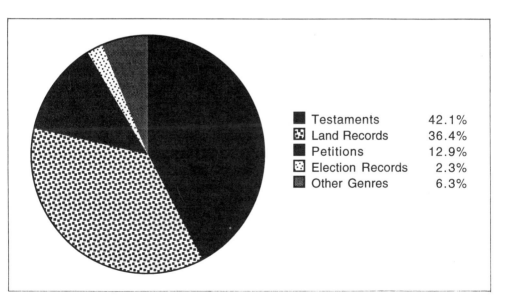

■ Testaments	42.1%
▣ Land Records	36.4%
■ Petitions	12.9%
▣ Election Records	2.3%
▨ Other Genres	6.3%

Fig. 18.3. Distribution of sources by genre.

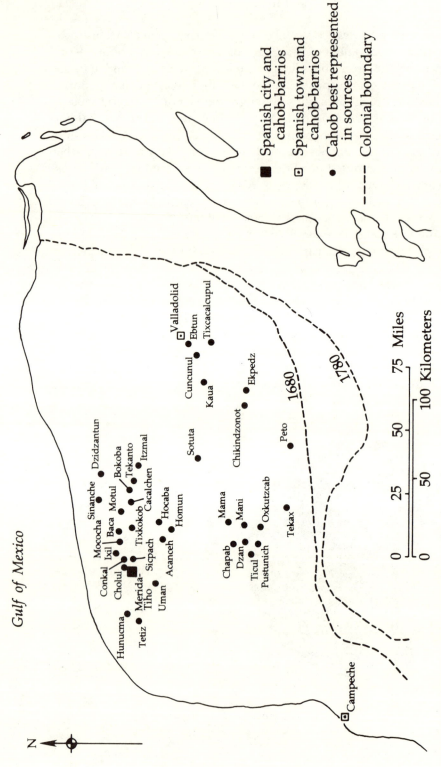

Map 18.1. Yucatan, 1557–1851: The cahob best represented in the Maya-language documentary sources. Cahob located using modern maps provided by INEGI; colonial boundaries after Farriss 1984: 17, 77; cahob shown are represented by five or more notarial documents in Maya between 1557 and 1851; this category includes the five cahob-barrios of Tihó, as well as Itzimná and Chuburná, whose location is shown in Maps 3.2 and 3.3.

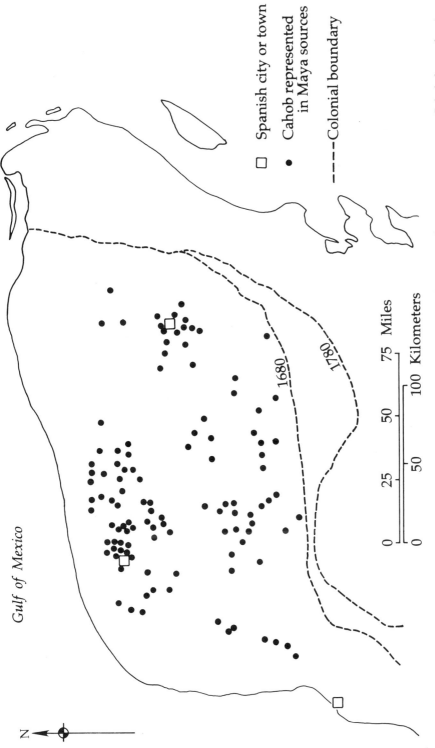

Map 18.2. Yucatan, 1557–1851: Distribution of all cahob represented in the Maya-language documentary sources. Cahob located using modern maps provided by INEGI; colonial boundaries after Farriss 1984: 17, 77; the 132 cahob shown are those that could be located and are represented by one or more notarial documents in Maya between 1557 and 1851; for location of cahob in and beside Mérida-Tihó, see Maps 3.2 and 3.3.

Maya legal and notarial activity after about 1720, when an upsurge in extant documentation begins. The greatest abundance of Maya material comes from the century 1720–1820, especially the second half of that period, which is the very time when Nahuatl notarial documentation went into a sharp numerical decline. The last Maya-language notarial document so far uncovered is dated 1851—a testimony to the tenacity of the Maya writing tradition.[48]

By the early eighteenth century there were just under 200 cahob under colonial rule; to date I have encountered Maya-language material from 80 percent of them (and growing). The combination of geographical and quantitative clustering in the extant documentation gives emphasis to four subregions within what was then the governable heart of the colony and is today the state of Yucatan. These clusters can be clearly seen in Maps 18.1 and 18.2, being the cahob that were the barrios and satellites of Mérida; these merge into the old Ceh Pech region, most of which became colonial La Costa, northeast of the capital (in particular Ixil, Cacalchen, and Tekanto, but also Izamal, Motul, and their neighbors); the area to the immediate southwest of Valladolid-Saci (especially Ebtun and its neighbors); and the populous cahob at the foot of the Puuc hills in Sierra Alta (primarily Maní, Oxkutzcab, Tekax, Ticul, and their neighbors).

Maya literacy, as expressed by mundane notarial material, was clearly one of the ways in which traditional indigenous methods of record and ritual were influenced by Spanish practices, the indigenous economy was documented to the benefit of Spaniards, and the Maya elite were used as a branch of colonial administrative rule. Yet Maya literacy also had profound nativist implications. Maya communities took advantage of alphabetic skills and Spanish recognition of indigenous notaries to resist colonial demands and obligations, the abuses of priests, and the threat of acquisitive Spanish landowners. Documents such as wills and land records may have contained seemingly mundane information, but the Maya made use of them to defend the integrity and territory of the cah and its families. Indeed, in many instances the very ordinariness of the text is what makes possible the transmission of cultural information, while the context and subtext help us to understand something of the political, economic, social, and cultural environment of the cah.

Petitions

Petitions in Maya were presented to the Spanish authorities with apparent regularity by indigenous cabildos throughout the colonial period. Although sometimes described by the Spanish *petición*, the Maya usually referred to this genre with their own term, *okotba than*, literally "statement of request." Revealing both Spanish and Maya roots and traits, this genre is a useful example of Maya notarial practice, as outlined in the preceding chapter.

The Language of Request

O Lord, Ruler, King, we are petitioning you, for the sake of our lord Dios,
we are kissing your hands and feet.
—cabildo of Dzaptun, 1605

Maya petitions can be organized into types, as shown in Table 19.1. Although all petitions involved requests of some kind, the first type (request) is differentiated from the other two (complaint, litigation) by the fact that accusation and antagonism were not involved. Naturally, the separation of petitions into discrete types can be artificial. For example, complaints against individual colonists often had to do with lawsuits between a Spaniard and a cah; complaints against priests often took the form of requests for the dismissal of the clergyman and sometimes turned out to be part of a broader dispute involving other parties.

All petitions were drawn up and validated by the cabildo, although specific representation might be corporate (complaints against overburden and against priests; requests for permission to sell cah land), factional (internal political conflict), or individual (petitions relating to privately held land). All petitions had in common certain traits of language and

TABLE 19.1

Typology of Maya Petitions

Type of petition	Object of petition
petitions of request	—to gain permission to sell land
petitions of complaint	—to reduce demands made by colonial officials or institutions
	—to gain redress or official action against individual Spaniards who are: (i) clergy; (ii) nonclergy (land disputes only)
petitions of litigation	—to gain official Spanish support in legal conflicts that are: (i) internal (inheritance or political disputes); (ii) with individual Spaniards (land disputes only)

SOURCES: AGEY, AGI, AGN, CCA, TE.

form that make these documents more than just a Maya imitation of a Spanish genre.

The formulas of Maya petitions revolved around the addressee, who was usually a high-ranking Spanish official. The language of reverence and respect tended to mix indigenous and Spanish terminology, with the result that the specific identity of the addressee was often obscured. This language, accompanied by self-deprecating descriptions of the petitioners, was undoubtedly descended from preconquest traditions of rulerly address. This style was not unique to the Maya; clear parallels can be seen between indigenous petitions from Yucatan and similar documents drawn up in Nahuatl during the colonial period. In a petition of 1605 the cabildo of Dzaptun declared:

yumile ahaue Reye okotbacacah	O lord, Ruler, King, we are petition-
tech yoklal ca yumil ti dios	ing you, for the sake of our lord Dios, we
uɔbentahcacah ta kab yetel a uoc	are kissing your hands and feet . . .
. . . licil coktic caba ta tan uchbal	we now present a petition before you
a uan ti con ta ɔayatzil yoklal	so that you protect us and take pity
techil ca yum cech ca noh	on us, for the sake of you our lord,
ahau cech uisoReye . . .	you our Great Ruler, our Viceroy . . .

In the same year the cabildo of Tahnab, a neighboring cah in the Campeche jurisdiction, used similar language:[1]

yume lay u chun licil ca noh oktic	O lord, this is why we humbly place
caba ta tan cech ca noh ahau ti	ourselves before you, our Great
Rey tu tzicil cah lohil ti Jesu	Ruler, the King, in honor of our
xpõ lic cuɔbenic a uoc yetel	redeemer, Jesus Christ, we kiss your
a kab con u kazil a mehene . . .	feet and hands, we the poorest of
	your children . . .

Compare these phrases with an example from central Mexico from the very same decade. Wrote the notary of the altepetl of Tezoyuca in 1607:[2]

| Mahuiztic tlahtohuaniye ma yehuatzin tlacatl tto dios mitzmotlacochicahuiltzinno totlacomahuiztlahtocatzinne mixpantzinco titonestiya timomacehualtzitzinhua cenca tictenamiqui y motlatocamatzin y motlatocaycxitzin . . . | O honored ruler, may our lord Dios give you health, our Precious Honored Ruler. We your poor vassals are appearing before you. We kiss your rulerly hands and feet . . . |

The elements of these examples of discourse are the same: the Spanish addressee, in these cases the provincial governor, receives the titles of and reverential language due preconquest rulers (in Nahuatl *tlatoani* and the traditional reference to god-given good health; in Maya *ahau* and *yum*, added to the appropriated and liberally applied Spanish terms for king and viceroy); the petitioners, though they are the elite of their communities, present themselves in the humblest terms ("poor vassals," or in Maya "children" as a juxtaposition to *yum*, which means "father" as well as "lord");[3] and both Mayas and Nahuas employ the exact same motif of deference, the kissing of hands and feet, a symbol of the Mesoamerican tradition of averting one's eyes in the ruler's presence. Keeping one's eyes lowered does not necessarily mean kissing, of course, and indeed a Maya variation on the theme substitutes mere groveling:[4]

| hokah in cah tin ba tu tan in noh tzicanil yum ti halach uinic gouernador uay ti noh cah Tihóe ti chinan en tzonan en yalan yoc yalan u kab . . . lic ca chinpultic caba tatan licix ca yabach lopix ti hatan tu tzil dios yalan a uoc yalan a kab | I am appearing in person before my Great Revered Lord, the Halach Uinic, Governor here in the great cah of Tihó, having abased and prostrated myself beneath his feet and hands . . . we now lower our heads before you, kneeling in great adoration in honor of Dios, beneath your feet and hands. |

What the petitioners expect in return for offering such reverence is, in general terms, a commitment to standard Mesoamerican obligations of rulership. The imagery of protection is especially strong, extending beyond the use of *an*, "to protect or aid" (used above), to the tree symbolism present also in Nahuatl references to rulership. Although Nahuas associated their rulers with specific trees—*in pochotl in ahuehuetl*, "the cypress and silk cotton tree"—such trees were clearly chosen because they provided shade, and it is this quality upon which the Maya also fix. One petition declares *katic tech ca a boybeson yalan u boy a kab*, "we ask you to protect us beneath the shade of your arm." The word *boy* (properly *booy*), "shade" is contained within *boybes*, "to protect," whose literal meaning is thus "to provide shade"; and the word *kab* means both "arm" and "tree branch."[5]

TABLE 19.2
Terminology of Maya Petitions

Term	Translation
Maya:	
hun	document (*u hunil petision*, petition paper)
kat	request (*yn kat*, my request; *yn katic*, I ask)
okotba	petition, plea (*okotba than*, petition statement)
Maya-written Spanish:	
auto	decree, edict
bando	proclamation
lisensia	(licencia) permit
petision	(petición) petition
sentensia definitamente	(sentencia definitiva) sentence, decision, final judgment
termino	(término) term of specified time period within which to present papers, etc.
testimonio	testimony
titulo	(título) [land] title

SOURCES: Same as Table 19.1

Another aspect of Maya reverential discourse seen in notarial petitions is the use of the language of love. A common opening formula to a Maya petition is *yn yamail . . .* , "my beloved . . ." In other words, some phrases go beyond deference to express loyalty in seemingly more affectionate terms; for example, *a noh tzicbenile yn yum ca yn mek yn kab yokol yn pucsikal*, "I embrace you in my heart, my Great Revered Lord."[6] Paul Sullivan made use of similar language in his analysis of letters written by semi-independent Maya leaders in the 1920's and 1930's to North American anthropologists, arguing that a rhetoric of courtship developed around the use of the word *yacunah*, which he glosses as ambiguously meaning "love," and such phrases as "I love you with all my heart."[7] Although Sullivan's study does not include the original Maya texts, it seems clear that this rhetoric might be better understood in the broader context of Maya discourse stretching back into colonial times, and indeed in the even broader context of Mesoamerican reverential language. To see in this genre information about Maya sexuality may be taking it too literally, just as the Maya would not have taken literally the bad translations into Maya of letters from Sylvanus Morley and colleagues. Such language does talk of embracing and kissing, of arms, hands, feet, hearts, but it was understood in purely metaphorical terms—surely by the Maya reading Morley's letters as much as by the colonial officials reading Maya petitions and by preconquest Nahua and Maya recipients of such address, whose literal meaning would have been given no more thought than we give to metaphorical idioms dating back to Middle English.[8]

The terminology the Maya used to describe the petition itself and the documents of decision sought by the petitioners (see Table 19.2) was bilingual. The Maya terms, however, indicate that the process was from the indigenous perspective relatively straightforward, perhaps reflecting a preconquest tradition in which requests for justice were presented orally or on paper, or both, resulting in a decision that was either favorable or not to the petitioning party. The Spanish legal terms borrowed by the Maya were, on the other hand, indicative of a different system, and were often used incorrectly, not to mention misspelled. Some Maya documents almost appear deliberately to pepper the text with as much Spanish legalese as possible, as though each word added to the validity of the paper regardless of how removed a term was from its meaningful legal context. This is not to denigrate Maya petitionary skills: the worst examples of the abuse of legal terminology come in late-colonial documents that claim to be copies of sixteenth-century land records.[9]

Petitionary Preoccupations

There are not enough of us to do so much work, and being few, neither can we manage our fields, not sustain our children.
—cabildo of Tahnab, 1605

Petitions are a genre especially rich in ethnohistorical information, and their substance has been discussed in earlier chapters on such subjects as political factionalism, land litigation, religion, and sexuality. But to give a fuller picture of the nature of the genre, in the pages that follow I discuss three categories of petition: complaints against the overburden of the colonial system, requests to sell land, and petitions against priests.

Petitions by cah cabildos that sought relief from colonial demands ranged from the specific to the broad, from perceived injustices that seem relatively innocuous to alleged abuses that appear to substantiate the horror of colonialism. At one end of the scale is a document presented in 1813 by don Leandro Can, batab of Tacchebichen, and five cabildo members, to "the Great and Respected Lord Subdelegate of the cabecera of Sotuta." Complained don Leandro:[10]

hachi manal chichil uɔaic u ba yn yum Alcalde ɔul u toc ten u llabeil u posito cah y u llabeil u cahail takin matan yn uol tic ca in kubee

it is an absolutely verified fact that m'lord the Spanish alcalde snatched from me and gave himself the keys to the cah depot and the cah silver chest; it is not my wish to deliver them to him

This alleged theft may have been officially sanctioned (in which case Tacchebichen's reverentially couched appeal to the local subdelegate would have been in vain), for the rapid changes in the way in which Yucatan was governed during this period of reform and revolt form the context of the above petition.[11]

The upheaval that marked the decades surrounding Independence is also the background to a petition of 1825 from Hocaba (a cabecera northwest of Sotuta), a document that likewise illustrates the Maya strategy of appealing to a higher authority, hoping to play one Spanish official off against another (a strategy also typical of the Spaniards themselves). The villain of the piece is again the local Spanish (or, since Spanish colonial rule is over, Ladino) alcalde, although he may only have been the messenger of "a decree that orders us to uproot trees, palms, breadnuts, and sapotes that are on stony ground." Such a decree indeed seems hard to fathom, which may be part of the artifice of the petition, unless the Hocaba cabildo genuinely misunderstood or were mystified by the alleged edict.[12]

More likely the petition's persuasive intent is at work here; the impression that the corpus of extant Maya petitions gives is that the petitioners usually knew exactly what they were doing, and this was true not just of the late-colonial period, as we shall see. In both the Tacchebichen and the Hocaba documents, the batabob emphasize why they are petitioning, with the cause of petition being not so much the perceived act of injustice itself as the reason why the act is unjust. The batab of Tacchebichen surely knew that his opposition to the seizing of the cah treasury keys was not enough, so he reminds the subdelegate that the cabildo access to cah funds has been jeopardized, implying a danger to the ability of the community to meet its fiscal obligations to the colony. The same strategy, based upon generations of experience in Spanish priorities, is employed by Hocaba, who point out that the threatened trees are the source of the sales tax fee— *tumen tan u tzabal u alcabalail*—and the reason is repeated—*tumen lay oxob batan conic u leob utial botic limosna y contribusion*, "for these breadnuts primarily are sold to pay alms and taxes." Therefore, states the batab, in the assertive tone that occasionally appears among the reverential phrases of Maya petitions, *bin ma c̆hace lay cheob*, "these trees will not be chopped down."

Three late-colonial petitions from Hunucmá and Tetiz illustrate the differences of approach that Maya complaints could take.[13] The point of contention is the demand for wood at the site of the construction of a new convent at Kimchil. The Hunucmá version blames the curate, a don José María Domínguez, for the fact that the cahnalob (cah residents) have not been paid, a violation of *caxic u thanuba yetel*, "that which was agreed upon." All "that is being asked," the cabildo conclude, "is that each work order be just and not forced"—*ca u kati tohol u meyah hunhuntul ma ɔalpachi*.

One Tetiz version, dated July 11, 1819, twelve days before its cousin document from Hunucmá, likewise blames the curate in Hunucmá, upon whose order the local priest underpaid the cah workers. Specific sums are provided: *ley lubche la uauacpel bara u chouacil u tohol tune ooxpel tumin yn tħox ma tupol . . . tune cu ɔabal u lak hunpel tumin tiob xan,* "a just [price] for these logs, six varas each in length, is 3 reales; I did not receive enough . . . let then the other one real be given to them also." The other Tetiz version is undated but is clearly part of the same case. It begins as *u cuentail lubche,* "the timber account," but quickly launches into a different tone that is more assertive and dramatic—and more typical of Maya petitionary style:

tumen tun ɔok u tzec con cat uas- kesah u taknil oxpel tumin yokol hebix cu ɔa cilace Bey tun xan yum bey tun xano yum binel cah tan u pachahal u cahal tiz yoklal mixbal yan u hantob uih cinsicob u real i medio u mutil yxim cu manicob hemax ti yane le Audencia Real . . . bey tuno yum ma tin chic yn cahal cex tu cimilobe . . .	Why then are we being punished? We ask that the money is returned to 3 reales as formerly given. For otherwise, lord, Tetiz cah will be ruined, since there'll be no food to eat. They'll die. A real and a half barely buys the measure of corn in the courthouse . . . However, lord, I shall not abandon [those of] my cah, although they are dying . . .

A compelling picture is presented of a town reduced to the last grains in community storage, whose cabildo shall defend it to the last, despite a cruel dependency upon the mercy of a dishonest colonial taskmaster. How close this picture came to reality we cannot be sure, beyond the general knowledge that famine and other woes periodically threatened the indigenous communities of Spanish America with decimation.[14] What we certainly have is an example of Maya discourse that, when compared with similar examples of two centuries earlier, suggests a well-established mechanism for dealing with hardship that was probably rooted in a preconquest tradition of interaction between ruler and ruled.

At the other end of the colonial era is the aforementioned pair of 1605 petitions from Tahnab and Dzaptun, cahob in the Campeche jurisdiction, whose sorry tales of hardship and moving (but presumably exaggerated) descriptions of misery and overburden are laced with reverential rhetoric and appeals for protection and justice. The link between these and the previous examples is not just one of style: the heart of Dzaptun's plea (see Appendix A) is an allegation of failure by the colony to pay for work carried out by the community—in effect, a petition against forced labor. Specifically the petitioners claim that they are cheated of fair payment for cutting wood, and are reduced to misery and death by excessive demands for the transportation of planks, firewood, and hay, and the raising of beams.

The crux of Tahnab's argument is that its location on the road to Campeche has been the cause of its great *numya,* "poverty":[15]

uay tu uol be lae yume tu kinil ti
yakabile lic ca pul cuch yetel chã
tziminob pul hunob ti licix ca kam
ti meson yetel anoria uay tu uol
belae yume hach nachix u lubil
tali ti villa canpeche lahunpiz u
lubil tali tac cahal licil u benel
cah cuchob cah pulhunob chã
tziminob ti kin ti akab ti
maix yab u xocan ca uinicile

Here at the heart of the road, O lord, day and night, we carry burdens, take horses, carry letters, and we also serve in the guest house and at the well. Here at the road's heart, O lord, it is really many leagues to the town of Campeche. Our porters, letter carriers, and horse takers go ten leagues as far as our cah, day and night. Nor are our people great in number.

These labor demands are presented as one of the pincers of the crab that is crushing Tahnab. The other pincer is taxation:

hehele lae ti mati chaanon ca kamab
u yabal meyah tumen mayx pimon
maix u chac ca tan lic ca mentic ca
col ca tzenticcal ca mehenob u noh
layli mayx u chac ca tanlic u cuch
ca patan yan cokol catzil yubte lic
ca ɔaic ichil hunppel hab yetel
cappiz yixmal huncot u lum huncot
ix caxtilla lic ca ɔaic be yume lay
tah oklal hach maix uchac ca tanlic
tumen u yabil meyah yan cokole

Every day there are not enough of us to do so much work, and being few, neither can we manage our fields, nor sustain our children. In particular we are unable to manage the tribute burden that is upon us. Within each year we give a tribute of two mantas, two measures of maize, one turkey, and one hen. This is what we give, O lord, and we really cannot manage it, because of our great work burden

As with the early-nineteenth-century cases above, the petitioners are quick to point out that overburden is counterproductive to the Spaniards, for in diminishing the population of the community—already "not great in number"—excessive demands reduce the ability of the cahnalob to provide services and pay taxes. Demographic reduction results from either death or flight. Tahnab implies that starvation is imminent, and Dzaptun makes such a catastrophe an explicit and present reality, stating that many have died already, and many of the cah's children "are dying from lack of food." The implied threat of flight is backed up by Tahnab in two explicit references to refugees from that cah: *u xocan ca uinic puɔantacobe yume lahuyoxkal u xocan u ppatahob yotochob tumen u yabal meyah yan cokole,* "fifty of our people have fled, O Lord, they've left their homes because we are burdened with so much work";[16] and by a statement to the effect that one Francisco de Magaña is advancing money to cahnalob for beeswax-collecting expeditions into the forest. This arrangement seems to be an illegal circumvention of colonial bureaucracy, denying the province revenue, as Tahnab artfully points out: *u takin halach uinic lic uɔaic tiob uinicob,* "the money he [Magaña] gives the men [the wax collectors] is really the Governor's."

The other Maya strategy apparent in the first examples above—citing Spaniards other than the addressee either as culprits or as authorities verifying the petition's claims—can be seen also in the Tahnab and Dzaptun documents. The villains in the former are Magaña, for luring Maya taxpayers into the forest, and an unnamed "lord governor marshal," for imposing the original "tanda" (labor obligation). This same governor has been the cause of Dzaptun's hardship. The wise Spaniards who also perceived Tahnab to be in such dire straits are "our Lord the oidor Doctor Palacio, who abolished our work burden, because of the great misery we experience," and "our priests who also know of our misery."[17] To these Spaniards are added, in the bicultural parallelism typical of Maya documentation, those authorities who would have meant most to the Maya themselves, *ca yumob ti halach uinicob lic u malelob uaye,* "our lords, the past governors here."[18]

The Dzaptun petition is ambiguous in its definition of who is being addressed directly, who indirectly, and who is being cited as a witness to the cah's misfortune. The original addressee is the King (*yumile ahaue Reye*), probably meaning the viceroy in Mexico City. But later the petition states: "You, O Lord (*yume*), you, O Ruler (*ahau*), likewise you, our Lord (*ca yum*), you O Oidor (*oydore*), you know our misery, you will help us, your children, before the Viceroy (*uiso Rey ahau*)." This is deliberate, for in one sense all these titles address one person, the reader. Or, to view it another way, the inclusion of all relevant authorities as addressees strengthens rather than dilutes the petition from the Maya perspective; their inclusion flatters them, as does the assumption that these authorities are acquainted with and understand the cah's position. The Maya thought of rulers as protectors—a Mesoamerican image, as we have seen—and it is in this spirit that the appeal of these petitions is made; in the ideal world of petitionary hopes, good rulers protect the people from the bad rulers, the latter defined in turn by their failure to protect. In using the future tense—"you will help us . . . you will do good things for us"—Dzaptun's cabildo are expressing their faith in the addressee's commitment to the obligations of rulership.

The claim of excessive poverty, a common feature of indigenous address to the authorities of New Spain, is likewise a pivot of the second category of petition under discussion, that of requests to the Spanish authorities to alienate communal land. As Chapter 16 discussed, Spanish law not only recognized indigenous community land, but in the interests of maintaining the tribute base of each cah, required Maya cabildos to file for permission to sell such land. Two examples of such petitions are revealing.

One involves a tripartite landholding by three associated communities, or complex cahob, the other a chibal property (land held by a patronym group within one cah) subject to the same Spanish laws regarding community tenure.

A sale petitioner was obliged to give a reason for selling. The types of such justifications forwarded by the Maya were essentially milder versions of those presented above to justify requests for the easing of the yoke of colonial demands. Three Maya communities in the Spanish villa of Campeche drew up a petition on August 13, 1737, requesting that a tract of forest be sold in order to pay debts to the provincial treasury, the Contaduría.[19] The three cabildos whose batabob and officers are the petitioners state that a purchaser has yet to be found—*yan mac cu hokol u mane lay,* "there is nobody committed to its purchase"—a possible deception considering that a bill of sale was drawn up only a week later. Perhaps the cabildos were afraid the authorities would think the land was being sold only because a generous offer for it had been made, and indeed the significant sum of 260 pesos is recorded in the sale document. This is not to say, of course, that the cahob's debt was not real, but it suggests that the following phrases were more a customary Maya petitionary rhetoric than an indication of any serious impoverishment of the communities:

tumen hetone u yabal u pax ma
cah . . . ychil numya y tukolal yan
ton . . . u paicuba lay cah lae otzilon

thus the cah has much debt . . . we are in a state of poverty and irritation . . . this cah is bankrupt, we are paupers

bay bic tanu chich tzabal ton hecen
paxan ti ca noh ahau lae lay tumen
mul cantah ca cone tumen minan
tux u talel ton takin botic lay paxan
ti contaduria uchben u talel

for now that which is owed to our Great Ruler is a considerable annoyance to us; thus we've jointly said we will sell, as nobody among us has the money to pay this long-due debt.

The first group of phrases is from the petition to sell; the second is from the bill of sale. Given this use of petitionary language in what is usually a dry and standardized genre, and the unlikelihood that the requested *licencia* was granted within a week, this bill of sale must be seen as a form of petition itself. Always the strategists, the Maya appear to have reversed tack. Either they decided to stop hiding the fact of the purchaser, or in the intervening week the offer was made. In any case, the sale is now presented to the Spanish authorities as a quick means for their treasury to acquire outstanding monies, with a don Joseph Claudio Méndez de Cisneros the fiscal savior: *ca supes u takinil tulacal ti ca kubic ti contadoria tulacal lae lay tumen betic u hunil kubic tu kabil yn yum*—"we'll lock up all the money that we'll deliver to the Contaduría, all of it; this is why we'll draw up the papers and deliver them to m'lord [the purchaser]."

Rebecca Horn's study of Nahua landholding observed that Spanish recognition of indigenous corporate rights to land meant in effect that indigenous farmers "possessed and worked land through membership in the community, with formal title resting with the corporate unit rather than the individual."[20] This describes the Yucatec situation precisely, and explains why lands whose tenure the Mayas clearly saw as being narrower than cah ownership could not be alienated without the permission of the colonial authorities. The Noh family, or members of the Noh chibal, in Homun, faced just such a process in the summer of 1804.[21] Eight named men and ten named women of the Noh, whose chibal was of noble status in Homun, appear as authors and witnesses to a request to alienate *lay u lumob tialob talahan ti u kilacabilob*, "these lands, the property used by their ancestors." The petition points out that, first, it is a joint statement, entered into *tu hunmol*, "together, as one"; second, it is witnessed also by relatives of the petitioners; third, the land is ancestral property; fourth, the boundaries have been marked—*cin chicultic lae*; and fifth, the land is being sold because the petitioners "find themselves in misery and poverty." The words used to describe this poverty—*otzil* and *numya*—are those used in the petitions from Campeche, Baca, and elsewhere, but they are used almost casually, as part of a formula.

Evidently the formula needed to be employed more vigorously, for after a week the Noh drew up a second petition. Of this we have only a Spanish translation of fifteen months later, but even after this is translated again (by myself, into English) the rhetorical force of Maya petitionary language can still be felt and the echoes of its repetitive formula still heard:

We miserable Indians here in this province . . . inform you of our petition . . . to obtain the Governor's superior permission for my poor subjects [names of Noh chibal members] to sell a strip of forest on their property so as to maintain themselves in the truly miserable poverty in which they now are, so as to sell to whatever vecino (i.e., Spaniard) of this town of Homun wants to buy it, for among us poor Indians nobody can afford it . . . so as to alienate it to some vecino . . . in order to buy corn to maintain themselves in the same wretchedness in which they are now.

The third category of petitions under discussion consists of complaints concerning local priests. These grievances can be summarized under three subheadings: accusations of violent conduct (with cah officials the usual victims), accusations of sexual misconduct, and accusations of malpractice (poor performance of sacerdotal duties). Of seven extant examples of such complaints (see Table 12.4), three alleged violence, two made accusations of sexual abuse, and six objected to the priests' offering of sacraments (primarily mass and confession).

A central characteristic of petitions alleging violent acts by priests is the naming of individual Maya victims, if not by patronym then by title of office; all such victims appear to be members of the privileged classes. In the Tihosuco complaint an alguacil of the cah was slandered (*chuc*) by the parish curate, who apparently ordered local militiamen (all non-Maya by this date)[22] to abuse the official:

in yum soldadooba cat u kaxhob	m'lord the soldiers then tied him up
y ca payɔub cat hopi u colcol[-]	and dragged him off, and he was then
payticob cat uɔahob bayoneta	whipped by them, and then they
tu xaxachalotil le algualsilo	stuck him [lit. made imprints] with
hebix u than yn yum curae lay	bayonets, as m'lord the curate
	ordered

The acts of violence of which the priest to Bolompoyche is accused fit a similar premeditated pattern, except in this case the priest, one José Gregorio Canto, does his own dirty work. This lengthy petition not only names sixteen individual Mayas victimized in specified ways by Canto, but states the number of blows given in most of the beatings, and builds a case against the Spaniard of systematic abuse. An example:

Bay xan seferino ɔib tu mentah u	Likewise he tied up Seferino Dzib
káxal cat u mentah u bisal ti mascab	and carried him off to jail in
samahil catun tu mentah u hatzal	Samahil where he beat him, and
samahil y calem u chic u bi[. . .]le	both times he carried him off he
arreal tu bota hunhunten u chic u	made him pay a real, each time he
bisal bey u chic u mentic Yn yum	carried him off m'lord the padre
padre u botic le uinico	made the man pay

The payment in question was probably not money extorted by the priest for himself, but the cost of journeying to Samahil, for Saturnino Balam was likewise made to pay a real on the two occasions when Canto took him to jail in Samahil, where he was given twenty-five and fifty blows, respectively, *yoklal oxɔac col u paxma ti yn yum padre*, "over three mecates of milpa he owed m'lord the padre." Nor did this priest welcome criticism of his actions: he beat Gregorio Piste for complaining about the beating of his brother Diego, an alcalde; another alcalde, Valentín Tun, received twenty-five blows for protesting the beating of a doña Marta Sel (who had missed catechism because her pigs or chickens had escaped from her solar). Similarly the pair of petitions against the local curate by Pustunich and Tinum both specify that a dozen blows were given each boy in catechism class.

The patterns of the complaint by Bolompoyche compare closely with those of a similar petition filed by the altepetl of Jalostotitlan (subject to

Guadalajara) in 1611. This Nahuatl document likewise gives details of the beatings of specific individuals who for the most part held local office (an alcalde, two fiscales, and an eight-year-old sacristan and his mother).[23] The alcalde also suffered the indignity of having his staff of office broken by the priest; in Yucatan two centuries later an ex-batab of Bolompoyche was similarly humiliated when the priest took from him the ceremonial staff and hat (*u Baston y u poc*) of the Assumption Day fiesta. The difference between these particular Nahuatl and Maya petitions is that the former is essentially a complaint by the alcalde over abuses personally suffered, with a second author and other victims mentioned as auxiliary to the petition. The Maya example is more typical of such petitions in both languages, in that it is drawn up and signed by the batab, escribano, an alcalde, and a regidor, none of whom is among the petition's list of victims, with only the batab adding at the end that he has been slandered by the priest.

In other words, the Maya cabildo is acting in its representative capacity. True, the direct or indirect connection of all victims to political office implies representation of the ruling classes alone, but perhaps the cabildo felt their case would be weakened by mention of any commoner victims (whose interests would still be served were the priest removed). The role of the Maya cabildo was to act as intermediary between the indigenous population and the various arms of colonial rule; this is demonstrated not only by the act of petition but also by the apparent fact of Maya officers and their families bearing what might have appeared to the Maya to be the brunt of Spanish brutality as manifested in Canto. When Valentín Tun spoke out against doña Marta Sel's beating he was simply performing his duty as a Maya cabildo officer, just as the cabildos of Tinum and Pustunich were fulfilling the obligations of their offices by complaining about the beating of their sons.[24]

The Nahuatl petition from Jalostotitlan also contains examples of the second subheading of complaint against priests: allegations of sexual impropriety. As we have seen, in petitions of this kind from Spanish America in general, these allegations tend to portray priests as illicit lovers and parents, as seducers of parish women, or simply as publicly lascivious.[25] The Jalostotitlan case includes two of these: a casual reference to the fact that the priest "keeps a lady there at the estancia," and an allegation that the priest seized the alcalde's daughter in the church "and wanted to have her."

This euphemistic reference to attempted rape also occurs in a 1589 petition in Yucatan by a group of five cahob. This document (discussed also in Chapter 11) is signed by don Juan Cool, governor of Peto, don Francisco Utz, governor of Tahdziu, and *alcaldesob tulacal*, "all the alcaldes," but it is written by don Pedro Xiu in his cah of Tixmeuac, and the *nucilob* (principal men) of Oxtzucon and Tetzal are also stated as present. These five cahob are brought together in a concerted effort to be rid of the curate they share, one Andrés Mejía. Three-fourths of the petition consist of introductory and reverential phrases to the addressee, fray Hernando de Sopuerta, an Inquisition commissioner, including the typical expressions of faith in the addressee's able commitment to the protection of the cahob. The nobles and officers produce their ace at the end:

he tilic uɔaic confesar ti	When he gives confession to women,
chuplalobe tilic yalic ua matan a	he then says, "If you do not give
ɔab aba tene matan y ɔab confesar	yourself to me, I will not confess you."
tech lay licil u payic chuplalti matan	This is how he abuses the women:
u ɔab confesar ti ua matan u talel	He won't confess them unless they
chuplal tamuk u pakic u keban	come to him, unless they recompense
chuplalob matan u ɔab confesarti	him with their sins.

Part of what makes this example noticeably Maya is the rhythm of the language, with *chuplal*, "woman," acting as a marker of repetition that simultaneously emphasizes that precious aspect of cah society under attack. Yet the terminology to describe exactly what is transpiring between priest and penitent is, like that of the Jalostotitlan petition, somewhat euphemistic: *ɔabab*, "to give oneself"; *pay*, "to pull, extract, borrow, deprecate, call"; *tal*, "to come"; *pak*, "to recompense, repair" (although with *keb* it can mean "fornicate"); and the final phrase *u coilob tu ɔacan*, which could be translated as "they are poisoned with madness" or "with lust," or even "they are driven to prostitute themselves." The similarity between these terms and those used in the Nahuatl example above suggests a style common to this petitionary subgenre that is not exclusively Maya. Either it is common to the Nahuas and the Maya as another possible Mesoamerican culture trait, or the influence is Spanish, presumably (ironically) clerical. The latter seems the more likely, based on the evidence of a second Maya petition, the anonymous 1774 petition discussed in previous chapters, the language of which is uncompromisingly graphic.

It is not clear whether the time span between these two petitions helps explain their difference of style. Certainly the explicit language of the 1774 document was in use in the sixteenth century.[26] Perhaps the political situation was too sensitive just a generation after Diego de Landa's pogrom of religious persecution for cahob on the edge of the colony (as Peto was, and was thus more suspect) to push their case too strongly. On the other hand, attacking Spanish priests was a risky business at any time, as reflected in the anonymity of the 1774 complaint. As we have seen, the explicit language of this petition, whose accusations were described by its translator of the time as "scathing, audacious . . . grossly excessive," represented a satirical moral protest by the Mayas against the hypocritical imposition of sexual repression by Spanish priests.

The concern for the women of the cah, and their identification as victims, evident in the 1589 complaint is not present in the 1774 petition. The latter, despite its anonymity, is clearly written on behalf of a particular cah—not in the defense of women abused by priests (indeed, the women, who are not Maya, are portrayed as accomplices to the crimes), nor in the interests of any individual residents, but for the sake of an entire community concerned (so the petition would have its readers believe) with high standards of clerical sacramental and social performance. The implication is that this concern originates in the fact that the cahnalob are all, like the *utzil maçehuale* who is punished by the hypocritical priest, good Maya subjects. Whether this was the real motive behind the attack need not be apparent. For although this petition is in many ways unusual, its testimony remains characteristically indigenous not only in its language (colloquial, explicit) and style (conversational, informal) but also in its authorship (collective) and intent (in the communal interest), which is fundamental and apparent even when it is merely implicit, as in this rare case.

Put another way, although the significance of the petitions alleging violence and sexual misconduct by priests is hard (even impossible) to gauge in terms of veracity and incidence, it is not necessary to know how widespread such accusations were in a given area such as Yucatan or how accurate they were. There are two facts apposite to our discussion.

One, curates are singled out in numbers totally disproportionate to their presence in the province, where for most of the colonial period they were a small minority. Assuming that seculars were not a vastly inferior breed more prone to lapses in conduct than Franciscans, this implies a general hostility for which specific grievances had to be either manufactured or exaggerated. Indigenous communities may have accused priests of sexual depravity not because priests so often failed to live up to the high standards expected of them by their parishioners, but because the sex strategy had long proved to be effective in gaining the attention of the Holy Office. Relationships between priests and housekeepers that violated chastity oaths were undoubtedly and not surprisingly common, but the very notion of priestly sexual predacity was sure to draw the attention of the Inquisition. Indeed it is in the files of the Holy Office that petitions of this nature have survived. Perhaps, then, these complaints represented attempts by indigenous peoples to use all means possible to control or resist the arm of colonial rule that was most among them—the parish priest (particular priests at least, if not priests in general).

The second apposite fact is that some of the complaints against priests seem to represent a genuine concern for due and proper sacramental process. Maya petitions may tell us less about the quality of priests in Yucatan (for example), less about the acceptance of the Church and of Christian values by the Maya, and more about the skill with which the Maya (like the Nahuas) exploited the insecurities and preoccupations of Church officials while working the Spanish legal system to their advantage. This still leaves us with the third and final category of complaint—malpractice. This has already been discussed to some extent in this chapter (solicitation of female penitents is obviously a malpractice of the sacrament of confession) as well as at length in Chapter 12. Suffice to reiterate here that Maya petitioners highlighted three sacraments in particular—mass, confession, and the last rites. Of these, the mass seems to have been the chief concern, especially if it was said in a "false" or "twisted" manner. These terms may refer either to the pace and pomp with which the service was (or was not) carried out, or to language: one cabildo complained of their priest's inability to speak Maya. The most common alleged cause of a priest's shortcomings was absenteeism. The fact that many priests were responsible for too many remote parishes to serve them adequately, especially before the increase in clerical numbers in the eighteenth century, never enters into the indigenous perspective of Maya-language petitions, in which a priest's absence is always caused by drunkenness or laziness or the sexual distractions of concubines or by the lack of food in the region or the desire to avoid settling a debt owed to the cah.

This tendency in petitions against priests reflects three main characteristics of all the categories of complaint reviewed above. One is the relentless hostility shown toward persons from outside the cah of authorship—primarily Spanish settlers and priests—that is tempered only by pleas for aid aimed at certain colonial officials. This is coupled with, second, a consistent expression of devotion and loyalty toward the institutions of the colonial period—Church and Crown, Christianity and provincial government—and, third, an unflagging portrait of Maya communities as impoverished, overburdened, and abused. This message—that the cahob were loyal subjects of a system whose health was threatened by the suffering of those subjects at the hands of corrupt and incompetent individuals—no doubt contained some tragic elements of truth. But it also served Maya purposes, being indicative of the strength of the cahob and the tenacious and often subtle strategies of resistance employed by their cabildos.

CHAPTER TWENTY

Election Records

The social and political context of election records is that of indigenous self-rule, as expressed from the Spanish perspective by municipal cabildo government and from the Maya perspective by the role of the cabildo and the larger body of cah notables. This context was given fuller treatment in Chapters 5 and 6; my purpose here is to examine the form and style of the records that Maya notaries made of cah elections.

Record and Process

Thus it is seen; we tell the notary as he writes in the book of our great lord, today, the 22 of December.
—cabildo of Cacalchen, 1690

The first indigenous-language election record from New Spain to be studied was a Nahuatl document of 1630, although the cabildo records of Tlaxcala, which include eleven Nahuatl election documents from the mid-sixteenth century, were known of before this.[1] The Tlaxcalan examples are detailed and structured in a way that suggests the practice was fully established by 1550 in central Mexico.

In possible contrast, the first example of a Maya election record comes from Ticul in 1611, in the form of an 1801 copy.[2] The existence of late-sixteenth-century notarial cah records, complete with the names of cabildo officers down to regidor, implies that some Spanish-approved system of election or appointment of officers was in effect long before 1611. Hernando Cortés is said to have given cabildo titles to local native notables as early as 1525,[3] and judging from the earliest surviving Maya notarial records, the colonial cabildo was in place in Yucatan within a generation after the conquest.[4] Yet the brevity of the 1611 election suggests that the ritual format of the written record of the process was still nascent:

Beluaalob utial haab de mil
seiscientos y dose años uay
ti Aud^a S^n Ant^o ticul

The appointment of officers
for the year 1612 here in San
Antonio Ticul's courthouse

This entry is followed by the names of the batab, escribano, two alcaldes, and four regidors, and then the following statement:

toon Batab th^e Jus^{as} Reg^s y
lix es^{no} uay ti auda Sn Ant^o
ticul lic alic than t ho chahi u
elec^l hab de mil seiscientos y
dose hebix yanil ychil u
libroil elecon ti maix hunpel
u letrail tin luksah maix tin
ɔah xan lay u hahil

We the Batab, Lieutenant, Magistrates, Regidors, and also the notary, here
in the courthouse of San Antonio
Ticul, send to Tihó the copy of the
election statement of the year 1612 as
it appears in the election book. I
neither took away nor added a single
letter. This is the truth.

The document then closes with the date and the names of the 1801 cabildo officers. Whether or not the brevity of the 1611 record was due to laziness on the part of the notary, Juan Ventura Dzul, is unclear. His denial of laziness smacks of formula; and the next extant records date from the 1680's, by which time a set of opening and closing phrases that are compa-rable to the Nahuatl election formulas is being used. The paucity of surviv-ing seventeenth-century election records (see Table 20.1) reflects the la-cuna in extant documentation rather than any cessation of record keeping on the part of the Maya. Probably during this time annual elections were notarized and kept in a discrete book, *u libroyl* (1690), or, *u libroil elecon* (1801). In 1666 the Spanish administration had lists drawn up of the senior cabildo officials in dozens of cahob (including Cacalchen and Tekanto) for the years 1659–65; the names were taken from the *"libro de las elecciones"* kept in each cah. The only extant example of what may have been a book comparable to the *libro de testamentos* fragments from Cacalchen, Ixil, and Tekanto is the run of consecutive late-seventeenth-century election records also from Tekanto—a sizable segment of the cah's "book of elections." The 1611 record only survives because, for some unspecified reason, it was copied and enclosed in the 188-folio compilation of evidence in the 1786–1820 lawsuit between a Spanish landowner and a Maya family over the Sabacche land tract.[5]

The word "election" as it describes the process of political accession or appointment among the colonial Maya carries none of the modern con-notations of popular democracy and means election only in its strict sense of "choose." I use the word because the Maya themselves use it, in loan-word form: *u libroil elec^{on}*, the election book (Ticul, 1611); *u thanil elecçion*, the election statement (Tekanto, 1706); *u gastoil elecçion*, the election cost (Maní, 1733); and so on.[6] It was also the term used by the Spanish authori-ties. However, the Maya had their own term too (see Table 20.2). In the

TABLE 20.1
Extant Maya Election Records and Related Documents

Origin	Election date	Remarks
Ticul	1611	Election of 8 officers; copy certified by 1801 cabildo
Tekanto	December 15, 1683	Election of 21 officers
Tekanto	December 17, 1684	Election of 21 officers
Tekanto	December 14, 1685	Election of 21 officers
Tekanto	December 14, 1686	Election of 21 officers
Tekanto	December 15, 1687	Election of 21 officers
Tekanto	December 14, 1688	Election of 21 officers
Tekanto	December 16, 1689	Election of 21 officers
Tekanto	December 15, 1690	Election of 21 officers
Cacalchen	December 22, 1690	Election of 28 officers
Tekanto	December 15, 1691	Election of 21 officers
Tekanto	December 15, 1692	Election of 21 officers
Tekanto	December 15, 1693	Election of 21 officers
Tekanto	December 15, 1694	Election of 21 officers
Tekanto	December 15, 1695	Election of 21 officers
Tekanto	December 16, 1696	Election of 21 officers
Tekanto	December 16, 1697	Election of 21 officers
Tekanto	December 16, 1698	Election of 21 officers
Tekanto	December 15, 1699	Election of 21 officers
Tekanto	December 19, 1700	Election of 21 officers
Tekanto	December 19, 1701	Election of 21 officers
Tekanto	December 19, 1702	Election of 21 officers
Tekanto	December 19, 1703	Election of 21 officers
Tekanto	November 9, 1704	Election of 21 officers
Tekanto	December 1706	Election of 21 officers
Ixil	1766–67	Wills showing new cabildo taking office in late November
26 cahob	September 1789	Maya translation of ordinance instructing October 30 elections and records delivery
Xcupilcacab	February 15, 1812	Example of a petition and *terna* reelection proposal to replace the batab
[illegible]	December 23, 1821	Election of at least 51 officers (including church choir posts)

SOURCES: TS: 62; DT: 28; AGEY-A, 1, 1; LC: 47; T-LAL-RMC, 1, 25, 2; MT: 49, 65.

Spanish translation of an 1812 reelection petition from Xcupilcacab,[7] the word election is used where the Maya uses *ãlic* (the *ã*, written with a tilde, is *aa*, the verb being *aal*, or *al*, to say or command). The implication is that the process was one of appointment rather than selection by voting.

It is tempting to see the verb *al* as one of the roots of *belnaalob* (1611), or *ah belnalob* (1690, Cacalchen), "the officers," though that is not the case. *Bel* means "office, tenure, occupation"; it appears in the Pío Pérez dictionary as *belnal*, "regidor," and *ah benal*, "officer,"[8] and in Cacalchen's seventeenth-century testaments as *u bel alcaldesob*, "the alcalde officers," and *antic u bel*, "the protecting officer." The *-nal* in belnal is the same agentivizing suffix that is in cahnal; thus the terms describe a person pertaining to an office or a cah.

In a clear example of cah-to-cah variation, Tekanto does not use *belnal*

TABLE 20.2

(a) Maya Election Verbs and Phrases

(1) The meeting

multuntic, to form a stone mound, to gather; belnal, officer
ti multumtic ah belnallob, "at the meeting of the appointed officers"
u multunticob tu mul, "they gathered at the meeting, they met"
u multunticob tu chacancunahob, "they gathered and appeared"
ti hun molon, "in one group, at the meeting"

(2) The appointing

*kaah, to agree; chich . . . nahi, to elect, choose; al/aal, to say; al/aal . . . than, to
make a statement, order; chicaan, to clarify, make evident*
u Kah lay ah Belnalob, "this the agreement of the appointed officers"
u tumutob cabildosob, "the appraisal/acceptance of the cabildo officers"
u yalahob u binsabalob, "to state and carry [i.e., to determine]"
tu chich cunahi xan u thanil calaacob, "to elect and to order the statement"
alic than . . . u elec¹, "to make the election statement"
u chiccanic u thanil eleccion, "to make clear the election statement"
u chebal u chich cunic . . . , "to corroborate/validate strongly . . . [an election]"

(3) The serving

*mektan, to govern, rule; tanlah, to serve; thanoklal, to make statements for,
represent; an, protect, aid; yacuntah, protect, defend, love*
bin mektanticob u tanlahil, "they shall govern as the servant of"
minan mamac than oklal, "there is nobody to represent us"
antic u bel, "the protecting officer"
hach malob u yacuntic cah, "he protects the cah very well"

(b) Nahuatl Election Verbs and Phrases

(1) The meeting

centlalia, to gather
otitocencauhque, "we prepared, arranged ourselves"
tonochintin totencopa omochiuh, "it was done by the order of all of us"

(2) The appointing

ixquetza, to elect, choose; pepena, to elect, choose; nonotza, to agree, deliberate
tictlalia yn toelecion, "we set down our election"
otictlalique yn aquin quimoyecanilis, "we ordered who is to lead"

(3) The serving

*tequipanoa, to serve; cuitlahuia, to care for; ipan motlatoltzinoa, to speak
  about something, to see to, to take care of*

SOURCES: Maya, same as Table 20.1, with the addition of LC: 30; Nahuatl, Haskett 1985:
121–22.

but rather a loan-based equivalent, *cabidosob*—the Spanish plural *cabildos*
treated as a singular, as was standard practice with most introduced office
titles, and given the *-ob* plural. The word is thus Mayanized in spelling,
grammar, and meaning (since the Maya included more offices in their
cabildos than the Spaniards did).⁹

In comparing Nahuatl election records with those in Maya, we find
that Maya municipal elections, in apparent contrast to those from central

Mexico, seem not to have had an electorate. Certainly there is no mention of voters in any of these documents, nor any record of actual ballot-taking, as if the process of nomination and election consisted of the sitting cabildo and cah principales choosing their successors from among their own number. Indeed, the presence and role of the outgoing cabildo is always stated, even emphasized, as is the cah itself, for the electoral process was part of what defined a cah. This is also the essence of what took place in the altepetl, with the difference that the Nahuas sometimes made reference to electorates and to voting.

The term *elección*, then, must have had different connotations at the indigenous and Spanish ends of the process. The colonial authorities received a record of the election of nominal officers or candidates, who were then confirmed more or less pro forma in their posts. Whether the Maya use of the term *aal* predates the conquest or not is unknown, but the indigenous method of gathering and selecting was certainly a Mesoamerican tradition. The existence, and colonial-era use, of a full election vocabulary in Maya presents a picture of preconquest precedent and suggests that traditional indigenous practice continued beneath the thin veil of Spanish procedure, among the Nahuas as among the Maya, as Table 20.2 demonstrates.

The postconquest act of selection took place in the cah *audiencia*, "courthouse," used by both Spaniards and Mayas to denote either the room or structure where the cabildo met, or simply the cabildo session itself (especially when there was no separate cabildo building). The use of *tu kunayl*, "in the church of," by Cacalchen and some other cahob seems to say that the election was held in the church. Perhaps Cacalchen could only afford one public building and used the church as audiencia. Because the Mayas normally used the Spanish *iglesia* to refer to the cah church, there may have evolved a colonial-era distinction between the two terms, with the Spanish loan carrying the full weight of the religious function of the church building, and the Mayas referring simply to the structure as used for secular purposes. An alternative theory is that, because the building is called "the church of our great lord the King," the phrase could be a reference to the "royal" in *autençia Real* (used by Spaniards only for the high court), and thus *kuna*—"holy (*ku*) house (*na*)"—becomes a reverential way to describe the courthouse. I am not aware of any other postconquest written conceptual links between "royal" and "holy," however. Most likely, cabildos met in churches until courthouse buildings were constructed in the eighteenth and nineteenth centuries, with a room in the church serving as the audiencia; the doors, tables, and chairs bought by the cabildo of Ebtun for their "audiencia" in 1811 may have been intended for just such a room.[10] In any case, even though the postconquest building where elections took place must have been different from the preconquest one, the language and the procedure can hardly have changed since the fifteenth century.

One obvious colonial innovation would have been the linking of the electoral cycle to the European calendar. The meeting of the cabildo to select officers was annual, toward the end of the year. The statement in the Cacalchen record below that officers were being selected for 1690 is presumably an error for 1691, although cabildos-elect seem to have assumed office immediately, which may be what the escribano is indicating here. This immediate transfer of power is suggested by evidence from eighteenth-century Ixil. In that cah the will of a Marta Coba, who died on December 3, 1766, was drawn up by the cabildo of 1767. Maya testaments record only the deathday, not the day the will was dictated, but obviously this particular will could not have been dictated *after* December 3. The new cabildo must have assumed office on or before that date. Another will, that of a Francisco Couoh who died December 23, 1766, is recorded by the 1766 cabildo, but Couoh could have held onto life for over a month after making his will—indeed it appears in the Ixil collection right before that of a man who died on November 12, implying that the 1767 Ixil cabildo took over between November 12 and December 3. There may have been a trend toward earlier elections in Yucatan, or, more typically, there were regional variations: Ixil, late November; Tekanto, mid-December; Cacalchen, late December. If this was so, a 1789 ordinance requiring elections on October 30 would have wrecked the pattern, although it is hard to imagine punctual compliance or the long-term insistence on this change by provincial authorities.[11]

Opening and Closing Phrases

The cabildo officers . . . while they are gathered publicly in meeting, shall declare who the alcaldes, regidores, majordomos, and alguaciles will be in the coming year.
                              —cabildo of Tekanto, 1690

A typical Maya election record, that of 1690 from Cacalchen, exhibits opening phrases stating time, place, and purpose, and a closing statement affirming and legitimizing the event and its record.[12] These paragraphs frame a simple list of officers for the coming year—not only the cabildo officers whose titles ratified most Maya notarial documents (batab, sometimes teniente, alcalde, regidor, and escribano), but also the body that I have termed fourth-tier officers (listed in Table 6.4). The Cacalchen record begins:

U Kah lay ah Belnalob cutalel
u yocolob ti yabil de 1690 añ
uay ti autençia Real tu kunayl
ca noh ahau ti Rey ah tepal ti
hun molon uay ti autençia
liciix ti multumtic ah
belnallob con cabido uay tu
canan cahil ca yumilan ti ah
bolon pixan san p° y san pª
cacalchen lay ilah liciix c alic
ti es^{no} ca u ɔibte tu libroyl
ca noh ahau hele en 22 de
ticiembre 1690 añ

The agreement of the appointment
of the officers to come for the year
1690, here in the royal courthouse,
the church of our great lord the
King Ruler, at the meeting here in
the courthouse, here at the gathering of appointed officers—we the
cabildo—here in Cacalchen, the cah
protected by our lords the blessed
St. Peter and St. Paul. Thus it is seen;
we tell the notary as he writes in the
book of our great lord, today, the 22
of December, 1690.

A comparison of this and the Tekanto record from the same year gives an idea of the general characteristics of the opening formula and the variations used by particular escribanos. Some of these characteristics of course apply in general terms to all colonial Maya notarial documents, since by definition such records needed to affirm place, date, and purpose in order to be valid; also, such affirmations anchored the document to the cabildo officers whose dutiful actions it was the record of. Except for changes in spelling and diacritics, Tekanto's election records from 1683 to 1706 all open (and close) with the same phrases.[13] The following is an except from the 1690 record that is reproduced in full in Appendix A:

hele 15 deçiembre de 1690 años
ti ocanobix ti audiençia Real ti
cabidosob . . . mahanquenile tamuk
u multunticob tu mul alcaldesob
Regidoresob mayoldomosob
aluasilesob bin u alacob ychil yabil
de 1691 años cutalele lay cah lemob
ti ca yumil ti dios yetel ca noh ahau
ah tepal hex cat ɔoci u multunticob
tu chacancunahob . . . tu chich
cunahi xan u thanil calaacob
bin mektanticob u tanlahil
Rey ah tepal

Today, December 15, 1690, having
entered the royal courthouse, the
cabildo officers . . . while they are
gathered publicly in meeting shall
declare who the alcaldes, regidors,
majordomos, and alguaciles will be
in the coming year, 1691, in this
cah entrusted to our lord Dios and
our great lord Ruler. Thus have
they just gathered and appeared . . .
to elect and order the statement of
[those who] shall govern in the
service of the King Ruler.

To complete the process of legitimation, the outgoing cabildo officers restated their business and the nature of the document, usually with phrases similar to those of the opening, and the notary recorded the officers' names and the date (in the Spanish manner). The purpose of election phrases was to link Maya election records intertextually to the greater body of cah notarial documents, for they were intended not only to satisfy the requirements of colonial law but also to confirm the legitimacy within the Maya community of the cah authorities and the process by which that power was perpetuated from one cabildo to another.

To detect Maya cultural elements in these documents we cannot make a direct textual comparison with a Spanish model document, because such a model does not exist.[14] Nevertheless, there are distinct patterns of language that are indigenous in character and, moreover, resemble traits visible in Nahuatl election documents. The following example is from the central Mexican altepetl of Cuernavaca, in 1673:[15]

Nica tictlalia y toleccion y tehuati	Here we set down our election, here
y nican ipa yn itlacoaltepetzin y	in the precious town of the noble-
cihuapilli Santa Maria Asupcion	woman Santa María de la Asunción,
nica vila quaugnahuac ...	here in the Villa Cuauhnahuac ...

A rhythm is established in the Cacalchen example by the repetition of *uay*, "here," and *liciix*, whose meaning is broader, as my translation above reflects, but I think conveys a sense of "now too" or simply "and." The pattern is uay-uay / liciix-uay-liciix, with the reference locations being audiencia-audiencia-cah-audiencia. This is much like the Nahuas' use of *nica(n)*, "here," to set up a repetitive rhythm of reference to altepetl (or audiencia)-altepetl-altepetl. Similarly, the reverential language used in Cuernavaca to describe the altepetl and its patron Virgin—language that is a classic indigenous hallmark—is paralleled by the terms of reverence used by the cabildo of Cacalchen to describe the community's patron saints and its audiencia (by association with the "King," which could be a reference to the governor of Yucatan or the viceroy of New Spain as much as the king of Spain).

The Nahuatl example also compares in a similar, though not identical, manner to the Tekanto phraseology. One of the basic traits of indigenous discourse in Mesoamerica was the use of semantic couplets. They are clearly visible above: Cuernavaca is described in parallel phrases as "the precious town of ..." and "the Villa ..."; Tekanto is given both its Christian and Maya names, and its location is described in terms of a pair of Spanish-Maya couplets—*u cuchcabal* with *u governaçionil*, and Mérida with Tihó. The Tekanto opening text continues with the couplet device to describe the various stages of the electoral process: the cabildo "gather and appear" to "elect and order" those who shall "govern and serve [lit. in the service of]."

Tekanto also conforms to the other rhetorical pattern described above. This cah is given reverential treatment not by way of the elevation of its courthouse or patron saint(s), but more directly, by its connection to Mérida and thus to the whole colony, and its link to God and the *ah tepal*—probably the provincial governor. In the latter case, the link is expressed simply by placing emphasis (*lem*) on the locative *ti*. Common to all three of these examples (Cacalchen, Tekanto, and Cuernavaca) is an assertion of importance by association with higher powers—self-promotion on the part of the altepetl or cah. This concern was fundamental to Mesoamerican politics and self-identity.

༺

CHAPTER TWENTY-ONE

Quasi-Notarial Genres

Most of the Maya-language sources that have been discussed here have been mundane, notarial documents that more or less follow the formats of Spanish official or legal genres. But there was also an important, smaller body of Maya documentary literature that was not mundane, and, from the Spanish perspective, was unofficial. This material might be termed quasi-notarial, in that the author may have been a cabildo or cofradía escribano or a maestro, or he may have been another Maya not recognized or sanctioned as a notary by the Spanish authorities. Unlike the material already discussed, these unofficial writings served no purpose in the colonial system; indeed, if discovered, they would most likely have been destroyed by the ecclesiastical authorities, who tended to associate unofficial writing with non-Christian religious practices, as they had done all pre-conquest manuscripts. At the very least, the civil authorities would have declared such material "invalid," as happened in the one known case when a portion of a quasi-notarial text, the Title of Yaxkukul, was submitted in 1793 to a court in support of a land claim.

Books, Titles, and Chronicles

> Thus, today, I declare and relate whatever occurred . . .
> I interpret what I heard . . .
> —Title of Chicxulub

The best known of the quasi-notarial genres are the Books of Chilam Balam, which contain a variety of fables and traditions that are mythical and historical, prophetic and calendrical, satirical, ritual, and curative or medicinal. Aside from the occasional signed note, the Books are anonymous, but they were maintained and guarded by the particular cah from which they are named (the Chumayel and Tizimin being the lengthiest examples). Indeed, most postconquest Maya communities may have kept such records along with the volumes of official, notarial documents. Maintaining and transcribing these compilations must have been considered in the cah as an official duty of the maestro or the notary of the cabildo or cofradía.[1]

The Chilam Balam have been mined and interpreted by scholars for a variety of purposes, but they have yet to be placed firmly in the context of other examples of colonial-era Maya literature, either other quasi-notarial material such as the "chronicles" or the large body of notarial documentation.[2] Table 21.1 outlines such a comparison, focusing on the three "chronicles" of Calkiní, Chicxulub, and Yaxkukul and also the Xiu "papers." I have dubbed all these documents "titles," because their purpose was to assert and maintain the titles to the privileges of specific chibalob and the territorial boundaries of the cahob in which these nobles were prominent. Furthermore, although these texts bear some resemblance to the annals of the Nahuas, such as passages with year-by-year entries, and authors of high status and some education, they are more closely comparable to the Nahua titles.[3]

A detailed comparison of Maya and Nahua examples of this genre follows below, but several points are worth making now. Titles in both languages share these features: they contain a community boundary survey dated very soon after the conquest, of which the title claims to be an original firsthand account, although other evidence indicates that titles were composed in the late-colonial period; the documents were usually preserved because they were submitted as legal evidence in land litigation; they include references to the adoption of Christianity under Spanish sponsorship; authorship can be inconsistent and chronology not always linear; and they are an expression of corporate ideology based on a traditional understanding of local myth-history. Inevitably there are also some basic differences between the genres in Yucatan and central Mexico: extant Nahua titles are far greater in number and far more varied than the four surviving Maya examples; the "popular" viewpoint of the Nahua texts is in their Maya counterparts more the lore of the nobility, even that of a particular family, thus contrasting altepetl-centrism with an emphasis on chibal as well as cah; and whereas (according to Lockhart) "Something insulated the titles genre from other kinds of [Nahua] writing,"[4] I wish to show that Yucatan's titles shared important common ground with the Books of Chilam Balam and notarial land records.

The basic structure of the title—a dynastic or community history with mythological overtones preceding a territorial survey—seems to have Mesoamerican cultural roots. Certainly the Yucatec-Nahua similarities are paralleled elsewhere in the Maya area. A close cousin is the Chontal Maya

TABLE 21.1
Comparison of Quasi-Notarial Texts

Text	Origin and Purpose	Intertextual links	View of time	Structure and style
Title of Yaxkukul (chibal: Pech)	Putative author: Ah Macan Pech. Compiled 18th c., by unknown, from earlier texts, to defend Pech status and cah boundaries.	Most of text parallels the Chicxulub. Mentions Nakuk Pech.	Mostly Christian calendar, also katun round. Vaguely linear.	Chibal's founding of cah; conquest account; land treaty. Episodic but repetitive.
Title of Chicxulub (chibal: Pech)	Putative author: Nakuk Pech. Compiled 18th c., by unknown, from earlier texts, to defend Pech status and cah boundaries.	Most of text parallels the Yaxkukul. Mentions Ah Macan Pech.	Mostly Christian calendar, also katun round. Vaguely linear.	Chibal's founding of cah; conquest account; land treaty. Episodic but repetitive.
Title of Calkiní (chibal: Canul)	Authors: cah notaries. Compiled 1821 from earlier texts, to defend cah boundaries.	Some textual parallels with Pech titles. Cites 1557 land treaty with Maní.	Christian calendar. Linear, but vaguely so in parts.	Founding of cah by several chibalob; conquest account; land treaties. Episodic but repetitive.
Title of the Xiu (cah: Maní)	Authors: cah notaries; some entries signed by Xiu nobles.	Some textual parallels with other titles. Includes 1557 land treaty with Calkiní.	Mostly Christian calendar and linear. Minimum use of katun round.	Chibal's founding of cah; conquest account; land treaty. Series of separate entries.
Books of Chilam Balam of Chumayel and Tizimin	Authors: cah maestros? Compiled 18th c. from earlier texts, to maintain cah record of myth, history, etc.	Stylistic and conceptual textual parallels with titles.	Pre-Christian calendar, including katun round. Cyclical.	Series of often unrelated episodes including accounts-myths to do with settlement, warfare, and land.
Notarial land records	Authors: cah notaries. Legal records, to defend cah interests.	Close parallels with titles' land treaties. Some conceptual links to Chilam Balam.	Christian calendar only. Fully linear.	Mostly Spanish legal formats, with Maya style and language of land description, survey, and original settlement.

SOURCES: TY, TCh, TC, TX, CBC, CBT. On notarial records, see Chap. 18.

Title of Acalan-Tixchel; also related are the Annals of the Cakchiquels, the Historia de los Xpantzay, and other, briefer Guatemalan titles. In terms of dynastic self-promotion rooted in myth-history, the Popol Vuh is also a related genre; it can be read as an extended history of the Cavek dynasty of the Quiché Maya.[5]

The structural and substantive similarities between the Maya titles suggest that they were copied and adapted over the centuries from earlier manuscripts, in a similar manner to the reproduction of the Books of Chilam Balam (for which, like the Pech and Canul titles, we have no pre-eighteenth-century examples). This is not to say that there was necessarily once an original model Chilam Balam and a model title, but there were probably local model versions of segments of these genres whose similarity can be accounted for by a common set of literary conventions (similar to those that have defined Western novels, plays, and so on). That these conventions have preconquest roots is suggested by evident elements of non-Western style and structure, by the appearance of some of these traits in the titles and the Chilam Balam and notarial land records, and by Juan Xiu's claim in 1685 that he was copying down a record in "*carácteres*" (he was probably copying down such a claim by an earlier author). In the case of the two Pech titles from near-neighboring cahob,[6] there are such close parallels—to the point of frequent identical sentences in near-identical paragraphs—that cross-fertilization or a common source seem certain. A fifth title, published as the Codex Mérida, may be the remnant of another such manuscript from this region, although it appears more to be a nineteenth-century copy of portions of the Pech accounts of the conquest.[7]

Among notarial documents this tradition of recopying earlier records takes on a clearer form and purpose, old wills and land agreements being proof of property ownership, which is reflected in some of the titles. The Calkiní is a sequence of records, some of them conventional notarial entries, that seem to have been copied down in 1821, when the cabildo also went to Maní to get a copy of the 1557 land agreement that is part of the Title of the Xiu—all this in preparation for land litigation. In the Xiu title, the sequence of entries is less cohesive for the copying was apparently not done at the same time; some documents were written by Xiu nobles asserting their status and privileges in the manner of the Pech; others were written by Maní's cofradía or cabildo notary and are more oriented toward the cah.

Because literacy was restricted in preconquest and colonial Maya society, and because Maya discourse, even on paper, carries a strong oral component, we might expect quasi-notarial texts to draw upon oral traditions as well as written sources. In fact, the two are intertwined; the text expresses the oral narrative, which is itself perpetuated by the copying and reading out of the text. The most succinct indication of this process is a phrase in the Chicxulub, in which the "author," Nakuk Pech, sums up the role of generations of quasi-notarial authors: *tin tzolah u xicinob. Tzol* is here a verb meaning "to organize, place in order, explain, interpret"; *xicin* is "ear, hearing." The phrase is thus "I place the hearings in order," or "I interpret what I heard."[8]

In terms of authorship and purpose, notarial records and the titles share important common ground. Generally speaking, all were corporately inspired, intended to defend cah and chibal, whose interests coincided in that the chibalob in question dominated their cahob. The 1567 petitions known as the "letters" to the Spanish monarch include examples from Canul, Pech, and Xiu batabs promoting themselves and their communities as much as do the later titles; in particular the Yaxkukul and Chicxulub use putative conquest-era authors, Ah Macan (christened don Pedro) Pech, and Nakuk (christened don Pablo) Pech, to promote the late-colonial noble representatives of the chibal.

The climactic passages of the titles are the portions describing mid-to-late-sixteenth-century land treaties; though these differ somewhat in style from notarial land records, their essential purpose is the same (defense), and so is their basic construction (a ritualized border walk). Something of the cross-genre parallels in descriptions of this ritual has been said in Chapter 15; here I wish simply to emphasize that these parallels show that the mythical-historical passages of the titles grow out of the border walks that they precede. At one end of the discourse scale are notarial land documents whose description of specific borders evokes post-Mayapan ancestral settlements and postconquest validations of boundaries; indigenous form is secondary to the substantive purpose of colonial legal format. At the other end of that scale are Chilam Balam passages having no colonial format or reference to specific points in space or time, which emphasize and play on the traditional form of the memory and description of migration and settlement.

In between lie the titles. They are concerned with specific land boundaries, when they were agreed upon and with whom, but these assertions of cah territorial integrity and the status of ruling noble families inspire the use of traditional descriptions of how such lands and privileges were established and confirmed. The walking of real land boundaries ritually represents an original migration and settlement that is mythically placed in the historical contexts of the recapitulation of boundaries after both the Mayapan wars and the conquest wars. This dual concern with colonial specifics and traditional forms of memory and discourse produces a mixture of linear chronology using Christian-calendar date entries (variously between 1511 and 1553) and references to the Maya calendar of katun rounds (the primary time reference of the Chilam Balam), with the events of the Mayapan and conquest wars and movements interspersed in such a way as to suggest cyclical continuity.

In the Calkiní, for example, the Canul and allied batabs present tribute to Montejo and welcome their new encomendero, in the middle of which the Canul leave Mayapan and establish the cahob of the Calkiní region, further details of which are provided after an account of the late-sixteenth-century land treaties between these cahob. The Chicxulub likewise inserts an account of post-Mayapan migration around the peninsula, ending in the Pech founding of the cah, within a description of the conquest and the cooperative and conquering role played by the Pech nobility; it too returns to repeat preconquest and conquest-era myth-history after describing a colonial treaty between the cahob of the region. The Yaxkukul is structurally a more pro-Spanish version of the Chicxulub, cutting most of the preconquest history and emphasizing the positive role of the Pech in the conquest.

This editing may have been done in preparation for the 1793 lawsuit. If this was so, it suggests a Maya awareness of the conflict between indigenous and Spanish cultures of political promotion in writing. For the Spanish authorities, Maya styles of historiographical manipulation and propaganda undermined the historical validity and legitimacy of a text, whereas for the Maya these very techniques were central to a written tradition of establishing historically rooted legitimacy, authority, and prestige. This tradition was thousands of years old; many of the characteristics of Mesoamerican hieroglyphic texts are also present in the colonial-era Maya titles—the preoccupations with genealogy and warfare, for example, and a willingness to falsify dates, telescope events, and reinterpret the past to serve the propagandistic ends of chibal and cah. The intended audience of preconquest propaganda by the dominant Maya elite—competing peers and subdominant commoners—is augmented in the colonial period by a new superdominant group to whom the propagandists must petition in order to receive recognition of status.[9]

A Quasi-Notarial Case Study: Yaxkukul

They will see the truth of the measuring of the land here around the cah.
—cabildo and principales in the Title of Yaxkukul

Since a comprehensive study of all these texts would require a volume of its own, I have selected a portion of one such manuscript to illustrate in detail some of the observations made above. This portion is the land treaty that ends the Title of Yaxkukul, the "Deslinde de las Tierras." I chose this portion on account of its comparative accessibility, its importance to the Maya (the text has survived in several versions and was submitted to the Spanish courts), and its contextual relationship to other genres (in particular Nahuatl titles, on the one hand, and Maya notarial land records, on the other).[10]

In 1793 a delegation of principales from the cah of Yaxkukul, under the leadership of their batab, a member of the Pech nobility, presented to a Spanish judge a lengthy Maya document that was said to be the record of a survey of Yaxkukul's territory that had allegedly occurred in 1544. A certified copy of 1769 was shown to the colonial authorities and was rejected by them as "having no validity, being in need of the authorization of magistrates and others."[11] The errors of the document, the judge implied, suggested that it had been fabricated, and without much ingenuity. That judgment on the Title of Yaxkukul, particularly the "Deslinde de las Tierras," is the starting point of the following analysis, which will explore some crucial aspects of the genre, including content, context, purpose, legitimacy, and effect.

The foundation for this exploration is a comparison between the features of the Deslinde and those of the central Mexican titles that have been the best studied among extant Mesoamerican examples. I have drawn ten characteristics of central Mexican titles from recent scholarship on the subject, primarily by Stephanie Wood,[12] and find all ten to apply to the titles in general, nine of the ten applying specifically to the Deslinde.

The first and second of these characteristics relate to the purpose of the document, the first being its style. The characteristic upon which the Deslinde and the other parts of the titles diverge indicates something of the relationship between annals and titles, and thus something of the purpose of the Deslinde. Broadly speaking, annals promoted their municipality (and sometimes dynasty)[13] of authorship by means of a date-entry narrative of sixteenth-century (and later) events; titles claimed to authenticate that community's territorial rights. The chief purpose of the two is very similar, and a similar style of writing might therefore be expected. Unlike a Nahua title, however, the Deslinde seems to be trying to address a nonindigenous audience, and it shows some differences of style. Nahua titles (and, to a lesser extent, annals) were usually not written in the tidy, formulaic, style of indigenous escribanos; their format is loose, their chronology is often inconsistent, and their orthography and vocabulary are sometimes aberrant. Such characteristics do not really apply to the Deslinde, although they do suit the titles, which have something of the feel of an oral performance, replete with the repetition and nonlinear chronology that is evident in the Chilam Balam texts (and indeed is characteristic of Mesoamerican discourse).

Late-eighteenth-century Pech notables must have been aware of the discrepancy between these titles promoting their version of sixteenth-century events—in the pre-Columbian tradition of self-promotion by the nobility—and contemporary notarial documentation that was considered legitimate by the judicial officers of the colony. As I have already suggested, the Deslinde may represent an attempt to strip the work of some of its indigenous elements to make it acceptable to the Spanish but without sacrificing the essence of its boundary claims and its reaffirmation of Pech status. In structure and style the Deslinde is at first glance a typical Maya notarial product. For example, it contains all the five defining features of a Maya notarial document (discussed in Chapter 18): a date of completion (albeit invented), a cah of origin, the names of authors and witnesses, an elaborate opening, and an explicit ending. But if this was an attempt to Hispanize the Pech document, it seems to have been a failure, in that the Spanish authorities immediately smelled an indigenous rat, peppering their judgment with phrases like *por carecer de autorizazion* ("for lack of authorization"), *suponiendo* ("supposing"), and *pretendiendo* ("claiming"). Reflecting this failure is the fact that the Deslinde reveals, upon closer inspection, most of the more specific characteristics (the remaining nine) of a colonial title.

The second characteristic has to do directly with land. The principal component of a title is the description of a sixteenth-century land survey of the territory claimed by the altepetl or cah. This is essentially what the Deslinde is: the description of an alleged journey on foot along the boundary of the Yaxkukul lands. Following the introductory phrases and the listing of witnesses, the bulk of the document walks the reader from the first boundary marker—the entrance to the well at Chacnicte—round the territory to the twenty-eighth—a stone marker at Yokmuux—which is adjacent to the first. It appears, in other words, to be a typical piece of ambulatory land description:[14]

xaman tan yn binel latulah u kuchul tu cacabil yaxycim nohoch mul tu lakin yan multun capel ca sutnac chikin tan u binel layli ah Kumcheelob yn lake ca kuchuc yokol chen piste ti yan multuni ca manac chikin tan . . .	I go north until one's arrival at the settlement at the great mound of Yaxicim; to its east are two stone mounds; we / one turn(s) westward where my friends the people of Kumche are; we arrive at the Piste well, where there is a stone mound; we go west . . .

Yet when compared closely with other ambulatory examples, the Deslinde seems less structured, less rhythmic. Take, for example, a 1735 description from the twin cahob of Dzibikal and Uman:[15]

. . . chikin tan u binel u lahcapis	. . . going westward to the 12th stone
alcab multun tu chun copo caye	mound at the base of a fig tree,
chumuc chikin tan u binel u	across the path, going westward to
yoxlahun alcab multun yok canal	the 13th stone mound on high land,
lum caye chumuc chikin tan u	across the path, going west-
binel u canlahun alcab multun	ward to the 14th stone mound
yicnal xan caye chumuc . . .	among palm trees, across the path . . .

Two contrasts stand out. First, pronominal reference in the Deslinde appears to shift almost at random, between first-person singular and possibly plural, and the third person. In the other example the pronominal reference is consistently third person. Second, the Dzibikal and Uman description is tightly tied to a pattern of repetition that hinges upon the progressive numbering of the stone mounds, the repetition of the cardinal direction whether the orientation of the surveyors has changed or not, and the repetition of the phrase *caye chumuc*. In other examples the Maya use the phrase *bay xan*, "likewise, then also," to itemize a survey.[16] The border description of the Deslinde uses the familiar markers, but its rhythm is jumpy and less easily caught. There are still cycles of description, but "they are not identical," as William Hanks pointed out in a linguistic study of the Deslinde, "varying somewhat in length, content and order of elements."[17] These are hints, then, of the anomalies of style (relative to mundane notarial genres) typical of titles.

The Deslinde was accompanied by a map, as were its comparable sections in the other titles. None of these maps has survived, but they might have been much like the maps discussed earlier—bird's-eye views of the land, with straight border lines dotted with circles to represent stone-mound markers or tree markers, and squares to represent abandoned or seasonal houses. Like the Deslinde, the Chicxulub title contains a detailed description of its border outline to accompany the map, but the description lacks the Deslinde's introduction, and the rhythm seems even less regular; it also emphasizes the presence during the survey of the neighboring batabs of Ixil, Conkal, Yaxkukul and Baca, as well as don Pablo of Chicxulub. Its date, of course dubious, is 1542.

The third through sixth of the genre characteristics are concerned with the Spaniards: as colonial authorities, as conquerors, as instigators of congregación, and as proselytizers. The survey of a title was supposed to have been conducted under official Spanish auspices, resulting in an explicit or implied confirmation of local indigenous territorial holdings by the colonial authorities. The Yaxkukul border walk is legitimized by references to a number of prominent Spaniards, one of the most significant in point being Tomás López, the oidor responsible for initiating in Yucatan the first of the congregaciones. At that time López also accompanied the principal men of a number of Maya communities on notarized border walks in an effort to prevent territorial disputes arising out of congregaciones. López acquired a certain notoriety as a result of this policy, which, together with a number of tribute reductions, made him highly unpopular among the encomenderos. Conversely he became a key authority for Maya claimants to cite, to wit a boundary agreement between the Maya governors of Tekom, Tixcacal, and Cuncunul in 1600, in which "our territorial limits were determined for us . . . by the great lord oidor Tomás López"—*u hol c luumob xotan toon . . . tumen halach uinic tomas Lopez oydor.*[18] Yaxkukul's reference is similar:[19]

ton con g^{or} y alcaldes Regidoresob y ess^{no} uay ti cah Sta Crus de mayo yaxkukul lae y tulacal u nucil uinicob no xibtacob yohellob u pach u tocoynailob cahanilob ca talob uay Sta Crus de mayo Ca tu yalah Ca yum alcalde mayor Dⁿ Thomas Lopes tali uattimara lay ulsavi tal nachil u thanil u pislahal luumob . . .	We, the governor, alcaldes, regidors, and notary here in the cah of Santa Cruz de Mayo Yaxkukul, with all the principal men, the elders, who know the borders of the houses abandoned when they were ordered to come here to Santa Cruz de Mayo by our lord the alcalde mayor don Tomás López, who came from Guatemala empowered to measure the lands for the sustenance of all residents without exception . . .

Later in the document, seven Spaniards are named as witnesses affirming:[20]

u hahil u pislahal luum tumen ca yum Juees Dn Thomas Lopes uay tu pach cah yaxkukul lae	the truth of the measuring of the land here around Yaxkukul by our lord judge don Tomás López.

References to other Spaniards are also intended to lend the document an air of validity, whether they be the five Spaniards considered most important by the Yaxkukul Maya—the king, the adelantado, the governor of the colony, the local encomendero, and the local priest—or Spanish witnesses assigned to legitimize the border survey.[21]

As accounts of the conquest complete with date entries spanning up to forty-two years, the titles repeatedly allude to the arrival and impact of the Spaniards on the status of cah and chibal. Description is fairly dispassionate, but subjects such as death in battle are not ignored; the violence of the conquest is often depicted in detail but placed in the context of "the misery imposed on us and the señor Spaniards by the Maya people formerly unwilling to deliver themselves to Dios." This is in contrast to central Mexican titles, which, in Stephanie Wood's words, "contain little informa-

tion on battles," and in which Spaniards are shown "considerable respect"
and the conquest itself is depicted as a distant "cosmic event with only
gradual repercussions."[22] Although references to the conquest in the Deslinde (our fourth characteristic) are more remote and neutral than such
references in other sections of the Maya titles, in the titles in general, the
conquest is in effect an event that had some factual bearing on the history
of the cah and its territorial holdings. In the portion that is the Deslinde,
the event serves largely to anchor the land survey in its alleged time frame
and display the legitimacy of the Pech and their document by mentioning,
somewhat obliquely, their reception of Spanish officials and institutions,
such as clergy and Christianity, encomendero and encomienda, oidor and
congregación:[23]

. . . tulacal uinicob noxibtacob hotuc- kallob layilob cuxanilob ti ma tac Señor espaniolesob uay tac lumil	all the elders, thirty-five of them, alive when the lord Spaniards had not yet come here to this land
. . . cu yahaulil ti Batabil kabansabi uay ti cah lae	. . . who was given a [Christian] name when ruling as batab here in this cah

The conquerors are described as "Spaniards," which is rarely the case in
Nahua titles, but, like its central Mexican equivalents, the Deslinde accords
to *the* conqueror the respect of his most important titles: *Señor D^n fran^{co} de
montejo g^{or} y Cp^n g^l Adelantado.*[24] The presence in Yucatan of these foreigners
is apparently a benign one; the Deslinde describes a peace accord between
Yaxkukul and those bordering on its lands as being an occasion when:[25]

. . . tu tanil ca yum encomidero tan u ɔaic u bendisio ca yum Padre fran^{co} hernades Clerigo yokol tulacal uinicob uay ti cah lae	. . . before our land encomendero, our lord Father Francisco Hernán- dez, cleric over all the people of this cah here, gave his blessing

The immediate context of the Deslinde may be the litigation of c. 1793
over a section of the border (possibly at the Chacnicte well between the
lands of Yaxkukul and Mococha), but its broader context is the Pech titles
and the ongoing Pech campaign to maintain hidalgo status and secure the
political and territorial integrity of Pech-dominated cahob. This campaign
included a presentation of the Pech role in the conquest as similar to that of
the Tlaxcalans in the Cortés campaign against the Mexica, namely, a cooperative one that was not only friendly but invaluable to the Spaniards.
Thus the tenor of association implied in the references to the arrival and
presence of Spaniards in the Deslinde is a faint echo of the bold claims of
association made explicit in its parent titles.

    Titles also tend to make light of another element of the Spanish in-
vasion: congregaciones (characteristic five). These relocation campaigns

were at first highly disruptive to Maya life, though it has been suggested that those indigenous communities receiving resettled families would gain from congregación in that a larger population would mean increased prestige.[26] Logically it would be these communities rather than the extinguished ones that would later be producing titles. Furthermore, the pain of resettlement would have been numbed by time, and, in Yucatan at least, offset by the Maya tendency to return to traditional landholdings, as well as by the broader context of agricultural, migration, and settlement patterns (see Chapter 13). In the Deslinde, congregación is alluded to only in a seemingly casual reference to the uninhabited properties on the edges of Yaxkukul's lands:[27]

... tu pach ca tocoynailob lay tux cahantacob to ma tac espaniolesob uay tac lumil lae	... around our abandoned houses, where we were settled when the Spaniards had not yet come here to this land.
Caix ti likon ca binon tu hool kaax tu pach ca tocoynailob ti maix yocol u yanal tocoynailobie	Thus we went to the edge of the forest around our abandoned houses, without entering the other abandoned houses.

The sixth characteristic of the title genre, in the same vein as the two preceding ones, consists of neutral, if not benign, references to the clergy and the spiritual conquest. This is evident in the excerpts from the Deslinde above describing the christening (it happens to be of Macan Pech) and the cleric's blessing (of Yaxkukul and its neighbors). Later the Deslinde declares that Yaxkukul works its lands for the sustenance of its people and to deliver tribute, which includes the feeding of the priests, *ah kinnob*—an unusual use of the Maya term if indeed the reference is to colonial times, as it apparently is. The passage continues:[28]

hach yab licil u talel yulellob uay ti xul u chi u luumil u pach cah yaxkukul lae tu yuchucil ca yumil ti Dios y ca noh ahau Rey ah tepal	there were many who came and arrived here at the edges of the lands around Yaxkukul, with the power of our lord Dios and our great Lord King Ruler

It is unclear whether these new arrivals are settlers of either ethnicity (because of the territorial references) or colonial clergy (because of the references to God and King), but if it is the latter, there is no indication of hostility. The implication may even be the opposite, that Yaxkukul's importance was reflected in the number of priests who came to its lands. Along these lines, Nahua titles characteristically mention the church of the altepetl as a symbol of its prestige, and indeed one passage in the Deslinde's second description of the López survey (quoted above) places emphasis on what may have been congregación and the relaying of the cah onto a grid of house plots.[29]

. . . u pisil u luumil yan hebal Sta yglesia Kuna y yotoch cah y solarlob uay lae	. . . the measuring of the land where the Holy Church and the cah homes and these house plots were

The final four title characteristics center on the Maya themselves, specifically self-promotion by the cah and by the Maya ruling classes, intraethnic rivalry, and Maya date-claims. In order to project the importance of the altepetl, titles in Nahuatl often included a wide range of information detailing the size, organization, and strengths and achievements of the altepetl of provenance; to this end the Xochimilcan titles drew upon the altepetl's annals for source material.[30] As discussed earlier, the Deslinde has a similar relationship to the Pech titles, being concerned with the status of the cah, into which the Pech have invested their political stock and future. From other eighteenth-century evidence, primarily Maya wills from Ixil, it is clear that Pech dominance in the region had been maintained through extensive landholding and political-marital alliances with the chibalob in the cah that had greatest wealth and cabildo representation. Although the Pech may have remained in a class of their own in terms of status in the community, under colonial rule they could not aspire to official positions beyond the indigenous cabildo. The sole avenues of colonial self-promotion open to the Pech were continued assurance of tax-exempt status (a central part of that campaign are the Pech titles, paralleled by the Xiu efforts in their title), and defense of the territorial boundaries of the cahob under their control—Yaxkukul and Chicxulub being fine examples, likewise Ixil, Conkal, and Baca, also protagonists in the narratives of the Pech titles and participants in the Chicxulub equivalent of the Deslinde.

The matter of authorship is complicated by the question of authenticity only if we are concerned to name the specific creator of each such document. In broader terms, the prominent, if not aristocratic, males of the community are responsible for titles (this is thus the eighth characteristic). The genre defends their interests, in terms of both their sixteenth- and eighteenth-century standing, their earlier status being used (in part, created) to advance their later position. The heroic central actors and sometime ostensible authors of the Pech titles drama are Nakuk Pech and Macan Pech, and the latter is clearly the most prominent of the notables behind the Deslinde. In an interesting reflection of the collusion (and perhaps priority) of interests that this document represents, the Deslinde lists the Maya signator-witnesses to the record as the seven members of the cabildo, followed by the four sons of the cah governor, don Alonso Pech (*tes-*

tigos yn mehenob, "[as] witnesses, my sons"), and lastly thirty-one named Maya males described as *testigosob u nucil uinicob*, "witnesses, men of importance." No Pech are listed among the thirty-one, although the patronyms on the cabildo reappear here. The hidalgo status of the Pech sons is made explicit—*lay hidalgos*, "they are hidalgos"—and their names are given "don" prefixes, which were reserved only for batabob or Maya hidalgos.

The previous two characteristics are essentially about defense—a primary purpose of the genre—and thus by extension a further characteristic element (the ninth) is that of hostility toward neighboring indigenous groups or persons of any ethnicity who threaten the interests of the cah. The Deslinde's strategic approach toward neighboring groups involves what might be described as reverse psychology. The authors are concerned to demonstrate to the Spaniards that the border claimed by Yaxkukul was agreed upon and sanctioned not only by Spanish authorities but also by the Maya residents on the other side of the border. The context of litigation suggests that the Deslinde was drawn up by Yaxkukul as a result of an eighteenth-century border dispute and was intended to convince colonial judges that peaceable, noble Yaxkukul was not the originator of the trouble. To this end the Deslinde is full of expressions of friendship for the neighboring people and their representatives on the survey: *ah mocochaob yn lake*, "my friends or companions, those of Mococha"; *lakin tan u binel layli nolo yn lake*, "to the east are my friends of Nolo." The asserted friendship with Conkal, Sicpach, and Kumcheel may have been genuine, since Pech are named as heads of these cahob, the governors of Mococha and Nolo being neither mentioned nor named. The border survey is thus a border agreement, culminating in a ritual expression of accord and brotherhood that is both a real event, "holding hands as brothers," *ɔin sucunil ti machlankabil*, before the encomendero and cleric as excerpted above, and a linguistic formula. The formula, of course, symbolizes the accord itself; its central phrase is:[31]

hunpelili u chi ca luumil yetelob Baix ah cumkallob	There is but one border between our lands and those of the people of Conkal

The phrase is repeated, with the name of the group making up the agreeing pair changed each time. The border is one, as opposed to two, which would be the case if the two peoples were to assert different boundary lines. To symbolize the union of each pair in agreement:[32]

cacanup u pictunil ti tulacal manic tu chi kaaxob	Two by two are all the stone mounds that pass along the forests' borders

The judgment of 1793 mentions survey documents presented by Mococha, strongly suggesting to us that it was this cah with which Yaxkukul was in dispute.

The tenth and final characteristic relates to dating. Charles Gibson defined a title as representing "an individual or collective memory of lands possessed or once possessed," a memory that "might be misguided or deliberately contrived to support a claim."[33] None of the extant versions of the Maya titles was written down before the eighteenth century, yet scholars have tended to accept on face value the claims of these titles to be copies of originals dating from between 1542 and 1562—in spite of the fact that the vocabulary, genre, and historical circumstances of the manuscripts strongly suggest post-1700 origins.[34] One version of the Deslinde claims to be an original record of a border survey conducted by the principal men of Yaxkukul on April 30, 1544—less than two years after the founding of Mérida. Barrera Vásquez suggests that this is a notarial error for 1554.[35] I suggest that the late-colonial authors of the document purposely chose this date to justify their claims; I further suggest that if such a survey was indeed conducted in the 1540's (one probably was), the Deslinde could not possibly be its original record. This is not to say that the Deslinde lacks all authenticity; it is an authentic contrivance, a late-colonial title that was spawned by necessity and purposefully misdated.

The Deslinde could not be a document of the sixteenth century for a number of reasons. First, no title of central Mexico is known to date before 1650, and because this knowledge is based on an appraisal of the characteristics of the genre,[36] late-colonial provenance is therefore one of those defining elements. Since the Deslinde shows most of the other title features, its date claim must be suspect. One of these features not yet discussed—the tendency to make glaring historical errors—pertains directly to dating. The oidor Tomás López was not in Yucatan until 1552; this fact alone therefore disqualifies 1544 as a Deslinde source date. If this was merely a copyist's error, the true date might just as easily be 1555, or, for that matter, 1644, since none of the document's witnesses claims to have been present at the time of the López ordinances. In fact, the date on the 1769 copy-version of the Deslinde is clearly 1522, which Barrera Vásquez explains as a not unusual confusion between 2 and 4 "in old documents."[37] But whose is the confusion? Earlier in the 1769 copy of the Chronicle the same notary appears to have had no difficulty distinguishing between the two numbers. Besides, is the "true" date not supposed to be 1554? Surely the point here is not one of error, but of perception and perspective. In the area of chronology, as Lockhart has written with respect to the Nahuas, "even more than with Spanish personae, offices, and procedural concepts, it seems as if the local people are using the Spanish paraphernalia as magic, as something efficacious rather than understood."[38] This is equally applicable to the Maya, whose understanding it was that the date served a validating, persuading function even when it had no linear chronological context.

Furthermore, a comparison of the Deslinde reference to López with that made by Tekom and others in 1600—both are presented above—reveals another error on the part of the Deslinde, when it not only fails to cite the judge's title of oidor but bestows upon him a "don." In fact López was only a licenciado at the time of his official visit to Yucatan, and he was never of "don" status; his social status was used by his encomendero opponents to ridicule him as an upstart and undermine his credibility as a competent and worthy official of the Crown.[39] Additional confusion over sixteenth-century Spaniards is evident in the naming of two different encomenderos in the different versions of the Yaxkukul border survey, Gonzalo Méndez (no "don") in the Deslinde, and don Julián Doncel in the 1769 version.[40]

Furthermore, the Spanish loanwords used in the titles, such as *conquista* and *historia*, are words that do not appear in other Maya texts until the eighteenth century and therefore point to a later date of origin, as does the use of *españolesob* in the titles and in the Deslinde.[41] Yaxkukul's Christian name of Santa Cruz de Mayo brings to mind the nineteenth-century Maya cross cult; certainly it jars with the normal early-colonial practice of ascribing a patron saint or Virgin to each Maya community.

The two arguments employed by Barrera Vásquez to suggest that the Deslinde is, if not from 1544, still sixteenth century, are in fact evidence to the contrary. The inconsistent use of diacritics and the irregular spelling of Spanish loanwords are both characteristics of Maya notarial writing from throughout the colonial period; the only generation that may have written Maya as the Franciscans originally taught it would have been the first alphabetically literate generation after the conquest. This generation might also have had a better understanding of the Spanish legal terminology that is misspelled and misused in the Deslinde—*ynformasionil derecho*; *ynformasio*; *ynpormasion*; *forma derecho de froseso*; *probision Real*. After the initial literacy campaigns of the sixteenth century the notary's skill was passed down from Maya to Maya, while the linguistic reach of Spanish became increasingly compromised by the reach of spoken Maya into the community of Spanish Yucatecans. Thus the process of the acquisition of Spanish loanwords by Maya was partly offset by the increasing Mayanization of those words.[42] The disregard for standard Spanish by the writer of the Deslinde proves very little, and suggests if anything a post-sixteenth-century provenance for the document.

The collective memory described by Gibson is present in the Deslinde—*noxibtacob yohellob u pach*, "the old men who know the borders"—and it was not an original recording of that memory that was presented in court in 1793 (and that has been passed down to us). If there ever was an original proof of landownership, it was converted over time into that particular genre that we call the title. The Deslinde of Yaxkukul projects a view of the conquest that is both immediate and distant; it purports to take us back among the events and people of the contact period, and yet its references to the traumas of that period are vague, politically neutral, devoid of any memory of disruption. The document reflects the conquest and its aftermath as it was seen from a couple of centuries later, when the Pech were still banking on a past association with the conqueror while simultaneously investing their future in the Maya community and its system of power centering on the cah and its territorial integrity. The Yaxkukul manuscript, like the Maya titles, demonstrates the Mayas' ability to appropriate aspects of the colonial world to suit indigenous ends, and to manipulate the past to secure the future.

◦·

CHAPTER TWENTY-TWO

Language

The study of language as a barometer of acculturation among the Nahuas has been explored in detail by James Lockhart, originally in collaboration with Frances Karttunen, who later produced a comparative study of Na-huatl and Maya and the impact upon them of Spanish.[1] However, as Kart-tunen recognized, the Maya part of this latter work was based on relatively few texts, and the conclusions were preliminary, leaving much to be done in this area. What is offered here is a brief analysis of Yucatec Maya as it was written during the colonial period.

Loanwords

> I, the *alcalde ordinario* . . . present the copy of the written document, the *auto*, the *título* . . .
> —alcalde with other cabildo officers of Maní, 1596

To judge from the conclusions (based primarily on Spanish sources) drawn by scholars of Yucatan with respect to the expansion of Spanish cultural influence in the seventeenth and eighteenth centuries, we might expect Maya sources to show a steadily if slowly increasing Spanish lexical influence during this period. Marta Hunt, for example, showed that the development of Spanish urban centers and an estate system was based on the same model as that of central Mexico, only temporally retarded by fifty to one hundred years; Robert Patch demonstrated the deep inroads made into Maya landholdings in the late eighteenth century, a trend confirmed by land documents in Maya; and the later period has been seen as the foundation for what Nancy Farriss called "The Second Conquest."[2] In accordance with these findings, the Maya language might be expected to have emerged from a mid-colonial phase of contact with Spanish—a phase

TABLE 22.1

Loanwords of 1557–1654 by Category and Proportion

Category	1557–1600		1605–54	
	Number	Percent	Number	Percent
Material				
Inanimate artifacts	1	1.6%	13	23.2%
Religious inanimate objects	2	3.3	1	1.8
Buildings	—	—	4	7.1
Animals	—	—	3	5.4
Quasi-material and abstract				
Titles and offices of individuals	28	45.9%	9	16.1%
Organizations, corporations	—	—	3	5.4
Religious	5	8.2%	11	19.6
Measurement, spatial divisions	6	9.8	4	7.1
Legal terms	14	23.0	5	8.9
Places	5	8.2	3	5.4
TOTAL	61	100 %	56	100 %

SOURCE: App. F. Note that each loanword is counted once; this table does not count incidence, or the number of times each loanword appears. To compare with Nahuatl, see tables in Lockhart 1992: 286–91; also Karttunen 1985: 51–78, which discusses the lexical impact of Spanish on Nahuatl and Maya in the colonial and modern periods.

that ended in central Mexico around 1640–50—only in the early or middle eighteenth century.

The evidence paints a slightly different picture. The loanword study included as Appendix F illustrates the pace and nature of what we might call the linguistic acculturation of the postconquest Maya. During the first few decades of contact, the Nahuas had resorted to using descriptions and various kinds of neologisms in indigenous vocabulary (as they have again over this past century). The Maya too may have gone through such a stage in the generation following the conquest (which was, for Yucatan, some two decades after central Mexico), but we have relatively little positive evidence of it, except for some terms for tools that bear the characteristics of neologisms and are still being used at the end of the colonial period (ɔopatan coch bol, "a blunt digging or planting stick"; *bronso licil u pabal tunich*, "a bronze tool for breaking stones"; and *lomob hobon mascab*, "a metal beehive-scraping or honey-extracting tool").[3]

Then, from the mid-sixteenth to the mid-seventeenth centuries in central Mexico, concepts and objects introduced by the Spaniards were described by borrowed Spanish nouns. The loanword table in Appendix F illustrates this process for Yucatan, highlighted by Table 22.1, which categorizes the words (all nouns) for the first century of extant sources. The reader should be aware that in spite of the precision of these numbers, they are based on a reading of a small body of *extant* notarial documents and therefore they give us a broad impression only. Having said that, it is clear that the initial impact of Spanish (and thus of Spanish culture) was heavily weighted toward the titles of office and legal terms that were a part of Spanish administrative process. This is to some extent a reflection of colonial conditions: the imposition of Spanish municipal government onto a similar preexisting system and the rapid conceptual reconciliation of the two; and the adoption of Spanish bookkeeping, measures, and divisions such as currency, weights, and the Christian calendar (dates are Spanish from the onset, but Maya words for year, month, and day continue to be used).

But these are also crucial aspects of the Spanish system that the Maya appropriated early in order to better engage that system in their own interests—how to write a legal document, what genre to claim and use, whom to address with what titles, what legal terms to cite, and what offices to place beside the names of the authors. The second half-century of colonial rule sees a more even distribution of new loanwords among categories, with a notable increase both in religious terms (abstract words such as "holy spirit" and quasi-material words such as "alms") and in inanimate objects (primarily furniture). Most of these words would have begun coming into use in the late sixteenth century, but it is in the seventeenth that such concepts and items became a fully absorbed part of the Maya world. During the course of that century (but often not appearing in extant records until early in the next), there is an extensive acquisition by Maya of Spanish nouns describing not only tools, clothing, and furniture, but also introduced plants and animals.

Nahuatl and Maya borrowed the same or similar Spanish nouns in the early colonial period; in fact, if we had a corpus of Maya wills from the turn of the sixteenth century to compare with the testaments of Culhuacan,[4] the list of loanwords would probably be closer than Table 22.1 implies. Nevertheless, looking at the colonial period as a whole, the experiences of Nahuatl and Maya undoubtedly diverge in the method of tempo and degree. Early-nineteenth-century examples from the Maya documentary base still answer to the characteristics of mid-colonial Nahuatl. Indeed, in many cases the Maya of this time barely conforms to even this stage, which Lockhart describes as being characterized by the Nahua borrowing of Spanish words readily and copiously.[5] The use of Spanish loanwords is often short of copious; a Maya election petition of 1812, for example, avoided the use of the word *elección*, although it had been in the language for at least two centuries.[6]

Such an example shows that the impression given by the loanword list in Appendix F of a cumulative acquisition of Spanish words can be misleading. Karttunen concludes that by the end of the colonial period, Maya had borrowed about half of the Spanish nouns that had entered Nahuatl.[7] If one compares the loanword list from the sources of this study with a

similar list from central Mexico, one might conclude that the Maya borrowed less than that.[8] The matter turns largely on the question of how to
evaluate dictionary attestations as opposed to text attestations.

An analytical reading of Maya-language sources suggests that many
aspects of lexical infusion that were early or transitional in postconquest
Nahuatl lingered much longer in Yucatec Maya. The earliest documents
display a high incidence of Spanish loanwords, increasing in number as
we move through the colonial period. But the more that documents surface from the century after contact, the more it becomes clear that it is in
this early period that most of the borrowing took place; the same phenomenon is seen in Nahuatl, but here it appears more pronounced. As in mid-
colonial Nahuatl, most of the words borrowed did not replace Maya words
but described what the Spaniards brought with them. The loanword evidence of the 1760's testaments of Ixil shows that the overwhelming majority of loans are to describe imported religious concepts and objects, imported political offices, and material goods and animals introduced by the
Spaniards (see Appendix E). The attestation dates in Appendix F are dependent upon the genres of document that have survived; wills, for example, are rich in religious terms and borrowed material objects, but the very
earliest extant wills are from the 1610's, and the first really useful corpus of
testaments dates from 1646–56, placing many words in these decades
when they may in fact have been used in the sixteenth century—note that
the first reference to a Maya testament is c. 1580.[9] In fact it is quite possible
that almost all legal, religious, and political terminology was adopted before 1600, and that most loanwords for imported material objects began to
be used well before 1646, if not by 1600. Much the same could be said for
Nahuatl, except that after the adoption of a core of words for basic material
objects in the mid-sixteenth century, that category continued to expand
indefinitely.

Grammatical change in colonial-era Maya appears to be virtually nil, as
in early-to-mid-colonial Nahuatl, although some Maya grammatical features may have disappeared very early in the colonial period. Karttunen
notes that Maya borrowed far fewer verbs than Nahuatl.[10] My evidence
suggests that even those few were more rarely used than in Nahuatl; to
date, I have found not a single inflected loan verb in my texts. Of the four
verbs found in colonial-era Maya texts that Karttunen surveyed, I have
discovered in the notarial texts only *confesar*, used as a noun—as in *u
confesaril*, "his confession."[11] Nor have I found any loan particles in this
source material. In general, the texts surveyed here show no evidence
of Maya borrowing at any time before Independence that would affect
syntax in the way that happens in Nahuatl from the late seventeenth century, although it is possible that evidence will surface of syntactic change
brought about by calquing.

The letter substitutions in the writing of loans by the Maya suggests something of their "Mayanization"—again a process paralleled in Nahuatl from the mid-sixteenth to mid-seventeenth centuries. Orthographic examples can be seen throughout this study, since all Maya documentation has been transcribed unaltered. Table 22.2 illustrates the process in a comparative context. There is no evidence of new sound classes added to the components of the Maya sound system (schematized in Table 22.3).[12] However, Maya speakers assimilated Spanish pronunciation to the Maya phonological system so that a Spanish loanword became comfortably Maya. Because the rules for concatenation of segments were different for the two languages (Spanish allowing syllable-initial and final consonant clusters, but Maya not), Mayas subjected loanwords to epenthesis (such as the vowel insertion that turned *cruz* into *curuz*) or dropped consonants—*yegua* became *yeua*, for example, and *encomendero* became *encometelo*. Maya speakers were approximating Spanish using the resources of their own phonological system, and they tended to ignore contrasts made by Spanish but not by Maya, and to identify Spanish consonants with the nearest Maya ones. Thus *iglesia* can be found as *ycreçia* (with the orthography indicating that the Maya did not make the *l/r* distinction), and *tanda* as *danta* (with *d* substituted by *t*, but the original *t* hypercorrected to *d*).

Put another way: although the Mayanization process followed the Maya phonological system, orthography was only standardized, following Spanish conventional spellings and abbreviations, for a few common words, such as *dios* and *alcalde*, and *juº* for Juan. In general, variations were plentiful; for example, I have noted nine different spellings of *conocimiento* ("acknowledgment") in Maya documents from Tekanto alone. The same process is visible in the use of Christian names by the Maya (see Table 4.2). The problem for Maya writers of Spanish words was twofold: such words contained unfamiliar sounds, some of which, such as *b*, *p*, and *f*, sounded the same to indigenous ears (the Maya had only a glottalized *b* before and during the colonial period); and Spaniards wrote them with letters that may not have been included in Maya alphabetic orthography. As a result, not only were letters substituted, as with the above examples, but indigenous notaries hypercorrected their spelling of loanwords. Such hypercorrections were usually mirror images of primary substitutions, with the Maya writers using letters not in their own alphabets: *publigo* for *público*, or, *tidroil* for *título*, an example of a double hypercorrection combined with vowel deletion and the addition of a Maya suffix.

This granting of the *-il* possessed suffix to Spanish nouns shows how the Maya treated these loanwords, morphologically speaking, as Maya nouns. Consider also the use of the Spanish name Pablo, feminized not as Pabla, but by the use of the Maya feminine prefix *ix*, to create "*xpab*."[13] Borrowed terms are often naturalized semantically as well. For example,

TABLE 22.2

Comparison of Spanish Alphabet, Spanish-based Nahuatl Alphabet, and Spanish-based Yucatec Maya Alphabet; with Primary Letter Substitutions and Hypercorrections made by Nahua and Maya Notaries

Spanish	Nahuatl[a]	Maya	Primary substitutions	Hypercorrections[b]
a	a	a		
b	—	—	p,u ([w])[c]	
—	—	b ([b'])		
c, ç ([s] before front vowels)	c, ç	s, z, ç		
c ([k] before back vowels)	c	c ([k])		g
ch	ch	ch		
—	—	cħ ([č'])		
d	—	—	t	
—	—	ɔ, dz ([ts'])		
e	e	e		
f	—	—	p	
g	—	—	c, x[d]	
h[e]	—	h		
hu ([w])	hu, uh	—		
i	i	i		
j	—	—	x[d]	
—	—	k ([k'])		
l	l	l		r
ll	—	—	y[c]	
m	m	m		
n	n	n		
ñ	—	—		
o	o	o		
p	p	p		b, f
—	—	pp, ᵽ ([p'])		
qu ([k] before front vowels)	qu	—		
qu ([kʷ])	qu	qu		
r	—	—	l	
s	—	—	x	j, g
t	t	t		d
—	—	th, ƫħ ([t'])		
—	tl	—		
—	tz	tz		
u	—	u[f]		
v	—	—	p	
v ([u], [w])	v	—		
x ([š])	x	x		
y ([i], [y])	y	y		ll[c]
z (syllable-final [s] and [s] before back vowels)	z	s, z, ç		

[a] Nahuatl alphabet is 16th century (Maya and Spanish 16th through 18th); Spanish/Nahuatl after Lockhart 1992: 336–41.

[b] Nahuatl writers appear only to have used hypercorrect letter substitutions in loanwords, whereas writers of Maya also used hypercorrections in Maya words.

[c] Maya only.

[d] Nahuatl only.

[e] Nahuatl writers occasionally used *h* for glottal stop; in Maya it could represent a velar or glottal fricative.

[f] Maya writers also used *u* as [w] before vowels (as Nahuatl writers occasionally did, in lieu of *hu* or *v*, neither of which was used in Maya for this purpose).

TABLE 22.3
*Comparison of Alphabetically Represented Segment Inventories
in Spanish, Nahuatl, and Yucatec Maya*

Spanish	Nahuatl	Maya
consonants		
p t k kʷ	p t k kʷ ʔ	p t k
		p' t' k'
	tˡ	
b d g gʷᵃ		b'
č	ts č	ts č
		ts' č'
f s šᵇ	s š	s š x h
m n	m nᶜ	m n
w y	w y	w y
r,r		
lᵈ	l	l
vowels		
i u	i,i	(*short*) i u
e o	e,e o,o	e o
a	a,a	a
		(*long high*) íi úu
		ée óo
		áa
		(*long low*) ìi ùu
		èe òo
		áa
		(*glottalized long*)ᵉ íʔi úʔu
		éʔe óʔo
		áʔa

NOTE: Time periods same as Table 22.2.
ᵃ These four pronounced as fricative variants intervocalically.
ᵇ ṣ and x in some dialects.
ᶜ Subject to contextual assimilation, including velarization.
ᵈ and ly in some dialects.
ᵉ In other words, long vowels with glottal interruption (redundantly high tone). Doubled vowels do occur in colonial-era Yucatec texts, but not consistently (as reflected in varying dictionary treatment; see Tozzer 1977: 20–21).

the Maya altered the Spanish *vaca*, "cow," both in form and in reference: *vacas*, "cows," is mutated into *uacax* (this exact form is often seen in Nahuatl), which is treated as a singular, and then may be qualified by an unaltered borrowing of the same word, *baca*, to indicate the female of the species. Thus *uacax* alone is a bull, or perhaps any bovine; *uacax baca* is a cow.[14]

Some of the late-colonial developments in Nahuatl orthography and letter substitutions also occurred in Maya, but far later and to a lesser degree. The substitution of *ll* for the y sound, which began in Nahuatl in the late seventeenth century, is an uncommon variant in Maya texts from the final decades of colonial rule, and though extreme examples of hypercorrection in Yucatan such as *tidroil* are restricted to earlier texts, new

words entering the language were still subject to Mayanized spelling. Furthermore, the late-colonial drift of Nahuatl writing closer to Spanish conventions is a much delayed and barely perceptible pattern in Maya writing: the *l/r* distinction that emerges in Nahuatl in the mid-seventeenth
century is still not in evidence at the end of the colonial period, and even if
the Maya writing of Christian names comes closer in the late eighteenth
century to conventionalization, there are still plenty of late examples of
spelling variants.

In Nahuatl the use of couplets of an indigenous word and a synonymous Spanish loan was characteristic of the late sixteenth century or of the
time of transition when that particular word was being introduced. The
double currency of a Spanish loan and its indigenous synonym even used
separately was generally a transitional phenomenon. In Maya, however,
this state of things continued indefinitely with many terms. The Maya
community at the heart of Spanish society in Yucatan was referred to
in a 1707 document as "Mérida Tihó"; in some eighteenth-century wills
phrases such as *puerta hol na* appear (both Spanish and Maya terms for
"door"). Yet these couplets do not seem to represent a transition to the
replacement of Maya terms with Spanish ones. For example, in an entry of
1801 the colony's capital is written as simply "t ho." In the 1640's Cacalchen used the Spanish loan for "ax," *hacha*, whereas in the century that
followed, nearby Ixil and Tekanto used the Maya term *bat*. Similar variation can be seen as late as the 1760's in Ixil, a cah just thirty kilometers from
Mérida. When declaring their property, some Ixil testators use no loans at
all, whereas one testator uses a Spanish loan seemingly at every opportunity, always choosing *puerta* over *hol na*, for example. In general these
two terms seem interchangeable, as do others such as *cama* and *poyche*
("bed").

The Maya appeared to recognize, in other words, that there was a
choice between two terms. In some instances the different terms may have
conveyed different meanings—a *casa* seems to have been a Spanish-style
house, different from the indigenous *na*—but in other cases the author of a
document seems to be demonstrating his position along an acculturative
continuum that ran between Spanish urban society and the world of the
cah. That such a continuum existed is clear; under Yucatec conditions it
may have been defined by person, class, and region as much as by time.
Individuals—rather than whole communities or regions—lived more or
less side by side in different linguistic phases or stages of language contact,
reflecting varying personal levels of bilingualism and biculturalism. An
example of this is the case of Pedro Mis, a mid-eighteenth-century Ixil
resident who seems to have acquired greater bicultural affiliations than his
fellow cahnalob—as discussed in Chapter 8. The bilingual semantic cou-

plets referred to in Chapter 18 appeared in both Maya and Nahuatl, providing a perfect medium for bicultural expression. But in Nahuatl they were a fleeting phenomenon during a period when either the Spanish term or its indigenous equivalent won out, whereas in Maya they are characteristic of the whole time studied here.

As in late-sixteenth-century Nahuatl texts, the metalanguage of much of Maya documentation is deliberately and functionally bilingual and bicultural. The classic example of this is the phrase *in takyahthan tin testamento*.[15] One of the two words used, the Spanish *testamento*, affirms the legitimacy of the document within the Spanish legal system. The word always occurs in the opening and closing formulas; it officializes the statement, and asserts the intertextual link to the greater body of the town's testaments. The same can be said of the Maya term *yn takyahthan*, "my final statement," which describes and validates the document within the local Maya context. The two words can be separated into Maya and Spanish, and their purpose can to a degree be separated, but ultimately their purpose is the same, and the closing testamentary phrase is quintessential colonial-era Maya: *"lay u xul yn takyahthan tin testamento,"* "here ends my final statement in my testament."

Another example of a slightly different nature comes in the Bacalar petition of 1838 against a priest. Though it is postcolonial, it nevertheless exhibits all the traits of colonial-era Maya notarial literature. The sacrament of confession is mentioned early in the document in the usual loan form, *confesare* (*confesar*, treated as a noun with a Maya referential suffix *-e*). Later it is referred to in Maya terms, in a descriptive phrase almost reminiscent of the neologisms of very early colonial Nahuatl:[16]

bix cu bin u yub c kebanob tu	How will a priest in a cah, who
pisinail u yalal tu le keban	passes wretched with drunkenness,
humpel p.ᵉ ti ychil hunpel cah	hear our sins in the sacristy where
cu mansal hilan yoklal calanil?	sins are declared? How will he
bix u bin u nat on ua ma tu	understand us if he has no
nuctic maya than?	grasp of the Maya language?

This is more than just rhetoric; it is a parallel and simultaneous means of saying "confession," in which Maya words convey the sense of what is supposed to occur in the act involving the bad priest and the Maya "us": *c kebanob*, "our sins"; *ub*, "to hear"; *al*, "to say, tell, declare"; *nat*, "to communicate, converse, understand"; and *nuc*, "to understand."

If, therefore, Maya accelerates into something like the early-to-midcolonial phase of the Nahuas within a decade or two of the conquest, and remains there well into the nineteenth century, and if the evidence shows the Maya borrowing Spanish words in a way that is inclusive rather than exclusive, additive rather than replacive, actively bilingual rather than passively acculturative, what does this say about the world of the cah? It supports the notion that Maya society was sufficiently vital and self-sustaining at the community level to justify characterizing the cah as a world unto itself, rather than a mere cog in the colonial wheel. In fact, just as the successive stages of Nahuatl turned out to be analogous to Nahua acculturation in general, so does the response of Maya to Spanish function as an indicator of Spanish influence on Maya society.

Regional Variation

From here it is very many leagues to the next cah . . .
—cabildo of Tahnab, 1605

The Maya documentary base here is drawn from a sufficiently dispersed variety of cahob to be of potential value to a dialectologist concerned to detect and map variation in postconquest Yucatan. Such a study would be a major undertaking unto itself; suffice to point out here that in the course of searching for sociohistorical information in these sources, I observed three forms of regional variation in language. Rather than indicating dialectal subregions consisting of blocks of cahob, these variations show different terminological traditions between individual communities.

One was the use of different terms to refer to the same object, often by drawing creatively upon Spanish. For example, the Tekanto records always refer to a mare as *na* or *tzimin na* (mother horse), whereas Ixil records always use the Spanish loan *yegua*: *yeua tzimin* (mare horse). Additional such comparisons can be seen in the comparative lists of Maya material possessions in Appendix E.

The second sign of dialectal differences is the use of spelling variations that do not involve Spanish loans or influence. The orthography of the written record cannot alone prove or disprove differences in pronunciation, but where different spellings occur that are consistent in each cah of attestation, some details of local pronunciation are strongly suggested. In Tekanto, a shawl or *rebozo* was a *box*; in Ixil a *boch*. In Ebtun children were *palalob*, in Ixil they were *palilob* (an example more likely to be morphological than phonological).

The third area of variation—one of lexical semantics—took the form of the same Maya word exhibiting different usages and therefore differing nuances of meaning from cah to cah. An example of this is the Ixil norm of using *kax* to denote nonsolar land in general, whether it is cultivated with citrus trees, turned into milpa for corn, beans, or squash, or lying fallow and waiting to be slashed and burned. For the inhabitants of Tekanto, on the other hand, *kax* has a more specific meaning, closer to what we find in the dictionaries: forest, bush, uncultivated land called *monte* by the Spaniards. Tekanto records show col being used specifically to denote milpa.

Many loci of these contrasting usages are communities that are not geographically far from each other. Ixil and Tekanto, for example, are in the same region of the province (just over fifty kilometers by today's roads, some of them unpaved; forty-three as the crow flies).[17] In other words, this evidence adds to the impression given elsewhere in this study that Maya society in Yucatan was divided by its cahob more than by any other geographical, sociopolitical, or cultural units. In the sense that the residents of different cahob referred to things in different ways, reflecting the fact that each cah had its own traditions and its own way of doing things, from cabildo composition to land descriptions, one can say that each cah had its own dialect.

The question of regional variations also relates to the question of acculturation as much as to patterns of loanword acquisition. These variants underscore the crucial role played by cah-centrism in Maya society and thus must modify any interpretative model of acculturative progression—perhaps helping to explain the slow pace of that progression—based on loanword acquisition and other linguistic changes.

The Maya notarial record indicates that the Spanish reforms of the final decades of colonial rule had little impact on the cah and its structure of self-rule, yet by the outbreak of ethnic war in the 1840's this structure had been severely weakened. This change did not occur suddenly in 1821; rather its foundations were gradually and partially laid in the decades before Independence, with accelerated change not beginning until after about 1830, and radical change dating from the Imán revolt of 1839 (which, in Rugeley's words, "shattered the already fragile stability of rural society"). In the 1840's two trends intensified: on the one hand, an increasing Maya expectation of the elimination of various political, social, and economic limitations and burdens; and on the other hand, a mounting Maya sense that the burdens of exploitation had passed formerly acceptable limits.[2]

Not surprisingly, the Maya continued to cling to all semblances of autonomy well into the Independence period. The documentary record shows that in some ways the functioning body of indigenous political officers continued to exist into the late nineteenth century as it had for centuries—for example, complete with minor variations from year to year and cah to cah. The first abolition of the repúblicas indígenas was in 1813–14. Technically, they were outlawed again in 1821, to be reinstated three years later (to facilitate tax collection), but with diminished authority and without the office of batab-governor. Although the repúblicas and their batabs seem to have survived these and other periods of "abolition," the loss of cofradía estates in 1832 and of most of the remaining cah-owned lands in 1843, followed by the development of the Ladino political conflict into a civil war, and its redefinition in the summer of 1847 as a Caste War, served to exacerbate the confusion and further reduce the power of Maya government in the cahob—along with the status of the noble and better-off chibalob who had dominated Maya cabildos and communities. Still, the system of cah government and its accompanying class hierarchy survived all this into the second half of the century.[3]

Comparing the eighteenth century with the early nineteenth, it appears that much of the stability of the colonial era lay in its apparent durability; the Maya cyclical view of the world was reinforced by alternating periods of prosperity and famine, Spanish moderation and excess, which were underpinned by the longevity of colonial society, with its overlapping Spanish and Maya worlds. Yet beginning in the 1810's the high and low points of this cycle grow further apart in degree, with exceptional demands made on cah residents quickly followed or even paralleled by millenarian expectations of an end to taxation. This millenarianism was fostered not only by periodic and temporary abolitions of tribute and forced labor, but also by the simultaneous and damaging attack on properties and on institutions (such as the repúblicas indígenas and the Tribunal de Indios) that had for centuries offered some protection and autonomy. Amid this complex pattern the documentary record shows the Mayas struggling to maintain continuity in spite of changes that appear radical if not devastating.

With respect to self-rule in the cah, the situation was analogous to the conquest. Just as the preconquest Maya batab becomes the colonial-era governor, in the end even regaining the title of batab, so does the colonial batab find a role in the postindependent cah as its senior official, often retaining that same title. Similarly, as we move further from the Hispanicized center, so do we find continuities increasingly profound and blatant. In the cahob-barrios of Mérida the Maya community officers simply elevate the offices of the two alcaldes to the rank previously held by batab and lieutenant, a practice consistent with new laws recognizing a "constitutional alcalde" as the senior officer of a municipality.[4] This allowed outward conformity, while at the same time preserving some of the substance of the traditional system. In contrast, cahob on the geographical edges of the former colony, such as Chichanhá, Tecoh, and Mopila, were able to maintain a "cacique" and lieutenant as late as the 1860's.[5]

Other cahob seemed to find less satisfactory solutions. Bacalar is an interesting case because it was one of the three Spanish villas, yet at the same time remote and isolated from the center of the peninsula.[6] An 1838 petition from this villa's Maya cabildo still lists a batab as one of its officers, but his positioning is ambiguous. "On behalf of all the cah residents," the document closes, "they [the officers] sign here:"[7]

> Yoklal tulacal u cahal lay firmaoba
>> Calisto Kumun alcalde 1°
>> Anselmo Canche alcalde 2°
> Regidores
>> Julian Chi 1°
>> Rafael Ku 2°
>> D. Juan Chuc Batab

The fact that this batab has retained his "don" status suggests that his office is still treated with traditional respect, and that within the Maya community he is still the senior officer and cah patriarch. But on the document, destined for Mérida and addressed to its bishop, don Juan appears relegated, in partial conformity to federal regulations, to the rank of regidor.

Similarly, the 1851 bill of sale for a solar in Maxcanú contains in its opening formulas the standard phrase *toon batab ten^{te} Justisia Reg^s y escribano uay tu mektan cahil ca cilich yumbil San Miguel Acangel Patron uay ti cah Maxcanu*, "we the batab, lieutenant, magistrate(s), regidores, and notary, here in the jurisdiction of our holy father San Miguel Arcángel, patron here in the cah of Maxcanú." The body of the document is also typical of solar sales, containing no new examples of Spanish loanwords, and including a stationary land description of the kind detailed in Chapter 15. However, instead of the customary list of cabildo offices and officers, there are but three names at the foot of the text, with *caciq^e* (and no "don") written after the second.[8]

Such change is also indicated in an 1821 election record written partly in Maya. The worm and water-rot damage prevents us from knowing not only the provenance of the document but also whether there was a closing phrase; the opening phrase has been reduced to one line, of which a single word has been left by the worms: *chicbesic,* "indicate, show, appoint." What follows is merely a list of names, with the officer titles introduced in Spanish: *"Para Regidor primero . . ."* and so on. This unusual bilingual document seems caught in the transition of the decades between Independence and the Caste War.

The fate of election records in the cah can be read as indicative of the fate of the indigenous cabildo. After 1770 the new regulations on indigenous elections that the Viceroy sought to impose meant that the authorities of New Spain would cease accepting as valid elections recorded in indigenous languages. The specific ordinance has yet to be uncovered, but its effect in central Mexico was to cause the disappearance during the 1770's of election documentation in Nahuatl.[9] Owing to the paucity of extant post-1706 election records in Maya, we cannot be sure that Maya escribanos were not likewise obliged to begin recording elections in Spanish. Yet it seems unlikely that they were, for a number of reasons.

First of all, there is little reason to suppose that ordinances issued in Mexico City were always applied in Yucatan. If the local encomienda could survive two centuries beyond its official abolition, record-keeping practices out in the Yucatec hinterland could easily resist change. Maya was not only close to being the lingua franca in Yucatan, but by the end of the colonial period it was not yet heavily infused with Spanish, as Nahuatl was by 1770. Unlike many Nahua notaries in the late period, Maya notaries lacked the bilingualism that would have allowed them to continue their practice in Spanish. Therefore forcing Maya escribanos to begin writing in Spanish might have created more problems than solutions, a consideration that obviously would not hinder the passing of an ordinance (far from it), but might well obstruct its application. Second, the 1821 election record mentioned above largely resembles a colonial-period Maya election document with a severely truncated formula, and an election record written in Spanish and lacking the characteristic listing of officers does not appear in Ebtun, for example, until 1823.[10] As we shall see, postindependence election records in Spanish from other cahob continue to exhibit indigenous traits.

Third, cah cabildo records of other genres written in Spanish do not appear before Independence except in the cahob-barrios of Mérida-Tihó (all are sales of house plots), and the majority of cahob continue to record in Maya through the 1820's and into the 1830's. The existence of a more or less typical Maya notarial record of 1851 from Maxcanú suggests that the archives may yet yield mid-nineteenth-century Maya documents from a number of cahob.[11]

One imagines that the 1821 fragment comes from a cah further removed from Hispanic influence than Ebtun, for the Ebtun election record of December 1823, written in Spanish, has a completely new format, and it describes a process of ballot-taking quite alien to the practices of the colonial period.[12] Yet there are still signs of continuity. The same patronyms dominate the political scene, and the nine "electors" are clearly the principales who are selecting the new cabildo from among their own class, every nominee receiving a suspiciously unanimous nine votes.

Election records from more remote cahob exhibit less disguised continuities. From 1832, 1837, 1854, and 1867 there have survived election records from fourteen cahob on the southeast edge of what is now Yucatan state, all in a format remarkably close to that of their Maya ancestor-documents.[13] Compare the following examples with each other and with the examples of opening formula presented in Chapter 20:

[*translated from Maya*]	[*translated from Spanish*]
Here in the town of San Agustín	In the town of Sotuta on the
Tekanto . . . on this day, the 15th of	18th day of November, 1867,
December, 1706, meeting here in	gathered in the town hall of
court are the members of the	the cabecera, the cacique C.
cabildo, Francisco Ku [etc.].	Policarpo Poot and most of the
Before the notary appeared [the	Indians, who met to proceed
cabildo officers] appointed for	with the election . . . for the
the coming year, 1707 . . . they are	year 1868, in conformity
assembled before . . . the governor	with the law which resulted
here in this town . . . [and] shall be	in the election of the
the next to serve . . .	following individuals . . .

The nineteenth-century records in Spanish go on to list the officers and close with a statement ratifying and verifying the process of appointment and the recording of it, all very similar to the colonial tradition. There then follows a statement of ratification by the local Spanish priest, a departure from the colonial norm, but consistent with the post-1770 laws that took effect in central Mexico. To some extent, control of the procedure seems to have passed into non-Maya hands. Whereas the Maya records were signed off pro forma by the secretary of the provincial governor and probably returned to the safekeeping of the local cabildos, the records in Spanish are forwarded to Mérida for good. However, it is possible that the reach of the authorities in Mérida was shorter after 1847 than it had been during colonial rule, at least for a while, so that many cahob were able to continue traditional practices of power politics and office appointment without having to keep any records at all.[14]

One of the most remarkable indicators of continuity in these nineteenth-century election records is a single word. Yaxcabá's election record dated December 5, 1867, lists the following nine officers:[15]

Teniente	José Ma Poot
Alcalde 1°	José Dolores Bahac
Alcalde 2°	Toribio Chuc
Chun than	Juan Yah
Alguacil	Juan Sulu
Topiles	José Sima, Miguel Ac, Andrés Chuc, Nicolás Coba

The reader will be able to spot the word in question. Its diacritics are wrong—it should be *chun than*; the notary barred the wrong *h*—and its meaning has apparently changed over the centuries, but the term is heavy with indigenous imagery. Pío Pérez gives it the sense of "president," but its roots are "trunk, base, bottom, cause, source" (*chun*), and "word" (*than*), evoking the concept of the representative foundation of indigenous rule. *Chun* can mean seat, in the sense of the traditional seating of the preconquest Maya ruler on the mat of authority and the seating—in time and space—of the katun round of the Maya calendar.[16] *Chun than* is used in the colonial period simply to mean "officer," but originally it had been one of the traditional titles of the local ruler; that ruler spoke for his cah, his words represented their needs and desires—as manifested in the colonial period in petitions filed by cahob in the names of their batabs and cabildo officers. When, in their petition discussed in earlier chapters, Xcupilcacab claims that its batab is ineffective, they assert that *minan mamac than oklal*, "there is nobody to speak for us [i.e., represent us]." Yaxcabá's positioning of *chun than* below *alcalde* implies an office equated with regidor in rank; certainly it is hard to see this chun than as the cah's senior official, especially since the record is signed by two additional untitled officers, presumably the "cacique" and notary.

Yaxcabá's use of *chun than* in 1867 is symbolic of a pattern of compromised continuity in Maya self-government that has emerged in the present analysis. The Maya adapted the form and structure of the Spanish-indigenous governmental system of New Spain to allow them to fulfill their obligations both to the colonial authorities and to the cah members they represented, all the while practicing local politics more or less in the preconquest tradition. The Yaxcabá example reveals that 325 years after the founding of Mérida, the principal men of a Maya community are still using a Maya title of political office whose original meaning evokes imagery of rule that is unmistakably indigenous.

Yet this example also symbolizes the impending demise of the world of the cah. For the title appears to have lost its original meaning and is being used to describe a lesser, perhaps uncertain, office, in a Spanish document that records a process whose significance has become compromised. In fact, in the year that Juan Yah served as chun than in Yaxcabá, Maya cabildos and the Maya electoral tradition were abolished once and for all and permanently vanish from documentary history. The cah survived, but it was never to be the same world again.

Spatial Context: Nahuas and Mayas

Let the officials of Santiago verify what I say.
—Nahuatl testimony before the cabildo of the altepetl of Tulancingo, 1584

The similarities and differences between Maya and Nahua responses to Spanish are representative of common and contrasting social experiences. Many aspects and principles of Maya culture, both preconquest in origin and colonial in context, were not unique but were paralleled by similar traits found not only among the Nahuas but also, as is now becoming increasingly apparent, among other Mesoamerican peoples. Although Mayas and Nahuas differed in certain specific respects, much of the contrast between these two societies after the conquest is related to the fact that the Nahuas soon entered an acculturative stage not reached by the Mayas until after Independence (and, in some respects, not yet reached today). In other words, what was said about language in the preceding chapter is generally applicable to Maya society.

The most significant Maya-Nahua parallel is that of the cah and altepetl. The similarities in the structure and significance of these two units, as seen from both indigenous and Spanish perspectives, show that the Mayas and the Nahuas shared many other details of the postconquest experience. For example, the nobles and principles of both communities (led by the tlatoani and batab) continued to govern as before, both loosely within the structure of the offices and electoral procedures of the (Spanish-style but semi-indigenized) cabildo. Cah and altepetl assumed identical positions in the combined Spanish-indigenous system of colonial administration, with one indigenous unit becoming one encomienda and one parish. (The encomienda system lasted well over two centuries in Yucatan, but in central Mexico it was superseded by other arrangements in less than half the time; the initial paucity of Spaniards in Yucatan meant that at first some encomiendas and parishes contained more than one cah.) The altepetl and the nature of its government began to fragment toward the late colonial period; the cah showed no signs of this, save to a limited degree in the cahob-barrios that became absorbed by Mérida.

The role of one indigenous officer in particular—the notary—was crucial and closely parallel in cah and altepetl alike. Notarial documents in Maya and Nahuatl were drawn up in the same genres, show the same balance toward testaments and matters of land, reflect the same commitment to litigation, and exhibit many of the same features of style and format. As we have seen, some of these features, like those of the opening formulas of wills, are European in origin; but many, such as the use of semantic couplets and admonitions, and the characteristics of reverential address, are distinctly indigenous. Nahuatl notarial records date from the mid-sixteenth century to the late eighteenth, those in Maya from the late sixteenth to the mid-nineteenth centuries; this contrast is tied to differing dates of conquest and greater strength of Spanish influence in central Mexico in the final years of the colonial period (the time, ironically, of most extant Maya documentation). Interestingly, the Maya appear to have taken to alphabetic record keeping even quicker than the Nahuas, who did not abandon pictorial elements altogether until the seventeenth century, and in a few genres even later. The apparent contrasts between the titles (the so-called Chronicles) and the Books of Chilam Balam of the Yucatec Maya, and the annals, titles, and similar genres of the Nahuas, in fact turn out to be slightly different representations of similar views of history and a similar preoccupation with the promotion of the altepetl and cah and their ruling families.

The cah and altepetl were not identical, of course. Two important and related differences in internal social organization stand out in particular. One is the fact that the altepetl subdivisions called calpolli had no apparent direct equivalent in Yucatan, where political power sharing among the Maya was even more closely tied to batab regimes than Nahua (often calpolli-linked) factionalism was to tlatoani rule. Maya internal social groupings and identities were also determined to a large degree by patronym—naming patterns being another major contrast between these two societies. The Nahuas lacked a patronym tradition, and in the colonial period they developed a highly complex naming system that served to rank individuals socially with great precision. As a result, the preconquest terminology of nobility withered away in central Mexico. In Yucatan, Maya terms of social rank persisted, along with a patronym system that was so important to the Maya that it has not been abandoned to this day; the chibal system thus acted as an internal organization that largely filled the vacuum that would otherwise have been left by the absence of a calpolli-type subunit. The fact that the Maya adopted very few Spanish kin terms, whereas the Nahuas adopted significantly more beginning in the mid-seventeenth century, may be related to this contrast in social organization, although the general trends of language change were probably more influential. Despite these differences, it should still be emphasized that both the Mayas and Nahuas maintained a class society in which status was determined by interacting combinations of birth, wealth, affiliation (to faction and calpolli or chibal), and cabildo service.

Two other areas bear final, brief comparison. One is that of land. Geographical circumstances determined different methods of land use in Yucatan (shifting cultivation) and central Mexico (permanent intensive agriculture), and this appears to have influenced practices ranging from measurement (the Nahuas measured land to a smaller denomination) to terminology (the Nahuas did not adopt the term "solar" to the extent that the Maya did until later in the colonial period). Still, the complex classification of land by various criteria was similar among both peoples, as were many of the rituals of exchange.

The Maya practice of placing land in the nominal or titular hands of a male household head, who represented the group that in essence owned the property, relates to the other final area of contrast, that of organizational principle in the broadest sense. Again, this has much to do with land use and the need of households and chibalob for access to areas of cultivable land far larger than those needed by Nahua social groups. Maya-language evidence suggests that the tendency toward subdivision among the Nahuas is present in Yucatan but greatly tempered by the principle of representation. In the end, this contrast may simply be a question of emphasis; after all, organizing individuals into interlocking groups headed by representatives at each social level was simply a different form of subdivision, though one lacking the balanced and clearly separate constituent parts of Nahua organizational units.

Conclusion

Here in the cah . . .
—characteristic opening phrase of a postconquest Maya notarial record

Maya-language evidence confirms that the use of indigenous-language documents is not only desirable and feasible, but necessary, to the study of major indigenous groups in Spanish America. The Maya majority in postconquest Yucatan constituted a society that was far from rendered dysfunctional by colonial rule, but was sophisticated, largely self-governing, and in many ways culturally independent. This society not only must be studied on its own terms, but indeed can be; the considerable and increasingly available corpus of Maya-language notarial documentation that has been the rich base of the present work remains an important source of future scholarly analysis. This book has discussed these sources in the context of their Spanish-derived genres, and has identified indigenous characteristics of the documents that are both general and specific to those aspects of Maya society that they reflect—petitions by or elections in Maya communities, for example, Maya inheritance patterns or land descriptions. Of the various themes that emerge from the reading of some 1,600 Maya documents, one seemed so pervasive that it cried out to be made the very anchor of the study, simply because it was clearly the anchor of Maya society itself—namely, the cah.

The cah was the Maya community. More than just a pueblo or town, it was the primary sociopolitical unit of the Maya, consisting of both a residential core and dispersed parcels of land held by the community and its members. More than just a geographical or organizational unit, it was the focus of Maya self-identity. A Maya who was to the Spaniards a mere "indio" was to his own people a "cahnal," a resident and member of a particular cah. He or she was also a member of a particular patronym group or chibal, but the importance of each chibal was localized, determined not regionally but by cah. In spite of the existence of cahob tied to neighboring units or to Spanish municipalities—what I have termed complex cahob—and in spite of the existence of the cah-to-cah variations that are in evidence in almost every chapter, the centrality of the cah and its common characteristics throughout the province of Yucatan helped allow this study to embrace most of the region for a time period roughly corresponding to the colonial era.

The similarity between the cah and the altepetl might prompt one to expect the documentation to reveal a sociopolitical subunit in the cah equivalent to the calpolli of the Nahuas. No such unit was found. Instead, social and political organization within the cah turned out to have been based on the principle of representation. Indeed, this was one of the fundamental organizing principles of Maya culture. It manifested itself in the language of the documentation, which reflected the role of the batab—the nobleman who governed the cah—who represented the whole body of community officers—the cabildo—all of whom represented all other members of the cah. These citizens, in turn, were organized into two lesser representational kinship units: the broader groups identified by patronym, sometimes called chibalob, that constituted intermediary units whose sense of common identity may have varied; and the smaller kin groups that were households.

Representation implies hierarchy, and indeed this was a class society. The traditional view of the Maya nobility as suffering an inexorable decline under Spanish rule is contradicted by Maya-language evidence. It was assumed that indigenous dynasties were obliterated by the conquest—decimated by the pre-1542 fighting, by the repression of the 1545–46 revolt, by the *auto* of 1562, and finally by the imposition of elected Maya cah governors to replace the dynastic batabob and halach uinicob. In fact, Maya postcontact demographic decline was more a result of introduced (class-blind) disease than of slaughter by the Spaniards, and repression by the colonial authorities sought not to eliminate the indigenous nobility but exactly the opposite, to coerce that nobility by means of selective punitive example and eventually to coopt by confirmation of status.[17] Continued Spanish recognition of a Maya nobility and of the governing officers of the cah was reflected in the continued acceptance of such a hierarchy within cah society, a hierarchy fortified by heredity, wealth, access to political office, and gender. The interrelation and correlation between these factors has been demonstrated above, in part using the case study of Ixil in the 1760's, whose dominant chibal turned out to be the same patronym group that dominated the area before the conquest: the Pech.

If representation was one side of the Maya cultural coin, the other side was participation. This was not necessarily direct: women did not hold cabildo offices; the batabil was reserved for the nobility; men played minor roles, if any at all, in solar-based cultivation and cloth-clothing production. On the other hand, at both levels of social organization—the cah, as manifested in cabildo action, and the household—a full body of participants can be detected behind the titular representative authority. On the occasion of the dictation of a testament, the batab, as the initial primary author of the document, is soon joined by the officers of the cabildo (the Maya version of which includes the entire body of "principal men" in the cah), before ceding authorship to the testator, who is in turn often joined by various household members and relatives. The enterprise was, in the end, a community affair. The same was true of the exchange of land, a drama whose protagonists included not only the batab and cabildo, but vendor and purchaser and neighbors and witnesses, all of whom literally or figuratively walked the boundary of the property as a practical and ritual means of passing possession to the new owner—the complete process reflected in its Maya-language record. In both cases (wills and land sales), a plot of land might be referred to as pertaining to a single named male, but when such a plot came to be sold or bequeathed, this was revealed as a façade behind which was the participation of the whole household—into the documents stepped wives, siblings, children, even the occasional parent. Sometimes property was declared as "ancestral," and the participants formed not just the household of the senior male but were the representatives, male and female, of that particular chibal in that particular cah.

The position of women can be taken as indicative of these broader patterns, in that women played roles that were determined by gender (and were often subservient or exclusionary), while also being participants in the tenure and exchange (by will and sale) of property, in the cah class system (in which status was determined largely by wealth and birth), and in the cah defense system (which took the form of cabildo legal action in the Spanish courts). There is considerable symbolic significance in the fact that, amid the many extant cases of litigation undertaken by cah cabildos against priests and colonial officials over a range of alleged abuses, among the victims and witnesses can be found commoner indigenous women whose inclusion in the cah system—whose membership in the world of the cah—provided them with the representation of their own government in their own language. In short, they were given a voice; these pages have been an attempt to listen to that voice.

Maya sources are so rich as to offer food for decades of scholarly thought and to allow students of the Maya to move in the future beyond studies of change in the language over space and time to the question of the impact of the postconquest centuries on Maya semantic systems. In due course, we shall fully grasp the links between the preconquest Maya of hieroglyphic texts, the postconquest Maya of notarial records and Chilam Balam literature, and modern spoken Maya. Further work can be done to confirm or qualify the details presented above of social life in the cah—such as the ladder pattern of cabildo officer careers and the role of batab "regimes," the succession of batabob and the persistence of the nobility, the patterns of even distribution and joint inheritance, the rituals of property exchange, the layout of the cah and the solar, the influence of labor division by gender on household interaction—all of which are here conveyed in the distinctly Maya terms (sometimes borrowed from Spanish and Mayanized) that appear in the written record.

This new stage of Maya ethnohistorical investigation needs to be placed not only in the Nahua comparative context but against work in progress or yet to be done on colonial-era documentation in Ñudzahui (Mixtec), Zapotec, Cakchiquel, Quechua, and other available indigenous-language sources. The idea that sources in these and perhaps a dozen other indigenous languages in Spanish America either do not exist or cannot be profitably understood is no longer acceptable. Already it is becoming clear that documents in Ñudzahui and Cakchiquel, just to start with, reveal many of the cultural characteristics of the Nahua-Maya post-conquest nexus of traits and responses.[18]

The ultimate goal, of course, is the whole picture; the emphasis on indigenous groups by the new school of ethnohistorians is driven by a concern to balance a traditionally Hispanocentric historiography, not by a lack of interest in the Spaniards. In the case of Yucatan, then, the Spanish and Maya perspectives need to be reconciled in a way that accurately reflects the highly complex nature of three centuries of interaction between Spanish society and the world of the cah. Aspects of this phenomenon have been studied here, as well as in other historical studies of the field.[19] Much of it is also to do with the fact of convergence; cultural features shared by Spaniards and Nahuas alike were mostly Mesoamerican characteristics also shared by the Maya—territorial states, kingship-governorship, state religion, the noble-commoner distinction, tax obligations, both individual and communal land rights, markets and commerce, female inheritance and property rights, and record keeping on paper.[20]

Yet there were also profound differences. In the end, at the heart of Spanish-Maya interaction is the nature and porosity of the cultural frontier. Maya perceptions of the borders that surrounded their own land plots and territorial tracts might be taken as illustrative of that cultural frontier. Maya borders were marked by stone mounds either in series or located at prominent points such as clearly identifiable trees. There may have been a path that followed the border in some cases, but there was no continuing physical line such as a fence or wall. In effect, the border was a dotted line. The easy passage to and fro that such a border allows might be viewed, therefore, as symbolic of the way in which the postconquest Maya passed in and out of the world of the cah, without sacrificing its cultural integrity. This passage was literal—migration between Spanish communities and cahob—but it also affected to varying degrees the ways in which things were done in the cahob, from ritual formulas of testament dictation to the use of kinship terminology, from the recording of traditional histories, prophecies, and cures in the Chilam Balam to techniques of well digging, from methods of proving land ownership to aspects of animal husbandry.

In no way can Maya society be said to have been totally isolated from the society of the conquerors, but from the late sixteenth to the early nineteenth centuries the cah exhibited a remarkable ability to expose itself to Spanish influence with the least amount of cultural compromise. This was not an attitude of active resistance, but an instinctive rejection of whatever was perceived as not useful, and a habitual tendency to witness ways that were different without changing one's own. For a person from Ixil, the strange practices may have included not only those of Mérida, but those, say, of Tekanto. More than this, the Maya emphasis on the cah meant that methods of describing or doing things were invariably perceived within a cah-centric context that fosters a subconscious Mayanization and localization of every practice, regardless of its origin. Thus, in spite of the forced linking of Yucatan to the Hispanic world, initiated with violence in the sixteenth century, there still existed by the early nineteenth century a socially complex and culturally vital Maya world.

Appendixes

Six Maya Notarial Documents

These six documents have been selected because they are in many ways typical of the sources discussed in the body of the book, as well as being prominent among those documents specifically quoted, cited, and analyzed. They have also been included because, aside from the Titles of Ebtun (Roys 1939) and the Testaments of Ixil (Restall 1995a), Yucatec Maya notarial records are not available in print as Nahuatl sources now are. Orthographic conventions are the same as those of the text above (see Chapters 18 and 22).

1. Petition by the cabildo of Dzaptun, 1605 [AGN-CI, 2013, 1, 6]

Uay ti cah ti San Juan batista ɔaptun heleac tu hunkal u kinil julio ti hab 1605 años licix ca lic u hahil ca than licil ca mançabal ti ya tumen halach uinic mariscal yumile ahaue Reye okotba ca cah tech yoklal ca yumil ti dios u ɔben tah ca cah ta kab yetel a uoc ca a ubi ca than licil ca ma[n]çabal ti ya tu yabal meyahob yetel cħac che ti mayx u tulil licil u botic tumen u tuxchi juez cu talel uay tac cahal tu tuxchie lay mançicon ti ya cech ca yum cech Reye uchebal a uoheltic u numçabal ti ya cahob ti manan u colob u hantan teob yetel yal u mehenob pimix çatac tiob tumen mananil u hanalob lay tah men licil coktic caba ta tan uchbal a uanticon ta ɔayatzil yoklal techil ca yum cech ca noh ahaue cech visoReye catac ylabil ca num ya yetel cutzilil ta men yoklal dios cech ca yume ɔayatzil bin a cibtunal tac numya con a mehene pimix cuçimil tun tumenel u numçah ya gonve'dor tumenel u canal uinicob yoklal u cutz cheob calub oxlub cu likil che bigas yetel çuc yetel çi tulacal nunya lic u ɔayc ton cech ca yume cech ahaue bay xan cech ca yum cech oydore a uohelte ca numya con a mehene ca uan ton tutan visoRey ahau lay ca than yan tac pidiçione con a mehene yoklal dios bin a uutzcin ton ta ɔayatzil yoklal ca yumil ti dios ca a uan ton yohelix ca yum pᵉ ca numya ti cutzilil lay uchun licil coktic caba techal cech ca yume cech ahaue licix ca patcantic ca numya ta tan con uayal uinice tu cuchcabal canpech con u provinçiae yume ma tobal u yanal ca than ca yumil ti dios bin yana u cici than a uokol

Lonrenço ch procurador	Luis na alcalde	tintanix cen
diego chuc Regidor	Ju° pol alcalde	Antonio kuil
Ju° cante Regidor	Ju° pot alcalde	escr°
gaspar may Regidor		fran^co to
		gaspar pol

Here in the cah of San Juan Bautista Dzaptun, today on the 20th day of July of the year 1605. The following words of ours are true, that we are forced to undergo hardship by the Governor Marshal. O father, great King, we are petitioning to you for the sake of our lord Dios, we are kissing your hands and feet; hear our words! We are made to suffer hardship and a great deal of work, and also we cut wood for them but they do not give us our rightful payment. For this reason they sent a judge who came here to our cah. We are made to suffer hardship. You our father, you the King, know of the troubles of your cahob! They have no fields to feed them, and many of their children will die from lack of food. This is why we make a petition in your presence, so that you protect us and take pity, for the sake of you, our father, you, our great lord, you, the Viceroy, so our misery and poverty be seen by you, for the sake of Dios. You, our father, take pity on us, alleviate our misery. There are many deaths among us, your children, because the governor causes troubles, because of the fatigue of the people, because they carry planks of wood two or three leagues and raise up beams, and because we carry hay and firewood. All these miseries he gives to us. May you, our father, O lord, and also you, our father, the oidor, know the miseries of us, your children, and intercede for us before the lord Viceroy! This is our statement and the petition of us, your children. For the sake of Dios you are to do good to us and take pity. It is for the sake of our father, Dios, that you should help us. Our father, the padre, also knows our suffering and poverty. This is the reason that we make a petition to you, our father, you, our lord, and why we are telling you of our suffering, we, the local people of the jurisdiction of, we of the province of, Campeche. O father, our statement is over. May the blessing of our lord Dios be upon you.

Lorenzo Chi, procurador; Diego Chuc, regidor; Juan Cante, regidor; Gaspar May, regidor; Luis Na, alcalde; Juan Pol, alcalde; Juan Poot, alcalde; also in the presence of me, Antonio Kuil, notary; Francisco To; Gaspar Pol.

2. Election record, Tekanto, 1690 [AGEY-A, 1, 1]

Uay ti cah santo agustin tekanto u tabal u cuchcabal u gouernaçionil Merida tiho u hol u prouiniçianil yucatan hele 15 deçiembre de 1690 años ti ocanobix ti audiença Real ti cabidosob geronimo cach feliciano canul fran^co noh fran^co koh Regidoresob = an^to camal hasinto balam alcaldesob = tin tanil cen mathe° couoh escriban° = mahanquenile tamuk u multunticob tu mul alcaldesob Regidoresob mayoldomosob aluasilesob bin u alacob ychil yabil de 1691 años cu talele lay cah lemob ti ca yumil ti dios yetel ca noh ahau ah tepal hex cat ɔoci u multunticob tu chacancunahob tu tan almehen don Juan ɔib gue^or uay ti cah lae tu chichcunahi xan u

thanil c alaacob bin mektanticob u tanlahil Rey ah tepal hek lay ti tun tabob uay ti
audiençia Real chumu[c] cah lae ɔiban u kabaob uay cabale

= antᵒ camal————————————gaspar oy————————alcaldesob
= pascual balam————————————alcalde meson————————
= feliçiano ɔib = josep hau = glegᵒ ɔib = agustin pech = Regidoresob————
= matheᵒ batun————————————procurador————————————
= agustin couoh————————————aluasil mayol————————
= pᵒ kantun————————————mayoldomo————————
= Juᵒ ake=andres canul=pᵒ canul=pᵒ chan=francᶜᵒ ɔib=francᶜᵒ hau-
aluasilesob
= Josep bacab————————————madamiento meson————————
= agustin chable————————————madamiento meson————————
————————————————ARancel————————————
= matheᵒ couoh————————escribano————7 pesᵒ 12 cargas yxim u serallo——
= Juᵒ may————————————maestro——7 pesᵒ 12 cargas yxim u serallo——
= francᶜᵒ hau————————————tupil dotrina madamientas————————

lay ti ɔoci u tu mutob cabildosob y alcaldesob caix tu yalahob u binsabalob tutan ca
noh tzicanil yum ti sr gueor u chebal u chichcunic u thanil elecçion uay ti audiençia
Real ti santo agustin tekanto hele en 15 deçiembre de 1690 años————————

= antᵒ camal alldᵉ   Don Juᵒ ɔib   = geroᵐᵒ cach————————
= hasinto balam alldᵉ   gueᵒʳ   = feliçiano canul————————
                          matheᵒ couoh   = francᶜᵒ noh————————
                          esnᵒ   = francᶜᵒ koh————————
                                          Regidoresob————————

Here in the cah of San Agustín Tekanto, rooted in the jurisdiction of, the governorship of Mérida-Tihó, the gateway to the province of Yucatan, today December 15,
1690, having entered the royal courthouse, the cabildo officers, Gerónimo Cach,
Feliciano Canul, Francisco Noh, Francisco Koh, regidores, Antonio Camal, Jacinto
Balam, alcaldes, in the presence of me, Mateo Couoh, while they are gathered
publicly in meeting shall declare who the alcaldes, regidors, majordomos, and
alguaciles will be in the coming year 1691, in this cah entrusted to our lord Dios
and our great lord Ruler. Thus have they just gathered and appeared before the
noble don Juan Dzib, Governor here in this cah, to elect and order the statement of
[those who] shall govern in the service of the King Ruler. These, then, are the
members of the royal court in the center of the cah; their names are written here
below.

Antonio Camal, Gaspar Oy, alcaldes; Pasqual Balam, alcalde mesón; Feliciano
Dzib, Josef Hau, Gregorio Dzib, Agustín Pech, regidores; Mateo Batun, procurador;
Agustín Couoh, alguacil mayor; Pedro Kantun, mayordomo; Juan Ake, Andrés
Canul, Pedro Canul, Pedro Chan, Francisco Dzib, Francisco Hau, alguaciles; Josef
Cab, Agustín Chable, mandamiento mesón.

Salaried: The salary of Mateo Couoh, notary, is 7 pesos, 12 loads of corn; the salary of Juan May, maestro, is 7 pesos, 12 loads of corn; Francisco Hau, tupil doctrina mandamiento.

Thus ends the acceptance of the cabildo officers and alcaldes as determined before our great respected lord, the señor Governor, who strongly corroborated the election statement here in the royal courthouse of San Agustín Tekanto, today, December 15, 1690.

Don Juan Dzib, governor; Antonio Camal, Jacinto Balam, alcaldes; Gerónimo Cach, Feliciano Canul, Francisco Noh, Francisco Koh, regidores; Mateo Couoh, notary.

3. Bill of sale and land title, Santiago Tihó, 1741 [ANE-Y, 1776, 256, 257]

Carta de uenta Santiago

Oheltabac tumemen (sic) tulacal lauacmac ti uinicil yetel lauacmac ti Justisiasil bin ylic U ɔibil Junil conol carta de venta donasio[n] u kaba hebicil ca ɔaic U hahil than conic hunac solar ti seniora fransisca del balle yoklal 12 p^s ti hach takin atpuli xan lay ilic ca kubic ti U hahal y yallob tu tan kin cutalel loe tumenel U tulul U takin U bote tu mançal tix mama pecolalil ti mama bin u ɔa u yanal thani lay lic ɔaic U posisinil con Justisias y Cabildosob y ess^{no} p^{co} tu tanil U Batabil Cah licix ɔaic U carta de uentail ti tu k[a]ba Dios y ca noh ahau Rey nuestro señior ah tepal heyx lay solar lae lay yan tu chikin U solar mrõ Juan felis Juchim pakte u cotil y tu nohol U solar maselo chac Caye real chumuc ta noh be tu lakin [U] solar cah tocoy na caye chumuc tu xaman U solar felis pot hun pakte U cotil yetel heyx lay solar lae cotan U pach y u chun cot tu [. .] titzil yanix U chenil xan yanix pakal xani lay cu kamic u posisionnil señiora fran^{ca} del Balle tu tanil U testigo felipe tolosa tu kaba dios y ca noh ahau Uhahatial licil U kuchahal ti tumen tu mannah yoklal dose pesos lay licil U ɔabal U posisionil tu ɔoc carta uenta donasion U kaba licil U ɔaic U firma Justisiasob y cabildosob [y] ess^{no} p^{co} y testigo tu tanil U batabil Cah santiago hele ag^{to} 12 de 1741 años————————

niColas garsia th^e	Capp^n D^n Manuel pot	
manuel cauich ~~alde~~	g^{or} santiago	
florensio chable ~~alde~~	Alonso mo essno p^{co}	Juan segura reg^{or} ma^{or}
		pedro chel ygnasio mex
		diego pech Josep chel
Josep ek ess^{no} segundo		Josep chabel pedro chay
Ju^o santo mendosa		Diego pot Ju^o Uc ygnasio Joyl
marselo chac felis pot testigosob		Ber^{no} cah Reg^{or}sob
	Juan de Dios ɔul	
	procurador	

titulo santiago

uay ti cahal santiago nak lic U noh cahal siudad de meridae tu probinsias yucatan corona real ti noh ahau Rey nuestro señior ah tepal hele ag^{to} 12 de 1741 años to[n] con Batab y Justisiasob y cabildosob y ess^{no} p^{co} lic ca ɔaic hunpel titulo Auto ti seniora franᶜᵃ del Balle y u posisionil tumen conah Junac solar ti Utial cah heyx Bahun conah loe yoklal 12 ps ti hach takin atpuli xan lay lic ca ɔaic U tituloyl tu kaba ca yumil ti Dios y ca noh ahau Rey nuestro señior ah tepal heyx lay solar lae lay yan tan noh Be bel Junucma = tu chikin u solar maestro Juᵒ felis Juchim hun pakte U cotil y tu nohol u solar marselo chac caye real chumuc = tu lakin tocoy solar cah santiago caye chumuc = tu xaman U solar felis pot pake y u cotil yan u chenil yan u chun cot tu pach lay licil ɔaic u firma Jusᵃˢsob y cabildosob y essno y testigosob tutanil U Batab Cah Uay tu ɔoc titulo solar cabal he u kinil ɔiban canal loe =————————————

Cappⁿ Dⁿ Manuel pot	niColas garsia thᵉ
gᵒʳ santiago	manuel cauich a̶l̶lde
	florensio chable a̶l̶lde

Juᵒ segura regᵒʳ maᵒʳ
p.ᵒ chel   peᵒ chay   Alonso mo ess*no* pᶜᵒ
diego pech Regᵒʳsob   Josep ek   Juᵒ de Dˢ ɔul procurador
                        ess*no* segundo
Juᵒ santos mendosa marselo chac feliz pot testigosob

Bill of sale. Santiago.
It shall be known by all, by whoever of the men, whoever of the magistrates, that shall see the written document of the sale—the bill of sale and donation, it is called. Wherefore we give the true statement of the sale of one house plot to Señora Francisca del Valle for 12 pesos in valid money, to be paid immediately. As seen, we deliver it, in validity, with benefits, from this day on, because the payment of money is just. It passes to her neither with misgivings, nor shall she give another statement. Thus we give her possession of it, we the magistrates and cabildo officers and notary, before the batab of the cah. Likewise we give its bill of sale, in the name of Dios and our great lord King, our lord Ruler. To the west, then, of this house plot here, is the house plot of maestro Juan Félix Huchim together with his stony land; and to the south the house plot of Marcelo Chac, across the street at the main road; to the east an abandoned house on a cah house plot, across the street; to the north the house plot of Félix Poot, together with his stony land, which borders up to the corner the stony land that goes with the house plot in question, where there is also a well and an orchard. Thus Señora Francisca del Valle receives its possession before the witness Felipe Tolosa, in the name of Dios and our great lord. Now it is truly hers, it is certain, because she purchased it for 12 pesos. Thus its possession has been given. The bill of sale and donation, as it is called, is finished. The magistrates and cabildo officers, the notary public and witness, give their signatures before the batab of Santiago cah, today, August 12, of the year 1741.

Captain don Manuel Poot, governor of Santiago; Nicolás García, lieutenant; Manuel Cauich, Florencio Chable, alcaldes; Juan Segura, regidor mayor; Pedro Chel, Ignacio Mex, Diego Pech, Josef Chel, Josef Chable, Pedro Chay, Diego Poot, Juan Uc, Ignacio Hoil, regidors; Juan de Dios Dzul, procurador; Alonso Mo, notary public; Josef Ek, second notary; Juan Santos Mendoza, Marcelo Chac, Félix Poot, witnesses.

Title. Santiago.

Here in the cah of Santiago, beside the great cah, the city, of Mérida, in the province of Yucatan, under the royal crown of our great lord King, our lord Ruler, today, August 12, of the year 1741, we the batab, magistrates, cabildo officers, and notary public, now give a decree of title to Señora Francisca del Valle, with its possession, because we sold one house plot of cah property to her. Here is what it was sold for: 12 pesos in valid money, to be paid immediately. Thus we now give her its title in the name of our lord Dios and our great lord King, our Ruler. This house plot, then, is toward the main road to Hunucmá; to its west is the house plot of maestro Juan Félix Huchim, together with his stony land; and to the south Marcelo Chac's house plot, across the street; to the east an abandoned house plot of Santiago cah, across the street; to the north the house plot of Félix Poot, together with his stony ground. It has a well at the bottom of the stony ground that goes with it. The magistrates, cabildo officers, notary, and witnesses now give their signatures before the cah batab. Here, today, below, ends the title of the house plot written above.

Captain don Manuel Poot, governor of Santiago; Nicolás García, lieutenant; Manuel Cauich, Florencio Chable, alcaldes; Juan Segura, regidor mayor; Pedro Chel, Diego Pech, Pedro Chay, regidors; Juan de Dios Dzul, procurador; Alonso Mo, notary public; Josef Ek, second notary; Juan Santos Mendoza, Marcelo Chac, Félix Poot, witnesses.

4. Will of Mateo Canche, Ixil, 1766 [TI: 41]

Cimi Mathe.° canche en 26 de nobiem.ᵉ de 1766 ã

tu kaba D.ˢ yumbil y D.ˢ mehenbil y D.ˢ esspilitu santo oxtur perzonas huntulili hahar D.ˢ Vchuc tumen tusinil mayx pimobi lay bin ylabac V Junil yn thakyahthan tin testamento hibicil tenil cen mathe.° canche V meheNen franᶜᵒ canche V yalen Malia tec ah caharnalob Vay ti cah yxil lae bay xan cin uoktic ynba ti ca pixanil yum p.ᵉ Van xul in Cuxtar uay yokol cab rae Volah mucul yn culutil ti santa ygressia y ca yalab Junpeɔ missa Rezada bin ɔabac V limosnayl uacper tumin y hunper tumin gielusalem = y ca u mansen tu payalchi ychil u missa antabar yn pixan tu nuMiayl purgatorliol = Bay xan Junpet kax yan tu hor cah t lub be ber chicxulub mul kax yan tu tzayar potoob yn parte lae cin patic tu kab yn uixmehenob rae luissa canche y Martha canche Bay xan hunper caha utial yn uixmehe[n] luissa canche Bay xan caɔit machete y Junɔit cuchio Vtial [y]n uixmehen martha canche = halili V xul yn than kah ten xan hunpet kax yn conma ti Joseph canul yan tixcacar lae Bay tun lae tin uaskahsah oxper tostones ti marⁿ canul Vmehen Joseph canul bay bic tun puɔan Marⁿ canul lae hebikin bin chicanac Marⁿ canul lae ca uɔoc uaskes u taknil tres pesso lay luiss canche y martha canche catun culac lay kax tu kabbob yn uixmehenob rae halili u xul yn thakyahthan tin testamento cin uaCuntic Juntul al mehen Jassinto pech albasseas = 6 rrˢ y gielusalem 1 rˢ

D.ⁿ ygn.° tec

Diego coot alcarᵈ   Batab   gaspar chan gaspar ek

gaspar yam alcar^d   Andres tec then^e   sebas.^n chim xtouar[na]
                            Marcos pot essno   Regidorlessob rae

Dijose esta missa resada y lo firm[e]   fr Juan de Hoyos

Mateo Canche died on the 26 of November of the year 1766.
In the name of God the Father, God the Son, and God the Holy Spirit, three persons, one true God, Almighty. The document of my last will and testament will be made public, inasmuch as I am Mateo Canche, the son of Francisco Canche and Maria Tec, residents here of the cah of Ixil. Wherefore I supplicate our blessed lord the Padre that when my life here on this earth ends, I wish my body to be buried in the holy church; and that one low mass be said, the fee for which will be given, six tomins, and one tomin for Jerusalem; and that a prayer be said for me in the mass so that my soul be helped in the suffering of purgatory. Item: There is a forest at the entrance to the cah, a league along the Chicxulub road, adjacent to the forest of the Poot family, my share of which I leave in the hands of my daughters, Luisa Canche and Marta Canche; likewise one chest for my daughter Luisa Canche; likewise two machetes and one spoon for my daughter Marta Canche. This is the end of my statement—also I remember a forest. I sold it to Josef Canul. It is at Tixcacal. However, I returned three tostones to Josef Canul's son, Martín Canul. Then that Martín Canul ran away. On this day let it be recorded that when Luisa Canche and Marta Canche have fully returned his money, the three pesos, to the aforementioned Martín Canul, then this forest will be placed in the hands of these daughters of mine. There is no more; this is the end of my final statement in my testament. I appoint a nobleman, Jacinto Pech, as executor.
Six reales, with one real for Jerusalem.

Don Ignacio Tec, batab; Andrés Tec, lieutenant; Marcos Poot, notary; Diego Coot, Gaspar Yam, alcaldes; Gaspar Chan, Gaspar Ek, Sebastián Chim, Cristóbal Na, regidores.
I said this recited mass and signed, fray Juan de Hoyos

5. Settling of the estate of Josef Cab by the cabildo of Ixil, 1767 [TI: 45]

testimonio Vtial = Joseph Cab = cimi en 30 de mayo de 1767 ã Ma tu yalah u than lae = cimi tiJoo = toon con Batab y then^e = y Jus.^as Reg.^orlessob rae y ess^no ti audiensia lae lic Multumtic ti tulacal on yoklal lay solal yl u chenil lic kubic tu palillob Joseph cab y ti yiɔinob ti u palilob tulacar y yixmehen Marcos cab u yumob tumen cimi Marcos cab minan u testamento cimi u mehen xan ma tu yalah u than xan lay Joseph cab Bay tun lae ɔoc ylic u testamento u kilacabillob rae yoklal lay solal lae tu testamento Joseph cab cimi tu habil 726 ã u kilacabillob rae u yummob tumen max bin tuclic Uanbar ma u tzil lae ca ylac u testamento Joseph cab rae he u yarl u mehennob = lic oc lic ychil lay solal tulacarlob = Dominga cab y malia cab = fran^ca cab lossa cab y fran^co cab = y yixmehenob Joseph cab cimi lae ysidro cab Anna cab y Simona cab = Bay xan hunper baat y sarga y hunper chete y Junper camissa y Junper ex y kaxnak utial ysidro cab = lay u hahil ɔoc tzoli tulacar toon Batab y Jus^as Reg.^orlessob y ess^no heren 30 de mayo de 1767 ã

Capp.ⁿD.ⁿygn.ᵒtec Batab
Diego cot alcardes   Andres tec thenᵉ   gaspar chan gaspar
gaspar yam alcarᵉ   ek Sebas.ⁿchim xtoua
                                  Marcos Poot essno   r Na Reg.ᵒʳlessob rae
                                  Joseph mis cuch cab

Testimony regarding Josef Cab, [who] died on May 30, of the year 1767. He had not
made his statement. He died in Tihó. We who are the batab, lieutenant, magistrates,
regidores, and notary are now gathered together, all of us, in court, in order to deliver this house plot with its well to the children of Josef Cab and to his younger siblings; to all his children and the daughters of Marcos Cab, as their fathers are dead.
Marcos Cab had no testament. His son, this Josef Cab, also died without making his
statement. Therefore, we have just seen the will of their ancestors with respect to this
house plot, in the testament of Josef Cab, who died in the year 1726, that it belonged
to their ancestors, their fathers. For whosoever thinks this is not good, let them see
Josef Cab's will. His children will affirm it. All of them use this house plot: Dominga
Cab and Maria Cab, Francisca Cab, Rosa Cab, and Francisco Cab; and the daughters
of this deceased Joseph Cab—Isidro Cab, Ana Cab, and Simona Cab. Also one ax,
one blanket, one machete, one shirt, one pair of trousers, and one belt, [now] the
property of Isidro Cab. This is the truth, the end of the arrangement of everything
[by] us, the batab, magistrates, regidores, and notary, today, May 30, of the year 1767.

Captain don Ignacio Tec, batab; Andrés Tec, lieutenant; Diego Cot, Gaspar Yam,
alcaldes; Gaspar Chan, Gaspar Ek, Sebastián Chim, Cristóbal Na, regidores; Marcos Poot, notary; Josef Mis, ah cuch cab.

6. Anonymous petition, 1774 [AGN-I, 1187, 2, 59–61]

ten cen ah hahal than cin ualic techex hebaxile a uohelex yoklal Pᵉ torres pᵉ Dias
cabo de escuadra Pᵉ granado sargento yetel pᵉ maldonado layob la ma hahal caput
sihil ma hahal confisar ma hahal estremacion ma hahal misa cu yalicobi maix tan u
yemel hahal Dios ti lay ostia licil u yalicob misae tumenel tutuchci u cepob sansa-
mal kin chenbel u chekic ueyob cu tuculicob he tu yahalcabe manal tuil u kabob
licil u baxtic u ueyob he pᵉ torrese chenbel u pel kakas cisin Rita box cu baxtic y u
moch kabi mai moch u cep ualelob ix ɔoc cantul u mehenob ti lay box cisin la baixan
pᵉ Diaz cabo de escuadra tu kaba u cumaleil antonia aluarado xbolonchen tan u
lolomic u pel u cumale tutan tulacal cah y pᵉ granado sargento humab akab tan u
pechic u pel manuela pacheco hetun pᵉ maldonadoe tunɔoc u lahchekic u mek-
tanilobe uay cutalel u chucbes u cheke yohel tulacal cah ti cutalel u ah semana uinic
y xchup ti pencuyute utial yoch pelil pᵉ maldonado xpab gomes u kabah chenbel
Padresob ian u sipitolal u penob matan u than yoklalob uaca u ment utzil maçeuale
tusebal helelac ium cura u ɔaic u tzucte hetun lae tutac u kabob yetel pel lay
yaxcacbachob tumen u pen cech penob la caxuob yal misa bailo u yoli Dios ca oc
inglesob uaye ix ma aci ah penob u padreilobi hetun layob lae tei hunima u topob u
yit uinicobe yoli Dios ca haiac kak tu pol cepob amen

ten yumil ah hahal than

I, the informer of the truth, tell you what you should know about Fr. Torres, Fr. Díaz, squad corporal, Fr. Granado, sergeant, and Fr. Maldonado: they say false baptism, false confession, false last rites, false mass; nor does the true God descend in the host when they say mass, because they have erections. Every day all they think of is intercourse with their girl friends. In the morning their hands smell bad from playing with their girl friends. Fr. Torres, he only plays with the vagina of that really ugly black devil Rita. He whose hand is disabled does not have a disabled penis; it is said he has up to four children by this black devil. Likewise Fr. Díaz, squad corporal, has a woman from Bolonchen called Antonia Alvarado, with whom he repeatedly has intercourse (lit. penetrates her vagina) before the whole town, and Fr. Granado screws Manuela Pacheco (lit. bruises her vagina) all night. Fr. Maldonado has just finished fornicating with everyone in his jurisdiction. He has now come here to carry out his fornication, as the whole cah knows. When he comes each week (lit. as a *semanero*), a woman from Pencuyut provides Fr. Maldonado with her vagina; her name is Fabiana Gómez. Only the priests are allowed to fornicate without so much as a word about it. If a good Maya (*macehual*) does it, the priest punishes him immediately, every time. But look at their excessive fornication, putting their hands on these prostitutes' vaginas, even saying mass like this. God willing, when the English come may they not be fornicators equal to these priests, who stop short only at sodomy (lit. only lack carnal acts with men's arses). God willing that smallpox be rubbed into their penis heads. Amen.

I, father, the informer of the truth.

Incidence of Maya Patronyms in Nine Cahob

(Cacalchen, Ebtun, Ixil, Tekanto, and the Five Cahob-Barrios of Tihó, 1590–1835)

Ab					
Aban					
Abnal					
Ac					Tihó
Ake	Cacalchen	Ebtun	Ixil	Tekanto	Tihó
Akhol					
Ay					
Ayi					
Ba(a)					
Bacab				Tekanto	Tihó
Bacal					
Bak					
Balam		Ebtun		Tekanto	
Balche					
Batun				Tekanto	Tihó
Baz			Ixil		Tihó
Be					
Bil					
Bolon					
Cab			Ixil		Tihó
Ca(a)ch					
Cahum/n				Tekanto	
Cal					
Camal		Ebtun		Tekanto	Tihó
Can					Tihó
Canche	Cacalchen		Ixil	Tekanto	Tihó
Cante			Ixil		
Canul		Ebtun	Ixil	Tekanto	Tihó
Catzim					Tihó
Cauich		Ebtun			Tihó
Cayut					
Cech					Tihó
Ceh					Tihó
Cel					Tihó
Celiz					
Ceme					
Cen		Ebtun		Tekanto	Tihó

	Cacalchen	Ebtun	Ixil	Tekanto	Tihó
Cetz			Ixil	Tekanto	
Cetzal					
Ci					Tihó
Ciau					
Cime			Ixil		Tihó
Cituk					
Cob					
Coba			Ixil		Tihó
Cochuah					
Cocom	Cacalchen				Tihó
Coh					
Co(o)l					Tihó
Copo					
Cot			Ixil		
Couoh	Cacalchen	Ebtun	Ixil	Tekanto	Tihó
Cox					Tihó
Coyi			Ixil		Tihó
Cucab					
Culua					
Cumii					
Cumux					
Cupul					
Cutis		Ebtun			
Cutz			Ixil		Tihó
Cuxim					
Cuxum					
Cuy					
Cuytun					
Chab					
Chable	Cacalchen				Tihó
Chac					Tihó
Chala					
Chan	Cacalchen	Ebtun	Ixil	Tekanto	Tihó
Chay		Ebtun			Tihó
Che	Cacalchen				
Chi		Ebtun		Tekanto	Tihó
Chicil					
Chiclin					
Chicmul					
Chim			Ixil		Tihó
Chimal					
Chinab					
Chuan					
Chuc				Tekanto	Tihó
Chuil					
Chul					
Chulim				Tekanto	Tihó
Chunab					
Ch'e					Tihó
Ch'el					Tihó
Ch'oben					
Ch'oo					
Ch'uy					
Eb	Cacalchen				
Ek		Ebtun	Ixil	Tekanto	Tihó
Euan	Cacalchen				Tihó
Ez					
Ha					

Haban					
Habnal					
Hau				Tekanto	Tihó
He					
Hoil					Tihó
Homa					
Huchim		Ebtun	Ixil		Tihó
Huh					
Human					
Hun					
Ich					
Icte					
Itz	Cacalchen				
Itza			Ixil		Tihó
Iuit					
Ix				Tekanto	
Iz					
Ibincab		Ebtun			
Ka(a)k					
Kancab					
Kantun				Tekanto	
Kanxoc					
Kauil					Tihó
Ke					
Keb					
Keuel					
Kinich					
Kinil					
Koh	Cacalchen			Tekanto	
Ku	Cacalchen		Ixil	Tekanto	Tihó
Kuk					
Kumun					
Kutz					
Kuxeb					
Kuyoc		Ebtun			Tihó
Mac					
Matu			Ixil		
May	Cacalchen	Ebtun	Ixil	Tekanto	Tihó
Ma(a)z	Cacalchen		Ixil		Tihó
Mazte					
Mazum/n					
Mex			Ixil		Tihó
Mian					
Miz		Ebtun	Ixil		
Mo(o)			Ixil		Tihó
Moan					
Moh					
Muan					
Mucuy					
Mukul	Cacalchen	Ebtun	Ixil		
Mu(u)l					
Mut					
Mutul				Tekanto	Tihó
Muy					
Na			Ixil	Tekanto	Tihó
Nabte					
Nacan					
Nah					

	Cacalchen	Ebtun	Ixil	Tekanto	Tihó
Na(a)l					Tihó
Nauat		Ebtun			
Nayal					
Nic					
Noh		Ebtun		Tekanto	Tihó
Nuch					
Och					
Oxte					
Oy					
Pacab					
Palib					
Pan					
Panti					
Pat	Cacalchen	Ebtun		Tekanto	
Patun				Tekanto	
Pauo					
Pech	Cacalchen	Ebtun	Ixil		Tihó
Pet					
Peu					
Pez					
Pib					
Pitz					
Pix					
Pol		Ebtun			
Pomol					
Po(o)t		Ebtun	Ixil	Tekanto	Tihó
Pox					
Puc	Cacalchen	Ebtun		Tekanto	Tihó
Puch				Tekanto	Tihó
Ppencech					
Ppizte			Ixil		Tihó
Ppol				Tekanto	
Ta					
Tacu					
Tah					
Tamay		Ebtun			
Tax					
Tayu					
Te					
Tec			Ixil		
Tep					
Tepal					
Tinaal					
To					
Tox					
Tuc					
Tucech					Tihó
Tucuch					Tihó
Tuin					
Tulum					
Tun			Ixil		Tihó
Tu(u)t					Tihó
Tutul					
Tuyu					Tihó
Tuz					Tihó
Tzab					Tihó
Tzabnal					
Tzakum/n					

	Cacalchen	Ebtun	Ixil	Tekanto	Tihó
Tzama					
Tzek					
Tzel					
Tzimil					
Tziu					
Tzotz					
Tzuc					
Tzul					
Tzum/n					
Uacal					
Uc		Ebtun			Tihó
Ucan		Ebtun			Tihó
Uech					
Ueuet					
Uex					
Uh	Cacalchen		Ixil		
Uicab				Tekanto	
Uitz(il)	Cacalchen				Tihó
Uluac		Ebtun			
Uman					
Un		Ebtun			
Ux					
Uxul					
Uz					
Xaman					
Xamancab					
Xan					Tihó
Xicum					
Xiu					
Xix					
Xoc				Tekanto	
Xo(o)l					Tihó
Xuch					
Xul	Cacalchen				Tihó
Xuluc					
Ya(a)					
Yah					Tihó
Yam		Ebtun	Ixil	Tekanto	Tihó
Yama					
Ye					
Yix					
Yoc					
Yupit					
Zak					
Zalu					
Zel					
Zima					Tihó
Zulu					
Zum					
ɔacab					
ɔahe					
ɔal					
ɔay					
ɔib		Ebtun		Tekanto	Tihó
ɔiɔ					
ɔul		Ebtun		Tekanto	Tihó
TOTAL	21	33	34	36	75

SOURCES: LC, TE, TI, DT, ANE-Y libros 1776–1839.

APPENDIX C

⟡

Cabildo Officers of Eight Cahob

SOURCES: Tekanto: AGEY-A, 1, 1; Ixil: TI and ANEY-1819iv, 37; Cacalchen: LC; Tihó's five cahob-barrios: ANEY, various volumes cited in the text.

TABLE C.1
Cabildo Officers of Tekanto, 1683–1707

	1683	1684	1685	1686	1687	1688	1689	1690	1691
BATAB	Don Juan Dzib	Don Juan Dzib	Don Juan Dzib	Don Juan Dzib	Don Juan Dzib	Don Juan Dzib	Don Juan Dzib	Don Juan Dzib	Don Juan Dzib
THENIENTE									
ESCRIBANO	Mateo Couoh	Mateo Couoh	Mateo Couoh	Mateo Couoh	Mateo Couoh	Mateo Couoh	Mateo Couoh	Mateo Couoh	Mateo Couoh
ALCALDE MAYOR	Gaspar Chan	Mateo Ppol	Marcos Mex	Mateo Ppol	Mateo Ppol	Mateo Ppol	Francisco Canul	Antonio Camal	Antonio Camal
ALCALDE 2º	Francisco Canul	Antonio Camal	Agustín Dzib	Andrés Canul	Antonio Camal	Pedro Canul	Andrés Canul	Jacinto Balam	Gaspar Oy
REGIDOR MAYOR		Domingo Batun	Joseph Uc	Francisco Canul	Juan Balam	Francisco Chable	Agustín Dzib	Gerónimo Cach	Feliciano Dzib
REGIDOR 2º	Francisco ...	Andrés Canul	Pedro Canul	Antonio Poot	Jacinto Balam	Antonio Balam	Joseph Uc	Feliciano Canul	Joseph Hau
REGIDOR 3º	Gaspar ...	Lucas Hau	Francisco Bacab	Andrés Canul	Lucas Hau	Gregorio Dzib	Lucas Hix	Francisco Noh	Gregorio Dzib
REGIDOR 4º	Joseph May	Francisco Bacab	Agustín Poot	Antonio Balam	Gerónimo Cach	Lorenzo Koh	Gaspar Koh	Francisco Koh	Agustín Pech
ALCALDE MESON		Gaspar Koh	Francisco Noh	Lorenzo Koh	Mateo Batun	Francisco Koh	Antonio Hau	Agustín Poot	Pasqual Balam
PROCURADOR		Pedro May	Gaspar Baz	Francisco Chable	Gaspar Koh	Joseph Hau	Feliciano Dzib	Antonio Canche	Matheo Batun
MAYORDOMO		Pedro Balam	Diego May	Francisco Koh	Feliciano Dzib	Francisco Ek	Pasqual Balam	Gregorio Pech	Pedro Kantun
ALGUACIL MAYOR		Lorenzo Koh	Francisco Kantun	Antonio Hau	Agustín Poot	Antonio Canche	Juan Batun	Francisco Canche	Agustín Couoh
ALGUACIL		Feliciano Dzib	Agustín Poot	Leonardo Balam	Diego Pech	Diego Pech	Juan Puch	Juan Ku	Juan Ake
ALGUACIL		Cristóbal Noh	Francisco Puch	Lucas Canul	Bonifacio Couoh	Pedro Kantun	Joseph Uicab	Bernardo Baz	Andrés Canul
ALGUACIL		Baltesar May	Pasqual Balam	Juan Batun	Diego Balam	Juan Hau	Lucas Canul	Pedro Ppol	Pedro Canul
ALGUACIL		Pedro Poot	Gerónimo Uicab	Francisco Koh	Francisco Hau	Diego Poot	Antonio Poot	Agustín Pat	Pedro Chan
ALGUACIL		Antonio Cante	Lucas Hix	Joseph Canche	Pedro Ku	Francisco Puch	Diego Chan	Juan Chan	Francisco Chan
ALGUACIL			Felipe Baz	Andrés Ku	Francisco Hau	Francisco >ib	Andrés To	Ygnacio May	Francisco Hau
MANDAMIENTO MESON		Francisco ...	Agustín Poot	Aparicio Balam	Pedro Ppol	Gaspar Uicab	Gaspar Uicab	Gaspar Uc	Joseph Bacab
MANDAMIENTO MESON	Tomás ...	Bernardo Baz	Bernardo Baz	Diego Chan	Andrés To	Juan Chan	Juan Baz	Antonio Xoc	Agustín Chable
MAESTRO	Nicolás Chan	Nicolás Chan	Nicolás Chan	Nicolás Chan	Nicolás Chan	Juan May	Juan May	Juan May	Juan May
TUPIL DOCTRINA MANDAMIENTO	Pedro Dzib	Lucas Camal	Pedro Dzib	Pedro Dzib	Cristóbal May	Pedro Dzib	Andrés Balam	Andrés Balam	Francisco Hau

	1692	1693	1694	1695	1696	1697	1698	1699
BATAB	Don Juan Dzib	Don Juan Dzib	Don Juan Dzib	Don Juan Dzib	Don Juan Dzib	Don Juan Dzib	Don Juan Dzib	[no batab]
THENIENTE								
ESCRIBANO	Mateo Couoh	Mateo Couoh	Mateo Couoh	Mateo Couoh	Antonio Ake	Mateo Couoh	Mateo Couoh	Mateo Couoh
ALCALDE MAYOR	Mateo Ppol	Jacinto Balam	Francisco Canul	Marcos Mex	Felipe Chan	Antonio Canul	Francisco Noh	Gerónimo Cach
ALCALDE 2º	Francisco Noh	Francisco Camal	Feliciano Dzib	Juan Batun	Gerónimo Canul	Bartolome Balam	Feliciano Dzib	Gregorio Dzib
REGIDOR MAYOR	Lorenso Koh	Andrés Canche	Marcos Balam	Ygnacio Canul	Juan Ek	Gerónimo Cach	Joseph Hau	Pedro Pool
REGIDOR 2º	Juan Ek	Diego Puc	Bonifacio Couoh	Joseph Hau	Francisco Koh	Diego May	Gregorio Couoh	Mateo Batun
REGIDOR 3º	Antonio Hau	Agustin Puch	Hernando Ake	Cristóbal Ku	Gregorio Dzib	Hernando Ake	Agustín Hau	Juan May
REGIDOR 4º	Francisco Canche	Antonio Canche	Sebastian Ku	Juan Puch	Alonso Balam	Pedro Camal	Pedro Kantun	Diego Poot
ALCALDE MESON	Juan Batun	Pedro Kantun	Joseph Canche	Cristóbal May	Diego Chan	Bonifacio Couoh	Lucas Hix	Antonio Pat
PROCURADOR	Cristóbal May	Diego Camal	Cristóbal Oy	Pedro Kantun	Diego Hix	Gaspar Uicab	Alonso Balam	Francisco Poot
MAYORDOMO	Andrés Ku	Aparicio Balam	Francisco Canche	Mateo Batun	Andrés To	Diego Poot	Juan Ake	Agustín Couoh
ALGUACIL MAYOR	Juan Puch	Andrés To	Lucas Canul	Diego Poot	Ygnacio May	Pedro Chan	Tomás May	Alonso Couoh
ALGUACIL	Francisco Ek	Antonio Xoc	Antonio Pat	Pedro Ku	Tomás Ake	Salvador Puch	Pedro Ku	Bernardino Batun
ALGUACIL	Antonio Baz	Joseph May	Juan Ake	Diego Ppol	Francisco Mukul	Gaspar Ppol	Andrés Baz	Gaspar Batun
ALGUACIL	Pedro Ku	Diego Poot	Joseph Uicab	Juan Ku	Alonso Couoh	Juan Canul	Nicolás Bacab	Cristóbal Baz
ALGUACIL	Juan Baz	Diego Baz	Marcos Hau	Gregorio Couoh	Juan Camal	Domingo Balam	Estebán Hau	Agustín Canul
ALGUACIL	Diego Chan	Andrés Ku	Joseph Bacab	Andrés Ku	Bernardo Dzib	Marcos Bacab	Juan Chan	Juan Baz
ALGUACIL	Jacinto Balam	Bernardo Dzib	Agustín Hau	Juan Chan	Gaspar Canche	Joseph Hau	Francisco Canul	Francisco Uicab
MANDAM. MESON	Pablo Canul	Nicolás Bacab	Agustín Couoh	Agustín Canul	Francisco Balam	Sebastian Ake	Antonio Mena	Gaspar Canche
MANDAM. MESON	Diego Poot	Bernardino Xoc	Cristóbal Baz	Francisco Uicab	Andrés Na	Joseph Hau	Gaspar Batun	Cristóbal May
MAESTRO	Juan May	Juan May	Juan May	Juan May	Juan May	Juan May	Juan May	Juan May
TUPIL DOC. MAND.	Francisco Hau	Lucas Camal	Bernardo Chan	Andrés Balam	Pedro Chan	Miguel Poot	Gaspar Couoh	Bartolome Bacab

339

TABLE C.1
Continued

	1700	1701	1702	1703	1704	1705	1706	1707
BATAB	Don Antonio Camal	D. Antonio Camal	D. Antonio Camal	D. Agustín de Palensuela	D. Agustín de P.	D. Agustín de P.	D. Agustín de P.	D. Mateo Ppol [?]
THENIENTE				Gerónimo Cach				Antonio Hau
ESCRIBANO	Mateo Couoh	Mateo Couoh	Mateo Couoh	Lucas Camal	Lucas Camal	Lucas Camal		
ALCALDE MAYOR	Juan Ek	Feliciano Dzib	Diego Poot	Francisco Canul	Gregorio Dzib	Gregorio Couoh	Gerónimo Cach	Alonso Couoh
ALCALDE 2º	Bartolome Balam	Pedro Ppol	Agustín Couoh	Lucas Hix	Luis Pech	Nicolás Canche	Agustín Pat	Juan Camal
REGIDOR MAYOR	Antonio Balam	Diego Poot	Pasqual Couoh	Francisco Noh	Alonso Couoh	Tomás Ake	Francisco Ku	Antonio Hau
REGIDOR 2º	Francisco Koh	Diego Puc	Agustín Hau	Pedro Ppol	Pablo Canul	Joseph Uicab	Juan Puch	Bernardo Baz
REGIDOR 3º	Ygnacio May	Gerónimo May	Marcos Puch	Pedro Kantun	Gerónimo Bacab	Bartolome Bacab	Diego Puch	Francisco Canul
REGIDOR 4º	Pasqual Couon	Joseph Uicab	Andrés Batun	Antonio Pat	Cristóbal May	Mateo Yam	Gaspar …	Francisco Puch
ALCALDE MESON	Pedro Chan	Lucas Canul	Ambrosio Balam	Juan Puch	Bartolomeo Chan	Andrés Ku		Juan Tep
PROCURADOR	Diego Camal	Nicolás Canul	Francisco Mukul	Francisco Mukul	Agustín Pat	Juan Puch		Pedro Ku
MAYORDOMO	Diego Chan	Bernardo Baz	Andrés Batun	Pedro May	Gaspar Dzib	Francisco Ku		Andrés Baz
ALGUACIL MAYOR	Bernardo Dzib	Francisco Chan	Aparicio Balam	Francisco Koh	Andrés Baz	Juan Chan		Andrés May
ALGUACIL	Francisco Koh	Pedro Ku	Diego Na	Lucas Canul	Agustín Balam	Andrés Batun		Felipe May
ALGUACIL	Joseph Balam	Antonio Mena	Cristóbal Bacab	Matias Na	Agustín Ku	Francisco Batun		Bernardino Hau
ALGUACIL	Bernabe Camal	Pedro Chim	Ventura Ku	Gaspar Batun	Pedro Bacab	Bernardo Canche		Gaspar Hau
ALGUACIL	Andrés Na	Joseph Ppol	Cristóbal May	Gaspar Hau	Juan Castro	Diego Ake		Mateo P…
ALGUACIL	Ygnacio Canul	Gaspar Canche	Andrés Ku	Mateo Pat	Andrés Baz	Mateo Poot		Antonio Canche
ALGUACIL	Baltesar Poot	Joseph Bacab	Gaspar Camal	Gaspar Ppol	Gregorio Camal	Gaspar Camal		Pablo Hau
MANDAM. MESON	Francisco Canul	Andrés Baz	Bernardo Canche	Gaspar Puch	Bernardo Chan	Bernardo Dzul		Diego Balam
MANDAM. MESON	Andrés Balam	Andrés May	Gaspar Hau	Juan Cetz	Nicolás Yam	Felipe May		Lucas Balam
MAESTRO	Juan May	Juan May	Juan May	Juan May	Juan May	Juan May	Juan May	Juan May
TUPIL DOC. MAND.	Miguel Poot	Agustín Uicab	Miguel Poot	Bartolome Bacab	Cristóbal Balam	Miguel Poot		Juan Chan

TABLE C.2
Cabildo Officers of Ixil, 1765–1807

	1765	1766	1767	1768	1769	1773	1777	1779	1786	1798	1807
BATAB	Dn Ygnasio Tec	Dn Ygnasio Tec	Dn Ygnasio Tec	Dn Ygnasio Tec	Dn Ygnasio Tec	Dn Joseph Cob	Dn Joseph Cob	Dn José Cab(?)	Dn Estebán Tep		Dn Estebán Tep
THENIENTE		Gaspar Coba	Andrés Tec					Felipe Canche	JndelaCr Chan	Franco Coba	JndelaCr Chan
ESCRIBANOS	Joseph Cob	Pablo Tec	Marcos Pot	Pablo Tec	Alonso Cob	Diego Chim	Marcos Pot	Domingo Ytza	Jsé Maria Chim	Estebán Yam	Ysidro Cob
	Marcos Pot										
ALCALDES	Andrés Pech	Joseph Pech	Diego Coot	Salvador Coba	Juan Pech	Gaspar Pech	Gaspar Yam	Sebastián Chim	Nicolás Tun	Franco Tec	Pedro Mis
	Nicolás Couoh	Diego May	Gaspar Yam	Clemente Cante	Franco May	Pedro Canul	Nicolás Ytza	Mathec Uh	Franco Yam	Manuel Tec	Pedro Pan
REGIDORES	Pasqual Coba	Antto Tec	Gaspar Chan	Juan Matu	Pasqual Canche	Gaspar Yam	Diego Tun	Franco May	Juan Coba	Simón Chim	Estebán Cutz
	Marcos Couoh	Franco Canul	Gaspar Ek	Juan Coba	Pasqual Na	Salvador Cante	Diego Poot	Pedro Coba	Gabriel Poot	Pasqual Coba	Pablo Chale
	Pasqual Pech	Antto Pech	Sebastián Chim	Franco Huchim	Nicolás Euan	Barme Pech	Pasqual Yam	Gaspar Cob	Alexandro Yam	Leonardo Tec	Jn Gaspar Chan
	Pasqual Canche	Pedro Canul	Cristóbal Na	Pasqual Canche	Antonio Kinil	Joseph Pech	Barme Matu	Felipe Canul	JndelaCr Couoh	Salvadr Canche	Marsel Matu
AH CUCH CAB								Joseph Pech			
								Diego Poot			
ALBACEAS	Joseph Mis		Joseph Mis		Joseph Cob						
	Matheo Canul	Dn Gaspar Canul	Dn Gaspar Canul	Dn Gaspar Canul							
		Pedro Poot	Pedro Poot	Pedro Poot							
		Jasinto Pech	Jasinto Pech								
		Pedro Mis	Bena Coba								
		Sebastian Yam	Agustin Cante								
		Pedro Cob	Juan Chale								
		Diego Pech	Gaspar Coba								
		Andrés Tec	Matheo Canul								
		Andrés Cob	Franco Coba								
		Joseph Cob	Juan Matu								
		Gaspar Ek									
		Marcos Pot									
		Don Andrés Pech									
		Gregorio Pech									

TABLE C.3

Cabildo Officers of Cacalchen, 1646–1656

	1646	1647	1648	1649	1650	1653	1654	1655	1656
BATAB									
THENIENTE						Don Miguel Canche	Don Miguel Canche		
ESCRIBANO					Antonio Chi		Antonio Chi		
ALCALDES	Don Gonzalo Kuk	Pedro Chi	Pedro Chi	Pedro Chi	Diego Canche	Don Gerónimo Pat	Francisco Chi	Francisco Na	Mateo Kuk
	Martín Euan	Martín Euan		Joseph Couoh		Francisco Uicab	Agustín Cox	Mateo Kuk	
	Martín May					Francisco Chi			
						... Cocom			
REGIDORES	Diego Pat	Mateo Kuk	Agustín Cox	Joseph Couoh	Antonio Ac	Francisco ...	Antonio Eb	Gaspar Tzox	Pedro Koh
	Diego Ake	Cristóbal Yuit	Juan Euan	Francisco Na		Andrés Couoh			Andrés Euan
		Antonio Ac	Diego Chable	Felipe Kuk		Andrés ...			
		Agustín Cox		Cristóbal Yuit		Gaspar Kuk			
		Pedro Canche				Lorenso Yam			
		Luis Cocom							
AH CUCH CAB				Francisco ...					
ALBACEAS	Diego Pech	Diego Balam	Andrés Euan	Juan Tun	Diego Yuit	Thomas Ake	Mateo Kuk	Antonio Chi	Pedro Koh
	Andrés Kantun	Diego Ake	Antonio Ac	Francisco Pech	Juan Kantun	Gregorio Pat	Antonio Xool	Antonio Eb	Gaspar Couoh
	Melchor Ac	Andrés Cocom	Pedro Pat	Francisco Uicab	Felipe Chi	Andrés Euan	Andrés Cocom		
	Francisco Uicab	Manuel Pat	Miguel Matu	Lorenso Euan			Gaspar Tzox		
	Francisco Na	Ventura Pat	Mateo Eb						
		Luis Pat							
		Joseph Pat							
		Pedro Matu							
		Miguel Uh							
		Mateo Kuk							
		Bartolome Chable							
TESTIGO	Juan Uitzil								
	Francisco Na								

TABLE C.4
Cabildo Officers of Santiago Tihó, 1741–1835

	1741	1744	1753	1755	1764	1765	1769	1778	1779	1780
BATAB	Don Manuel Pot	Don Manuel Poot	Don Alonso Euan	Don Alonso Euan	Don Alonso Euan	D. Juan E.S. Chable	Don Diego Uluac	Don Marcelo Bacab	D. Silvestre Chable	D. Silvestre Chable
THENIENTE	Nicolás Garsia	Manuel Cauich	Ygnasio Pech	Nicolas Chel	Juan Antonio Canul	Theodoro Poot	Marcelo Yx	Matias Can	Carlos Poot	Dionisio Uc
ESCRIBANO PUBLICO	Alonso Mo	Alonso Mo	Marcelo Pech	Alonso Mo	Alonso Mo	Marcelo Pech	Marcelo Pech	Dionisio Euan	Antonio Pech	Juan Coba
ESCRIBANO 2°	Josep Ek			Juan Baut'a Chable					Feliciano Cauich	
ALCALDE 1°	Manuel Cauich	Florensio Chable	Felipe Hau	Bartolome Pech	Matias Can	Lorenzo Pech	Simón Canche		Ylario Chable	
ALCALDE 2°	Florensio Chable	Antonio Uicab	Valentín Garcia	Theodoro Poot	Jacinto Chay	Francisco Canche	Pablo Chable			Valentín Canche
REGIDOR MAYOR	Juan Segura	Pedro Chel	Baltesar Bacab	Diego Hau	Leonardo Yuit	Joseph Chan	Lorenzo Pech	Juan de Dios Chable	Teodoro Poot	
REGIDOR 2°	Pedro Chel	Ygnasio Mex	Agustín Chan	Matias Can	Theodoro Poot	Simón Canche	Tomás Canche		Ylario Poot	
REGIDOR 3°	Pedro Chay	Joseph Chel		Manuel Ek	Gregorio Na	Felis Camal	Pablo Chel		Pablo Chable	Silvestre Cime
REGIDOR 4°	Diego Pech	Juan Uc			Felis Cach	Pablo Dzib	Santiago Bas		Santiago Pech	Marcos Xul
REGIDOR	Josep Chel	Juan Segura							Rafael Ku	
REGIDOR	Josep Chabel	Pedro Chay								
REGIDOR	Ygnasio Mex									
REGIDOR	Diego Poot									
REGIDOR	Juan Uc									
REGIDOR	Ygnasio Joyl									
REGIDOR	Bernardino Cab									
PROCURADOR	Juan de Dios Dzul					Bartolome Pech				

	1781	1782	1786	1789	1793	1797	1802	1806	1835
									[CACIQUE & ALCALDE AUXILIAR]
BATAB		D. Silvestre Chable	D. Marcelo Bacab	Don Marcelo Bacab	Don Marcelo Bacab	D. Marcelino Bacab	D. Juan de la C.	D. Marcelino Bacab	
THENIENTE		Santiago Pech	Carlos Poot			Leonardo Sisneros	Pablo Xol		
ESCRIBANO PUBLICO	Juan Coba	Juan Coba		Toribio Coba	Joseph Venancio Chan	Joseph Ven. Chan	Esteban Chan	Joseph Venan. Chan	José Buenfis
ESCRIBANO 2°									
ALCALDE 1°	Felis Cauich	Pablo Chable		Manuel Canche	Agustín Na	Pedro Canche	Eusebio Pech		
ALCALDE 2°	Julian Ek	Antonio Chable							
REGIDOR MAYOR	Carlos Pot	Ylario Chable		Ygnacio Poot	Juan de Dios Chable	Gaspar Naal	Pasqual Chable		
REGIDOR 2°	Miguel Chan			...n Canul	Leonardo Rosado	Reymundo Yah	Carlos Pech		
REGIDOR 3°						Pablo Poot	Marcelo Chable		
REGIDOR 4°							Jose Poot		

343

TABLE C.5
Cabildo Officers of San Sebastián Tihó, 1749–1815

	1749	1752	1756	1758	1760	1762	1764	1765	1766
BATAB	D. Francisco Dzul	D. Francisco Dzul	D. Francisco Dzul	D. Francisco Dzul	Don Francisco Cox	Don Francisco Cox	D. Francisco Cox	D. Francisco Cox	D. Francisco Cox
THENIENTE		Hernando Can	Andrés Coyi	Ventura Kuyoc	Juan Ramos Kuyoc	Bonifacio Kuyoc	Ventura Kuyoc	Juan Ramos Kuyoc	Juan Cosme Batun
ESCRIBANO PUBLICO	Joseph Chan	Joseph Chan	Joseph Chan	Feliciano Mex	Feliciano Mex	Joseph Chan	Feliciano Mex	Feliciano Mex	Feliciano Mex
ESCRIBANO 2º			Feliciano Mex			Feliciano Mex			
ALCALDE 1º	Antonio Mex	Cristóbal Che			Lucas Pech	Tribusio Dzul	Pasqual Chan	Ylario Coyi	Salvador Cox
ALCALDE 2º	Mateo Uc				Juan Batun	Luis Puc		Juan de la C. Cech	
REGIDOR MAYOR	Andrés Couoh	Juan Santos	Bernardino Chan	Cristóbal Chi	Juan de la C. Cech	Bernardino Chan	Juan Batun		Lucas Pech
REGIDOR 2º	Juan Chuc	Gaspar Dzul	Mateo Yam		Francisco Pech	Pedro Chan	Pasqual Santos		Ambrocio ...
REGIDOR 3º		Baltesar Mas	Juan Cosme Batun			Juan Santos Kuyoc			
REGIDOR 4º		Eusebio Mutul	Joseph Yah			Ylario Coyi			
REGIDOR		Pablo Pech				Juan Tucech			
REGIDOR						Lauriano Ku			

	1773	1775	1776	1778	1781	1782	1809	1815
BATAB	Don Claudio Ku	Don Claudio Ku	Don Claudio Ku	Don Claudio Ku	Don Claudio Ku	Don Claudio Ku		D. José María Kumun
THENIENTE			Tribucio Dzul	Juan Batun	Lauriano Puch	Juan Batun	Estebán Dzul	Lucas Na
ESCRIBANO PUBLICO	Juan Pio V Kuyoc	Juan Pio V Kuyoc	Juan Pio V Kuyoc	Juan Pio V Kuyoc	Juan Pio V Kuyoc	Juan Pio V Kuyoc		Estanislao Kuyoc
ESCRIBANO 2º								
ALCALDE 1º	Tribucio Dzul	Bernardino Chu	Simón Kuyoc	Domingo Ku	Tomás Uitz	Domingo Kuyoc	José María Kuyoc	Juan Kuyoc
ALCALDE 2º	Lauriano Puch	Juan Batun	Mauricio Poot	Antonio Camal	Pablo Chim	Pedro Chan	Lucas Na	Antonio Yah
REGIDOR MAYOR	Tribucio Puc	Juan Santos Kuyoc	Juan Mex	Bernardino Chu	Julian Chan	Juan Santos Kuyoc	Sebastián Chim	Menehildo Ac
REGIDOR 2º	Pedro Camal	Juan Thomas Chan	Bonifacio Osorio	Joseph Manzum	Luis Pech	Juan Tomas Chan	Lazaro Kuyoc	Ventura Uc
REGIDOR 3º			Pedro Camal	Tomás Uitz	Lauriano ...	Mauricio Poot		
REGIDOR 4º			Lauriano Puch			Estevan Kuyoc		
TESTIGOS			Bernardino Chan					
			Antonio Dzul					

344

TABLE C.6

Cabildo Officers of San Cristóbal Tihó, 1713–1830

	1713	1766	1767	1770	1781	1783	1784
BATAB	Don ... Pech	Don Domingo Sima	Don Martin Ek	Don Martin Ek	Don Martin Ek	D. Antonio Poot	Don Antonio Poot
THENIENTE	Juan Chan	Sebastian Poot	Asensio Chuc	Pasqual Camal		Pedro Franco	Gregorio Chay
ESCRIBANO	Nicolás Chan	Juan Xol	Juan Xol	Juan Xol	Juan Xol		
ALCALDE MAYOR		Pasqual Chi	Cristóbal Pizte		Cristóbal Sima	Felisto May	Felipe Chan
ALCALDE 2º			Bonisio Cauich				
REGIDOR MAYOR	Andrés Puc	Carlos Chi		Ventura Chan	Manuel Kuyoc	Pasqual Poot	
REGIDOR 2º		Juan Chi	Pasqual Uc			Juan Canul	
REGIDOR 3º		Juan Antonio Can	Sebastián Argaes			Baltasar Chan	
REGIDOR 4º			Francisco Poot				
REGIDOR 5º		Ventura Chan					

	1810	1815	1819	1820	1822	1830
BATAB	Don Pedro Nolasco Camal		Don Basilio Pan			Miguel Chi
THENIENTE	Joaquin Xol	Reymundo Poot	Mauricio Poot			
ESCRIBANO	Juan Casimiro May	Seferino Ku	Seferino Ku	[ALCALDES AUXILIARES]		Sisto Uc
ALCALDE MAYOR	José Tzab	Gerónimo Chan	Patricio Poot	Pedro N. Camal	D. Juan Lino Angulo	
ALCALDE 2º	Dionisio Couoh	Casimiro Canul	Tomás Chi	Juan Pablo Chim		[TESTIGOS]
REGIDOR MAYOR	Pedro Canche	Pablo Chi	Matias Tus	Juan Tomás Suares		Bernardino Ponti
REGIDOR 2º	Lucas Chan	Atanasio Ek	Teodoro Tun	Juan Lino Angulo		Pedro Tus
REGIDOR 3º	Roman ...	Pablo Canche	Martin Chan			Dionisio Couoh

345

TABLE C.7

Cabildo Officers of La Mejorada Tihó, 1769–1825

	1769	1770	1771	1774	1776	1783
BATAB	Don Toribio Tuyu	Don Toribio Tuyu	Don Toribio Tuyu		Don Ygnacio Muños	Don Ygnacio Muños
THENIENTE						
ESCRIBANO PUBLICO	Santiago Chan	Santiago Chan	Santiago Chan	Santiago Chan	Santiago Chan	Santiago Chan
ALCALDE MAYOR	Roque Chan	Roque Chan	Pedro Chan	Lorenso Dzul	Juan Cosme Cauich	Juan Cosme Cauich
ALCALDE 2º	Julian Cen	Nicolas Cocom		Felipe de la C. Puc		Siprian Chan
REGIDOR MAYOR		Manuel Chable	Pasqual Dzul	Juan de la C. Chan	Joseph Ci	Pasqual Yam
REGIDOR 2º	Pedro Kuyoc	Pasqual Chan		Teodoro Canche	Antonio Chan	Bernardino Ek
REGIDOR 3º	Salvador Balche	Julian Canche				
REGIDOR 4º	Ventura Cob	Pasqual Yam				
ALGUASIL MAYOR		Jn Ambrosio Canche				
					Pedro Uc	

	1787	1790	1791	1793	1825 [ALCALDE AUXILIAR]
BATAB	Don Juan May	José Ci	Nicolás Couoh	Antonio Ek	
THENIENTE					
ESCRIBANO PUBLICO	Santiago Chan	Santiago Chan	Santiago Chan	Santiago Chan	
ALCALDE MAYOR	Pedro Chan	Manuel Dzul	Jacinto Canche	Ysidro Noh	Mariano Vega
ALCALDE 2º		Sebastián Kuyoc			
REGIDOR MAYOR	Juan Cosme Cauich	Pedro Chan	Pedro Col	Lorenso Canche	
REGIDOR 2º	Marcos Xol		Pedro Chable	Manuel Aban	
REGIDOR 3º			Atanasio Chan	Antonio Pan	
REGIDOR 4º					
ALGUASIL MAYOR		Marcos Xol			

TABLE C.8

Cabildo Officers of Santa Ana Tihó, 1748–1822

	1748	1766	1770	1781	1783	1794
BATAB	Don Juan Canche	Don Dionisio Kauil	D. Marcos Canche	D. Eusebio Kauil	D. Eusebio Kauil	D. Alexandro Ake
THENIENTE	Marselo Dzul	Asensio Pech		Tiburcio Couoh	Sebastián Couoh	Francisco Peh
ESCRIBANO PUBLICO	Alonso Mo		Felipe Chable	Mariano Couoh	Mariano Couoh	Gregorio Camal
ESCRIBANO 2º	Gerónimo Ek					
ALCALDE 1º	Pasqual Dzul	Miguel Asueta		Francisco Can	Pablo Chan	Narciso Chable
ALCALDE 2º	Mechor Cocom	Juan Chan				Marcelo Chan
REGIDOR MAYOR	Dionisio Kauil	Dionisio Dzib		Pablo Poot		Bernardo Chim
REGIDOR 2º	Pedro Tun	Pasqual Setina				
REGIDOR 3º	Santiago Pech	Gregorio Dzib				
REGIDOR 4º	Pasqual Dzib					
REGIDOR	… Canche					
REGIDOR	Joseph Chan					Marcelo Couoh
ALGUACIL						
		1822				
[BATAB]						
[THENIENTE]						
SECRETARIO	Faustino Chan					
[ESCRIBANO 2º]						
ALCALDE 1º ELECTION	Don Valentín Canche					
ALCALDE 2º ELECTION	D. Pedro Celestino Chan					
REGIDOR MAYOR	Don Tribucio Chable					
REGIDOR 2º	Don Agustín Yam					

⌀

Wealth and Inheritance in Ixil, Cacalchen, and Nine Other Cahob

Table D.1. Index of Ixil testators, 1765–1768

Table D.2. Index of Cacalchen testators, 1646–1679

Table D.3. Wealth in Ixil, 1765–1768: male testators

Table D.4. Wealth in Ixil, 1765–1768: female testators

Table D.5. Wealth in Cacalchen, 1646–1656: male testators

Table D.6. Wealth in Cacalchen, 1646–1656: female testators

Table D.7. Inheritance in Ixil, 1765–1768: goods bequeathed, by category, and recipients, by kin relation to testator: 31 male donors

Table D.8. Inheritance in Ixil, 1765–1769: goods bequeathed, by category, and recipients, by kin relation to testator: 20 female donors

Table D.9. Inheritance in Cacalchen, 1646–1656: goods bequeathed, by category, and recipients, by kin relation to testator: 16 male donors

Table D.10. Inheritance in Cacalchen, 1646–1678: goods bequeathed, by category, and recipients, by kin relation to testator: 11 female donors

Table D.11. Inheritance in Ebtun, 1785–1813: goods bequeathed and recipients, by kin relation to testator: 9 donors

Table D.12. Inheritance in various other cahob, 1629–1784: goods bequeathed and recipients, by kin relation to testator: 8 donors

NOTE: The numbers along the top of Tables 3–6 are testament numbers; to match a testament number to a name and date, see Tables 1 and 2. The property items listed in Tables 3–12 are presented in translation, with the Maya (or Spanish terms used by the Maya) in parentheses and in the original orthography.

TABLE D.1
Index of Ixil Testators, 1765–1768

Doc.	Testator	Folio	Date
1	Gaspar Matu	1r	[1765]
2	Antonia Cante	v	[1765]
3	Manuel Cab	2r	[1765]
4	Pedro Couoh		11-28-1765
5	Andrés Coba	v	[1765]
6	Gregorio Canche		1-12-1766
7	Ignacio Canul	3r	1-3-1766
8	Josef Uitz	v	10-15-1765
9	Antonia Coba	6r	1-10-1766
10	Felipe Coba		1-12-1766
11	Pedro Matu	v	1-26-1766
12	Maria Canche	7r	1-28-1766
13	Petrona Na	v	2-12-1766
14	Diego Chan, maestro	8r	1-24-1766
15	Gabriel Tec	v	1-30-1766
16	Joseph Couoh	9r	1-5-1766
17	Gerónimo Tec		2-15-1766
18	Bernardina Couoh	v	3-5-1766
19	Gaspar Poot		3-10-1766
20	Nicolasa Tec	10r	3-28-1766
21	Simón Chan	v	4-4-1766
22	Ventura Yam	11r	4-4-1766
23	Viviana Canche	v	4-28-1766
24	Bernardino Cot	12r	4-29-1766
25	Bernardino Coba	v	5-2-1766
26	Maria Chan		5-7-1766
27	Juan Tacu	13r	7-20-1766
28	Juan de la Cruz Poot		6-15-1766
29	Pasquala Matu	v	8-25-1766
30	Pedro Mis	14r	8-17-1766
31	Marta Coba	v	8-6-1766
32	Josef Poot	15r	9-17-1766
33	Josef Yam	v	11-20-1766
34	Marta Chan	16r	11-8-1766
35	Francisco Couoh	v	12-23-1766
36	Juan de la Cruz Coba	17r	11-12-1766
37	Antonio Huchim	v	12-20-1766
38	Marta Coba	18r	12-3-1766
39	Diego Coba		1-14-1767
40	Sebastián Uh	v	1-10-1767
41	Mateo Canche	20r	11-26-1766
42	Pasqual Huchim	21r	2-11-1767
43	Diego Canul	v	2-30-1767[sic]
44	Pasquala Balam	22r	5-5-1767
45	Josef Cab	v	5-30-1767
46	Thomasa Tec	23r	6-9-1767
47	Juana Mo	v	6-9-1767
48	Juana Tun		6-1..-1767
49	Salvador Poot	24r	6-24-1767
50	Lorensa Yam	v	7-18-1767
51	Pasquala Tec	25r	7-18-1767
52	Micaela Tec	v	8-9-1767
53	Pasqual Coba	26r	9-20-1767

TABLE D.1
Continued

Doc.	Testator	Folio	Date
54	Pasqual Ku, almehen	v	10-8-1767
55	Antonia Coba	27r	10-21-1767
56	Luisa Tec	v	11-2-1767
57	Pedro Huchim	28r	11-20-1767
58	Antonio Coba		11-11-1767
59	Monica Na	v	12-4-[1767]
60	Nicolás Chan		n.d.
61	Jacinto Poot	29r	12-14-1767
62	Lorensa Canul	v	12-27-1767
63	Ignacia Coba		1-8-176[8]
64	Mateo Yam	30r	11-15-1767
65	Luisa Couoh	v	1-13-1768
	Marta Mis		10-14-1769

SOURCES: TI (save for Marta Mis: ANE-Y, 1819(iv), 37r). For identification purposes I have numbered the wills in the order in which they appear in the surviving *libro* fragment. This was presumably the order in which they were written. The dates, written at the top of each will, record the day of the testator's death. It appears that the year and month were written at the time the will was dictated, and the day added upon the testator's death. Thrice the testator appears to have hung on longer than expected, and the escribano has had to change the month—always to the next. Year dates in brackets [] indicate where the year is illegible but can be deduced from the list of cabildo officers.

TABLE D.2
Index of Cacalchen Testators, 1646–1679

Folio	Testator	Date	Folio	Testator	Date
1	Pedro Koh	6-22-1646	18	Francisco Kuk	7-28-1647
2	Hernando Ku	6-26-1646	19	Luisa May	4-19-1647
3	Juana Mukul	6-26-1646	20	Gaspar Euan	4-28-1647
5	Gaspar May	3-18-1647	21	Clara Che	6-24-1650
6	Gaspar Uh	3-22-1647	22	Juan Eb	6-30-1650
6	Magdalena Uh	3-28-1647	23	Viviana Pat	4-16-1653
7	Bonaventura Canche	7-6-1647	24	Juana Eb	5-6-1653
8	Cecilia Couoh	7-19-1647	25	Julián Koh	4-..-1654
9	Andrés Pat	6-8-1647	26	. . .	6-..-1654
10	Francisca Ytz	6-12-1647	27	Andrés Uitz	9-30-1654
11	Alonso Couoh	1-28-1648	28	Sebastián Ake	11-2-1654
12	Baltesar Puc	2-8-1648	29	Catalina Chan	..-19-[1655]
13	Diego Eb	9-2-1649	30	Agustín Pat	2-16-1656
14	Francisco May	9-4-1649	31	Doña Francisca Uitz	5-18-1678
15	Francisco Pech	6-29-1649	32	Doña Francisca Uitz	5-..-1678
16	Ursula Ake	6-27-1649	33	Ana Xul	..-..-1678
17	Lucia Cocom	7-19-1649	34	Gaspar May	2-4-1679

SOURCE: LC.

TABLE D.3

Wealth in Ixil, 1765–1768: Male Testators

28 MALE TESTATORS:	1	4	6	7	10	14	15	19	21	24	30	32	33	35	36	37	39	40	41	42	43	45	49	53	54	58	61	64	totals
LAND																													
house plot (solar)							1				1													1		1			4
solar with well	1	1	1	2	2	2	1		1	1	1		3	1	1	3		2			1	1	1		1			1	28
well (chen)																	1	2									1		4
productive land/forest (kax)	1	2		2	1	2	2				4		3		1	4		1	1		1		1		1		1	2	30
kax with well						1							1																2
FLORA																													
sapote orchard											1																		1
henequen orchard				1																									1
sapote (ya)														1															1
henequen (ci)				50																									50
red mamey (chacal haaz)			1																										1
plantain (prantano)																									50				50
seed (ynah)								1																					1
vegetable garden (payera)								2																					2
FAUNA																													
beehive (cab [etc.])													85		7														92
horse (tzimin)													1														4		5
gelding (capon tzimin)				2		1		2					1																6
colt (potro)				1						1	1																		3
mare (yeua tzimin)				1		7	1				1	3	2	1									1						17
filly (al yeua)											1																		1
foal (al)				2																									2
donkey (burro)				1																									1
female mule (mula)	1			3																									4
male mule or goat (macho)			1	2																									3
cow (uacax baca/baca)				6		1	4																						11
calf (chichan uacax)	1																												1
RESIDENTIAL																													
house (na)											2																1		3
house door (hol na)			1					1								2											1		5
house door & frame (marco)					4					2	2														1				9
door lock & key (yabe)											2																		2
beam (bac)		1																											1
FURNITURE																													
bed (cama)											1									1									2
bed (poyche)																										1			1
chest (caja)			2		2	3	1	1	1	2	1			1			1				1		1	1	1	1			20
table (mesa/tabron)						2		1			1					1									1				6
writing desk (papirera)											1																		1
bench (banco)											1														1				2
chair (sia kanche)										2	2													1					5
seat (nuc)											1																		1

TABLE D.3
Continued

	1	4	6	7	10	14	15	19	21	24	30	32	33	35	36	37	39	40	41	42	43	45	49	53	54	58	61	64	totals
TOOLS																													
ax (bat)		1	1		1			1	1	1						1				1	1	1			1			1	12
small bar, bullet (baleta)	1																												1
iron tool (xul mascab)																					1								1
iron-tipped stick (lobche mascab)									1																				1
planting stick (>opatan coch bol)										1																			1
VALUABLES																													
Virgin image & tabernacle									2				1																3
San Diego image (ca yum San Diego)										1																			1
rosary (rosario)							1																						1
coral necklace (corales)						1	1																						2
coin (peso)												2																	2
gold coin (cueta de oro)							1																						1
silver spoon (cuchala takin)				1						1					1										1				4
knife (cuchio)																			1										1
jar (botihuela)						2				1																			3
dish (batea)																									1				1
gourd (ca)							1																						1
CLOTHING (MALE)																													
shirt (camisa)		1		2				1		2												1							7
trousers (ex)		1		2				1		4												1							9
cloak (tilma)		1						1									1												3
CLOTHING (M/F)																													
belt/sash (kaxnak)		1		1																		1			1				4
CLOTHING (FEMALE)																													
huipil (ypil)									1																				1
undergarment (pic)							1		1																				2
shawl (boch)								1																					1
CLOTH																													
blanket (sarga)			1	1			1													1		1					1		6
length of cloth (paño)	1																												1
crude cloth (jerga)			1	1																									2
fur (tzotz)																									1				1

TABLE D.4
Wealth in Ixil, 1765–1768: Female Testators

18 FEMALE TESTATORS:	2	12	13	18	20	23	29	34	46	48	50	51	52	55	56	63	65	totals
LAND																		
house plot (solar)															1			1
solar with well		1	1	1	2	1	1	1				1			1			10
well (chen)				1			1											2
productive land/forest (kax)					1								1	1	2			5
FLORA																		
palm for roofs (xan)															38			38
sapote (ya)															2			2
FAUNA																		
beehive (cab [etc.])	6																	6
gelding (capon tzimin)		1																1
mare (yeua tzimin)						1									1			2
filly (al yeua)						1												1
mule (mula)															1			1
male mule or goat (macho)															1			1
pig (keken)		1																1
cockrel (pot)															1			1
RESIDENTIAL																		
house door & frame (marco)		1										1						2
FURNITURE																		
bed (poyche)	1																	1
chest (caja)	1	1	1								1	1			2	2		9
chair (sia kanche)												1						1
VALUABLES																		
saddle (sia tzimin)															1			1
coral beads or necklaces (corales)							4				20			1		1		26
a pair of earrings (hun>am tup)									1									1
bronze stonebreaker (bronso licil u pabal tunich)												1						1
small bar or bullet (baleta)															1			1
jar (botihuela)															2			2
clothes washing bowl (akal luch)															1			1
loom (akal kuch)															2			2
CLOTHING (MALE)																		
shirt (camisa)	1	1					11			3					1			17
trousers (ex)							11			3								14
CLOTHING (M/F)																		
belt/sash (kaxnak)							4			3								7
CLOTHING (FEMALE)																		
huipil, dress (ypil)		2					5				1	1		1				10
petticoat (pic)		3	1				5				1	1		1		3		15
shawl (boch)				1	1		2		1		1		3					9
toca (headscarf)																1		1
CLOTH																		
yarn (kuch)	1																	1
length of cloth (paño)							2											2
length of cloth (hebal nok)										2	3							5
crude cloth (jerga)																1		1

Wealth in Cacalchen, 1646–1656: Male Testators

16 MALE TESTATORS:	1	2	6	7	9	11	12	13	14	15	18	20	22	25	28	30	totals
LAND																	
field (col) [by quantity or mecates]	30	170				110	60	3	230	140	150	280			60	30+1	1260+4
forest (kax)																	
FLORA																	
palm for hats (bom)							3										3
sapote (ya)		2										2					4
tree (yxche)												1					
measure of corn (yxim)															1	1	2
yuca (>in)																	
vegetable garden (kanche)																	
medicinal plant (halab)																	
FAUNA																	
beehive (cab [etc.])					10	50		12	9								81
horse (tzimin)								2	4	1	2		1				10
foal (al tzimin)											1						1
colt (potro)						4					1				1		6
mare (yeua/na tzimin)						4				1	1						6
female pig (na keken)		1			1	1	1				2						6
piglet (chichan/chupul keken)					4	3					2						9
chicken ([na] castilla)													1				1
cockrel (castilla u yum)																1	1
turkey ([na/chachan] ulum)												2			3	1	6
RESIDENTIAL																	
abandoned house (ducuy na)						1											1
[door] frame (marco)																	
FURNITURE																	
bed (cama)			2														2
bed (poyche)										2							2
mattress (tas)																	
chest (caja/caxa)	1	2		1	1	2			3		1					1	12
table (mesa)						1				1	1						3
bench (banco)											1					1	2
chair (sia [kanche])						3		1		1	3					1	9

	1	2	6	7	9	11	12	13	14	15	18	20	22	25	28	30	totals
TOOLS																	
machete (machete)			1	1	1	1			2						1	1	7
ax (hacha)						1				1					1	1	4
shoe iron (pakam)																	
iron-tipped stick (lobche mascab)					1												1
digging stick (xolal)		1				1	2		1			1				1	7
honey extractor (lomob hobon mascab)					1												1
shotgun (>on)					1					1	2						4
saddle (sia tzimin)						1									1		2
bridle (freno tzimin)															1		1
VALUABLES																	
coin (peso, toston, tomin)							1					1	6	3	6	1	18
spoon (cuchara)					1												1
plate (plato, frado)						3											3
jar (botihuela)						1											1
gourd (luch)										3							3
CLOTHING (male)																	
shirt (camisa)			2	1	1	1					1	1			1	1	9
trousers (es)				1	1	1	1				1	1			1	2	9
cloak (ziyem)					1	1					1	1				1	5
CLOTHING (female)																	
huipil, dress (ypil)														1		1	2
petticoat (pic)														1			1
shawl (boch)																	
CLOTH																	
length of cloth (hebal nok)					3	6	1										10
piece of cloth (xet u hebal nok)																	
large piece of cloth (nohoch nok)																	
small piece of cloth (chachanok)						1											1
tribute manta (yubte)							1									1	2
cloth bag (chuh)										2							2

355

TABLE D.6
Wealth in Cacalchen, 1646–1656: Female Testators

11 FEMALE TESTATORS:	3	8	10	16	17	21	23	24	29	31/32	33	totals
LAND												
field (col) [by quantity or mecates]		1					1	50	5			50+7
forest (kax)		1				1						2
FLORA												
sapote (ya)			1									1
bursera wood (ze chacah)								1				1
tree (yxche)				10								10
henequen (ci)		1	1									2
measure of corn (yxim)						1						1
measure of cotton (>in)						6		10	13			29
vegetable garden (kanche)						1						1
medicinal plant (halab)									1			
FAUNA												
beehive (cab [etc.])		20		58		10	3			15		106
horse (tzimin)		1			1	2						4
colt (potro)				1		1						2
mare (yeua/na tzimin)						1						1
piglet (chichan/chupul keken)				2+								2+
RESIDENTIAL												
[door] frame (marco)							1					1
FURNITURE												
bed (cama)				1	1					1		3
bed (poyche)							1		1			2
mattress (tas)									1			1
chest (caja/caxa)		1	1	1			1		1	2		7
chair (sia [kanche])				2						1		3
TOOLS												
shoe iron (pakam)		1										1
digging stick (xolal)						1	1					2
VALUABLES												
coin (peso, toston, tomin)	1			5		14						20
gourd (luch)		1				1						2
CLOTHING (female)												
kub (dress)								1				1
huipil, dress (ypil)	2		1	1	1	1	2	1	2	2	4	17
petticoat (pic)	2	1		1	2		2	1	2	2	4	17
shawl (boch)	1	1	1	1		1			1	2	2	10
CLOTH												
length of cloth (hebal nok)											1	1
large piece of cloth (nohoch nok)											1+	1+
yarn (kuch) [by item or measure]				120		6					1	120+7
tribute manta (yubte)						2			1		5	8
fur (tzotz)						1						1

TABLE D.7

Inheritance in Ixil, 1765–1768: Goods Bequeathed, by Category, and Recipients,
by Kin Relation to Testator: 31 Male Donors

	land (solar /kax)	flora	bee-hives	horses/ mules	cattle	houses/build-ing materials	furni-ture	valuables	tools	men's clothing	women's clothing	cloth
MALE INDIVIDUALS												
son (mehen)	4		41	3		5	4	7	12	18		3
son-in-law	1			2	2		2					
adopted son (tzenpal)	1			3		3	4	3	1			
brother	1											
grandson (mam, ui>in)	3			1	1		1	1				
(mam)	3			3		1	1	1		3		
(mekpal) infant/grandson										2		
FEMALE INDIVIDUALS												
wife (atan)	2	5	37	13	1	4	11	2			1	
daughter (ixmehen)	9		14	5	3	3	5	4	8			
(mam) [female]				1								
(ui>in) [female]				1								
(tzenpal) [mistress]	1											
granddaughter	1											
MALE GROUPS												
sons (mehenob)	7						2		2	3		
sons-in-law	1					1						
nephews	1											
(mamob)							1					
younger bro (ui>in) + uncle	1											
FEMALE GROUPS												
daughters (ixmehenob)	7	1					1		2		1	2
wife + daughter[s]	5	1					1		1			2
MIXED GENDER GROUPS												
wife + 2 sons [diff. mother]	1											
wife + (mam)		1										
wife + adopted son	1											
wife + children				6		2	2					
children (palilob)	16			2	4	4	3					
children + sisters	1											
children + niece					1							
son + his wife	1											
2 daughters + 2 male cousins	1											
daughter + grandson (ui>in)	1											
ditto + uncle + younger bro.	1											
grandchildren	2											
2 uncles + an aunt	1											
[unspecified male + female]	1											
totals	75	8	92	40	12	23	38	18	26	26	2	7

Inheritance in Ixil, 1765–1769: Goods Bequeathed, by Category, and Recipients, by Kin Relation to Testator: 20 Female Donors

	land (solar/kax)	flora	beehives	horses/ mules	saddles	pigs	houses/building materials	furniture	valuables	men's clothing	women's clothing	cloth
FEMALE INDIVIDUALS												
daughter (al/chuplal)			5	3	1			3	7	9	29	2
daughter-in-law (lib)											6	
granddaughter	1										1	
aunt (tilla)						1						
MALE INDIVIDUALS												
husband (icham)	1			1				1	1	14	3	2
son (al/al xib)	6	2	1				2	5	5	15		4
son-in-law	1											
adopted son (tzenpal)								1				
MALE GROUPS												
sons	2							1				
husband + son				2			2					
MIXED GENDER GROUPS												
children (alob)	9							1				
husband + niece	1											
husband + (al) + uncle +												
older brother + (ui>in)	1											
totals	22	2	6	6	1	1	4	12	13	38	39	8

Inheritance in Cacalchen, 1646–1656: Goods Bequeathed by Category, and Recipients, by Kin Relation to Testator: 16 Male Donors

	land (col)	flora	beehives	horses	pigs	fowl	houses/building materials	furniture	tools	valuables	men's clothing	women's clothing	cloth
MALE INDIVIDUALS													
son (mehen)	8	1		10	3			15	21	5	5		9
son-in-law	2	1	4	2									
grandson (mam)	1		1										
maternal uncle (acan)										1		2	
[kinship unspecified]		3		1		3			4	3	4		
FEMALE INDIVIDUALS													
wife (chuplil)	1	5	14	3	8	5	1	6		1	5	1	5
daughter (ixmehen, al)	3		9	3	2			2					
granddaughter (chich)											1		
[kinship unspecified]			4								2		
MALE GROUPS													
sons (mehenob)	2			5					1				
son + son-in-law									1				
FEMALE GROUPS													
daughters (ixmehenob)	1												
MIXED GENDER GROUPS													
wife + son	2												
wife + children			50 [1]										
children (palilob)	3									6			
[heirs unspecified]	1							2	1		4		
totals	24	10	32	24	13	8	1	25	28	16	21	3	14

TABLE D.10

Inheritance in Cacalchen, 1646–1678: Goods Bequeathed, by Category, and Recipients, by Kin Relation to Testator: 11 Female Donors

	land (kax)	land (col)	flora	beehives	horses	pigs	houses/building materials	furniture	tools	valuables	men's clothing	women's clothing	cloth
FEMALE INDIVIDUALS													
daughter (al/chuplal)		1	11	6		2		7				9	2
daughter-in-law (ilib)			5									6	
granddaughter (abil)		1										5	
sister			10							1			
elder sister (cic)				5						1			
younger sister (i>in)				6	1					7		1	
sister-in-law (hauan)			5										2
paternal aunt (ixcit)										1		6	
[kinship unspecified]			8							1		1	2
MALE INDIVIDUALS													
husband (icham)	1		5	1	1				1	1	1	3	2
son (al/al xib)		2		20	4		3	6	1			6	5
son-in-law (haan)	1		11	4				1			1	2	
brother-in-law (mu)		1							1		1		
paternal uncle (>eyum)										1			
[kinship unspecified]				7						6		2	3
FEMALE GROUPS													
daughters (ixmehenob)		1											
MALE GROUPS													
sons (alob, mehenob)				40									
MIXED GENDER GROUPS													
children (alob)					1	2							
totals	2	7	55	89	7	4	3	14	3	19	3	41	16

TABLE D.11

Inheritance in Ebtun, 1785–1813: Goods Bequeathed and Recipients, by Kin Relation to Testator: 9 Donors

TESTATORS	Rosa Camal 1785	Antonio >ul 1811	Francisco Un 1811	[?] Couoh [f] 1811	Dionisio Huchim 1811	Manuel Un 1811	[?] Couoh [m] 1812	Rosa Balam 1812	Felipa Couoh 1813
LAND									
house plot (solar)		2 (me,ix)	2 (ix)			2 (ob)	2 (ob)		
well (chen)			1 (ix)				1 (ob)		
forest (kax)				1 (ob)		3 (ob)	3 (ob)	4 (ob)	4 (ob)
milpa field (col)			1 (at)			1 (at)			
FLORA									
measure of corn (yxim)						4 (me,ix)			
FAUNA									
horse (tzimin)	1 (ob)								
colt (tzimin potro)	1 (ob)								
cow (baca)			1 (ix)						
goat or male mule (macho)			1 (ix)						
APICULTURE									
beehives	10 (ob)	40 (me,ix)	83 (at,ix,ti)	25+ (ob,ix,[m])	19 (at,me,ix)	5+ (me,ix)	29 (at,me,ix)	6 (me)	39 (ich,me,ix)
arrobas [of wax or honey]		8 (me,ix)	1 (ix)				1 (me)	1 (me)	
honey extractor (lomob hobon mascab)									1 (ich)
wire mask (careta)							1 (ix)	1 (me)	
RESIDENTIAL									
house door (hol na)					1 (ix)			1 (ix)	
(hol na) & frame (marco)			3 (ix)						
FURNITURE									
bed (cama)			2 (ix)	1 ([?])			1 (me)	1 (ix)	
wood table (mesa che)			1 (ix)						
small table (chichan mesa)					1 (me)				
wooden bench (banco che)								1 (me)	
metate (bancoil sacan)			1 (ix)				3 (me)		
wooden chair (silla che)					1 (me)			1 (me)	
stool (taborete)			1 (ix)		1 (me)				
chest (caxa/caja)		5 (at,me,ix)	2 (ix)	1 ([?])	2 (me,ix)		2 (at,ix)	2 (me,ix)	2 (me,ix)
chest & lock (kalbil)	1 (ob)								

361

TABLE D.11
Continued

TESTATORS (cont.)	Rosa Camal	Antonio >ul	Francisco Un	[?] Couoh [f]	Dionisio Huchim	Manuel Un	[?] Couoh [m]	Rosa Balam	Felipa Couoh
	1785	1811	1811	1811	1811	1811	1812	1812	1813
TOOLS									
iron bar or bullet (bareta)		4 (me,ix)	1 (ix)						
hammer (matilo)									
VALUABLES									
rosary of coral & gold	1 (ob)								
coin (peso takin)		238 (at,ix,me,mam)							
spoon (cuchara)									2 (me,ix)
silver spoon (cuchara takin)		4 (me,ix,mam)		2 (ix,[m])	1 (at)	1 (ix)			1 (me)
plate (plato)			3 (ix,ti)				1 (ix)	1 (me)	1 (me)
flask (frasco)	1 (ob)	4 (me,ix)	1 (ix)		1 (me)	1 (me)			
jar (bothuela)		13 (at,me,ix)	2 (ix)	2 (ix,[?])	3 (at,me,ix)	2 (me)	5 (me,ix)	4 (me,ix)	
bottle (limeta)		1 (ix)	1 (ix)		2 (me,ix)	3 (ix)	4 (me)		4 (ich, me,ix)
black calabash cups (ek luch)								6 (me)	
CLOTHING									
dress/huipil (ypil)									1 (ix)
slip (pic)									1 (ix)
shawl (boch)							2 (ix)		3 (me,ix)
length of cloth (hebal nok)									2 (ich)
pieces of cloth (xet u hebal nok)									6 (me)

SOURCES: TE: 195, 224, 230, 233, 234, 235, 238, 239, 242.

ABBREVIATIONS: (at) atan, wife; (ich) ichan, husband; (ix) ixmehen, daughter; (me) mehen, man's son; also used for al, woman's son; (ob) palalob, man's children; alob, woman's children; (ti) tiyo, tio, uncle; (mam) mam, male kin via a female (above case: probably daughter's son); (jml) male of unspecified kin; ([?]) recipient unclear.

NOTES: [?] before testator's patronym indicates unclear Christian name; [m] or [f] indicates gender. The table does not show numbers of relatives or the distribution of goods where there are multiple recipients to a particular property type, but note that the number of children declared by each testator is 4, 5, 3, 2, 6, 8, 4, and 3, respectively (average: 4.2); distribution is discussed in the text.

TABLE D.12

Inheritance in Various Other Cahob, 1629–1784: Goods Bequeathed and Recipients, by Kin Relation to Testator: 8 Donors

TESTATORS	Diego Mul Mani 1629	doña Maria Ca-tzim Tekax 1689	don Lucas Tun Cuncunul 1699	Fabiana Cardoza Santiago 1741	Matias Ku Itzimná 1756	Juan Cutz Motul 1762	Felipe Noh Homun 1763	Ventura Uitz Bokoba 1784
LAND								
house plot (solar)		2 (me+chi)	1 (me)	0.5 (me)		4 (me, ix)	2 (at, ob)	
well (chen)		1 (me)	1 (me)				1 (at)	
forest (kax)	1 (at+me)	2 (me+chi)	2 (me)		2 (me)		3 (me, ob, mam)	
milpa field (col)			1 (at)			4 (me)		
FLORA								
orchard (pakal)						1 (me)	1 [plantain] (at)	
sapote tree (ya)							3 (at)	
measure of corn (yxim)							15 ([m])	
FAUNA								
mare (yeua tzimin)						1 (me)		2 (me)
gelding (capon tzimin)					1 (me)			
female mule (mula)					1 (me)			1 (me)
cow (baca)						1 (me)		
calf (u yal [baca])						1 (me)		
APICULTURE								
beehives					7 (me, ix)			65 (me, at)
arrobas [of wax or honey]					1 (me)			
honey extractor (lomob hobon)					1 (me)			
RESIDENTIAL								
house+goods (na+u bal)				1 (me)				
house door (hol na)			1 (me)		1 (me)			
(hol na) & frame (marco)					1 (me)	1 (me)		
FURNITURE								
bed (cama)					1 (ix)			
wood table (mesa che)			1 (me)					
large table (noh mesa)					1 (ob)			
wooden bench (banco che)					1 (me)			
stool (taberte [taborete])					2 (me)			
chest (caxa/caja)			1 (at)		1 (ix)	1 (me)		
TOOLS								
iron bar or bullet (bareta)			1 (at)					
hammer (matilo)			1 (at)					
VALUABLES								
silver spoon (cuchara takin)						1 (me)		
plate (plato)				1 (ix-in-law)				
flask (parasco [frasco])					1 (me)			
jar (butihuera [botihuela])					1 (me)		2 ([m], at)	
CLOTHING								
dress/huipil (ypil)				1 (ix-in-law)				
slip (pic)				1 (ix-in-law)				
shawl (toca)				1 (ix-in-law)				

SOURCES: TT: 13; ANEY, 1826ii, 301–2; TE: 28; ANEY, 1810i, 256; ANEY, 1835, 193; ANEY, 1796–97, 205; AGN-T, 1359, 5, 19–22; ANEY, 1828–30iii, 8.

NOTES: The table does not show numbers of relatives or the distribution of goods where there are multiple recipients to a particular property type; distribution is discussed in the text.

ABBREVIATIONS: (at) atan, wife; (ix) ixmehen, daughter; (me) mehen, man's son; also used for al, woman's son; (ob) palalob, man's children; alob, woman's children; (mam) mam, male kin via a female (above case: probably son's son); (chi) chibalob, descendants; ([m]) male of unspecified kin.

⚭

The Material World of the Cah

Property Items in Maya Testaments from Four Cahob, 1646–1835

PROPERTY ITEM	TERM USED BY MAYA	CACALCHEN	EBTUN	IXIL	TEKANTO
LAND					
house plot	solar		√	√	√
forest	kax	√	√	√	√
field	col	√	√		√
plot	sitio				√
well	chen		√	√	
FLORA					
palm for roofs	xan			√	√
palm for hats	bom	√			√
fig	copo				√
sapote	ya	√		√	√
plum	abal				√
plantain	prantano			√	
banana	haaz				√
red mamey	chacal haaz			√	
bursera	chacah	√			
ramón	ox				√
henequen	ci	√		√	√
tree	yxche	√			
tall tree seed	canal che ynah			√	
measure of corn	yxim	√	√		
yuca	>in	√			
vegetable garden	payera			√	
vegetable garden	kanche	√			
medicinal herb	halab	√			

TABLE E.1
Continued

PROPERTY ITEM	TERM USED BY MAYA	CACALCHEN	EBTUN	IXIL	TEKANTO
FAUNA					
bees, beehives	cab [etc.]	√	√	√	√
horse	tzimin	√	√	√	√
gelding	capon tzimin			√	√
colt	potro, podro, podoro	√	√	√	√
mare	yeua tzimin	√		√	
mare	na (in) tzimin				√
filly	al yeua			√	
foal	al, al tzimin			√	√
donkey	burro			√	
female mule	mula			√	√
male mule	macho		√	√	√
cow	baca, uacax baca		√	√	√
bull	uacax toro				√
calf	chichan uacax			√	
pig	kek, keken	√		√	
female pig	na keken, chupul keken	√			
piglet	chichan keken	√			
cockrel	pot			√	
chicken	castilla	√			
turkey	ulum	√			
female turkey	na ulum	√			
turkey chicks	chachan ulum	√			
RESIDENTIAL					
house	na			√	√
abandoned house	ducuy na	√			
house door	hol na		√	√	√
with frame	yetel u marcoil		√	√	√
with key	yetel u yabeil			√	√
frame	marco	√			
beam	bac			√	
FURNITURE					
bed	cama	√	√	√	√
bed	poyche	√		√	
mattress	tas	√			
chest	caja, caxa	√	√	√	√
with key	yetel u llabeil				√
with lock	yetel u kalbil	√			
table	mesa, tabron	√		√	√
small table	chichan mesa		√		
wood table	mesa che		√		
writing desk	papirera			√	
bench	banco	√		√	
wooden bench	banco che		√		
metate	u bancoil sacan		√		
metate	u bancoil huch				√
metate	u yucail huch				√
wooden chair	sia, silla, kanche, che	√	√	√	√
seat	nuc			√	
stool	taborete		√		

TABLE E.1
Continued

PROPERTY ITEM	TERM USED BY MAYA	CACALCHEN	EBTUN	IXIL	TEKANTO
TOOLS					
machete	machete, mache	√		√	√
ax	hacha	√			
ax	bat			√	√
pike-ax	pico				√
hammer	matilo		√		
small bar, bullet	bareta		√	√	√
iron tool	xul mascab			√	
shoe iron	pakam	√			
iron-tipped stick	lobche mascab	√		√	
digging stick	xolal	√			
planting stick	>opatan coch bol			√	
bronze stonebreaker	bronso licil u pabal tunich			√	
well pulley	carrillo				√
weight	plomo				√
branding iron	u llero uacax				√
shotgun	>on	√			√
wax and honey	arroba [of]		√		√
honey extractor	lomob hobon mascab	√	√		
wire mask	careta		√		
saddle	sia (in) tzimin	√		√	√
bridle	freno/plenoil in tzimin	√			√
loom	akal kuch			√	
VALUABLES					
Virgin image	ca cilich colel/colebil			√	√
with tabernacle	yetel u tabernacoil			√	√
San Diego image	ca yum san Diego			√	
saint image	ca yum santo				√
rosary	rosario			√	
of coral and gold	corares oro		√		
coral necklace	corales			√	
pair of earrings	hun>am tup			√	
gold chain	alaja				√
coin	toston, peso, real, tomin	√	√	√	√
gold coin	cueta de oro			√	
bronze coin	bronso			√	
spoon	cuchara	√	√		√
silver spoon	cuchala takin		√	√	√
knife	cuchio			√	
plate	plato, frado	√	√		√
silver plate	plato takin				√
dish	batea			√	
jar	botihuela, botixuela		√	√	
flask	frasco		√		√
bottle	limeta		√		√
gourd	ca			√	
gourd/calabash cup	luch	√			
black gourd	ek luch		√		
washing bowl	akal luch			√	

TABLE E.1
Continued

PROPERTY ITEM	TERM USED BY MAYA	CACALCHEN	EBTUN	IXIL	TEKANTO
CLOTHING (male)					
shirt	camisa	√		√	
trousers	es	√			
trousers	ex			√	
cloak	ziyem	√			
cloak	tilma			√	
CLOTHING (female)					
dress	kub	√			
huipil, dress	ypil	√	√	√	√
petticoat	pic	√	√	√	√
shawl	boch	√	√	√	
shawl	box				√
head scarf	toca			√	
CLOTHING (m/f)					
clothes	ropa				√
belt/sash	kaxnak			√	
CLOTH					
cloth, clothes	nok				√
length of cloth	paño, panio, panilloyl			√	
length of cloth	hebal nok	√	√	√	
large piece of cloth	nohoch nok	√			
piece of cloth	xet u hebal nok		√		
small piece of cloth	chachanok	√			
crude cloth	jerga, jergueta			√	
yarn	kuch	√		√	
blanket	sarga			√	
tribute manta	yubte	√			
cloth bag	chuh	√			
fur	tzotz	√		√	

SOURCES: LC, TE, TI, DT.

৩

Spanish Loanwords and Phrases in Maya Notarial Documents

1557

[Spanish Christian names]
[Spanish month names, years, and numbers]

aroba	arroba [weight]
audiençia	audiencia, "court"
en. . .años	"in the year. . ."
cruz	"cross"
dios	"God"
don (1650 doña)	"sir"
escriuano	escribano, "notary"
gouernador	gobernador, "governor"
juez (1669 juueç, juuez)	"judge, magistrate"
juez de comission	juez de comisión, "commissioner"
provinçia	provincia, "province"
sanct. (1567 san, sant.)	santo, "saint"
señor	"mister"
su mãg	Su Magestad, "your majesty"

1561

testigosob, texgos	testigo, "witness"
tidroil (1596 tiduroil)	título, "[land] title"

1567

alcalde	"municipal judge or councilman"
castilla	Castilla, "Castile"
çiudad de merida	cuidad de Mérida, "city of Merida"
clerigosob	clérigo, "secular priest"
cristianoil, cristo, xpianosob	Cristiano, "Christian"
defensorob	defensor [judicial post]
doctrinas	doctrina, "[Franciscan] parish"
españae	España, "Spain"
evangelio	Evangelio, "the Gospel"
firmasob (1733 filma)	firma, "signature"
frai	"fray" [title]
frailes	"friars"
franciscos	Franciscan
justiçia (1587 justicia, 1595 justiçias)	justicia, "justice; magistrate"

obispo	"bishop"
oyador	oidor
missa	misa, "mass"
p^e, padresob	padre, "father" [priest]
Toledo	Toledo
yucatan	Yucatán, "Yucatan"

1569

españoles	"Spaniards"
denienda	teniente, "lieutenant"

c. 1580

almoneda	"auction"
casadaobi	casada, "married women"
inventario	"inventory"
mandamiento	"order"
notificaçion (1587 notificazion)	notificación, "notice, notification"
testamento (c. 1600 textamentoob)	testamento, "testament, will"
tiniente genelar	teniente general, "lieutenant general"

1587

ofisioe	oficio, "occupation, trade"
pesion (1591 petision, 1605 pidiçione)	petición, "petition"

1589

[Spanish weekday names]	
confesar (1774 confisar)	"to confess" (always used as a noun, to mean "confession")
	regidor, "municipal councilman"
regidoresob (1786 rehildro)	

1590

carta	"letter, bill"
juramento	"oath"
alcalde ordinario	[rank of municipal judge]

1591

procurador	"lawyer"

1595

capp^n	capitán, "captain"
peso	[coin]

1596

encometero (1669 encomidero, 1762 enconenderroe)	encomendero
gouernaçionil	gobernación, "government"

1600

alguacil	"constable"
estancias	estancia, "agricultural holding"
maestro	"teacher"
mesa (1647 mexa)	"table"
Rey	"king"

c. 1600

conoçamento	conocimiento, "acknowledgment"

1605

anoria	"well"
bigas	viga, "beam"

cabildo — "town council"
caxtilla (1647 cax) — "chicken" [i.e., fowl from Castile]
danta — tanda
doctor — [title]
Jesu xp̃o — Jesu Cristo, "Jesus Christ"
mariscal — "marshal"
meson — "guest house"
mexico — México, "Mexico City"
uisoReye — virrey, "viceroy"

1610

comunidad — "community"
mayordomoil — mayordomo, "steward, majordomo"
prata — plata, "silver"
testimonioil — testimonio, "testimony"
toxton (1629 testones, 1646 tostones) — tostón [coin]

1611

elecon (1683 elecçion) — elección, "election"
libro — "book"

1616

personas (1646 presonas, personas, 1766 personnas) — "persons" [only used in religious formulas]
real — [coin]
tumin — tomín, "coin" [used to mean "real"]

1629

albaseas (1646 aluaseas, aluaçeas, albaçeas) — albacea, "executor"
cantollesob — cantor, "singer," cantores, "choir"
cofradesil — cofrade, "member of a sodality"
gloria — "[religious] glory"
libras — libra, "pound"
monesterio — monasterio, "monastery"
Romae — Roma, "Rome"
santa bera cruz de la penitencia — Santa Veracruz de la Penitencia [the saint of penitence]
santa ygreçia catolicae — Santa Iglesia Catolica, "Holy Catholic Church"
señora de la conçepçion — Señora de la Concepción [the Virgin]
uigillail — vigilia, "vigil"
ygreçia (1646 yglesia, ygressia) — iglesia, "church"

1642

corona real — Royal Crown [the institution]
essno publico — escribano publico, "public notary"

1646

caja, caha (1765 caxa) — caja, "chest"
candelas — candela, "candle"
conbento — convento, "convent"
espir santo — espiritu santo, "holy spirit, soul"
gelusalem, gielusalem (1765 jelusalem) — Jerusalem
limosnayl — limosna, "alms"

1647

banco — "bench"
cama — "bed"
camisa, camissa, canisa — camisa, "shirt"

machete (1656 macħe)
"machete"

missa re^da (1654 resada, 1766 resar, rezar, ressae)
misa resada, "recited, said mass"

1648

botixuera (1766 botihuela)
botihuela, "jar"

sia, silla
silla, "chair, seat"

yeua
yegua, "mare"

1649

guardian
guardián, "custodian" [priest]

hacħa
hacha, "ax"

potro
colt

1650

carta de uenda
carta de venta, "bill of sale"

1651

pormayl derechos
informe de derechos, "statement of rights" [a legal document]

1654

missa cantata
misa cantada, "sung mass"

pleno
freno, "brake, bit" [bridle]

1669

amen
"amen"

concistadoresob (1670 cunquistadro, cuncistahhob, cuncistaltahhob)
conquistador, "conqueror"

hiro, hilo
hilo, "thread"

jabon
"soap"

memorya
memoria, "statement, report"

promisia
promesa, "offering"

rexitençia
residencia, "investigation, trial" [held at the end of a term of office]

vesitador, visitador
visitador, "inspector"

1670

hidalgos
hidalgo, "noble"

probansa
probanza

c. 1675

sobrino
"nephew"

1678

cassa
casa, "house"

u yabeil
llave, "key"

1683

arançel
arancel, "tariff, fee"

regidor mayor
"senior regidor"

patron
patrón, "patron [saint of a cah]"

serallo, serario
salario, "salary"

1688

auto
"judicial edict"

1708

cargas
carga, "measure, load"

diputadosob
diputado, "deputy"

priostesob	prioste [cofradía official]
santa maria Assupcion	Santa Maria Asunción [the Virgin]

[c. 1725]

baca, uacax	vaca, "cow"
baleta	bareta, "small metal bar" or "bullet"
capon	capón, "neutered male animal"
cuchara, cuchala	cuchara, "spoon"
macho	"male mule"
marcoyl	marco, "frame"
mula	"female mule"
sitillo	sitio, "site, parcel of land"
solar, soral, solal	solar, "house plot"
tabernacoil, tabernacula	tabernáculo, "tabernacle"

1733

alféres	alférez, "ensign" [title]
autos ynformaçion	auto de información [legal document]
gastoil	gasto, "cost"
hentençia, jentençia	sentencia, "sentence, decision"
nuestro Rey	"our king"
oras	hora, "hour"
posisionil	posesión, "possession"
salhento	sargento, "sergeant"
termino	término, "deadline [for producing specified legal documents]"

1736

santisimo trinidad	"Holy Trinity"
sta fe catolica Romana	"Holy Roman Catholic Faith"

1738

essno repormado	escribano reformado, "assistant notary"

[c. 1767]

animas	anima, "soul"
anjos	ajo, "garlic [plant]"
batella	batea, "tray"
bronso	"copper coin"
burro	"donkey"
corales, colales, colares, colalles	coral, "coral" [necklace]
cuchio	cuchillo, "knife"
cueta de oro a medio	cuenta de oro a medio, [gold coin, 50% pure]
gerga, gergeta, hergeta, jergueta	jerga, "crude cloth, serge"
gilon	jirón, "piece, part, parcel [of land]"
panio, panillo	paño, "cloth"
papirera	papelera, "writing desk"
parte	parte, "part, share"
payera	pajera, "straw loft" [used to mean "straw-covered trestle for vegetable cultivation"]
prantanos	platano, "plantain [tree]"
puertail	puerta, "door"
pulgatorio, purgatorio	purgatorio, "purgatory"
rosario	"rosary"
sarga	sarga, "blanket"
sebollas	cebolla, "onion [plant]"
sinta	cinta, "ribbon"

tabronil	tablón, "large plank, table"
tio, tillo, tilla	tío, tía, "uncle," "aunt"
tirma	tilma [orig. Nahuatl], "cloak"
toca	"head scarf"

1769

quentail	cuenta, "account" [behalf]

1771

posito	depósito, "deposit, deposit box"
semilla	"seed"
ynterino	interino, "interim, provisional"

1774

cabo de escuadra	"squadron leader"
cura	"curate"
estremacion	estremación, "last rites"
inglesob	inglés, "English"
ostia	"host" [in mass]

1812

Baston	bastón, "baton"

1814

erencia	herencia, "inheritance," or residencia [see 1669]
kirillos	carrillo, "well pulley"

1819

archiboil	archivo, "archive, record"
mutil	almud [grain measure]
patio	"patio"

1838

exemplo	"example" [legal document]
pisinail	piscina, "pool" [used to mean "sacristy"]

SOURCE: Maya notarial documents, e.g.: AGI-E, 315b–318a; AGN-BN, 69, 5 and AGN-CI, 2013, 1; DT; TE; TI; LC; TT; TC; TX; also consulted: Hanks 1986; Karttunen 1985; Thompson 1978. The spelling variations given are examples, not comprehensive lists.

Reference Matter

Notes

For complete information on secondary works cited in the Notes, see Works Cited. The following abbreviations for archives and primary sources are used in the Notes:

AGI   Archivo General de las Indias, Seville, Spain
            -E   Escribanía
            -M   México
AGEY   Archivo General del Estado de Yucatán, Mérida, Yucatan
            -A   Ayuntamiento
            -CP   Censos y Padrones
            -CR   Criminal
            -E   Empleos
            -G   Gobierno
            -T   Tierras
            -V   Varios
AGN   Archivo General de la Nación, Mexico City
            -BN   Bienes Nacionales
            -CI   Civil
            -CR   Criminal
            -I   Inquisición
            -IN   Indios
            -T   Tierras
ANEY   Archivo Notarial del Estado de Yucatán, Mérida, Yucatan
            -P   Protocolos
            DT   Documentos de Tekanto
CAIHY   Centro de Apoyo a la Investigación Historica de Yucatán, Mérida, Yucatan
            CCA   Colección Carrillo y Ancona
                    TI   Testaments of Ixil [cited numbers follow document numbers in Restall 1995a]

BNM   Biblioteca Nacional de México, Mexico City
           -FF   Fondo Franciscano
CBC   Book of Chilam Balam of Chumayel [cited numbers follow pages in Roys 1967]
CBT   Book of Chilam Balam of Tizimin [cited numbers follow pages in Edmonson 1982]
DTY   Deslinde de Tierras en Yaxkukul [part of TY; cited numbers follow line numbers in Barrera Vázquez 1984; also published as Martínez Hernández 1926]
RY   Relaciones de Yucatán [cited numbers follow pages in Garza 1983]
TAT   Title of Acalan-Tixchel [cited numbers follow pages in Scholes and Roys 1968]
TC   Title of Calkiní [also Códice, Codex, Chronicle; cited numbers follow pages in Barrera Vásquez 1957; also published as Gates 1935]
TCh   Title of Chicxulub [also Códice, Chronicle, Crónica de Nakuk-Pech; cited numbers follow pages in Brinton 1882]
TE   Titles of Ebtun [cited numbers follow document numbers in Roys 1939]
T-LAL   Latin American Library, Tulane University, New Orleans
           -RBC / RMC Rare Book / Manuscript Collection
           DTi   Documentos de Ticul
           LC   Libro de Cacalchen
           MT   Montes de Tsek [et al.]
           TS   Tierras de Sabacche
           TT   Tierras de Tabi
           TX   Titles of the Xiu [also Papers; see Gates 1978]
           TY   Title of Yaxkukul [also Chronicle]

Cited numbers in Notes are folio numbers unless otherwise indicated above.

Chapter One

1. These ideas are discussed by Carroll 1991: 32 and Cope 1994: 4.

2. On Gaspar Antonio Chi, see Karttunen 1994: 84–114, 165–69, 308. The Xiu letter that describes the 1562 persecution by Landa is reproduced (in translation only) in Gates 1978: 115–17. On the conquest of Yucatan (including the 1560's), see Blom 1929; Chamberlain 1948; Farriss 1984: 12–25; Clendinnen 1987; Karttunen 1994: 84–105. Landa's version is in Landa 1982: 6–11, 20–34 (Gates 1978: 4–8, 19–31); Chi's account is in his 1580 *probanza* in AGI-M 104. Maya-language accounts are cited below. On the conquest along the southern Yucatec frontier, see Jones 1989. On the "second conquest" that began at the end of the eighteenth century, see Farriss 1984: 355–95; Rugeley n.d.; and parts of Chaps. 17 and 23 below.

3. TCh: 199, 204–7, 193; TY: 3.

4. TCh: 213–14; CBC: 20. For further discussion of these sources and their genres, see Chap. 21. I am presently working on a larger treatment of Maya views

of the conquest; now in draft form, the book manuscript is titled *This Change of Rulers: Maya Accounts of the Spanish Conquest of Yucatan.*

5. TAT: 391, 400–405; TT: 32r; TCh: 198; DTY: 17.

6. Stephens 1963 [1843].

7. In spite of his romantic attachment to the ancient Maya, Sylvanus Morley's attitude toward the postconquest Maya was unashamedly utilitarian: Morley 1983 [1946]; see also, Roys 1972 [1943]; Sullivan 1989.

8. This historiographical line runs from Lizana 1893 [1633] and López de Cogolludo 1867–68 [1688] to Ancona 1878–79, Molina Solís 1904–13, Means 1917, Blom 1929, and Chamberlain 1948.

9. Landa 1982 [1566]; Tozzer 1941; Brinton 1882; Tozzer 1977 [1921].

10. Clendinnen 1987: xiii.

11. Scholes and Roys 1968 [1948]; quote in J. Thompson 1967: 98.

12. For a complete bibliography of Roys's published and unpublished works, see Ventur 1978.

13. P. Thompson 1978: 5–11 is an excellent survey of the early historical literature from an anthropological perspective; Thompson's coverage of Roys also influenced my own.

14. Gibson 1964; Anderson, Berdan, and Lockhart 1976; Karttunen and Lockhart 1976; various articles eventually republished together as Lockhart 1991; Lockhart 1992.

15. García Bernal 1972, 1978; Hunt 1974 (see also 1976); Patch 1979, 1993. Also important are a series of articles by García Bernal: 1979, 1984, 1991a, 1991b, 1992, 1994.

16. Clendinnen 1987; Farriss 1984; Jones 1989. Rugeley n.d., which also recognizes the need to use Maya-language sources when writing about Maya society, is a skillful attempt to weave Spanish and Maya sources together to this end with respect to the early nineteenth century.

17. Reed 1964. Clendinnen's (1987) partial reappraisal of Ricard's apologia for the Franciscans in New Spain (Ricard 1933) embodies a sensitive interpretation of divergent views of a Christianized Yucatan in its presentation of a cruel side to Landa that complements the Pacheco Cruz mural of Landa in Mérida's Palacio de Gobierno and at the same time contradicts the mild, scholarly Landa of his *Relación* (1982 [1566]). Still, the author of this encyclopedic study of the Maya is not easily reconciled with the author of a policy of systematic torture and indiscriminate persecution of Maya men and women.

18. Farriss 1984: 400.

19. Since the publication of *Maya Society* four other scholars from four different nations have made noteworthy efforts to reconstruct aspects of postconquest Maya life using Spanish-language sources, each with specific concerns and approaches. Three of these have turned to the question of sixteenth-century Maya political organization, their work as much concerned with native structures before as after the conquest. Riese's (1981) doctoral study analyzed the famous Maní map and its close relations, and the doctoral research currently being undertaken in Mexico by Tsubasa Okoshi (Ochiai 1991; Quezada personal communication) challenges

Roys's interpretation of Maya political entities at the time of Contact. The best work presently being done by a scholar from Yucatan itself is Sergio Quezada's forthcoming revision of his doctoral dissertation (1990), which modifies the traditional Roys-based view of Maya leadership immediately after the conquest with archival evidence from Seville. The fourth of these recent contributions is the thorough investigation of the southern frontier conducted by Jones (1989), who finally shatters the colonial Spanish perspective of a "civilized" northern Yucatan and a south that was the dark refuge of intractable pagans. The study of the colonial-era Maya from various anthropological perspectives during the 1980's has also illuminated certain aspects of the field. A debate on the nature of "frontier" in postconquest Yucatan was deliberately introduced into the heart of Jones's *Maya Resistance* (1989); it was also the implied substance of Paul Sullivan's (1989) account of anthropologists' encounters with the Quintana Roo Maya between the two world wars; and the subject has been given a linguistic treatment by one of the leading scholars of the Yucatec Maya language (Hanks 1987). The conceptual links between Jones 1989 and Sullivan 1989 are discussed in reviews by Hanks (*American Anthropologist* 93 [1991]: 178–79) and by Restall (*UCLA Historical Journal* 11 [1991]: 159–64).

20. Quote in Lockhart 1992: 427.

21. Jones 1989: 7–8.

22. Bricker 1981, 1986, 1989; Edmonson 1982, 1986; Burns 1991b; Hanks 1986, 1987, 1988, 1989a, 1989b, 1990 (1988 and 1989b discuss Chilam Balam passages).

23. Process traced in Lockhart 1991: part III, and 1989. The notables of this historiographical evolution include: Taylor 1972; Bakewell 1971; Brading 1971; Russell-Wood 1968; Schwartz 1973; Spalding 1967; Lockhart 1968 and 1972. The New Philologists include the early Nahuatlatos, published as Anderson, Berdan, and Lockhart 1976; Lockhart, Berdan, and Anderson 1986; and Karttunen and Lockhart 1976 and 1987; as well as the new generation of ethnohistorians: Burkhart 1989; Cline 1986; Haskett 1985; Horn 1989; Kellogg 1995; Schroeder 1991; Sigal 1995; Terraciano 1994; and Wood 1984. Quotes from Lockhart 1991: 200. For comparative purposes in this study I have mostly used Cline 1986; Lockhart 1992; Haskett 1985, 1991; Horn 1989; Kellogg 1979, 1995; Terraciano 1994; and Wood 1984.

Chapter Two

1. Bacalar petition of 1838: AGN-BN, 5, 35, 5; Calkiní petition of 1669 listing tax items: AGI-E, 317b, 9, 9.

2. Edmonson 1982: 169; 1986: 100 (*Maya Ah Itzae*), 109 (*Maya uinice*), 132, 138, 143, 153, 178, 207, 210 (*Maya uinicob[i]*); Roys 1967 [1933].

3. TCh: 193, 213, 214.

4. AGI-E, 317a, 2, 147 (petition by the cah governor or *batab*, don Diego Poot, and the cabildo of Baca, 1669, against *repartimiento* or forced-sales demands).

5. *Dzul* was obviously a term in use before the Spaniards arrived, and it is used several times in the Chilam Balam literature (see, for example, the Tizimin: Edmonson 1982: 32, 33).

6. TE: 274.

7. AGN-BN, 26, 55, 20.

8. Cline 1986: 155; Lockhart 1992: 115.

9. TT: 13 (will of Diego Mul, Maní, 1629). Spaniards were also called *caxtillan uinicob*, "people of Castile," and *kul uinicob*, "people in authority," but *españolesob* was used only at the end of the colonial period (Karttunen 1985: 53). There is no evidence that Maya speakers (or indeed Nahuas and Mixtecs; see Terraciano 1994: 497–98) ever referred to Spaniards as "whites" or "white people."

10. The use of cah in verbal form is pervasive, but examples are in AGN-T, 1359, 5, 19–22; TI; DT. On the distinction between the two terms *cah*: Bricker, personal communication.

11. On clans, lineages, and *lignages*, see Goody 1983: 229–39. On chibalob names, see Chap. 4; on chibal and class, see Chap. 7; and on marriage within and between chibalob, see Chap. 10.

12. Terraciano 1994: 463–523.

13. For published cruzob text, see the 1850 proclamation and an 1851 letter by Juan de la Cruz in Bricker 1981: 187–218; a significant number of similar letters are catalogued in the CCA, with others reputed to have been sold into private hands, and some of 1844 and 1850 are in T-LAL-RMC, 2:7 and C454.

Chapter Three

1. For Nahua contrast: Lockhart 1992: 14 (for the broader contrast: chaps. 2, 3, 5). I infer from Terraciano (1994), though he does not specifically state this, that the Ñuu, the Ñudzahui (Mixtec) equivalent of the cah and altepetl, is closer to the altepetl in this respect.

2. Coe 1965; Roys 1972: 11, 63; P. Thompson 1978: 298, 321.

3. In postconquest towns, the church was usually constructed upon the foundations of the old temple, and was often built of the same stones (the convent at Maní being a notable example). One exception, Acanceh, provides the visitor today with a remarkable illustration of Yucatec history: a central plaza delineated by the preconquest temple mound, the sixteenth-century church, some colonial residences whose front rooms are now (and probably always have been) general stores, and the cabildo building rebuilt in the nineteenth century but still housing the municipal authorities. On preconquest plazas, see Marcus 1983. For a discussion of the confluence of Mesoamerican and Spanish plaza traditions, see Low 1995.

4. Vogt 1983: 89–114. Patrilineal clans and swidden agriculture are discussed elsewhere in this study.

5. Kubler 1948: 1, 90; Kostof 1991: 115. Kostof (111–24) points out that the grid pattern resurgence of the Renaissance did not result in the immediate rebuilding of the relatively formless medieval European city; the three regions where sixteenth- and seventeenth-century Europeans were able to build the new urban order were Sicily, Scandinavia, and the New World. McAlister's view (1984: 149–50) is that the grid had late-medieval European origins but was also influenced by the layout of pre-Columbian New World cities.

6. LC; and DT, TE, TI, TT, etc. Dictionary terms that come closest to meaning solar are all general or ambiguous references to land that may or may not be cultivated or located near or beside the house (Barrera Vásquez 1991).

7. Vogt 1983; Kurjack 1974: 73–89; Redfield 1941, 1950. One cluster equals one block in concept but not necessarily in size. Clusters were larger than both colonial and modern blocks, as reflected in the greater number of residential compounds they contained, and in their number; Late Classic Dzibilchaltun had about 30 clusters, and the community was much larger than colonial Ixil, which even today has about 50 blocks. Thus the transition to the grid would have been influenced by many local variants. The question of the acquisition of "pueblo" status by indigenous communities, the subject of much of Wood 1984 (with respect to the Toluca region), has received scant attention by historians of Yucatan. I have found Maya documentation to shed little light on the matter, but there are Spanish records in AGEY-A, 1, 11, and 16 concerning the granting of cabildos to cahob in the final decades of the colonial period.

8. Field notes on modern cahob: Jan.–Mar. 1991, May 1992. Maya solars are also discussed in Chaps. 8, 15, and 16.

9. On the altepetl, see Lockhart 1992, chap. 2; Wood 1984. On the ñuu, see Terraciano 1994, chap. 4.

10. Farriss 1984: 163, which largely follows Coe 1965; Quezada 1990.

11. Barrera Vásquez 1991: 867; Lockhart 1992: 14 (on *altepetl*). The general Mesoamerican association of towns with images of hills and water is treated in Marcus 1992, chap. 6. The Ñudzahui sometimes used the term *yucunduta*, which is semantically equivalent to altepetl; *yucu* ("hill") began many ñuu names (Terraciano 1994: 246, 253).

12. Gibson 1964; Lockhart 1991 and 1992; and the doctoral work of: Haskett 1985; Horn 1989; and Wood 1984.

13. Both Gibson (1964) and Farriss (1984) did use a small number of indigenous-language sources, but mostly in contemporaneous Spanish translations.

14. Lockhart 1992: 14 (in reference to the altepetl).

15. Franciscan parishes were called *doctrinas*, and secular parishes *curatos*. The cahob that made up each parish were called *visitas*, with each parish headed by its cabecera (Farriss 1984: 149). For listings of encomenderos and the communities they received, see García Bernal 1978; app. 1 and 2; and Quezada 1990, app. 1. Much of this information is also in Hunt 1974 and in the RY. Hunt 1974, chap. 3; García Bernal 1978, chaps. 6–11; and Quezada 1990, chap. 2, are all discussions of the encomienda in Yucatan, the first an unequaled study of seventeenth-century encomienda society, the second a treatment of the encomienda as an institution (also focusing on the seventeenth century), and the third a brief analysis of the sixteenth-century establishment of the encomienda (with some comment on the correlation between encomienda organization and preconquest native political structure). Patch 1993 discusses the transition from encomienda to other forms of labor procurement in the context of the eighteenth-century growth in Spanish cattle enterprises and other estates.

16. Farriss 1984: 149.

17. Ibid., 149–51; Quezada 1990. Batabil refers in the colonial period to the senior office of the cah (see Chap. 6), but Quezada uses it to denote preconquest sociopolitical units larger than the cah. The discussion of the "provinces" is not the only instance of the tendency of recent scholars in this field to rely less upon primary sources than upon Roys's speculative imagination (in this case, passages in 1957).

18. Example from ANEY, 1828, 7 (sale record of 1782). See Chap. 6 for discussion of ah cuch cab in context of Maya political office.

19. TCh: 193, etc.

20. For the claim of disappearance, see Farriss 1984: 163. A Spanish translation of a Maya land document of 1815 uses the term "parcialidad" (AGN-T, 1419, 2, 55, 6; also discussed briefly below); and the word also appears in reference to Maya communities in files of the 1810's in AGEY-A, 1, but the late-colonial usage seems to be in reference to "reduced" communities.

21. On congregación in Spanish America, see Lockhart and Schwartz 1983: 72–73, 116–17; in Yucatan: Quezada 1990: 98–126; Farriss 1984: 158–64, 206–10; Patch 1993: 48–56. Also see Chap. 13 below.

22. For example, Maní in 1629 enjoyed the protection of both San Juan and San Miguel Arcángel (TT: 13), and Nohcacab in the 1770's had both San Mateo and Santa Barbara as its patrons (CCA-I). These facts do seem to point to the existence of calpolli-type subunits, but until other evidence surfaces to support this interpretation, we can only assume that these two cases are explicable in terms as yet unknown to us—having to do, for example, with anomalous local secular-Franciscan arrangements.

23. AGN-IN, 82, 1, 146–67.

24. RY: I, 65; Roys 1972: 11–12.

25. Quezada's interpretation (1990) is that although the dominance of one chibal (which he sees as lineages called tzucub) over each province is patchy, each community head was answerable to a provincial overlord, the *halach uinic*. I see halach uinic not as a separate office but simply as a title bestowed upon a dominant batab; the flexible use of Spanish rulership titles by the Maya may not reflect a lack of understanding on their part, but rather a tradition in which titles were not specific (like today's "president") but reverential (like "sir"): see Chaps. 6 and 19.

26. Okoshi's studies of the Ecab region and of the Calkiní "Codex" (title) are known to me in the form of unpublished papers presented in Chiapas (1989) and Campeche (1990), described briefly by Ochiai 1991.

27. Bacalar and Campeche are Hispanizations of the Maya names Bakhalal and Canpech, although they appear in Maya documents in or close to the Hispanized forms.

28. Altman 1991: 442; Calnek 1972; Gibson 1964: 371.

29. For example, AGN-BN, 5, 35, 4–5 (Bacalar) and ANEY, 1736–37, 277; 1766–69, 141; 1812i, 230; 1818iii, 1–4 and 12 (Itzmal). The ANEY has dozens of cah documents from other cabeceras, such as Maní, Motul, Ticul, and Tekax (where the Spanish-Maya population ratio was 11,255:35,648 by 1811: AGEY-CP, 2, 3). There is no evidence that Spanish cabildos were established in cabeceras during the colonial period.

30. Census records: AGEY-CP, 2, 4, 1–5 (Valladolid, 1811) and 2, 1 (Campeche, 1810). Campeche cahob-barrio sale: ANEY, 1736–37, c. 400–404 (discussed in Chap. 19).

31. Piña Chan 1977: 56, 65. See also Magaña Toledano 1984: 36–37, who points out that "Naboríos mexicanos" refers to Nahua dependents of the Adelantado Montejo, brought from his central Mexican encomienda at Azcapotzalco; *naboría* (as it was originally) is an Arawak-derived term the Spaniards used to describe indigenous dependents throughout Spanish America (Lockhart and Schwartz 1983: 71).

32. Magaña Toledano 1984, for example. Hunt 1974, chap. 2, is the partial exception to this remark; rather than belaboring the inconsistency of the sources, she makes some tentative suggestions about the ethnicity or ethnic-organizational status of certain barrios.

33. ANEY, examples in volumes dating from 1748 to 1838, documents dating from 1713 to 1809, from La Mejorada, San Cristóbal, San Sebastián, Santa Ana, and Santiago. These documents are uncatalogued and have not so far been used or even mentioned in the scholarly literature.

34. Edmonson 1986: 101; Brinton 1882: 242. Victoria Bricker (personal communication) has pointed out that the *ho* in Tihó is *ho'*, not the *hó'o* meaning "five." However, the five-cahob evidence makes me reluctant to abandon the idea of some toponymic connection here. The *ti* locative on Maya toponyms was often dropped when the name was not being used in a locative context—for example, as an adjective, as in *batab kanto*, "the batab of Tekanto." Or it could be dropped when used with a verb of motion; a Maya today might say, *tin bin chac*, "I'm going to Chac / Techac." Another example is the simple contraction, often written in Maya documentation, of Tihó as *t ho*. Note that Nahua toponyms also include locatives, the *co* in Mexico being the most obvious example, although Nahuatl does not allow the locatives to be dropped as Maya does.

35. Hunt 1974: 154, 159. The Franciscan convent was built on the mound to the southeast of the plaza mayor.

36. ANEY 1826ii, 34–36v; AGN-T 1419, 2, 55–56.

37. Examples, respectively, are ANEY, 1813ii, 13; 1798ii, 8 (see also the opening phrase of the second half of document 3 in App. A); and 1828–30iii, 10. A document might be headed *Tihóo*, and then state its provenance at the end as *Santa Anna* (1748–50, f.?), or headed *S^ntiago* or *santiago ti hoo*, later stating the presence of the cabildo and *u batabil cah*, or simply including the formula *uay ti cah* (1766–69, 261; 1818i, 173).

38. The remarks on Mérida in this and succeeding paragraphs based on Spanish sources are drawn from Hunt 1974, chap. 2. My interpretation of the history of Mérida-Tihó is offered as a modifying update or complement to Hunt's study, which drew upon solely Spanish-language primary sources.

39. Cárdenas Valencia (in 1636) and Cogolludo (in 1656), cited in Hunt 1974: 207–8.

40. The climate of Yucatan has had serious effects over time on archival material, but though very few records have survived from before 1700 in the peninsula

itself, archives in Seville contain Maya-language records from the Mérida-Tihó cahob-barrios from the late 1660's, for example (AGI-E, 315b, 31), and possibly from earlier still.

41. Hunt 1974: 221. The only extant Maya-language evidence of Santa Catalina and its apparent status as a satellite of some sort is from 1670 (AGI-E, 315b, 31, 70), in the form of a cabildo petition requesting payment for work done on the citadel; note that the labor demands that went to the cahob-barrios extended to the satellite cahob of Santa Catalina, Kanasín, and Chuburná. Chuburná and Itzimná, two cahob that were not barrios but were eventually absorbed by Mérida, are well documented in the Maya-language sources; in the case of Itzimná, the cah appears to have fallen under the jurisdiction of La Mejorada at the end of the colonial period (see Chap. 16 and Map 3.3).

42. This interpretation of Maya migration (Hunt 1974: 226) is supported by the analysis of Maya patronyms in Tihó and other cahob in Chap. 4, which shows a greater variety of patronyms in the cahob-barrios than in other cahob. On the various migration patterns, see Chap. 13.

43. Hunt 1974: 233.

44. These are described in a broad context in Chap. 2 above, and in Chap. 6 they are presented in detail in the context of the discussion on land. Two examples of sales of land outside the residential core come from Santa Ana, 1748 (ANEY, 1748–50, f.?), and Santiago [?], 1759 (ANEY, 1813i; 70). The relative rarity of such sales may reflect the fact that cah-barrio residents relied more on salaried domestic service than rural cah dwellers did.

45. ANEY 1800, 211; 1816–17, f.?; 1819i, 70; 1822–23, 33; 1827–28, 278; 1828–30, 74. The last Maya-language sale: 1810ii, 99. I have not looked closely at the form of sales in these communities after 1840, but the records are in the ANEY.

46. ANEY 1824–25, 171; 1826i, 114–16; 1826i, f.?; 1828–30, 74. It is not clear, but neither is it ruled out by the language of some of the sales, whether don Marcelino was selling off community property (as one Nahua ruler had been accused of doing—Lockhart 1991: 93); a few decades earlier Santiago had certainly owned cah house plots (ANEY 1776, 257).

47. ANEY 1741–42, n.f; AGN-T 1419, 2, 1–7 (discussed below).

48. Marcus 1983: 226.

49. In 1991 this feud caused great scandal when Hunucmá failed to return the Virgin to Tetiz on the scheduled day, prompting state police to enter the church at Hunucmá, seize the image, and transport it in a police vehicle the eight kilometers to Tetiz (author's field notes, Feb. 1991).

50. Uman et al.: the 1815 document is a six-cah land boundary agreement: AGN-T, 1419, 2, 55, 6; I take the -il in tzucil to be the collective suffix used on nouns (-il has many purposes), which thus obviates the need for a plural suffix on cah. Dzibikal: AGI-E, 317b, 9, 1–3. Calkiní: TC: 85 (Barrera Vásquez translates tzuc as parcialidad, but elsewhere in TC these three "tzucob" are also called cahob). Espita and Tzabcanul: AGEY-A, 1, 28. Examples from twin cahob: AGN-T, 1419, 2, 1–7; AGN-CR, 316, 1; 335, 1; 336, 1; AGN-T, 1421, 13, 15–16; AGN-BN, 26, 55, 2–4/ 19/20–25; AGN-I, 82, 1; ANEY, 1741–42, n.f. Examples of other multi-cah docu-

ments: Maní MS in T-LAL-RMC; AGN-I, 69, 5, 277; ANEY, 1736–37, c. 400. TE also contains examples of documents drawn up by two, three, and four cahob.

51. This is shown by twentieth-century forced resettlement programs under circumstances as different and in countries as distinct as Malaysia, Guatemala, South Africa, and Tibet.

52. Returns to original sites are shown on the maps accompanying Quezada 1990, who discusses congregación (98–126). See also: Farriss 1984: 158–64, 206–10; Patch 1993: 48–56, 225–26; and with respect to colonial Spanish America, Lockhart and Schwartz 1983: 72–73, 116–17; and Chap. 13 below. Patch 1993: 51 is a list of "parcialidades"; where Maya-language documentation is extant for these communities they are shown to be cahob, which is no doubt the case with them all.

53. Farriss 1984: 164, 207, for example, comments on settlement continuity.

54. By taking the Nahuacentric perspective offered her by Nahuatl sources Wood (1984: cap. 2) came to a similar conclusion with regard to the impact of congregaciones on the Toluca region. Terraciano (1994: 297–99) similarly concludes, with respect to Oaxaca, that Ñudzahui communities "were not moved very far and retained their separate identity, names, and lands throughout the [sixteenth] century and beyond."

Chapter Four

1. Roys 1940: 38; TC.

2. Roys 1940: 39, on Owl Face; the other translation is mine.

3. Landa 1982 [1566]: 58; Gates 1978: 56; translation mine.

4. The repetition of complete names within one family was more common among the postconquest Nahuas; Cline (1986: 119–20) poses the question, "What were these women actually called?" and tentatively suggests that the use of Nahuatl first names was practiced in speech to the end of the sixteenth century at least.

5. Field notes, 1991–92; William Hanks, personal communication. It hardly seems worth pointing out the obvious, that most, if not all, cultures employ nicknames of some kind.

6. ANE-Y, 1839, 2 (Camal); ANE-Y, 1810(ii), 70 (Canche). Juan Ramos would be a typical low-status postconquest Nahua name. Some other examples of names the Maya added to Juan: Ambrocio, de Dios, de la Cruz, Espiritu Santo, Pio Quinto (or Pio V), Santo, Tomás. Such "extensions" were also added to the equally common female name Maria.

7. Cline 1986: 117 on early evidence; caveat of later pattern from Horn 1989.

8. AGN-I, 1187, 2, 59. TI: 51, etc. for examples of patterns described. Note that we have more individual male examples because women were excluded from cabildos and fewer women drew up wills than did men. Spaniards, like Mayas, were often named after their grandfathers.

9. DTY/TY; TC; TCh; Brinton 1882; T-LAL-RMC, 26.

10. TT: 32–33; CCA, Chichí, I, 29.

11. Cogolludo 1867–68 [1654]; Scholes and Adams 1938; Miller and Farriss 1979; Clendinnen 1987; Farriss 1984. That the name change was not swift and

unresisted is implied in Tomás López's ordinances of 1552, in which the oidor instructed, "No one shall give a heathen name to his children," presumably a reference to non-Christian first names. What is more, "Many Indians having been told that their children will die if baptised, I command that all children be brought for baptism" (Gates 1937: 157–58).

12. Lockhart 1992: 118–19. It may be possible that the actual disappearance of *na* names was not as sudden as it is in the historical record, and that it faded out gradually just as the use of Hispanic-style matronyms and patronyms faded during the twentieth century.

13. Farriss 1984: 94 (translation hers). The bishop's "names from pagan times" were presumably either Maya pronunciations of Christian names or Maya nicknames. Roys's (1939: 23) identification of "pagan group-names" in some of the Ebtun sources reflects his unawareness of the widespread use of the chibal collective in colonial times; the document in question (TE: 25) is also very damaged, and it is written in an unusual opaque style.

14. Karttunen 1985: 103–4.

15. See Chap. 7.

16. On the Nahuas, see Lockhart 1992: 117–30; on the Ñudzahui, Terraciano 1994: 427–44.

17. Written: *D^n Montejo Xiu* (ANE-Y, 1826ii, 301–2).

18. Cline 1986: 121 (on the Nahuas); P. Thompson 1978, chap. 4 (on Tekanto); see also Chap. 7 below.

19. Landa 1982 [1566]: 41–42; Gates 1937: 40; Roys 1940: 35; translation mine.

20. See Chap. 10, n. 29.

21. See Landa excerpt above; RY, I: 269; Roys 1967 [1933]: 63–64 (the Chilam Balam of Chumayel) and 1940: 35.

22. Farriss, for example, 1984: 57–79.

23. Roys 1940, citing tax lists in "AGI-1688" (the citation is incomplete); Roys, Scholes, and Adams 1940.

24. I list the cahob-barrios of Santa Ana, San Cristóbal, San Sebastián, Santiago, and La Mejorada together as Tihó for convenience; also, because some are better represented in the documentation than others, separate listing would be no more useful than listing names from rural cahob with a dozen or so extant documents (such as Conkal or Oxkutzcab). Because they are also geographically contiguous, I have assumed (rightly or wrongly) that they are less contained, in terms of marriage and settlement patterns, than rural cahob. See Chap. 18 for the distribution of extant Maya records, and Chap. 3 for a study of these cahob-barrios.

Chapter Five

1. On Flores de Aldana, see AGI-E, 315a–327; also García Bernal 1979; Farriss 1984: 78–85; Patch 1993: 124; and various references throughout this book. I am currently working on a separate study of the Flores de Aldana period, as part of a book project titled *Identity and Interaction: Maya, Spaniard, and African in Colonial Yucatan*.

2. AGN-CI, 2013, 1, 4.

3. See, for example, Farriss 1984, chaps. 1 and 2; and Patch 1993, chaps. 2 and 4.

4. ANEY, libro 1736–37, c. 400. The Nahua community treasury was a similar insurance policy; Haskett 1985: 204–7.

5. My point is not that the 1761 revolt did not occur, but that it was directly created by Spanish hysteria rather than by Maya conspiracy; see especially Bricker 1981, chap. 6; also Farriss 1984: 68–72; Villanueva 1992; Patch 1993: 156–57, 228–29; Patch n.d.

6. CCA, *libros de cuentas y depositos*. My translation of some of the phrases is tentative. Patch (1993: 208–24) cites the same archival file, but he is interested in how it relates to his analysis of the colonial economy. One of the points he emphasizes is the sale of grain by Maya farmers to Mérida's pósito agents (at prices he convincingly argues cheated the Maya); the Maya-language records show that such sales were conducted by way of the representative structure of indigenous cabildos.

7. AGN-BN, 26, 71, 16 (Tihólop, 1813) and 26, 55, 2–4 (Tetiz, 1819). For more detail on the nature of Yucatan's granary system, especially the relationship between rural production and urban demand, see Patch 1993, chaps. 7 and 8; see also Chap. 14 below.

8. TE: 275; TI: 35a (in which Maria Huchim went before the cabildo to win possession of a mare that was given her in her husband's will seven years earlier but was being held by one of his brothers) and 40a–b; DT; ANEY, 1826ii, 9v; T-LAL: Xcupilcacab, 2; TT: 32–36.

9. Tlaxcala's cabildo records reproduced in part in Lockhart, Berdan, and Anderson 1986. Ebtun example: TE: 276. Tixpeual example: DT: [II] 47. On the altepetl's official buildings: Haskett 1985: 213–14. Audiencias within churches in Yucatan are implied by the use of *kuna*, "church," to describe the locations of cabildo meetings, as discussed below.

10. AGN-CI, 2052, 6, 9.

11. AGN-IN, 82, 1, 158.

12. The purpose of the Spanish imperial judicial system was the subject of continuous debate throughout the early modern period. The existence of advocates for a system of justice that protected all men, including the indigenous subjects of the Crown, resulted in laws that provided ethnic groups such as the Maya with funds to cover legal expenses as well as a colonial official—"the Defender/Protector of the Indians"—who, theoretically, would oversee their interests (Borah 1982; Farriss 1984). Maya communities did not consistently benefit from this system; the parish priest of Seye, for example, complained in 1817 that local hacendados were infringing on indigenous lands but the attorneys appointed to defend the "Indians looked upon their cause with indifference" (AGEY-T, 1, 17, 2). The *defensor* in the 1660's was subsequently prosecuted for his participation in the Flores de Aldana administration's economic exploitation of the cahob (AGI-E, 315b).

13. AGN-BN, 5, 35: 5.

14. TI: 45, 54; TE: 230, 234.

15. TI: 36.

16. Haskett 1985: 253.

17. TI; the Spanish *testigo*, with Maya pl. ending *-ob*. TT: 2.

18. For example, TI: 32.

19. See ANEY in volumes dated between 1716 and 1777.

20. Rugeley n.d. has demonstrated the central role played by Spanish priests in the rural economy in the first half of the nineteenth century.

21. ANEY, 1775: 5v.

22. ANEY, 1758–60: 338.

Chapter Six

1. Gibson 1964: 167–68; Haskett 1985: 31; Horn 1989: 74–75; Lockhart and Schwartz 1983: 114–15.

2. Cisteil and Nenelá, for example; evidence from the investigation into the 1761 "rebellion" (Patch 1993: 229).

3. Morelos study: Haskett 1985, especially cap. 2; 1991; other studies: Gibson 1964: 188; Horn 1989: 95–123; Spores 1967: 121; Terraciano 1994: 314–38.

4. Horn 1989: 75–81.

5. Terraciano 1994: 274–96, 314–27.

6. Roys 1972 [1943]: 134–41. Whether hereditary lordship was meant to be implied or not, the use of the term cacique by Spaniards conveys no reliable and specific information to us. There is no evidence that the Spaniards using the term were concerned with heredity, a concept that the Maya were only concerned with in group terms, in the way that batabs were chosen from a pool of eligible families.

7. Farriss 1984: 232–35. The question of the separation of the offices of governor and traditional ruler is also important in the Oaxaca region; the Ñudzahui *yya toniñe* there was the equivalent of the Maya batab and the Nahua tlatoani, and it compared more closely in this respect to central Mexico than to Yucatan (Terraciano 1994: 321–26).

8. Farriss 1984: 232–35. The only Maya sources among these are late-seventeenth-century election records from LC and AGEY, 1, 1 (Tekanto) that do not address this question. Roys's (1972, chap. 20) portrayal of a Xiu petition of 1640 as an attempt to assure a "succession of caciqueship" founders on his use of terminology: the petition aims at acquiring or maintaining *indio hidalgo* privileges for certain Xiu chibal members, and clearly relates to social and economic status rather than to political office (Xiu papers, or TX, are in T-LAL).

9. For central Mexico, see Haskett 1985: caps 2–4; Horn 1989: 75–95. The reelection of a Nahua governor was, of course, commonplace.

10. For example, the case in RY, 1: 279, 281 of the batabs in Tixkokob and Mococha being replaced by governors could easily have represented a factional conflict misunderstood by the Spaniards, rather than a Maya recognition of the bifurcation of offices (as read by Farriss 1984: 243).

11. ANE-Y, 1776, 257 (see App. A).

12. DTY; RY, I: 147; Roys 1972: 135.

13. TC: 81.

14. Roys 1967: 83ff; Farriss 1984: 246–55. Edmonson's interpretation (1986: 168)

and Marcus's (1992: 78–79) are similar to Roys's; Burns (1991b: 35) persuasively argues that the passage is "a repository of riddles that function to question and mock authority, not celebrate it."

15. P. Thompson 1978, chaps. 5 and 6.   16. Laws cited by Haskett 1985: 32.

17. P. Thompson 1978: 347–48.   18. See Farriss 1984: 184.

19. Documents of 1578 and 1589: AGN-I, 69, 5, 199/275.

20. Some examples of *(u) chun than*: T-LAL-TT, 37; DT: 30; T-LAL, Maní MS (TX); AGI-E, 315b, 17.

21. The family tree of sources in this case seems to have as its trunk Diego de Landa (1982 [1566]), who, as a primary source on the Maya, needs to be treated gingerly, and as its branches Roys (1943), Coe (1965), Thompson (1978), and Farriss (1984).

22. An example of each: TC: 77; TI: 45.

23. DT: 29.

24. For example, *u chun thanob* and *u nucil/noh/xib uinicob*; some of these are included in Table 2.1. The Maní MS (TX) contains many of the most commonly used Maya terms for political and sociopolitical units (i.e., office titles, ruling bodies, provinces, districts, etc.).

25. *Noh* means "large" (example from Chikindzonot, 1775: ANE-Y libro 1775, 5v; *chichan* means "small" (from Bolompoyche, 1812: AGN-BN, 21, 20, 4). Note that these are *late* colonial examples.

26. TT: 28–30.

27. Farriss 1984: 234. (fig. 8.1, which contrasts somewhat with my Table 6.4). Also see my Table 12.1.

28. Nahua-Spanish pattern described by Haskett 1985: 364; the quote describing the Tlaxcalan system, actually follows Lockhart, Berdan, and Anderson 1986. The quote would also apply to the Ñudzahui version of cabildo government (Terraciano 1994: 314–38).

29. P. Thompson 1978, chap. 5. I repeat my gratitude to Philip Thompson for his generous sharing with me of the Tekanto election documents more than a year before I could get to the originals in the AGEY.

30. I estimate that ten to twelve names represent two or three individual careers, and that 20 of the 88 names appearing once (and in the first three or last four years of the sample) were officers with careers outside this period.

31. Haskett 1985, chap. 4.

32. P. Thompson 1978, chap. 6.

33. On the 1549: Haskett 1985: 65, who cites José Miranda, *Las ideas y las instituciones políticas mexicanas* (Mexico City: Instituto del derecho comparado, 1952). The Yucatec ordenanzas were in 1552 (Tomás Lopez Medel), 1567 (Céspedes), and 1584 (Dr. Palacios). The Cacalchen ordenanzas (LC: 35–46) appear to be a 1729 translation of the Palacios regulations, if not a similar series of laws; election requirements are not detailed beyond stipulations that they be held annually in each cah, with justice and without dispute.

34. On Nahua election records, see Haskett 1985, chap. 3. For a fuller discussion of Maya election records, see Chap. 20 below.

35. TE: 283.

36. T-LAL-RMC, 1, 25, 2.

37. Haskett 1985: 102–17.

38. There are terna proposals all through AGEY-A, all in Spanish. Examples of the relatively few Maya-language terna documents are the Xcupilcacab case discussed here, and one from Ekpedz of 1830 (the latest in Maya of which I am aware; AGEY-E, II, 57).

39. Farriss 1984: 246–48.

40. P. Thompson 1978: 361–63.

41. The 1732 will (ANEY, 1729, 255) of Valenzuela's widow, Mauricia Suárez, shows that the couple owned property and lived in Izamal, although she naturally claimed that in spite of being local residents they were "of" Mérida. Something of the couple's status is indicated by their residency in Izamal, and by the fact that Suárez had no *doña*: even in the Maya ratification of the will by the Ytzmal (Maya Izamal) cabildo she is called respectfully, but only, *yn colel* (m'lady, or señora) *mablisia suares*.

42. In arousing Spanish intervention this dispute is comparable to the Tekax dispute of 1610 between an Uz and Xiu candidate that led to an alleged riot of the inhabitants; see note 43 below.

43. Farriss 1984: 192–94, 429 n. 48; AGI-E, 305a (Tekax); 318a, 9 (Tzotzil); 317a, 2 (1669 Maya-language statements against and by batabs from Baca, Mococha, Pencuyut, and Sinanche, over repartimiento abuses); 318a, 13 (nearly 400 folios of testimony, much of it in Maya, regarding repartimiento demands involving Flores de Aldana agents and local batabs; see Chap. 5, n. 1 above).

44. TT: 33.

45. AGN-BN, 5, 35: 5.

Chapter Seven

1. Farriss states that "the leveling process failed to close the gap between nobles and commoners entirely" (1984: 165) and she provides some evidence to that fact, but she gives greater emphasis to "the leveling process" itself. This is in the Gibsonian tradition, in which colonial rule equalized and compressed indigenous class society (1964: 153, for example).

2. Roys 1972 [1943]; Morley 1983 [1946]; Farriss 1984.

3. ANEY, 1832–33ii, 161–65.

4. Farriss 1984: 245. For contrary evidence, see note 10 below.

5. Similarly, Terraciano (1994: 359–92, 436–46) found that among the Ñudzahui "social differentiation was complex and dynamic and evolved gradually throughout the colonial period, rather than collapsing dramatically after the Conquest" (445).

6. Foucault 1980: 93–94.

7. P. Thompson 1978: 232; Farriss 1984: 239. Roys was also vague on class terminology (1943: 129–71).

8. DTY: line 450 (and *lay hidalgos*: 78). Farriss (1984) emphasizes the perspective,

based largely on Spanish-language sources, that sees the Maya use of titles of nobility as increasingly hollow and removed from social realities.

9. See Farriss 1984: 231.

10. AGI-M, 367, 62–71; RY, I: 65, 78, 129, 221, 278; Quezada 1990, app. 1; AGI-E, 316b, 51, 1; TI; TY.

11. See P. Thompson 1978: 200.

12. Tihó, App. C; Ebtun, App. B; TE; Roys 1939: 48–49; Tekanto, App. B; DT; P. Thompson 1978: 353–54. The other examples: TI, LC, TE, DT, DTY, and various records in AGN and ANEY.

13. AGI-E, 315a–318a; Rugeley n.d., intro. and chaps. 5 and 8. See also Chap. 6 on the batabil and Chap. 14 on repartimientos.

14. Lockhart 1992, chap. 4; MT: 65.

15. Maya class and title are given an interesting insight by the case discussed in Chap. 6 (unique in extant records) of a Spaniard, don Agustín de Valenzuela ("Palensuela"), being imposed as a cah governor during a factional dispute: Maya records refer to him not only as don, although he himself signs his name without the don, but also as almehen; even though he is an outsider and a *dzul* (meaning non-Maya, not Dzul), the principales of Tekanto see him as the occupant of a *Maya* office and lend him the appropriate titles of status and respect (AGEY-A, 1, 1).

16. Examples from TI and DTY; see also Chap. 2.

17. It is worth remarking here that these patterns call into question the notion that the survival or decline of Maya dynasties after the conquest was determined in part by the extent to which that chibal was a preconquest parvenu on the peninsula (suggested by Farriss 1984: 22–23, 244–45); the postconquest survival of ruling chibalob in each cah now seems to have been far more widespread than previously thought, to the extent that the conquest may have had a negligible effect on a process that would in any case have included a certain amount of attrition. Furthermore, not only is the historical evidence of these foreign dynasties, in particular their arrival dates, unreliable, but also, if certain chibalob achieved dominance in a majority of cahob in certain areas, with leading batabob earning the additional reverential title of halach uinic, "dynasty" and "province" may not be the most accurate terms to describe this situation.

18. Goody 1976: 23.

19. Of the 65 wills of Ixil (1765–68), 20 include bequests of kax, and 15 name the neighboring kax owners. The total number of kaxob mentioned (as bequests and as neighbors) is actually 97, but by cross-referencing the wills I have identified three kaxob as mentioned twice. It is possible there were a few others; Mateo Yam the neighbor, for example, may be the same man as Mateo Yam the testator, but the incomplete descriptions of the kaxob ascribed to them suggest three separate pieces of land, so I have recorded it as such.

20. TI: 36. Two of the Ixil wills are in App. A; the entire corpus is in Restall 1995a.

21. Up to eight family members are listed as joint heirs to land in the Ixil wills; TI: 45, for example.

22. The Pech are not immortal: Pech wills from 1738 and 1779 have survived (ANEY, 1819(iv), 19r and 19v). I do not include them in this analysis because they

do not fit the time frame, but such an inclusion would, of course, skew the picture even more in the Pech favor.

Chapter Eight

1. P. Thompson 1978: 155.

2. Ibid., 106 on the quadripartite nature of Maya kinship. The paucity of collective terms and words to describe the family has a parallel in Nahua kinship: Lockhart, 1992: 72.

3. Goody 1983; Stone 1977; Wall, Robin, and Laslett 1983.

4. Wills in DT, LC, and TE. Holmes (1977: 336) observed that in the 1970's "the major organizing principle of a woman's life" was kinship, yet the nuclear family was fragile, offset in part by the importance of sibling ties and by the role of gender-specific kin-based neighborhood "networks." These networks look very similar to the kind of chibal alliances that were fundamental to social subdivision in the postconquest cah.

5. On the Nahuas: Lockhart 1992: 72–85. Hanks (1990: 95–110) shows the extent to which the modern Yucatec Maya sense of family is also based on solar residence patterns.

6. The nal suffix is the adjective; cahnal might translate as "cah native": see Table 3.1 and the accompanying discussion in Chap. 3. Otochnal reminds one of the current American street slang "homeboy," "homegirl," "homey," and "homes" to describe a fellow member of the neighborhood. Indeed one Maya dictionary defines otochnal as "neighborhood" (Pío Pérez 1866: 259).

7. Because I use colonial Maya, not modern, orthography, the reader may be justified in confusing this na with the hard, or glottalized na (na'), meaning "mother." I doubt there is a semantic relationship between the two, although the idea is tempting.

8. TI: 30 (1766).

9. Roys 1972 [1943]: 21, citing Bienvenida, published in *Cartas de Indias [1877]*; Roys, Scholes, and Adams 1959: 205.

10. For a comprehensive discussion of Maya kinship, including a presentation of all terms in the colonial dictionaries, see P. Thompson 1978, chap. 2. For kinship terms in use today, see Hanks 1990: 102–4. For a less systematic look at kinship, from the viewpoint of contemporary Maya women, see Holmes 1977.

11. TI: 49 for attestation of sobrino; I have yet to see "sobrina."

12. TI: 56; ANE-Y, 1819(iv), 19r. The observant reader will spot that Pablo Tec should not have the same patronym as his mother, although she clearly states that he is yn ual, "my child." Luisa's other heirs are three males named Tec, whose relation to her is unstated. It seems unlikely that all four were illegitimate sons, or sons-in-law from the same chibal. My guess is that the other three were Luisa's brothers and Pablo her son by an extramarital relationship, an arrangement that was apparently not uncommon in eighteenth-century Ixil. The only other solution, that Luisa took the name of her husband (she does not say if she has ever had one), is not borne out by the general evidence of Maya naming patterns.

13. I refer here to the Annales-school conjunctive descent from the first his-

torical level (demography) to the second (social structure) to the third (culture) (Chaunu 1978; Darnton 1985), although my approach is more consciously influenced by anthropological methodology and the history-anthropology debate represented by, for example, Chartier 1982; Darnton 1985; Geertz 1973; and Thomas 1963.

14. On a gun in a Maya will: LC: 9. On the weapon ban, see Gates 1978: 159; Roys 1972: 168; Reed 1964; on tapir, etc., see Morley 1983: 194.

15. Roys 1972: 19, citing *Documentos inéditos del archivo de las Indias.*

16. AGN-BN, 21, 20, 2–8.

17. For Maya land sales, see Chap. 16 below; today's practice observed in Oxkutzcab (Feb. 1991) and Telchaquillo (May 1992), where the solar is still often called *soral*, as in the colonial-era documentation.

18. LC; and DT, TE, TI, TT, etc.

19. Roys 1972: 20, citing the RY; he also points out the Motul dictionary's listing of *cocolche*, "wooden fence," and *tulumche*, "wattle [?] fence," but I have not seen either term in the Maya notarial record. Because the Spanish word *corral* appears in colonial-era Nahua texts to mean "animal pen" it has occurred to me that the term *coral* (with r's and l's interchangeably used) in Maya wills could have the same sense, although context and the accompanying numerical classifiers strongly suggest that "necklace" is meant.

20. Brief entry buried in TC: 111–12. The phrase "many batabs collaborated" in this project suggests the possibility that the road also, or instead of, went between Calkiní and other cahob.

21. This comparison may be explained by the fact that Maya communities were less densely settled than Nahua communities, their layouts unhindered by rivers, ravines, or mountains; differences in building materials may have had something to do with the existence of two-storied Nahua houses. On Nahua houses: Lockhart 1992: 59–72. On (preconquest) Maya houses: Wauchope 1938; Morley 1983: 207–10.

22. The balance between the two shapes is unknown, but Roys (1972: 21) implies that apsidals existed at least from early-colonial times and were the most common by the early nineteenth century. Kurjack's (1974: 53–59) survey of late Classic Dzibilchaltun revealed a considerable number of structures in various forms of the Preclassic and apsidal style.

23. The best examples of this were in Ek Balam, a tiny community northeast of Valladolid and adjacent to the ruins of the same name. Many of these reception-storage houses contained pre-Columbian images, taken in recent times from the ruins, which were displayed on tables beside Catholic images. Aside from this, and the prominence of bicycles and radios, such structures appeared entirely premodern (visit of Feb. 1991). It is tempting to see a link between this modern conception of a reception space to interact with guests and Landa's (1941 [1566]: 86) description of the division of noble Maya houses into a private back and a front for "lodging their guests." For an evocative analysis of domestic space in modern Oxkutzcab, see Hanks 1990: 313–51.

24. This information is presented broadly in App. E, and also in more detail in Tables 1–6 in App. D.

25. See Farriss 1984: 178.

26. The postconquest Maya bed is a subject of some mystery, as P. Thompson (1978: 111) has pointed out: there is no mention in the colonial record of the hammock, which at some point was introduced from the Caribbean by the Spaniards and today is the standard form of Maya bedding, as well as a staple of the local economy. The colonial-era use of the Spanish *cama* implies that another form of bedding was introduced before the hammock, perhaps a form similar to the Maya *poyche*, whose name implies a wooden structure of some kind. I find another bedding item in the Cacalchen wills, *tas*, "mattress," but the reader should be advised that this reading of the word is not absolutely certain and the word does not appear elsewhere.

27. Gruzinski 1989: 78.

28. TI: 30. This account is based on a comparison between the Pedro Mis will and the body of 65 wills from Ixil, 1765–68, not the entire body of colonial Maya wills.

Chapter Nine

1. TI: 23.

2. Inanimate nouns in the plural do not always need the plural *-ob* ending (thus the first mention of well and solar could be singular or plural), and when following numbers with classifiers never have an *-ob* (thus in the second mention the *oxac* could govern just the *chen* or both *chen* and *solalae*—an elision of *solar/l* and *lae*). See Karttunen 1985: 20 on the plural in Maya.

3. Not dissimilar from the Nahuatl *huel* (Karttunen 1985: 86; Lockhart, unpublished guide to Nahuatl).

4. P. Thompson 1978: 182–83. Thompson also reads references in two Tekanto wills to property previously being owned by the testator's *kilacabil* as showing a pattern of patrilineal descent that had changed by the eighteenth century to bilateral, as evidenced by Tekanto's nonsexist inheritance patterns. I read *kilacabil* as simply "ancestry, ancestors," and its references strengthen my interpretation of even-but-joint ownership as a long-standing Maya practice. Reference to *kilacabillob* in an Ixil will (TI: 45) is made in a context similar to that of Viviana Canche's mention of her father's will. On *kilacabil* and similar terms, see Chap. 7. On the rise of estancias-haciendas, see Chap. 17 and Patch 1993: 96–122.

5. TE: 234 (will dated 1810).

6. TE: 195 (will dated 1785).

7. LC: 14. The seven movables were three chests, two machetes, a digging stick, and a seventh item whose identity has been lost to document wear-and-tear (recipient: a daughter).

8. LC: 14, 18.

9. TI: 40 (Uh will of 1767); LC: 22 (Eb will of 1650).

10. TI: 29 (will dated 1766). This same will is discussed further in Chap. 10.

11. TI: 33.

12. DT, I: 61–62 (Manuel Chan); TI: 51 (Pasquala Tec).

13. ANE-Y, 1819(iv), 19r; will reproduced in part in Chap. 10.

14. TI: 54, 45.   15. TE: 234, 230.

16. TT: 33.   17. TI: 64.

18. Ah Pootob is in TI: 41 (reproduced in App. A); Uh's will is TI: 40; "owner-ship" might be put in quotation marks, since I am making assumptions about tenure based on who actually works the land and whom it sustains. This question is explored in Chap. 16. Similar to Uh's statement are references made in a will from Homun (AGN-T, 1359, 5, 19–22), in which a Felipe Noh asserts *ley chen lae ma manbil talan ti kilacabil u chi,* "this well was not purchased, but came from all the ancestors"—along with an item of kax, it is to be left *tu kab yn mehenob yetel tulacal kilacabob hecex sihanob tu kilacabil ah nohil uinicobe ti bin katnacob u tzentiubaob te tutan kin uchmale,* "in the hands of my children and all their descendents to be born, the Noh descendents who shall successively sustain themselves with it in the future."

19. TI: 7, 14, 20, 21 (Simón Chan), 32, 64. There is one instance in Ixil of a testator naming a coresident whose kin relation to her is unclear: *heix lay chen y solal yn cah lic lae yan u hahal than Rosa coyi yn uetel u chic,* "Here is the well and solar where I live with Rosa Coyi, she and I together; this is the truth" (TI: 20).

20. The sole exception to this (TI: 32) seems to be self-consciously an exception, as though the testator is concerned to prove, with cabildo confirmation, that he acquired a solar of the Chuc patrimony only—*chen*—for his economic needs, not in order to shift the plot from Chuc into Poot hands: *heix solar yn cah lice mantiali utial ah chucob lae chen ɔan ten tumen Yn tzentic Ynba lae bay Yohelil Yn yum batab y Jus.ᵃˢ lae,* "Here is the solar where I live, property purchased from the Chuc family; it was given to me [i.e., placed in my hands] only so that I may support myself, as m'lord the batab and magistrates know."

21. The entire document (TI: 45) is reproduced in App. A; my translation of a few of its phrases is tentative. Note the hypercorrective consonant insertion in *yarl* (*yal,* "child"); see Chaps. 18 and 22.

22. Kellogg's analysis (1995: 135–59) of Mexica wills suggests that in the vicere-gal capital from the late sixteenth to late seventeenth centuries Nahua testament writing and inheritance practices rapidly evolved under Spanish influence and the pressures of economic and demographic decline. Although Kellogg's observation that indigenous testaments were not static in form and content is widely pertinent, my sense of the evidence is that such levels of acculturation did not occur outside Mexico City until later in the colonial period or, in the case of Yucatan, later still.

23. Lockhart 1992: 90–93 on comparison of Nahua inheritance with Spanish practice; on Nahua inheritance see Cline 1986: 75–85 (late-sixteenth-century Cul-huacan) and Kellogg 1995: 104–59 (early-to-mid-colonial Mexico City).

Chapter Ten

1. ANE-Y, 1819(iv), 19r.   2. AGN-I, 69, 5, 275.

3. Lockhart and Schwartz 1983: 130.   4. Elmendorf 1985: 1.

5. Ibid., 124.   6. Schlegel 1977: 34.

7. Schele and Freidel 1990: 33, passim.

8. Hanks 1990: 166–75, 184–91; AGI-E, 317a, 2, 82.

9. TI: 54 (Francisco Canul); AGN-T, 1359, 5, 9 (Noh chibal); there are many other examples of women appearing in land sale records along with their male relations as vendors or purchasers (e.g.: Maria Canche with Felipe and Ventura Chable, vendors from Cholul, 1719; CCA-Chichí, III, 111v); see Chap. 15 for discussion of land description. For a discussion of sixteenth-century female Maya roles based on Landa's comments (1982 [1566]), see Clendinnen 1982. For a complementary analysis of some of the present chapter's sources, see Restall 1995b.

10. LC, TE, TI, DT, and P. Thompson 1978.

11. O'Brien 1977: 122–23. These sex roles and the division of labor by gender are similar in Maya communities today: Holmes 1977, chap. 4; Hanks 1990: 110–12; my field notes from Telchaquillo, May 1992 and June 1994.

12. There appears to be no gender pattern to beekeeping in modern cahob, with both men and women apparently keeping bees, although predictably men seem to be responsible for selling the wax and honey outside the cah (field notes, May 1992). Neither Holmes (1977) nor Hanks (1990) discusses apiculture.

13. As P. Thompson (1978: 176) observes.

14. Luisa Tec has a pair of looms (TI: 56); she and Pasquala Tec (TI: 51) have stone-breaking tools. For more detail on tools, see Chap. 14.

15. TI: 6, 10, 41, 43.

16. TI: 64.

17. TI: 42.

18. TI: 29—the terms used are *camissa* (shirt), *ex* (trousers), *ypil* ("huipil," or dress), and *pic* (slip); also TE: 242.

19. Farriss 1984: 167; Patch 1993.   20. TI: 21 (Chan); TI: 19 (Poot).

21. TI: 24.   22. Cline 1986: 114.

23. For a somewhat different set of emphases on Tekanto, see P. Thompson 1978: 154–76.

24. LC: 11. Note that although this distribution is gender balanced, it is still prejudicial to the two female heirs.

25. LC: 23 is one example.

26. Postconquest Maya population is briefly covered in Chap. 13.

27. TI: 29.

28. The status of the Pech in Ixil is treated in detail in Chap. 7.

29. There is some evidence that the taboo on chibal endogamy was occasionally broken, but, significantly, only by elite chibalob, presumably because at the top of the socioeconomic pyramid the taboo narrowed the already-limited choices available to nobles unwilling to marry down. Thus shortly after the conquest, the batab of Maní, the aforementioned don Francisco de Montejo Xiu, married the newly baptized María Xiu, daughter of the Xiu batab of nearby Calotmul (Roys 1965: 667). Two later examples from Ixil may not reflect the same level of power politics, but the principle of exception is the same: at the beginning of the eighteenth century, Agustín Pech and Viviana Pech married and later had two sons who survived childhood, one of whom, don Pedro, was destined to become batab and die in 1779 when the Pech chibal still dominated the cah; during this same time, two members

of a noble chibal, Antonio Yam and Petrona Yam, were also a married couple (ANEY-1819iv, 19; Restall 1995a; TI: 50; Chap. 7 above on class and chibal in Ixil).

30. LC

31. TI: 30, 36.

32. TE: 284.

33. TT: 32–33.

34. This is according to Holmes 1977: 245.

35. AGN-I, 69, 5, 277.

36. AGN-I, 1187, 2, 59–61; also see Chap. 11 below.

37. Bolompoyche petition: AGN-BN, 21, 20, 2–8; Ebtun example: TE: 275.

38. In their campaign for separation from Mérida in the late nineteenth century the people of Campeche cited the fact that for centuries Merideños had been nursed by "Indians," ate "Indian" food, spoke Maya, and many more had Maya blood than were willing to admit (Marta Hunt, personal communication; Manuel A. Lanz, *Compendio de Historia de Campeche*; Hunt and Restall n.d.). Spanish sources sometimes reveal unexpected little insights into the Mayanization of Hispanic Yucatec culture: for example, a young woman from a well-off Mérida family at the end of the colonial period sitting in her huipil in the backyard in the evening drinking chocolate (AGEY-CR, 1, 7A).

39. In one such case the Maya servant failed to show the expected amount of gratitude, and the donor filed legal papers to have the gift taken back and given to another of her female Maya domestics (AGEY-T, 1, 22).

40. The examples of the preceding four paragraphs are drawn from Hunt and Restall (n.d.) having originated in Mérida's Archivo del Registro de la Propriedad and the Baeza papers of the Archivo de Notarías. See also Hunt 1974. I repeat my gratitude to Marta Hunt, specifically for her generous sharing of this material.

41. ANEY libros dating 1748–1838, documents dating 1725–1813, discussed in Chap. 3.

42. ANEY, 1815–17, 87; 1828, 7; and 1810ii, 91.

43. Baeza papers, Dec. 27, 1692 (see note 39 above).

44. Schlegel 1977: 354–55.

45. Cline 1986: 122–23.

46. Kellogg 1979: 85 (repeated on 99; see also Kellogg 1995, chap. 3).

Chapter Eleven

1. On Hocaba, Holmes 1977, chap. 6; on Oxkutzcab (based on 1977–87 fieldwork), Hanks 1990: 120–22 (note that, for reasons of consistency, I have rewritten *baxal than* in colonial orthography); on the colonial period, Burns 1991b, and Sigal 1995. For comparative context, see Gutiérrez 1991 and some of the contributions to Lavrín 1989.

2. AGN-I, 1187, 2, 59–61.

3. See AGN-I, 69, 5, 277; TT: 32–33. Both documents are also discussed in Restall 1995b.

4. CBC: 59, 50; CBT: 62, 84, 107. See also, Restall and Sigal 1992: 107–13; and Sigal 1995. Note, however, that translating *tzintzin* as "anus" does not explain the reduplication in the term. Nahuatl also has a suffix *-tzin*, used both as an affection-

ate diminutive and as an honorific, which partially reduplicates as -tzi-tzin in the plural (Karttunen, personal communication).

5. CBC: 44.

Chapter Twelve

1. The exception is Dennis Tedlock, who, in a brilliant essay (1993: 145–46) traced this historiographical leitmotif from Scholes and Roys (1938: 599–600) through Tozzer (1941: 80n–81n), Roys again (1972: 83), J. E. S. Thompson (1977: 29), Bricker (1981: 20), and Farriss (1984: 291), to Clendinnen (1987: 188).

2. Scholes and Roys 1938; D. Tedlock 1993; Kamen 1985: 15–16.

3. CBC: 20, 22; TCh: 193, 213.

4. For example: Farriss 1984: 286–87.

5. On the maestro, see ibid., 233–36, 335–37; and Collins 1977.

6. Field notes of Feb. 1991 and June 1994.

7. There were also efforts to maintain parallel such structures that lacked a Spanish-recognized connection to the official church; these range from two Mayas proclaiming allegedly themselves "pope" and "bishop" and performing mass (Tipu region, 1610; Farriss 1984: 318) to the existence in probably every cah of an *ah men* (today's *h-men*), a medical practitioner or shaman whose practices and the Maya belief in their efficacy had a spiritual and religious-ritual component that arguably places the ah men in the category of a parallel religious official—although, of course, Spaniards also believed in many of the "superstitions" in which shamans dealt (Farriss 1984: 288–89, 296–99). Today's shamans practice in competition with modern medical doctors and their clinics (field notes of June 1994; Elmendorf 1985; Hanks 1990).

8. Patch 1993: 114; Farriss 1984: 233–34, 265–66. See also Chap. 14 below.

9. CCA, I, 1700–1702; T-LAL-RMC.

10. Farriss 1984, chap. 11; includes details of fiestas and other aspects of saint maintenance. Note that her emphasis on saint cults as the glue that held communities together, rather than vice versa, differs from mine.

11. Not all saint cults were cah cults; some were regional, and some were created and maintained by groups other than the cah officers and elite. Regional cults based in pilgrimage centers such as Itzmal and Ichmul effectively promoted the importance of the cahob that controlled the saint images; the unofficial saint cults within communities (see, with respect to the early nineteenth century, Rugeley n.d., chap. 6) were relatively rare and short-lived, mostly because they tended to lack the support of the cah authorities and also came under the censoring scrutiny of the Spanish authorities.

12. The possibility of a gender shift in image-holding during the colonial period is suggested by evidence from Nahuatl wills from Mexico City, in which an early-colonial female majority is replaced by a late-colonial male majority (Kellogg 1979, and 1995: 135–59; there does not appear to be additional evidence in two other obvious secondary sources, Cline 1986, and Lockhart 1992); note that evidence of Maya image-holding is mostly eighteenth century.

13. TI, DT. The latter phrase, *ca cilich colebil*, must have evolved to become the specific reference to the Virgin; it is in the late dictionaries (for example, Pío Pérez 1866–77: 55). Another variant is *ca cilich colebil consepcion* (e.g.: will of Lucas Euan, Sicpach, 1709; CCA-Chichí, III, 107v). Sometimes the Maya term for "virgin" is used, as in *ca cilich colel tu suhuy santa maria* (DT: i, 27). Because this rare naming of Mary is an early example (a land record of 1616), I suspect that Mayas ceased using the Virgin's Spanish name sometime in the seventeenth century.

14. For example, AGI-E, 317b, 9, 1 (Dzibikal, 1669).

15. And, in some cases (Hunucmá and Tetiz, for example), continue to do so today; see the discussion in Chap. 3 on "complex cahob." Of course, household, workplace, and even vehicle images are common today in Yucatan, as in most of Spanish America.

16. Landa 1982: 42.

17. Seoane 1985: 95–106. See also the first section of Chap. 18 below.

18. The bishop outlines the system of fees for posthumous masses and notes that this was made clear "on the previous visit" but is not being strictly observed. The charge for a said mass was six reales, with an additional real for Jerusalem—a fund that would have been fairly lucrative for its guardian had he received donations from the dying throughout the empire; local priests probably kept most of them. Jerusalem received two reales from a testator asking for a high, or sung, mass, which itself cost twelve reales. The veracity of the bishop's complaint is hard to determine, since the escribanos of Tekanto tended to write simply *misa rezada* or *cantada* at the top of the will, dispensing with the formulaic detail employed in Ixil. The testators in Ixil in the 1760's did accurately observe these mass fees, but the donations to Jerusalem appear to fluctuate randomly between two reales and nothing. In some cases (almost always in Ixil: see TI) the Spanish priest, who always notes in his own hand that he has received the fee and has said or sung the mass, writes a total in the margin indicating that the testator has donated to Jerusalem, although the escribano does not always bother to mention it in the will. I suspect that in Ixil and Tekanto the system of fees was so commonly understood that the testator left it to the escribano to fill in the formula correctly; when the escribano neglected to do so, the bishop interpreted this as a failure on the part of the community to conform to specific instructions—and "an intolerable abuse." (The three inspections are folios 153r, 180v, and 205v–206r.) Note that whereas Ixil and Tekanto testators of the eighteenth century almost always leave money to pay for masses, testators from the previous century commonly left fowl and other consumables (LC; TT: 13).

19. I view the individual variations in opening religious formulas as insignificant relative to the variations between communities; however, Terraciano (n.d.) does see evidence of personal piety in his interpretation of these formulas in Ñudzahui-language (Mixtec) wills.

20. Uayma case: AGEY-V, 1, 18 (quotes on f.3v); other cases: Rugeley n.d., chap. 3, largely based on documents published in Dumond and Dumond 1982. During the 1839–42 Imán revolt some priests feared another outbreak of hostility from their Maya parishioners (Rugeley n.d., chap. 7). Although the detailed assertions of

Cogolludo (1867–68) suggest that early in the colonial period some Maya religious practices on the fringes of the colony were indeed "idolatrous," we should be wary of general Spanish assumptions that outside the colony Mayas lived in a primitive pagan state in which naked "Indians" practiced "witchcraft" and lived in trees (for a 1669 example, see AGI-E, 315a, 3, 208).

21. For reasons of space and of analytical consistency, I have not included cases whose records are in Spanish, but the types of complaints are the same; for example, the curate of Hampolon was accused by the cah cabildo in 1816 of giving the maestro "a hundred blows" (AGEY-V, 1, 25).

22. General studies include Sánchez 1972; European studies include Bennassar 1979; Christian 1981; González 1985.

23. Anderson, Berdan, and Lockhart 1976 (example used below); Huston 1993 and personal communication of documents in the Archivo Nacionál de Asunción detailing alleged misconduct by priests in early-nineteenth-century Paraguayan parishes, particularly the keeping of indigenous "concubines."

24. Bennassar 1979; Christian 1981: 253, n. 37; González 1985.

25. AGN-I, 69, 5, 199 (Xecpes) and 275 (Tetzal).

26. AGN-I, 1187, 2, 59–60; see also App. A.

27. In 1582 there were 23 Franciscan and 4 secular parishes; by 1737, 29 Franciscan and 31 secular; by 1766, 20 Franciscan and 40 secular, but the friars still held the best parishes and some 36 percent of the Maya population (Farriss 1984: 92, 149). Also see note 33 below.

28. There are rumored to be other accusations against priests, dating back through the colonial period, in the archives of the Church in Mérida, where they are closely guarded and denied to visiting scholars. If this is true, it indicates how sensitive such material still is. However, Terry Rugeley, who has spent many hours in these archives, doubts the existence of such material (personal communication).

29. For example, Chapab's expenditures of 1800 (AGN-CI, 2052, 6, 9); see Chap. 5.

30. The Maya of this document is unusually difficult; my translation here is the best I can offer at present.

31. The Yucatec population was badly hit by a series of famines and European disease epidemics in the 1560's and 1570's, which caused a demographic decline of up to 50 percent between the surveys of 1549 and 1580–86 (Farriss 1984: 57–79).

32. Scholes et al. 1936–38, 2: 48–50. In Sopuerta's letter there is no mention of Peto or its neighbors. The implication is that the area was one of the four curatos, and indeed in a letter of 1582 from the governor of Yucatan to the king the "Vicaría de San Andrés de Petu" is listed as the only clerical zone in the province of Mérida (ibid., 51–65). The letter lists six towns subsidiary to Peto, all between two and twelve leagues from it. These are Tahdziu ("Taçiu"), Tetzal ("Tiçal"), and four others that do not appear in the above three documents. The question of the size of the visitas is not fully answered, but suffice it to say that in another letter of 1582 (ibid.) to the king, the bishop of Yucatan states that Peto has a single priest.

33. By 1580 there were 38 friars at most for the whole peninsula of Yucatan, half of whom were at any one time residing in Mérida or Campeche. The "pacified"

area was divided into 22 *doctrinas*, of which only the most compact could be toured once a week. Only a third of the Maya in the diocese of Yucatan actually lived inside the doctrinas. On the southern and eastern fringes a year might pass between a priest's visits. In addition to the Franciscan presence there were four secular *curatos* (curacies), manned by a modest seventeen priests, most of them attached to the cathedral in Mérida (Farriss 1984: 93, 304).

34. Unfortunately the RY entry for Tahdziu (I, 389) makes no mention of any priests. That all three Maya documents in this case ended up in Mexico City, in the files of the Inquisition, implies that Mejía's file was taken seriously enough to be brought before the Holy Office with all relevant documentation gathered together as evidence.

35. AGI-I, 69, 5, 275.

36. To wit, a Paraguayan example of a native community complaining about a local official to his superior, in response to which the local official had the petitioners whipped (Huston 1993: 70).

37. For a more comprehensive survey of religion in colonial Maya society, based primarily on a different set of sources and with some differences of emphasis, see Farriss 1984: 286–351.

Chapter Thirteen

1. On Yucatan's geography, see Morley 1983, chap. 7. On the "exceptions": Patch 1993: 61–62.

2. Horn 1989: 208, 240.

3. AGI-M, 1035 (Matrícula, 1700); Patch 1993: 53, 55; Lockhart 1992: 52–58 (on central Mexico).

4. TE: 153 (Roys's transcription; my translation); TT: 32. Another example that falls between the above two is a 1616 statement by Tekanto's cabildo affirming the cah's purchase of a land tract from a cah nobleman during the first postconquest batabship (DT: i, 27). See Chap. 21 for comparison between notarial land documents such as these examples and quasi-notarial texts such as the Titles and the Books of Chilam Balam.

5. On the incidence of plague and famine, see Farriss 1984: 61–62.

6. AGN-C, 2013, 1, 4–6; TE: 192; T-LAL-TT: 32–36.

7. Rugeley n.d. Patch 1991 and 1993 emphasize the continuities between late-eighteenth-century patterns in the northwest and the patterns of postindependence henequen production. "Second conquest" is Farriss's phrase (1984, chap. 12).

8. Farriss 1984: 200.

9. Burns 1991a.

10. Farriss 1984: 199.

11. Vogt 1983.

12. Wightman 1990: 5. The work of both Wightman and Powers (1995) goes beyond this "duality." See also, Robinson 1990.

13. For example, Farriss 1984: 205. In fact, even in the Andes, migration and the maintenance of indigenous communities were not necessarily incompatible, as shown by Saignes 1985 and Powers 1995 (whose thesis contains the important caveats that Quito's Andean communities were reproduced in new locations in

the early colonial period and transformed by the colonial experience in the late seventeenth-century).

14. The 1721 percentages are of adults: Patch 1993: 60 (using source in AGI-M, 1039). Robinson's work has seen various presentations, the most recent, to my knowledge, being Robinson 1987 (also see Robinson 1990 for related studies). Gosner 1979 provides an example of high percentages of nonnative residents in Uman and neighboring cahob in the 1770's. (In my discussion of migration I use "native" to refer to a member of a particular cah, not to mean "indigenous" or "Maya.")

15. Additional Ixil data derived from TI (the two nonnatives are in documents 8 and 26; the deaths outside Ixil in 15 and 45).

16. Barth 1969: 21 (also quoted by Farriss 1984: 223, who uses the point far more tentatively, in accordance with her interpretation of colonial movements as essentially disruptive to "the fabric of Maya society"). As Patch recognizes (1993: 65), the well-worn analytical tool of open-closed corporate communities, as archetypically defined by Wolf 1957, is not helpful with regard to the Yucatec Maya.

Chapter Fourteen

1. In response to the introduction of a new series of technologies in the late nineteenth and twentieth centuries, the Nahuas have returned enthusiastically to neologisms (Hill and Hill 1986: 122–41; Van Zantwijk 1965).

2. Because every Maya man may have worked land does not mean that all were reduced to the same social level (Farriss 1984: 160–67). As Vogt (1983: 90) has pointed out, there is not necessarily a contradiction in the existence of a class society (see my Chap. 7) that is at the same time a society of farmers.

3. Maya will examples: LC: 9; TI: 1. Nahuatl example: Lockhart 1992: 268. On native Yucatec animals: Morley 1983: 194.

4. LC.

5. On today's livestock diseases: Philip Thompson, personal communication (based on his fieldwork in Yucatan in the mid-1970's). Also mentioned in Holmes 1977.

6. Hunt 1974; Patch 1993: 81–92, 155–61; Farriss 1984: 39, 43–45. The colonial honey trade may have been conducted much as it is today; I observed (May 1992) a merchant from Mérida work a net of cahob between Mérida and Tecoh using prominent locals to go door to door buying surplus honey; the task took several days each month (one hive produces about 25 kilos of honey every fortnight).

7. TE; see also Table 11 in App. D.   8. ANEY, 1796–97, 205.

9. CCA-XI, 1819, 010, 2.   10. TI: 19; Lockhart 1992: 180.

11. LC: 33; TI: 29.

12. Canche: TI: 41. Nahuas: Lockhart 1992: 177–85. Note that Stephens (1963: 115 or 1988: 102) claimed to have seen cacao beans being used as currency at the 1841 market fair in Halachó.

13. Patch 1993: 90.

14. For example, TI: 42.

15. On Nahuatl words in Maya: Karttunen 1985: 4–14. On flora and floral

designs: Patterson 1992. On preconquest female tattoos and dress: Landa 1982: 55 (Gates 1978: 53–54).

16. On López: Cogolludo 1867–68: book 5, vol. 1, chaps. 16–19. On the tianquiztli: Lockhart 1992: 185–98. On the Yucatec and Guatemalan ecosystems: Harrison and Turner 1978; Flannery 1982; Morley 1983: 20–44.

17. Farriss 1984: 155–56; Hunt 1974; Lockhart and Schwartz 1983: 99. The itinerant traders were usually called *tratantes*.

18. TT: 33.

19. *Discurso Sobre la constitución de las Provincias de Yucatán y Campeche* (BNM, FF, 1150); the report is a major source of Farriss 1984.

20. TE: 192 (Ebtun); Patch 1993: 44 (entrada); AGI-E, 315a–318b (Aldana).

21. AGN-C, 2013, 1, 4–6 (1605). Patch 1993: 92 also quotes a Spanish source in which a curate claims the "cacique" (batab) of Bolonchenticul had threatened to lead his community into the forests if repartimientos were reintroduced.

22. Farriss 1984: 266–67.

23. Maya sources: CCA, *Cuentas y Depositos* (see also Chap. 5); Spanish sources: used by Patch 1993: 75–81.

24. Patch 1993: 81–92; García Bernal 1979 and AGI-E, 315–27 on the extensive repartimientos under Flores de Aldana (see Chap. 5, n. 1 above).

25. Ibid., 92.

Chapter Fifteen

1. Hanks 1987: 674; Yaxkukul segment in question reproduced in Barrera Vázquez 1984.

2. The Maya terms for east and west are of course also related to the position of the sun and, when translated literally, seem equally poetic to an English-speaker—lakin being "next sun," and chikin "eaten sun." Quiché and Kekchí refer to these directions in terms that translate more as the Nahuatl ones do (B. Tedlock 1982: 2, 176); in other Mayan languages such as Chorti, Cholti, Chol, Tzeltal, and Tzotzil, the terms are as "efficient" as in Yucatec (Schele and Freidel 1990: 426), although all convey a Mesoamerican conception of direction as oriented toward the sun—i.e., time.

3. Horn 1989.

4. Ibid., 149 (based on bills of sale, 1567–1641).

5. On preconquest cardinal iconography, see Schele and Freidel 1990: 66–67; Tedlock 1982: 173–76; and Morley 1983: 472, 488, 524. On the northeast tilt of Maya "archaeological sites and contemporary towns," see Vogt 1983, who gives the pattern a Mesoamerican spin and cites a dozen related publications.

6. There is evidence of a counterclockwise preference in other parts of Mesoamerica (Marcus 1992: 180).

7. TI: 20, 37; see Table 3.1.

8. TI: 33.

9. ANEY, 1812ii, 8 and 1814ii, 111.

10. Schele and Freidel 1990: 66–67 (on the World Tree). B. Tedlock (1982: 82)

discusses a modern-day Quiché ritual "sowing and planting" of a town that consists of a sacred circuit of the four directions. On the pre- and postconquest Nahua world view as cellular and quincunx-related, see Clendinnen 1991: 234–35; Van Zantwijk 1985; Lockhart 1985; 1992: 436–42; and Florescano 1994: 11–22.

11. B. Tedlock's study of the modern Quiché (1982: 177–78) complements the impression given by colonial Yucatec sources; she describes Maya directions as "sides" or "trajectories."

12. TE: 28 (i[n] mehen . . . u yoher u multumil lae). Cabildo assertions that "we know all the stone mounds" are common (DT: i, 27, for example).

13. AGN-T, 1419, 2, 1–7.

14. TE: 166. Another good example of this Ebtun style, showing it unchanged in over a century, is TE: 221.

15. TE: app.; ANEY 1826ii, 34–36.

16. ANEY 1826ii, 387 (Saclum, 1732; I have left my reading of prosecioonil ambiguous because, though it is tempting to read it as "procession," the Spanish procesión does not appear as a loan in any other notarial document in Maya, or in Nahuatl [Lockhart, personal communication], whereas posesión often does, and in just this context); TT: 41 (Pustunich, 1740); DT: i, 27. The following remarks made by Vogt (1983: 101) on the modern Maya seem apposite: "For the Maya we know today ethnographically, it is clear that the procession is one of the most basic forms of ritual . . . rituals are modeled on some essential features of everyday life in a society. Maya spend much of their time each day traveling single file along trails to and from their fields [and] water holes. . . . The ritual procession appears to be based on this commonplace, but essential, fact about Maya daily life."

17. AGN-T, 1419, 2, 1–5. I have presented this excerpt in series and added the solidus to separate phrases and help the reader isolate the characteristics of the description.

18. ANEY, 1826ii, 9.

19. I do not suggest that the Maya were culturally unique in this respect; since first making this analysis, I have read Certeau 1984: 115–30, who argues that most cultures have tended to represent land cartographically in two ways, the "tableau" and the "tour," into which categories the stationary and ambulatory land descriptions of the Maya would seem to fit.

20. First and second passages: Roys 1967: 15–19. I have taken out the punctuation Roys added to the Maya, but otherwise use his transcriptions; the translations are mine. The second passage is also in Edmonson 1986: 79ff. Compare this ancestral journey with that of the quoted notarial document in Chap. 13; also see Chap. 21. Third passage: Roys 1967: 38.

21. Chatwin 1987.

22. Examples of maps in or attached to Maya records are: Roys 1939, plates 5–7 (Cuncunul, 1797, Ebtun, 1784, 1802, and map of 1820); ANEY, 1832–33ii, 161–65 (Sotuta, 1821); MT: 39 (Chichimila, c. 1820); TC: 39 (Ticul, 1760); TS: 90, 134 (Sabacche, 1809, c. 1800); AGN-T, 833, 2, 35 (Chalmuch, documents mostly in Spanish, c. 1800); ANEY, 1828ii, 74, n.f. (Mérida-Tihó, documents mostly in Spanish, 1819, 1828). T-LAL-RMC has two well-known examples: the Tabi map of 1817, and the

Maní-Oxkutzcab map with the circular horizon. Marcus (1992: 179) states that Maya maps were called *pepet dzibil*, "circular writing," but I have not found such a phrase in colonial-era sources. For reproductions of the Maní-Oxkutzcab map versions: Riese 1981: 168, etc.; Stephens 1988: 274; Gates 1978: 133; Marcus 1992: 181. On Nahua maps: Lockhart 1992: 345–64; Leibsohn 1993: chaps. 4 and 5; and 1994; Gruzinski 1987. On Mesoamerican-European map traditions in general: Leibsohn, personal communication.

23. Roys 1939: 267, 55. I suggest that a similar confusion was at the root of the Brinton-Landa muddle described by Marcus 1982: 254–56.

24. P. Thompson 1978: 120.

25. DT: i, 56.

26. Horn 1989: 203–7. What is written as *kan* in colonial orthography is written as *kaan* in orthography that recognizes vowel-length distinctions.

27. Marcus 1982: 254.

28. My attempt to correlate numeral classifier definitions in the "Cordemex" dictionary (Barrera Vásquez 1991) and in Tozzer's grammar (1977, app. 3) with incidence in eighteenth-century Maya sources was undermined by an apparent inconsistency of usage, with cah variations apparently overriding "rules" of usage; further investigation may isolate some determinative factors and point to the start of an attrition in numeral classifier usage that has resulted in today's use of mainly *tul* for human beings and *pel* for everything else (field notes, 1991–94; Frances Karttunen, personal communication).

29. P. Thompson 1978: 118–24 (Tekanto); LC (Cacalchen).

30. Lockhart 1992: 145. Although it is not known how far back the twenty-unit land measure goes, the vigesimal system was apparently used by Zapotecs and Mayas as early as 600 B.C. (Marcus 1992: 96). The system may hark all the way back to counting on one's fingers and toes and thus be older still.

31. Lockhart 1992: 143–46.

32. These three measures consisted of *xoth* ("pieces")—144 to a sapal–arm span, 16 to an oc-foot, 9 to a kab-hand: see O'Brien and Christiansen 1986. I can find no occurrences of the *auat* ("earshot") that Roys (1939: 55) states was equal to a quarter-league.

33. Roys 1939: 307.

34. Marcus 1982: 249.

35. Patterson 1992.

Chapter Sixteen

1. P. Thompson 1978, chap. 3 is a major contribution, although some of the analysis is left to the reader; the Spanish-language source bases of Farriss 1984 (especially 272–85) and Patch 1993 (especially 67–73) make them very useful for Maya-Spanish relations over land but less so for Maya concepts of tenure.

2. Used with kax in TI and with pak in TE.

3. ANEY, 1826ii, 387 (Saclum, 1732); and DT: ii, 29 (Ytzmal, 1792), respectively.

4. TE: 158. Note in the 1670 Ebtun excerpt that the vendor pays the *cahob*, which

I translate as cah, though it is probably a reference to the people of the cah—an underscoring of the communal function of cah property. Note, however, that when cah property is purchased, it is often noblemen and cabildo officers who ritually take possession of it—as cah and chibal representatives (DT: i, 27, for example). The 1803 excerpt that follows appears again in slightly different wording as TE: 209–10. As with all TE excerpts, transcriptions are Roys's, translations are mine.

5. TE: 191. In stating "repair" I follow Roys's "restore," the Maya being *ca tulis kaxic u pach*, literally "we tie its edge(s) whole"; it is possible, but less likely, that the meaning is, "we agree whole its possession," i.e., "we all agree to take possession of it."

6. ANEY, 1736–37, c. 400–402. These documents are also discussed in Chap. 19.

7. A reference in a will from Cacalchen to "the batab's field"—*u col batab*—probably meant property owned privately by the batab in office rather than land that pertained to the office itself (LC: 11). I have found no example in the Maya record of the so-called *u hanal batab*, "the batab's food," the 60-mecate field cultivated *for* the batab that is mentioned by Marcus 1982: 258 and Roys 1939: 45; the allusion seems to have originated in the Motul Dictionary (Martínez Hernández 1926: 642) and it may therefore be apocryphal, or strictly preconquest, or limited to a particular cah and time period.

8. Far rarer was *quauhtlalli*, either "wooded land" or "eagle land." Information on Nahuas principally from Horn 1989, chap. 5, but also Cline 1986, chap. 8. There is also an overview of Nahua land categories in Lockhart 1992, chap. 5.

9. DT: i, 79.

10. Lockhart 1992: 168–69. "Saint's land" was apparently common to the Spanish world; it also appears in Paraguay, for example (personal communication, Richard Huston).

11. CCA-XI, 1819, 010, 2; TI: 40a.

12. Examples from ANEY: 1826ii, 354 (Dzan, 1819) and ANEY: 1826ii, 135 (Tekax, 1788).

13. ANEY, 1776, 256 (also in App. A).

14. DT, I: 50. I believe *hokes* is a "translation" (in the sense that this is a Spanish legal form) of the Spanish *sacar*, and thus could also mean "copy," as I have glossed it elsewhere.

15. ANEY, 1798ii, 212. The document's date is lost where the page is damaged, but related documentation suggests the sale date was 1792.

16. ANEY, 1826ii, 34–36.

17. ANEY, 1805–6, 198–99. The only reminder of Maya Itzimná is the simple little church (dated 1719) in the center of the main plaza. I believe the community was not an original cah, but a satellite cah of Mejorada, hence the lack of a large church facing the plaza. The entry of Spaniards in the eighteenth century foreshadowed the later recreation of Itzimná as a wealthy suburb of Mérida, and many of the mansions of the henequen boom still stand in what is today regarded as one of the more desirable neighborhoods of the city.

18. Horn 1989: 185.

19. ANEY, 1826ii, 65 (sale of 1811).

Chapter Seventeen

1. Lockhart 1992: 176.

2. On loanwords, see Chap. 22; on Maya cabildo record keeping, see Chap. 18.

3. For example, TE; DT; ANEY, 1826ii, 134.

4. AGN-T, 1419, 2, 1–5.

5. ANEY, 1826ii, 387 (Saclum, 1732).

6. ANEY, 1826ii, 243v. The -*ob* on *conosimientoob* is a plural possessive: "their false acknowledgments."

7. Roys 1939, chap. 1 (treaties of 1600); CCA, Chichí, III (1786); AGN-T, 1419, 2, 55–56 (1815; note that Dzibikak, Dzibikal, and Uman constituted a complex cah; see Chap. 3). It is worth pointing out the considerable distances between these cahob (symptomatic of the shifting nature of Maya cultivation): Ebtun, Cuncunul, Kaua, Tekom, and Tinum are all within an area of about 300 square km some 40 km from Yaxcaba; the cahob of the 1815 treaty are also in a 300-square-km area (see Maps 3.1 and 3.2).

8. Roys 1939: part 2 and 21–38.

9. Farriss 1984: 281–83 includes a quote by a Spaniard that the Maya were "by nature prone to litigation."

10. TE: 45.

11. TS (includes 180 folios in Spanish, and ten Maya documents dated from 1596 [probably not "genuine"] to 1809). A similar but briefer case from the same area has survived in photostat form (DTi), and many other lawsuit records involving Spanish-Maya conflict over land can be found in the ANEY and among the private papers pertaining to surviving estates (some, like those of Chichí discussed below, are uncatalogued in CCA).

12. ANEY; examples in Chaps. 15 and 16 above, this chapter, and Chap. 19; Patch 1993: 69 lists fourteen sales of cah plots to Spaniards between 1689 and 1737, and mentions others in the text of his chaps. 4 and 5.

13. ANEY, 1835ii, 99–101.

14. Lockhart and Schwartz 1983: 68–71, 92–97.

15. Patch 1993, chap. 5.

16. The 1912 statistic is from Patch 1993: 112; otherwise source on Chichí is CCA, Chichí (uncatalogued) (170 folios in Spanish and Maya, 1626–1786). The 1786 border walk (Chichí, III) must have been quite an affair: preparations took ten days and involved the collection of seventeen notarized statements, some in cahob and in estancieros' homes in Mérida; in addition to Maya cabildo participants from Cholul, Itzimná, Nolo, and Sicpach, and various Spanish officials and estancieros, there were also Maya estancia workers acting as witnesses and some as representatives of their employers (of the three estancieras involved, only one of the women joined the walk). The event was also symbolic of Maya-Spanish relations; both Spaniards and Mayas participated in a common legal exercise recognized by both as meaningful and legitimate, and yet each drew up validating statements in their own languages and formats, reflecting the fact that each viewed the process from somewhat different cultural angles.

Chapter Eighteen

1. The Mexican census of 1980 returned 665,377 Yucatec speakers and 1,376,989 Nahuatl speakers. Although some argue that many indigenous-language speakers have a poor command of their language, using Spanish at home and in public settings, Yucatecans today usually opine that a million people speak Maya. There is no doubt that Yucatec Maya has been assisted by the physical features of the peninsula, lacking the mountains of the Guatemalan highlands, for example, where almost every valley evolved a separate dialect, most of which have disappeared. The movement in Yucatan to preserve spoken and written Maya seems as strong today as ever, with bilingual elementary and secondary education on the rise in some parts of the peninsula. (Barrutia 1991; personal communication 1991 with Fernando Peón Molina, Regidor de Cultura of Mérida at the time, and with Armando Dzul Ek, a bilingual maestro in Maní; and in 1994 with Moises Díaz Alcocer, a bilingual maestro in Teabo.)

2. Schele and Freidel 1990: 52–55; Marcus 1992: 18–19, 87.

3. Fash 1991: 139–51 (Copán); D. Tedlock 1985 (Popol Vuh); Roys 1967 and Edmonson 1982, 1986 (Chilam Balam).

4. Bricker 1989: 48. See also the work of Kathryn Josserand (Schele and Freidel 1990: 421).

5. For example, where a final *l* is followed by the pronoun *u*, another *l* is sometimes added to that *u*; occasionally, the first *l* will be changed to an *r*, an example of simultaneous hypercorrection and consonant insertion (see Chap. 22 below).

6. Marcus 1992.

7. The earliest extant documents in Maya whose dates are uncontested are the following: 1557, land boundary agreement, Maní (TX); 1561, land title, Kochila (Ebtun) (TE: 240); 1567, letters to the King, various cahob (AGI-M, 367, 62–88); 1569, land title, Dzan (TT: 32); 1578, petition vs. parish priest, Xecpes (AGN-I, 69, 5, 199). The "letters" (petitions) are reproduced in part and discussed in Zimmerman 1970 and in Hanks 1986. A Spanish-language record of the 1545 Sotuta border survey states that it is a "translation of the papers of the towns," but no Maya originals are extant (Roys 1939, app.). The earliest *claim* is the *Documento No. 1 del Deslinde de Tierras de Yaxkukul*, self-dated 1544 (Barrera Vásquez 1984), but probably seventeenth or eighteenth century. Brinton (1882: 68) states, "An official document in Maya, still extant, dates from 1542, and from that time on there were natives who wrote their tongue with fluency," but he provides no further information about this seminal MS, unless it is the section of the Title ("Chronicle") of Chicxulub dated either 1522 or 1542, but probably only as old as the Yaxkukul document, itself part of a title (TY); see Chap. 21 below.

8. The Spanish equivalent might be *escribiente* (or, in the nineteenth century, *escribano de ración*: Ramón Arzápalo, personal communication). There is also the Maya *uooh* for "write," but I have never seen it used to describe the notarial process. As Marcus (1992: 79–80) suggest, *ɔib* and *uooh* were used before the conquest in different contexts; it seems that the context of *ɔib* correlated best with that of postconquest notarial writing. Sometimes Maya notaries used substitute verbs for

"write" such as *chicbes*, "show, mark," and ɔa, "give." To distinguish *hun*, "paper, document," from *hun*, "book," the Maya use *libro*, which has the added legitimizing attraction of being a Spanish legal term, like *información* and *auto*. The Maya word *hoch* described a copy, or copied document.

9. The other creative adoptions were the addition of a horizontal line through the *h* of *ch* to indicate glottal constriction, *cħ*; the use of a horizontal or a parallel vertical line on *p* to denote glottal constriction, *p̃*; the use of *th* to indicate a glottalized *t*; the use of *k* to mark a glottalized *c*; and a horizontal through a *y* when it represents *yetel*, "and, with": y̵. (For a comparison of Spanish and Spanish-based indigenous alphabets see Chap. 22 below, particularly Tables 22.2 and 22.3.) Note that Landa (1982: 32) mentions the rapid acquisition of alphabetic skills by the Maya, but asserts that no new letters were created. This may have been a simple error on his part, or perhaps he was thinking of the 1540's (from which period no documents are extant), and the full orthography did not become widely used until the 1550's or later. The unusual use of *tz* instead of ɔ by the notary of Xecpes in 1579 (in the word ɔa, "to give") may indicate either cah variation or the fact that the invented letter was not yet fully conventional (AGN-I, 69, 5, 199).

10. Karttunen 1985: 79–90. The lack of vowel-series differentiation is more of a problem for present-day students of such texts; likewise, the inconsistency or lack of divisions between words in Maya documents can hinder decipherment.

11. In the last few decades of the colonial period up to half the total Maya population of parishes in the northwest (the postindependence henequen zone) lived on Spanish estates (Patch 1993: 148–54). I believe that these people were still tied to the world of the cah by cultural if not personal and kin ties, since there is no evidence that they were acculturated to Spanish society, living as they did on estates owned largely by absentee landlords.

12. Cacalchen sample: 35 wills, 1646–53, 1678–79 (LC). Ebtun sample: 10 wills, 1699–1813 (TE). Ixil sample: 65 wills, 1765–68 (TI). Culhuacan sample: 63 wills, 1572–99 (Cline 1981: 75). Tekanto sample: 332 wills, 1724–59 (ANEY)—statistic also reflects the gender balance of lists of the dead for two epidemic years in Tekanto, 1724 and 1725. The Mexica wills studied by Kellogg (1979, 1995) show a testator gender balance of 1:1.36, but the significance of this cannot be determined without more information on the source sample.

13. Horn 1989: 130.

14. Anderson, Berdan, and Lockhart 1976; Borah 1982; Cline 1986; Horn 1989; Lockhart 1992.

15. Altogether there are ten Maya documents in the Sabacche file (TS).

16. Cline and Léon-Portilla 1984: 4. Cline (1986: 16) suggests that the preconquest Nahua testament tradition was oral; Kellogg (1995: 129–35) minimizes the possibility of preconquest precedent. I have seen wills not only in Nahuatl and Yucatec but also in Mixtec and Cakchiquel. For sample wills in these languages, see Roys 1939; Anderson, Berdan, and Lockhart 1976; Cline and Léon-Portilla 1984; Hill 1989; Lockhart 1991 and 1992; Offutt 1992; Terraciano 1994; Restall 1995a; and Restall and Kellogg n.d. (which includes sample wills in all four of these languages). Testaments in a number of other Mesoamerican languages also exist.

17. Landa 1982: 42.

18. TE: 239.

19. Seoane 1985: 95–106.

20. Kellogg 1995: 130–34; Lockhart 1992, app. B.

21. There were visits to the La Costa district, for example, in 1737, 1746, and 1751 (DT: 153r, 180v and 205v–206r); see Chap. 12.

22. See the example of the intestate Josef Cab of Ixil (TI: 45), as well as the intestate Dionisio Huchim of Ebtun (TE: 234), and Viviana Canche (TI: 23), who declares, "It may be seen in my father's will" (*te bin ylabac tu testamento yn Yum lae*) why she settles her estate as she does.

23. See Patch 1993 (for a clear analysis of this development, based on Spanish documentation); also Part Three above.

24. See Chaps. 6 and 20.

25. Hill (1991: 127 and 1992) referring to the colonial-era Cakchiquel. He adds, "Having in a sense let the genie of writing out of the bottle, the Spaniards were unable to control the range of uses to which the Cakchiquel . . . put writing."

26. Hanks 1987: 672.

27. Gabriel Tec's will is TI: 15. In TI: 45 (transcribed and translated in App. A) Ixil's cabildo settle the estate of Josef Cab, who died intestate.

28. AGN-I, 1187, 2, 59–61; reproduced in full in App. A and discussed at some length in Chap. 11.

29. This point is well demonstrated by the 1708 Cakchiquel will photographically reproduced in Hill 1991: 134 (text and translation in 1989); the Guatemalan national archive, Archivo General de Centroamérica (AGCA), contains many other native wills—AGCA-G, 4551, 38560, for example.

30. McGee 1991: 10. Note that there is another *tun* (*tuùn*, as opposed to *túun*) that means "stone." It is tempting to see a link of meaning between these two words, but, as Frances Karttunen has pointed out (personal communication), "both Maya and Nahuatl studies have been plagued by false etymologizing and claims of virtuoso punning based not on fact but on colonial-period orthographic under-representation."

31. Horn 1989: 160; Lockhart 1992: 368–69.

32. Hanks 1986: 730 is one example; he cites the others. See also, Edmonson 1982 and 1986; and Edmonson and Bricker 1985: 60.

33. See App. A for the "Mérida" example; see Table 12.1 for the "testament" example; and Chap. 15 for the "walk of possession" (including an alternative reading of the phrase). For another cluster of examples, see the discussion of "Opening and closing phrases" in Chap. 20. The phenomenon of bilingual couplets, which also occurred among the Nahuas, is discussed in the context of postconquest Maya language change in Chap. 22.

34. "The dialogue, based on two words brought together through a conversation, is the core concept of Mayan literature" (Burns 1991b: 36).

35. TI: 45, 51.

36. DT, I: 62.

37. TI: 41. This will is transcribed and translated in App. A.

38. ANEY, 1819 iv, 37. William Hanks, personal communication, recognized the Maya phrase as also being contemporary.

39. AGN-I, 1187, 2, 59–61; reproduced in full in App. A.

40. AGN-I, 69, 5, 199 and 277; AGN-BN 5, 35, 4–5; all three documents are discussed in Chap. 12.

41. TT; TS.

42. LC; TI (Restall 1995a); DT.

43. TE: 279, 168. In 1819 the notary of Sicpach used the loanword *archivo*, but the context indicates that its meaning was not "archive" but "record" (specifically a land transaction of 1750 and other documents): *in kubic u archiboil u bal u ba Almehen Gregorio Chi*, "I deliver the record of the nobleman Gregorio Chi's household property" (CCA-XI, 1819, 010, 2).

44. As of March 1991 the original collections of both the Ebtun and Tekanto papers had disappeared, the former from the town itself, the latter from the Archivo Notarial in Mérida. Until they resurface, we are fortunate to have Roys's published transcriptions of the Ebtun papers, and photographs of the Tekanto material are in safe, private hands (to whom I am indebted and profoundly grateful).

45. TI: 45 (reproduced in App. A).

46. List of epidemics in Farriss 1984: 61. Wills: LC, TI, and DT.

47. The sources are from archives in the United States (T-LAL-RBC/RMC), Spain (AGI), and Mexico (AGN, AGEY, ANEY, BNM, CCA) and, in two instances, from published transcriptions (Barrera Vásquez 1984; Roys 1939); see Works Cited.

48. Nahuatl begins to be replaced by Spanish as the notarial language of the altepetl after 1770, and post-1800 Nahuatl examples are very rare (Karttunen 1985: 47). I suspect that, with ongoing searches by myself and others, more mid-nineteenth-century Maya-language sources will surface.

Chapter Nineteen

1. Dzaptun petition transliterated and translated in full in App. A; this and Tahnab petition: AGN-CI, 2013, 1, 4–6.

2. Haskett 1985: 248; and 1991: 80 (his translation; original Nahuatl in 1985 only). For an example of another Nahua petition (reproduced in full and translated) using the kissing-hands-and-feet metaphor, see Anderson, Berdan, and Lockhart 1976: 174–75.

3. The inversion leitmotif in Mesoamerican reverential language means that not only are Maya subjects children to the lords-fathers of colonial rule, but the lords-fathers of the cahob, the principales, also become children through the filter of petition discourse—for example, *u nucilob cah y[etel] tulacal u mehenilob cah*, "those of intelligence in the cah and all the children of the cah," is a semantic couplet describing the principales (CCA-I).

4. TT: 33 (Tabi, c. 1580); AGN-C, 2013, 1, 4 (Tahnab, 1605). There are many other examples of this rhetoric; such as that of the 1567 letter from a group of batabob to the Crown: *con chambel uinic . . . hach thonanoon taclacal yalan a uoc yalan a kab*, "we lowly men . . . are all truly humbled beneath your hands and feet" (AGI-M, 367, 62,

etc.). Portions of this text are also published in Zimmerman 1970: 32 and in Hanks 1986: 731. The hands-and-feet motif was also a Spanish image of deference; this may be a case of coincidental social forms, of which there are many other examples, but if the Nahuas and Maya did borrow the image from the Spaniards, they certainly gave it a logical place in the structure of indigenous address.

5. Nahua example from Haskett 1985: 88; Maya example from ANEY, 1736–37, c. 400. The connection between rulership and the shade of tree branches is also made in the Popol Vuh, for among the emblems of lordship is a canopy, *muh*, which is a Quiché term for "shade" (D. Tedlock 1985: 329). Note also that one Yucatec Maya term for the preconquest ruling group was *nucteil*, "great trees" (Hanks 1989b). Indeed the Classic Maya of Palenque portrayed the rulers that had preceded Pacal as his orchard of ancestors, and past rulers of Copán were immortalized on "tree stones," inspiring Schele and Freidel (1990: 71, 220) to title their collaborative work *A Forest of Kings*. The Mixtec (or Ñudzahui) made similar links between trees and prominent men (Furst 1977). For a broader discussion of the role trees played in postconquest Maya society, see Chap. 15.

6. CCA-VIII, 1811, 09, *Documentos Hocaba* (contains three items c. 1810–25).

7. Sullivan 1989: 108–20. In colonial Maya, which does not differ greatly from early-twentieth-century Maya, *yacunah* could also mean "appreciation" or "favorable or appreciative words" (colonial-era texts; Pío Pérez 1866–77: 403).

8. Where contemporary Spanish translations exist of Maya documents using metaphors of reverence and affection such phrases are literally translated—e.g., AGN-C, 336, 1, 159–60 (Chikindzonot, 1794).

9. Examples of excessive use of Spanish legal terms are DTY / TY and TS: 41v–43; this genre is treated in Chap. 21.

10. CCA-VIII-1811, partially miscatalogued as *Memorial en lengua Maya, 1808–9*.

11. The alleged thief, in the Maya literally "the foreign alcalde," was either a Spanish official appointed to Tacchebichen's cabildo as a result of empire-wide reforms, or the Spanish alcalde mayor, often also called corregidor, an administrative and judicial official appointed from outside to a jurisdiction covering a number of cahob. (See Chap. 23 on the nineteenth-century changes in governmental organization.)

12. CCA-VIII, 1811, 09. The breadnut is the *ramón* (Maya: *ox*; botanical Latin: *Brosimum alicastrum*), the sapote is *zapote* (*ya; Manilkara zapota*), and the palm is the kind whose fronds are used for roofs (*xan; Nypa fruticans*): see Table 15.6.

13. AGN-BN, 26, 55, 2–4; 19; 20. My translation of the Tetiz excerpt is tentative; the final sentence in particular is problematic.

14. Farriss 1984: 39–85; Wightman 1990, chaps. 2, 7.

15. AGN-CI, 2013, 1, 4–6.

16. Literally, "the count of our fled people, O Lord, is fifty, the count of those who have left their homes, because there is much work upon us." The argument that if the petition's requests are not granted taxpayers will flee is also used by the Nahuas—e.g., 1611 petition demanding removal of a priest (reproduced in Anderson, Berdan, and Lockhart 1976: 173). Protestations of poverty are evident in other Maya petitions, usually conveyed in the semantic couplet *otzilil y numya*, as in a

1790 complaint by Baca against the burden of four years of church construction; the Baca petition is also typical in arguing that by laboring on the church the local Maya have no time to earn "money to pay my [our] fees and church taxes and tribute" (*takin utial Botic tzaul y botic limosna y yn patan*), let alone tend to their crops (AGEY-A, 1, 3).

17. The Maya texts: *ca tuli ɔocan ix u lukçabal meyah cokol tumen ca yum ti oydor doctor paraçio tumen hach yabil numya lic ca mançic*; and *yohelob ix ca yumob ti peob xan.*

18. The usage of officially obsolete Maya titles of office in the colonial period can be ambiguous; halach uinic is usually applied to the provincial governor, but in this case I believe it is a reference to past batabob of the cah, who may indeed have been halach uinic at the time of the conquest six decades before this petition (see Chap. 6).

19. ANEY, 1736–37, c. 400–402.   20. Horn 1989: 185.

21. AGN-T, 1359, 5, 9.   22. Farriss 1984: 175.

23. Reproduced in Anderson, Berdan, and Lockhart 1976: 166–73.

24. For additional comparison with Nahuatl petitions in this subgenre, see a case dating from 1652 from what is now the state of Nayarit, consisting of a series of complaints alleging violent acts and threats by the local priest against named alcaldes and other named residents of three neighboring indigenous communities: originals in the McAfee Collection in the Research Library of UCLA; one petition transcribed and translated in Braun, Sell, and Terraciano 1989. Maya complaints of beatings by priests are paralleled by similar accusations against civil officials, with a typical victim again being a named Maya alcalde (for example, TE: 274).

25. The fact that concubinage was too widespread or even tolerated to be an effective charge on its own is demonstrated by the addition of more serious accusations in the Nahuatl and Maya examples, and by a Paraguayan case of a priest who was prosecuted by the authorities only after he attacked his housekeeper (by whom he had had three children) in an alleged fit of jealous rage over her relationship with another man (Archivo Nacionál de Asunción, SJC 1742-36/81, document dated 1841, personal courtesy of Richard Huston; see Huston 1993).

26. As evidenced by a rare noncabildo petition from Dzan, c. 1580, in which a Diego Pox accuses his batab of *can muc u kuchul ychil u otoch u chochopayte in chuplil u pakic keban yetel*, "coming four times inside my house to grab my wife by force to fornicate with her" (TT: 32–33; also discussed in Chap. 11).

Chapter Twenty

1. Haskett 1985, chap. 3, is the only detailed substantiated discussion of Nahuatl election procedures, although Lockhart, Berdan, and Anderson 1976: 5, 111 includes a brief coverage of the subject and a sample election document of 1561, one of the Tlaxcalan corpus first mentioned in Gibson 1952.

2. TS: 62.

3. Haskett 1985: 31, who cites Gonzalo Aguirre Beltrán, *Formas de gobierno indígena* (Mexico: Imprenta Universitaria, 1953: 32).

4. Maní, 1557 (TX); documents beginning 1560 in Roys 1939.

5. AGI-E, 318b, 44, 1, and 88, 1 (1666 lists); TS (1611 record).

6. TS: 62; DT: 28; TT: 15 (there is no mention here or, so far as I know, elsewhere, of *how much* elections cost, or what that cost involved).

7. T-LAL-RMC, 1, 25, 2.

8. Pío Pérez, 1866–77: 23, 4.

9. LC: 26, 30.

10. TE: 278. The reference in a Spanish document twelve years later to Ebtun's audiencia as the "sala" only adds to the ambiguity (TE: 283).

11. MT: 49.

12. LC: 47.

13. AGEY-A, 1, 1 for 1683–1704, and DT: 29 for 1706.

14. The closest thing to a model for indigenous election phrases is not Spanish at all, but the Nahuatl of Sahagún's informants in the Florentine Codex (Book 8: 61, reproduced by Haskett 1985: 78), in which the process of meeting and choosing is described in terminology similar to that in the Cuernavaca example given here. The connection to Yucatan, however, is not Sahagún, but the common pool of Meso-american culture.

15. Nahuatl text and English translation from Haskett 1985: 67.

Chapter Twenty-one

1. Some communities still maintain such books (Dzitnup, for example), and their anthropological and political value today has inspired at least one cah (Xocen in 1994) to create its own "libro sagrado" compiled from Chilam Balam and modern works of scholarship published in Mexico and the United States. Some of the Chilam Balam are available as Roys 1967; Barrera Vásquez 1948; Craine and Reindorp 1979; Edmonson, 1982, 1986. Copies of the Ixil, Kaua, and Tusik are in T-LAL-RMC.

2. Clendinnen 1987, for example, searched the Chumayel for insight into Maya views of the persecution of the 1560's; Sigal 1995 uses the Chilam Balam for information on Maya perceptions of the body and of sexuality; Edmonson and Bricker 1985 place the Chilam Balam in the context of a brief overview of Maya literature.

3. Maya titles cited as TY, TCh, TC, and TX. Neither examples nor analysis of the titles is readily available. A small part of TY is published in Spanish as Martínez Hernandez 1926 and in Barrera Vásquez 1984 (given linguistic analysis in Hanks 1987 and n.d.), and complete eighteenth- and nineteenth-century copies of the manuscript are in T-LAL-RMC. Part of TCh is published in English in Brinton 1882 and is preserved in a Gates facsimile in T-LAL-RBC (there is also an 1864 Spanish translation by Manuel Encarnación Avila, and a 1936 Mexican edition by Hector Pérez Martínez). TC is preserved in facsimile in Gates 1935, in translation in Barrera Vásquez 1957; a transcription by Ralph Roys is in T-LAL-RBC and a Willard photostat is in the Southwest Museum in Pasadena, Calif. TX is also in T-LAL-RMC, and parts of it are summarized in Gates 1978. I intend to publish translations of the passages in these documents that recount the conquest (see Chap. 1, note 4). On Nahua titles, see Lockhart 1992: 410–18; Wood 1991. Earlier, less comprehensive

discussions are in Taylor 1972; Gibson 1975; Lockhart 1991, chap. 3. A word about the term "title," or *título*: Spaniards, and in imitation indigenous escribanos, used *título* to describe any document that laid claim, or title, to a piece of land. Modern scholars have adopted the word to label a narrower genre of colonial document, the indigenous-language "primordial titles" written as informal municipal histories by speakers of Nahuatl, Mixtec, Chontal, Quiché, Cakchiquel, and no doubt other Mesoamerican languages. It is in this sense that I use the word here.

4. Lockhart 1992: 413.

5. TAT; Guatemalan texts: Berlin 1950; Crespo 1956; D. Tedlock 1985; discussed in Carmack 1973; Hill 1991; and, most usefully, in Hill 1992.

6. Chicxulub is 14 kilometers northwest of Yaxkukul. Both are in the preconquest Ceh Pech (colonial La Costa) area northeast of Mérida (see Map 18.1).

7. Stacy-Judd 1940.

8. TCh: 213.

9. On preconquest Mesoamerican text and propaganda, see Marcus 1992, especially chap. 12.

10. The text has been published by Barrera Vásquez 1984 as "Deslinde de las Tierras de Yaxkukul"—not, I fear, easy to find. To avoid confusion, I have followed Barrera Vásquez's name for this portion of TY, referring to it as the Deslinde, and citing it as DTY and by line number in Barrera Vásquez 1984.

11. TY: 16; Barrera Vásquez 1984: 98.

12. Wood 1991.

13. Chimalpahin's promotion of the dynastic line of Tzaqualtitlan Tenanco, for example (Schroeder 1991), compares interestingly with the self-promotional propaganda of the Pech's own titles.

14. DTY: 235–44.

15. AGN-T, 1419, 2, 1–5; also discussed in Chaps. 15 and 19.

16. See Chap. 15, especially Table 15.5.

17. Hanks 1987: 674.   18. TE: 5.

19. DTY: 39–52.   20. DTY: 344–48.

21. References to the King (DTY: 3, 11, 304–5); the Adelantado don Francisco de Montejo (9–10); the Governor in Mérida (361–62, 398–400); the encomendero Gonzalo Méndez (in the version of the 1769 copy, don Julián Doncel) (7, 333, 389); the priest, Francisco Hernández (391); the Spanish witnesses (336–43).

22. TCh: 213; Wood 1991: 180, 186, 188.

23. DTY: 12–15, 30–32. Barrera Vásquez has some difficulty with his numbers here: his footnote (1984: 51) is confused and *hotuckallob* is not 25 but *ho-tu-ca-kal-ob*, five before two twenties, which is 35, the number of extracabildo Maya witnesses (31 "important men" plus four Pech sons).

24. DTY: 9–10.   25. DTY: 388–93.

26. Wood 1991: 184.   27. DTY: 20–24, 33–38.

28. DTY: 299–305.

29. DTY: 349–53. Note that the church is referred to in a typical Spanish-Maya bilingual couplet—*kuna,* "holy house," essentially being a translation of *santa iglesia* (see Chaps. 18 and 22).

30. Wood 1991: 179–80.

31. DTY: 368–82.

32. DTY: 385–86.

33. Gibson 1975: 321.

34. See Brinton 1882: 189ff; Barrera Vásquez 1984: Hanks 1987.

35. Barrera Vásquez (1984: 11, 106) repeating Martínez Hernandez (1926: 37).

36. Lockhart 1992: 411.

37. Barrera Vásquez 1984: 98.

38. Lockhart 1991: 61.

39. Hanks 1987: 668–69; Roys 1939.

40. The 1769 version is the one named *Nº2* by Barrera Vásquez 1984; it mentions both Méndez and Doncel as *u hahil concixtador*, "true conquistadors."

41. Karttunen 1985: 54. I note that the *Chicxulub* uses *cax* for chicken; this form appears in the Pío Pérez dictionary, whose sources are eighteenth and nineteenth century, whereas mid-seventeenth-century Maya testaments from Cacalchen (LC) use what must be the earlier full form, *caxtilla* (from *castilla*; chickens were introduced from Castille); Nahuas made a similar loan.

42. See Farriss 1984: 110–12 on Maya spoken by Spaniards. See Chap. 22 on loanwords. As Karttunen has pointed out (1985: 104), in general reference to colonial-era Maya documents and in specific reference to the Pech titles, the substitution of *s* for *c* places these documents firmly in the eighteenth century.

Chapter Twenty-two

1. Karttunen and Lockhart 1976; Karttunen 1985; Lockhart 1991 and 1992.

2. Hunt 1974: 588–89, and 1976; Patch 1979 and 1993; Farriss 1984.

3. TI: 30, 51, 56; TE: 242.

4. See Cline 1981 and 1986; Cline and Léon-Portilla 1984; Lockhart 1992: 290.

5. Lockhart 1992: 284–304. See also Karttunen 1985: 51–71 on colonial-era loans of Spanish words into Nahuatl and Maya.

6. T-LAL-RMC, 1, 25, 2.

7. Karttunen 1985: 53.

8. Karttunen and Lockhart 1976.

9. Karttunen (1985: 15) has pointed out that there are at least 139 Spanish loans in the Motul dictionary of the 1580's. However, as Karttunen recognizes, we cannot assume that all these loans were in common Maya usage by these dates (even though this would support my argument above) and I have therefore ignored dictionary claims and used solely Maya sources. A number of Spanish loans appear only in the Books of Chilam Balam (particularly the passages to do with herbal curing) but because these sources cannot be accurately dated, such loans are not included in this chapter's analysis.

10. Ibid., 53.

11. Ibid., 59. Another verb found by Karttunen is *firmar*; the form *ca firma* (sometimes *ca firmasob*) is extremely common, but as a noun loan, "our signature(s)." The discrepancies between my findings and those of Karttunen (which are presented in far greater detail and within a linguistic analytical framework) are minor, indicating not contradictory conclusions but rather the need for a more comprehensive study.

12. I would like to thank Victoria Bricker, William Hanks, and Frances Kart-

tunen for invaluable comments made on Tables 22.2 and 22.3; the latter is based on Karttunen, personal communication (although any errors in either table remain my responsibility). I should also note that both Bricker and Hanks observed that there is an *r* in Maya; however, as shown in my tables and as noted later in this chapter, it is my reading of colonial-era texts that at this time there was only an *l*, and that incidences of *r* are hypercorrections.

13. AGN-I, 1187, 2, 59–61.

14. TI. Also from TI: the Maya *tzimin*, originally a tapir but used to describe the European horse, appears on its own to mean the male of the species, whereas *yeua tzimin*, using the Spanish *yegua*, means mare.

15. See Chap. 18. Testamento is always possessed in the first or third person, *yn testamento* or *u testamento*, sometimes with the possessive noun suffix, *u testamentoil*.

16. AGN-BN, 5, 35, 5.

17. When we consider that at this time in highland Guatemala such a distance could divide dialects or languages that were mutually unintelligible, and that con-temporaneous English towns equally close to each other used dialects with greater differentiations than those above, and that in both cases these variations have largely survived to the present, the existence of minor dialects in Yucatan seems expected.

Chapter Twenty-three

1. Rugeley n.d.

2. Ibid., intro. and chap. 7.

3. The state confiscated Maya cofradía estates in 1832, and in 1843 it seized and sold cah lands outside a one-square-league perimeter of the cah plaza. On the buildup to the Caste War: Reed 1964; Farriss 1984, chap. 12; Rugeley n.d.

4. ANEY: group of documents from "cahob-barrios" discussed in Chap. 3 above. TE: 283 shows Ebtun, for example, conforming likewise.

5. It is not clear from the sources whether these cah governors were now called caciques by the Mayas or whether the title was only used on paper, with batab persisting as the title of use in the cahob; I suspect the latter (AGEY-G and AGEY-CP, various years from 1826 through 1867). Rugeley (n.d., chap. 5) maintains that batabs were able to maneuver and parlay their role as intermediaries between Ladinos and Mayas into ongoing positions of status through the 1820's and 1830's, before being caught (perhaps fatally) between the demands of state and church and increasing Maya peasant unwillingness to meet those demands. The Chi-chanhá above must be a different cah from the Chichanhá near Bacalar—identified by Rugeley (personal communication) as a *pacífico* postwar community led by a series of "commandantes."

6. Jones 1989.

7. AGN-BN, 5, 35: 5.

8. MT: 46.

9. Nahuatl was superseded by a Nahuatl-influenced Spanish, called Nahuañol by Haskett, who describes the transition in detail (1985: 102–25).

10. MT: 65 (of which only a poor 50-year-old Gates photostat of the original seems to have survived); TE: 283.

11. MT: 46. I am convinced, in fact, that more Maya material from this period will surface. The apparent rapid drop-off in extant Maya-language sources after 1830 may reflect my own time-determined research decisions, since I could not review post-1840 volumes in the ANEY, for example, as thoroughly and as many times as the pre-1840 material. It also may be due to the increasing use of an acidic ink that ate away at paper. In a larger way, it probably reflects the gradual completion of the transition to Spanish discussed above, either as the language used by cah notaries, or (as Rugeley has suggested, personal communication) as a result of local officials or priests translating cah documents that have not survived.

12. TE: 283.

13. The cahob are Baca, Chichanhá, Huhi, Mopila, Nenela, Sotuta, Sahcaba, Sanahcat, Tacchibichen, Tecoh, Tixcacaltuyu, Tixkuncheil, Yaxcabá, and Yaxkukul: AGEY-G, above dates.

14. The end of the paper trail makes it hard for the historian to trace the process of Maya political continuity beyond the final abolition of the repúblicas indígenas on January 1, 1869—one begins to rely on the journals of foreign scholars and travelers, as did Paul Sullivan (1989)—and the methodology, let alone the time period, takes us well beyond the scope of the present study. However, as stated earlier, there is more than ample room for further research and study.

15. AGEY-G 1867(b), 1 (transcription courtesy of Philip Thompson, personal communication).

16. Edmonson 1982, 1986; Roys 1967 [1933], 1972.

17. Roys recognized this over 50 years ago (1972 [1943]: 129), but his perspective has yet to become conventional wisdom.

18. On Ñudzahui: Terraciano 1994 (some Maya-Ñudzahui comparisons on specific matters have been drawn in the course of this book using Terraciano's work). On Cakchiquel: Hill 1991; Cakchiquel documents from the Archivo General de Centroamérica, Guatemala City, courtesy of Robinson Herrera.

19. Particularly Hunt 1974; Farriss 1984; Clendinnen 1987; Jones 1989; Patch 1993.

20. Lockhart 1992: 436.

Glossary

Albacea (Sp). Executor of a testament

Alcalde (Sp). A rank of judge and a cabildo member

Almehen (M). Maya noble

Altepetl (Nahuatl). Nahua municipal community, equivalent to cah and ñuu

Audiencia (Sp). Spanish High Court and its jurisdiction; used by Maya notaries to refer to a cah cabildo session and / or the room or building where the meetings took place

Batab (M). Cah governor (batabil: governorship)

Cabecera (Sp). Head town of a Spanish administrative district

Cabildo (Sp). Spanish-style municipal council

Cah (M). Maya municipal community (cahob in the plural)

Cah-barrio (M / Sp). Cahob that were barrios (subdistricts) of Mérida, Campeche, and Valladolid; term constructed by the author

Cahnal (M). Cah resident and member

Calpolli (Nahuatl). Subdistrict of an altepetl

Cetil (M). Even distribution, primarily of property to heirs

Chibal (M). Patronym group

Chilam Balam (M). Mythical Maya prophet and reputed original author of Maya-language books copied alphabetically in colonial period

Cofradía (Sp). Lay religious brotherhood

Col (M). Field, usually cultivated

Congregación (Sp). Forced resettlement to central site

Despoblado (Sp). Literally "uninhabited"; Spaniards' misnomer for the "unpacified" (unconquered) southeastern regions of the Yucatan

Don, doña (Sp). Title prefixed to first name; like English "sir" and "lady"

Dzul (M). Foreigner, non-Maya, including Spanish Yucatecans

Encomendero (Sp). Holder of an encomienda (grant of labor and tribute from a cah, altepetl, ñuu, etc.)

Entrada (Sp). Spanish military expedition aimed at conquest or at returning indigenous refugees to cahob under colonial rule

Escribano (Sp). Notary

Estancia (Sp). Cattle ranch

Halach uinic (M). Preconquest regional ruler (literally, true man)

Henequen (Sp). Plant and the fiber it produces, used for making cordage

Huipil (Sp). Indigenous woman's dress (from Nahuatl, huipilli; in Maya, ypil)

Indio (Sp). Spanish term for all indigenous people, who did not use it

Indio hidalgo (Sp). Category of indigenous nobility recognized by Spanish authorities and exempt from tribute

Kax (M). Forested land; also used in some cahob for cultivated land

Macehual (M). Indigenous commoner (from Nahuatl macehualli)

Maestro (Sp). Teacher, choirmaster; Maya official in charge of liturgy and catechism in the cah

Manta (Sp). Length of cotton cloth, used as an indigenous tribute unit

Multial (M). Joint or group ownership

Nahuas (from Nahuatl). Nahuatl-speaking indigenous central Mexicans (Mexica: Nahuas from Tenochtitlán-Mexico City) (Aztecs: primarily a modern term applied variously to the Mexica and Nahuas)

Ñudzahui. Term used by the Mixtecs for themselves and for their language

Ñuu (Ñudzahui). Ñudzahui municipal community, equivalent to cah and altepetl

-ob (M). Yucatec Maya plural suffix

Oidor (Sp). A judge of an audiencia (in the sense of the Spanish imperial High Court and its jurisdiction, such as those of Mexico City and Guatemala)

Peso (Sp). Primary monetary unit, consisting of eight reales or tomines

Principales (Sp). Indigenous community elders or prominent men

Regidor (Sp). Councilman, cabildo member

Repartimiento (Sp). In Yucatan, forced purchase of goods from cahob

Solar (Sp). House plot

Teniente (Sp). Lieutenant; office attached to Maya cabildo

Tomín (Sp). A coin worth one-eighth of a peso; in Maya and Nahuatl a term for coin or money; usually written "tumin" in Maya

Tupil (M). Lower-level municipal officer

Tupil doctrina mandamiento (M/Sp). Assistant, sometimes apprentice, to maestro and sometimes escribano

Vecino (Sp). Nonindigenous resident

Yum (M). Father, lord; used reverentially

Works Cited

Altman, Ida. 1991. "Spanish Society in Mexico City After the Conquest." *Hispanic American Historical Review* 71, no. 3: 413–46.

Ancona, Eligio. 1878–79. *Historia de Yucatan desde la época más remota hasta nuestras días.* 3 vols. Mérida: Manuel Heredia Argüelles.

Anderson, Arthur, Frances Berdan, and James Lockhart. 1976. *Beyond the Codices.* Berkeley and Los Angeles: University of California Press.

Bakewell, Peter J. 1971. *Silver Mining and Society in Colonial Mexico: Zacatecas, 1546–1700.* Cambridge: Cambridge University Press.

Barrera Vásquez, Alfredo. 1948. (with Silvia Rendón) *El libro de los libros de Chilam Balam.* Mexico City: Fondo de Cultura Económica.

——. 1957. *Códice de Calkini.* Campeche: Biblioteca Campechana.

——. 1984. *Documento No. 1 del Deslinde de Tierras en Yaxkukul, Yucatán.* Colección científica, Linguistica 125. Mexico City: INAH.

——. 1991 [1980]. *Diccionario Maya.* 2d ed. Mexico City: Editorial Porrua.

Barrutia, Richard, 1991. "Comparative Research on Bilingual Education in Mexico and the US." Paper presented at the 9th International Symposium of the Latin American Indian Literatures Association, Quito, Ecuador.

Barth, Frederick, ed. 1969. *Ethnic Groups and Boundaries: The Social Organization of Culture Difference.* Oslo and London: Universitets Forlaget and Allen & Unwin.

Bennassar, Bartolomé. 1979. *L'Inquisition espagnole (xv–xvi siècles).* Paris: Hachette.

Berlin, Heinrich. 1950. "La Historia de los Xpantzay." *Antropología e Historia de Guatemala* 2, no. 2.

Blom, Frans. 1929. *The Conquest of Yucatan.* Cambridge, Mass.: Riverside Press.

Borah, Woodrow. 1982. "The Spanish and Indian Law: New Spain." In George Collier, Renato Rosaldo, and John Wirth, eds., *Inca and Aztec States, 1400–1800: Anthropology and History,* pp. 265–88. New York: Academic Press.

Brading, David A. 1971. *Miners and Merchants in Bourbon Mexico, 1763–1810.* Cambridge: Cambridge University Press.

Braun, James, Barry Sell, and Kevin Terraciano. 1989. "The Northwest of New Spain: Nahuatl in Nayarit, 1652." *UCLA Historical Journal* 9: 80–90.

Bricker, Victoria R. 1981. *The Indian Christ, the Indian King: The Historical Substrate of Maya Myth and Ritual*. Austin: University of Texas Press.

———. 1986. *A Grammar of Maya Hieroglyphs*. New Orleans: Middle American Research Institute, Tulane University (Publication 56).

———. 1989. "The Last Gasp of Maya Hieroglyphic Writing in the Books of Chilam Balam of Chumayel and Chan Kan." In William F. Hanks and Don S. Rice, eds., *Word and Image in Maya Culture: Explorations in Language, Writing, and Representation*, pp. 39–50. Salt Lake City: University of Utah Press.

Brinton, Daniel G. 1882. *The Maya Chronicles*. Philadelphia. Reprinted 1969. New York: AMS Press.

Burkhart, Louise. 1989. *The Slippery Earth: Nahua-Christian Moral Dialogue in Sixteenth-Century Mexico*. Tucson: University of Arizona Press.

Burns, Allan F. 1991a. "From Maize to Medicine: Cultural Persistence in Yucatec Maya Migration to Mérida." Paper presented at the 47th International Congress of Americanists, New Orleans.

———. 1991b. "The Language of Zuyua: Yucatec Maya Riddles and Their Interpretation." In Mary H. Preuss, ed., *Past, Present, and Future: Selected Papers on Latin American Indian Literatures*, pp. 35–40. Culver City, Calif.: Labyrinthos.

Calnek, Edward. 1972. "Settlement Patterns and Chinampa Agriculture in Tenochtitlán." *American Antiquity* 37, no. 1.

Carmack, Robert. 1973. *Quichean Civilization: The Ethnohistoric, Ethnographic, and Archaeological Sources*. Berkeley and Los Angeles: University of California Press.

Carroll, Patrick J. 1991. *Blacks in Colonial Veracruz: Race, Ethnicity, and Regional Development*. Austin: University of Texas Press.

Certeau, Michel de. 1984. *The Practice of Everyday Life*. Translated by Stephen Rendall. Berkeley and Los Angeles: University of California Press.

Chamberlain, Robert S. 1948. *The Conquest and Colonization of Yucatan, 1517–1550*. Washington, D.C.: Carnegie Institution.

Chartier, Roger. 1982. "Intellectual or Socio-cultural History? The French Trajectories." In Dominick La Capra and Steven L. Kaplan, eds., *Modern European Intellectual History: Reappraisals and New Perspectives*. Ithaca, N.Y.: Cornell University Press.

Chatwin, Bruce. 1987. *The Songlines*. New York: Viking.

Chaunu, Pierre. 1978. "Un Nouveau Champ pour l'histoire sérielle: Le Quantitatif au troisième niveau." In Pierre Chaunu, *Histoire quantitative, histoire sérielle*, pp. 216–30. Paris: Fayard.

Christian, William A., Jr. 1981. *Local Religion in Sixteenth-Century Spain*. Princeton, N.J.: Princeton University Press.

Clendinnen, Inga. 1982. "Yucatec Maya Women and the Spanish Conquest: Role and Ritual in Historical Reconstruction." *Journal of Social History*, Summer 1982: 427–42.

———. 1987. *Ambivalent Conquests. Maya and Spaniard in Yucatan, 1517–1570*. Cambridge: Cambridge University Press.

———. 1991. *Aztecs: An Interpretation*. Cambridge: Cambridge University Press.

Cline, S. L. 1981. "Culhuacan 1572–1599: An Investigation Through Mexican Indian Testaments." Ph.D. dissertation, University of California, Los Angeles.

———. 1986. *Colonial Culhuacan, 1580–1600: A Social History of an Aztec Town*. Albuquerque: University of New Mexico Press.

Cline, S. L., and Miguel Léon-Portilla. 1984. *The Testaments of Culhuacan*. Nahuatl Studies Series, no. 1. Los Angeles: UCLA Latin American Center Publications.

Coe, Michael D. 1965. "A Model of Ancient Community Structure in the Maya Lowlands." *Southwestern Journal of Anthropology*, 21: 91–114.

Cogolludo, Diego López de. 1867–68 [1654]. *Los tres siglos de la dominación española en Yucatán o sea Historia de Esta Provincia*, 2 vols. Mérida: Manuel Aldana Rivas. First published 1688 as *Historia de Yucatán*. Madrid: J. García Infanzón.

Collins, Anne C. 1977. "The *Maestros Cantores* in Yucatan." In Grant D. Jones, ed., *Anthropology and History in Yucatán*, pp. 233–47. Austin: University of Texas Press.

Cope, R. Douglas. 1994. *The Limits of Racial Domination: Plebeian Society in Colonial Mexico City, 1660–1720*. Madison: University of Wisconsin Press.

Craine, Eugene R., and Reginald C. Reindorp. 1979. *The Codex Pérez and the Book of Chilam Balam of Maní*. Norman: University of Oklahoma Press.

Crespo, Mario. 1956. "Títulos Indígenas de Tierras." *Antropología e Historia de Guatemala* 8, no. 2.

Cross, Claire. 1989. *York Clergy Wills 1520–1600: II, City Clergy*. Borthwick Institute of Historical Research, Text 15. York: University of York Press.

Darnton, Robert. 1985. *The Great Cat Massacre and Other Episodes in French Cultural History*. New York: Vintage.

Dumond, Carol S., and Don E. Dumond, eds. 1982. *Demography and Parish Affairs in Yucatan, 1797–1879: Documents from the Archivo de la Mitra Emeritense, Selected by Joaquin de Arrigunaga Peon*. Portland: University of Oregon Press (Anthropological Papers, 27).

Edmonson, Munro S., trans. and ed. 1982. *The Ancient Future of the Itza: The Book of Chilam Balam of Tizimin*. Austin: University of Texas Press.

———. 1986. *Heaven Born Mérida and Its Destiny: The Book of Chilam Balam of Chumayel*. Austin: University of Texas Press.

Edmonson, Munro S., and Victoria R. Bricker. 1985. "Yucatecan Mayan Literature." In Munro S. Edmonson and Victoria R. Bricker, eds., *Supplement to the Handbook of Middle American Indians*, vol. 3, *Literatures*, pp. 44–63. Austin: University of Texas Press.

Elmendorf, Mary. 1985. *Nine Mayan Women. A Village Faces Change*. Rochester, Vt.: Schenkman.

Everton, MacDuff. 1991. *The Modern Maya: A Culture in Transition*. Albuquerque: University of New Mexico Press.

Farriss, Nancy M. 1984. *Maya Society Under Colonial Rule. The Collective Enterprise of Survival*. Princeton, N.J.: Princeton University Press.

Fash, William L. 1991. *Scribes, Warriors, and Kings: The City of Copán and the Ancient Maya*. London: Thames and Hudson.

Flannery, Kent V., ed. 1982. *Maya Subsistence*. New York: Academic Press.

Florescano, Enrique. 1994. *Memory, Myth, and Time in Mexico: From the Aztecs to Independence*. Austin: University of Texas Press.

Foucault, Michel. 1980. *The History of Sexuality*, vol. 1, *An Introduction*. New York.

Furst, Jill Leslie. 1977. "The Tree Birth Tradition in the Mixteca, Mexico." *Journal of Latin American Lore* 3, no. 2: 183–226.

García Bernal, Manuela Cristina. 1972. *La Sociedad de Yucatán, 1700–1750*. Seville: Escuela de Estudios Hispano-Americanos.

——. 1978. *Yucatán: Población y encomienda bajo los Austrias*. Seville: Escuela de Estudios Hispano-Americanos.

——. 1979. "El Gobernador de Yucatán Rodrigo Flores de Aldana." In *Homenaje al Dr. Muro Orejón*. Seville: Escuela de Estudios Hispano-Americanos, pp. 123–72.

——. 1984. "Los comerciantes estancieros en Yucatán y la gran propriedad de Nohpat." *Temas Americanistas* 4: 8–14.

——. 1991a. "La pérdida de la propriedad indígena ante la expansión de las estancias yucatecas (siglo XVI)." In *Actas de la VIII Jornadas de Andalucía y América: Propriedad de la tierra, latifundios y movimientos campesinos*, Seville, pp. 55–90.

——. 1991b. "Un posible modelo de explotación pecuaria en Yucatán: El caso de la propriedad de Tziskal-Chacsinkin." Seville: Publications of the Escuela de Estudios Hispano-Americanos, 48: 283–348.

——. 1992. "Indios y Españoles en Yucatán: Utopia y Realidad del Proyecto Colonizador." Seville: Published proceedings of the Congreso de Historia del Descubrimiento, 2: 387–427.

——. 1994. "Desarollos Indígena y Ganadero en Yucatán." *Historia Mexicana* 63, no. 3: 373–400.

Garza, Mercedes de la, ed. 1983 [1581]. *Relaciones Histórico-Geográficas de la Gobernación de Yucatán*. Mexico City: UNAM.

Gates, William. 1978 [1937]. *Yucatan Before and After the Conquest, by Friar Diego de Landa*. Reprint. New York: Dover.

——, trans. and ed. 1935. *The Maya Calkiní Chronicle, or Documents Concerning the Descent of the Ah-Canul, or Men of the Serpent, Their Arrival and Territory*. Baltimore: The Maya Society.

Geertz, Clifford. 1973. *The Interpretation of Cultures*. New York: Basic Books.

Gibson, Charles. 1952. *Tlaxcala in the Sixteenth Century*. New Haven, Conn.: Yale University Press.

——. 1964. *The Aztecs Under Spanish Rule: A History of the Indians of the Valley of Mexico, 1519–1810*. Stanford, Calif.: Stanford University Press.

——. 1975. "Survey of Middle American Prose Manuscripts in the Native Historical Tradition." In Howard F. Cline, ed., *Handbook of Middle American Indians, 15, no. 4, Guide to Ethnohistorical Sources*, pp. 311–21. Austin: University of Texas Press.

González N., Jorge René. 1985. "Clérigos solicitantes, perversos de la confesión." In Sergio Ortega, ed., *De la santidad a la perversión*, pp. 239–52. Mexico City: Editorial Grijalbo.

Goody, Jack. 1976. *Production and Reproduction: A Comparative Study of the Domestic Domain*. Cambridge: Cambridge University Press.

——. 1983. *The Development of the Family and Marriage in Europe*. Cambridge: Cambridge University Press.

Gosner, Kevin. 1979. "Uman Parish: Open, Corporate Communities in Eighteenth-Century Yucatan." Paper presented before the Association of American Geographers, Philadelphia.

Gruzinski, Serge. 1987. "Colonial Maps in Sixteenth-Century Mexico." *Res* 13: 46–61.

———. 1989. *Man-Gods in the Mexican Highlands: Indian Power and Colonial Society, 1520–1800*. Stanford, Calif.: Stanford University Press.

Gubler, Ruth. 1991. "Concepts of Illness and the Tradition of Herbal Curing in the Book of Chilam Balam of Nah." *Latin American Indian Literatures Journal* 7, no. 2: 192–214.

Gutiérrez, Ramon A. 1991. *When Jesus Came, the Corn Mothers Went Away: Marriage, Sexuality, and Power in New Mexico, 1500–1846*. Stanford, Calif.: Stanford University Press.

Hanks, William F. 1986. "Authenticity and Ambivalence in the Text: A Colonial Maya Case." *American Ethnologist* 13, no. 4: 721–44.

———. 1987. "Discourse Genres in a Theory of Practice." *American Ethnologist* 14, no. 4: 668–92.

———. 1988. "Grammar, Style, and Meaning in a Maya Manuscript." *International Journal of American Linguistics* 54, no. 3: 331–69.

———. 1989a. "Elements of Maya Style." In William F. Hanks and Don S. Rice, eds., *Word and Image in Maya Culture: Explorations in Language, Writing, and Representation*. Salt Lake City: University of Utah Press.

———. 1989b. "Rhetoric of Royal Address in Sixteenth-Century Yucatec Maya." Unpublished MS.

———. 1990. *Referential Practice: Language and Lived Space Among the Maya*. Chicago: University of Chicago Press.

———. n.d. "L'intertextualité de l'espace au Yucatán." Unpublished MS.

Harrison, Peter D., and B. L. Turner, eds. 1978. *Pre-Hispanic Maya Agriculture*. Albuquerque: University of New Mexico Press.

Haskett, Robert S. 1985. "A Social History of Indian Town Government in the Colonial Cuernavaca Jurisdiction, Mexico." Ph.D. dissertation, University of California, Los Angeles.

———. 1991. *Indigenous Rulers: An Ethnohistory of Town Government in Colonial Cuernavaca*. Albuquerque: University of New Mexico Press.

Hill, Jane H., and Kenneth C. Hill. 1986. *Speaking Mexicano: Dynamics of Syncretic Language in Central Mexico*. Tucson: University of Arizona Press.

Hill, Robert M., II. 1989. *The Pirir Papers and Other Colonial Period Cakchiquel-Maya Testamentos*. Publications in Anthropology 37. Nashville, Tenn.: Vanderbilt University Press.

———. 1991. *Colonial Cakchiquels: Highland Maya Adaptations to Spanish Rule, 1600–1700*. Orlando, Fla.: Brace Jovanovich (Case Studies in Cultural Anthropology).

———. 1992. "The Social Uses of Writing Among the Colonial Cakchiquel Maya: Nativism, Resistance, and Innovation." In David Hurst Thomas, ed., *Columbian Consequences*, 3: 283–99. Washington, D.C.: Smithsonian Institution Press.

Holmes, Barbara E. 1977. "Women and Yucatec Kinship." Ph.D. dissertation, Tulane University.

Horn, Rebecca. 1989. "Postconquest Coyoacan: Aspects of Indigenous Sociopolitical and Economic Organization in Central Mexico, 1550–1650." Ph.D. dissertation, University of California, Los Angeles.

Hunt, Marta Espejo-Ponce. 1974. "Colonial Yucatan: Town and Region in the Seventeenth Century." Ph.D. dissertation, University of California, Los Angeles.

———. 1976. "The Process of the Development of Yucatan, 1600–1700." In Ida Altman and James Lockhart, eds., *Provinces of Early Mexico*, pp. 33–62. Los Angeles: UCLA Latin American Center Publications.

Hunt, Marta Espejo-Ponce, and Matthew B. Restall. n.d. "Indigenous Women of Colonial Yucatan." In Susan Schroeder, Stephanie Wood, and Robert Haskett, eds., *Indian Women of Colonial Mexico*. Norman: University of Oklahoma Press, forthcoming.

Huston, Richard P. 1993. "Folk and State in Paraguay: Political Order and Social Disorder, 1810–40." Ph.D. dissertation, University of California, Los Angeles.

Jones, Grant. 1989. *Maya Resistance to Spanish Rule: Time and History on a Colonial Frontier*. Albuquerque: University of New Mexico Press.

Kamen, Henry B. 1985. *Inquisition and Society in Spain in the Sixteenth and Seventeenth Centuries*. London: Weidenfeld & Nicolson.

Karttunen, Frances. 1982. "Nahuatl Literacy." In George Collier, Renato Rosaldo, and John Wirth, eds., *The Inca and Aztec States, 1400–1800: Anthropology and History*, pp. 395–417. New York: Academic Press.

———. 1985. *Nahuatl and Maya in Contact with Spanish*. Texas Linguistic Forum, 26. Austin: University of Texas Department of Linguistics.

———. 1994. *Between Worlds: Interpreters, Guides, and Survivors*. New Brunswick, N.J.: Rutgers University Press.

Karttunen, Frances, and James Lockhart. 1976. *Nahuatl in the Middle Years: Language Contact Phenomena in Texts of the Colonial Period*. University of California Publications in Linguistics, 85. Berkeley and Los Angeles: University of California Press.

———, eds. 1987. *The Art of Nahuatl Speech: The Bancroft Dialogues*. UCLA Latin American Center Nahuatl Studies Series, 2. Los Angeles: UCLA Latin American Center Publications.

Kellogg, Susan M. 1979. "Social Organization in Early Colonial Tenochtitlán-Tlatelolco." Ph.D. dissertation, University of Rochester.

———. 1995. *Law and the Transformation of Aztec Culture, 1500–1700*. Norman: University of Oklahoma Press.

Kostof, Spiro. 1991. *The City Shaped: Urban Patterns and Meanings Through History*. London: Bulfinch Press.

Kubler, George. 1948. *Mexican Architecture of the Sixteenth Century*. New Haven, Conn.: Yale University Press.

Kurjack, Edward B. 1974. *Prehistoric Lowland Maya Community and Social Organization. A Case Study at Dzibilchaltun, Yucatan, Mexico*. New Orleans: Middle American Research Institute, Tulane University (Publication 38).

Landa, Diego de. 1982 [1566]. *Relación de las Cosas de Yucatán*. Mexico City: Editorial Porrua.

Lavrín, Asunción, ed. 1989. *Sexuality and Marriage in Colonial Latin America*. Lincoln: University of Nebraska Press.

Leibsohn, Dana. 1993. "The Historia Tolteca-Chichimeca: Recollecting Identity in a Nahua Manuscript." Ph.D. dissertation, University of California, Los Angeles.

———. 1994. "Primers for Memory: Cartographic Histories and Nahua Identity." In Elizabeth Hill Boone and Walter D. Mignolo, eds. *Writing Without Words: Alternative Literacies in Mesoamerica and the Andes*, pp. 161–87. Durham, N.C.: Duke University Press.

Lizana, Bernardo de. 1893 [1633]. *Historia de Yucatán*. 2d ed. Mexico City: Museo Nacional.

Lockhart, James. 1968. *Spanish Peru, 1532–1560*. Madison: University of Wisconsin Press. Reprinted 1994.

———. 1972. *The Men of Cajamarca: A Social and Biographical Study of the First Conquerors of Peru*. Austin: University of Texas Press.

———. 1985. "Some Nahua Concepts in Postconquest Guise." *History of European Ideas* 6: 465–82.

———. 1989. "The Social History of Early Latin America: Evolution and Potential." Unpublished MS.

———. 1991. *Nahuas and Spaniards: Postconquest Central Mexican History and Philology*. Stanford and Los Angeles: Stanford University Press and UCLA Latin American Center Publications.

———. 1992. *The Nahuas After the Conquest: A Social and Cultural History of the Indians of Central Mexico, Sixteenth Through Eighteenth Centuries*. Stanford, Calif.: Stanford University Press.

Lockhart, James, Frances Berdan, and Arthur J. O. Anderson. 1986. *The Tlaxcalan Actas: A Compendium of the Records of the Cabildo of Tlaxcala (1545–1627)*. Salt Lake City: University of Utah Press.

Lockhart, James, and Stuart B. Schwartz. 1983. *Early Latin America: A History of Colonial Spanish America and Brazil*. Cambridge: Cambridge University Press (Latin American Studies 46).

Low, Setha M. 1995. "Indigenous Architecture and the Spanish American Plaza in Mesoamerica and the Caribbean." *American Anthropologist* 97, no. 4: 748–62.

McAlister, Lyle N. 1984. *Spain and Portugal in the New World*. Minneapolis: University of Minnesota Press.

McGee, R. Jon. 1991. "A Structural Comparison of 16th Century Mayan Texts with Contemporary Mayan Mythology." Paper presented at the annual meeting of the American Society for Ethnohistory, Tulsa, Okla.

Magaña Toledano, José Carlos. 1984. "Historia Demográfica de las Ciudades de Mérida y Campeche. 1809–1810." Licenciatura thesis, Universidad de Yucatán.

Marcus, Joyce. 1982. "The Plant World of the Sixteenth- and Seventeenth-Century Lowland Maya." In Kent V. Flannery, ed., *Maya Subsistence*, pp. 239–73. New York: Academic Press.

———. 1983. "On the Nature of the Mesoamerican City." In Evon Z. Vogt and Richard M. Leventhal, eds., *Prehistoric Settlement Patterns: Essays in Honor of Gor-*

don R. Willey, pp. 195–242. Cambridge and Albuquerque: Peabody Museum of
   Harvard University and University of New Mexico Press.
———. 1992. *Mesoamerican Writing Systems: Propaganda, Myth, and History in Four
   Ancient Civilizations*. Princeton, N.J.: Princeton University Press.
Martínez Hernández, Juan. 1926. *Crónica de Yaxkukul*. Mérida: Nuevos Talleres de la
   Cia. Tipográfica Yucateca.
Means, Philip A. 1917. *A History of the Spanish Conquest of Yucatan and of the Itzas*.
   Cambridge, Mass.: Peabody Museum, Harvard University.
Miller, Arthur G., and Nancy M. Farriss. 1979. "Religious Syncretism in Colonial
   Yucatan: The Archeological and Ethnohistorical Evidence from Tancah, Quin-
   tana Roo." In Norman Hammond and Gordon R. Willey, eds., *Maya Archaeology
   and Ethnohistory*, pp. 223–40. Austin: University of Texas Press.
Molina Solís, Juan Francisco. 1904–13. *Historia de Yucatán durante la dominación
   española*. 3 vols. Mérida: Imprenta de la Lotería del Estado.
Morley, Sylvanus G. 1983 [1946]. *The Ancient Maya*. 4th ed., revised by G. W. Brain-
   erd and R. J. Sharer. Stanford, Calif.: Stanford University Press.
O'Brien, Denise. 1977. "Female Husbands in Southern Bantu Societies." In Alice
   Schlegel, ed., *Sexual Stratification: A Cross-Cultural View*. New York: Columbia
   University Press.
O'Brien, Patricia, and Hanne Christiansen. 1986. "An Ancient Maya Measurement
   System." *American Antiquity* 51, no. 1: 136–51.
Ochiai, Kazuyasu. 1991. "Recent Ethnohistorical Publications by Japanese Latin
   Americanists." *Latin American Indian Literatures Journal* 7, no. 2: 215–19.
Offutt, Leslie S. 1992. "Levels of Acculturation in Northeastern New Spain: San
   Esteban Testaments of the Seventeenth and Eighteenth Centuries." *Estudios de
   cultura náhuatl* 22: 409–43.
Patch, Robert W. 1979. "A Colonial Regime: Maya and Spaniard in Yucatan." Ph.D.
   dissertation, Princeton University.
———. 1991. "Decolonization, the Agrarian Problem, and the Origins of the Caste
   War, 1812–1847." In Jeffrey T. Brannon and Gilbert M. Joseph, eds., *Land, Labor,
   and Capital in Modern Yucatán: Essays in Regional History and Political Economy*.
   Tuscaloosa: University of Alabama Press.
———. 1993. *Maya and Spaniard in Yucatan, 1648–1812*. Stanford, Calif.: Stanford University Press.
———. n.d. "Culture, Community, and 'Rebellion' in the Yucatec Maya Uprising of
   1761." In Susan Schroeder, ed., *The Pax Colonial and Native Resistance in New
   Spain*. Lincoln: University of Nebraska Press, forthcoming.
Patterson, Steven. 1992. "In Search of a Mesoamerican Floricultural Tradition: Ceremonial and Ornamental Plants Among the Yucatecan Maya." Ph.D. dissertation, University of California, Los Angeles.
Piña Chan, Román. 1977. *Campeche durante el período colonial*. Mexico City: INAH.
Pío Pérez, Juan. 1866–77. *Diccionario de la Lengua Maya*. Mérida: Imprenta Literaria
   de Juan F. Molina Solís.
Powers, Karen Vieira. 1995. *Andean Journeys: Migration, Ethnogenesis, and the State in
   Colonial Quito*. Albuquerque: University of New Mexico Press.

Quezada, Sergio P. A. 1990. "Pueblos y Caciques Yucatecos, 1550–1580." Dissertation for Doctorate in History, El Colegio de México, Mexico City.

Reder Gadow, Marion. 1986. *Morir en Malaga: Testamentos malagueños del siglo XVIII*. Malaga: Universidad de Malaga.

Redfield, Robert. 1941. *The Folk Culture of Yucatan*. Chicago: University of Chicago Press.

——. 1950. *A Village That Chose Progress: Chan Kom Revisited*. Chicago: University of Chicago Press.

Reed, Nelson. 1964. *The Caste War of Yucatan*. Stanford, Calif.: Stanford University Press.

Restall, Matthew. 1995a. *Life and Death in a Maya Community: The Ixil Testaments of the 1760s*. Lancaster, Calif.: Labyrinthos.

——. 1995b. " 'He Wished It in Vain': Subordination and Resistance Among Maya Women in Post-Conquest Yucatan." *Ethnohistory* 42, no. 4: 577–94.

Restall, Matthew, and Susan Kellogg, eds. n.d. *Dead Giveaways: Indigenous Testaments of Colonial Mesoamerica and the Andes*. Salt Lake City: University of Utah Press, forthcoming.

Restall, Matthew, and Pete Sigal. 1992. " 'May They Not Be Fornicators Equal to These Priests': Postconquest Yucatec Maya Sexual Attitudes." In Lisa Sousa, ed., *Indigenous Writing in the Spanish Indies*, pp. 91–121. Los Angeles: UCLA Historical Journal Special Issue.

Restall, Matthew, and Kevin Terraciano. 1992. "Indigenous Writing and Literacy in Colonial Mexico." In Lisa Sousa, ed., *Indigenous Writing in the Spanish Indies*, pp. 8–28. Los Angeles: UCLA Historical Journal Special Issue.

Ricard, Robert. 1933. *La "conquête spirituelle" du Mexique*. Travaux et mémoires de l'Institut d'ethnologie, 20. Paris: Université de Paris.

Riese, Frauke Johanna. 1981. *Indianische Landrechte in Yukatan um die Mitte des 16. Jahrhunderts: Dokumentenanalyse und Konstruktion von Wirklichkeitsmodellen am Fall des Landvertrages von Mani*. Hamburg: Hamburgischen Museum für Völkerkunde.

Robinson, David J. 1987. "Migration Patterns in Colonial Yucatan." Paper presented at the International Conference of Latin American Geographers, Mérida.

——, ed. 1990. *Migration in Colonial Spanish America*. Cambridge: Cambridge University Press.

Roys, Ralph L. 1931. *The Ethno-Botany of the Maya*. New Orleans: Middle American Research Institute, Tulane University.

——. 1939. *The Titles of Ebtun*. Washington, D.C.: Carnegie Institution.

——. 1940. "Personal Names of the Maya of Yucatan." In *Contributions to American Anthropology and History* 6: 31–48. Washington, D.C.: Carnegie Institution.

——. 1957. *The Political Geography of the Yucatan Maya*. Washington, D.C.: Carnegie Institution.

——. 1965. "Lowland Maya Native Society at Spanish Contact." In *Handbook of Middle American Indians*, 3: 659–78. Austin: University of Texas Press.

——. 1967 [1933]. *The Book of Chilam Balam of Chumayel*. Norman: University of Oklahoma Press. Reprint. First published Washington, D.C.: Carnegie Institution.

——. 1972 [1943]. *The Indian Background of Colonial Yucatan.* Norman: University of Oklahoma Press. Reprint. First published Washington, D.C.: Carnegie Institution.

Roys, Ralph L., France V. Scholes, and Eleanor B. Adams, eds. 1940. "Report and Census on the Indians of Cozumel, 1570." In *Contributions to American Anthropology and History* 6: 1–30. Washington, D.C.: Carnegie Institution.

——. 1959. "Census and Inspection of the Town of Pencuyut, Yucatan, in 1583 by Diego García de Palacio, Oidor of the Audiencia of Guatemala." *Ethnohistory* 6: 195–225.

Rugeley, Terry. n.d. *Men of Audacity: Yucatan's Maya Peasantry and the Origins of the Caste War, 1800–1847.* Austin: University of Texas Press, forthcoming.

Russell-Wood, A. J. R. 1968. *Fidalgos and Philanthropists: The Santa Casa da Misericórdia of Bahia, 1550–1755.* Berkeley and Los Angeles: University of California Press.

Saignes, Thierry. 1985. *Caciques, Tribute, and Migration in the Southern Andes: Indian Society and the Seventeenth Century Colonial Order.* London: University of London Press.

Sánchez, José M. 1972. *Anticlericalism: A Brief History.* Notre Dame, Ind.: University of Notre Dame Press.

Schele, Linda, and David Freidel. 1990. *A Forest of Kings: The Untold Story of the Ancient Maya.* New York: Morrow.

Schlegel, Alice, ed. 1977. *Sexual Stratification: A Cross-Cultural View.* New York: Columbia University Press.

Scholes, France V., and Eleanor B. Adams, eds. 1938. *Don Diego Quijada, Alcalde Mayor de Yucatán, 1561–1565.* 2 vols. Mexico City: Editorial Porrua.

Scholes, France V., Carlos R. Menéndez, J. Ignacio Rubio Mañé, and Eleanor B. Adams, eds. 1936–38. *Documentos para la historia de Yucatán.* 3 vols. Mérida: Compañía Tipográfica Yucateca.

Scholes, France V., and Ralph L. Roys. 1938. *Fray Diego de Landa and the Problem of Idolatry in Yucatan.* Washington, D.C.: Carnegie Institution.

——. 1968 [1948]. *The Maya Chontal Indians of Acalan-Tixchel.* Norman: University of Oklahoma Press.

Schroeder, Susan. 1991. *Chimalpahin and the Kingdoms of Chalco.* Tucson: University of Arizona Press.

Schwartz, Stuart B. 1973. *Sovereignty and Society in Colonial Brazil: The High Court of Bahia and Its Judges, 1609–1751.* Berkeley and Los Angeles: University of California Press.

Seoane, Maria Isabe. 1985. *Sentido Espiritual del Testamento Indiano.* Buenos Aires: Fundación para la Educación, la Ciencia y la Cultura.

Sigal, Pete. 1995. "Passions of the Mind: Yucatecan Maya Thoughts on the Body, Pleasures, Sexuality, and the Self, Sixteenth to Eighteenth Centuries." Ph.D. dissertation, University of California, Los Angeles.

Spalding, Karen. 1967. "Indian Rural Society in Colonial Peru: The Example of Huarochirí." Ph.D. dissertation, University of California, Berkeley.

Spores, Ronald. 1967. *The Mixtec Kings and Their People.* Norman: University of Oklahoma Press.

Stacy-Judd, Robert B., trans. 1940. *A Maya Manuscript (Codex Mérida)*. Los Angeles: Philosophical Research Society.

Stephens, John L. 1963 [1843]. *Incidents of Travel in Yucatan*. 2 vols. New York: Dover. Also 1988. Mexico City: Panorama Editorial.

Stone, Lawrence. 1977. *The Family, Sex, and Marriage in England, 1500–1800*. New York: Harper & Row.

Sullivan, Paul. 1989. *Unfinished Conversations: Mayas and Foreigners Between Two Wars*. New York: Knopf.

Taylor, William. 1972. *Landlord and Peasant in Colonial Oaxaca*. Stanford, Calif.: Stanford University Press.

Tedlock, Barbara. 1982. *Time and the Highland Maya*. Albuquerque: University of New Mexico Press.

Tedlock, Dennis. 1985. *Popol Vuh. The Mayan Book of the Dawn of Life*. New York: Touchstone.

———. 1993. "Torture in the Archives: Mayans Meet Europeans." *American Anthropologist* 91, no. 1: 139–52.

Terraciano, Kevin. 1994. "Ñudzahui History: Mixtec Writing and Culture in Colonial Oaxaca." Ph.D. dissertation, University of California, Los Angeles.

———. n.d. "Colonial Ñudzahui-Language (Mixtec) Testaments from Oaxaca, Mexico." In Matthew Restall and Susan Kellogg, eds., *Dead Giveaways: Indigenous Testaments of Colonial Mesoamerica and the Andes*. Salt Lake City: University of Utah Press, forthcoming.

Thomas, Keith. 1963. "History and Anthropology." *Past and Present* 24: 3–24.

Thompson, J. Eric S. 1967. "Ralph Loveland Roys, 1879–1965. *American Antiquity* 32, no. 1.

———. 1977. "A Proposal for Constituting a Maya Subgroup, Cultural and Linguistic, in the Petén and Adjacent Regions." In Grant D. Jones, ed., *Anthropology and History in Yucatán*, pp. 3–42. Austin: University of Texas Press.

Thompson, Philip C. 1978. "Tekanto in the Eighteenth Century." Ph.D. dissertation, Tulane University.

Tozzer, Alfred M. 1941. *Relación de las cosas de Yucatán, by fray Diego de Landa*. Cambridge, Mass.: Peabody Museum of Harvard University (American Archaeology and Ethnology Paper 18).

———. 1977 [1921]. *A Maya Grammar*. Reprint. New York: Dover.

Van Zantwijk, Rudolf. 1965. "La tendencia purista en el náhuatl del centro de México." *Estudios de cultura náhuatl* 5: 129–42.

———. 1985. *The Aztec Arrangement: The Social History of Pre-Spanish Mexico*. Norman: University of Oklahoma Press.

Ventur, Pierre. 1978. *Maya Ethnohistorian: The Ralph L. Roys Papers*. Nashville, Tenn.: Vanderbilt University Press.

Villanueva C., Carlos R. 1992. "Jacinto Can Ek: heroicidad e infamia." *Por Esto!* 2, no. 53, *Unicornio*, pp. 14–17. Mérida.

Vogt, Evon Z. 1983. "Ancient and Contemporary Maya Settlement Patterns: A New Look from the Chiapas Highlands." In Evon Z. Vogt and Richard M. Leventhal, eds., *Prehistoric Settlement Patterns: Essays in Honor of Gordon R. Willey*. Cambridge and Albuquerque: Peabody Museum of Harvard University and University of New Mexico Press.

Wall, Richard, Jean Robin, and Peter Laslett. 1983. *Family Forms in Historic Europe.* Cambridge: Cambridge University Press.

Wauchope, Robert. 1938. *Modern Maya Houses: A Study of Their Significance.* Washington, D.C.: Carnegie Institution.

Wightman, Ann M. 1990. *Indigenous Migration and Social Change. The Forasteros of Cuzco, 1520–1720.* Durham, N.C.: Duke University Press.

Wolf, Eric R. 1957. "Closed Corporate Communities in Meso-America and Central Java." *Southwestern Journal of Anthropology* 13: 1–18.

Wood, Stephanie. 1984. "Corporate Adjustments in Colonial Mexican Indian Towns: Toluca Region." Ph.D. dissertation, University of California, Los Angeles.

——. 1991. "The Cosmic Conquest: Late-Colonial Views of the Sword and Cross in Central Mexican Títulos." *Ethnohistory* 38, no. 2: 176–95.

Zimmermann, Günter. 1970. *Briefe der indianischen Nobilität aus Neuspanien an Karl V um die Mitte des 16. Jahrhunderts.* Munich: Kommissionsverlag Klaus Renner.

Index

In this index an "f" after a number indicates a separate reference on the next page, and an "ff" indicates separate references on the next two pages. A continuous discussion over two or more pages is indicated by a span of page numbers, e.g., "57–59." *Passim* is used for a cluster of references in close but not consecutive sequence.

Library of Congress Cataloging-in-Publication Data
Restall, Matthew, 1964–
    The Maya world : Yucatec culture and society, 1560–1850 / Matthew
Restall.
      p.   cm.
    Includes bibliographical references and index.
    ISBN 0-8047-2745-7 (cloth)   :   ISBN 0-8047-3658-8 (pbk.)
    1. Mayas—Social life and customs.   2. Mayas—Politics and
government.   3. Mayas—History—Sources.   I. Title.
F1434.2.S63R47   1997
972.81′016—dc20   96-26167
                                                               CIP

⊛ This book is printed on acid-free, recycled paper.
Original printing 1997
Last figure below indicates year of this printing:
06   05   04   03   02   01   00   99